PRIMORDIAL ENGINIZATION

ISBN: 979-8-234-00426-0

TABLE OF CONTENTS

Two things opposed don't stand opposite
Beliefs aren't made, they're discovered
Everything comes with tradeoffs
Observation is punishment
Your soul is your struggle
Stern belief invites irony
Good is a circumstance
There are no simplicities
Reinforcement is destiny
With order comes disorder
A gift is a curse and vice-versa
Pity is poison no matter the context
To fail to admit mistakes is to inhibit growth
An interaction is more complex than either member alone

I

EVOLUTION & ECONOMICS

1.1 The Value of Interaction

If you dig deep enough in the right places, you find rare metals that can fetch a pretty penny. Finding and extracting them can make for a lucrative business. As you may know, these things have forever been a part of the same planet we've always inhabited, but our knowledge to assess their worth and make use of their properties was harder to extract than the metals themselves. As not only do we extract materials from our surroundings, we extract lessons from everything we interact with. We extract wisdom from observing the results of cyclic events over the course of history, as well as interesting physical properties from creatures that have grown them for their own survival. Store enough wisdom and you can extract inspiration from even the worst of circumstances. There's a use for everything as long as you can find it. We find more value in finding ways to find value than we do in finding value itself.

Of all the places you could, where might one look for the most valuable lessons to learn? This question has an evolving answer, it always has. Perhaps you could look to find the most complex thing you don't fully understand. In that case, you can grab a mirror and the resulting staring contest would lead down a rabbit hole where you'll end up completely lost. Maybe there are simpler examples? Even if you found a dumber person, you still wouldn't be able to answer many questions because the problem of what to infer wouldn't change with differences in intellect, the answers are lost to millions of years of evolution. Luckily, it might serve you well that there's plenty of other organisms to choose from.

What exactly might one learn from studying organisms? The evolutionary history of our planet has fostered a vast plethora of examples, whose interactions with their own environment are facilitated by features which aid them in extremely specific modes of survival. If you're looking for complexity, an interaction is more complex than either member alone.

The most fundamental interactions make for the most obvious functions, does something walk, swim, fly, or something else? Among these examples are multitudes of details about efficient structures for moving while minimizing impact and wasted energy. To continue going in this obvious direction, as many already have, you'll eventually come to the conclusion that if you want to build an airplane, then you may want to understand how birds fly. Biomimicry has proven to be one of the greatest sources of engineering wisdom, inspiring designs that work far outside their organismal context, as well as providing the basis for wheels that then didn't need to be reinvented at great cost and energy.

So what else might one learn from biology if not the utility of structure and interactions? Is there a deeper underlying philosophy? A design principle, if you will? That would be an interesting discussion to have, but how would you approach it? The answer to this question moves us in a direction distinct from the structures of biological function, and more towards the creation of that function. It points towards evolution. What kind of things can, realistically, be learned from evolution? To even attempt this would require snapshots across time rather than the organismal cross-sections one might normally observe. Is there a well-studied yet simple enough concept where wisdom can be extracted? Wisdom that's generally applicable, wisdom that can find parallels across different areas of life?

1.2 An Evomimetic Model

The idea of organisms being models of their environment has a long philosophical history. Leibniz's *living mirrors of the universe*[1] and

1. Gottfried Wilhelm Leibniz. *The Monadology*. Johann Meyers sel. Witwe, 1720

Kant's *objects of experience*[2] are basically the precursors to this revelation. Afterwards, multiple biologists and psychologists went on to all say the same thing for the next couple hundred years using their own inventive terminology. Richard Dawkins eventually made a significant shift in this mode of thinking in that *"any animal, is a model or description of its own world"*[3]. It's an accurate statement that the features of an organism are sculpted to garner advantages that are purely complementary to their environment. Even the concept of convergent evolution offers examples of multiple different organisms conforming to the same structure for this very reason[4], presenting the same exact form, such as crabs, which have multiple species of unrelated origins that all arrived at the same general body structure because they inhabited similar habitats. There's a lot of information you can play with, as this is a hefty idea with a lot of literature to it, but I'd like to take a rather different swing at this concept. Multiple, actually.

Geese have a compass built into their head in order to navigate their flight, sharks have skin that can cut you should you brush up against them, but I don't find these to be particularly interesting areas to apply the lessons of the knowledge of evolution. Not because it couldn't be useful for someone, but because there isn't much of a mystery. What entices me more is the mystery of humans, what we are, how we got to this state of supreme intelligence, and what kind of environment are we actually supposed to be models of?

People often point to dexterous hands that can use tools, to take advantage of any object, and traverse any environment. A jaw structure that evolved to make more intricate vocal distinctions, allowing for complex communication. Upright walking, which allowed for roaming away from the trees we were born from. Slow speed but great stamina, for chasing animals until they tire out. But none of these provide an answer to the question of what *exactly* is so special about the human brain to be able to grasp so many concepts so well? What brought that into fruition in the same light that jumping led to gliding, which eventually became flight? The answers to these questions will take some time to flesh out, you might even say it could take a whole book. To approach the topic, let's start by delving into the nature of

2. Immanuel Kant. *Critique of Pure Reason.* Johann Friedrich Hartknoch, 1781
3. Richard Dawkins. *Unweaving the Rainbow.* Allen Lane, 1998
4. Arthur Willey. *Convergence in Evolution.* John Murray, 1911

evolution using examples similar to what I'd previously brushed off as uninteresting.

There's an underlying pattern through the evolution of nearly every physical structure you can imagine. It starts with an addition of new features, which is oftentimes a replication, then it moves towards a specialization of those features, and finally ends with a reduction of redundancy, in order to finish the process. Which is a dazzlingly interesting pattern if you're able to see the value in it. It's called Williston's law[5], named after the man who first recognized this throughout the fossil record.

Take for example the general pattern of the evolution of various crustaceans, more specifically their appendages. Antennae which became sensory organs. Front-facing claws, for hunting and self-defence. Mandibles that crush and grind prey, as a parallel to chewing. Some limbs are used for shoveling food into their mouths, some aid in movement, others in swimming, and the list goes on. You can do your own research if you're truly interested in all the specifics, the point I'm presenting isn't in the fine details but rather the big picture. There are very specific roles for each limb. Each appendage started out as just a plain leg, of sorts. A mutation event occurred where its basic legs were then repeated across its body, and their extreme differences in structure came from the specialization each limb eventually acquired over time. Some even ceased being true limbs, like the antennae. Once the specialization process was finished, extra limbs were discarded through the next phase of natural selection. Why have 4 limbs for a job that 2 can accomplish? It would only be a waste of energy.

Considering this hypothetical crustacean as a design, what has it accomplished? Rather than a simple reconfiguration of advantages and disadvantages, the art of design is that which tries to lose less capability than it gains through whichever tradeoffs take place. Harnessing an overall advantage in capability. Despite the many generations it took to make these changes, it's accomplished an optimization. The end result? This organism has modeled its environment.

But what is a model? It's an extremely general term. And what exactly was the transgression that allowed for an improved modeling

5. Samuel Wendell Williston. *Water Reptiles of the Past and Present*. University of Chicago Press, 1914

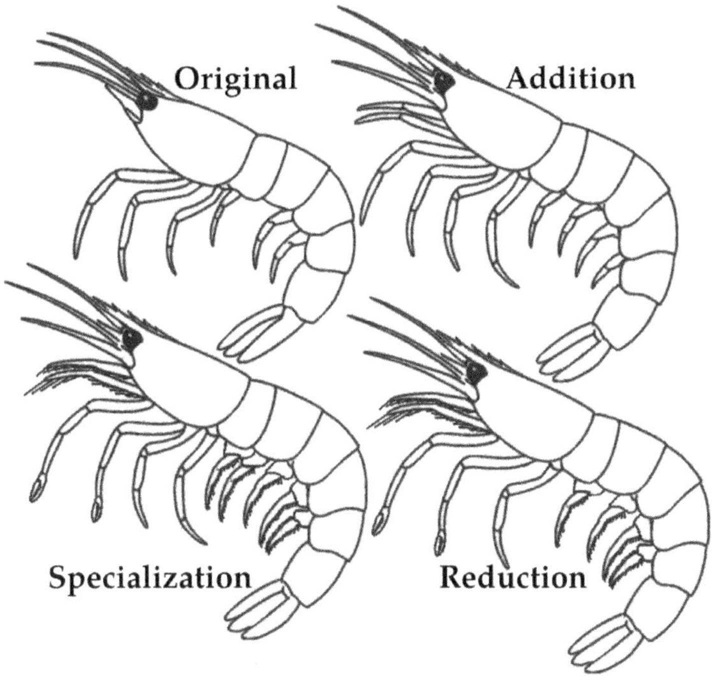

Figure 1: The Basic Concept of Williston's Law

of its environment? What yielded such different results on limbs that were typically less than a centimeter away from each other?

A model is an attempt to describe as much complexity in as few amount of terms as possible. Crustaceans aren't known for verbally describing much, as they've refused to speak with us for quite a while, likely because of a grudge. But the features of the legs themselves reflect their own purpose. They describe themselves through their own function. The claws used for self-defence don't have eyeballs in between either side because they would be crushed. There isn't a mouth on the bottom of your foot, because dirt and garbage would enter your system too easily. Likewise, your brain isn't inside the soft tissue of your stomach, it's cased inside a hard skull that acts as a primary helmet should your brain not work as intended.

Design principles require a kind of backwards thinking, like trying to predict a problem then coming up with a scenario that aims to prevent it from happening. It's similar to the basic concepts of calculus, where you have a derivative function and need to solve for an integral.

The derivative is easy to find if you start with an integral, but the reverse can be either difficult or impossible. Stating an organism that breathes directly into its own eyeballs will likely suffer from ridiculous infections if this problem isn't addressed, or its dental hygiene isn't perfect, doesn't offer much of a challenge to arrive at. The integral in this case isn't simply forcefully changing the shape of every eye-breathing organism with something akin to braces for human teeth, it would require a redesign at its most important layer of genetics. The hurdle of overcoming this is much more difficult than simply stating the problem. Hence, why it's an integral to solve. Looking through a purely mathematical lens, some integrals are simply not solvable. Although from a design perspective, there's usually a way around any theoretically unsolvable problem. As the realm of practicality doesn't hinder itself through the hard-coded limitations of mathematics, but that still doesn't make it easy. Through the lens of practicality, solving an integral is thinking backwards far enough to learn to utilize a principle that's more fundamental than any prior advantage could confer. Moving in the direction of derivatives guarantees all functions eventually bottom out into straight lines, but moving in the direction of integrals may as well be infinite, and reveal a pattern of evolving complexity. It's unknown if there's a limit to integration due to the difficulty in solving each one, but it's unlikely that they do. There's also cases of cyclic derivatives, where they continually circle back to form the same equations over and over again. I'll continue to use the terms integral and derivative throughout this book in this manner, strictly referring to a use analogous to the concepts known from calculus in order to model the complexity that will be explored on many topics.

So this explains a general design constraint. The difficulty of arriving at good answers and the energy it takes to maintain them. When it comes to human development, is there anything else we can expand upon to infer what elements had both hindered and enabled growth?

1.3 Developmental Lockstep

Lamarckism[6] is the idea that animals adapt their features in response to their environment. That giraffes grew long necks because they needed to pick food off tall trees. Lamarck assumed that animals would adapt to their environment through forms of exercise, and that

6. Jean-Baptiste Lamarck. *Zoological Philosophy*. Dentu et L'Auteur, 1809

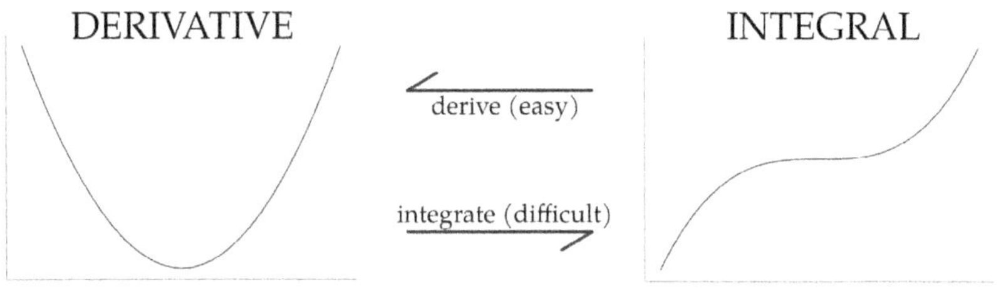

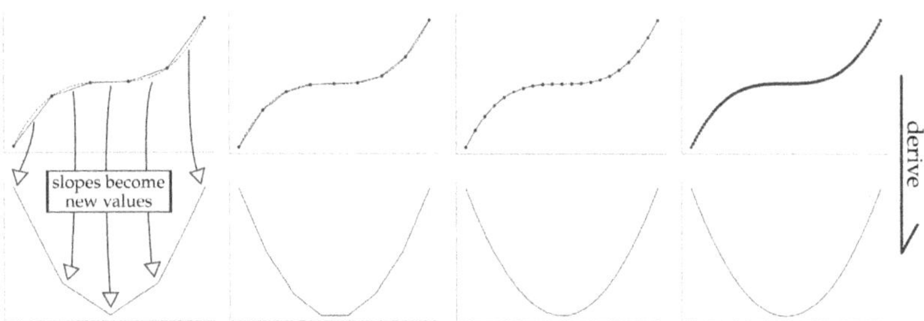

The slope of a line between any two points along a function can be used to find the value of its derivative function at that specific point. The value of the slope becomes the value of the newly transformed derivative function.

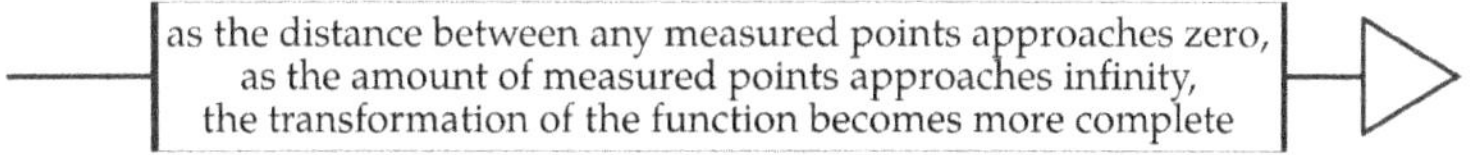

The area under a function can be estimated using various shapes, rectangles are commonly used. The area of the shape beneath the function accumulates into the value of the newly transformed integral function.

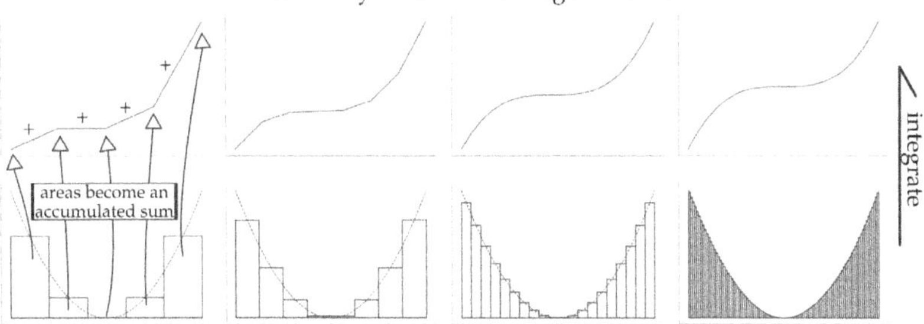

Figure 2: The Basic Functionality of Calculus

these adaptations would automatically be present in their own children as a default form of inheritance. It's a slight play on causality compared to Darwin's theory of natural selection, which views inheritance as the primary driving force behind adaptation[7]. Neither Darwin nor Lamarck would have known about DNA and its tendency to mutate. Darwinism is the base of the evolutionary pyramid in today's world, but the heart of Lamarck's transformist ideas are still alive in some academic circles. The chances of Lamarckian elements being intertwined with the driving factors behind the evolution of modern organisms are not zero.

You can cite thousands of papers, books, and whatever else to explain why Lamarck wasn't technically wrong. Eugene Koonin argues that DNA and mutations aren't enough to explain the whole picture of some organism's evolutionary history, that there's a multi-faceted nature to the development of every population that would follow Darwinian, Lamarckian, and quasi-Lamarckian mechanics running in parallel[8]. His arguments include small-scale pseudoimmune responses to foreign invaders of single-celled organisms. Denis Noble has made the case that DNA is like any other piece of the cell, forever being affected by its own inner workings, and doesn't enjoy absolute causal primacy from atop any throne[9]. There's various other claims, and the full list can go on for quite a while. But I consider this to be rather boring, this is just chasing smaller and smaller targets. The game of cat and mouse with Lamarckism shouldn't only yield results that become more minuscule and specific if it's to be true Lamarckism at all.

In questioning which was the true evolutionary paradigm, Lamarckism was initially seen as an opposing idea to the Darwinian school of thought. Rather than being anti-Darwinian, Lamarckism essentially fits into the Darwinian worldview. Lamarckism *is* a Darwinian process. It just so happens the complexity of the truth was not being properly modeled by the simplistic nature of the questions posed at the time.

Which points in a fascinating direction, the nature of evolving complexity. The problem wasn't just about being right or wrong, the orientation was misframed. The question was wrong. Even when you try

7. Charles Darwin. *On the Origin of Species.* John Murray, 1859

8. Eugene Koonin. *The Logic of Chance.* FT Press, 2011

9. Denis Noble. *Dance to the Tune of Life.* Cambridge University Press, 2016

to approach a subject that seems straightforward, you're always prone to take unexpected turns when dealing with something more complex than you can understand. Biologists who argued over which theory was more realistic, as an evolutionary basis, didn't consider that there needed to be a more complicated question, because they didn't know the age of the Earth. Estimates at the time were still ranging between tens to hundreds of millions of years. Of course they didn't understand the significance of billions of years of evolution. Basic concepts of chemistry were barely elucidated, the origins of life were an absolute mystery. The evolution of our ideas were, and will always be, in this perpetual lockstep with one another.

In that same regard, human development is in lockstep with technology. The salability of metals, the ability to use them as money, granted by the ability to melt and combine them, grew the potential for better economic exchange. Awarding greater potential for economic growth, as having a suitable form of currency to act as a store of value increases the value of value itself. The increased efficiency of storing such value enables all kinds of interactions amongst individuals that would otherwise never be possible.

More interestingly, the material of exchange needed to match this specific preordained task represents a pure concept in search of the physical properties to contain it. That there's an inherent role most appropriately modeled by the chemical properties of something like gold is a stroke of luck as grand as the formation of life itself. Its chemical stability, portability, universal uniformity, recognizability, scarcity, and divisibility all make it ideal as a proxy for value through trade. The big picture may change as more truth comes to light some day, but the amount of time throughout which gold was a standard for exchange roughly coincides as starting with the building of the Great Pyramids, and ending with the World Wars. It lasted for so long, and encompassed multiple technological revolutions, periods of philosophical enlightenment, civilizational collapses, and all sorts of societal advancements. The context of where we now find ourselves, now having salable goods aside from gold, isn't just in a blooming age of technology, but also a burgeoning age of value exchange. One might even call it a golden age.

There's been commentary on the evolution of humans, suggesting that most of their evolution over the past tens of thousands of years has been purely in the metabolic realm. People attempting to study whether there's evidence for an increase in intelligence during that same time period run into the problem of having to use something as a proxy for intelligence, which doesn't tend to offer much insight. There's good evidence for the evolution of metabolism amongst adaptations for lactase[10], starch[11], and lipids[12], to name a few key examples. Yet, even if you wanted to link improvements in intelligence to dietary intake and metabolism, these examples don't provide arguments that support that case specifically. A notable facilitation in the intelligence of humans is more likely the consequence of a tradeoff in gut size relative to brain size, an adaptation that was able to take root due to improved culinary preparation[13]. Observing traits across primates displays a decrease in gut size coinciding with an increase in brain size, a pattern found in other vertebrates but not in other mammals. Rather than being of some pure genetic origin, advancements to our pre-existing intelligence, likely among other things, were in lockstep with our diet.

Strategic directed mutations are the white whale of the Lamarckian world, and they aren't real. From single-celled organisms to humans, there are no cellular processes that target specific nucleotides for mutation across the entire genome. There are no cells capable of *engineering* the proteins of their entire genome for improved functionality, they don't have the ability to *target* specific nucleotides for alteration. The clearest evidence of the impossibility of this is within the immune system. If it were possible for a cell to engineer its own proteins, it would occur during the production of antibodies.

The somatic hypermutations of antibodies are some of the furthest away anything has gotten from true randomness, yet they're simultaneously not deterministic either. This process starts by filtering against B-cells that produce antibodies with too strong an affinity for binding to host proteins, that then undergo multiple iterations of life and

10. Todd Bersaglieri et al. *Genetic Signatures of Strong Recent Positive Selection at the Lactase Gene.* American Journal of Human Genetics, 2004

11. George H Perry et al. *Diet and the Evolution of Human Amylase Gene Copy Number Variation.* Nature Genetics, 2007

12. Sara Mathieson and Iain Mathieson. *FADS1 and the Timing of Human Adaptation to Agriculture.* Molecular Biology and Evolution, 2018

13. Leslie C Aiello and Peter Wheeler. *The Expensive Tissue Hypothesis: The Brain and the Digestive System in Human and Primate Evolution.* Current Anthropology, 1995

death selection for B-cells that produce an antibody that appropriately binds to a target. Their life and death cycles are dependent upon the binding affinities of the antibody they produce, and should they pass each subsequent stage of this process, they replicate themselves and this entire process repeats until the immune response defeats the population of invading pathogens. If such a directed protein engineering process were possible, it would occur here. But it doesn't, and successfully doing this requires multiple iterations that include actual tests of the protein itself, so there's no way for organisms to get this right in just a single attempt, and using only genetic information. If such a thing couldn't happen in the most specific context possible, where there's just one single job to do, which is bind to something, then it's not possible for the rest of the genome either. As a cell or body certainly wouldn't be able to track the functionality of any other mutations it made to any other gene because it's unable to properly perceive them. Even if such a targeted process were possible, trying to account for such things would only be a massive energy requirement. It would still be energetically unfeasible.

Random mutations are the primary driving force behind genetic adaptation, so it's randomness itself that's used for introducing adaptation when and where necessary. Some areas of the genome experience a lower, or higher, mutation rate, depending on where they're located[14,15]. Some genetic neighborhoods are more protected than others, based on the importance of the information they hold. Even then, there's still screwups in some of the safer neighborhoods. Even Hox genes, arguably the most important genes for organismal development, still experience mutations, resulting in unviable offspring. If mutations didn't occur in such places, then evolution would never have happened in the first place, the flaws of genetic machinery are both a feature and a bug.

Not only does the mutation rate differ across genetic localities, the mutation rate itself can be increased. Cells respond to stress by caus-

14. Kenneth H Wolfe, Paul M Sharp, and Wen-Hsiung Li. *Mutation Rates Differ Among Regions of the Mammalian Genome*. Nature, 1989

15. Peter F Arndt, Terence Hwa, and Dmitri A Petrov. *Substantial Regional Variation in Substitution Rates in the Human Genome: Importance of GC Content, Gene Density, and Telomere-Specific Effects*. Journal of Molecular Evolution, 2005

ing random mutations to take place across their genome[16], this is the most evident form of Lamarckian response. The more progenitors some organism had that were exposed to such stressors, the higher their mutation rate will be, and the more novelty many of their mutations will have[17], and this is the true Lamarckian engineering process. Any specific strategic mutation would be impossible, and a population of organisms would eventually converge upon all the same mutations if this were true. Genetic variation itself would decrease if mutations weren't entirely random. Stress-triggered mutations allows for only parts of a population that were under stress to undergo changes, meaning separate enclaves of a population are able to act as a sort of control group against potentially deficient outcomes. It's not only unfeasible, at an individual level, to impose targeted mutations on any genome, it's a surefire way to destroy an entire population through what becomes directed inbreeding if it were to somehow be successful.

So what does this strategy of randomness accomplish under a more philosophical interpretation? What lesson might we learn from the fact that evolution has adopted this as an answer to the problem of adaptation itself? That the a priori determination of a *correct* answer isn't physically possible. Nor is it worth guessing. All the best choices can only be recognized in hindsight, you may have a general idea of where they may be, but you'll never know exactly what they are beforehand. Making a scattershot of random changes, and simply determining where more change could be useful, is more valuable to the group as a whole than to aim at some specific target. It's not aiming for correctness, it's avoiding that concept altogether. It's aiming to *not be incorrect*. Lamarckist genetic responses feed the random mutations required for Darwinian selection. Their nexus doesn't need to rely on specificity.

Mutation rates seem to dance in lockstep with stress. But is that the only form of Lamarckian response? Possibly not. If you want to uncover some grand Lamarckian mechanism, it might be best to determine what it dances in lockstep with. Surely there's a larger Lamarckian mechanism to find if this idea is to have any dignity? Like the

16. John Cairns, Julie Overbaugh, and Stephan Miller. *The Origin of Mutants.* Nature, 1988

17. Ying Zhao et al. *Parental Folate Deficiency Induces Birth Defects in Mice Accompanied with Increased De Novo Mutations.* Cell Discovery, 2022

preparation of food and the salability of cash, is the evolution of our intelligence in lockstep with other physical limitations outside our biology? Aside from stress, and aside from the genome, is there any other kind of Lamarckian response to be found in complex organisms? If so, how might these limitations lift themselves, and where might they take hold?

Surely, inherited information isn't only found in the realm of DNA? There must be some process, and method of its activation, where Lamarckian adaptation circumvents genetic inheritance. DNA is what's used to pass on genetics, do we have anything else that we pass on? Is this relevant to all animals? All mammals? Humans deal in information specifically. Culture, information, and other forms of knowledge are human specialties. This arrives at the crossroads of nature and nurture, we inherit information the same way we inherit DNA. Fish, amphibians, reptiles, and invertebrates certainly don't do this, any examples of the sort would be incredibly nuanced and lacking the same depth. Animals that can't be released into the wild without preparation, after having been raised in captivity, likely share this ability to inherit information. Those that do would be other mammals like cats, primates, cetaceans, and even certain birds. Needless to say, you couldn't release an untrained human into the wild with any hope for their survival. The journey that uninformed, unraised, neglected humans would undergo just to survive very likely wouldn't yield success. It's almost like we've superceded our own ability to do so thanks to our reliance on the intergenerational sharing of information. Secondary transmittance of information by intelligence is both a gift and a curse. So you could say the potential for our intelligence is in lockstep with our ability to inherit it. Then the question becomes, at what point did the inheritance of our knowledge circumvent the inheritance of our genetics?

Any reasonable assumption would look at the history of human evolution to indicate there *must* be something the evolution of this process dances in lockstep with. One might also assume there's great similarity between how evolution in general dances with this concept, and how the basis for intelligence itself might also do the same. After all, if there's outward facing intelligence, you can fairly assume the nature of inward facing autonomous processes act with just as much prudence. This book will arrive at what that process is, and how it operates, as well as the complexities of human civilization that can be modeled by understanding it. So to start on that, let's explore the basis for evolutionary advancement outside organismal design.

1.4 Global Diffusion

Like heat dissipating from a source, the movement of highly successful organisms across the planet is a natural phenomenon that occurs when something is able to spread out beyond its original niche, and finds success in many others. We see this in many organisms across the planet. Arthropods and mammals, among some others, have successfully conquered the globe we see today. Things like large cats are found on every continent minus Australia.

Regarding hominid success, the same thing likely happened long before the earliest known datings of any remains we've found of any cousins, or progenitors, to modern humans. It probably happened again quickly enough that they could interbreed and produce viable offspring. The way of determining whether two related animals are still the same species is whether they can have children that can successfully reproduce, which tends not to be the case for the hybrids of many animals. Technically a lot of large cats can do the same, but with large cats the only viable offspring they can produce tends to be female, which is indicative of a larger genetic distance. Hominids are likely the first terrestrial mammals to achieve this diffusion across the globe at a speed in which their subsequent waves of global exploration were still able to mate, and produce viable offspring, with the last waves living in whatever distant location had been arrived at.

This spreading across the globe isn't dissimilar to the addition step considered in the context of Williston's law. It's the indication of a pioneering effort. In today's world, this pattern of global diffusion is carried on via knowledge and technology, as humans have progressed to the point of no longer needing to be a passive player in their own game of evolutionary development. Rightfully so, as at the forefront of evolution is human engineering.

Global diffusion was originally a means of navigating around the problems of any single locality, or a way of expanding from success. It's interesting that we now find ourselves stuck in our respective corners, countries, their boundaries, and the consequences it bares. So what new problems arise across closed systems and their individual economies?

1.5 Foundations of Value Creation

I'm going to start by comparing the US economic system with that of China under Xi Jinping. In particular, I aim to compare their flaws and inefficiencies, and to specifically use the flaws of the Chinese system to create an understanding of economic flaws in general. I'll then apply that understanding to the US economy to present where improvements can be made. Am I aiming to fix the Chinese system with this book? No, it's not my problem. Simple yet fundamental improvements to the Chinese system have been offered time and time again by more worthy people whose advice continues to be ignored. Offering the basis for fundamental improvements to the American system, on the other hand, would be of great importance to the global system as a whole.

Allow me to be more specific on what I mean by flaws. You could say the economy of the US is reliant on wars, and the threats created by the existence of its military, alongside the money printed while maintaining itself. You might criticize the thought that the US can retain its economic dominance by giving money away to foreign nations, arguing against granting increasingly more leverage to people who want it bankrupt because it needs to constantly appease their need for more leverage else they use it against the US, as this isn't an economic theory, it's a hostage situation. You could even say the US budget is as overweight as its citizens. You'd probably be right no matter which one you pick, despite their contradiction, it's a very complicated system after all. But these aren't the aspects of the economy I wish to focus on. I'm interested instead in what areas can be modified, most legitimately, to provide the most benefit. To build on top of what already exists, to make it into a better form of itself. I'm looking to narrow in on value creation where it truly starts.

Let's start by painting a picture of the Chinese system from the perspective of value creation. Unlike in the West, where the private sector steers the ship of bottom-up investment, and the government plays a stabilizing role, the Chinese government makes top-down decisions where it lends money, and its private sector innovates within predefined boundaries dictated by their government. The Chinese economic shackles lie in being unable to fully adopt a consumption-based model, with the consumer-level economy being what's built atop of agriculture, resource extraction, and manufacturing as well as the industries these lead to. This is due somewhat to a multitude of reasons, as people living in China prefer to save their money rather than spend it. It's also due to the fact that their heavy investment in industry and extraction roles, which tend to require less people to fulfill them over time as technology advances, means less people have money to spend on the consumption of their own products[18].

A consumer-based economy is one whose main engine for growth relies on service industries such as retail, restaurant, and entertainment work among others. The service sector tends to carry the majority of employment, as well as revenue generation, for all developed countries, China included. Missing out on the true potential of consumption from their service sector is a loss of serious opportunity for the Chinese economy. Growth of internal consumption hasn't been an attractive model compared to the exporting of goods, in contrast to the consumption-led economy of the US. This creates a vicious cycle where less money is spent generating returns in their own market, and is instead invested in manufacturing plants that focus on exporting more consumer goods.

This top-down nature is somewhat parallel to another communist story. Under the Soviet economy, the production of tools were valued over other kinds of products because it was seen that tools could be used to produce anything else that was needed. Having an abundance of tools was seen as a form of sovereign security. This strategy didn't last very long, as it was a poor decision in the long run to consider such a simple idea as the basis for an economy. Regardless of this resulting in an overproduction of tools and an underproduction of badly needed goods elsewhere, this wasn't the only thing wrong with communism. In fact, I think this single idea was rather clever, that tools offered a doorway to making more things, which in the context of freedom and independence seems quite valuable. Producing the means of producing means itself is not unwise. It's all basic scalability, and it's a highly valuable concept.

But what about this makes something scalable? Intuitively, it makes sense, but how would one describe this? I would again borrow from the concepts of calculus to notate one as an integral, and the other its derivative. The tool and the manufacturing plant are integral to the end product, which is the derivative. As you integrate further,

18. Michael Pettis. *The Great Rebalancing*. Princeton University Press, 2013

which is in the direction of difficulty, you become more scalable. This, in economic terms, would generally make things cheaper and more efficient to produce.

Due to the Chinese inability to solve the integral of consumption within their society, their economic potential has yet to be fully unlocked. They've been unable to transition their value creation pipeline from general industries into entities that respond to economic demand because there's such low demand in the first place. Meaning their government has to continue investing in industries instead of generating entities that do this investing for them. None of this is a death sentence, but there's potential for improvement through the nature of the distributed calculations that an economy naturally performs. That being said, it's obviously not the intentions of the ruling Chinese political class to allow these kind of improvements to happen, so their system stagnates for different reasons than would otherwise be assumed looking only through an economic lens.

Overall, being unable to solve this integral is analogous to the crustacean being unable to reduce the number of its own limbs after specializing them. This is easy to see from an American perspective, as we've studied our own economy in more depth and it's reached a point where it's progressed further than the Chinese in terms of value creation. The flaws of the Chinese system are known flaws, rather than unknown flaws. Which makes it a useful case for the introduction of a model of description based on the concepts of derivatives and integrals. Such a model can be used to frame the inherent inefficiencies of a system relative to their potential for greater general scalability. The advantage offered by this is that if the model is general enough, where you can infer the same manner of flaw, such as a lack of scalability, and from both systems despite having different circumstances, then all that's left to assume a path of improvement is to determine which components of either system can be adjusted to allow for the next phase of growth to flourish.

So to continue, what kind of flaw would you uncover if you were to apply this kind of thinking to the American system? The answer isn't going to be obvious at first, because unlike the Chinese system there isn't a more advanced example to compare it to. But I can provide an answer throughout the course of this book, and summarize the ideas here in ways not unlike the philosophy behind the value perceived in the utility of Soviet tools.

You might protest that this clearly aligns with the flaw of dictating demand rather than allowing it to speak for itself, a key failure of communist systems. I don't intend to introduce such a flaw. However, allowing this flaw to exist within the analogy makes for an interesting point of comparison across the US and Chinese economies. Because if the model holds any value, it would reveal the potential to describe a flaw in the US economy parallel to the failings of the Chinese system in being unable to transition to a consumer based economy. But would it actually indicate something worth changing? In order to find a worthwhile target for this concept, because it operates under the assumption of constant demand, it would need to be something that's constantly active, and that the US economy can absolutely not do without. It would need to be a component of civilization that continually fuels the economy. What could that possibly be?

Like the potential for the Soviets to continue to climb their own economic ladder by fueling integrals, as the American system pipelines its value creation mechanisms through private entities capable of spurring growth, its flaw focuses around its inability to create more and improved entities capable of carrying this torch. The American shackles lie in being unable to translate material from the high quality knowledge base of its rich academic fields to the lower rungs of its attainment ladder. Doing so more effectively would improve upon the basis of entity creation capable of spurring growth. So the problem is the school system.

Much like how human development has been in lockstep with the salability of currency, the technological and psychosocial development of young children is in lockstep with the environment of their upbringing because they model their environment. What would benefit the American system is to grow higher-skill individuals capable of doing more on their own. Which is the principle of distributed scalability itself. A major obstacle to bringing about this improvement is the failing public school system typically offered across the entire country. Any conceptual improvements are met with heavy regulations, and quite often schools are forced to fit into the mold of state laws despite the fact that these state laws are the source of so many downstream flaws.

The process to establish a school is often severely hindered depending on the state, you typically need a large wallet and a huge compliance process just to be able to raise children. Even homeschooling is often forced to comply with state mandated curriculums. But this is so odd, hominids have been raising children for longer than humans have existed. This is an instinct derived from millions of years of evolutionary development. You can try to out-engineer the biological machine, and you would fail. Much like how disrespecting the concept of economic demand and reward under communist regimes eventually broke down their social and political fabric, the forced orchestration of specific upbringing standards independent of the wishes of parents and the best interest of children has destroyed the ability of the American public to have children that are themselves capable of doing the same. This fact is visible in the decrepit American birth rate, and is the same in every country that's integrated American standards in their upbringing process.

There's no innovation in education, but there always seems to be plenty of room for corruption and plagiarism. The never-ending array of grievance studies, the Ponzi scheme nature of student loans, and the ever-increasing prices offered by the college cartels is an obvious sign that the education system is a failed institution that pipelines children into an academic scam that has grown, in many ways, to subvert its own purpose.

I find the curriculum generally offered by schools to be underwhelming, and the culture to be stagnant from unimpressive and toxic individuals. The nature of these school systems seems designed to inhibit growth rather than enable it. Should this be surprising? It's a Marxist system, the state is raising your children, and everything related to this form of system has been proven time and time again to produce disastrous results. Teachers, who they work for, and the nature of the bureaucracy above them are all products of a failed university system. These are people who genuinely *believe* Marxist schools are the answer to all of life's problems, while ignoring the problems they themselves create. This societal class of teachers can't even do anything to change the nature of the schooling they participate in, yet it's strange to find individuals that actually believe such bureaucratic stagnation offers any benefit. At best they can alter whatever courses they might offer, but not the framework they operate on. The problem is derived from big picture cultural and societal norms for education. Expecting to make a serious difference in the lives of children by changing a few factors inside a modern classroom is like dumping bottled water into a muddy swamp with the expectation of making it clear enough to see the bottom.

So many factors of young lives are instilled through the education system. Political opinions, culture, beliefs, and the basis for cooperating with the rest of society are inevitably related to where someone went to school. Yet I find it odd that, when functioning properly, a school would offer the advice that a wise person can learn something from just about anyone they interact with. But that same system is caught up in a regulatory torrent of restricting, at every level, who a child is able to learn from, what they're able to learn, and how that learning takes place.

The weakness of the Chinese economy, the failure of the Soviet Union, and the undermining of so many public schools in the US are all due to a failure to properly model the complexity presented in their respective environments. Integrals are not being solved, scale is not being achieved, and end results are squandered in the face of many factors that would otherwise present better results had regulations not hindered innovation for the sake of bureaucracy.

With the abundance of information, and its complexity in our lives, so much history and culture have transpired to the point where it's easily forgotten that parenting is an evolutionary strategy based around yielding an advantage to the children who have the opportunity to learn directly from their predecessors. The problem with the school system is that children are not learning from someone who has experience in what they'll be doing for the rest of their lives. It's a fruitless apprenticeship. It even at some point crossed a threshold where it's turned into insidious indoctrination. Teachers in your child's school are likely the target of online ad campaigns that feed them rage bait in order to force their opinions in a specific direction. These algorithms can identify everything about you, they can determine when a woman is pregnant before she herself is even aware of it. These then go on to affect the children in their classroom, as a strategic interference in your life that you're not even aware of. Even if you want to claim this is crazy talk, the potential for this exploitation exists nonetheless. It's even more likely to happen with teachers who would laugh at this idea. There are much more insidious political and financial interventions that happen on a daily basis throughout our lives, by comparison this one would be extremely simple to pull off and I don't have faith in the established institutions to prevent it.

In fact, I'd like to see the evolution of the school system progress in a manner similar to that of Williston's law. Schools have been widely rolled out across the country to the point where they've become a cultural norm, and a legal requirement for every child to attend, the addition step has been satisfied. This is a step up from what had existed before it, but the approach is still very homogeneous. Specialization isn't yet widely implemented, and the best forms of deviation are likely the most expensive if you're not lucky enough to live in a locality with a great public school. You might feel the urge to argue that the specialization step comes during *college*. But let's be honest, there are multitudes of children who can do 4th grade work in kindergarten, and who can do college level work in middle school. Yet they can also be denied that opportunity. Any school system where this is even a possibility has completely failed its purpose.

The education process costs too much, takes too long, and doesn't provide enough for people who are ambitious and competitive at a young age. What better time to develop your advantages in life if not childhood itself? I would argue we're programmed to be that way at a young age, so as to not waste the rest of our lives trying to grow, and learn, when these make for but a single priority across the vast breadth of adulthood itself. It's such an easy feat for a young developing brain to learn as much as possible. The average school system instead sucks the soul out of your body through repetitive busywork intended more for the function of a daycare than for that of an honest academic pursuit. Perhaps you don't share this opinion, perhaps it's because the school you went to was different from that being described. Good for you, I'm happy for you. That's how it should be.

I'm not looking to force changes on every school system that's functioning properly. I'm not even looking to force changes at all, especially to people who don't want them. I want to point out the flaws in our current system, propose the legal grounds to fix them, and in the process do justice to the American economy as well as those who inhabit it. Put simply, to enable competition.

1.6 The Interactions of Organisms

It's strange what we call parasitism, competitive behavior, and symbiotic behavior amongst organisms. In the short term, a symbiote that cleans the teeth of a large mammal will yield a health benefit for that mammal, and protection plus a meal for itself. But in the long term, this could make the population of said large mammals vulnerable to foregoing selection for oral cleanliness. Providing a problem should those symbiotes ever disappear. Even if they don't, the long-term incentive for the symbiote may be to become a parasite. What was supposedly a mutually beneficial act of cooperation might actually become a toxic relationship through this *relaxed selection*.

What's denoted as parasitism seems more like a curse than a legitimate lifestyle. Parasites become extremely adapted to the internal environment of their hosts. If it was such a bad idea to be one, there wouldn't be so many around. It's a free ride, after all. You don't need to think much, don't need to do much. Something exists and you attach to it while it does all the work for you. But it's rarely anything other than an evolutionary dead end. There are a few examples of parasites becoming free-living, and some becoming symbiotes, but very rarely might such an overadapted organism survive the pressure of losing its host population. Becoming a parasite is truly the most unfortunate outcome, organisms are best off avoiding this path.

Brutal rivalries between a venomous predator and the immunity of its prey leads to benefits for either population involved. This kind of relationship usually develops over thousands of years from the same process repeating itself. The predator population making a more effective venom to subdue its prey with less energy. The prey population developing a stronger resistance to such venom every time one manages to survive. To the benefit of both, the advantages gained by either tend to even work outside this relationship. The predator has a weapon that maybe won't work on every potential opponent it could come across, but will generally work on more than just what it's been developed for due to large overlaps in the biochemical pathways affected. Likewise, the prey that developed an immunity to venom will likely fare better against other venoms, and they perhaps gained more than just that one trick along the way. What at face value seems like a purely antagonistic relationship confers unique advantages to either population involved. It's almost like fierce competition is more rewarding than cooperation.

Which is ironic. It seems natural to perceive it as something with more animosity, a brutal blood rivalry of thousands of years. But under a different light it's more like a partnership, whether the organisms involved understand that or not. A lot of medical and technological advancements were made during WWII, at the height of historical antagonism, so it's not like this concept is wrong, it's just that these benefits come at a cost. It's moreso that nothing we characterize is ever only as it appears. There are no simplicities, and everything has tradeoffs.

Likewise, the nature of the free market offers widespread benefit as a result of fierce competition. It's the constant innovation and pushback between entities that brings us better goods over time. By comparison, if such an entity were to be propped up by the government, it would fail as an institution. An entity that's always been forced to win real competitions will always outperform something that hasn't ever participated in one. Everything from the design of the operation, to the people in charge, are optimal for the performance of a competitive entity. So wherever possible, it would be wise to replace propped-up entities with competitive ones. Where in our society do we see this propping? Many places, but no doubt in education specifically. The schools don't compete with each other the way that businesses would. If hominids hadn't competed against each other, we would in no way have ever become intelligent in the first place. Competition breeds healthy complexity, as the economic machine is a largely non-zero-sum game.

The idea of a non-zero-sum game is an interesting one, to have your cake and eat it too. An even more interesting game is determining where and why certain aspects of life are non-zero-sum. After all, the more non-zero-sum games we play, the better off people should be. Part of the problem is in the lockstep of not understanding whether something necessarily qualifies as truly non-zero-sum. But what's easily identifiable are avenues of competition. The complex infrastructure delivered through competition is more beneficial for large swaths of people. So is this the case everywhere that we find growing complexity? If we find a decreasing complexity, is that a bad sign for societal cooperation? To start, let's look back into the mirror and approach some of the grandest unexplained complexities of our time.

We can offer a description for nearly any organ. A kidney filters blood, a lung exchanges gas. But what is a brain? A central node of the nervous system? That doesn't explain what goes on inside of it. Is it analogous to a computer? Calling it a computer doesn't really add up, even in the age of AI we have no computers completely capable of doing what the human brain is able to. Your computer won't be sad over your tardiness, but a brain experiences all kinds of emotions. It's a great mystery, possibly the greatest we'll ever come across.

You might think that which encompasses something is thereby more complex than what it encompasses. I would argue the opposite. A bowl is not more complex than the infinite combination of things you can place within it, nor is it more complex than what can be done inside of it. So something more complex than the brain might be that which the brain facilitates. That which stands directly between the most complex mystery ever known and the forefront of biological pioneering.

II

INTELLIGENCE

2.1 The Mystery of Intelligence

One definition of intelligence is *"the ability to acquire and apply knowledge and skills"*, according to the Oxford Dictionary. Which doesn't seem like a bad definition. It's a thorough seeming description. Offering even face value insight as to how one might measure such a thing. But I wonder if this statement is fair enough to encompass the entirety of intelligence? It certainly falls short of describing where it came from.

Would it be a skill to predict which knowledge and skills would be most advantageous? I think to consider this a kind of knowledge or skill leaves a gray area for how it's acquired. Acquiring it may be luck, depending on personal experience. If luck plays such a role in intelligence, then the acquisition thereof seems too extrinsic rather than intrinsic. But that's not what's assumed by the nature of intelligence, it's meant to be intrinsic to an individual.

Would determining a minimal set of skills that offers the most benefit for the least effort be considered intelligent? Certainly, but when you think of someone being *more* intelligent, you would naturally assume they acquire skills easier, and hold more knowledge. Whereas assuming the advantage of a minimal set implies a cost-benefit trade-off. Painting a picture that the scale is not simply linear, more may not necessarily be better. So if being more intelligent isn't a more intelligent choice, then what exactly is happening here?

In the society we live in, acquiring skills and applying knowledge is the bare minimum you offer for your survival. You might add *appropriately* at the end of the definition above to avoid the conundrum that civil engineering will do you no good if you're stranded in a desert. Or perhaps you could instead tack on *strategically* if you wanted to make a case for the smallest amount of effort in exchange for the most amount of value gained. But if either of these seem like too much time wasted, then maybe you'd add *wisely* while putting in as little effort possible to still get by while maintaining rich relationships with a loving family. Let me ask you now, which one is the intelligent choice? Without giving credence to your answer, I can predict that people will tend to answer differently. Meaning it's not easily agreed upon. I could bring up more definitions, I could fill the entire chapter with them. But they would ultimately fall to similar criticisms.

There's multiple poorly understood concepts that go on inside people's heads. At worst you might argue these things, either some or all, aren't necessarily intelligence. That they're just some aspect of consciousness. But how do you distinguish intelligence from consciousness? How do you separate any aspect of the mind from consciousness? Whether a survival instinct, an innate curiosity, or a lifelong habit, it may as well have something to do with intelligence if neither can be clearly delineated from consciousness. That's basically everything to do with the mind, no matter how you slice the pie.

We characterize intelligence the best we can, but the deeper you go the further it carries a pervasive mystery. It might be more interesting to define it by a threshold, such as being able to fully understand what intelligence actually is, which perhaps is more a level of *enlightenment* than intelligence. It seems like the original definition presented is more like an outside observer's idea of intelligence. So before we go deeper into what the insider's perspective might be, what's the absolute best that the outside observer's perspective has to offer? As this could still provide some keen insights.

2.2 Measurements of Intelligence

It's fair to say that intelligence isn't unidimensional. So if the metric of IQ is, then something is naturally wrong with it. You might then argue that some number of metrics, from some number of distinct tests, could then replace it to show a map of how one's skills perform. The problem being that there are plenty of baseline intelligent people with their head up their ass. They're littered all over the university system, like garbage on a sidewalk. So does scoring well on a test really measure intelligence? Well, tests, by their very nature, are fake. But are they useless?

If you follow people who study IQ, they would describe a few key patterns that basically make up the core of the information learned from studying it. The population of men displays slightly greater variability than the population of women, both higher highs and lower lows, and that the average of either population is basically the same[19]. That those on the extremes tend to be extremely rare. They would tell you there's more variation within races than across [20], arguing more widespread similarities than differences. That people's ability in one area of expertise tends to correlate with the performance they would give in any other area[21]. Most of all, they'll say intelligence doesn't change throughout someone's lifetime[22], and that intelligence is roughly 70% genetic[23].

There are problems with IQ as a metric that stem from problems with tests being a proxy for intelligence in general. In short, there's too much capability inherited throughout history that isn't accurately represented by some oversimplified metric being applied to an incredibly complex environment. Your brain didn't evolve to see the number 2 written on the inside of your eyelids in order to perceive there being two people in front of you. The perceptual input to your brain isn't simple. So if we're using simple perceptions to test something complex like human intelligence, it would indicate these tests aren't modeling the environments that people have modeled throughout their evolution.

People who study intelligence make theories about it, then attempt to characterize it through measurements. They build evidence based on a statistical bridge between predictions and outcomes, then revise their understandings whenever the evidence suggests doing so, which

19. Larry V Hedges and Amy Nowell. *Sex Differences in Mental Test Scores, Variability, and Numbers of High-Scoring Individuals.* Science, 1995

20. Richard J Herrnstein and Charles Murray. *The Bell Curve.* The Free Press, 1994

21. Charles Spearman. *General Intelligence, Objectively Determined and Measured.* American Journal of Psychology, 1904

22. Ian J Deary et al. *The Stability of Individual Differences in Mental Ability from Childhood to Old Age: Follow-up of the 1932 Scottish Mental Survey.* Intelligence, 2000

23. Thomas J Bouchard et al. *Sources of Human Psychological Differences.* Science, 1990

is much more comprehensive than any dictionary definition. But there's also no agreed upon classification of intelligence. Some people in this field argue grades are representative of IQ, that they're basically the same thing. You can argue this is scientific, and fair, and thereby a reasonable interpretation of the concept of intelligence. Maybe you'd argue that grades are more indicative of effort, and time spent studying, and this also has merit. But what I find most disagreeable with tests themselves are their repetitive use within schools. Just because some test of intelligence is *fair* in a scientific sense, doesn't mean its utility is valuable in an educational environment when used so aggressively. Even though you can practice to perform well on a test, does the information on a test always provide something useful to someone? Does repetitive testing actually offer more benefit to people's lives over learning real skills, making things, and judging a book by its contents rather than some average thereof? When taken to their extreme, tests themselves fall into the trap described by Goodhart's law: *when a measure becomes a target, it ceases to be a good measure.*

Statistics are often oversimplified in nature. Why is this? The field of statistics was founded in a day and age when computers weren't present, and calculations were done by hand. Many of the summarizing techniques were meant to simplify data to the point where they could be interpreted at all, because handling large datasets was another problem in itself for people looking to understand phenomena that required a lot of measurements. It's forced a lot of fields handling information into the culture of oversimplifying on a purely historical basis. These oversimplifications have been mixed in with philosophies of science and measurement to yield questionable methodology. It's not like statistics could be reinvented any differently in the modern day, there's nothing wrong with the math, per se, but the culture of applying statistics follows a specific pattern that seems out of place. Modern scientific endeavors tend to favor simple tests within complex environments that yield small correlations to justify even smaller discoveries from highly context-dependent scenarios. In science that involves studying people and their behavior, or intelligence, these correlations are laughably bad, typically falling flat with an R^2 of no more than 0.3. This result would be interpreted to mean that 30% of the variation in the measurements can be explained through the function used to model to any data presented, that function usually being that of a straight line.

The problem is that these statistics are being applied to situations where the potential number of confounding factors are too abundant to be accounted for. I'd even say they may be accounted for in ways that are either wrong or only half-correct, it's impossible to know. It would be convenient to say that there's never some foolproof indicator that all factors have been handled to their fullest potential, but there actually is, it would be seeing strong correlations from simple questions of these extremely complex scenarios. The problem being, that's not what we see at all. From these failed measurements it's evident that their statistics are failing to properly model these environments. A more artistic approach would use complex testing of complex environments that yields simple, elegant answers. To model complexity with complexity would mean to receive a confirmation far more acceptable than only some minority of variation. But that's only if these concepts are measurable at all.

A person's potential, and motivation for furthering it, are granted by experience rather than studying. You might argue that IQ tests are filled with pattern-matching, and are designed to be taken by people who don't have any academic background. Of which I would criticize that focusing on either a screen, or a piece of paper, is not where you'll find the apex of someone's pattern-matching abilities. The measurements aren't necessarily measuring what you'd expect them to, as they have rather inherent flaws. The patterns aren't hidden the way they are in real life. Even if you want to cling to the assessment of patterns as a utility, you would need to utilize more than just pattern-matching to get by in life. You can even obsessively search for every and any potential pattern that may or may not exist, but in navigating the patterns of patterns one would still need to assess which patterns are the most valuable to make use of. Whatever behavior acts to determine the value of those patterns is thereby a more appropriate classification of intelligence, I would even reason the assessment of value itself is that very classification.

We live in an ever-changing world, technology advances and new opportunities always arise. The art of engineering outpaces any classification thereof. Why should we measure for what was deemed useful 50 years ago? Rather, if you're *not* changing what you're measuring for in any meaningful way, then are you measuring anything meaningful?

I don't mean to imply that tests would make subtle changes to keep up with technological advancements. I would instead directly articulate, to leave no misunderstanding, that the ability to build is more useful than to follow the dogma of an older technological paradigm. The need for such tests is superceded by the knowledge that growth provides in a functioning economy that spurs civilizational advancement. The usefulness of any metric is outweighed, in practicality, by the door left open from the latent potential of never-ending novelties. The ceiling on knowledge simply doesn't exist, we live in a realm of infinite possibilities. Alongside the luck of experience, the real-world implications of measuring intelligence would only be correlated with success in an environment controlled by compulsive credentialism. Even with as much as has been accomplished through this long line of academic dogma, there's always a looming disaster waiting should you place too much trust in it. Stern belief invites irony.

The implied value of a test is that it measures value itself, but intelligence is not that which is inherently valuable, it's that which finds what's valuable. To mistake one for the other is to mistake a derivative for its integral. Perhaps you'd argue this difference is trivial. I would argue raising individuals to believe all these things about intelligence is as non-trivial as the outcomes of their very lives. To not find value in your own ability to find value is to have been subverted by those who sabotage your success. It's brainwashing. If these institutions are failing to produce people who have the proper amount of meaning in life to go on to be successful enough to buy a home and reproduce, then one might surmise that it's the environment they're modeling that's become oversimplified. It's become that way because the one thing these classes all have in common are grades, it's the measurement that supposedly acts as the basis for the scientific understanding of intelligence. These environments have come to model the oversimplified statistics that aren't respectful of complex environments. This blatant incomprehension of complexity is an affront to the nature of intelligence.

You can dumb people down to a measurement, then that just reduces their worth to their measurement. Whereas I believe intelligence encompasses something more akin to value-finding, and I find more value in giving these children, intelligent or not, a better environment to model. Their future isn't so set in stone that some single number will determine their life's outcome decades in advance. If there's a way to make sure that's not the case, to best ensure they can perform beyond what some numbers might indicate, it would be to not have them model the environment of such oversimplified measurements in the first place. The measurement, being so philosophically empty, basically inhibits people from reaching their maximum capacity. If for all the years you spent telling someone that they're stupid, or that they didn't work hard enough to get better scores on a test, they could have spent that time honing a trade or craft that they could use to make money and otherwise be more successful, or to make valuable things for other people, then it's not that person that's stupid. It's the school system.

Your potential, and how adept you are at using it, is a matter of practice. If you believe someone less intelligent, from today, could technologically outmaneuver a more intelligent adversary from 2000 years ago, if you believe in the progress of time, then you believe that any baseline inherited ability is negligible when compared to the fullest potential of those abilities. Then in believing this you'd also acknowledge that beliefs themselves play a part in harnessing this potential to its fullest. So what beliefs are we putting in the minds of children through these oversimplified metrics? Your potential matters as much as the philosophy used to ignite it. Do schools discuss this philosophy? Is a child judged on their ability to articulate theirs? Aside from the oversimplified nature of these metrics, the monolithic respect they garner in place of anything else that might be deemed valuable seems negligent of the multifaceted nature of life itself and what these skills are meant to accomplish.

The very purpose of intelligence is finding value. To measure for it independent of its purpose is a betrayal of its function. This very betrayal has become the primary export of the existing schooling paradigm. Just because you can calculate and predict something, does it mean you understand it? We can calculate all sorts of things about the cosmos, yet we still know practically nothing about it. Measuring intelligence independent of its proper context has only served to either stifle people's belief in their own abilities or to frustrate them with disagreement. Which, either way, then goes on to prevent them from reaching their full potential.

Finding value is not a unidimensional game. Even intelligence is only one avenue towards doing so. Part of it can be physical, explorational, and parts of it can require bravery, or kindness. In fact, just about every aspect of human existence can be said to be valuable for finding value. So why has intelligence, as a graded measurement, become so hyperfixated upon in schools? Are schools even doing a good job at measuring intelligence?

If a scientific article cited its methods as demoralizing large groups of teenagers in a prison-like environment, would anyone believe it was a worthwhile measure of their abilities? Where they sit down all day instead of exercise. Where they only follow directions rather than think for themselves. Where they're penalized for behaving in ways that humans have behaved for thousands of years. Where human nature itself is denied in favor of some ideal delusion. Would anyone consider that measurement to be valuable? Or rather, can you think of any way to make that measurement, as well as the outcomes of those children, even more valuable by tapping into the wisdom you've likely gained from going through this process yourself? Of course you can, because your instincts already know how. The school system has just been denying them.

A more sophisticated means of finding value isn't necessarily a more valuable way of finding value. Even something as widely appreciated as music is relatively easy to make proportional to how much it's worth. Sophisticated means can find amazing things. They can also run large risks, and finding things that run extremely large risks is not just a risk, it's a perpetual responsibility. If you disagree, then consider that North Korea has nuclear weapons.

People who study IQ would still argue that measurements of intelligence correlate with life outcomes, such as salary. Yet so many of these outcomes are gatekept by tests that are no different than those measurements. Even despite this, the R^2 of this correlation has only a single digit when written as a percentage, so should this be a surprise? Is there a better measurement to use? I would think so, and it has more to do with cultural doctrines rather than scientific observations. As neither IQ tests nor any other metric to measure such things can be derived from purely truthful information any more than they're based on religious beliefs. Finding value is not a test you sit down to prove your ability at, it's a lifelong endeavor. This topic will be further elaborated on later.

2.3 Boundaries of Convergence

Regardless of what anyone says, people will always try to approach an answer to what they don't understand, it's instinctual. Because some things are not easily definable, they're not easily understandable. It's only natural that people attempt to come to an understanding regardless of any obfuscations to their view. In fact, throughout this book I'll aim to better define some well known mysteries that I don't believe anyone has offered clear answers for. First, let's build on what we've already set out to do.

So what is intelligence, really? It's super intuitive to understand. Yet it's never simple to characterize. Do you think of what books someone's read? Their educational attainment? Whether they've built their own car? None of these will be perfectly representative, and you know that. But why is it so intuitive to know that none of them are perfect? You might say nothing other than intelligence is capable of defining. That intelligence is that which defines. But the concepts being defined exist independent of intelligence, they're not made, they're discovered.

Recognizing these axioms we've discovered so far isn't as impressive as using them well, and using them covers such a wide breadth of behavior that it only brings us back to wondering how best to distinguish the capabilities of any use from every other potential alternative, which is still the same as the problem of defining intelligence. Does the problem lie solely with understanding intelligence? Sure, but that itself is another oversimplification. When you don't understand something it leads you to a paradoxical lack of information. There's a failure in understanding the concept of intelligence that isn't describable due to the failure in understanding the concept of intelligence... It's the nature of defining itself that's meant to overcome this paradox, but that alone doesn't generate answers.

To try and describe the paradox, the simple understanding of intelligence spans a breadth not easily definable. It's *too* observable relative to any descriptions offered for it, they fail to encompass what's representative of the concept. So where might we look to better define it?

Instead of simply redefining intelligence, to arrive at all the same flaws, I'll reinterpret the basis of its integral and redefine definitions themselves. Boundaries of convergence are the approach of a definition from *two* different perspectives. In extreme cases they can be suicidal nihilism and conspiratorial paranoia. The truth would be somewhere in the middle, but still not concisely distinguishable. Either one alone could even be a form of extremism, but together they make a method of refining the domain of uncertainty. After all, does it make sense that measurements are always denoted with their errors, yet definitions are purely singular? That won't work well for things we barely understand. To ascribe definitions as concise monoliths can easily assume their meaning is created, rather than discovered.

A wide boundary can mean two things, either a lack of information or a great complexity. It could also represent a lot of social disagreement. But unlike what you might expect, the art of defining isn't necessarily in aiming for correctness. In aiming to define *to define* I'll simply say it's to *not be incorrect*.

It's not that the core aspects of intelligence even need to be changed, but its definition needs a reformatting. I want to rearrange what factors are intrinsic and extrinsic to the concept of intelligence provided. Much like how I'm claiming this is an insider's perspective, as opposed to that of an outsider's, I want to approach the definition from two different directions. To arrive at a definition through convergence of the aspects inherent to the concept itself, the same way multiple independent species had converged on the phenotype of a crab. Much like the two directions one could use to approach a function they're trying to model, through either derivation or integration. I'm looking for what's in between the two. Intelligence, in its widest reaching yet most generalizable functionality, aims to grasp knowledge of known factors, analysis of known unknown factors, and the perception of unknown unknowns and beyond. Or more simply, the boundaries we arrive at are *knowns* and *unknowns*.

There aren't disagreements on how to deal with known factors of life, dogma comes from the existing solutions to known problems. But measuring people on how well they perform some dogmatic function is just a failed test of aptitude. So it's generally not well understood information that differentiates one person from another, given that either isn't lacking. Rather, it's the handling of unknowns that further differentiates behavior across individuals in ways I would classify as differences in intelligence. The coherence to work with known factors, and the depth of which one can question the unknown. Intelligence is the utilization of a library of known factors that expands into a network of unknown factors and beyond.

Networks, like expansive maps of nodes and connections, can be made and utilized in ways equally flexible to the nature of intelligence itself. So the nature of questioning unknowns is as much an art form as it is a calculation. The depth to which one can question, and the rate at which one's questioning leads to accurate understandings, operates as advantages should they perform well. Regarding properties of the network, I would state it's the magnitude of unknowns that sit at the pinnacle of what intelligence itself attempts to create defining boundaries for. As these concepts are discovered, and not made, intelligence is a manner of approximating the boundaries of concepts we've yet to understand.

2.4 Elites and Selection

If you want to improve a population, you pick off the weak. If you want to destroy a population, you pick off the strong. A lion only needs to catch the slowest gazelle. But every time it does, the population of gazelles hypothetically become a little faster, and the lion then has to match this improvement. It's no different to the predator-prey dynamic discussed previously. But what if the lion caught the fastest, gazelle every time it hunted? Selection would dictate the population of gazelles would in fact be slower. When you remove the strong, fast, and/or smart from a population, the population suffers at the genetic and sociological levels. Which perfectly describes the effects of extreme game hunting without limitation, as well as communism.

The gazelle's speed doesn't increase forever, neither does the lion's ability to hunt. There comes a point where evolution caps out at physical limitations dependent on the size of the animal. If either of these factors change, something else also would. A faster gazelle might mean a smaller, or lighter, gazelle, which would cause their population to lose more members in order to feed the same number of lions. There's no free lunch, and tradeoffs can exist at either the individual and/or group level.

Likewise, the changes to human intelligence have probably improved in a number of ways through competition both within and across groups. Throughout this process, the evolution of the group would then be in lockstep with the evolution of individuals. Intelligence is not something that developed independent of collective wellbeing.

The general deduction regarding extinct hominids is that they were less intelligent than modern humans. There's been attempts to support the case for Neanderthals being less intelligent based on skull physiology. But the same can't yet be said for Denisovans as we don't have these fossils. In fact, if we can't find any of their remains, one might conclude they were fairly intelligent. It could suggest they held rituals for their dead in some way that either hid, or destroyed their bodies.

Does human intelligence even need to grow infinitely? The growth of human knowledge has likely far outpaced the growth of human intelligence, the former making up for the latter. Human cooperation and technological advancement will probably supercede knowledge as the primary mode of growth for civilizational development, they may even be in lockstep with one another. That's not to say we're free from selection, however. Independent of upper or lower limits, the population at large can become more or less intelligent. This is dependent on where societal reinforcements are directing people.

Forcefully imposing some standard of selection has been called eugenics. It isn't popular, and it's got a major flaw that by aiming for something, you have to first determine what to aim for. The concept of eugenics might work in a lab with a few animals, but for hundreds of millions to billions of people, that govern themselves, this process would inevitably become political. Whatever target they aim for is only going to come back to haunt them. The opposite would be even worse, a dysgenic outcome where all the worst behaviors are rewarded, and the traits and culture passed on become self-destructive. Yet these aren't even opposites, they're one and the same. Any form of eugenics automatically becomes dysgenic. The solution to this dilemma was highlighted earlier. Just as in aiming for correctness, the answer is not to be correct but rather to *not be incorrect*. Like with genetic mutations, insisting you already know best will only guarantee you make terrible decisions. *Correct* in this instance isn't a real concept, because there's no way of targeting an ideal due to there being no legitimate way to, a healthy target to aim for is to be non-dysgenic. Which simultaneously enables any and all avenues of success to come to fruition organically, whatever they may be.

Are differences in intelligence zero-sum? No, differences across a population are like hedged bets. You can never be sure of what's actually advantageous, and how much it takes for something to become a bad thing. Variations in intelligence are a hedged bet on the survival of the group any person belongs to. Elite level intelligence is useful until there's too many elites, and not enough of something else. Whichever traits are advantageous at any given time are not obvious, despite that people tend to believe in the modern day that intelligence will lead you to a better job, and therefore a better life. It may also lead you to never-ending responsibility, or a job market that isn't hiring.

Intelligence isn't necessarily everything. So what's on the other side of its coin? A proper counterbalance, not something like stupidity. Two things opposed don't stand opposite. What's something that comes in handy when intelligence doesn't? I would say it's resilience, it's the ability to put up with something you can't or don't need to solve. For when you may not have intelligence as a possible avenue to solve your problems, resilience then becomes the natural solution. Willingness to overcomplicate your problems might be a disadvantage relative to those who can put up with them.

So this presents an interesting conundrum. People tend to want their children to utilize their intelligence more than they, as parents, may have been able to in order to succeed in life. History doesn't really provide much in the way of suggesting a successful and humane method of societal selection outside fair laws and economic development. But it does specify that too much of anything is a bad thing, including elites.

So what exactly are *elites*, and do you want your child to be one? Every advantage comes with a disadvantage. Everything consists of tradeoffs to the point where it may as well be a physical rule. So what's the tradeoffs of intelligence? It looks like highly specialized fields consist of people who work in derivatives at the end of a long chain of integrals, which often seems to block their worldview. Elites also carry more risk, which is why they tend to be replaced in revolutions[24]. Throughout the cycles of history, elites go into and out of power. They get overthrown, and thrown out. To be a part of a failed elite class means to lose everything.

The purpose of the university system seemed to be to produce elites, but printing diplomas didn't cure stupidity. The US and

24. Crane Brinton. *The Anatomy of Revolution*. WW Norton & Company, 1938

many other countries who employ similar systems all share the same disastrous birth rate. Elites can't be made through production, they can only be selected for. Or can they? If knowledge growth outpaces intellectual growth, and both are dwarfed by technological growth, then maybe production is possible to some degree that wouldn't otherwise be accessible in a less scalable economy. Even though this may be the case, we don't currently have a societal implementation that achieves this goal. This book will address this possibility.

In the US, the university students at large are going into obscene debt to get diplomas that are worth less than the paper they're printed on. For many graduates, the selection mechanism has been cast onto them as debt, and the circumstances to pay it off. It seems like an extremely zero-sum method, which shouldn't be necessary. Regardless, it came into existence through the federal government issuing debt to anyone who asked. For the ones who pass the selection, it seems highly likely they were already born into families that came from actual elite selection mechanisms of the past.

Perhaps it's a good thing that elite production is such a difficult process, that selection doesn't bend the knee to uniformity. For the sake of civilizational development, let's assume greater population intelligence is a good thing. That even if you have dirty jobs, there's always a smarter way to do them. It then seems to be genuinely mysterious that multiple systems of elite selection had most definitely existed in the past, and are lost to history. How were these systems made in the first place? Is it really possible for a society to, perhaps over hundreds of years, assemble itself into a mechanism favorable for not just elite selection, but elite production?

I can offer some answers which will come in later chapters. For now, let's figure out how intelligent, or not, organisms assemble themselves in ways that make sense for their own selection. Is it possible to find mechanisms by which elite selection methods spontaneously arise?

2.5 The Broken Compass

Try, fail, and fail again. As where there's opportunity, there's failure. When a man and a woman really love each other, it means the woman's done what's called a shit-test. It's there to test someone's confidence. To check whether their character is stable under pressure. This doesn't just happen with individuals. Civilization was not born by luck, it was born by a civilization-building mechanism akin to a shit-test.

As the scale of communication grew over the decades, starting with telephones and becoming social media, this process had been scaling itself up. Maybe even since the invention of the printing press. As the uncertainty of the effects of the scale of social media became apparent, this uncertainty was reflected throughout the portion of the population sensitive to these changes. It triggered an instinctual response en masse. Throughout the last decade, podcasters, content creators, and individuals of great character stood up and voiced their opinions in the face of censorship, corruption, and malicious tyranny. I don't wish to speak too soon, but it seems we're on the blooming end of a new era where confidence in media can be restored due to it resting faithfully on the reputations of those who weathered the storm publicly, and without flinching. Society itself seems to have also decided upon this, where the most popular mode of communication is no longer in the hands of now deprecated media outlets. But I feel there's something that's been overlooked. Most people have, and in a lot of cases rightfully so, assumed the extreme left-wing that had festered over the last decade had grown from genuine evils. In some cases this isn't entirely wrong, but I also see this through a different lens. It was a civilizational shit-test. Making this festering reaction a feature, not a bug.

From the perspective granted from this very rare age in time, where uncertainty itself was so widespread that it caused this group to be able to collectively shake our civilizational foundations, we learn a very important lesson about human instincts. A lesson that shows us where we came from. That through the most chaotic of circumstances, the right people will stand their ground and prevail. This is an instinctual civilization-building process. Some people might refer to this as a kind of hero's journey. But in the case where the heroes are abundant, and the villains are ambiguous, I'll refer to this as the broken compass.

Rather than focusing on the journey of a hero, I would focus on the mistakes of their opposition. As I find a fascinating nuance in where they went wrong. They didn't just fail, they failed in a spectacular way. These people, a lot of the time, have good intentions. They don't want to bankrupt society, or tear it down, despite the fact that many of them have claimed these things publicly. In every area where they tried to exert power, there was once a power vacuum. The gravitation towards it was a feature, not a bug.

Should this vacuum have never been approached, it could have invited worse figures to seize the same ground. Or worse, the stability that may now be built upon it would never have come into place. Leftists had basically pointed out every area where a serious societal weakness was exposed. They were able to lock onto all the flaws that would have otherwise not been addressed. As the communists, censors, and tyrants, were defeated by way of losing popularity, every space they occupied began to be inhabited by a more worthy hegemon. The reputations of those who challenged them grew, and the credibility of those who stood firm against their demands are now widely known for their bravery. Like a woman finally finding a stable man to settle down with.

This broken compass does a number of important things. It creates problems, and gives people an occasion to rise to. It points out structural flaws in the existing social fabric. I can't understate the rarity of this age enough, where we've had the opportunity to observe this. Never would we have ever had what was essentially a social collapse, all while still having a functioning economy. At no point prior would there have ever been the technology to actually view the breakdown of our own social fabric, in real time, the way we have with social media and video. It would be like if credit scores were invented just a single year after the Great Depression, while simultaneously assigning the appropriate reputations of every businessman and banker in the country. It's created a media ecosystem resistant to communists, censorship, and tyrants. Like it kept forcing rounds of the prisoner's dilemma until it found people not willing to defect on each other. No propped-up private or public initiative could have accomplished this in just 10 years. Because the only way to accomplish it is not to aim at this goal, but to try to *not* accomplish its opposite. Like walking up a mountain backwards, like steering a ship blindfolded, like solving an integral.

So while many are probably still caught up in this mess, and its aftermath, I actually find this astounding. I'd like to write this section in dedication to this process. This civilization-building mechanism forces intelligence, character, and the selection thereof, to the forefront of human attention. This is not luck, this is by design. There's an extremely intricate instinct packed inside this event, and it's something that's always been around, yet is naturally elusive.

The broken compass is specifically designed to fail for the same reason that we implement such concepts in our engineering designs. If something fails predictably, it presents the opportunity to cause the least amount of harm to anything involved. The predictability is key to more than just failure. It leads us in the wrong direction both philosophically and practically, pointing us towards the most optimal lessons for us to learn based on a momentary predicament. It does this by forcing us to make mistakes. From these mistakes come predictable lessons. Though these lessons are much more predictable in hindsight, which is what's rather amazing about it as this starts to describe what exactly the human machine is. The lessons learned from those mistakes are integrals to some derivative. The incorrect directions you end up being pointed in are derivatives of the wrong integral. To solve this puzzle is to find the answers to a question that no one knows to ask. The broken compass is a mechanism for deriving what the true first principles of a conundrum actually are, when you're not even aware of the conundrum nor its problems to begin with. Which is its main function, blind problem-finding.

It facilitates the slow removal of doubt in people's minds about how to improve whatever failing aspects of society are becoming increasingly obvious. The people who can find the solution to these problems aren't the same demographic as those who can point towards the need for the problem to be solved in the first place. It's like one set of people are acting as direction finders, and always pointing towards a problem. They basically build something resembling a half decent idea in the wrong place as a starting point for the next civilizational structure to take shape, like a multifaceted devil's advocate. It catalyzes an increase in the complexity of your ignorance to be higher than the solution requires so that the relative simplicity of the truth becomes clear. It's no different to how even inaccurate scientific assessments lead people towards constructive debunkings that go on to spur the making of better ideas.

The broken compass doesn't just point you in one wrong direction, it points you in every wrong direction. You can even say it's not just designed to fail in a certain way, it's *meant* to fail in every way. That failing *is* its function. Because the broken compass iterates unknowns. It attempts a constant boundary formation of the unknown, it's a hard-coded simulation of that very function.

Having highlighted a societal selection mechanism on the basis of competence, it's likely opened more doors than were opened previously. Which is befitting of mysteries in general. How did this process form? Will truth even help us in understanding this? Surprisingly, probably not. But perhaps there's something more appropriate to use than truth itself. Maybe truth is too simple for the basis of something as intricate as intelligence. Where truth is ill-defined, where else can we look?

III

IRONY

3.1 A Unit of Reality

Truth is thought of as this rigid and unchanging structure. Like every piece of truth is supposed to be a permanent fixture of the universe. But truth itself always depends upon some requirement, some precursor to its existence. Even molecular forces exist *because* of some phenomenon, the world around us follows a chain of causality, which is how anything exists in the first place. If truth has any requirements at all, then truth itself is emergent, where emergence is what yields some inevitable consequence that arises as a phenomenon from a system of interactions. But it would subsequently argue that just because something can happen doesn't mean it must happen, the universe would then be governed by chance rather than truths. Which only surrounds this idea of truth in paradox. One might then proceed to notice the only way to wrangle truth out of its own emergent paradox is to embrace the emergence of this irony.

Even if you insist the universe is still ultimately governed by underlying truths, the interactions thereof spawn a combinatoric explosion of potential outcomes. All of which are then emergent when they *do* occur. The potential outcomes that don't occur can't even lay claim to their own existence, they would remain a possibility until they do. But incidentality isn't a realistic interpretation of everything we see around us, there was no alternative to planets, stars, and black holes. There was no other manifestation of celestial bodies likely to form besides that which we've obsessively observed for thousands of years. So is it a truth that black holes are inevitable? No matter how much effort you exert, they're not leaving, and you're not going to prevent their formation. The existence of black holes, even if transient, is not optional. Why should atoms be any different?

I think truth itself isn't so well-defined to handle these cases. If black holes are inevitable, it may as well be a truth that they *will* exist. But something existing isn't seen as a truth, a truth is usually a principle used by things that *do* exist. Which I feel muddies this line to the point where we need to find an entirely new basis for classifying information. Truth was meant to be a contract with reality, an honesty of the universe, but now I feel the universe is lying to me about the concept of truth. Jordan Peterson has broken this down between Newtonian truth and Darwinian truth. Meaning it's a Newtonian truth that black holes *can* form, and a Darwinian truth that they *do*. But the fact that there now needs to be this stratified understanding of truth, isn't that ironic? On the essence of what's supposed to be an axiom of clear pictures, there are no clear pictures, and that's entirely truthful.

It seems factual that truth is always present to spawn irony, and irony to spawn truth. Like cyclic derivatives. But is this just a matter of semantics? The point of truth, the reason we rely on facts, is for the interpretation of information. And information, like the emergence of truth, has a *sequentiality*.

As conceptually alternative philosophical cornerstones, truth and irony operate at alternating levels of consistency. Truth dictates within the bounds of an increasingly linear display of a non-linear function, as you decrease the scale of visual range. Whereas irony is the bridge that links multiple concepts across large swaths of truth.

The inherent structures of information will always lead towards truth when investigated. You can believe in truth when you want practical reliance on something tangible, and information will lead the way to it as long as you respect its interpretation as an art. The concept of truth is real, and you can find it where we're still naive enough to need it. Otherwise, you'd be better off looking for irony.

Looked at unidimensionally, irony exists as a string of continual contradictions. Which may itself seem contradictory as a utility of interpretation, but this pattern happens to better illustrate the nature of information more than truth ever could. There's always an exception to every rule. There are endless exceptions that prevent causal uniformity. Reality doesn't prefer exceptions, yet always makes way for them.

Irony itself is intrinsic to information, that which we are creatures of. Natural selection itself is a process of continually adapting along ironic circumstances. Irony is the currency of adaptation.

Irony is a better descriptor of reality than truth, it's the fabric of interaction. Irony stands guard at the toll that time takes as it leads things towards their natural destruction. It dictates not only that nothing is entirely black nor white, but moreso that we live amongst a myriad of tradeoffs. In the context of where it exists, irony is to complexity what money is to a market economy.

Irony is basically a unit of reality, like an inch, or a second. It's something we all understand but can't physically observe. The abstraction of information follows that truth is to irony as irony is to paradox. Any further abstraction wouldn't make sense to us, it wouldn't make sense at all. But this doesn't mean a paradox presented is truly a paradox, it's more likely that a paradox presents itself when the information to grasp it hasn't yet been achieved. So which came first, the chicken or the egg? Without the concept of evolution it's a very difficult question to understand. To grasp the paradox requires the acknowledgement that regardless of whichever came first, that life itself had a beginning and grew to become the form it holds today. That life itself is ever-changing, and at some point the laying of hard-shelled eggs came to replace the soft-shelled eggs that came before them.

3.2 Symbolic Origins of Life

So where did life begin? To answer that question we're going to take the scenic route. I'm going to ignore highly specific details both here and throughout this book, as I'm not looking to explain specific structures and reactions. I'm looking to explain the big picture that I feel is lacking in the modern day, and all the valuable parallels that can be found along the way. I'll introduce, conceptually, the manner in which life began without considering the exact moment it occurred (which will be in the next chapter).

The mixture of various molecules spread across the early ocean of Earth, that eventually formed life, was known as the primordial soup, where we can expect these events to take place. I'll speak vaguely about a hypothetical structure that existed either before or during its lifetime. Because structure is an interesting topic, structure bestows function. With a keen eye, function can be inferred from structure. A non-exhaustive list of the evolution of this form of thinking would include reasoning that was used by Plato when describing human collectives [25], explanations of organismal utility by Aristotle and Galen to understand the body designs of organisms[26,27], as well as the systematizations of Georges Cuvier who realized that anatomical structures offer both forward and reversible predictive gateways to understanding everything from the habits to habitats of an organism[28,29]. Cuvier went further to insist that there must be a correlation between the parts of an organism, that teeth made to chew specific kinds of food need to be matched with the organs required to digest it. This is a central underpinning to every practical device in our daily lives, and all the same in the nature of molecular interactions. Function is something that can be subverted, and subversion itself can also be a function.

Let's say you have a molecule, prior to the formation of life, that's been made through some natural process. It's floating around the ocean, just like all the other molecules, and it's not the only one of its kind. It has a specific function, a catalytic function. It alters other molecules if they have a specific structure. From this scenario, there's multiple ways its function can be subverted. It can run out of things to alter, and therefore have no function left to perform. This wouldn't affect it directly, but it would effectively be subverted. It could subvert itself by altering its own catalytic site as a part of the reaction, preventing it from accelerating any other reactions until its own structure is remodified. It could be altered by some other molecule also acting as a catalyst, preventing it from catalyzing other reactions. Or it could do the most ironic thing possible and fuel its own doom loop, where a chain of multiple reactions, originating with our friendly neighborhood catalyst, end up causing another molecule to be modified, that then comes and modifies the original in a way that prevents its catalytic properties from being used. Or something could destroy it altogether.

When talking about the molecules that eventually formed life, the opportunities for these molecules were abundant. There was a lot of potential energy in the form of potential subversion. There was also

25. Plato. *The Republic*. 375 BCE
26. Aristotle. *The Parts of Animals*. 350 BCE
27. Galen. *On the Usefulness of the Parts of the Body*. 165
28. Georges Cuvier. *Lectures on Comparative Anatomy*. Baudouin, 1800–1805
29. Georges Cuvier. *Research on the Fossil Bones of Quadrupeds*. Deterville, 1812

the potential for them to work together, of which the opportunities for would have arguably been much scarcer than the number of potential subversions. This coordinated option would be the opposite of a doom loop, where one catalyst feeds a reaction towards the next catalyst, which feeds an entire loop that in some way provides energy to fuel its own reinitiation. The opportunity for their organized coordination would have been a subversion of the available individual subversions.

Classifying reactions as a form of subversion is a somewhat interpretive choice, yet it seems like a fair enough description to broadly classify networks of enzymatic interactions. You might argue an alternate perspective based around the term *modification*. So why must this all need to be viewed through the lens of subversion? Because irony is a subversion of expectations. Where's the expectation? It's momentary. Think of yourself as an outside observer to the process. There's multiple kinds of outside observers. One can be outside the occurrence, and one can be outside its time frame. As you're reading this, you're outside of the time frame. But to an observer only outside the occurrence, someone who's independent of the actions taking place but who simultaneously witnesses them occurring in real time, the basic routes of subversion I just described are the boom and bust cycle of this molecule and its function at a population level. Throughout these prior routes of individual subversion there would be an increase in the amount of catalysis taking place, followed by an eventual dying off. Whether these individual subversions are permanent or not is somewhat irrelevant, because the end result of the big picture is the coordinated outcome.

We all know the end of the story, the subversion of subversions won out. Defeating the defeat of expectations, and here we are. Life became a self-designing chemical reaction. Although instead of an actual cyclic reaction, it may have been made up of physical functions that reinforced the existence of one another through the same metaphor. It's difficult to know the truth, but irony can shed light in places where truth can't reach. The nature of the subversion of subversions was undeniably the key. Subversion is the core implementation of life, and it seems to model irony itself.

3.3 Competition

Those who play better games, win better prizes. Competition is a game that nurtures complexity. True selection *must* come from competition, it has no other source. To inhibit competition is to cripple society from both the bottom-up and top-down. All the most important and intricate mechanisms, societally and biologically, have constant pushback from opposition. Competition is *sacred.*

What makes something sacred? It's a representation of a fundamental axiom of the universe. In the simplest terms it's a *scalable truth*, where one need not feel like their estimation is but a small linear portion of a non-linear function, but can instead rest assured the function is truly just a straight line. Competition is the lifeblood of interactions themselves. Economies don't survive without it, the most convenient examples being the controlled economies of communism. There would be no ecosystem for which organisms could thrive if not for the competing behaviors of every species acting in their own best interest.

But too much of anything can be a bad thing, you wouldn't want to have to fight to the death every time you shop at a grocery store. Like the growth of complexity throughout the history of our planet, our competitions have come to refine themselves in ways analogous to the complexity of modern organisms. We compete in order to survive, so any competitions should be respectful of that very fact. To subvert competition is to insist on unfairness.

Enabling competition is no different than enabling complexity. Western culture has come to view people as equals under the law, which is a fine balance. It's the right choice to enable competition across individuals that doesn't undermine basic fairness. But that's all it should be. There should *only* be equality under the law, any other form would only inhibit competition. Any other forms of *equality* only results in discrimination. If you treat people fairly, you win the best possible rewards. If you force someone to treat people *fairly* regardless of their behavior, you undermine any potential mutual benefit.

The evolutionary strategies of men are vastly different from the evolutionary strategies of women, they play different games, perceive different threats, and have been selected for different behaviors. Likewise, people in different environments, separated for thousands of years, will develop different characteristics, like any other organism. They develop different cultures, different religions, and will often value and respect different behaviors. Even more, they tend to arrive at different interpretations of their purpose in life. Certain groups aren't replaceable with others, and it makes no sense to believe this when imagining how these groups formed in the first place. The prevailing insistence of their total equality has only come to hurt the goals of the people who stand so staunchly for upholding this lie. We don't pretend people are equals when it comes to athleticism, artistic talent, or the ability to cook edible food. People aren't even equal *within* any of these classifications, because people are never equal in general. The term *equal* isn't even the right term to use in some of these cases, as it's implying some grand unidimensional hierarchy where you're either better or worse than everyone else.

A better word is just *different*, they've had to survive in different environments, overcome different problems, and throughout time became different people. There's no need to put people down over there being differences, it just makes more sense to set these expectations early in life, rather than living a lie only to become frustrated when later faced with reality. It's *because* people aren't equal in life that we find reason to treat them equally under the law, it's why we interact with courtesy and respect. People have been hostile to anyone speaking on this topic for decades, because they assume truth to be nihilistic. Yet that preference for nihilism is a religious choice, the truth of the matter is that truth isn't nihilistic. Truth has been the saving grace of civilization for thousands of years, the way we've chosen to not only disregarded it but to ostracize it in the modern day is an outright catastrophe, it means we've completely lost track of it. The truth is, like everything else, these differences confer neither pure advantage nor disadvantage, everything is made of tradeoffs.

This mindset has persisted since at least the American Civil War, perhaps longer, and although so much time has passed since, people still hold this too close to their heart for a war they didn't participate in, and for circumstances they've never lived under. Too many aren't able to realize that the truth has evolved. Unlike how the sentiment of who *won* WWII had changed from being the Soviets to the Americans over the course of multiple decades, the rightful interpretation of the American Civil War continues to be ignored by people who have proven, over multiple decades, to be no better than the supposed *racists* they rally against. When an American proudly claims the North had defeated racism in the civil war, it stands to be a testament to the lack of evolution in this realm of thinking. The North had done more than defeat the South, they *saved* them from the cruelties of slavery, and from the lesser potential they were crafting of their own future. Now, there are new groups crafting the same lack of potential for themselves, and it's worth dragging them out of that hole they dig for themselves. Political motivations for citing instances of legitimate racial inequality and discrimination in the 20th century have transformed into astroturfing instances of discrimination with false victimhood in the modern day[30]. The messaging has yet to evolve towards an appropriate understanding of human nature by refusing to admit that people are flawed, despite the glaring flaws in character of the groups in the modern day who chant these slogans about equality, paint victims out of criminals, and patronize every demographic they supposedly support. Think of this what you will, but surely you won't tell me it isn't ironic?

The concept of irony rules so many of the interactions we have, especially those of great tension. Both individual interactions, and across populations. The so-called *anti-racists* of the universities have found themselves gazing into an abyss by demanding equality that already exists. The ideologies of these groups are funded by actors far disconnected from their consequences, and they've essentially formed a religion over this very cause. If the universities are an entirely separate universe from the rest of the country, then the school systems are failing to model their environment. Competition in the religious realm would force them to turn heel and adopt a more reasonable message. It would result in an equilibrium better for all parties involved. Amongst many other things, this is a book aimed at describing the nature intelligence, **this is also the formal establishment of a religion.** As for the basis of the religion, you're already reading it. For every aspect of our academic dogma, legal precedents, and cultural baseline that stands unquestioned, I'm going to introduce competition. A lack of competition breeds bad outcomes, so throughout this book I'll challenge ideas that other people refuse to.

3.4 Spawning Complexity

In the modern day we explain people's consciousness through the lens of psychology, at the level of an individual. But ideologies, polit-

30. Wilfred Reilly. *Hate Crime Hoax*. Regnery Publishing, 2019

ical beliefs, and philosophies all have clear lines of inheritance from a predecessor. Most people don't exactly make their own beliefs, those who do run a large risk of being less likely to be successful. Descriptions like these make way for the thought that such things belong more to groups than individuals, which seems to not be incorrect.

People obviously want to find axioms to live their lives by, they're prone to doing so. As that would be easiest, like a path of least resistance. Bad ideas fail to model the complexity of our environment, and it's hard not to arrive at them as it's the act of attempting to define *good*. These definitions tend to become the justification for some form of action. But *good* isn't something you do, good isn't an action, it's a circumstance. From so many learning bad ideas in the school system, bad ideas have run rampant for more than a decade. It's not that anyone is necessarily in search of an oversimplification of the concept of *good*, they're in search of a proper philosophy and likely haven't heard one. Perhaps they're in search of a good leader, or role model, and have never met one.

Living life based on an oversimplification, instead of a genuine philosophy and religion, is self-destructive. But let's try twisting the truth with some irony, there should still be one lone oversimplification to live your life by that acts as the exception to that rule. Which specifically, would be to not live life based on any one rule, any oversimplifications. It's to appropriately respect the complexity of every scenario you find yourself in. Which isn't just ironic, it's poetic. It leverages irony to the point where the simplest thing to live your life by is to never live life by any mode of oversimplification. It spurs changes that are orders of magnitude more rewarding than the initial effort. This leveraging actually spawns complexity out of thin air from something as simple as a personal decision. Which needs to be matched with responsibility, as the reward will match the game.

Everything will come back to either help you or haunt you, depending on your choices. Much like the subversions of individual biomolecules, the same outcomes befall people and their groups. A refusal to appropriately model complexity invites oversimplifications that form the basis for belief structures that are unable to adapt to new information and ultimately meet their subversion. Stern belief invites irony. It's why gazing into an abyss is a cyclic prophecy. Emulating the subversion of subversions means to back away from racism. To claim to be the *opposite* of a racist, like aiming for correctness, is to eventually meet with the subversion of that oversimplification. You can impose your morality on others, you can even impose your morality about imposing morality on others, this would be the nature of irony meeting complexity to make a self-destructive machine that's destined to fail. It's all another act of Goodhart's law.

The First Amendment is a great example of these principles being used well. To not make laws about speech is wise. Because it gets stupid for politicians to waste time bickering about language instead of doing their job. Secondly, it's a law that enables other laws to be more respectable. Because you're always able to express dissent. A society that makes something taboo to speak about ends up making those taboo topics into the most needed conversations to have. Making something more forbidden only makes it more desirable, and eventually necessary.

The same mechanisms cause cyclic events all throughout the world and its history. Like the *flippenings* of the cryptocurrency community reflected on by Balaji Srinivasan[**31**]. Balaji highlights multiple changes to economic paradigms throughout recent history, that see their course reversed across different continents at the same time. He also highlights the changing of institutions, culture, and trade through the alternation of centralization and decentralization. Which are basically the same things as individual subversions, but at a civilizational level. They're like macroironic civilizational restructurings.

The dawn of a new geopolitical paradigm often comes through a manifestation of complacency overtaken by that of determination. With vices comes virtue, almost as if there isn't enough determination to go around. Which is not unlike how a shrinking economy can reverse its fate with a new wave of its own global competitiveness due to the opportunity granted to foreign investors from favorable currency exchange rates. Anyone with less to lose always has more to gain.

The McCarthyism of the 1950s was seen as problematic for the world of journalism at the time. Yet the only form of news available from the 1990s through the early 2020s was basically McCarthyian. Despite being astroturfed, it was such a strong force that it extended into people's professional and social lives through cancellation. Yet

---

31. Balaji Srinivasan. *The Network State.* Balaji Srinivasan, 2022

these trends have largely been rejected through voting. Forces of change will spark the light of their most suitable opposition.

It's for the same reason why hospitals, of all places, end up becoming breeding grounds for antibiotic-resistant strains of pathogens, like MRSA. It's not even that the people operating these places don't understand how it happens, but their hands are tied. They must administer antibiotics to those who need them. Which, over time, creates antibiotic-resistant strains of pathogens, that then grow and spread inside hospitals where these drugs are quite often administered. Because who can ask a doctor to consider whether they're growing antibiotic-resistant MRSA when someone they're treating needs an antibiotic?

Likewise, this is similar to the problem of C-sections. An increasing amount of babies are born with heads too big to be born naturally now. Because when they're born we keep giving them C-sections, so those genes are spreading. Realistically, none of this is wise. Yet, the hands of those in charge are tied by sociomoral obligations and ethical codes. All of this will inevitably come back to haunt us.

The flaw here is that we're approaching the mosquito as if it were a giant. You can kill a giant with brute force as it's one large target. There probably aren't any other giants around as, metaphorically, it's representative of a monolith. But mosquitoes come in swarms, there are millions of them. If you can kill a few thousand using one approach, then by the merit of whichever ones escape, you start breeding mosquitoes resistant to the approach you just used. It's the hydra, you cut off its head and two more grow back. Even if you need to kill it, you must do so in entirety. To try and fail is to train it to fight against you.

I don't mean this as a dose of extreme pessimism. I speak these words implying the message that liability needs to be taken out of the hands of instant gratification. People need to be liable for their own actions. In some cases they may need to be both liable and capable of their own recovery from a simple infection. That's really not a great solution. Especially considering C-sections, what exactly is the best advice? To not have a child because its head is too big? I don't know what the answer is, hindsight can only be granted in time. I just see the problem and want to avoid making any more problems of the same nature.

Personal responsibility for children within the context of a school, as opposed to potential liability of the adults in their lives, is an excellent way to raise them, as well as prepare them for a future where they'll need to use that personal responsibility they'd practiced. Children should not be given social curses in the name of gifts such as safetyism. We even seem to naturally become over-reliant on our own technological innovations. Just because we expand the limits of what's biologically possible doesn't make it a good thing for the longevity of our children and grandchildren. To be cognizant of this pattern that we make for ourselves is going to be the key to our survival. These are the bricks of the Tower of Babel we're currently placing. Where we can, let's aim for placement and not complacency.

3.5 The Endless Walk

The Old Testament tells the story of Adam and Eve. A snake tricks a woman into eating fruit which she shares with her husband, and it bestows them self-awareness. The fruit taken from the tree is representative of intelligence, and comes at a cost. This is supposed to be a metaphor for the birth of mankind, and while this interpretation of the story is classic, I'm of the opinion that there's generally more than one way to read these kinds of stories to find them applicable to modernity.

Detectives try to piece together the sequence of events from a crime scene using the evidence left behind. Archeologists and historians do the same using remnants of the past to enlighten ourselves about the nature of our predecessors. Geologists acquire the history of the Earth through the layers of soil and sediment beneath our feet, the markings on rocks, and even the isotopes within either. It's these leftover scars of the past that explain the history of the world around us. When it comes to organisms, the remnants of our history and its leftover pieces don't just exist around us, they're left within us. More complex processes produce more complex traces of behavior. No different than how one can infer the nature of the digestive system of an animal from its teeth alone, we can infer the political nature and history of humanity from the relaxed selection of metabolites we can no longer make for ourselves.

The cost of the sustenance of the fruit coincides with the concept of relaxed selection. Relaxed selection occurs in organisms where evolutionary pressure is no longer applied to a specific gene or structure, and its function is lost over time. Humans, or an ancestor to them, lost the ability to produce vitamin C at some point because it was supplemented through their diet. Meaning, our hominid ancestors had then eaten so much fruit, that they lost the ability to synthesize their own vitamin C. So when the genes responsible for its production mutated, it didn't result in any disadvantage. The need to make it became unimportant when you could just eat something that had vitamin C to get your supply, like fruit from a tree. Dogs, by comparison, can still make it for themselves.

To take the fruit from the tree means success for both the fruit and its consumer. But that's not the entire story. Sure, it's an easier acquisition of something that previously required more effort for production. The plant does all the work for you, the Sun provides its energy. But for the consumer, it's simultaneously an imprisonment. A reliance so long-lasting that it hooked your ancestors at the genetic level. This dependence became somewhat permanent, with little chance of reversing. A gift is a curse. You may think this is rather dramatic when considering just a single example. But in how many different ways has this happened?

This isn't unlike the economic position we find ourselves in, where you may live and die by what specialized role you have in society. If the job you've made into a profession becomes automated, finding another career is going to be stressful. Is that not a dangerous dependency? Because the answer isn't to never advance, it's not to resist societal improvement with scalable technologies that would otherwise grant us greater efficiency. Increased efficiency offers such a great reward that it's not just hard to turn it down, it's foolish.

Amongst a myriad of biochemical, social, economic, and environmental dependencies, we constantly exchange what amounts to being a piece of our soul for an advantage in survival. This isn't necessarily a bad trade, but it requires a balancing. With every automated process you use comes the necessity for greater responsibility. To not eat vitamin C is to get scurvy. To have a layer of cultural inheritance that can circumvent genetic inheritance means to be reliant upon receiving that information at a young age for the sake of survival. As you find throughout the evolution of organisms, everything is a tradeoff. In this instance, it's not simply transforming an existing body part using one's own development and energy to get something beneficial. It's the sacrificing of a slower and less efficient version of an older process to gain a new advantage in a rapid and efficient manner. In the genetic case, over time that older process is lost, typically forever. In an economic case, it might not be lost permanently but requires motivation, time, money, and energy to reacquire should it be found worthwhile to backtrack. In the case of schooling, we sacrifice our childhood to gain an advantage in survival, but this process needs to be updated to respectfully acknowledge this fact. Even amongst the fruit of a tree there is no free lunch.

These tradeoffs aren't always easily determined. It can take time to realize they're either not optimal, or that the success being offered creates a whole new problem. For the former, it's the case of the broken compass. But for the latter, it might still be a good choice, perhaps the job just isn't finished. Because nothing good is ever finished. There's always room for improvement. There's always more work to do. For every little thing you end up making easier for yourself, you bring in something difficult that requires further optimization. The story of human development is no different, advantages are subversions of our difficulties. It's the balance of novel subversion with the old order that describes the majority of growth. Each step of the staircase within the Tower of Babel is carved out of irony.

Because that's all this is, the constant growing of abilities, and technology, until the layers built in the Tower of Babel are stable enough to build more layers atop. There seems to be an interpretation of this story that the tower should never have been built, which is why it was destroyed by God in the end. But I see it as a cautionary tale. Each brick in the tower needs to be placed carefully, and in the right location. The story of life is one in which we can't see the tower we're building. Every brick is a unique piece of information. The understanding of where to put each one can be figured out through either intuition or trial and error. The tower will crash down over placing smaller bricks below larger ones, or from inconsistent stacking, like population collapse, like economic crashes, like wars that arise from political differences. Yet from each disaster comes a new lesson on modeling the concepts of life.

The analogy of the tower has an underlying truth, that you must give up something you have in return for something you want. Take this example, imagine you have a computer program that can perform any feat of mathematics. To raise children, engineers even, using this, instead of teaching them to do math, and for generations, might rapidly improve the infrastructure of your society relies upon, but might genuinely deprive your civilization of any ability to do math in the case of a solar flare that causes the widespread destruction of electronics. It's obviously an oversimplified example, but it's not dissimilar to the use of large language models. To want to raise children doing both math and using advantageous technology, to tackle projects that time would otherwise not allow without it, has a very simple solution. You want the children to become the designers of such a program or model. There's no way to be able to make it without knowing how to do the math in the first place, and it replaces the need for the senseless practice while supplanting their ability to exceed normal technology-free expectations. The use of technology should not make children unproductive, children should become productive by forging their own technology. It's a reversal of the basic irony presented that offers a clear path forward, it's modeling the environment they find themselves in.

Intelligence is the process of the estimation of endless complexity that *is* the Tower of Babel. This isn't just a human thing. Plants respond to stimuli in many ways that seem intelligent. Whether they're intelligent in the manner in which humans would agree or not is irrelevant. If their actions mimic intelligence, it's because they model the same concepts that our evolution also has, regardless of whether plants exist with a state of consciousness.

Darwin concluded his book remarking *"endless forms most beautiful"* as a description of life itself. But convergent evolution seems to imply that if there's a limited number of potential environments for organisms to develop in, then there's also a limited number of optimal forms. There might be some added nuance regarding interactions with other organisms living in the same environment, but even the dynamics between different organisms in some niche habitat should be no less inevitable than everything else that already adapts to it. Likewise, there's a specific set of answers, scalable truths, that act as sacred principles that can genuinely guide us through the forays of our own advancement. As growth doesn't often present itself as a purely advantageous gift.

My message isn't anti-technological. We can gain the abilities of technology, but it requires a cultural balancing of every factor. We've been experimenting with that ever since it's been possible by widening our horizons and loosening the grip of our morality inherited from older times. The opening up of our culture through various forms of liberalization, also granted in part by technology and the industrial revolution, has performed this role. The attempts to declare every new political goal as some kind of *human right*, based on the triumphs of the past, as a cheap imitation of how one might truly learn from history, have become abundant towards the ends of this process of loosening morality.

The liberalization of society has acted like a fitting algorithm that's reapproached many topics almost predictably. After all, we're able to support many more walks of life, as a civilization, without our collective survival being dependent upon desperate enough circumstances to warrant a justified form of social tyranny. Which will likely come back to offer gifts in return. What's on the other side of this algorithmic optimization? It could be war, it could be renaissance, depending on how history develops.

The approach of complexity moves forward in an endless walk. Just like the inevitability of bipedal organisms developing stairs, human development arrived at an eventual move towards trade and the concept of money. Then towards nations and economies of scale. As we try not to let the important aspects of our survival drift away, the never-ending balancing act of gifts with curses remains on a precarious perch. We must recognize that growth itself is a filter. Even success doesn't guarantee survival. Sometimes, success is an error, and all errors will eventually be self-correcting. Just as the selection of a non-salable currency would crash an economy, any tower built on a mistaken block will fall much further below its original point of collapse.

Irony guides life, its optimizations, and all of its interactions. It arrives at truths that are as reliable as the inevitability of black holes, whether through convergence or obvious functionality. But then you must ask, perhaps to retain enough dignity to actually believe any of this, by what process? Irony seems to be a form of potential, but not a mechanism. What acts as a conduit to these optimizations?

IV
ENTROPY

4.1 Concept or Mechanism?

They say entropy is a measure of molecular freedom. What does freedom accomplish? Specifically, it's a concept that allows other concepts to arise naturally, and thrive within some context. The Earth takes in heat from the Sun then subsequently releases it, the amount of either must be equal. In the process of releasing the heat to space, it transforms the many mediums that it radiates through, with these transforming mediums being what eventually became life. Freedom is to transformation as irony is to evolution.

The substrates that heat enters on its way through Earth undergo both interactions and transformations. These two factors enable changes to any molecule this heat has been excited or absorbed by. As these changes accumulate, the potential for interaction becomes more competitive, and the directionality of transformation follows incentives towards greater complexity. Primordial complexity would have held a function that maintained a structure capable of best taking advantage of this absorption and dissipation of heat from the planet in a manner that seemingly competed with any neighboring forms attempting the same, much like how trees grow taller to compete for sunlight.

Sadi Carnot first analogized entropy through the power generated from a waterfall[32], his analogy was improved upon over time by other contributors to explain that entropy tends to increase the same way that water in a waterfall tends to decrease. It might land and rest

32. Sadi Carnot. *Reflections on the Motive Power of Heat*. Bachelier, 1824

at some intermediary point without reaching the bottom. The final destination may be the ocean, if it has a path. Otherwise, water will accumulate in the lowest place it can find. The source of the waterfall is a source of potential energy.

In modernity, entropy is seen as a concept that's used as a measurement. There's a few ways to summarize it, either through the lens of heat, information, or structural conformation. Throughout this chapter I'm going to use two specific kinds of entropy as descriptive tools, thermodynamic and statistical entropy. Thermodynamic entropy is a measure of wasted energy, it's heat given off by a process[33]. It could be from something like an engine, or your body. Something gives off heat that it has no further ability to retain due to diffusion. More heat lost is representative of higher entropy. Statistical entropy is a measure of structural conformation, which determines how many ways you can rearrange every component of some object, its atoms even, while retaining the same shape and properties[34]. That is, the number of microstate rearrangements that can be made to the macrostate without changing the actual object. Where any defect offers an increase in the number of possible microstates, thereby increasing the entropy.

Why is this necessary? Well, it's hard to characterize what entropy is in a classical sense, it's just *disorder*. Philosophically, people like to link it to the irreversibility of time. Measuring disorder isn't always straightforward, and you can get very creative with how you might do it. To many, it's an entirely man-made term, purely a concept. I'm going to explain, throughout this book, why it's not just a concept, but a mechanism.

I'd also like to address the nature of nihilism and why it exists. Nihilism is existential negativity, it's a pathway to understanding that which can be mistaken for wisdom. The second law of thermodynamics claims that entropy tends to increase over time, and it seems in the modern day there are people who take this to a nihilistic extreme, assuming that there's no ending for the universe except its own heat death. But this is just one boundary of the definition of what we understand of the universe. It's as naive as it is premature, and it's parallel to what a lot of people believe about the climate.

33. Rudolf Clausius. *The Mechanical Theory of Heat.* Friedrich Vieweg & Sohn, 1864–1867

34. Ludwig Boltzmann. *Lectures on Gas Theory.* Johann Ambrosius Barth, 1896–1898

Sometimes the second law of thermodynamics is written in regard to an experiment taking place in a glass tube, or from the perspective of watching things decay inside a glass box. Some people extrapolate this and pretend the universe is encased inside a glass box itself. Experiments under controlled conditions definitely tend to perform differently than everything we see around us. I would argue the nature of the universe is the blatant opposite of a controlled experiment.

No matter how many Nobel laureates say otherwise, no matter how many climate scientists declare it not true, there will always be extremists who believe we live in the age of an impending climate disaster. It's simply that for every 10 years that go by, another doomsday prediction pops out of some new corner of academia that's been funded for the sake of perpetuating this lie. The real reason for this is propagandistic control of the energy sector. Irresponsibility would be met with such a disaster, surely, but that's not what the world seems to be doing. In general, people seem to respond wisely to danger, and the world is both at and moving towards what seems to be its lowest points of atmospheric pollution yet[35,36,37,38,39].

A completely optimistic view would be irresponsible, it would ignore the problem. Likewise, a completely nihilistic view would be dangerous by way of inducing no fear of drastic action. The blissful ignorance, and lack of expertise, of extremists is a dose of optimism, as they have neither participation nor control of any related technical implementations of the topic.

The nihilistic perspective tends to be simpler throughout itself, like the addition step of Williston's law. Each component it holds is as sim-

---

35. Chi Li et al. *Reversal of Trends in Global Fine Particulate Matter Air Pollution.* Nature Communications, 2023

36. Wenche Aas et al. *Global and Regional Trends of Atmospheric Sulfur.* Scientific Reports, 2019

37. Jeffrey A Geddes et al. *Long-Term Trends Worldwide in Ambient NO2 Concentrations Inferred from Satellite Observations.* Environmental Health Perspectives, 2015

38. Rebecca R Buchholz et al. *Air Pollution Trends Measured from Terra: CO and AOD Over Industrial, Fire-Prone, and Background Regions.* Remote Sensing of Environment, 2021

39. Haolin Wang et al. *Global Tropospheric Ozone Trends, Attributions, and Radiative Impacts in 1995–2017: An Integrated Analysis Using Aircraft (IAGOS) Observations, Ozonesonde, and Multi-Decadal Chemical Model Simulations.* Atmospheric Chemistry and Physics, 2022

ple as possible, like pessimism tends to be more uniform. Which makes things easier to grasp as a natural first step into anything. It's the ledge you pull yourself upon to see the bigger picture. It's almost like perception itself is something one accumulates until we end up renaming it as experience, or knowledge. That first dose is always simple and thereby the most nihilistic. Which means those two tend to naturally coincide. Yielding, at the very least, a significant indicator of widespread ignorance where you find it in abundance.

As we try to define the boundaries of the dangers we come across, there's often a wide range of uncertainty, much like throughout the complex subjects we fail to find monolithic definitions for. Even though the heat death of the universe is not a threat to our environment, there's a reason the nihilistic interpretation has come before any dose of optimism. That reason is the broken compass. The nihilistic bound of uncertainty allows one to mechanically step towards optimism by transforming the unknown into the known.

Just as there's no climate disaster, there will be no heat death. The prevailing view that disorder is some continually increasing result of the existence of life is false. Life does not purely increase the disorder of its environment in exchange for maintaining internal order. The interactions and transformations brought about through the fluctuations of heat from the Sun inevitably cause an increase in complexity above all else.

4.2 Between Order and Disorder

An economy is something made between human potential and the Earth's resources. Organisms are made between the Sun and the potential of Earth's resources. In some cases they might even be between other organisms and the Earth's resources if you consider the specifics of an ecosystem. Our lives are caught between order and disorder, agreement and disagreement. Your thoughts and intelligence are caught between knowns and unknowns. All of which are basically the same analogy. Physically, we're caught between two sources of disorder and one is always going to be relatively more ordered than the other.

Life came about by the interactions of multiple forms of potential energy. Each can be, in their own right, described as a form of disorder. There was potential energy available in the minerals and basic organic molecules floating around Earth's oceans. There was the potential for the heat from the Sun to interact with all of these things. In the most basic way, without either of these, there would be no life on Earth. Without the input of two forms of disorder, there would be no complexity. Complexity doesn't emerge instantaneously, nor is it ever going to emerge unidimensionally from just one source of disorder. Unidimensional complexity would be an oxymoron, it emerges via multiple interacting dimensions of potential energy. Complexity arises at neither low nor high entropy, it arises between these two boundaries.

The capturing of the Sun's heat transformed the primordial ocean into the primordial soup by acting as a broad kind of catalyst that could be applied to anything and everything. Maybe you'd want to say it was hydrothermal vents specifically, which could definitely at least be part of it. From the interactions of these processes came the widened scope of potential interactions altogether, as interactions are always more complex than either member alone. You can consider the heat of the Sun as a factor in just about any primordial reaction, like it's one side of a multiplication table that yields a 2-dimensional plane out of two existing 1-dimensional arrays. Which leads the way towards the network of subversions mentioned previously.

Any interacting forms of disorder can be seen as competing over their shared potential. Imagine two waterfalls falling into the same area, but neither is actually water, as primary sources of disorder. One of the waterfalls is a new phenomenon and brings something that reacts with the original source. The reaction causes their collective pool to expand, due to a decrease in density or some other figment of your imagination, which then is able to overcome its surrounding inclines to begin flowing downhill. It might even flow in more than one direction. Yielding a very dynamic process, pools of entropy interacting to not only form new pools, but forming new means of forming new pools. Being more than just an analogy, pools of entropy represent the networking function of a nervous system. They also represent the geographic instability of large river systems. It's a network of disorder that changes like a self-evolving computer chip. They're the changing environment downstream of personal and political shifts, caused by the connectedness brought by the internet, as it once was for the printing press. The signaling networks of cells have come to model pools of entropy in both form and function. Like a river always looking for the lowest ground to equilibrate to, always changing whenever there's a reason. When would a network of these pools of entropy re-optimize? When it becomes saturated with the homogeneity of an old optimization. Which then yields a vantage that can better delineate a new ratio of advantages to disadvantages, as these pools are metaphors of concepts that model their own environment.

As integrals are solved, these networks of pools grow closer to the principles of their own source of energy. They start to better take advantage of the potential in their pool, and the disorder flowing into it. **Order models disorder.** That's what integrals represent physically, the subversion of a source of energy. No different than how we one day dream of harnessing the energy of the Sun to power all of civilization.

These layers of disorder we're sandwiched between become apparent from their levels of stability. Black holes are estimated to last between 10^{70} and 10^{100} years. The larger something gets, the more stable it seems to be. Or rather, something is only able to become so large through having such unrivaled stability in the first place. Which is destined to far outlive anything we actually know of in our own lives. Likewise, the microcosm has the same tremendous stability as the macrocosm. Not every piece of it is, but an electron itself supposedly lasts for more than 10^{29} years, and protons are understood to last for more than 10^{34} years. For something to be derived from some source of disorder, you might expect such disorder to be much more stable than any of its derivatives.

With competition comes optimized entropy, brought about by the free movement of the pools within this analogy. Which is how life came about in the first place, all of our greatest innovations too, there was a lack of their inhibition. Everything great is brought about through freely competing entities. Between order and disorder is the birth of complexity, and something can only be a source of disorder by having a lack of inhibitions specifically. Freedom is a necessity in order to create the benefits of competition. Whether it's a market by free trade, or political disagreement by freedom of speech, nothing we know would be the same without either one of these. You end up getting optimized outcomes *because* of these things simply not being inhibited. To learn from these examples, perhaps we could even raise children through freedom of religion.

4.3 Internal Order Optimizations

How does complexity arise between order and disorder? From any flaws in some structural order there comes the potential for a utilization of disorder through every potential exploitation. From within these structural flaws comes the potential to utilize any advantage they could come to represent. A gift is a curse, and irony governs the interactions of the components of any system. Any structural failing can always be turned into a blessing, as disorder is a space of latent potential. Irony delivers competitive evolution over time, and society folds like a protein to find a more ordered and advantageous form. It's the makings of a more optimized structure. Just as a windmill takes energy from the wind, so does order from disorder. Order provides structure and thereby function, while disorder provides energy. Order would be most closely related to physical states, like that which is considered by statistical entropy. Disorder is generally caused by heat given off, that which is measured via thermodynamic entropy. Meaning, any kind of complexity to arise must use these basic mechanisms. Between dancing the line of needing order for structure and needing disorder for function, complexity forms a specific entity which is capable of adaptation. Where order is the integral to its respective derivative of disorder.

Metaphorically, the optimization of internal order is a process of solving integrals. Physically, it's how the dispersion of heat and chemical energy becomes more sophisticated. Increasing sophistication, in this sense, is like having a waterfall start at a greater and greater height as you progress. It's being able to take better advantage of the energy you have, becoming better at finding energy, and finding better energy to use all at the same time. Imagine collecting energy from the source of a waterfall where you spin turbines as the water falls down. More potential energy can be taken advantage of if you can make the water fall from a greater height. Over time, you can alter the setup so that it becomes capable of taking full advantage of the entire scenario. In a more finished design there wouldn't be any falling water exposed to the air, there would be a vacuum sealed system fully optimized to collect of every piece of energy available. Then imagine making a defence system against invaders who wanted to steal water. Where the energy from the water would fuel weaponry placed on the outside that responds to threats when detected. Which would be a better use of that energy than losing it altogether. Imagine wanting to either preserve the chemical purity of the water, or adding specific catalysts to it, so that you can further harness its chemical properties to generate even more power as it moves. It's all no different than an organism developing a body over billions of years.

Solving an integral is a lot like swimming up the waterfall. Like getting closer to the source of energy for that pool of entropy. The process requires using the energy delivered at the source in order to subvert the source. Life, as a self-designing reaction, has solved a multitude of integrals to get where it is today, some probably a multitude of times. This is the primary function of the self-designing reaction, to subvert sources of disorder to grow the complexity of its own internal pools of entropy.

Just like organisms in an ecosystem, as members of an environment learn to utilize its potential, and this can be an industry or country like our own, it increases its order while outputting some effect on its surrounding environment. It's commonly believed this always increases the disorder of the environment, but that's not necessarily the case. It might be the case at first, and it's easily more true locally than globally. But when you add enough disorder to an environment over time, it can then become an opportunity for some external entity to grow in complexity. In the case of most organisms, they may as well be adapted to waiting for a new form of disorder to take advantage of. The existence of disorder becomes an integral for something else to solve. Which is no longer purely an addition of disorder to an environment, but an addition of complexity.

These kinds of outcomes are littered all over the place, there's prevalent internal order, and complexity that takes advantage of disorder, throughout every part of our environment. Routine chores like cleaning wards off invasive complexity like mold. We maintain our order all the same when we sleep at night to put our brains and bodies back together. The distributions of roles in a family and a society are in their own right a form of internal order. Any goal you set out to accomplish most likely starts with research, or information gathering, as the basis for which you then assemble a plan. A consolidation of internal order is even why the internet went from being a lot of random disconnected webpages to being centralized by a few large social media websites. Afterwards, the transformation of all text on the internet went from being valuable yet too vast for deep encyclopedization, to being highly valuable training data for large language models that then went on to contribute complexity to the surrounding environment. Product assembly is of the same nature at many levels, assembly over time becomes cheaper, faster, and easier, while any product itself becomes more widespread, and thereby an added complexity to the external environment. Cell phones are popular because you can get texts, notes, pictures, videos, and a near endless array of functionality all in one. If it took 5 devices to do all of these things, none of them would be as handy. Think of the hurdles it took to generate nuclear power, where utilizing the most complex principles of the time were the most difficult task yet to be undertaken. Which makes sense, as nuclear power is a much more powerful source of energy to tap into, requiring a more difficult integral to be solved. Convergent evolution exists *because* organisms are optimizing internal order relative to their environment. That's *why* they're models of their environment. Because the environment incentivizes certain models.

The point of having an internal order is that you have an in-group preference. You have something that you're preserving internally. A population of some kind, a metabolism, etc. It's to delineate from externalities for the sake of that preservation. It's why we form governments and civilizations, and it's why they keep evolving. It's why we delineate ourselves into ethnicities, cities, families, and so on. Most of all, it's what an upbringing is adapted for. Children grow up learning to order themselves and their habits, childhood is one massive internal order optimization process. Childhood itself is basically selected for high-speed internal order optimization, it's a slingshot built for exactly that when you consider the capabilities and learning rates achievable by the youngest of us. They've become highly optimized to approach their source of potential energy, of knowledge and skills, at a young age. When an order optimizing step is overemphasized, like education taking too long, you end up with a massive burnout of individuals when they're older. They would've generally had more potential than they were able to take advantage of, yet it was destroyed by a credential mill. As when it's overdone at a societal scale, you end up with millions of people who refuse to work, alongside many who never get around to having children.

A question that's left over is, are entropic optimizations zero-sum? Some forms can be once they're solved, but in general the nature of optimizations never end. First and foremost, the environment you live in is something like a food supply chain, a transportation infrastructure, a business environment that funds your government, an academic environment for building knowledge, a legal system that deters harm, and the list goes on. These are not easily changeable. They've been somewhat optimized to be the way they are over long periods of time. Sometimes for good reasons, and sometimes these good reasons can become outdated. With structures already inhabiting these niches, change would not likely be accomplished overnight. There isn't a huge need for anyone to design a different transportation network. Roads, cars, trains, planes, and boats all seem to be working just fine. Meaning it's zero-sum in that no other paradigm is going to be built alongside it without careful deliberation. The point of having an agreed upon form of governance is to implement a zero-sum game in specific niches so as to not harbor redundant optimizations, as such a thing wouldn't be an optimization at all. Where is it non-zero-sum? At smaller scales, and in areas where innovation can thrive. Perhaps you invent a kind of car that can hover 30 feet off the ground without crashing into buildings. As things become outdated, there comes an inevitable cycle that forces modern interpretations to update prior beliefs.

4.4 Transformations of Complexity

While an increase in entropy may be a primary function of some simpler interactions, once you get enough disorder interacting with itself, complexity tends to systematically arise from it. This describes a number of things at a basic level, like the formation of both celestial bodies and life. Both can be analogized through Williston's law. Stars that have formed since the expected beginning of the universe are divided into three main groups. What are called Population III stars were formed early in the universe. They were made of mostly helium and hydrogen, because these should have been the only elements that were around. A lot of these were large, and died quickly compared to the stars we have now, their resulting supernovae created elements like magnesium, oxygen, neon, silicon, calcium, and iron. You can consider this the addition step, which created the conditions for these elements to then specialize newer stars that are considered to be Population II. These Population II stars had accumulated small amounts of metals, which granted them greater overall stability. The same process repeated itself, where these stars created even more elements, and much more of them. Population I stars are what we have around us today, they are rich in metal, and are highly specialized compared to anything that came prior. The variety of different kinds of stars grew, and their lifespans greatly increased due to the amount of metal inside them. What reduced in abundance were the older hydrogen stars, they don't even exist anymore. The rate at which new stars form was also reduced, granted by the increased stability brought about by metals being dispersed across the universe. As a result of these transformations, like with organisms, they actually allowed for greater survivability for the stars, there are expected to be more stars now than there ever were, and their numbers keep growing. While these classifications are more rightly considered a continuum rather than rigid boundaries, not only does the same general story of Williston's law apply, but the same general story was already applied within the communities that study these phenomena.

Put more simply, stars emerge as the addition. New elements are born in these stars, as the specialization. As newer stars are made out of newer elements, the older more basic stars reduce in abundance, as the reduction. This recurring theme of the utility of Williston's law seems to represent a process that spawns complexity. But what is complexity? A unidimensional answer is an accumulation of irony, where more irony tends to compound as more complexity. The multidimensional equivalent would be disorder within order, a very ironic combination. The encapsulation of disorder is basically the core mechanism of entropy, it's the inevitability of it. In a purely physical sense, complexity would be something like the impact derived over time relative to the space something occupies at any moment. If disorder is not a state but an action, whereas order is a state, then complexity is the utilization of both.

Complexity requires selection, which requires competition, which requires growth. If you get in the way of this pipeline, you stifle growth, and you'll have no birth rate. Growth allows for increased competition, which allows for increased selection, which allows for increased complexity. But even this has multiple layers, we have biological growth and economic growth. For the sake of simplicity let's encompass technological growth within economic growth. The economic growth can help biological growth, which is the point of everything else. Although you can unfortunately favor economic growth to the point where you stifle biological growth, because too much of anything is a bad thing. The conditions for growth exist in a natural balance with other things around you, an equilibrium, which is just a form of order itself.

Everything in the universe has an order to it. Molecules, atoms, and subatomic particles, all have internal order. Within their internal order is the internal order of the next on that list. Because complexity is the norm, and simplicity is the exception. Even what one might assume are simple planets can't evade this. A planetary core forms over millions of years by way of a density gradient reflective of its gravity, and typically yields some manner of electromagnetic effects from where concentrated metals meet the heat of the core, and frequent some cycle derived from a relationship with the planet's rotation. Even if those electromagnetic effects are weak, even if the planet is small, likely even if its composition is somewhat uniform, there's still an internal order that it possesses through optimizations that have been made. As a part of its internal order optimization it cleared its own orbit. Reflective of its internal order it maintains its own atmosphere, and has geologic structures, and patterns, reflective of its internal forces. As is with an ecosystem, an orbiting moon, a solar system, a galaxy, and beyond. Optimized order is the norm. Where it isn't, it eventually becomes so. But at what point does this internal order begin to exist, and for continually evolving forms of complexity, when does it completely distinguish itself from any of its related predecessors to become something entirely different?

Looking at entropy in a closed system with no influence from space, time, energy, or abundance of different elements is like trying to understand human nature without considering evolution. Thinking that people only respect nurture without nature, that you can have them model whatever you like if you raise them as such, is like recreating the concept of civilization bereft of its history. There's never maximization for either order or disorder alone that isn't extreme, optimization happens between the two to form complexity. Order lets up to allow for greater disorder, and that disorder is funneled through an ordered enough system to make functional use of it. Assuming that the disorder of any environment only ever increases completely avoids the fact that life exists at all. The reason complexity hasn't been a factor in the classical equations of entropy is that while disorder is able to be quantified, complexity is as difficult to quantify as irony. Modern science doesn't have an understanding of entropy that's able to quantify evolving forms of complexity, especially the products of billions of years of transformations. Which is to say, it's difficult to have a complex representation of complexity.

So where exactly is the inevitable increase in disorder provided by organisms, is it the fecal matter they excrete? Well that fertilizes plants, and is eaten by microbes. Is it the waste products we bury in the ground? Wood wasn't digestible for 40 million years until fungi found a way to do so, and now the remnants of these sit in the ground as coal, a major source of energy for civilization. A few hundred years of landfills is nothing by comparison. Disorder should mean high free energy and thereby being impractical to harness, more broadly it implies waste and destruction, but there's always new opportunities for old materials. Someday these landfills won't be any different. Even as we send satellites and ships out into space, it's not merely maximizing disorder. It's one less unsophisticated rock, and one more complicated device. Organisms don't simply increase some external disorder around them. They maximize complexity with every interaction, they incentivize it.

But in what turn of events does complexity begin to take shape as a target? And at what moment did life begin, exactly? The moment when some process of disorder was enveloped by a form of order. Likely into what was a metabolic process, plus the genetic material to create it, encapsulated by something a bit more advanced than a micelle. Where the force of an optimizing internal order pushed back and forth against its own disorder like a heartbeat, as the competition between order (low entropy) and disorder (high entropy) isn't just structural, it's temporal.

An entropy-based definition of life is a fitting baseline, I do consider viruses to be alive. They're more reliant on other kinds of organisms for their reproduction, but not any more than a seed's reliance on dirt. Being alive means something is capable of holding a balance between internal order and an external environment for the sake of producing more of itself. By this definition, you might rightly point out that it would seem prions can be considered alive. So are we anything like them? Obviously not. The complexity of our being alive is on an unaccountably higher level than that of viruses or prions. Life has a definition that allows for stratifications, rather, it requires them. The boundaries of convergence for life should not be set as spanning from microbes to humans. It should encompass every living process, and grow in complexity as the organisms that transcend lower states of existence grow into modeling universal concepts themselves. *Being alive* is much too simple of an explanation for what humans actually accomplish just by existing.

Along the different stratifications are all the other definitions of a biochemical, evolutionary, and autopoietic basis, and then some. Organisms are, truthfully, no different than some automaton with billions, perhaps trillions, of microscopic gears all forming bifurcations that act as competing internal decision-making processes. You could say life itself is between the bounds of order and disorder, but there's an even more appropriate arrangement of those same terms, the encapsulation of disorder by order is a more fitting description. Once disorder sits inside order, order learns to make disorder even more disordered, to its advantage, and the two begin to push against each other while co-maximizing each other's function.

When a derivative is being integrated, it's like a model is forming from shifting metaphysical pools of entropy. The weight applied to a model stems from a piece of irony. Irony accumulates in the form of weights to impact the conformation of the pools being modeled, which is where its utility as a unit of reality takes flight. The only quality of a unit irony has is none other than the fact that it's capable of acting as one. Rather than being some form of complexity that's difficult to define, irony seems to be more consistently inconsistent enough to avoid being quantifiable. Like the concept of irony itself is resistant to the nature of counting, falling short of any monolithic characterization. Instead, it maintains a non-uniform yet ubiquitous presence. Big and small, obvious yet hidden. The perpetual adjustment of weights of a model, via the various forms of irony it interacts with, determine both the underlying nature of the concept being modeled, as well as the modeling of any concept itself. Which, by sheer circumstance, makes it an excellent unit by model standards, insurpassable even.

When relating to the math itself, the underlying characteristic of a transformation of complexity, of integration and derivation, is a transcending of infinity, it's taking another step through the staircase in the Tower of Babel. It's not the continuous chore-like cleaning of an internal order optimization, it's breaking ground on new internal areas to maintain and optimize. Such as when a state of matter becomes saturated with energy to the point where it changes states, like solids becoming liquid, or liquid becoming gas. The concept of infinity is the same as the concept of the number 1. You can count infinities, so any countable number can be seen as the same conceptual framework. Transcending infinity is metaphorically analogous to taking a scale that spans between 0 and 1, and transforming it to a scale that spans between 1 and infinity. Either process requires a division of 1 by any value being transformed. They're essentially the same representations, the former is of fractions of a whole, whereas the latter represents a multitude of wholes. But the scaling of one to the other is the relevant change.

There's two useful aspects to the interpretation of transcending infinity. Its first state is an *approach* of infinity, the second is the transformation it yields after properly transcending it. In the context of calculus, the concept of an approach of infinite refinement is what occurs when something is continually altered in smaller and smaller ways albeit more broadly. Functions change due to a distance of refinements *approaching* zero while the number of refinements *approaches* infinity. A transformation won't always occur in some immediate step, but it's possible to know when it's something that will eventually occur if you can identify the approach.

Disease and disorders are everything that can go wrong in the automatons. If a vulnerability exists, it's likely the niche has been filled throughout time by something that takes advantage of it in these forms. More complex infiltration agents, like parasites, act as penetration testers. As even vulnerabilities themselves naturally become more complex.

What is a parasite? It's something that feeds off some fraction of its host. Parasites try and squeeze themselves between two pools to make a third, an invasive pool of entropy. They adapt to be dependent on a larger pool that does all the work for them. This is a natural byproduct of the reaction of life. But if the amount stolen from the host increased, from 0.1 for example, to be larger than 1, it would no longer be a parasite. It means the parasite would have more than one host. Because it's not killing like a predator would, it's feeding off of living hosts. Making it, conceptually, a vampire. The transcending of infinity is a transformation of complexity, and an organism modeling an environment is done through this same mechanism. It's not just the occurrence of organisms modeling their environment, it's a fundamental improvement in their ability to do so. It's the basis for evolution, which is always done in the context of tradeoffs. A parasite can hide on its host because of its small size, but a vampire has to take different measures in order to hide in plain sight.

So is every transcending of infinity worthwhile? No, and in your life you have a limited supply of them, simply because your time and effort aren't infinite. They form much easier when young, and it can be tricky to reverse bad habits when you're older. It's a garden of your own wisdom. Like anything else, weeds grow from negligence.

A black hole is a transcending of infinity of transcending infinities, it isn't anything like matter that has some kind of state change. The process of internal optimization itself is transformed. A black hole is like if a car engine ran out of control and somehow changed into an entirely new concept. Which is the very idea of transcendence. Luckily, there's still enough in common between a black hole and the star it started off as to be able to make sense of it in the first place.

It's very difficult, impossible probably, to properly compare the complexity of two extremely different things. You can manage a comparison of different organisms as they're all phylogenetically related at some level. Yet comparing a human to a black hole doesn't yield any fruitful wisdom no matter how hard you try. Irony, as a unit, isn't very quantifiable, so comparisons aren't simple when classification is so distant. Is it possible to instead use entropy as a tool to make this comparison?

The classic understanding of statistical and thermodynamic entropy is that they're interchangeable, that they represent the same thing. If you were to view a small sliver of time, a finite cross-section of reality very similar to the infinitely small differences and distances being assessed during an integral or derivative, this would be true. You would find either one of these concepts to be representative of the other. But once you step outside that sliver of time, it stops being true. One must consider that time is constantly moving. These two concepts aren't simply interchangeable in reality, they're sequential. This sequentiality becomes more true at more extreme examples such as life and black holes, and the extremes aren't just hot and cold, big and small, or alive and dead because two things opposed don't stand opposite. The statistical state of organisms derives their thermodynamic state. Meaning, the orderliness of their conformational macrostate determines the efficiency of their energy use. That rule should generally hold true for just about everything complex enough to manifest such a state. The only case where this is different are black holes.

For a black hole, the thermodynamic state is trapped. The trapped heat and particles, extreme density of the environment, and gravitational pressure involved, all act in concert as forces that unlock alternate paradigms of stability in the local microcosm. What would be heat, given off via thermodynamic entropy, is never given off. It then goes on to be recycled into influencing the nature of the statistical state of its microcosm. Making the thermodynamic state and statistical state exist in a kind of deadlock with each other. All the various forms of trapped energy are put into maintaining this paradoxical stalemate. Which acts like a sponge to heat, and energy in general, explaining the near absolute zero kelvin temperature of the event horizon, and also the fact that larger black holes are colder than smaller ones. As there's basically no limit to which any energy will be used. It's never lost, any small amount of energy given off by Hawking radiation is largely irrelevant to the macrostate of a black hole. All energy is invested in the quantum, sub-quantum, or microcosmic states even further beyond that, unlocked by this energy.

Traditionally, entropy has been seen as just a tool we use to describe the universe, and not necessarily a part of its underlying mechanics. But I disagree, we've arrived at the basis for the mechanics itself by forming tools to understand it. It's of reasonable expectation that humans, too, model their environment in any way they can. The concepts we arrive at are not by coincidence. Statistical and thermodynamic entropy carry significant meaning in the physical world.

It would require one to refuse the evidence seen through their own eyes to be shocked that life is the process of order taking advantage of disorder to maximize complexity. The path towards disorder is not a prophecy, the final state of any pool of entropy would be environmentally optimal. People say this always results in an increase in disorder for the environment of whatever organisms undergo this change. That even cells take in energy and expel it into their environment in the form of heat, which should increase the disorder of their environment. Disorder, at best, is an intermediate step. The ejection of heat and chemical energy is a very stratified process, it moves through every compartment that it must until it finally exits an organism. Then it finds itself in an environment where it might yet again be taken advantage of by some other organism. Whether trees above, a bush it gets blown towards, microbes floating in the air, or some other opportunist waiting for its chance. It's always possible to take advantage of any heat being dispersed to become energy for another valuable process. There's a minimization of dead ends where there's a maximization of complexity. Even the stars themselves transformed before complex life was likely ever possible.

Optimized internal order will harness external disorder to embrace complexity, changing the nature of the universe time and time again. Life will undergo its endless walk to conquer planets and stars, eventually transcending the limitations of the universe itself as yet another act in the never-ending play of entropic optimization. Where energy again percolates through to the next pool of entropy to build yet another layer of complexity upon everything that's come before it. That's basically the meaning of life and its inevitable result, optimization driven entropic transcendence. Which, in layman's terms, means infinite growth. It may seem like science fiction, but it's possible through the scalable wisdom granted by solving integrals of the most impactful derivatives, and it's inevitable.

Complexity utilizes its own output, or else it wouldn't be complex at all. If what heat is lost from the planet even goes to the microbes living in our atmosphere before radiating itself throughout our solar system, then whatever quantity of heat that was lost had been utilized probably multitudes more than any simple system ever could have. Complexity is a hedged bet against heat dissipation with built-in risk neutralization. It's a bet against pure disorder, as even disorder feeds back into complexity and we continue this process in our own inventions and endeavors. There's plenty to add about environmental pollutants, which can be problematic, but these problems can be handled. By some feat of *magic*, to anyone who doesn't believe in an ever-increasing complexity, humans were able to detect pollutants when no such thing had ever been of concern. Which then followed up with laws and measures to prevent their misuse, all without the need for violence. Because the final determinant of our environment is us. The tradeoff of taking this step in the Tower of Babel is the responsibility that comes with it.

A basic reason why disorder is always subvertible is because chemistry and physics are not unidimensional. They're complex, because the universe generates complexities. There isn't a one-way ticket from order to disorder. There's many ways to go from A to B. Some of them are reversible, some of them are slower, and some rides from B to A are faster and cheaper. Technological advancements, coupled with capital growth as a mechanism of economic development, can win the battle against the seemingly rate-limiting concepts of physical laws because resources are superabundant[40], and chemistry is largely versatile. Superabundance refers to the fact that having more people in our civilization brings us cheaper goods and resources that become more plentiful per person. Though you might argue this pushes the boundary of our limited supply of resources down to the level of subatomic particles, rather than finding an *infinite money glitch* in chemistry, and you would be right. Any rate-limiting factors of that boundary will be contested too, as will the next after that.

4.5 Limits of Perception

The concept of spacetime is an interesting one. That the 3-dimensional space we perceive has some hidden component to it that becomes distorted by gravity. Time somehow nestles itself in without being invited. Yet the only time *time* seems to show itself is under special circumstances, and as a special circumstance gravity is already confusing enough. Your body doesn't have some inherent property that causes it to be attracted to the planet. There's no manner of object, smooth or abrasive, acidic or basic, sturdy or frail, that's free from its effects. Even small objects like dust particles experience gravity the same as everything else, they just also experience drag and the viscosity of air. Things fall downward, and it at first seems like the most obvious expectation, until you learn the Earth is round. So if it's not actually obvious, then what exactly is *falling*, and how can we intuit what a 4th dimension looks like when we perceive everything in three?

General Relativity describes gravity from the perspective of mass-energy density[41,42]. That when denser objects form, they distort

40. Marian L Tupy and Gale L Pooley. *Superabundance*. Cato Institute, 2022

41. Albert Einstein. *The Foundation of the General Theory of Relativity*. Annalen der Physik, 1916

42. Albert Einstein. *The Field Equations of Gravitation*. Proceedings of the Prussian Academy of Sciences, 1915

the 4-dimensional space around them. It describes gravity as curving the geometry of spacetime, where objects affected by it follow a path towards the center of gravity. Here, gravity isn't a force, it's described as a kind of geometry.

On a planet with stronger gravity, you experience time relatively slower. To an outside observer, time passes faster than it would to the people they see on that planet. It's also the case that you experience time slower when you're moving faster. The problem that's hard to grasp is how to interpret 4-dimensional spacetime using this information. There's no unified philosophical conceptualization of time, and various physical modelings utilize different facets of time under different circumstances. In case you thought this book was only about education, religion, and intelligence, you're about to find out that it's also about time. As the source of our misunderstandings about any one of these is the same as the rest.

There's a lot of trouble in interpreting the 4th dimension of spacetime. But I think the answer tends to be written in layman's terms for us to see. Large celestial bodies move fast, but we perceive them as slow because we perceive their angular motion. While some small subatomic particles are so short-lived they're nearly impossible to track accurately. This axis isn't a typical kind of 4th dimension, but it does point to the basis for time itself.

Physicists have stopped short of the full interpretation of 4-dimensional spacetime, simply not knowing how to think outside of their own box. The nature of this interpretation is an art, not a science. Thinking the 4th dimension can't exist within the 3-dimensional framework itself is a form of nihilism, which acts as a mental trap to those who instead turn to admire the problem rather than understand the solution. This kind of thinking is bad for society. It's necessary, but bad to dwell on. The frontiers of academia are limited more by an unchanging culture than a lack of ability.

To make things more complicated, we don't simply have one understanding of the universe around us. General Relativity has a lot of agreement with, but also stands unreconciled in some ways to, Quantum Field Theory. To truly understand what's going on, I'm going to use both frameworks.

Gravity, through the lens of Quantum Field Theory, is made up of an entrenching field of particles called gravitons brought about by objects in space[43,44]. Gravitons are assumed to be emitted as particles from larger bodies when agitated by disturbances, but they otherwise remain in a dormant state that seems to create the effects of a weak field around every object. In this light, gravity is a force that's supposed to affect everything everywhere.

Gravitons have been indirectly detected in the form of gravitational waves[45], but directly detecting actual gravitons is a large technical hurdle that's not been passed. Quantum Field Theory suggests a gravitational field is something that hooks onto anything with energy, most notably matter[46]. That's why every form of matter, and radiation, feels the same gravitational pull independent of any properties. Gravitons are technically unproven concepts, but are predictable at a theoretical level. In the context of a planet, gravity behaves less like a force and more like a well that things become trapped in. Gravitons as a gravity well become small wrinkles in space. Together, all the wrinkles add up into a larger and larger well to form the effects of the gravity of a planet, or something larger.

Gilbert Lewis and Richard Tolman used the concept of a traveling light clock to explain parts of Einstein's framework[47]. Point a light source facing down that blinks every second, and aim it at a mirror that reflects right back at the source. The flash of light will reflect off the mirror back to the source at the speed of light. Anyone within the inertial frame of this apparatus will see the same process. Next, put that clock on a spaceship where the process is visible from the outside. Fly the ship at 90% of the speed of light, and to any outside observer they won't see the straight up-and-down flash that people inside the spaceship see. The outside observers will see a diagonal line going down, and a diagonal line going back up after hitting the mirror. Even the

---

43. Marcus Fierz and Wolfgang Ernst Pauli. *On Relativistic Wave Equations for Particles of Arbitrary Spin in an Electromagnetic Field.* Proceedings of the Royal Society A, 1939

44. Suraj N Gupta. *Gravitation and Electromagnetism.* Physical Review, 1954

45. LIGO Scientific Collaboration and Virgo Collaboration. *Observation of Gravitational Waves from a Binary Black Hole Merger.* Physical Review Letters, 2016

46. Steven Weinberg. *Photons and Gravitons in Perturbation Theory: Derivation of Maxwell's and Einstein's Equations.* Physical Review, 1965

47. Gilbert N Lewis and Richard C Tolman. *The Principle of Relativity, and Non-Newtonian Mechanics.* Proceedings of the American Academy of Arts and Sciences, 1909

distance of the diagonal lines will be different for the outsiders. If the length between the light source and the mirror is 1m, the length of the diagonal line seen by the outside observer would be ~2.29m. The mechanics of what happens on the ship is slower to the outside observer, and seeing as the speed of light acts as a physical limitation of the universe, the outside observer must experience the elongated flash of light at the speed of light itself. Every point of time this outside observer experiences relative to those on the ship becomes longer by this same representation. Meanwhile, the travelers inside the ship experience less time than an outside observer. If they both started with synchronized clocks, the clock inside the ship would have experienced less time after the event took place. Their clocks would no longer be synchronized. Einstein insisted this was a universal speed limit, and that nothing can travel faster than the speed of light.

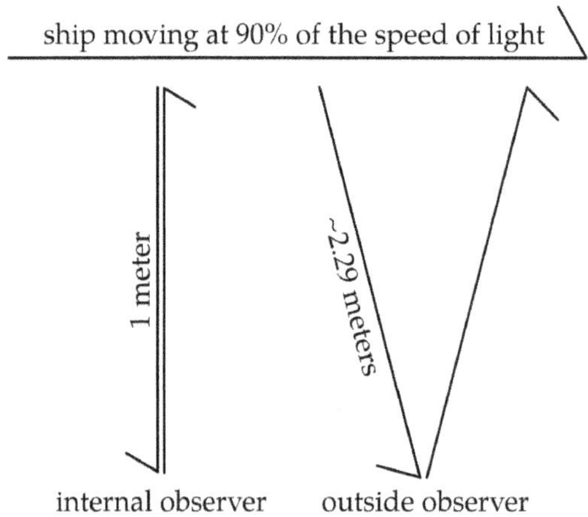

Figure 3: Observations of a Traveling Light Clock

But is this accurate? While it seems from our perspective that nothing can transcend the speed of light, and that light itself has a limit to how fast it can travel, this may just be in the eye of the perceiver. There's nothing wrong with the measurements, there's something strange about the universe for behaving this way. Light definitely travels at that speed relative to anyone who observes it, but it's because there's more likely a universal limit to perception. Which would lead one to question, how exactly can perception be the problem? How would perception limit the universe based on the nature of observation? It's nothing to do with our observations specifically, the most likely reason is because the nature of observation is an intrinsic part of the universe.

Even the idea of a hypothetical observer isn't free from the same physical limitations of the universe. Calculations can be made independent of some observer, but an observer becomes necessary when making predictions about physical phenomena. To theorize the signal some detector will receive requires the context of an observer within the calculations in order to offer a prediction for what one might measure from a real experiment. In this light, perception translates calculation to expectation. Interestingly, if one wanted to make a gigantic observer, like a gigantic human with gigantic eyeballs that were the size of a galaxy, the perception of this observer wouldn't match that of our own senses. The time it takes light to reach these eyeballs, the time it takes blood to flow, nerves to send signals, and its body to move, would all be at odds with one another because even light wouldn't travel fast enough to make this body adept at understanding its own movements and positioning. The universal speed limit acts as a limit of perception, as the ability to receive and understand such signals requires a specific size range in exchange for effectiveness. If a body at this size, or even larger, were to somehow be feasible, it would need to rely on completely different physical principles. But even if supermacrocosmic perception is possible, perceiving these forces from our own scale might not be. To what would find the largest celestial bodies we know of to be akin to a piece of sand to us, or an atom even, would operate on entirely different utilizations of the same laws we're familiar with. From our perspective, from our scale, matter's interaction with its surroundings is more dependent upon its temperature than its molecular structure, changing its state from solid to liquid or gas. With the scaling of structure comes a scaling of principles that result in novel interactions that operate under completely different paradigms than what would seem familiar to us, and likely analogous to how different they operate in the microcosms beneath us. Throughout the effects of what we can't perceive may as well be the reason for the limit to the speed of light. Because it's nonsensical that one even exists, under classic Newtonian mechanics if light is massless then it should have infinite speed. What actually causes this limit is highly likely to be completely outside the limits of our perception.

You're obviously familiar with how 3-dimensional space works or you wouldn't be able to hold this book in your hand. These three dimensions aren't wrong, you're not being deceived by spacetime. To understand the distortion of spacetime, you have to make the distinction of something *having* time, rather than *being* time. Because to us time is something we interact with, as a perceiver is someone who witnesses time before their eyes. Time experienced happens in the most finite and distributed form possible, and this is with relation to both organisms and inorganic objects, it happens at a much smaller physical scale than we're used to perceiving. Similarly, a culmination of all time experienced is what accumulates into *history*, which is more like a network of lots of smaller distributed occurrences. The state of your body would be analogous to this interpretation of history, where the collective aging, or damage of each individual cell, are what produce a matured, or dying organism. Time experienced is a bottom-up phenomenon, but time perceived is a top-down experience.

We normally envision an axis in 3-dimensional space as a direction, to translate this understanding through the idea of a limit of perception, time would be the dimension of scale. Just as physical laws transform into different paradigms at different scales, time, as the 4th dimensional axis, extends in and out of the microcosm. You can think of every continuous piece of space having a microcosm of its own wherever there's matter, and on that scale of size comes the axis of time. Likewise, you can extend it in the direction of the macrocosm and it would point in every direction simultaneously, as strange as that is. **The axis of time is spherical.** Where there's but one macrocosm to extend to, and an infinite number of potential microcosms that stand opposed to it. A single *stabilizing* point that stands opposed to an infinite amount of infinitely *fragmentive* counterparts. Traveling along this axis to the macrocosm is simple, and operates as expected. As any 2 initial microcosmic spheres grow larger and larger, as they approach having an infinite volume, they approach becoming the same sphere independent of their starting positions. Regardless of their initial distance, the difference in starting positions becomes infinitesimally small, and negligible. But moving in the opposite direction, towards the microcosm, would force you to pick just one final point in an infinite sea of possible choices.

When it comes to celestial bodies, gravity affects spacetime to distort the axis of time in a single direction, towards the center of gravity. When you fall, you're not *experiencing* gravity, so to speak, you're moving in the direction of time. Which is why relativity sees gravity as a form of curved geometry, a sphere is just the culmination of what these curves result in. The core of a source of gravity becomes the most locally respected axis of time. Gravity is time that's being redirected to align with space, they're the same thing. Time *is* gravity, more specifically it's the large-scale centralization of time experienced, its compartmentalization. This takes shape as a local reference frame, specifically it spurs the creation of these frames within itself, which for practical purposes are no different than inertial frames. All the same it's an inertial frame that's on the traveling ship that's capable of acting like a separate block of time.

Explaining time through spherical coordinates isn't a new idea. It was first used around the same time Einstein came up with his ideas on relativity. Herman Minkowski first used this concept to explain time as a factor of the universe, he actually used 4-dimensional cones to explain a measure of distance across spacetime[48]. The same way that to slice a 3-dimensional cone into 2-dimensional pieces would yield a host of circles, any 3-dimensional slice of a 4-dimensional cone would then generate a sphere within 3-dimensional space. These resulting spherical shells then explain a distance of spacetime in a perceivable format to anyone looking to understand the topic in an intuitive manner. Consider a span of time where an occurrence takes place, the occurrence could be a signal that's sent from one location to another. The final instance of that occurrence could be visualized as a large sphere whose radius expands from its starting location to its final destination, representing the maximum distance that something could have traveled from its starting position in any direction within that time. If you trace the entirety of the occurrence across time, you would get a set of these spheres representing each individual instance. The 4-dimensional cone would be a representation of all of those spheres together, with each axis of time encompassing its own potential within this same exact framework.

Even the idea of time as a spatially distributed physical concept has been forged across decades. Shin'ichirō Tomonaga first reasoned for a spatially distributed concept of time, and purposed an equation to do so[49]. It had reconciled discrepancies between Schrödinger's

48. Hendrik Lorentz et al. *The Principle of Relativity*. Methuen and Company, 1923

49. Shin'ichirō Tomonaga. *On a Relativistically Invariant Formulation of the Quantum Theory of Wave Fields*. Riken Iho, 1943

equation, which demanded a universal concept of time, and Special Relativity, which insisted there's no single time that every observer can agree on. Julian Schwinger independently derived the same equation some years later and purposed it into the greater frameworks of Quantum Field Theory[50]. Richard Arnowitt, Stanley Deser, and Charles W. Misner then rewrote General Relativity into a form that allowed each piece of space to carry its own mathematical clock[51,52, 53]. Their framework being built atop of the concept of time being spatially distributed in every piece of matter allowed for the proper simulation of space. Any snapshot of some physical scenario could be moved forward, step by step, and accurately understood through this framework. Bryce DeWitt then took a step towards making such simulations in Quantum Field Theory[54]. He applied the style of framework offered by Arnowitt, Deser, and Misner to Quantum Field Theory in order to treat the whole geometry of spacetime as a single quantum object. In his picture there's no single master clock that applies to the universe at large. Instead, every piece of matter experiences time independently from every other, yet the time of each would still simultaneously connect to every other piece of space in its proximity, like molecules of water moving in an ocean. Eventually, Stephen Hawking and James Hartle transformed this concept into something that could take advantage of all these principles while not requiring there to be mathematical clocks embedded at the hypothetical beginning of the universe, which allowed for the formulation of a novel starting condition for the Big Bang[55].

It's no coincidence that the theories of physics became more coherent as the concept of time became a more intrinsic part of space and matter itself from within its calculations. The field was undergoing an *approach* of infinite refinement no different than that found within

50. Julian Schwinger. *The Theory of Quantized Fields I*. Physical Review, 1951
51. Richard Arnowitt and Stanley Deser. *Quantum Theory of Gravitation: General Formulation and Linearized Theory*. Physical Review, 1959
52. Richard Arnowitt, Stanley Deser, and Charles W Misner. *Canonical Variables for General Relativity*. Physical Review, 1960
53. Richard Arnowitt, Stanley Deser, and Charles W Misner. *Coordinate Invariance and Energy Expressions in General Relativity*. Physical Review, 1961
54. Bryce DeWitt. *Quantum Theory of Gravity. I. The Canonical Theory*. Physical Review, 1967
55. James Hartle and Stephen Hawking. *Wave Function of the Universe*. Physical Review, 1983

the framework of calculus. Increasingly useful gateways were opened through these detailed incorporations of a spatially distributed concept of time *because* a spatially distributed concept of time is the way in which the universe operates. It wouldn't provide valuable results if it weren't true, it wouldn't model this environment successfully.

The nature of the axis of time is that of scale, it's what differentiates a small observer from a large one. Likewise, a giant clock would experience similar problems. To take this even further, imagine you have an analog clock with just one arm. It can spin once per second, or thousands of times per second if you wish it so. Next, imagine there's a small embedded clock sitting at the end of its arm, and there would then be another clock embedded within that sub-clock's arm. You can either imagine this in a finite manner to prevent the clocks from caving in due to gravity, or you can go further to envision this hypothetical problem with an infinite number of clocks. Each sub-clock would experience a staggered time dilation, producing different elapsed times in order of their physical embeddings, and relative to the frequency of the arms. Despite occupying the same space, and even being inside one another, they would record time differently, because an ideal clock only exists in mathematics. That's to say, the measurement of time within a measurement of time yields an offset across both measurements. Real clocks undergo the effects of time experienced, and that demonstrates the compartmentalization of time. To not differentiate time experienced from time perceived would present this analogy as saying that the measurement of time is dependent on time itself, which poses a contradiction. To even allow the gravity of clocks to influence everything within the example would then imply that time affects time. But when you can clarify that it's time perceived which is dependent on time experienced, one can note that time perceived is a psychological phenomenon that has brought forth an idealized modeling of time experienced that doesn't exist in the real world, and that's because time experienced is a local phenomenon of deep compartmentalization no different than the nature of our tellings of history.

Time perceived is the perspective of a detector, it's a directionally opposite representation of the actual physical phenomenon, so it shouldn't be the base layer of a physical model as if it were the real thing. Our sense of time is a detection, which is why Einstein insisted upon time being relative, time perceived is a detected phenomenon that only applies to an observer, no different than needs to be considered for any other detector within these same physical models. Explaining physics from the perspective of a detector would only yield a flawed model compared to deriving the output of the detector from the model. Like the modeling of any other detector, it should be the *product* of physical models, not a core principle of them.

Our perception of 3-dimensional space is made from a perceived lack of this spherical coordinate system. In the backdrop of an infinite number of microcosms, viewed from the scale of our perception, there's an implied straightness to the 3 dimensions we visualize. The norm is actually the spherical coordinate system, our 3-dimensional perception of reality being rectangular is more of a trick. We can't see this nature of the microcosms around us because of their size. Lots of small spheres next to each other form what seem like straight lines, which is just another form of interaction that occurs differently as structures scale.

Every notable object in the universe tends to be spherical. Even the limits of what we can observe emerges in a spherical shape. You might try arguing the reason for these things, in defence of rectangular geometry, and the reasons can either be cast aside or brought to the forefront of the argument, it doesn't matter. Everything around us respects a spherical geometry, therefore so should we.

I find it to be a misconception that the speed of light is a universal speed limit, I don't believe it's light or anything else that has a limit to how fast it moves. Instead, it would seem that spacetime, as the medium by which things pass through, enforces what seems like a speed limit. Rather, it limits perception, as a speed limit to observation itself. Light probably experiences relativistic-like slowdowns no different than what an outside observer notices of a planet. It wouldn't be relativistic itself, as light seems to travel at the speed of light regardless of any inertial frame, but with the possibility of slowing down time at all comes the potential for the same occurring in other physical contexts. What we perceive through observation is independent of what actually occurs simply because we can't observe every layer of every microcosm with our eyes or instruments. It would seem that *time* is a perception wherever it's observed, independent of where it's experienced. It's perception, relative to some location along the axis of time itself, that enables a gestalt of limitation.

Time itself is as much a perception as it is a phenomenon, your brain is a sense for time the same way your eyes are a sense for your surroundings. Assuming there's the implied extreme difficulty of Einstein's limitation in something traveling faster than the speed of light, is there some way to turn this into a possibility? General Relativity insists one would need infinite energy in order to do so, but this doesn't mean it isn't possible. If something could break this speed limit, what would it be and how would it do so? That answer will be in a later chapter.

4.6 Infinite Universe

We live under some pretty obvious contradictions, I'd like to clear away some of what I think are blatant lies, and some of what are reasonable untruths. They say there's no such thing as perpetual motion. But isn't that what we are? We are the objects that don't stop moving. You might say there's a lot of reason behind why it's not technically perpetual motion, and you can bring out details from all of biology, chemistry, and physics just to reason that we do eventually stop moving. But then I would add, that before that, we end up giving birth to the next thing that doesn't stop moving. Perhaps you would shoot back to say that only works until we run out of resources on our planet. To which I would argue that there are resources all over the universe, which we haven't yet found any limits to, and this argument can continue indefinitely. Then I would insist, much like the nature of this debate, that the universe itself is also infinite.

Maybe you'd bite back, and say there's no *evidence* that the universe is infinite. That I've brought a baseless claim to the table. So then propose a mechanism by which the planets, stars, and galaxies all stop moving. Then propose a mechanism by which every molecule in the universe approaches 0 degrees kelvin the way heat death would. Well there's certainly no *evidence* of that being possible, yet it's widely believed that it will definitely happen. Based on the transformations of matter across the universe, it would seem the idea of heat death doesn't need to only consider an unchanging universe, it needs to wrestle with the fact that transformations of complexity actively resist such ends. No one has managed to achieve 0K with even a single atom yet, and that's not for a lack of trying, so of course there's no mechanism for it. The latest record achieved 38 picokelvin[56], comparable to

56. Christian Deppner et al. *Collective-Mode Enhanced Matter-Wave Optics*. Physical Review Letters, 2021

the surface temperatures of supermassive black holes. Is 0K achievable? It might be possible, although there's an asymptotic difficulty in achieving even fractional differences in this realm. Newton's limitation doesn't measure up to reality. In fact, it's reality that seems to be getting in the way.

You might argue that due to the continually increasing nature of entropy, that the eventual heat death of the universe is inevitable, and everything *will* at some point stop moving. You might even argue that certain objects, and their aggregate molecules, will at some point stop moving and destabilize long before then. But is there a point to caring if any one motion isn't perpetual? Motion *itself* is perpetual. There's always motion somewhere. It seems there will always be moving components of the universe, as well as whatever greater stage it seems to be dancing on. As saying perpetual motion doesn't exist is also stating that perpetuity doesn't exist.

I'd also like to argue against this decrepit dogma, that the universe is a finite number of particles trapped in a glass box where entropy only ever increases and nothing happens afterwards. These imposed artificial constraints don't exist in nature. The simple dogmatic scheme of basic entropy is not respectful of the complexity of the universe, and implies it has limiting boundaries. By natural entropic development, complexity is an inevitable feature of the universe. As is what you find on Earth, as is what you'll find throughout the universe, there are no simplicities. An all-encompassing boundary is much too simple of an idea. Any imposition of finitism would be done by disaster, some natural calamity, that prevents further exploration like the oceans once used to. Not some glass wall.

With no boundaries comes no finale. There will be no heat death of the universe just as there will be no climate catastrophe on Earth. Both of these beliefs are the same kind of lower bound nihilism, a necessary precaution that comes with an insidious trap that's not to be mistaken for an end result. The insidious trap leads down the same route that nihilism warns about, nihilists will claim to have all the answers but are just as ignorant as they assume others careless. So why are nihilists consistently incorrect? They're meant to be, it's a feature, not a bug. They oversimplify, and that's an instinctual mechanism for caution. It acts as a speed bump, the caution is meant to be overcome when found appropriate to do so once someone can pass its test. Oversimplifications tend to lose out in the long run, because they fail to model complexity where it's comprehensible. So are there any other oversimplifications we can fish out of this scheme?

Believing in the eventual heat death of the universe relies on the idea that matter and energy are somehow finite, which allows for the idea that a finite amount of things will eventually stop moving if you wait long enough. The problem with this is the story of creation, and our own technological shortcomings. Mass and energy seemed to have spawned out of nowhere, so it's possible there's a yet unobserved mechanism somewhere, throughout the cosmos, that could be operating right now, spewing more of it out. But I'd prefer to avoid relying on an unobserved concept. Still, there's no creation model that seems to contradict this, whether you want to abide by the Big Bang, or whether you believe it was the work of God.

We haven't observed any limits to the universe, only limits to our observations. It would be intellectually dishonest to assume any exist. Everywhere we look there are new celestial bodies. By refuting the concept of heat death in favor of the infinite nature of reality, you can embrace a philosophy of infinite complexity. This opens the door to finding the latent universal parallels that exist around us. It seems reasonable, and acts as a basis for integrating as close to a first principle understanding as possible using background knowledge with no calculations, after having been thrown into this chaotic array of life with never-ending streams of information all around and no clear point of origin for neither sanity nor existence.

We've made estimates of the age of the universe, but that doesn't mean we've been measuring the age of the universe. This approach is likely nowhere near finished, the universe is likely of infinite age. By the time we understand the full breadth of what was originally attempted in these measurements, we'll find this age doesn't apply to the new layers of complexity that emerge from our increased abilities in measurement brought about by our expanded wisdom.

In measuring the age of the universe, I can somewhat predict how it will turn out. The current estimate of the age of the universe is roughly 13.8 billion years. But the idea that this measurement is incorrect isn't even the flaw I wish to pick at most, it's the concept of what's being measured. Even the measurement of the age of the Earth was slowly refined over many years until a realistic value was finally arrived at. The same is happening with the picture of human evolution as we uncover more archeological findings. Our understanding of the age, vastness, and history of the universe will constantly expand in a manner more complex than what had originally occurred for the age of the Earth. Those who are implying that there's a limit to the size of the universe are wrong, and likewise regarding its age.

The Big Bang as an origin story is probably wrong, though not unreasonable. It's more likely that it's a premature idea of what humanity will later come to expand upon. As we expand our powers of observation, and by the time the next major theory of how our universe likely came about comes around, either the theory arrived at will show little to no resemblance to the nature of the Big Bang, or a concept resembling the Big Bang will be merely an embedded piece inside a larger picture. Then another theory will then expand these concepts again, embedding yet another layer. Why is this? Because wherever we gain better powers of observation we can expect to find more complexity. It's already looking like the inside of a proton has an extraordinarily complicated set of factors and interactions[**57**,**58**]. We'll likely find things that become increasingly more complex in either direction we look.

For one to think it's insane to believe God is the creator of the universe, only to claim there was some massive expansionary force of unexplainable origins to incite the Big Bang, you may as well believe it was Santa Claus who lit it off with a firework because all three of these scenarios are equally as absurd. Saying nothing existed, then something did, is missing way too many details. Our clearest picture of a creation story still isn't anything different than a myth, even if you want to add in some measurements and scientific credibility. Whether the universe was hypothetically filled with a bunch of hydrogen doesn't avert the same criticism. Obviously no one can know the real answer, that's the point. Modern science can't escape the ridiculously fictitious sounding narrative that gets forced upon itself. It's not that anyone's stupid for trying to understand it. Quite the opposite. The urge to understand it is as much a biological necessity as it is an existential search. But

57. H1 Collaboration and ZEUS Collaborations. *Combination of Measurements of Inclusive Deep Inelastic e±p Scattering Cross Sections and QCD Analysis of HERA Data.* European Physical Journal C, 2015

58. VD Burkert, L Elouadrhiri, and FX Girod. *The Pressure Distribution Inside the Proton.* Nature, 2018

it's equally as stupid to assign worth beyond that which may have been dreamed up millennia ago. As even our best scientific understanding is likely closer to absurd fiction than it is to absolute truth.

No matter the context, it's the act of creation itself that defies all laws. It's more likely there was no creation. As absurd as it sounds. Saying *things exist because they always have* seems to make slightly more sense than saying *things suddenly started existing*. But even that's still absurd, which doesn't do a good job at reducing the size of the problem. In dealing with these absurdities, maybe it's better to embrace the absurdity. Is there a way to argue *both* that things have always existed and that they have a starting point?

The idea of the creation of the universe is a paradox no matter how you spell it out, and the creation of creation itself is a paradox of a paradox. If a paradox is just truth we can't yet grasp, then we may as well look for a better paradox to explain creation. If you consider the universe to have been created, then you must ask how it was created. The problem with this is that it results in an infinite loop, where the creation process must somehow itself be created. So any singular point of creation seems to be unrealistic, and also leads to the postulation for a lack thereof. Then it seems more reasonable to say it's infinite, has always existed, and will always exist independent of a starting point. Which has problems in itself, because a timescale without a starting point seems unintuitive. On the other hand, it may be reasonably intuitive to note the self-assembling nature of life may find a parallel in the assembly of the universe itself.

It seems our planet, star, and solar system all came from material that has a cosmic origin, born from celestial bodies across billions of years. We will undoubtedly someday build a telescope more powerful than the James Webb, and we'll yet again find out that everything is even more vast and unexplainable than we previously believed. Finding more anomalies every time. It might be your intuition that looking amongst and beyond subatomic particles might not lead you to a measurement about the entire universe, but it was isotopes of lead that were used to determine the age of the Earth[59]. I find it likely to be ironic that we look out towards the stars when considering creation, towards the macrocosm rather than the microcosm.

59. Claire Patterson. *Age of Meteorites and the Earth*. Geochimica et Cosmochimica Acta, 1956

What I'd suggest, that instead of looking towards the infinite, as all you'll find is the infinite, in particles as you would throughout the stars, I find it more reasonable to consider our known universe is, just as everything else, between two sources of disorder. Like oppositional pushback between that of the micro and macrocosms. Where once they were of some independent origin, they eventually grew in the same direction and acted as opposing forces that created a balance residing in where we now find ourselves. You might think that the largest entities are always made up of everything down to elementary particles and beyond. So this probably, reasonably, seems like an odd understanding. What I consider is that there are two layers to our universe. One that constructs from the top-down, and the other from the bottom-up. Just as life had with order and disorder, respectively.

It's the goal of the modern scientific apparatus to find *one* first principle. The underlying rule that will derive everything else. But either there are some serious missing pieces, or that it actually takes two to tango, as it does with pools of entropy. I think the separate rules for what derives from the microcosm versus the macrocosm will continue to elucidate themselves as such, I suspect there's a different set of bottom-up rules than top-down rules. As you scale a phenomenon, it interacts under a different set of rules for massive objects, or even clusters of massive objects. It seems to be that within the realm of physics there is currently no unifying principle to explain both the macro and microcosm together. Or more specifically, there's no reconciling the different ways to describe the curvature of spacetime under both Quantum Field Theory and General Relativity[**60,61**]. Physics, as a field, will not find a unifying principle in general. Even if so for spacetime curvature someday, there will again be a divide, or a divide will always eventually re-emerge. The occurrence of this divide is inevitable. For what has been uncovered, those at work have generally arrived at the correct answers. There are two guiding conceptual forces as explained through the modern theories. Beyond that, it seems more reasonable to state it doesn't create the universe specifically, it creates complexity. Complexity is the apex of the results of this collision between two sets of rules, and it's just as difficult for the universe to create it as it is for us to elucidate it. Whether greater complexity for the universe, or greater

60. Léon Rosenfeld. *On the Quantization of Wave Fields*. Annalen der Physik, 1930
61. Matvei Bronstein. *Quantum Theory of Weak Gravitational Fields*. Physikalische Zeitschrift der Sowjetunion, 1936

elucidations of physics, the complete reconciliation of both sides, the estimation of this center value, this core truth, is always of the greatest difficulty. As there are two sets of rules that collide, and together they've fueled the creation of this universe.

There you have it, both a starting point for this universe as well as the basis for a likely infinite timescale for whatever came before it by the same paradoxical technicality. Where an acceptance of two ideas, General Relativity and Quantum Field Theory, evolves from initially assuming their natural contradiction, like the meshing of Lamarckism into Darwinism.

It's hard to comment on the true nature of either of these, but their origins are probably achieved by a concept most parallel to that which brought about life. The more we look towards either scale, detecting microcosms beyond subatomic particles, or peering further out into the universe itself to find even larger structures, the grounds upon which we search are likely to be infinite. But if it's infinite, then can anything ever be characterized from a causal-deterministic point of view? Can we ever find a first principle of everything in the universe? Of anything? We may not be currently savvy enough to arrive at any form of explanation to this for now through exact scientific rigor, and whether that can be done in the future is to be determined, but without any research I can still answer the question. In characterizing not the first principle that's expected to be sought out, but instead an integral of this derivative of infinite age, size, and character, the further one peers towards either scale of the cosmos, the more rational it will be to agree that the foundational principles of the universe arrive to us through the transformations and interactions of entropy and irony.

4.7 Recursions

Optimized entropy comes to optimized solutions, many of which mirror the same solutions found in other areas of life due to the problems being parallel in nature. Parallel solutions from parallel problems are not surprising. In fact, when the same solution exists within a context that's a subcontext of the same solution, you end up with an interesting array of recursions. It's similar to convergent evolution. An example for the sake of enlightenment on this topic would be the bacterial transmembrane protein complex that looks and functions exactly like an electric motor[62,63]. The electric motor was invented independent of knowing it existed in nature. As odd as it may seem, much like how our conceptualizations of entropy are not a coincidence, this motor design is the exact same mechanism used by many bacteria to control their flagella. While this might not seem like a true recursion, because these flagella don't have a purpose inside a real electric motor, it's still temporally recursive. Human civilization, and all of its precursors, would have only ever been built atop a world of microbes that had already formed such contraptions throughout their evolution, and there's strong evidence to suggest this protein complex came about before the advent of multicellular life[64,65].

In general, the exact same solutions are arrived at in broadly different situations, this protein complex is a crisp example of what kind of recursions are possible, as would be something like a cell's nucleus and a brain. These patterns repeat because they're solutions to the same problem that arose in multiple contexts. But these aren't in the same form as what's normally referred to as recursions, normally they're something that comes from inside of something else, which would be endobolic. In most instances of our biology, their evolving formations across time, and even philosophies of complex life forms, the recursions are outward forming, they're epibolic.

Normally these recursions would grow biologically, as layers of tissue. But we grow our philosophies, religions, and intellectual pursuits in the same fashion, because these forms of intellectual growth are just recursions of biological growth itself. This is the nature of life, it's what makes life possible. So it doesn't seem strange that life forms then eventually learn the same tricks that formed themselves in the first place, to leverage energy through every possible dimension for benefit. This leverage will provide the opportunity to transcend limitations rather than be left helpless in the face of the heat death of the universe. From

---

62. Howard C Berg and Robert A Anderson. *Bacteria Swim by Rotating their Flagellar Filaments*. Nature, 1973
63. Prashant K Singh et al. *CryoEM Structures Reveal how the Bacterial Flagellum Rotates and Switches Direction*. Nature Microbiology, 2024
64. Renyi Liu and Howard Ochman. *Stepwise Formation of the Bacterial Flagellar System*. Proceedings of the National Academy of Sciences of the United States of America, 2007
65. Adrián A Davín et al. *A Geological Timescale for Bacterial Evolution and Oxygen Adaptation*. Science, 2025

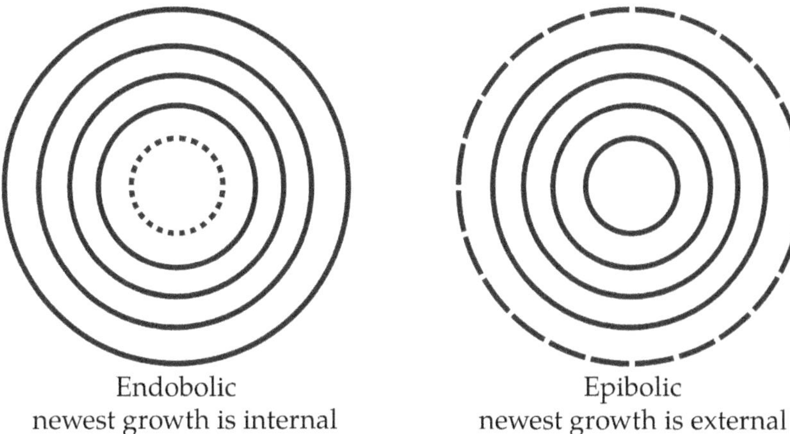

Figure 4: Directionality of Recursions

the nature of these repeating embedded patterns, these recursions, we can find extremely successful states of circumstance that are not where they are by chance. In discovering them, we can attempt to incorporate them into our own culture and society at large should it prove beneficial, for the end goal of increased benefit for those who participate. The largest example would be that of Williston's law, and it's resemblance to the transformation of stars across the time span of the universe.

Transcendence, in this case, would mean to rise above the recursions that you were born within. To escape out of them like a creation having mastered its own nature. Like a child out of their mother's womb, which is itself a literal recursion. Just as the meaning of heat is to disperse throughout the universe, the meaning of life is to disperse beyond it.

Describing life as something that came about once order could encapsulate disorder misses a requirement. It must somehow persist. This isn't just repetitive. Life itself is not an infinite loop of behavior, nor is this just something elongating its own life either. Its reproduction is recursive by way of its own success. When considering an entire species, the most successful microstates go on to determine the future of their collective macrostate.

What exactly is statistical entropy in the context of a living organism? People insist that you must only consider rearrangements of something in ways that retains its original form and function. In that case, this definition becomes difficult to apply to an organism conceptually as you would need to work through atoms, molecules, cellular machinery, and cells either individually or together. Maybe even to different sections of organs if you rearrange them carefully enough to preserve functionality. What exactly is the micro and macrostate of an organism? Take a piece of steel for example, you can imagine its statistical entropy would be highest if it's all beat up and broken. Its statistical entropy would be smallest when every piece of it is in some uniform conformation with every other piece. The ideal macrostate of an organism is one in which compartmentalized functions, of extremely uniform processes, all play out as efficiently as one another in completely separate environments. It has layers to its microstates which are defined by functionality as much as they are structure, yet compartmentalization is the most significant functionality of all, as it functions as a structure. The integrity of compartmentalization itself is the most fitting biological parallel to physical statistical entropy.

You can consider a species, or ecosystem, to be a kind of macrostate. Likewise, modern organisms are made up of more than just one set of encapsulated disorder. Cells have multiple compartmentalized organelles, bodies have multiple compartmentalized organs. Which reflects how successful the paradigm of recursive encapsulation really is. Could it be a modeling of something?

In living things, microstates seem to have microstates of their own. The purpose of that recursive compartmentalization is to resist any increase in entropy. All the same, if you put a dead animal in a glass box you'll find it there for much longer than if you left it in a forest. The universe is made up of the same kind of structures, but it's hard to envision every layer of the physical world due to the obscurity of its nature. Organisms have uniquely large microstates called cells, and organs, where it's possible to imagine this process more vividly. Understanding the microstates of particles hasn't proven to be simple, but they undoubtedly exist in some understandable form.

In general, we see these different forms of optimized internal order stemming up from the microcosm. What else stems from the microcosm? The axis of time! Recursive compartmentalization is a modeling of the interaction of time across cosmic scales. Whether cells, organs, or even countries, compartmentalization itself is a hedge against the effects of time. Entropy, and its creations, are undeniably a reflection of the nature of the 4th dimension. Just as subatomic particles became parts of atoms, atoms became parts of molecules, molecules made organic automatons, and humans as organisms came to understand all of these things together, entropy is a bridge that allows the transcendence of complexity along the axis of time. These hedges succeeded, and so will we in our own transcendence through economy, governance, religion, and anything else that will take us towards escaping the heat death, or destruction, of the universe itself.

It's consciousness that acts as the bridge of the last known leg of this problem. But what is consciousness? It derives from the automaton. Instead of being just a simple counting process, it has two opposing sides that push back and forth against each other, as recursions of order and disorder, each one aiming to prioritize its own counting process. Each individual count leads to a different regulatory conformation, a paradigm at every step. As it grows more advanced, each individual bifurcation grows its recursive tree of subcomponents. Each subcomponent then grows its depth based on the energy required to perform its task well enough relative to the importance of ever other mechanism at the automaton's disposal. Eventually, with enough awareness of the surrounding world, it transcends towards awareness of itself.

At some point, the exact bifurcating structures probably grew so complex that they began to overlap, and became non-trivial to directly recognize through protein interaction networks. Regardless, it's possible to know these bifurcations are real because they transcend the automaton, they're visible in the most core aspect of human society. Where arguments of for and against mimic that exact same bifurcated structure.

V
POLITICS & GOVERNANCE

5.1 Left and Right

Everything is political. You might believe there was once a time where this wasn't the case. But it was actually that most topics were less important. The food you put on your table isn't political until you can't find any.

Politicized systems always consist of two main opposing forces. You might object, claiming there are political systems with multiple parties, and some with only one. No matter the party, they're always defined as either left- or right-wing in some regard. So-called centrists are just relatively centrist, not absolutely so. If it does ever seem that a third option appears, it's more likely because what used to be two sides have mellowed, and become more similar than different. Other exceptions would be that a situation is militant, rather than civil, or that even deeper bifurcations are drawn around ethnic lines. Even countries with one predominant political party have two internal factions beneath the surface. This rule is never violated in spirit, and political machines where these bifurcations don't arise make for less efficient governance.

Why does this surface in human populations? From a mechanical point of view, it would be the social manifestations of the bifurcations of the automaton, being social manifestations means they've transcended individual nodes to become parts of a distributed calculation across a population. The reason these bifurcations emerge is because it makes for the most efficient prioritization process, and it arises because it's a recursion of the same prioritizations that occur within organisms. Does either side play a special function? Do the two sides together find some kind of final harmony, where either one would be worse off should they eventually endeavor alone? Ultimately, one wing is built on ideas independent of reality, and the other on reality independent of ideas. Both are entirely legitimate ways of viewing the world, and most individuals are a complicated mix of both. Governance acts as the balance between the two.

People will betray their own principles just to punish someone else for seemingly betraying theirs. In the process, either side will ignore their own stance, stand on their opponents' principles, and accuse each other of hypocrisy. Often times they even use words entirely separate from their actions in order to do so. Where words are reversed from actions, actions are distant from principles, and either side takes a stance they don't actually stand by, the simple word to describe this is *politics*. It's the embodiment of deliberation. Making it the most monumental conduit of irony. But why must they always argue back and forth? Why can't any individual society ever agree on what's actually good for themselves?

Deliberation, like definitions, comes between two boundaries of convergence because it's the art of the estimation of a center value. The bounds in this case become the individuals who uphold their values. The highest complexity is neither at the upper nor lower bound, like it's neither at the highest nor lowest entropy, it's between the two. Achieving an estimate of this center value takes more energy than it does to perceive this problem's existence, which means it ultimately takes more time to solve. The automaton is that which has two opposing forces, two competing modes of functionality. Like the two competing paradigms at the cutting edge of physics, reconciling the difference between either side is a problem that can only be solved with time.

People on either wing view each other as fundamentally backwards. This is directly related to the derivative-integral basis rather than any simple linear relationship, two things opposed don't stand opposite. For further explanation I'll borrow descriptions of the left- and right-brain from Iain McGilchrist[66]. McGilchrist avoids a political classi-

66. Iain McGilchrist. *The Master and His Emissary*. Yale University Press, 2009

fication in his descriptions, which I think is somewhat correct yet not entirely accurate all at the same time. He describes a right-brain that sees the big picture, and a left-brain that is hyperfocused on a goal. The best description he offers paints a solid evolutionary origin, the left-brain predation functionality, and the right-brain predator avoidance functionality. Where the right-brain maintains an awareness of its surroundings, and the left-brain is used for attaining things of great value when needed.

Across any political preferences, the core functionality of either hemisphere can be preserved while simultaneously manifesting in different ways because the two groups play different roles in society. Each relying on their relevant hemisphere to a greater degree through philosophy and lifestyle. Either, through relation to the earlier classification of intelligence, is modeling either the known or the unknown more heavily than the other. McGilchrist speaks in somewhat opposite terms to what I'm going to use, so allow me to reconcile them as they don't actually contradict. He regards the left-brain as being focused on what's known, and the right-brain as being attuned to the unknown. The way I see this, the political left is actually modeling the unknown using the specifics of what has previously been uncovered, the known, the derivative. Put plainly, it's modeling the unknown by using the known. The political left are constantly trying to match puzzle pieces of what's known into empty spaces of the unknown for the sake of matching a familiar understanding to an unfamiliar environment. While the political right is modeling the known as a way of navigating the unknown and the constant uncertainties of life through the worldview they hold, the integral. Modeling the known to navigate the unknown. The former is constantly asking what worldview is appropriate, the latter is continually testing whether they can trust their worldview.

This doesn't mean a politically left person doesn't see the big picture of the world, but it's not where their main interest lies. Likewise, a politically right person isn't incapable of hyperfocusing on details, they're just more tuned to watching the movements of society in relation to its big picture. There's a kind of infinite recursion that occurs within these concepts. The deeper the classification goes, the more recursions you see, and the more irony you can incorporate. While I limit my descriptions to a depth that presents the pair, a single classification could use the words *known* and *unknown* together fourteen times for a single description and one could still go further while describing smaller and smaller groups in society. This alternating functionality is more akin to two people peering over each other's shoulder to watch the other's back. Human societies always have this functionality, it's an evolved feature. The societal structure of humans mimics the bifurcation of their brain hemispheres. Which is a recursion of this bifurcation, and where there's a recursion you're bound to find some kind of underlying truth.

Western society has found a balance between these two forces that combine into the most desirable traits of either side. Liberal values center themselves most strongly around Voltaire's call for freedom of expression[**67**], Montesquieu's separation of power[**68**], John Locke's consent of the governed[**69**], Thomas Jefferson's inalienable rights[**70**, **71**], and the concept of equality before the law, which had been around before the Magna Carta. None of these were entirely original, having predecessors from thousands of years prior. People like Cicero, Aristotle, Polybius, Socrates, and more had covered less matured precursors to all the same topics. The fact that they've come back to be re-emphasized over and over is testament that a functional society can't be established without them. The power of operating on these values, and the widespread fairness and prosperity they bring, would lead anyone with functional brain hemispheres to assume they're naturally occurring axioms *because* of the success they deliver upon implementation.

The other major force in Western society is religion, but that will be addressed in a different chapter. Put briefly, it's the preservation of tradition, family, and their continuance that make up the core of conservative values. These are the two groups you must deal with in society. Naturally, like the functionality of the hemispheres, no one consists of purely one or the other. Both aspects were difficult to develop to fruition, but politics is largely about the refinement of interactions across large societies. Fair exchange was a political challenge to

---

67. Voltaire. *Treatise on Tolerance.* Cramer Brothers, 1763

68. Montesquieu. *The Spirit of the Laws.* Barrillot & Fils, 1748

69. John Locke. *Two Treatises of Government.* Awnsham Churchill, 1689

70. Thomas Jefferson. *A Summary View of the Rights of British America.* Clementina Rind, 1774

71. Second Continental Congress. *The Declaration of Independence.* John Dunlap, 1776

perfect throughout the course of history. This problem gets more difficult with more people, as well as with higher connectivity amongst them.

They say there's a pendulum that swings back and forth between left and right. I see it as more of an optimization process. The left digs a hole only to not find what they expected. The right comes in and uses the hole as a foundation to build something more appropriate. Without the left, the right wouldn't build anything. Without the right, the left would be stuck digging their own grave. The left can be right about the need for an idea, and wrong about its implementation. The left can dream but they can't implement. The right can implement, but they won't seek changes if they aren't provoked, especially in social structures. All of this together matches the description of the broken compass.

A commonly used theme in storytelling is the king and his two advisors, each with a different point of view. Neither is necessarily incorrect, but it's the king's job to find middle ground between the two. The point of a functional political system is that you have a liberal arm on a conservative body. If successful, the liberal arm eventually becomes a functional part of the body and persists. This is, physically, what happens when insects and animals evolve new limbs or wings.

Insects evolved wings through small steps. They didn't directly change their limbs into wings. The limb was typically lost after a wing was gained. Before flying, you have gliding, and prior to that you have jumping. Why are the steps so small and steady? Because each liberal arm is always an experiment.

In humans it's not the arm that's liberal, it's the ideas. It's always changes in philosophy, thought, and culture that bring about experimentation in human society. Like large-scale poison testers across a population, the left and the right together make a hedged bet. The purpose of the right is risk neutralization. This pattern isn't unique, in fact it's recursive with regard to men and women being of the same nature. Men are high risk and high reward, as both individuals and collectives. The bell curve of male behavior is much wider than for women, as men can succeed massively or fail terribly. Women risk-neutralize, their bell curve is much shorter, as there's a narrower band of evolutionary success associated with the role of growing a child.

Liberals and conservatives together form a hedged bet. I'm willing to bet, and as you can probably imagine, throughout human history there have consistently been groups of people always experimenting with new foods, breaking away from dogmatic norms, building new things, and exploring new places. They were likely people who either had something to prove, nothing to lose, or were pushed to the brink of desperation. Others played the part of being aware of the general dangers of not following cultural norms, knowing that they tended to exist for a reason, and chose to not participate in such excessive risk-taking. One side experiments to make sure those ventures are reasonable, while the other doesn't, like an experimental and control group. If an experiment turns out to be worthwhile, it can be of great benefit to the group as a whole. Which obviously works, because these experimental and control groups are built into our innate socioevolutionary behavior.

Another example of the conservative body and liberal arm can be found in the evolution of corporations. There was, once upon a time, an age where software companies were a specific kind of company, and many companies didn't have IT departments. But since the advent of technological advancement, every company has its own technological wing of some kind. Because where in the modern day would you find yourself without at least a few software engineers? It's a necessity. Having passed the test of time, now no one can compete without it.

Another way to view the socioevolutionary hedged bet is through the lens of antagonism. With no true external rivalry, any society would turn to compete with itself. Normally, there would be a risk neutralizing control group staying at home maintaining the birth rate. With the experimental wing being weaponized for defending against some enemy, the control group grows and maintains the society. But with the defeat of a major adversary, the experimental wing turns on its own society. The left, in this case, has acted as an overactive immune system to the right where their movements gained great traction roughly 25 years after both the victory of WWII and the collapse of the Soviet Union. Like perpetual penetration testers looking to find the flaws that any parasite might take advantage of, like a woman shit-testing a man.

In a social system, the left acts as pseudopredators to the right, and tries to find any vulnerabilities within their stability so it can be addressed and fixed. The left would be making sure the right is well practiced at its function and not susceptible to falling prey to predators. Like a real immune system, they can become too aggressive and kill their host, or severely impede it. This is the nature of left-wing extremism, the analogy of the angry swarm of millions of mosquitoes. With each individual bug being a single flaw that could be exploited, it's antithetical to any uniform description. On a practical level, this behavior is not easily generalizable except from a very big picture perspective. Likewise, when an extreme right-wing backlash occurs, they've historically blamed their problems on some scapegoat because it's often been so difficult for them to classify what they're actually fighting against. It's a militaristic fight for survival after losing control of their own fate to the swarm.

Why does either side go extreme? Liberalism and conservatism are static points on a line, these definitions can't be changed. Despite many in the modern day attempting to do so. But on the contrary, the positions of either side's constituents are always moving. They're never still. So if one side suddenly disappears, weakens, or fails, the other tends to go overboard.

Aside from being left or right, there's two ways to play the game of politics. You can fight fair, or you can fight dirty. Playing honest in the open, or by being insidious and secretive. There are public champions who speak well on an open stage and win people over, and there are shadowy figures who consolidate power quietly without the need for even becoming a political figure themselves. Both are necessary, refusing to honor one just makes your society weak to an external version of it. Even if one sounds better, as many tend to find in either side of some embroiled argument, the tradeoffs received from any single stance generally always mean either more false positives, or more false negatives, in some resulting circumstance. Taking a stance on something is equivalent to picking which edge cases you decide to care more or less about, like the construction of the universe it's a competition between a bottom-up and top-down process. For those cases that you disregard, they're the responsibility of the other side who peers over your shoulder. So it would seem natural that extremism takes over should a co-reliance change into an individual endeavor, as not doing so would open the door to a potential major vulnerability. The point of such extremism is to convince others to take the opposite stance. But where extremism can take root isn't always obvious, even if it's right in front of you.

5.2 The State of the West

The US Constitution did an amazing job learning from the failings of British rule. A constitution by nature is a set of rules for rules, an integral to any derived legislation. But this doesn't mean it's destined to continue operating as one if it's badly designed, or completely disrespected. Pretending there's no new mistakes to learn from is nothing but a source of entitlement, to fail to admit mistakes is to inhibit growth. The world is an ever-changing place, it will not stop growing even if you yourself do. To neglect this is to allow old norms to become new tyrannies.

It's important to not over-romanticize old victories, or enemies that don't exist anymore. A focus on the future with an eye on the past is a reasonable path through life. We, in the US, love to embrace the opposite of the people we defeat. Perhaps the reason this culture took root is that the US had a founding story around learning from the mistakes of their oppressive opposition. Or maybe it's just pride, normal human pride. Regardless, after some major military victories the story of those victories took root in the culture. It soon became fashionable to not just *not* embrace the philosophy of the defeated, but to oppose it in some kind of public loyalty ritual. Learning from the mistakes of those you oppose is not the same as becoming their antithesis. Trying to be the opposite of racists and Nazis has only left many gazing into the abyss of either. People who want to oppose something they believe to be evil end up embodying it while believing in their own moral superiority to lead them down a different path, but this is attempting to solve the same integral and expecting a different result.

People seem to have evolved extreme sensitivities to specific kinds of information, this process happened a long time ago, but is showing itself today in such a form due to the scalable communication of social media. In the modern day, it appears to be a solved problem on how to evoke innate civilizational defence mechanisms through messaging alone. There's even a chilling effect in what some groups refuse to acknowledge. While these propagandistic mechanisms played a significant part of the last 10^{+} years, integrity has proven to be an equally competitive form of long-term messaging.

Civilizational defence sensitivity is the driving force behind the shift in the order of leadership in the Western world and beyond. It's why candidates all around the world, who are savvy on social media, and spend orders of magnitude less money campaigning than their established opponents, have challenged the establishment quo so successfully. Messaging from the media sphere has transformed the never-ending accusations of racism into crying wolf. The eventual backlash of this propaganda is an example of why aiming directly for something you perceive to be a good thing is actually a terrible strategy. Because you have no idea whether something is *actually* a good target to aim for. To avoid the target is to avoid gazing into the abyss. Aiming to not be incorrect is more fruitful than believing you're always right.

It's hard to predict what the future of politics will look like, making any prediction even 10 years out is always a long shot. In the current day, it looks to be that the products of social media will continue opposing widespread state propaganda, slowly eating the corpse of the establishment. But this is misunderstanding the nature of the establishment. The entrenched political establishment is a machine that was born half out of sticky relations, and the other half out of necessity. This world of politics is a game of mutual benefit, and business relations. It's, without a doubt, something that maintains the homeostasis of the world. To dislodge it, even if for the best, would take substantial effort. As for a prediction, it would seem likely, with social media making it very obvious who is and isn't a competent leader, that integrity begins to play a core role in the elections of supreme executive offices throughout many countries in the future. Which leads the establishment towards the form of a shadow government, where they'll acquire new faces controlled by old actors. The future of politics will consist of these kinds of actors facing off against new players in the game who have visible integrity, and large social media clout. As for the landscape being argued over, it's likely going to consist of the establishment clinging to old mistakes to cater to older generations, with newer voices coming in to argue for reasonable changes where these historical ideals have come to be misplaced.

With the insistence upon equal rights for every person in the West, came an opening of the country's citizenship to people of completely different backgrounds, and the entering of women into the workforce prior to their having children. The former began to replace the maintaining of our population, and it's now become the role of politicians to instead impregnate their districts with imported voters rather than enable their own citizens to be able to start families of their own. In the work place, large amounts of roles began to be taken over by women, and this shows itself very clearly as the collective behavior of these institutions stopped resembling their traditional predecessors. Western institutions have tended to be upheld by the disagreements of the male demographics that invented them, it was suited to their behavior. Helen Andrews has noted that with women coming to replace men in these roles, has come a preference for consensus rather than disagreement[72]. Constant agreement destroys the value of agreement itself. The agreement of rivals is leagues more valuable than the agreement of co-conspirators, but if those rivals don't exist, then this value becomes inaccessible. They've also adopted the feminine temperament of compassion, and have applied this liberally, especially to foreigners.

As women entered the work force, housing prices came to respect the increase in household members capable of paying for them, and going into the workforce was no longer a luxury for women, it became a requirement. As the difficulty in achieving the baseline conditions granted to prior generations for starting a family became less feasible, more women had to work more, plan their careers further in advance, and set their expectations for men even higher. Men, on the other hand, had been increasingly forced out of what would normally be fair competitions in favor of diversity initiatives, affirmative action quotas, and corporate interests, as not having enough women or other demographics could open institutions up to expensive discrimination lawsuits.

As one would expect, the increase in female positions resulted in a decrease in our birth rate, and a decrease in high-earning men turned into a decrease in marriage. The collective ability for women to band together to protect their own interests isn't something available to men, whose instincts insist on being self-sufficient. With the decrease in population affecting liberal areas the most, as their living standards are higher, it's the liberal cities who would begin to lose power in the House of Representatives and the presidential election. Not wanting to give up political power, politicians replaced the population-sustaining role of women with the near-unlimited supply of foreigners that were interested in coming here. With living standards being so high, these politicians leveraged the compassion

72. Helen Andrews. *The Great Feminization.* Compact, 2025

of their successful female demographics to support giving welfare to the foreigners, and at accelerating rates. The politicians found a way to maintain their power while luring in voters under the banner of diversity, and the hook of dependency.

These groups have doubled down by opening every border they ever could, despite never communicating this when running for office. Because if the migrants are so-called *asylum seekers*, then it's painted as saving those in need rather than the human trafficking operation that it's become. It's well known that many of these asylum seekers go home to vacation in their own country[73], which doesn't sound like their life is at risk when they go there, and should disqualify their asylum claim. Most asylum seekers to Europe over the last 10^{+} years were young men rather than women and families, and the people who brought this information to the forefront of everyone's attention have had their lives destroyed by whatever groups that were trying to brush it under the rug. This isn't even just a problem for people of European ancestry, the US has all sorts of demographics at risk from this very idea of becoming a borderless welfare state. Just because you call someone a refugee or asylum seeker doesn't make them innocent. It's a specific description being applied in a broad context, and it doesn't always match the outcome of their arrival. People who are genuinely fleeing from danger don't then become the danger in whatever host country takes them in.

Feminine compassion has continued to be weaponized against the populace by painting opposition to this failed civilizational strategy as racist, and from these accusations rang the same traumas of liability from lawsuits over discrimination felt in the wallets of nearly every organization. To circumvent these problems came the rise of credentialism to guarantee quality, bureaucracy to avoid liability, and forced agreement on political issues to avoid confrontation with the now abundant amounts of women who have come to inhabit roles that were intended to be upheld by disagreement.

Many of these women now find themselves unable to find a man capable of living up to their standards, and our institutions continue to be occupied by women who have been let down by an inherently

---

73. Alex Alma. *Bulletin/Novus: Nio av tio utrikesfödda har semestrat i sitt födelseland [Bulletin/Novus: Nine out of ten foreign-born have vacationed in their country of birth].* Bulletin, 2022

flawed system. Both men and women have come to revert to their own primal instincts in the face of this ongoing mismatch of intentions with priorities. In the process, our population is being replaced by foreigners, some of which come with hostile intentions, our currency is inflating from the increased propensity of our government to become a distribution center, and our politicians have become so far separated from our own best interests because those are no longer requirements for their continued abuse of our government's dignity.

Normally, when you do something badly, you aim to correct your mistake. It's culturally normal across the entire world to apologize and fix what you've done wrong. If someone continues to do a bad enough job, they even get fired. But this has not been the case across broad swaths of the West that have mixed ideological beliefs about humanity with immigration. Across many parts of the West, prosecution for heinous violations of the law have not been equally prosecuted, it's become dependent on race and immigration status. Widespread sexual assault of young girls across Europe has been covered up for decades. These girls tend to be low-class and are written off by the establishment so badly that the girls themselves, or their fathers standing up for them, end up being imprisoned instead[74]. In a sane world the worst immigrants would be deported, and we would find other excellent candidates to come fill their now vacant spot. This has *not* been the response to the crimes of violence, pedophilia, torture, mutilation, branding, and rape across Europe. Being against such things is a perfectly normal opinion to hold, especially considering that **immigration and mass migration are not the same thing**. People are publicly shamed and fired from their jobs, over an opinion such as this, over mere words and thoughts.

These anti-discrimination laws came with the best of intentions, as did granting rights and the ability for people to work regardless of whatever they were born as, but we have to question the nature of how we've come to organize ourselves, and whether or not this even produces outcomes that every member of society is actually able to appreciate. This obviously isn't to suggest we bring back discrimination, or prevent people from working, but with the rise in status of demographics like women, and the second-order effects that come with them, is every single aspect of these anti-discrimination laws working

74. Triggernometry. *Grooming Gang Survivor Tells Her Story*. YouTube, 2025

as intended? Discrimination itself has come to be interpreted in a misconstrued way that's come to enforce quotas. While I wouldn't want any actual discrimination to result from this, these quotas have only acted as disruptions to the cohesion that people would normally find amongst themselves. These laws came into play because it was mostly white men that inhabited important roles, and they tended to hire other white men. Which seems like a fair reason to introduce these laws, doubly so because the educational institutions were no different. But this isn't where we find ourselves now, and with the implementation of these laws coinciding with hostile narratives around white men, it seems these laws have come full circle to now be used as vehicles for discrimination itself. With every demographic being educated, and more equally than ever before, have these laws come to create the problems they were meant to solve? I write this for the sake of asking the question, are we clinging to these anti-discrimination laws too tightly?

In the post-WWII era, America has attempted to break down barriers between every group that exists within its borders. This started with the civil rights act, and continued in good faith for the sake of cultural cohesion. But there's an unaddressed flaw that's continued to be ignored in every part of where this aspect of American culture has come to tear down its own walls.

The Jim Crow era was an abomination, it had obnoxious levels of segregation that didn't provide a level playing field for civilizational advancement of all its members. Due to this sequence of events, America has become largely anti-segregation, but this is a product of history, not a timeless facet of human existence. History could have emerged differently, and segregation could have become the solution rather than the problem. After all, South Africa ended up finding some level of segregation that they continue to abide by. This isn't to suggest we change what we do, whether people appreciate the answer or not is more important than the exact direction society moves in. But it does indicate that this isn't some universal principle that can never go wrong, too much of anything can be a bad thing, and a refusal to acknowledge this would only lead to the same problems such a system intended to prevent in the first place.

This idea of anti-segregation has transformed into a kind of forced association on the American public, and ideologies have taken it to an extreme. The problem being, that any group that becomes unable to maintain their own internal order is writing their own death certificate. In the process of embracing this oversimplification, societal delineations have been trampled. If we want to better preserve aspects of American culture so that its members can continue to exist, and not just as a cultural skin worn by others, what is the line we should draw, and where should it be made?

In places where it acts like a religion, some of the most dedicated members of the creed of diversity and inclusion, that spawned out of the school system, have come to desire an exclusion of *white people*. Some groups have insisted on having their own segregated spaces, and other notable events, like the *Day of Absence* at Evergreen State College, insisted that white people and professors should stay home for a day so that everyone else can have an event that caters to them specifically. Which is incredibly racist, but they're a product of this system that enabled them to be this way in the first place. There's two basic reasons this happened, one is an institutional incentive, and the other has its roots in evolution. These institutions, trying to level the playing field across different groups within the US, enabled a different kind of racism, decentralized even. It used to be that racism was used to discriminate against people, and bully them. In the modern day, the racists cover themselves in DEI and weaponize accusations of racism against others as a form of discrimination itself. This ironic change was the product of institutions addressing racism the way they had, with dedicated bureaucrats and ideologies. The obvious flaws of such an implementation meant this was an inevitable end result. The second reason this racism appeared is because it's instinctual to people.

Our entire evolutionary history consists of belonging to stratified layers of a family, a society, and various groups that become larger and larger as you incorporate more people within some expanding frame of association. Various ancient Greek city-states still considered each other Greek, despite having loyalty to different factions. It's a kind of internal order that's typically been preserved in human groups, this was fruit that we've picked off a tree. It's normal to want to delineate yourself, your friends and family, and anyone else you relate to into these layered groups who depend on each other. On the other hand, the government forcing these relationships to be completely open would be detrimental to those who inhabit these layers. These DEI groups that insist on having segregated spaces have arrived at this same core human instinct meant to preserve internal order, they find themselves needing a form of self-reliance they're not able to provide for themselves.

So in navigating our anti-discrimination laws, how might these layers of societal structure be better respected, to give people what their instincts are asking for, while still upholding the state's right to dictate a level playing field that hedges against racism in general? To answer this, let's consider the various aspects of internal order that we maintain in our society. How many foreigners can you let into your country before it becomes theirs instead of yours? Immigrants have no problem delineating themselves from others, they have their language and culture. It's this ability to delineate themselves from others that becomes an advantage for them. Often times, an immigrant parent not speaking English as well as their child will grant that child a level of freedom that becomes beneficial for their development. These families don't have to work to exclude others, this delineation is natural, and these laws work to their advantage.

Without cultural delineations, generational improvements to communities and individuals become more difficult. America used to maintain the quality of its own population through capitalism, those that couldn't survive here would self-deport. In the process, we maintained the internal order of the country by ensuring people were self-reliant enough to survive without government assistance. Welfare given to immigrants has destroyed this process, and with this, the internal order of the US has been dislodged. Anti-discrimination has been the backbone of the political ideologies that have brought the country to a state of inherent social injustice, it's the reason why we now give welfare to every person that comes here from a foreign country.

All across Europe, people who simply share opinions against mass migration are often given longer prison sentences than migrants who violently gang rape underage girls[75]. The pattern is that of obscene racist violence against the native population, and the murder of young girls by older men. These stories have been generated non-stop across Europe, they coincide with hundreds to thousands of churches being

75. R v Melia. *Far-right organiser found guilty of intent to stir up racial hatred through distribution of stickers.* Crown Prosecution Service, 2024

burned down[76,77], and foreigners driving cars into crowded marketplaces on Christmas[78]. Hate crimes have continually been covered up by a political and media establishment who, for some incoherent reason, want to pretend not to notice. The same thing has happened in the US to some degree, although with better self-defence laws, clear cultural boundaries around minding your own business, and a history of taking in immigrants, this doesn't offer the same magnitude of problems as seen in modern Europe. Still, entire police departments will seemingly refuse to go after certain foreign pedophiles, as they're either loyal to the political order that brought them here, or completely demoralized by a judiciary who works against them[79,80, 81]. Or maybe I'm wrong, maybe it's all kinds of pedophiles equally, because who can really tell? Either way, it's clear that the reason people have been imported into Western countries isn't for the benefit of the West, it's for the benefit of politicians.

So where would it be most appropriate to curb this ideology, while still allowing the US to continue as the largely open-minded and open-hearted society that's capable of maintaining its own unity so well? To ask the same question in another way, where do people deserve to be the most selective? Where do they *need* to be selective? Which is an easy question to answer, it's with their own children, because their survival hinges upon their upbringing. Any group incapable of maintaining their own internal order is at an inherent disadvantage to any who can. The government doesn't interfere in people's social lives, this job of anti-discrimination occurs in jobs, in business, and it currently makes its largest impact in schools. But should it be the role of the government to dictate this relationship to children?

---

76. Yvette Harding. *Hundreds of Churches Burned in Europe.* Assist News, 2024
77. Heather Tomlinson. *Churches Are Burning Across Europe. But Why?* Premier Christianity, 2024
78. Kamuran Samar. *Timeline: Deadly attacks on Christmas markets in Europe.* Euronews, 2024
79. *ICE Boston, federal partners arrests illegal Ecuadoran national charged with more than 20 sex crimes against Massachusetts minor.* US Immigration and Customs Enforcement, 2025
80. *ICE Boston arrests illegal Guatemalan national charged with forcibly raping Massachusetts minor.* US Immigration and Customs Enforcement, 2025
81. *ICE arrests illegal Guatemalan alien charged with sex crime against Massachusetts child.* US Immigration and Customs Enforcement, 2025

Some people have large families, some people even have what they consider to be an extended family of close relationships with people they're unrelated to. But *everyone* has limits. You wouldn't give pedophiles access to your children, you wouldn't want racists of some other race to destroy the lives of your family members. If your family had the same open border policy as many Western governments have imposed on their citizens, your family wouldn't be able to feed themselves. You wouldn't give strangers access to your bank account, and it's a good thing the government doesn't force you to. But how would one learn from these examples? To paint a less extreme version of these scenarios, in a much more general manner these descriptions give rise to what would be described as a forced association, and it's already the case that the government can't force you to incorporate anyone into your family structure. But these forced associations do show up in other parts of your family's life, it's in the school system. Maybe you're already understanding of the need for delineations without any of these examples, but one has to ask, is family the only level of delineation we need to have across society? Should the relationship between the government and its citizens go directly to their family, to their children, to the most important individuals in their lives, with nothing else in between?

There's been a great breadth of explanatory significance from the comparison between the *state* of China and the *society* of India, because of the precariousness of these constructs in human nature[**82**, **83**]. It's often said China is a strong state with a weak society, where the tentacles of the state extend into nearly every social structure[**84**]. In that same light, India is often noted as a weak state with a strong society, where the state is afloat in a river of competing currents representative of social groups and historical legacies that the Indian government must appease, rather than command[**85**]. This axis of state and society are the most key comparative forces between the two largest civilizations on the planet, and that's because the importance of these

82. Joel S Migdal. *Strong Societies and Weak States.* Princeton University Press, 1988

83. Joel S Migdal, Atul Kohli, and Vivienne Shue, eds. *State Power and Social Forces.* Cambridge University Press, 1994

84. Vivienne Shue. *The Reach of the State.* Stanford University Press, 1988

85. Lloyd I Rudolph and Susanne Hoeber Rudolph. *In Pursuit of Lakshmi.* University of Chicago Press, 1987

concepts are the most core to any functioning civilization. This line between state and society is no different than the idea of Jefferson's wall between church and state. The US striking the right balance between the two is a matter of life and death. The US can undergo an internal order optimization, unique to its culture and laws, that allows for a reciprocating relationship to be held between its state and its society, rather than one where the state sells off its society in an attempt to maintain the political hegemony of politicians who led the country down such a questionable path in the first place. The strong US economic machine can be downstream of a competitive child-rearing environment.

This added delineation would be most useful for the least capable of us, for those who are still getting their bearings in life, for children. The schooling of children doesn't need to be discriminatory, but it shouldn't be the state that's allowed to delineate between our children and the world around them, that deserves to be a role reserved for the parents. Admission to schools deserves to be a matter of free association, rather than one of anti-discrimination.

Anti-discrimination is a factor the state imposes on its citizens, but is it what's best for children? It could be, but the right to determine whether it is or not needs to be a personal decision for parents, because in the modern day these anti-discrimination laws have incentivized the creation of racists that weaponize these laws and accusations against others due to the historical narratives associated with their creation, and these people tend to inhabit the school systems. Children have too easily become the victims of this insidious psychological warfare, and parents deserve the right to determine whether or not it's happening to them. There's even incredibly condescending, disrespectful forms of pity and coddling that's often disguised as compassion. In many cases, forms of instant gratification, marketed as generational promises of improvements to intelligence, have been sold by people absent of any understanding for what it takes to achieve these changes, and this book will further discuss how to successfully implement these mechanisms in a later chapter. Parents deserve to control the layer of association that forms between their child's family and the world governed by our state, and that territory in between the two is a school.

The existing schooling infrastructure favors certain groups so much that it damages others, ultimately creating a form of insidious discrimination. Instead of forcing everyone together, or getting rid of the benefits incurred by allowing people to be part of a group that favors them, we should just allow people to find groups that favor them in general. That would be what's best for everyone, and wouldn't force insidious discrimination against anyone.

The push for diversity and multiculturalism is similar to polytheism, and its widespread acceptance of many forms of worship under one roof. Yet those who push for it will usually deny others the right to have a homogeneous society, the same way a race purist would deny race mixing. Many people don't seem to understand that one isn't better than the other, they're just extreme representations of centralization and decentralization within human society. These two beliefs are equally as racist, even racism exists across these same axes of centralization and decentralization. You have purity-racism, where people attempt to remove others along the lines of race, ethnicity, religion, or some other delineation. Then you have diversity-racism, which attempts to dissolve all ethnic lines, religious lines, and so on. Both are evil when taken to an extreme. Diversity-racism aims to destroy lines and delineations that people would be better off preserving, the only fair stance is that of neutrality. They're two sides of the same coin, two boundaries of the same definition. Yet we live in the lie that one is completely acceptable, and the other is uniquely heinous. They're both derivatives of excess pride. If this bothers you, I have bad news. Bickering isn't going to help, if justice is what you're looking for then politics isn't where you'll find it.

To the people who think America is terrible, that it's built on colonialism, genocide, or slavery, these narratives are built on obtuse oversimplifications. Stop indulging in its luxuries if you hate it so much. The people who want to burn it down are the most heavily invested in ideological multiculturalism. Yet ironically, if the US were to fall, it would ultimately be seen as a failure of multiculturalism. It's not actually an ending they want, but they're not looking in that direction. They need someone peering over their shoulder to be the warning system for this, as their focus is elsewhere.

These delineations don't just need to be made to protect your child from bad families, they need to protect your child from bad teachers. Schools were never meant to turn children into radical political activists, they were never supposed to have any political bias in the first place. I would argue that parents should be the ones to decide whether they want this to be an aspect of their schooling as well. If people want their admission standard to be DEI, they should be able to have that too.

Bias in the admission of students to schools already happens, and they don't seem to be going anywhere, many universities even seem to continue disrespecting the Supreme Court on this issue. With these laws coming full circle to cause what they were meant to prevent, we should acknowledge the impossibility of achieving this specific goal. Doing things the way we have has allowed for a new insidious kind of racism, where the worst people have become enabled to throw accusations of racism at others despite their own racist behavior. One side of our political system built up a massive and litigious anti-discrimination infrastructure, and the other didn't. Which is why these laws have become a one-way street for abuse and discrimination itself, they're antithetical to their own causes. Does it make sense that laws aiming for fairness have become weaponized? Instead of pushing the needle back in the other direction only to achieve the same result, let's just break these standards off where they currently lie, and let people admit who they want. If that means some universities want to implement DEI, this ends up being a better deal for everyone involved.

In a broader sense, there seems to be the intention of a forced push for ethnic diversity, but any realistic solution to multiculturalism would need to acknowledge that most people tend to marry within their race, and that's not by coincidence[86]. These individual races are always going to exist. The same occurs within political parties. While there's nothing wrong with living in a multicultural society, and by marrying whoever you wish, it seems there's often times some proxy to blame in order to expand upon the goal of either form of racism. For the Nazis, it was the Jews. For those who embrace diversity like a cult, it's white men, successful individuals, and people who speak their opposition to it openly. There's been an attack on European history because of this, as destroying the history of a people works to sabotage their population. It seems too many academics, and teachers, all have what seems like an aversion to the greatest books

86. Gretchen Livingston and Anna Brown. *Intermarriage in the US 50 Years After Loving v. Virginia*. Pew Research Center, 2017

ever written simply because they were written by white men. Yet the only way multiculturalism is going to work is if people embrace successful cultures, regardless of origin. There's something to learn from anyone, even your enemies can become your greatest teacher.

In the land of common sense, where I wish more people would come to live, we need neither these goals nor these targets. It's not extreme to yearn for either kind of society. Clearly a lot of people do, and that's mostly due to evolutionary reasons. However, it's most definitely extreme to push it onto others, that's the line in the sand. Dealing with the cards you've been dealt is one thing, rigging the deck is another. Pushing for some specific goal that you *believe* to be right is inferior, in every way, to simply aiming to not be incorrect. It's often said differently, that the road to hell is paved with good intentions, but I would argue some of the intentions aren't so great either. To force diversity through mass migration is ethnic disintegration.

Mass-importing migrants simply ignores the problems we have with our own intergenerational stability. The US can realistically take in 0.1% of its population, in immigrants, per year. But we should only be doing so if most of our age ranges are growing. Otherwise it's unethical to both the migrants and the natives, it creates a population churn. The asylum system has been abused to allow this, and we've reached the point where we can't faithfully continue to have one. The push for immigration, that turned itself into mass migration, is a leftover mindset from the baby boomers who thought they could simply *help* everyone, and that the entire world would be like them if they just had the same laws and technology. Not every country wants to be ran through democracy. These places don't tend to want to *be* Western, they just want to gain the level of technological and sociopolitical advancement visible throughout the West.

Opponents of what I have to say on this topic would want to paint this as a hatred for immigrants. It's not a hatred of anyone. They've simply labeled the concept of *hatred* as their enemy, as they believe themselves to be loving. But these actions bring about neither loving nor compassionate outcomes, it's yet another abyss they gaze into. The people who push for such *compassion* will go on entire tirades about how every stateless people deserve their own country to live in, yet join in supporting the attempt to force nearly every single European ethnicity to become stateless in their own countries.

It's not compassionate to the people born in these European countries to continue this process of destroying their heritage in front of their very eyes. This brings an entirely unfair imposition on people who never voted for this in the first place. It's become an unfair game meant to impose an unfair set of rules, and it's clearly meant to subvert democracy itself. Doubly so by paying welfare to migrants, as they'll naturally vote for whoever gives them that welfare. The mistake being made by the liberals who push for this is that to warp the board to forever be in their favor isn't to find perpetual victory, it's to incentivize civil war. Fairness is something that must be preserved across the two groups that are meant to balance each other out. Otherwise it's no longer a game, it's a fight for survival. This game is meant to continue into the future, so there's an infinite number of incentives to be made and used. If any one of them leads to a bad result, then one simply needs to admit fault, move on, and find a better way of competing that doesn't incentivize the destruction of the board. America doesn't need to end up like Europe. Westerners are so often used to politicizing human rights abuses abroad that they've become complacent in believing it could never happen to them.

Proponents of immigration say it's good for the economy. Studies coming out of the EU beg to differ, showing that on average, immigrants are costing the entire system more money than they return due to crime and welfare[**87**,**88**]. Proponents say it's to pad the birth rate, and prevent a complete economic collapse as populations dwindle. But this is based on conjecture, neither science nor history provide evidence of this claim that padding will help the outcome. In fact, it seems more natural to embrace the decline in preparation for the next phase of growth. I would argue the children of the previous generations have been betrayed. The education system could have prepared people for an economy of scale, for individuals skilled in automation, and programming, to carry the jobs of multiple retirees. Instead, most are indebted to a fraudulent university system where interest grows so fast their loans can never be paid off, purely for the intention of funding more wars. Which is what the government used to pay for

87. Jan H van de Beek et al. *Borderless Welfare State.* University of Amsterdam, 2021

88. Finansministeriet Makropolitisk Center. *Indvandreres nettobidrag til de offentlige finanser i 2019.* Finansministeriet, 2023

through raising the interest on mortgages, but seeing as most young people can't afford homes they had to switch strategies.

The welfare dollars given to immigrants, that compete with wages of the young and lower class, could have easily been paid to young American couples looking to start a family, money could have been given for them to have children, so they could buy a house, and produce the population we need in the future. Or it could have just as easily been used to subsidize the wages of those working at companies who weren't earning enough to desire the work after the massive wave of inflation brought about by Covid spending. Wage suppression instead acts to prevent young people from being able to afford a home and to have children. It leaves many people with few options. If you're from the West, then it's fair to say that it's your right to claim your heritage rather than allow the government to sell it off.

This insidious political globalism is treating the declining population as a problem. But a declining population isn't the primary problem we face. The problem is raising the birth rate. We're not trying to decrease the population, nor to deal with a decreasing one. Which is why this is such deceptive rhetoric. Politicians insist it's needed for every democratic Western country, yet it was never put up for vote. Across Europe, the consequences were that police, for some reason, cared more about policing the speech of native citizens than the actual crimes of immigrants, and judges simultaneously followed suit. Yet it's somehow seen as immoral to want them to leave. It's not immoral. If laws were not respected in bringing them there, then laws need not be respected in kicking them out, and that should be a law.

Alongside the shutdown of discussion of immigration, came a scaling of this behavior around the events of Covid. The shutdown of debate regarding treatments for Covid seemed to be abused as an opportunity to make money off vaccines. The imposition of shutting down entire global economies seemed to have largely negative consequences for the youth, who now find themselves with even larger government debts to bear in the future. Sweden was the only Western country to have any real variation in their strategic response. Fear and hatred were weaponized in a cruel and unusual manner, where blame was cast onto people unwilling to take a vaccine that was rightfully called experimental. Even worse, if you opposed lockdowns or vaccinations, you were labeled as wanting to *"kill old people"*. This kind of gaslighting, mixed with a demand for compliance, does us more harm than any naturally varied response ever would have. If you, in your personal life, lived by such a singular, monolithic, and narrow-minded philosophy, you'd be completely dysfunctional. It's playing a Darwinian game as if it were Newtonian. Governance is more complicated than any individual life, as it deals with a plethora of lives, and these demonizations are societally destructive.

How did we get here, where the more that time progresses, the less that conversation matters, and the more that urgency gets to displace deliberation? Causing us to fall into increasingly worse civilizational traps. How did we find ourselves using fear, gaslighting, and a questionable sense of urgency, to dictate plans that govern hundreds of millions of people? Attributing this all to the feminine temperament seems overblown. People think money is the source of political corruption, money is the reason for it, but agreement is its source. Our political system was already fairly saturated with such kinds of agreements prior to women taking these roles, but it's now accelerated as a process because of their placement. To be perfectly honest, women themselves aren't even the problem, they're behaving as intended. The problem is, they tend to represent their own interests so well that any competing priorities are never invited to the table, this forms an inherently unstable government structure by neglecting the need for balance between two opposing parties. The function of this structure is a cult, and it becomes particularly notable within bureaucracies. These cults maintain their psychological borders no different than how a country maintains its physical borders.

When given enough room to act, bureaucracy becomes a parasite that spawns other parasites. Demanding the government, like a person, eat more in order to feed every leech that's latched onto its skin. More importantly, they attempt to put an invasive pool of entropy between every existing pool it can find. A never-ending array of middlemen, that insist on managing every interaction, despite that evolution has found ways to allow us to manage our interactions already. It drains the complexity of every interaction in exchange for being expensive and confusing. To avoid this general problem, any government position that can be replaced by either a laptop or a website, should be. Simply removing these people from government positions, and disconnecting them from the host that feeds them will cure everyone else.

If you want to do an honest job as a bureaucrat, you would ultimately finish your own job, and either close up the agency once it was finished, or maintain the size needed to function. But if you wanted to do a worse job, then you would be rewarded for it, with constant employment. Even worse than that, if you wanted to make sure a problem was never fixed, you could invent a problem that's impossible to fix, such as various social and environmental issues, and you would be rewarded for that not only with prolonged employment but with a larger department that hires more people who also have prolonged employment in order to solve this unsolvable problem. Even worse than *that*, if you wanted to prolong not only the sanctity of your lie of an unsolvable problem, but aim to hide your lie like a tree in a forest, you would aim to create even more lies that create more unsolvable problems alongside that of your own, and you would still be rewarded yet again with even more job security. The long story short, is they become a burden on those who pay their wages. So if you had to summarize what they do, what would you call it?

Well, if you had to make an unsolvable problem, why not base it around an immeasurable concept? That sounds convenient, let's base it around feelings. Then you can feel bad for people forever. Let's call it the politics of pity. It comes with an endless supply of injustice, which becomes a motte-and-bailey for everything you could ever need.

Pity is the monster that gazes into every abyss. It's a form of weaponized empathy. Pity is a complex form of psychological warfare, a weapon of mass psychological destruction. It can weaponize the naive who believe it's compassionate, mobilize the vindictive who see it as an opportunity, and fool the innocent into believing it's beneficial. It's the art of making someone's instincts betray them, an act of sabotage that enables an ironic self-fulfilling prophecy of destruction at every scale. Though to be fair, it's a form of competition. But one you need not fight fairly. You don't box with a parasite, you cover it in salt and make it shrivel.

In an environment filled with people you're unfamiliar with, respect is a balance held between not showing disdain, and not granting awards. Pity throws off this balance to demand people can only ever be over or underprivileged. It's a desire to psychologically balance reality with a false perception. Every demand of undue equality is a form of microcommunism.

Communism is a reversion of society back to the more nihilistic steps it took to get to where we currently are. It's a rejection of complexity, and by proxy a rejection of reality. Considered in a modular context, it's a left-brain process that people, in general, aim to do frequently, and at different scales. It's aiming to climb back down the ladder of integrals, towards derivatives, and reverse course. We've recently had, and hopefully just finished, a multi-generation reversion over climate issues. Which is essentially the broken compass with technical replicates. It's making sure we have our facts straight on a civilizational and socioevolutionary level. Despite how tedious this reversion has been, despite how brainwashed some children may have become over the climate, and despite how crazy some of society may have gone over this topic in general, I would argue this is still a feature and not a bug. More open-ended problems require more serious reversions. It forces people to go back to square one, through childhood indoctrination, and motivate children to try to find a variety of different answers to an urgent problem. Aside from the indoctrination, which can at times be extraordinarily questionable, this strategy attempts to create maximal variation from a source of uncertainty, which is actually a brilliant evolutionary strategy, and mirrors the spawning of complexity. It might not have ever necessarily been an option for every young child to even figure something out in the first place, but it's the instinct of doing this that's brought enough people to the table of this gigantic anomaly, the atmosphere, that we collectively did not know enough about relative to how we were polluting it. The complexity of the atmosphere, and our overall climate, is still very difficult to predict far into the future, as both its scale and chaotic nature are quite impressive. But we've made outstanding strides in doing so, weather predictions have improved magnificently. We can say for sure that we've passed peak pollution, and that the consequences of our actions are better understood for the sake of our prolonged survival.

On the milder end, why does this behavior lead towards indoctrination and microcommunism? It's an attempt to do the same thing multiple times, to shit-test society to make sure civilization is absolutely confident in the direction it's moving in. If the safety checks pass, it gives people more confidence to assume they've found the right answer, so that a new brick can be placed in the Tower of Babel. But in the extreme case, of pushes for genuine communism, and the insidious games that come with it, the only way to pass this specific test is to avoid the reversion altogether, as it's more a test of leadership than direction. Any aspect of any human process can become extreme. These are built-in evolutionary behaviors, and they've not been designed to be self-limiting. They've been modeled around the fact that there's always an opposing force that pushes back, so the desire to push in any direction can usually be quite fervent.

It's important to know that when people push back on these issues of race, climate, and immigration, it's not simply a denial of everything the left is offering for the sake of some petty goal. It's because pushback is the game of politics. That's the point. Many of these causes have gone terribly awry, and the pushback is more than warranted. It seems with the release of files from the now defunded USAID, that many of these movements were funded through the government to influence foreign politics in the most insidious and corrupt racket imaginable. It's justified to want to stop immigration, and even send many of them back to wherever they came from. To push too far in one direction requires a reciprocation of equal force, to say otherwise is to only encourage your opposition to go even further, as they learn their actions bear no consequences. It's the nature of one side to bring a plethora of new ideas to the table, and it's the job of the other side to push against it unless it belongs. To deny this right is to deny autonomy.

Freedom and control are the antithetical pairing born when you cross life with autonomy. People tend to want control as a kind of security, and safety, against unhinged freedom, thinking that freedom enables unpredictable danger. But obsessive control poses the same exact danger, it just centralizes power while allowing it to operate in secret. Centralized control is just centralized integrity, and it comes with tradeoffs of its own. Independent of a context neither is technically better than the other, but practically speaking there's a clear difference that arises when applied to different scenarios. For a body, control is more favorable than freedom, because otherwise your body would run its course faster, and with less preservation in mind. For a society, freedom is more favorable because it allows for the freedom of cooperation, rather than the forced cooperation that comes with control, which always generates worse outcomes. Cells can't run away from your body, they might flake off and die but that's a normal life cycle. However if people are running away from your government, your government is dysfunctional.

A great example of this dysfunction is the UK, and they've managed to do the impossible. They've turned towards successfully inflicting the resource curse upon themselves by deindustrializing, albeit they've replaced resources with corporate interest. It's punishing their most successful citizens, driving the least successful into the ground, and overall making it more difficult to be successful in the first place. Meaning, the successful people flee to somewhere else, as they have been for years. The UK was previously attempting to position itself as a financial hub of the world, while needlessly sacrificing home-grown industries to their own folly. The irony is, this only makes other places more likely to fill that role than the soon-to-be decrepit UK.

With many countries copying the American paradigm, instead of a single dying empire, we're left with every country in the world being in decline due to a lack of accountability. This doesn't happen due to negligence of some simple trick that could be implemented to fix everything. It happens because accountability is the law of the land when it comes to interactions and exchanging value, and that's independent of the governments which think they control either. It's no stroke of luck that the world's population is collapsing, living standards are collapsing, financial credibility is collapsing, and that the firestarters for major wars have been flickering throughout the last few years. So-called *experts* have believed for decades that the debts incurred by governments don't need to be held to the same level of accountability as they would for any individual. The US government, among many others, has grown too accustomed to misusing its money printer, and this habit has gone on to fund all the problems society is now dealing with. Having the world's reserve currency confers unique advantages, but also unique disadvantages, as a gift is a curse. Money we've spent decades ago has come back to hurt us through both inflation and terrorism, and we soon might not have a choice but to continue printing to deal with either.

Currency is a tool of exchange, and a measure of its own ability for exchange. To abuse it in one dimension destroys it in the other. Value exists independent of human interaction because it's a universal axiom in the first place. It's reflected through us in ways that mediates fair exchange amongst us. Those who pay the price of foreign wars, foreign aid, and funding the enemies that then attack us again, are the American mortgage payers, taxpayers, and those who went to college and will forever owe money as their interest outpaces their ability to repay their loans.

Maybe it would be good for businesses if young employees weren't covered in mountains of debt. If there were young people who had stable lives and could buy houses to start families, these companies would likely be worth much more. Unstable employees, people who waste their 20s without getting to start a family, and not even save $100k in their own name, have no way of delivering quality work to any employer for prolonged periods of time. College is definitely not the answer for most, but it's been sold so heavily as a requirement. It's the biggest hole the US government has ever shot in its own foot. Broke and indebted, childless individuals will not continue funding wars when their life is unfulfilling. If you have to pay to get a job, it's a scam. The state of the West is a mess, and the schools are responsible.

Likewise, the EU is a project that tricked multiple democratic countries into trading their financial independence and border security into being part of a bureaucratic dictatorship. The EU is the most insidiously anti-democratic machine on the planet, the euro as a currency should be dissolved, and the individual countries should manage their own banks in competition with one another rather than cooperation. Otherwise, their currencies will continue to be used for weaponized political money laundering just as the US dollar was through an entrenched federal bureaucracy. The EU has been a one-way ticket to the importation of American gaslighting and mass migration, despite not being a settler society, and having neither the culture nor the laws to make it work as one. They handed over their freedom for security, and now have neither. It was as foolish as it would be to trust a machine to count votes.

5.3 On the Wings of Freedom

When enabling competition, you don't often need to worry about how to make competition work. The way to make competition work is to enable freedom, competition will come on its own. Success by freedom is not a coincidence. The hierarchical modularity of the American system, combined with the ability for Americans to move freely to different localities within the country, creates a valuable means of enabling competition across multiple dimensions. Competition across businesses, across localities for business, for the types of regulations on businesses, and the ability to steal all of these things away from other localities exist as points of dynamism that allow the American system to flourish. It's specifically the talent poaching nature of competition that keeps the economic backbone of the US surviving the abuse of the government's money printer. Without it, we would likely have shifted towards a completely state-controlled economy. Free competition allows for modeling complexity via distributed calculations at finer levels, and in more apt locations. Because what does competition accomplish? It's a competitive interaction, as interactions tend to be, that forces complexity on all parties involved.

But surely the government has done some good in funding, and initiating novel industries that would otherwise be too expensive and difficult to make, and in such a short amount of time? Where does the government go right in trying to initiate competition? When it tries to push the boundaries of innovation.

The human genome project was funded by the government, as was the first space program, as has been many things that were difficult to achieve yet desirable. All good investments eventually found a home within the economy, independent of government aid. Yet it's a shame this kind of thinking is never applied to the healthcare market at large. It seems like a natural pattern, where these difficult projects are first aggregated by a common need, then dispersed out to the private sector where they're handled more cost effectively and for greater benefit.

The subsequent initiation and handing off of projects to those who are incentivized to continue them proves to be a wise investment both civilizationally and economically. But where might this be going wrong? If you repeat any pattern long enough, you eventually attract parasites who attempt the same things, people with a larger propensity for spending money, but without any of the same proclivity for success. Even worse, they'll work for the government.

What makes democracy so great if it keeps spawning bureaucracies? Originally, democratic governments having more accountability than others gave the more accountable government an edge in deal making. Because it had more skin in the game, more feelers around to figure out what made sense and what didn't. But if the whole world is filled with bureaucracies and assemblies, then that becomes the new form of dictatorship, and it clearly has. These unelected forms of government are prone to crashing unpredictably, because they won't admit their mistakes, all the same as a bad dictator. Something isn't bad because it's a dictatorship, it's bad because it's a tyranny.

Since time changes every rule, turning exceptions into norms, we have a need to adapt towards a system that better involves and represents actual citizens. This is possible now, due to scalable technology causing a saturation of the means of communication to the point where we can solve an integral. Likewise the same saturation exists within the education system, there's a great opportunity to transform it into something better. Democracy has become the new tyranny because it doesn't properly model the complexity it's come to enable. Why is this? The problem with dictatorships isn't just due to lone rulers. It's the growth of control over freedom, rather than that of freedom itself. Which can be seen as global bureaucratic cooperation, and the coordination that comes with it.

Dictatorship isn't necessarily a bad form of government, it's a bad method of passing on governance. Even if it's rare, a dictator might be an amazing leader. It can even be necessary under certain circumstances. But ultimately, it's fair to say that democracy is usually the best choice for what a successful dictatorship can become. If a dictatorship creates a growth phase, and manages it well, it can entrust its civilization to those that it's grown. Mirroring the pattern of governments funding innovation.

Politicians tend to be the embodiment of the status quo. If that weren't so, they wouldn't be politicians. They simply copy what's worked in the past, and some try to listen to what people might want in the future. This is why savvy businessmen come into American politics and tip the scales every now and then. Career politicians can't innovate, they're physically incapable of it. They tend to have loyalties that are tied in a more complicated web than that of the diplomatic alliances that dragged every country into WWI. Both of these are a feature, not a bug. For the most part they represent people's interests, and that can mostly only happen in a free system. Love them or hate them, they're not as bad as bureaucrats.

Bureaucracy is a semi-dictatorship within a democracy. You can cooperatively choose to allow for bureaucracy to exist, but if you can't cooperatively choose to get rid of it, then you live in a controlled state. Why are there so few doctors speaking up about the corruption in the medical system? If they came out, there would probably be a push to fire them, because bureaucracies hate people who stand out. This has happened to people whistleblowing sex-change operations on children that weren't supposed to occur at hospitals that had claimed they stopped doing them[89,90]. Everything becomes a liability to the bureaucracy. Why must entire professions, that our civilization relies on, be under the territory of those who wish to keep conversations behind closed doors? Why are they allowed to have a *territory* in the first place? It's too painful that people operating within a public system aren't allowed to criticize it publicly, when these are the voices that everyone else in the country needs to hear from the most. It prevents a natural hierarchy of leadership from forming across these professions outside of that which exists in the form of bureaucracy.

No matter how important your bureaucracy is, if it's filled with just one political ideology then there's a great chance your entire department will be attacked, and possibly destroyed by your political opposition when your party eventually goes too far. If federal agencies have no honest balance between themselves, then it's too big an opportunity for insidious political corruption and sabotage to not be destroyed by opposition. If people care so much about some cause that they feel a federal bureau is absolutely necessary to enact protections for it, then they absolutely can't discriminate politically when hiring their employees, otherwise it will eventually cease to exist. Because if you make yourself into a villain, then your opponent will rise to become the hero that opposes you. Likewise, if the discrimination is happening in the universities prior to being hired, the same result will occur. The best way to ensure the persistence of such a thing is the same strategy used by the human race in general, hedge your bets across different political wings. The same problem exists with regard to the school system in a lot of places, by some entrenched group entirely controlling either certifications, accreditations, or topics, that every child must learn. Even dishing out tons of cash for your child to attend private schools might not be enough to escape it. It's extremely problematic for the entire country, especially those who disagree with the political leanings of those who belong to this class of education professionals.

But don't we need bureaucracy? How else will we manage our relation to the reality we live in? We need to somehow manage vehicle

89. Steve Alder. *DOJ Unseals Criminal HIPAA Charges Against Surgeon Who Exposed Transgender Care at Texas Children's.* The HIPAA Journal, 2024

90. Steve Alder. *DOJ Drops Charges Against Surgeon Who Exposed Continuing Transgender Care at Texas Children's.* The HIPAA Journal, 2025

safety, railways, pollution, and so on. These are intended to subvert the dangers of what we understand. It's human instinct to want to manage danger. Another danger we understand is that of entrenched bureaucracies, and how they can destroy entire civilizations from the inside. All the same, gigantic hordes of nonprofit organizations act as an indirect bureaucracy that controls more of our government's actions than its own citizens. The management of this, along with everything else, requires another estimation of some center value, which comes about through elections. For these problems to continue to fix themselves naturally, we simply need transparency.

Most people don't manage the federal government, most people don't make vaccines, most people don't run banks, so of course it's natural that distrust is spread across demographics reflective of their distance to these core societal underpinnings. The more we can enlighten, the better a grasp on reality we'll have at the various complications it creates. It's of the utmost importance to fully expand the capabilities of individuals at as young of an age as possible. In the age of scalable communication, clear communication itself is all it takes to gain people's trust. For those afraid to step out into the sunlight, it's probably because they're sucking blood.

5.4 Modeling American Complexity

People who play stupid games win stupid prizes. So what's to be said about people who play fair and interesting games? Why should you want complexity to be modeled appropriately? Fairness is something to be enshrined for great mutual benefit. It was done well at the founding of the country and century after century we reap the benefits of this wisdom. Likewise, at every point in the future our actions will have consequences. How can we balance this need for fairness and complexity in the political realm?

If an American institution set up by Congress isn't delivering on its intended goal, then there needs to be an opportunity to rename them, either for accuracy or for shame. It's currently supposed to require an act of Congress. The president of the US should have the sole power to rename the federal bureaucracies set up by Congress, in order to make it apparent to the American people what's actually happening in these institutions.

We must stop giving nearly 3 months for an ex-President and the former Congress to sabotage the state of the government for the incoming winners of an election as it creates an atrocious culture within political parties. There absolutely needs to be a 2-term limit for the Senate, and a 5-term limit for the House of Representatives. And the tradition of pretending that electorates still need to be people, and that ballots need to take months to count, are only aiding in fraud.

There are countries that manage to vote with paper and count everything in one day, and we can accomplish the same. The only reason this wouldn't happen would be because of widespread vote rigging, which is very likely, as this has been happening in the US for a long time[**91**,**92**,**93**]. Anyone who cares about this process should accept no other explanation, it's because of vote rigging. There's no reason every voter can't confirm their citizenship, no reason every counting process in the US can't be livestreamed, with every ballot in plain view of a camera, where anyone can see every piece of paper, other than vote rigging.

The best solutions are ones that provide benefit for every party involved. They call that a win-win situation. The reason this is the case is that modeling complexity is the art of tying multiple problems together in order to come to a solution. But these notions above are all basic, it's usually what children think of when they see the glaring problems of the first few elections they experience. Let's tackle some bigger fish, more specifically those of the problems noted throughout this chapter. A few ideas will be saved for later chapters.

5.4.1 Federal Polls

It's a shame polls are only done privately at the national level. Often times some small town will be determined to be representative of the entire country, and that town will be asked questions that only they have the privilege of answering, but this ought to be considered fraud. Sampling only thousands to represent hundreds of millions may as well not be accurate if people can't trust the pollsters. Supreme executive elections are an excellent opportunity to poll the nation. Questions on this poll give the chance for the candidates to reflect on what they would do should any question go in some specific

91. Tracy Campbell. *Deliver the Vote*. Carroll & Graf Publishers, 2005
92. Edward B Foley. *Ballot Battles*. Oxford University Press, 2016
93. John Fund and Hans von Spakovsky. *Who's Counting?* Encounter Books, 2012

direction. If the winning candidate ran on issues that showed a lot of support from the polling, then the mandate becomes that much stronger. It would also prevent issues like voter ID for elections, where supposedly 80% of the American public agrees should exist, from being problematic at a large scale. Is that 80% real? An official federal poll would help us find out. It could also allow a losing candidate to still gain a cultural victory on some specific topic.

It's a mode of communication for the general public, not just with their politicians but with each other, in order to make sure their politicians are actually representing them the way they're supposed to. Quantitative answer formats, rather than strictly yes or no answers, could also be welcomed. The questions could come in a number of ways, but would need to be limited so that voting doesn't take 2 hours per individual. If each party could put 3-5 questions on the ballot, it might make sense that an incumbent could ask 5 questions to the public, but a challenger would carry questions from the opponents they've defeated in their primary and gathered endorsements from. This opportunity presents a rare chance to ask the entire American public their opinion on some specific issue. To prevent a random slew of independent candidates adding infinite questions every year there can just be a required 10% of the prior elections popular vote for any party or individual that wants to get questions on the ballot.

We have sophisticated legislative channels that are able to make and destroy laws, but these legislators are meant to represent voters. There's no reason that voters shouldn't have the chance to directly participate in the legislative process. Federal polls can also act as a voter's veto to repeal certain laws that they don't like anymore, should such a thing be put on the ballot. It wouldn't require an act of Congress or anyone to approve it, just a 2/3 majority, if the vote wins then it happens, period.

As each incoming candidate may have motives behind the questions they ask, they should be put under more pressure. Any outgoing president that's ineligible to run due to reaching their term limit should also be able to put 3-5 questions on the ballot. They have a unique perspective, and may have an interesting way of mixing up the game of elections. Federal polling will help with the problems of communication caused by social media. We need this now *because* of social media, otherwise all communication remains hindered by bots and algorithms.

5.4.2 Representative Electorate Strength

The US has experimented with various ways of getting an increase in voter participation, and it usually boils down to government money being wasted on programs that throw parties and give out food while registering people to vote. Instead, we should make voter participation a part of the game of elections. People don't often have the power to vote against every politician when they don't like the choices. A dissenting vote would only go to some third party candidate, with little to no support, and zero chances of winning. Not voting is the only real choice, and it doesn't do anything to challenge the system. This has the unfortunate side effect of allowing corruption to fester unchallenged due to people not being able to take power away from whatever establishment might be entrenched.

We currently use the census to determine electoral power for districts, while allowing the amount of people living somewhere to designate the strength of winning that district. There's also a tedious and repetitive nature to presidential elections that tends to focus on the same places, the same swing states, and it ultimately becomes a stale competition that's easier to game. The way I see it, we could incentivize increased voter turnout, reward that turnout, and even challenge the power of any simultaneously unpopular, yet entrenched, establishment in areas that have been demotivated away from voting, while granting the many neglected states a reason to be visited by presidential campaigns out of necessity. We could also prevent the demotivation of voter participation from being an insidious political strategy. Otherwise, parties won't have any reason to address this. If we dynamically modify electorate strength based on the number of people who vote in a district and state during that specific election, then this system can add a layer of complexity that disavows parties who demotivate their voter base due to a lack of good choices. Willpower should be real power.

We play a game of getting to 270 electorates, but this part of the competition isn't necessary. It's actually a bad idea that the old members of the House of Representatives, who may have been voted out in that same election, get to decide who becomes president should 270 electorates not be reached. The competition may as well be turned into a race to get the most electorates instead. If the electorates are tied, then simply turn to the popular vote to break the tie.

Commonly, less than half the country ever votes in a presidential election. This pattern is similar, and sometimes worse at every level, for governors, house seats, and so on. The solution is a punishment and reward system. For governors who win their state in a race where a high percentage of the population voted, the electorates applied in the next, or current, presidential race increase. Likewise, for districts whose congressional representative does the same, the electorates of that district apply in the same weighted manner.

To fix the system from being inflexible, and never bringing presidential campaigns to any states other than the existing swing states, who basically decide our elections in place of the entire country, apply the percentage of eligible voters who voted in both the gubernatorial and house elections to the electorates of each district. Total electorates, determined by the census, would be multiplied by both of these percentages to yield the number of electorates for that district applicable to the presidential race. The number of electorates in a state is equal to the number of house representatives it has plus its two senators, the two electorates representing the senator seats can apply just the gubernatorial percentage. Each governor's race would apply across the entirety of each state, as they fit within the 4-year presidential election cycle. Whereas Senate terms don't line up well with this election cycle, so these races can be excluded from this voting paradigm. States and districts tend to have party preferences, so people can give up in order to penalize their opponents. Some gubernatorial elections don't co-occur with the presidential election, but in the states where they do the process can happen in real time, otherwise the voter percentage from the last race can be used. House seats are always up for election at the same time as every presidential election, so these can be done in real time. Big turnout and high intensity competition would yield greater representation in the presidential election, and politicians would become incentivized to reach out to underserved demographics of voters at every level.

On the other hand, it may become strategic in certain places to *not* vote for the same reason. You may wonder, why should a vote be a gamble? As that's essentially what this would turn it into. Only someone with a chance of winning would want to continue to run, else they might hurt their party's presidential race. It should be a gamble because everyone gets to vote, there's no real requirement other than age. You should need to stake something if you're going to play. Governors and Representatives become incentivized to be more appealing to their own voter base, and people simultaneously have a way of shunning the system should they feel it's punishing them. This offers more sophisticated voter dynamics, better feedback, better rewards voters for their participation, and should make for a fairer game.

This doesn't need to be implemented before being studied either. We tend to have very simplistic channels of change, and this level of simplicity and abrupt change, or the frustration that would come with it, isn't even necessary. To observe the outcomes of such a system for 3-4 elections would allow us to then later have citizens directly vote on whether we want to implement such a system through a federal poll. We could even vote again 1-2 election cycles later to determine whether or not to still keep it.

5.4.3 The Economics of Homes and Birth

Not enough young people are able to buy a home, which becomes problematic for the birth rate. Instead of young men competing over young women to have children with, the young men are competing over young women, who are competing with both young men and women for jobs to be able to afford to save money for a home, to someday use to be able to have a small amount of children before they get back to work because all of this is extremely expensive. Homes are expensive, children are expensive, and time off from work to raise children ends up being the same. A sensible form of competition has turned into a nonsensical one. Children didn't use to be so expensive.

Some blame foreign investment in the housing market, and large corporations doing the same. Saying either is able to outcompete families in buying homes, raising the prices much higher than would otherwise be possible to put a down payment towards in your 20s. This is true in a lot of places. Some people point out that we've had a failing birth rate since women started participating in the workforce, but it's not unreasonable for them to want a form of financial independence. Other reasons turn out to be a lack of wage growth relative to housing prices. Can young Americans, Westerners even, at least have some way of competing with the vast plethora of entities interested in buying homes in their own country?

It's problematic that people tend to need housing to start families, and that you can only start families while young. But it's very hard to save enough to buy when young while also having the job, the credentials to get the job, and even time to raise children. In a world where couples had commonly pushed out upwards of 10 children, most that can actually afford them only end up having 2. Which is far above average at this point. Wouldn't it be nice if the people who create all the value in the American economy could actually have the children required to maintain this level of economic production in the future?

Of the nations that have a successful birth rate, they tend to rely on an orthodox class in order to achieve this. Which may in itself have drawbacks if every orthodox child then wishes to also be orthodox. Is there a solution for this problem to be found within the West, and all its modern accommodations?

There's a common suggestion that people tend to make. That incentivizing corporations, and foreign entities, to divest from the US housing market, and adding a continually accruing tax for each property owned based on some factor of its value, would make for a fair market for people to own houses, while preventing them from competing with people who just want to own property in order to make money off rent. Which might not be a bad idea, the saturation of the housing market coinciding with terrible birth rates might indicate a need for change. On the other hand this might introduce other problems, like a large collapse in housing prices, a lack of incentives to build new homes due to them not being profitable, and it might only end up in the creation of more apartment buildings. It's hard to tell which is more accurate, but it seems there's an inherent set of political interests that act towards maintaining housing prices. There's also many homeowners who would hate to see housing prices collapse, as they themselves would lose a lot of value. A lot of people would even be stuck paying off loans for property that isn't as valuable as what they're spending. Perhaps we can maintain their prices somehow? Even if this all worked it's still expensive to have children and to find the time to raise them. Is there a way to accomplish the impossible, to maintain prices while simultaneously opening up the market, granting parents enough time with their children, all while making housing affordable?

People want to be able to raise their children, but they need to work to pay for everything, and homes are expensive. Why is the down payment for most homes so high? It depends on the cost of the home, but is ultimately a way of showing you're invested in being able to pay off the loan. Yet the majority of the population won't be paid enough to achieve this level of savings in a reasonable amount of time before their fertility wanes, young women are typically forced into wasting their most opportune years for having children. Saving enough money for a home takes a long time before they can properly even attempt it, by the time this chance comes around some of them can no longer even have children. Is there any way out of this problematic conundrum for both the populace, who needs to reproduce, and the bankers, who need to lend money responsibly?

The incentives tried so far were focused around women working. Giving them tax-free labor, to incentivize the problem rather than the solution. Politicians publicly pretend there's no way to incentivize people to have children, because they can't wrap their heads around how families were ever made in the first place. It wasn't by having a woman leave the home to work a job, that's quite literally not how babies are made. You don't need to train a dog to eat apples by bribing it with carrots. You don't need to overcomplicate the reward structure. Then there's mass migration, as the supposed cure to this incompetent reward structure not doing its job. Is that governance, or a lack thereof?

Even if couples can manage to afford a home and children, daycare is still extremely expensive. Maternity leave is at most a year, and after that year you have to leave your child with someone else while they're still very young. None of this is ideal, and that's how we get into this mess of competing just to have children, rather than competing by making the best or the most children. It's a stupid game and we've won its prize.

Well, why must we only pay for housing with money? The reason one would want a house is to have children, I would hope. Otherwise you should live in a broom closet somewhere. Children are ultimately what keeps the economy moving in the future. As well as maintaining the status of your schools, and institutions of upbringing, which would otherwise collapse with a collapsing birth rate, only making the entire problem worse. When you buy a home, you tend to get a loan from a bank. They usually assess you on your ability to pay it off, but why can't they also factor in your ability to have children? We always think of exchange in terms of money, but money is just representative of value. It's not as if we don't already produce value biologically. For all the reasons stated above, a baby is a financial derivative, it's a call option.

In order to pay off a loan, married couples, and this needs to be restricted to married couples, would then have two options, cash and children. Having children is a method of value creation no different than participating in the economy in the first place. After all, having and taking care of young children *is* quite a lot of work, which seems to go underappreciated by the government. But it's also a major motivating factor for the workforce to stay employed to support the economy. Society will benefit from having those children to the point where the money granted to the homebuyer will come back to benefit others in society the same way that the bank would have originally done had it received its money. Having children would be incentivized. But how would the banks factor this in? Surely they can't operate at such a loss. Who invests in the baby?

That's a government investment, they can pay the current GDP per capita against the home loan. Which, in a growing economy, would be much less than the amount of value produced over the lifetime of that individual starting roughly 20 years later. Raising children then becomes both a viable path towards paying off a home, allows the mother to raise them as she wouldn't need a job to afford to, and the money earned by the other parent can support the family while actually having enough surplus to put into savings, investments, and their own future. Instead of the house, child, and time to raise a child all being extremely expensive, the mother could pay off at least part of the house through birthing children, depending on how many children they have. The time to raise them is available to the mother, who doesn't need to work during these years, and the money the family earns isn't spread so thin anymore. To boot, most couples wouldn't otherwise even contribute the value of the GDP per capita of the country towards their home loan, giving them equity, and a solid investment in the future of the country, which leads to wiser voting patterns. It would also allow young people to compete with others who buy multiple homes for the sake of being a landlord, and anyone else entering the housing market. With much higher guarantees of the loan being paid off, the down payment for younger couples could easily be lowered. A newborn baby can even act as the down payment, they can even accumulate as more are born.

So how does this look in terms of money printing? With roughly 3.6 million births in 2022 and a GDP per capita around $80k, this would cost the US government about $300 billion per year, assuming every one of these births goes towards a mortgage. Which comes out to less than the military, Social Security, Medicare, and education individually. Ideally, the cost would grow, but even that's a worthy use of our tax dollars. The constantly increasing per year student cost of education could even be decreased to compensate for this, as it's just another investment in a young child all the same. In fact, there's incredibly high daycare and babysitting subsidies in effect in various parts of the country that may as well be put to better use, by simply allowing mothers to actually be mothers. To disincentivize constant divorce and remarrying, the amount rewarded can half with each new marriage, and this would still be a worthwhile endeavor for at least 3 marriages. Printing money won't solve our debt crisis, but printing babies will.

We spend roughly $1 trillion annually on welfare. Yet many regard this as a mistake. Regardless, we now need to continue supporting people through government welfare now that we've started it. Though ideally, it would be great to reverse course. Even in wanting to do so, it still can't be done overnight. Paying off housing through childbirth also acts as a way of stopping welfare entirely. We may be able to replace one with the other for younger people, while phasing out welfare for future generations entirely. As welfare is an extremely complicated ship to bring back into port. If someone can't maintain their own relationship, then they can sell their house and gain the money given for their children. Any money needed to raise children after a relationship fails need not be given by the government, it can instead be taken from what the government has already given. This won't fix the existing welfare problem, but it can introduce a new set of rules to make sure we don't incentivize any more welfare dependencies in the future.

For a man to get his life together means to get a job, and work to improve himself. For a woman to do so doesn't mean to do the same, it means to start a family. This simply allows them to achieve this without the government becoming their primary benefactor, as one can't survive off of money that goes directly towards a mortgage if they wish to keep their home.

But this idea also makes for a continued problem with mass migration. Because immigration warfare is so easily used against the existing population, we must learn from this mistake and implement this policy only for people who were born here. There's simply no way around this, the point of this idea is to maintain the birth rate. It would be antithetical to offer the same benefits to foreigners.

Kids are expensive, and so are homes, but having one is invaluable when making the other. So why not push the arrow in the other direction? Formally recognize the value of childbirth, not just as something a family does for their own sake, but as a contribution to society. This value was always there prior to the formalization of economies, but it was hidden from plain sight. With no incorporation of this into the mechanisms of the formal economy, it's no wonder why every country to put their women to work has received a declining birth rate. Something that provides a value-added to society is being pushed at a multiplied cost to parents, which makes no sense. Parents should receive a fair offer in exchange for making this extremely difficult to attain value.

We will *all* eventually need children to inherit the Earth. Those same children would be a lot better off if they actually get to spend their first 3 years with their own mother instead of in a daycare or with a nanny, and the mortgage payoff would be enough to cover this time period. Those first 3 years are the most important developmental time in their life[94], without it, the futures of these children will crumble like our birth rate currently is. Even if a woman spends all of her 20s raising children without working, assuming she retires at 60, the economy retains 75% of what would otherwise be her expected amount of labor. If your complaint is that this might somehow result in too many children being born, you should know that there's already built-in evolutionary mechanisms to stop having kids, which is where such paranoia comes from in the first place, it will never need legislation. Failing birth rates seem to happen naturally at the peak of population booms, and there's a strong historic precedent for this. Compared to paying people raw cash in exchange for babies instead, which would incentivize a wider range of behaviors, this is much closer to a mechanism for curbing birth rates to incentivize family creation. The increased demand for home-building would spur a whole other industry for many within the country. Things are continually being outsourced

94. Erica Komisar. *Being There.* TarcherPerigee, 2017

to foreign countries, but this isn't possible for homebuilding. Much like how introducing credit scores allowed for the quick recovery of economies after a market bust, allowing for children to be counted as value-added to the economy will help retain populations after baby booms eventually die out.

Young women *must* be able to have children. If your young women can't afford to have children, then your stupid society won't be able to afford to keep existing. If someone else has to put in the work, the money, the time, the effort, the dedication, to raise the children that someone else refuses to have, that will take care of our society, our economy, our future, and who will pay the taxes to uphold everything that we use to survive, then the least we can do is subsidize it.

5.4.4 The Nature of Long-Term Planning

There's a prevalent criticism of the US, that China as a country is able to plan 100 years ahead, while the US is crippled with shortsightedness by its 4-year elections. The greatness of the American presidential position, from the fact that people are limited to 8 years, and checked at 4, is there can be a higher degree of new individuals who make unique mistakes. From the chaotic array of mistakes arises the most valuable lessons, as well as the people who realize what they are and know how to solve them. Which has proven somewhat crazy yet effective. The mistakes can be bad, but the victories are much greater in magnitude.

Long-term planning in America need not be outside the scope of the long-term planning of people's lives, which is the business of each individual. The short-term steering of the US is processed the right way, through its hierarchical government structure. This offers a kind of enhanced sensibility that totalitarianism can't compete with, and that authoritarianism generally can't reproduce. There's no need to be envious of the Chinese.

The 4-year term forces a President to focus on ideas that are attainable within this time frame, which works out well because there's a limited number of things that can be accomplished. The irony is, unless you're terraforming a planet, or building a giant structure, planning 100 years ahead is actually short-term thinking. Predicting even 10 years into the future is difficult, let alone guessing all the conditions that need to be met in order to gain some actual advantage from it. Believing you can succeed in planning 100 years in advance for anything other than a construction project is naive optimism.

Along this line of thinking comes the contradiction that the leadership of China can also somehow instantaneously snap its fingers, and act in a moment's notice. Which is also overblown. Neither ultra long-term planning nor immediate gratification works well for governance. The US moves on consensus, and with it comes a dynamic momentum. The US does, and is able to, act in the short term in the appropriate amount of time to respond to just about anything, and this is a wise doctrine. The model of political votes and opinions culminates into a moving average that continues to guide us in the best strategic direction.

In believing they were planning for the future, the CCP have overbuilt their housing infrastructure, they've overbuilt their rail infrastructure, and now they're currently in the process of overbuilding their electrical infrastructure. Their entire economy runs on building infrastructure that they will neither need, nor be able to maintain even 10 years later. No matter what they build, there's no regard for whether it's useful. It doesn't respect any concept of demand. Even in this age of AI, innovation for reducing energy use will outcompete the growing demand for electricity. Large models will be specialized in function and reduced in size, and will require less electricity in the process. Small models will become more competitive as large models hit a performance wall, and at no point will the projected electricity demand ever overlap with real demand.

Governments are terrible at making long-term plans for their own citizens. We can see this through the effects of the current university system, as well as the declining birth rate, the terrorism we've funded only to have it explode in our face, and the man-made virus we'd somehow managed to unleash upon ourselves. Will the US choose to be a state or a society? Or some finer distinction in between, some better estimation of a center? Believe it or not, the answer to this question isn't actually a matter of governance. The US, and Western governments around the world, have failed to plan for both the previous and upcoming generations. Of course they've failed, this isn't the job of government in the first place. The Chinese aren't good at this either. This is the job of an entirely separate institution. The US government just needs to stay out of its way to allow people to grow their own visions of what they want for themselves. Rather than enabling government institutions to force their views onto the populace.

VI
RELIGION

6.1 The Nature of Values

Beliefs are not made, they're discovered. They create structures in your head made out of knowledge. In the same way that convergent evolution arrives at a specific body plan suitable to an environment, emergence itself emerges in predictable ways. While calling crustaceans predictable might only seem appropriate in hindsight, their body structures were pre-determined by the nature of the emergence of their environment. Organismal design converges on a structure that matches their environment the same way human innovation converges on solutions to problems that expose their susceptibility to inevitability in hindsight. The circumstances of human history were as much a springboard towards specific innovations as some environments were springboards to specific organismal designs, as many of the lifestyles, inventions, and controversies of human history pertain to a Darwinistic inevitability. Whatever structures of knowledge that might lead to these innovations, that are rooted in some inevitable combination of beliefs, would naturally arise from a chain of inevitabilities together. Even the occurrences of history have timeless meanings that link across chains of causality brought about by inevitable forms of belief.

A definition of religion requiring a belief in the supernatural, or spirituality, is nonsensical. That's an embodiment of some religions, but not all. A description of its downstream manifestations at best, not a definition. To paint this definition in a more accurate light, religion is that which is intrinsically linked to belief. But even that's just one bound relative to values.

Religion is the operating system that runs on your brain's hardware. Everyone has a religion, because otherwise you wouldn't be able to function enough to read these words. Jordan Peterson's definition of religion is a wonderful way of exploring how different political mindsets come to be, he describes the basis for values and priorities ordering how we interact with the world[95]. He says religion is *"the basis for the hierarchy of values that you use to organize your perception"*. Values are individual nodes that govern interactions, and a hierarchy of values would be pools of entropy that use them in conjunction.

To break into explaining how a hierarchy of values can be used, let's look back to the example of modeling the known compared to modeling the unknown. Modeling the known via the unknown yields a single belief system, modeling the unknown via the known yields the live generation of different belief systems. These differences are analogous to the concepts found along the axis of time, a single *stabilizing* concept standing opposed to an infinite array of infinitely *fragmentive* concepts. Instead of stability and fragmentation, you might call it order and chaos to stay true to more classical roots, or chaotic and lawful as seen through a literary lens. Even the terms centralization and decentralization are the same exact analogy.

But where do these terms come from? Perhaps it almost seems random to bring them up as if they have any relevance whatsoever. Analogous to the microcosm, the very essence of fragmentation itself, which is everywhere yet somehow also independently so in every instance, would be the analogy of extreme left-wing behavior that pushes for infinitely increasing diversity. The microcosm leads towards an infinite fragmentation both into itself and amongst itself. There's a perceptually infinite number of microcosms that exist around us. It's the swarm of mosquitoes, it's the infinite number of puzzle pieces of those who model the unknown via the known.

Right-wing extremism is analogous to the macrocosm, like a single stable expanding encroachment of every direction pointing outward along the axis of time, symbolized by the lone man with a hammer who pushes for purity. It's the never-ending stream of questions that ask whether everything truly is as it seems, of those who model the known via the unknown. Even the way we interact with these expanses is of the same representative nature. You build a better telescope to peer

95. Jordan Peterson. *Maps of Meaning*. Routledge, 1999

into the macrocosm, and as difficult as that may be, one must use the widest variety of extremely complex technologies to barely peer into the seemingly chaotic feats of the microcosm.

To model the unknown via the known yields a chaotic landscape, because of the magnitude of different possibilities, as it's the fitting of known puzzle pieces into a void of the unknown. People who practice this art form mentally group things together that are sometimes from completely different instances of reality, as if trying to apply every possible pattern match available in order to understand something they don't. Within this kind of space, hypocrisies are allowed and so are contradictions. Inequalities in general are allowed because the equals sign in the middle of the equation has been broken. The two sides of any equation aren't equal when modeling the unknown via the known, because it's actually a comparison of inequalities. One would be trying to best organize things in order of some perceived value, because the purpose isn't to find balance, it's to rank order what's found for the sake of deciphering the unknown. In the face of an enemy, it works well for intelligence gathering and trying to find cracks in a fortress. Which is why it's capable of becoming a kind of societal autoimmune disorder when left without a rival. Unknowns are infinite, and the nature of modeling the infinite means you can fit an entire universe inside a microcosm. Where you think you know and understand 99.99% of how something works, that 0.1% can expand into a world larger than the original known factor. That's the insidious subversion that always lives on when approaching an understanding of life from this direction, it's the door that's always left open for irony to form greater complexity.

For example, imagine the biosphere of Earth and its many ecosystems, there's a lot of ways to destroy the environment and most of your thoughts would probably be directed at killing wildlife if you had to imagine it being done. But if you took something as seemingly irrelevant as viruses, and removed every single one of them from the planet, every ecosystem would probably go into a complete meltdown. That would likely be more impactful than if entire landmass-wide ecosystems collapsed on multiple continents at the same time. Viruses were an early byproduct of the reaction of life, every other ecosystem is either built on top of or intertwined with them. That seemingly irrelevant 0.1% would turn out to be rather important.

Modeling the unknown via the known, as a worldview, happens because one has more unanswered questions, more unknowns, than experiences to fill in those blanks. Which is why it's such a common mindset amongst young people and students who haven't participated in the real world, due to no fault of their own. Through having such a naive worldview, young people have been easily pushed towards mistaking interpretations of unknown factors they've learned about as both true and of great concern. These concerns are typically the products of nihilism, and this is a basic explanation for the origins of many political movements in recent years. It also implies a cure. Taking the immaturity out of the school system can be accomplished by giving people real-world experience and something to genuinely feel passionate about. This will deter people from going down these nonsensical rabbit holes of unknown factors, and submerging themselves in lies to the point where they can no longer find the surface.

Modeling the known via the unknown, is to consider the reliability of every piece of information available. It's to assume there's always something that isn't understood within an environment or lifestyle. Like a constant observer that wards off negligence. It's a process that considers the potential for broader misunderstandings, and aims to prevent them. Rather than relying on the known, it expects the unknown.

To model the known via the unknown is to look inward to find answers, to model the unknown via the known is to look outward. To the former, principles are independent of the environment. To the latter, the environment is independent of any principles. These are representative of the two ways of viewing nature, and the universe itself. One as an ecosystem regulated by deep and meaningful interactions, and the other as a cold heartless place where anything can happen. For the most part, both are true. Across a population, like values in a hierarchy, like organs in a body, not every member is going to have the same function.

To use a more realistic example, imagine the people in your life who prefer hearing the truth, compared to those who want to be reassured. The right-brain orientation, the stability oriented, wants accurate details, they want the truth. The left-brain orientation, the fragmentation oriented, those that are hyperfocused and not just on one thing but often on many, want to know everything behind them is fine, because they're not watching the big picture as keenly and are largely unaware of it. They want reassurance of the big picture. These explanations come at the cost of a bit of oversimplification, but the general pattern holds.

Both of these descriptions are able to find analogous counterparts within the framework of the hierarchy of values, as it can exist in nearly any form, it's a fully flexible format. To understand the direct relations of either with respect to such a hierarchy, let's break down its simplest components into two basic, rather extreme, forms that make it decipherable. The naive extreme is analogous to the nihilistic first step, it has both simple and homogeneous composition, where every potential value holds an equal standing, like sitting at a roundtable. This is the form of mentality found in young children, and it has a tendency to fragment. The process of maturation forces this naive form into a more optimized form, where each value holds a different standing. Other changes occur alongside this, such as an increase or decrease in the number of values, and a greater overall shift in the broader hierarchy itself. In general, the pattern of this transformation would follow Williston's law.

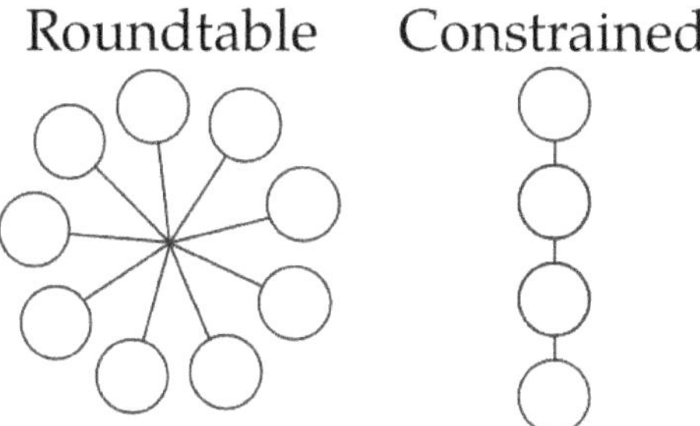

Figure 5: Basic Value Hierarchy Extremes

The other extreme would be one of a completely ordered hierarchy, with no splitting, and no complications. It would be the round table, but linearized and flipped into a pure unidirectional hierarchy with no twists or turns. This constrained hierarchy would exhibit one value at the head of a string of others, with each value having but one other value directly above and below it. This would be a completely principled individual, albeit in an extreme manner under this simplistic example, where any one piece of information becomes context-dependent. It's a hierarchy that's undergone one optimization after the next, and decided on its structure. You can imagine it being much more predictable, trustworthy, and otherwise unchanging as it's representative of stability. Any normal person probably holds a bit of either within their actual hierarchy, as they would be somewhere in the middle. Reality would find value in both of these conceptual forms, and any real hierarchy would be much more complex than either alone.

The constrained hierarchy is a hierarchy in the truest sense, where values are intertwined with each other, and there's a clear picture of what's at the top. Any further extension of values are constraints placed on every preceding point, as a way of addressing nuance and complexity. A violation of a hierarchy of this kind would tend to violate multiple principles at once, like being caught in a web that can be clearly articulated. It's set up for consistency, which is the nature of the right-wing, those modeling the known via the unknown focus on stability, which is why they're the control group. For this group, a specific kind of nurture matches their nature.

When it comes to the roundtable hierarchy, it's actually less like a hierarchy and more like a centralized network. The values are free-floating, without priority. Which generates flexibility in how they can be used. Their lack of prioritization turns each individual value into something more like a detector, able to be set off by any individual violation of whatever principle that value might represent. Every time one of these detectors is triggered, it's typically for the same reason: unfairness. These differences, in the articulation of violations, of a constrained hierarchy compared to the ubiquitous unfairness found by the roundtable, would be the same care-harm divide found in Jonathan Haidt's Moral Foundations Theory[**96**].

For the free-flowing roundtable, they take up a mindset of being more mendable with nurture than with any inherent nature they could possess in alternate circumstances. This kind of self-identification is just as fluid as the mechanisms by which they use their values. Those who use their values like this do so to reject what they perceive as an established conformity, fulfilling the role of an experimental group.

The transformation of a value hierarchy, from a young roundtable process to a more mature and constrained form, is simply a ranking

96. Jonathan Haidt. *The Righteous Mind.* Pantheon Books, 2012

of priorities. It's a strategic prioritization. It's an acknowledgement that treating each value in their roundtable as equal comes into conflict with a desired interest they have. Which is simply a process of maturation, an internal order optimization, a mental modeling of their environment. Maturation is the process of changing from having one reason that justifies multiple beliefs towards having multiple reasons to justify *every* belief. It tends to happen over time, which is why people get more conservative as they age.

But this is still an oversimplification. Everything in the brain is a first-class function, which is a term from computer science that implies all functionality can be passed around as a modulatable variable. You can view something as either a completely adaptive hierarchy or a completely determinant hierarchy. The nature of a hierarchy itself, within the mind of an individual, means it can transform into something less concrete. To superimpose the two basic examples into one, a round table of many constrained hierarchies can hypothetically take on the features of any of its contained subhierarchies, depending on the situation, and that would be a feature rather than a bug. Like an adaptation that can take place on the fly, while reverting back to its base form at the nearest convenience. This, more specifically, is the idea of fragmentation. Where the hierarchy is able to take on an adaptive array of forms, rather than a single determinate form. In this way, most people would realistically hold both abilities, it's a necessary part of life. The functionality of hierarchies would be equally as varying as any circumstance of life. Some things are non-negotiable, like protecting your children from atrocities. Whereas you might be more understanding of the need to adapt to other things, such as culture in a foreign country.

The governing force of what an individual's hierarchy becomes would ultimately be tied directly to their experiences as they age, and probably their evolutionary history as well. Roundtables are prone to fragmentation, as they're pre-adaptation. Constrained hierarchies are prone to stability as they're post-adaptation.

Overall, these two general strategies are part of the socioevolutionary hedged bet that humanity divides itself into. Those who model the unknown via the known *seek* principles. Those who model the known via the unknown, which is the process of *utilizing* principles, seek the utility of the unknown, as they're the ones who keep an eye on the big picture. Like two people watching over each other's shoulder, the same pattern as before, yet this is closer, descriptively, to the true reason behind it. There are things we're aware of, and things we aren't. There are always unknown factors in our environment that can either be a danger or advantage to us, and there are also problems we've known about for hundreds of years that can sneak up lest we forget them. Modeling both of these processes is necessary for group survival, and it's also a lifestyle. Which means society requires individuals to dedicate to either.

To reflect on how these characterizations scale, we can look at the typical sociopolitical differences between urban and rural areas. The virtue of cities is that they're able to foster greater creativity. But when people inhabit areas of lower population density, it's independence that becomes the key virtue. Stability and fragmentation are forms of adapting to an environment. You model your environment through these concepts. It's like a continual competition between the components of Williston's law where the stability orientated focuses more heavily on reduction and the fragmentation orientated focuses more heavily on addition. These are the internal characterizations of the transitions between centralization and decentralization that manifests at larger scales across the world illustrated by Balaji Srinivasan, as what we see happening at large scales across populations should ultimately be indicative of innate characteristics within people, and vice versa. Where do these differences come from? Looking at population density, in rural areas you have more people you directly rely on relative to how many you know and interact with. Interaction and reliance go hand in hand, which forges a more uniform set of principles across people in these kinds of areas. This has been the evolutionary history of isolated living.

In denser populated areas, there's a mixed bag of things that people tend to care about, being receptive to a broad set of values makes for an advantage in peacemaking. A more matured fragmentation orientation does something like going from a roundtable to different constrained hierarchies dynamically, depending on the context. They go back and forth, and rest at the roundtable as a means of using different perspectives like tools. Like favoring perspectives over principles, as opposed to principles over perspectives, which are the same descriptions given earlier regarding principles and environments, as well as principles and the utility of the unknown.

I only describe the two generalities when it comes to the hierarchy of values because it's too speculative to delve into more complicated examples. Regardless, the outcome across this divide, at the baseline, can be described independent of the exact values being used. Rather, it's the nature of the hierarchy they find themselves in that holds some initial effect over behavior. So if individual values of a hierarchy are baseline independent of the behavior exerted, can the behavior exerted from the hierarchy be baseline independent of the nature of the interaction it imposes across individuals?

6.2 The Model of Interactions

Any interaction is more complex than either member left alone. There's entire modalities around certain interactions that we call communication, and communication itself has a stratified definition because of it. Emotions operated as a language long before verbal communication was ever possible, and a method of fair exchange before the exchange of value was possible. It's usually said that emotions and logic don't bode together, or that emotions contradict reason. Which is nonsense, otherwise emotions wouldn't have developed the way they have, our interactions wouldn't have ever become comprehensible.

If organisms are a model of their environment, emotions are a model of life and interaction itself. Emotions *are* the very outcomes of the game we call life. There's a certain spark to stories that manage to come to a scenario of extreme depth, such as a beautiful vision that perhaps no one has ever experienced, a situation that you're unsure of whether anyone has ever truly experienced but is certainly possible, some novel fright in a horror movie, or to accomplish making people feel an emotion they're completely unfamiliar with. We usually call that good writing. The reason we do so is because they've modeled life well, and imagined a scenario they've perhaps never lived through to a degree that maintains the accuracy of feelings they might have never had.

I disagree with those who say people would be savage without law. It's true that people can be, but not that they must be. Groups are made to be naturally cohesive. The mechanisms for this are already built-in, we've evolved for the sake of cooperation with each other. Because those who couldn't cooperate were selected out through their own isolation. Whereas groups who grew to cooperate better eventually formed their own societies and civilizations.

I write this in opposition to the branches of game theory that offer oversimplified simulations as explanations to understand things like human and animal behavior. I also write this in opposition to the animal behaviorists who believe anthropomorphization to be a form of bias when interpreting the behavior of animals. The relationship between organisms is phylogenetic, and this relation negates the supposed barrier assumed in this proposed form of bias. Cooperation cannot be truly understood when simulated absent the entirety of the model of interactions, and the basic communication had in social animals. Those simulations mean close to nothing if they only present an outcome from an oversimplified context. The results of interactions, and the branching network effects they cause, are too much more complex than anything being modeled in these scenarios for any gained insight to be properly reflective of reality. At best, they offer some finite detail, independent of a context, absent of the true bigger picture that is also something to be interacted with.

Emotions are someone's ability to live throughout, and thrive, in the world. A transformation of emotions is the test you pass in order to proceed through the stages of life. You can absolutely destroy those of a young child, and damned be those who do as you're destroying the map they'll need to someday navigate the world. You may even be destroying the map they pass on to their own children, which is evil.

Emotions are an evolutionary history of everything that's happened in the lives that came before us. It's also important to note that emotions aren't functional at scale, as simple interactions don't work in that manner. That's what principles are for. Principles are methods of steering a ship blind that navigates through interactions with others at scale.

Regulating interaction was necessary, so it was done by nature, and was an improvement to the ecosystem. It's a safeguard against uprooting the entire system. When necessary, civil society will sacrifice its own members if it means not allowing abhorrent people, or bad groups to prevail. When someone succeeds at this goal, without themselves being sacrificed, that's the hero we know from our history of literature. An ecosystem that maintained interactions as meaningful, and with depth, persisted over those that didn't. Which is another way of saying that civilizations who lose their religion will die out.

Language certainly started as an integral of emotion, but they've both come to be cyclic derivatives of each other. Relative to irony, which has this cyclic relationship with truth, it paints irony as being more like a unit of interaction than that of reality. Which grants you, through your perspective, a way of quantifying what your priorities are. Because to love is to take priority for. Love is the most complex human experience, and the most complex experience for any animal. Love completely lays out the model of interaction of either of the two who are falling in love.

Love embodies every other aspect of your life. Love is the balance you walk with every fiber of your being. It takes influence from every piece of you, and demands more than anything else, while being able to reward in just as many dimensions. Love is the metaphysical model of every other emotion, a recursion of each within itself. It's the potential for ultimate cooperation between two people. But love is the least scalable manifestation of emotion. To fail to balance the necessary caution, and freedom, required to manage love, is to fail those you claim as your own. You can't over or under cook love and have it work out fine, it wouldn't be love. Love without regulation is menacing, it's a danger. It can destroy whatever you care about if you're not careful. Love is impervious to success by dogma. There are no simple rules for its management. Love is more complex than every other emotion combined. Taking an extraordinary effort is its hallmark. Love is both noble and humiliating, humbling and elevating. To oversimplify it is to curse your loved ones. To overcomplicate it is to doom yourself.

Love is the full combinatoric explosion offered by the interaction of two sets of emotions, two models of interaction. With the model of interaction being a representation of a model of life, love is just as complex as life itself. The most complicated thing you'll ever do being necessary for continued survival guarantees the need for sentience to be at the wheel of each individual body. As there's no automated process that can pull this off. The combinatorics of these interactions act as a deep inspection that determines whether every aspect of your sentience functions adequately to form a stable partnership, and this strategy is extremely successful. So much so that it's abundantly clear that the most intelligent life forms on the planet all work through the basis of sexual reproduction.

Many animals, and most mammals in particular, seem to have a layer of communication built on top of their emotions to further support communication through even more specific interactions than what might otherwise be understandable without something as clear-cut as human language. Human language is the most complex form of species-based communication that we're aware of, but it's still only a single framework. Language doesn't inform you of the best way to live your life, it doesn't give you the experience of those that have spoken it without some intermediary to do so, but it does necessitate you to find such things. So in order to communicate this across generations, there needs to be a communication of communication itself. Which means that given enough time, some form of religious text will inevitably come to fruition. Humans would, and will continue to, compile various forms of everything they've learned in order to better build layers of their Tower of Babel, because people would never be satisfied with constantly failing to do so. Without this, the complexity of human society becomes too large for it to be efficient for individuals, families, or even civilizations to continue growing without compiling the information needed to model their behavior. In fact it's a modeling of modeling itself, as the reflections on their own behavior are just epibolic recursions of that behavior itself, as it's now growing outside the organism in question. It's a guide for people in the future, and a historic account of where their actions took them in the past.

The art of communication reaches its peak when two people share a moment not easily described through basic emotions, being built on multiple layers of them. In this regard, both emotions and something like the Bible are actually recursions of one another. They both model the basis for interactions. But there may be more than one way of seeing it.

Earlier civilizations, born with the same skill, but less wisdom, built a functional model of the human brain 2000-3200 years ago based on the stories of their lives. LLMs are basically a modern version of that same process. It would seem that throughout history, we've come to continually model our interactions in order to find answers from it. Which gives an extreme value to interactions and behavior.

To clarify, it seems unreasonable to think the writers of the Bible set out with the intentions to make a model of the human brain specifically. Regardless, it's a fair interpretation of what they produced. They may have just wanted to record, and aggregate, the most notable lessons known that they felt painted the most important stories to learn from. It turns out that a model is a metaphor, so the recursion we call language actually allows us to communicate in models, which is the very basis for religion itself.

But even that eventually changes with time, a model of the brain can't last forever. Cultures change, and so does the brain with it. Considering the expanded field of interactions offered on social media, even the emotions you've grown like a garden, over billions of years, have come to an unnatural fork in the road, representative of the divides across most civilizations we see today. The need for stories is still there, but it's no longer the pinnacle of what can be used to model the brain. It was a structure of knowledge that formed core beliefs. The art of the interpretation of information is now dependent on an amount of truth that's never before been held, and simple stories will not do it justice.

As it's a religion I'm aiming to make, as well as other things, it would be worthwhile to acknowledge what this book aims to accomplish. As it wouldn't be fitting to attempt to only copy what was done thousands of years ago, but instead improve upon it, and perhaps offer some reflection. I aim to make this book a model of the complexity of human knowledge and existence. Not just the truth lived by those in the past, like what's in the Bible, but the truth we've accumulated after having found so much new truth that we submerge ourselves in it in ways that had only previously been possible as a submergence in lies. Because if they were lies, it would be easier. You could pick a side, become tribal, and hate the other. But now that we're swimming, feet off the ground, head underwater, in what are not just lies but also many hard truths, in which some are disputed, disputable, and some are even hated for what they represent, I wish to enlighten on the aspect of truth itself. That there's always a brighter interpretation of truth, and a much more enticing interpretation through irony. Despite any pessimism, or immediate misinterpretations that spread like wildfire igniting masses of people who march against some lone shimmer of non-falsity, that instead of rallying a cause against reality itself you should look to question whether or not it's reality that's really so terrible. You might just find that there's always a supreme optimism put there for you by grace of the evolution of your body modeling the world so that your mind could model the universe. By the struggles of everyone and everything that's come before you, placed into you as a crest of the model of interactions that's been won, by trial and error, by right and wrong, by every ancestor you've ever had. A gift they deliver to you, from history you'll never know. That justice does triumph, and that you have every reason to believe in those who believe in you. Both in their intentions, and in your cooperation with them. That no matter how long the fight, no matter how dark the trenches dug in disgust by a throne abdicated to those unworthy, their end result is destined for failure. The innocent are forever rectified, and those who take good will for granted will grant themselves a timely end. So it's not up to you to decide which is which beforehand. Let time decide, as it was time that gifted you the emotions you use to make your judgement. Time has not failed you in granting you this ability, time will not fail you in delivering it either.

6.3 The Basis of Religion

Religion belongs at the base of the Tower of Babel. It's where you set your widest layer, the absolute boundaries of every boundary you could ever find. It's at the heart of every model you have. The tower inevitably thins out as you go higher, symbolizing the refinement of complexity. Religion aims for a much wider goal than anything else, it's the big picture of big pictures. The first principle of first principles. The core of right-brain imbuity.

To make a broad but accurate generality, beliefs and values are the boundaries by which both groups and individuals optimize their internal order. The refinement of values is a refinement of interactions, meant for dealing with other people, other organisms, as well as aspects of our own physical environment. A refinement of beliefs is a refinement to the structure of one's own knowledge and their awareness of any lack thereof. Together, these act as delineations across individuals, families, groups, ethnicities, and religions. Which is why these two forms of metaphysical attributes are the most legitimate delineations by which one can define religion. They determine everything about each group as a whole. Which also then emphasizes that the entropic optimization of either is a religious process, both within groups and individuals.

We've lived through an era without a true main source of stability. Instead we've had mechanistic forces of growth that we relied on to supplant it, made up of the economy that keeps us alive and a pursuit of knowledge to improve this process. The alternation between either is a cycle that seems to repeat throughout history, and from this same cycle comes the inevitability of religion. Iain McGilchrist, alongside his idea of the left- and right-brain functionality, also paints a history where societal paradigms undergo this alternation that are represented by a resurgence of either functionality becoming more prominent. Through these cycles, religion, as an integral to a philosophy of growth, always eventually takes root and a new tower base is formed.

Religious texts are as inevitable as bipedal organisms designing stairs. Experience and wisdom need to be accumulated, and compiled, because life is too complicated for it not to. People all across time have spent their entire lives devoted to problems that we undoubtedly take the rewards of for granted, as they've become such simple second nature to us. Religious texts were like the moon landing of core principles, they were the basis for forming grander structures of knowledge out of beliefs. These books are hindsight on hindsight itself. They act as a savepoint for accumulated wisdom.

Why do civilizations tend to start off as polytheistic, then eventually transform into monotheism? It's yet another internal order optimization. Religion has its roots in antiquity and is likely to be the key signature of intelligent life. If nihilism is the first step one takes towards understanding any topic, then religion is the first step towards understanding what it is you're not aware of. It's the initiation of grasping the unknown.

The changes throughout the various ages of religion are, again, no different in nature than what we see in Williston's law. Animism, fueled by the transformation of grief from natural disasters into uncertain blame, would tack on new threats as entities as a form of keeping track of what forces were worth being wary of, and represents the addition step. That these forces of nature eventually became representative of and had human characteristics, as people became a larger threat than the less frequent natural disasters, is a representation of specialization. Then as polytheism turned into monotheism, there was a reduction of redundancy that completed this optimization.

Most major world religions have, at some point, probably had a serious denial of evolution. Religion aims to be the basis for human civilization to be able to pass the test of time. Ironically, this itself is within the realm of evolution. The basis for evolutionary history, and the world being older than some may have thought, was a story with the power to supercede a narrative of control. In reality, those who feared losing control should have feared that evolution would have provided wiser lessons to learn from than whatever holy books had been around. Their fear was right, but their reasoning was misplaced.

Likewise, in the modern day, it's the woke enforcement bureau that doesn't want anyone learning from human nature. The extreme left-wing of the West has an unnatural fear of Darwinian philosophy being applied to humans, because they're afraid of racism and eugenics like it's some boogeyman that lives under their bed. But that's just cover. People who want to control the origin story want power. Where there's a group attempting to sever your link to the past, your history, and the philosophies it's brought forth, they're attempting to sever you from your own civilization. It's civilizational sabotage.

I think the social differences, between now and when the Bible was written, are larger than the differences in the interpretations of the metaphors of that text across the same period. The metaphors still work where they're applicable, which means the Bible ended up being a pretty good model. A bad model, by comparison, is saying something like *all religion is stupid* because there were wars fought on a religious basis. Our existing culture war is basically a religious war, many people would undoubtedly hold the excuses for their beliefs much closer to their heart than they might for anyone they disagree with.

If I had to write a book, that would persist for thousands of years, without having truly grasped what religion was meant to accomplish, I would write it in metaphors. Across both time and translations, the metaphors would be the most likely aspect to survive. Seeing as it's worked for various religious texts, that was realistically the best avenue for both conveying and preserving the messages of those books through thousands of years. But unlike a lot of books written thousands of years ago, I can communicate much more concisely by intertwining the realm of literary metaphor with modern knowledge, the same way language intertwines with emotions to take on more complex forms of communication.

Religion functions by offering a clear vision, one that unites a connection to the past with a vision for the future. The connection to the past can be maintained through the handing down of tradition, the wisdom gained from evolution, the lessons learned from history, and the development of lawful rule and fair principles. The vision of the future can be built on technological improvement, an acknowledgement of the potential of the superabundance we live amongst, as well as the necessity of good leadership, open communication, freedom, and competition. We've barely tapped the resources of the Earth. Ideas of premature resource conservation only work to bring us backwards technologically, environmentally, and economically. Which is to say it would bring us back morally. We can transform our use of resources in order to learn to make better use of our resources, using less to get more.

Where interactions take precedence over claims of divinity, you have a family. Where claims of divinity take precedence over interactions, you have a cult or a scam. Where interactions and claims of divinity sit equal to each other's proportions, you have a religion.

The core tenets of a religion are bets on reality and human nature in the same way that an investment is a bet against the rest of the market. Why invest in one thing specifically? There's a lot of places to put your money, and they all technically compete with each other. A religion, made in good faith, is a gamble on the nature of humans, their interactions, and that of the universe itself. The expectation is to see a payout from the effects of an improved optimized internal order throughout society, one which comes from a successful alignment with universal principles, a modeling of their underlying existence despite our uncertainty of their true nature.

People have historically used God, and still do, as a part of formal reasoning to explain things in place of what they didn't understand. Throughout history, it's been used as a proxy for understanding evolution, the creation of the universe, and physical reality. These were things people intuitively understood, yet couldn't fully explain, and their uncertainties now lie exactly where our own certainties have grown. But they didn't arrive at the basis of those understandings free of charge, they had to grow their cumulative intellectual endeavors to the point of being able to ask those questions at all. We still find ourselves in those same shoes, where the questions we must ask to uncover new understandings, that require the next evolved religious proxy of our uncertainty, have now become as intricate as our understandings for any of these topics. There's no way to outgrow the need for such a proxy, and calling it a proxy quite honestly does it a disservice. It's a reversal of the nature of emergence, as emergence is a forward-moving phenomenon, it flows in one direction like the time we experience. Yet the more time moves forward, the harder it becomes to uncover. The further you go in unraveling its nature, the more you'll find this perpetually hidden concept only unveils its next disguise.

6.4 Philosophy of Religion

Religion is meant to be the compass that actually works. The problem being, the world has gotten a lot more complex since any major religions have been born. Not only that, it seems to be getting more complex at a faster and faster rate. There's so much nuance left unaddressed by dogma, and real-world scenarios not covered by these age-old cultures that truthfully no longer exist in the same form. If you had to make a religion, what aspects of life would be necessary to address in order to ensure that it meets the needs of what it's meant to accomplish?

Much like how a successful animal eventually migrates to different continents, the core achievements of the West have spread across the world in the same way. Technological advancements, codes of law, economic models, schooling paradigms, and every art form ever designed has made its way to every notable civilization on the planet due to the nature of its success. That success was originally derived from something central to Christianity, but the world changes. Success eventually becomes failure if it never adapts. As great as it is, sharing everything you've made just gives your advantages away to everyone else for free, and leaves you without any way to distinguish yourself. There's a need to adapt to the times once again.

We find ourselves at a crossroads of science and religion, of philosophy and governance. Having accumulated so many gifts from the dead, we now have the ability to do so much more than anyone from any preceding time period ever has that it requires a major organizational step to now use all of our own advantages well. I find it reasonable, desirable even, that religion should cover a breadth of topics as wide as possible, with as little complexity as required. It should aim to address problems that are present in the modern day, which cause the most undue stress, and it should be the formation of a lifestyle that makes individuals capable of withstanding nearly everything they might come across.

What are some core things a religion might then have? A creation myth? Some kind of model of human nature? Both of these seem reasonable. Should it be highly specific? Maybe not, there's a lot to be gained by having specific advice, but there's a lot to be lost by disregarding nuance. Specifics should be derivable, otherwise the religion wouldn't be modeling life very well. Because religion is the art of the big picture. You can't possibly take every situation into consideration, but some key ideas can at least be planted. So any further details should be derivable rather than explicit.

As for a core motivation, should it be God? God plays an interesting role in religion, but I would argue the core motivation should be children. God is what we approach as we move towards the future, God is the center value we estimate using the social bifurcations of the automaton. Without children, there will be no future, so children come before God. Rather, children *are* the path towards God. The point of perpetuating family values is for children. The point of having a stable society is for children. The point of having a religion, to hold society together, is so your children may one day do the same. After all, an economy is reliant upon two things, an upbringing process and competition, which are just metaphors for a mother and father.

Religion is infinitely flexible as a concept, it exists as a recursion of life in that it also carries a wide stratification of variations and characterizations. Life and religion, as performed by intelligent organisms, are potential answers to a question that asks *what's the best way to live and persist*? Like cultures, not all religions are equal. Just as you find across the stratifications of life, organisms that learned to manage sharing their environments through the model of interactions were able to coexist together in ecosystems with the bare minimum hostility that it took to survive. Which is why polar bears, hornets, and crocodiles don't just make bad pets, they make terrible neighbors. Likewise, bad cultures and bad religions do the same.

I don't want religion to be an institution so reliant on old dogma, there's too much value in innovation. Being truly grateful for something doesn't mean to show blind loyalty. Being grateful is being able to understand something so well that you can make the most honest, yet serious, criticism of it for the sake of its own improvement, otherwise it may never become better for itself and for others. It's the ungrateful who accept everything as it is and offer no recourse for improvement, especially while reprimanding others for speaking such things, denying dignity to whatever's left over, and making sure to leave the world without having made it any better than how they found it.

The point of religion isn't to enforce beliefs, it's to find what beliefs are worth upholding. The point of religion is to fuel relationships the way money fuels an economy. Having one globalized superstate rule the entire world would be a terrible idea, as would having *one true religion*. There should always be competition, as populations of people, and their beliefs, eventually wither, change, and bloom again. Those aiming to eradicate other people, their culture, and their religion, while claiming such a thing as their own culture, or religion, make for an atrocity worth fighting against. Religion is a means, not an end.

There always comes the question of which religion is correct. You shouldn't expect any of them to be correct, they're all trying to model the same thing and none of them have the answer. Some may be better at doing that than others, but none are perfect, mistakes are inevitable. Meaning there's always room for growth. When they all end up independently agreeing on something, then they may have found something valuable.

The ideas I've described so far aren't new ideas. They're the same ones that people always tend to find. Is karma not a form of irony? Are the Amish not wary of the curse of the gift of technology? The two opposing forces of order and disorder are the same as yin and yang, and competition is just a different representation of the balance they represent. Stability and fragmentation are also analogous to the archetypes of lawful and chaotic, which is still just order and disorder.

What kind of religion is worthy of having, should you aim to make one yourself? How can one establish a religion worthy of the level of human advancement that's been achieved both intellectually, and societally, and to pair that with a desirable path in life for children to flourish? The line between reality and science fiction is the most blurred it's ever been, our civilizational existential crises are reflective of this state. We can see in the modern day where religion hasn't made sense to people, who've come so long after both its creation and peak, and this is actually reasonable. A lot of it is metaphorical, but some of it is cryptic. Some of the stories just don't resonate when experienced side by side with the comparatively blooming art form of modern storytelling. But consider the history of religion, and what it's tried to accomplish. Religion has had the challenge of categorizing itself while simultaneously discovering the nature of what religion is even trying to discover in the first place. It's always been a step behind what it was chasing. Trying to solve an integral from a derivative, when it had access to neither, and that's a solid description of what our brains have been trying to do for thousands of years in various forms. It probably still is. I find it reasonable to believe that people would not become devout believers in something that didn't make sense to them. Religion, in its various forms, had something groundbreaking to offer people relative to what they had believed prior.

Religion is the art of being able to explain things that are just barely out of reach of a fair explanation. Trying to take an honest shot at making a religion is like describing the unknown with only the unknown. It's like playing a game where every shot you need to make has to come from out of bounds. You have to break every rule while you play.

Does that mean that religion acts as a delineator of what's known and what's unknown, or perhaps non-disprovable? That would be Karl Popper's philosophy of science[97]. Karl Popper's line of falsifiability is the most reasonable demarcation for the process of elucidating the known, but how does that help us with religion? Is there something that can be proven? When forming a religion one can't simply make use of Francis Bacon's call for controlled experimentation[98], nor can one adhere to John Locke's concept of empiricism[99]. That sounds more like science, but perhaps science and religion are what belong on either side of the delineation being formed.

Let's compare a couple examples. Planets can distort time relative to another location, changing the reference frame of observed events. Which means planets act as a device that distorts time, it can slow time down relative to an outside observer. Therefore we can definitively say that the technology to make some kind of time chamber to slow down time isn't science fiction, and this comes from observably true

97. Karl Popper. *The Logic of Scientific Discovery*. Verlag von Julius Springer, 1934
98. Francis Bacon. *Novum Organum*. John Bill, 1620
99. John Locke. *An Essay Concerning Humane Understanding*. Thomas Basset, 1689

information. The only people to disagree would need to do so on the most high-strung technicalities. Planets already *are* this technology, so this is a scientifically valid statement.

Within the realm of religion, one could posit that aliens would, without a doubt, share a functional paradigm of biochemistry very similar to our own, because it's quite unlikely for intelligent life to arise any other way. In fact, I will. The proteins, and even signaling pathways, found in alien biology would undoubtedly hold solutions to the same exact problems that arose in our own case. The core biochemical nodes within our bodies are all solutions to extremely specific problems, the most important active sites on one planet would remain as such on most others, even some tertiary and quaternary structures of alien proteins would undoubtedly match what we find throughout the biochemistry of our own world. Structures such as ribosomes, and modalities such as splicing, would undoubtedly exist. Other forms of successful intelligent life would also undoubtedly arrive at the same values, principles, and concepts as any successful civilization on Earth, because these values and physical principles are fundamental axioms of the universe itself. One might expect some slightly different base pairs, a slightly different set of codons, perhaps even slightly different amino acids, but the general patterns and mechanisms will be the same, the general chemistry won't differ too much, and there wouldn't be some wildly foreign form of organism based on something other than carbon. We'll likely find they share a generous portion of our biochemistry, and fundamental molecular clockwork, as these would be solutions to the same exact problems, and thereby not likely to yield entirely different answers. Other forms of intelligent life to emerge throughout the universe would even do so in humanoid form.

Organismal biochemistry, the concepts modeled from language, and emotions all consist of solutions to specific problems that have specific answers. There's even second order solutions that arise from these as ways to live your life, that then become represented by stories used to form religions. For these emergent pillars of interaction, there's axioms they follow through their emergence. Words are indicative of meaning that's intrinsic to the universe itself. Words aren't just randomly crafted concepts used to arbitrarily latch onto subjective meanings, they're representations of the structure of information inherent to the universe, which is why they can be used to interpret information at all, it's why languages are translatable. The concepts that words represent are universal axioms. Language is only capable of forming sensible frameworks *because* it's able to latch onto these axioms. We form systems of beliefs through the connective logic of the axioms represented in words to construct formal reasoning. You might think the words *"and"*, *"cloud"*, and *"crab"* are just descriptive representations of reality. But *"and"* is a logic gate. A cloud is an inevitability within another emergent framework that constructs the universe, one that's bound to form in the atmospheres of celestial bodies. Even the concept of a crab is a form of inevitability as it's a concept that's formed through a modeling of an arguably inevitable environment. A crab is as much an emergent universal axiom as a cloud or a black hole. Crabs are not a coincidence. Where do we actually find anything we can definitively label as *truth* throughout these layers of inevitabilities built upon other layers of inevitabilities? Even the laws of the universe are likely no different than emergent principles. Scientific elucidations would be uncovering the emergence of emergences, and this would eventually transform to an uncovering of the pattern of emergence rather than the emergences directly.

In his philosophy of science, Popper argues for reasoning over inference, and deduction over induction. But he was naive to consider one superfluous and the other as holy. If either of these weren't useful tools of decipherment, then our evolution wouldn't have allowed for their interpretive utility. Any line of reasoning can be principled, they would simply require a unique practice to be used well. The irony of living in this age, where centuries of scientific advancement have provided an environment filled with the products of deductive reasoning, has resulted in there being bountiful concisities ripe for the process of inductive inference.

But this still isn't entirely accurate, the nature of the universe doesn't fit cleanly into the induction, deduction, and abduction breakdown. They're fine as standalone thought processes, but they're more like if you had to explain extremely finite versions of thought to someone who's never had a thought in their life. I don't believe intelligent organisms developed modes of reasoning independent of the concept of transformation. This is where Popper's philosophy falls short, because it isn't able to see itself as a stepping stone, it prevents itself from transforming. The universe doesn't emerge from these concepts of deductive or inductive reasoning alone, so using only one of these to attempt to explain the universe in its entirety will lead to a dead end.

Independent of forms of reasoning, if falsifiability is meant to better delineate the line between fanciful dreams and demonstrable reality, then how is religion meant to offer a balance to this game, a competitive pushback on this mental monopoly on the interpretations of information itself? Two things opposed don't stand opposite. Healthy competition takes the form of a hedged bet, it's to keep one foot in your opponents camp in order to use their own knowledge against them. Without being able to address what competes across his line of falsifiability, without being able to address a formal utility of religion, Karl Popper's philosophy of science is incomplete. Any proper philosophy on the topic would be a philosophy of both science and religion together, as these two institutions are inherently linked to one another as scaled representations of the known and unknown respectively. To address how the institutions of religion can cohabitate the delineation of falsifiability with the institutions of science, I'm going to address where Popper falls short with his other major linchpin, objective truth.

Objectivity is the idea that if we can scientifically validate things, we can be sure of what we know. But we can never be sure of what we don't know, so we can't ever be sure that we know absolute truth. It's not that Popper is unforgivably far off the mark, but rather that I want to rearrange some of what's considered simple and what's considered complex as an update to this model. The replacing of all faith with the rigid pursuit of truth has only come to show us why powerful beliefs are valuable tools of truth finding, and why having faith in that truth can be more powerful than having formally articulated it. Those saying we can only deal with objective truth just states the impossibility of reaching absolute truth to be an absolute truth. Objective truth itself is contradictory, it's a denial of metaphysical validation, it's the belief that truth can ever be perfectly secretive. It's allowing truth to remain holy, yet the entire point of elucidating truth at all isn't to find what's holy, it's to understand how things work for the sake of survival. It requires a religious dedication to accept this contradiction, because one requires metaphysical validation to insist that we'll never understand absolute truth. Because it's a belief. The only way to skirt around this contradiction of objectivity is to accept Popper's concept of objectivity itself as a belief. Acknowledging it's a belief leads us somewhere unique in processing information, because with information it's desirable to seek truth, but with a system of beliefs it's worthwhile to seek utility.

Popper insists that works of science can never be treated as absolute truth. He claims theories can never be fully verified, that they're simply our best understanding of how the universe works. My problem with Popper is, aside from his bland flavoring of words, he speaks from the perspective of a prisoner of the universe. Reading any book written by Karl Popper will certainly make someone feel like they're in a jail cell, but the universe isn't a jail cell, it's a riddle. To approach truth from one single direction is to unnecessarily handicap yourself. It's like only ever looking at the sky through a telescope, forgetting the horizon is wider than it is deep.

If we're able to validate things at all, if we can speak, and reason, and make sense of the universe using the universe itself, then it's because the universe makes sense. So then whatever makes the universe exist also makes sense. Then if things that make sense make a pattern, if the emergence of emergence isn't entirely random, then the logical structures of such emergences should be predictable. Which is how we can predict the existence of things like gravitons via Quantum Field Theory, as was done with positrons before it. So there's reason to believe it can be completely understood, even without directly witnessing it.

We also have reason to believe the truth we do have is a part of the absolute truth, that's what validation is meant to deliver. Even if it exists in some grand misinterpretation, that misinterpretation itself is part of the truth, and it would probably become yet another emergent story for people to learn from. Even if we don't at any point have a perfect version of truth, we still *approach* it. In approaching it we learn to better approach more things, and this is a transformation. As we don't simply make small linear steps in our thinking that can never catch up with the universe, we grow, and we grow at growing. So if absolute truth is something that's at the end of a long line of thousands or millions of years of transformations, then not only is it achievable, the concept of absolute truth is no different than the concept of God. If people insist we can only ever know objective truth, that's just their belief. In refuting the attainability of absolute truth, one places objective truth in its place. But with absolute truth being a metaphor for God, this is essentially a slaying of God. Which is an overtly religious statement once you pull back this shroud of objectivity.

Worshipping unattainable truth is a denial of the potential of transformations. It's also the insistence that absolute truth comes in a form that can be hidden. Which is assuming the structure of absolute truth, yet we're supposedly not able to know that as it's purportedly unobtainable. It may as well come in a fragmented form and be dispersed into many smaller truths, like those which we collect. We may as well have pieces of absolute truth already, they're just layers of the entire whole. If truth is finite then it's attainable in its entirety as long as we never stop trying to understand it. If you assume it's infinite, then that's a form of belief because that's what's required to state anything can be infinite at all. You would need to *believe* some aspect of reality to be infinite because you can neither prove nor disprove the infinite nature of anything outside mathematics. We can't assume the universe is finite because we have a limited window to view it, but we're not inundated with so much scientific truth that we can't even parse it all individually.

If absolute truth is infinite then that's not truth. We use models and truncated forms of reasoning to understand things at scale. You don't need to characterize the shape of every speck of dust to verify that every piece is in fact a speck of dust, it's just small particles floating in the air or that build up on surfaces. Absolute truth can't be more infinite than the universe it creates, to interpret it as such is just an unrefined belief.

But we're not squashing ideas, we're rearranging them to fit in better positions. So where does this concept of unobtainability fit? There's two ways to paint some inevitably persistent scientific incompleteness. Incompleteness of breadth, and incompleteness of depth. Being incomplete in breadth means there's always going to be some missing information at large that was never accounted for. Being incomplete in depth means some ideas that are thought to be understood might not actually be fully understood. But these two formats are something we've already become familiar with. Assuming either of these forms of incompleteness is just modeling the unknown via the known, and the known via the unknown, respectively, and I find these to be instinctively compatible with how human thought actually behaves, as opposed to induction, deduction, and abduction.

There are many ways to question the integrity of what you know, or question the nature of what it is you don't, but your ability to question is never independent of what you're aware of. To rely on what you know in order to attempt to understand what you don't, to model the unknown via the known, is to accept what you rely on as truth. The lineage granted through inheriting information, or somehow finding and learning it yourself, is always a subjective process regardless of whether the information itself can be deemed objective. This isn't meant to offer the interpretation that all information is equal, it isn't, but granting awards to information for being supposedly *objective* is itself a subjective process. Something being objective truth or subjective truth is irrelevant. This also isn't meant to argue you can't attempt objectivity, but that's what it is, it's only ever an attempt. The point of stating all this isn't to say the approach of objectivity should be disregarded, rather it's to say that subjectivity itself shouldn't be discarded as worthless. It can even be embraced. Subjectivity may be useful in unexpected ways, or may be unexpectedly objective given that the high order logic we call emotions are actually innate survival mechanisms able to derive wisdom from information-dense interactions.

To believe our personal feelings only lead to faulty interpretations of information is to disregard whether people would appreciate dumb luck in understanding the universe. Answers found by dumb luck offer no story, it grants neither triumph nor inspiration. If discoveries were continually made through dumb luck, rather than through effort and accomplishment, people would never be motivated to discover anything at all, it wouldn't be necessary. In the face of this existential disappointment, what would then be properly inspiring would be to learn that such dumb luck wasn't actually dumb at all, that there was an extremely intricate reason as to why such luck ever occurred in the first place. There's meaning in discovering novelties, and your emotions guide you towards that meaning like the wings of a moth to a flame.

To seek the flaws of what you understand, to model the known via the unknown, would be to understand why dumb luck isn't so dumb after all. It's to question objectivity itself. Even if objectivity has value, there's always value in questioning what's ostensibly objective. In order to pose these questions, subjectivity isn't only inevitable, it's desirable.

Science isn't able to monopolize the pursuit of truth, it was originally inherited from the work of religious institutions to begin with.

Before having the ability to organize society into groups capable of partaking in formal scientific inquiries, religion was first able to understand human nature enough to organize people into societies at all. Philosophies like Popper's only acts to exclude the core underpinnings of belief entirely by deputizing empiricism to be the sole mechanism for the elucidation of truth. This disregards the nature of truth that was discovered prior to the formalization of science. Where Popper's naive is to assume the only path towards the elucidation of truth is an act of clarification.

Failing to acknowledge the nature of belief required to accept a form of truth as imperfect only acts to maintain a philosophical ambiguity around the concept of objective truth itself. Allowing any established thought to be simultaneously indisputable while also being acceptably imperfect only grants the concept of objective truth a throne much like religions grant to their most deeply held beliefs. This isn't to say any scientific theory is entirely indisputable, they're transiently indisputable. More specifically it's the simultaneity of being incontrovertible and yet offered unending forgiveness for what are assumed to be built-in errors that introduces a hypocrisy only acceptable through a religious dedication, as such a contradiction can't be rightfully called a respectable philosophy for seeking truth. You might protest, that Popper's philosophy doesn't rely on objective truth. He instead insists upon testing for errors and critical discussion. But what are these if not a means of *approaching* objectivity much like a transformation in calculus being made from approaching infinity? Within his philosophy of science, Popper inserts a religious worship towards objective truth, where he paints the impossibility of disagreeing with imperfection. To disagree with an imperfect consensus would normally be classified as a belief. Which is where his philosophy falls short, it fails to acknowledge the nature of his own belief, where he instead calls this a *methodology*. To rely on science as a library of truth requires a belief that it can be used as a tool to be depended upon in order to make further elucidations into the nature of the universe. To understand that scientific theories are imperfect requires belief in an inherent framework of truth that we ourselves are attempting to model.

Even outside of scientific pursuits, objectivity has taken people over like a disease and it isn't in the least bit desirable. It's been useful for the sake of analysis and clarity, but too much of anything becomes a bad thing. We *need* subjectivity, we *need* bias, we need to acknowledge differences amongst groups and ideas. The war against bias has allowed for Marxist ideas to slip into what are meant to be *functioning* parts of society. An idea paraphrased from Rudyard Lynch:

> Academics have been told for decades not to write in personable or interesting ways, because that's considered biased. If you write about how some people perceive consciousness compared to others, different tiers of consciousness, or different strengths and weaknesses thereof, that's considered biased. Which ultimately leads towards Marxism, because you're never allowed to say one worldview is better than any other. It's a tool for preventing judgement while upholding equality of any and all views independent of what those views entail.
>
> *Sex and Power in History*

This insistence on equality and unbiased analysis only serves as a gateway towards communist ideologies when incubated for decades. Bias is a necessary wall that allows for greater potential to one's internal order, as well as that of their group. The model of interactions exists *because* bias is necessary. Not all ideas are equal, not all cultures are equal, not all behaviors are equal, not all beliefs lead to the same place, and differing values certainly don't create replicable societies. Equality itself is the wrong lens to even look through when understanding these fundamentally *different* entities.

The concept of objective truth only acts as a point of worship for scientists who refuse to associate with the term *belief*. They want to believe to the best of their knowledge that something is true, but have no problem saying it could be false for the sake of not sounding religious. Yet to build upon an idea, one must believe in its utility in order to do so. So while someone can reap the benefits of believing the utility of something, Popper's philosophy of science allows one to escape the claim that they actually *believe* in anything by using the concept of objective truth as a shield against belief itself. Now it's not that scientists should be sued over their theories turning out to be incorrect in some way, but this presents a problem with the accountability of scientific pursuit itself. The same claims are made by religious figures about God. Popper turned science into a psychological weapon, a mental trap against belief itself, while simultaneously denying and still reaping the benefits of those same beliefs. Popper completely muddies the line between belief and truth.

Popper insists any form of truth also needs to be testable to be deemed true. We can't test that the universe was *created*, yet there's undeniable evidence in that we exist. Some might say there's methods of theorizing *how* the universe was created, but we can't go back in time to before that point and ask, *what happened*? Explaining the Big Bang, if you insist that was the beginning of the universe and not merely a stepping stone in our understandings of such, is never at any point an explanation for *how* the Big Bang itself ever was created. The creation of the universe doesn't need to be tested in order for it to be true. If it weren't true, we wouldn't be here arguing over the nature of elucidating truth. Does the evolutionary convergence on the body plan of a crab *prove* crabs are emergent axioms of the universe? No, emergence itself is an interpretation built upon truth. There's no way to prove or disprove it, it's a belief formed from a systematic understanding of how the universe assembles itself. But in understanding this interpretation, one finds an advantage in finding and interpreting the emergence of other truths, you must be brave enough to make such leaps, otherwise you'll trap yourself in Popper's jail cell. Axioms of emergence can't be proven to be such, they're extremely resistant to deduction-based elucidation. Yet their understanding is undeniably useful, and most likely required in order to fully understand the universe. Their utilization requires faith. The point of seeking truth was never meant to be abstinent of belief, and belief isn't purely a mode of inspiration. Belief fills in the gaps where experimentation can't reach. One must take the same leap of faith with their interpretations as would be needed to accept the nature of an infinite approach of some topic as being a transformative mechanism.

You might say a methodology of elucidating truth isn't a religion, and maybe even *because* it's a pursuit of truth. But that's all religion has ever tried to do. No matter how inefficient, that's what religion does and has attempted to do in its best light. Even Popper's system of beliefs has roots in religion, like every other academic pursuit.

Popper's failed acknowledgement of truth and belief forces his terminology to only ever approach a definition without reaching it, rather than accepting the utility of transformation to utilize what these definitions are objectively approaching. An objective truth can just be an accepted truth without all the philosophical entanglement. In elucidating the universe we should expect complexity, but to embrace it needlessly in our own lives only displays an inability to properly model our environment. It's an aversion to claim truth because of an aversion to belief. You can be wrong and change your beliefs later, and this is fine. Scientific thought accomplishes the same exact thing. But to claim neither belief nor truth to be legitimate, like claiming neither are axioms of the universe itself, is a religious denial of religious axioms. You may as well admit you believe something as true, to allow a belief to transform into a pillar for thought. The avoidance of this acceptance is an attempt to remove humanity itself from the process of truth-seeking, yet the only things that can operate a system of beliefs are things capable of having beliefs in the first place. In his attempt to avoid working around every sensible human convention, beliefs aren't acknowledged as beliefs, and the only truth about truth is that truth can never truly be understood. The only formal incorporation of truth he utilizes is a denial of truth itself. This is a dreamless religious paradigm. Karl Popper didn't make a methodology, he made a mental device. It's a belief system, you must believe that his methods work in order to trust them. Trust in his methods implies a belief in what they produce.

That's not to say there's anything wrong with it being a religion, or that his methodology is entirely dysfunctional, but to seek truth one must seek honesty. Karl Popper's *method* is actually a system of beliefs, stating it as anything else is fraudulent. You can name it a *methodology*, and use all the fanciful language you want, but the function of the structure of what he provides is essentially a system of beliefs, and this is inescapable. The truth of a statement is related to the structure it proposes, not the descriptions it insists upon.

True objectivity is only as approachable as the concept of absolute truth. While one may argue over the achievability of ever reaching true objectivity, or absolute truth, it's clear that we're able to approach either while rooting ourselves in what we believe to be true. Our abilities to reach such things aren't bereft of the potential transformations that reinvent our understanding of what an end goal actually looks like, so we don't actually have a need for such static ambivalence to replace our own basic flexibility of thought. In reality, people use beliefs to elucidate truth, where they leverage any truth elucidated to better elucidate other truths. Any attempt at doing so requires a system of belief. Any attempt at measurement, experiment, understanding, or reasoning at all, can only ever be built atop of a systematic belief structure. Beliefs are the structures that support every aspect of intellectual function. We can't find any first principles of the universe to base our elucidations on, and that's even the point of our elucidations in the first place, it's to base our thoughts on something more tangible than beliefs. In the process we've made systems of belief for doing so, and that's what they are. They're beliefs.

Anything and everything we understand is built upon beliefs. Beliefs are the primary mode of understanding itself. Any systematic attempt at clarifying any form of truth is automatically a system of belief. Understandings of truth are built atop of beliefs. Although it's not unfair to be unsure of whether something is either truth or belief, that would be representative of a formal uncertainty. Popper's philosophy claims to allow the ability to hold neither acceptance nor belief for pieces of information that are relied upon in a manner that one would typically rely on either belief or accepted truth. If everything in your repertoire is somehow always neither, then you've only fooled yourself into thinking you can use neither in your process. The word for that is dishonesty.

In accepting the incorporation of beliefs into scientific understandings themselves, without shying away from belief as a pillar of thought, we can rely on the elucidations of science and knowable truths rather than just concepts devoid of any concrete accountability. Science can be viewed as a tool for elucidating truth, as well as a library of truth that's been elucidated. To accept there being an absolute truth we seek, one must accept the intrinsic consistency of truth itself. In modeling the inherent framework of truth of the universe, which in its most refined state can't disagree with itself, the library of truth elucidated by science aims to follow the same standard. If absolute truth has no inconsistencies, then accepted truth can't be accepted as discrepant. This might annoy you, if you believe there are existing scientific disagreements, but there's no such thing as a scientific disagreement.

The framework of truth has no contradictions, any contradiction of understandings is an error in interpreting these axioms. A contradiction would only imply there's a misattributed axiom being represented by some word or concept that's introducing a logical error in reasoning under the same light that one can sneakily use algebra to divide by zero, incorrectly, to make it look like 2 = 1 is a true statement. Any belief in an inherent framework of truth of the universe holds the same proposition, a belief in truth is a denial of contradiction. It's to accept that the universe makes sense at all, which is why the embedded philosophical inconsistencies within Popper's idea of objectivity inevitably make for a defective attempt at modeling truth.

Any disagreement on elucidated truth, by the nature of its disagreement, becomes a religious disagreement. The disagreement falls in the realm of the unknown, not the known, so it can't yet be fully associated with *truth*. Science is the library of elucidated truth, the known, while religion represents the realm of what's unknown, can't be known, or what's currently considered an inconsistent form of truth. Under a proper acknowledgement of accepted truth, religion is able to compete with the ambiguity produced by any scientific field. Even whether some things are disprovable may be up to interpretation, and this would also be a religious dispute. Where there can be no question about interpretation, we have as close an elucidated truth as possible, and within many of these elucidations there should be no room for ambiguity whatsoever. Even if some theory holds unrivaled predictive power within some niche, any territory between that idea and any other that can't be entirely reconciled is most appropriately classified as religious territory until there can someday be a completed connection between the ideas in question.

Critics of Popper's line of falsifiability would state that not *everything* can be falsified, that there are limits to the ability to draw this conceptual line in the sand. But not everything needs to be, this is assuming the line to be a linear delineation of two sides. More truthfully, this line actually manifests more as a blob that grows outward, and you can even envision it growing towards both the micro and macrocosms. There's no doubt within the physics community that we can use batteries to transmit power to lightbulbs, the various aspects of this process are understood in fairly great detail. We might not completely understand what happens inside the individual electrons being transmitted through wires during this process, but it isn't a requirement for understanding the parts of the truth we already have. There are aspects of these processes that aren't understood, as we have no first principle, our understandings grasp at whatever truth we can find. As long as a line of falsifiability can be made *at all*, there can be a delineation between accepted truth and belief, as the line of falsifiability would surround an area consisting of accepted truth itself.

The culture in scientific institutions often presents itself as the *one true* hierarchy of truth, the same manner in which many religions over time have presented themselves as having the *one true* God, it's no different. But this existing club presents a false dichotomy. It's no different than the political gaslighting we constantly experience. Sure, there's good and bad science, where good and bad are indicative of value. But there isn't just one hierarchy involved here, there's two. There's also more and less valuable religious ideas. If science, as an institution, is going to use reasonable evidence to elucidate truth, then religion should take reasonable ideas and look for truth that supports it. Science is a mechanism for reaching the truth of the universe, religion is a mechanism for reaching the truth of our perception. At some point this will come in handy, there's two ways to approach any problem for a reason and this is analogous to the functions of the big picture and small details of our right- and left-brains. That reason being that there's certain problems that can only be approached from one of these directions, rather than the other. It's very likely certain problems can only be solved in some exact manner that might not be possible in the existing paradigms of scientific thought, many of which have even gone plenty beyond Popper's calls for deduction.

With that in mind, there's a difference between what's truly falsifiable, and what's feasibly falsifiable. The statement that alien biochemistry would follow the same paradigms of interaction as human biochemistry is truly disprovable if you believe aliens to exist, but it's not feasibly falsifiable as we currently have no aliens to use to determine this. But this isn't a new idea, one can claim that they believe this is true, this could even *be* true, but would this being hypothetically true qualify as *competing* with a scientific paradigm acting to prove or disprove it? In order to truly compete, and with even grander levels of distinction, there must be another interpretation we can use to stand in opposition to the elucidations of science, at an even larger scale. Otherwise, this is destined to be no different than the act of chasing finer and finer distinctions of cellular function to insist upon Lamarckism not being entirely wrong. You shouldn't need to chase progressively smaller targets just to be right about something.

Everything we don't understand belongs in the realm of religion because it requires belief to stand by it as true. Science is that which drags out both truth and falsity from the realm of belief to make grounded judgement. Any philosophy of science absent a philosophy of religion is incomplete, especially because institutions and philosophies of religion were the precursors all scientific work was eventually built upon. Otherwise, removing that block of the tower will only eventually lead to collapse.

In elucidating the structures of knowledge, we'll run into energy constraints that force us to estimate a value between our upper and lower estimates. This process tends to be difficult, and first estimating the bounds is a path of least resistance to either side of our hedged bet. The same duality presents itself in politics, as it does at the forefront of physics. Proper estimations of a center value will be found in each over time, and as they're always found, new divides will also emerge. The estimation of God is the same as the progression of all these factors together. But why do these two structures of information exist at all?

From any scientific work, there's generally two ways to interpret information. You can form ideas from within evidence, to assert empirical truths, or you can form ideas beyond evidence, to form beliefs. One is confining information to stay within the realm of concise elucidation, and the other allows information to be extrapolated into larger trends that data alone might not suggest. It's much more reliable to stay within the realm of empirical evidence, as it provides a layer of robustness. At its worst, staying within the realm of what's empirical can be too rigid to work with, and at its best it can provide solid ground to walk along. Going beyond evidence can take a bit of creativity, and willingness to believe. At its worst, going beyond evidence can be completely fanciful, but at its best it can provide entirely novel perspectives. To build on either is a different process. One offers a religious view based around the art of interpretation itself, and the other, a minimally realistic view built on concise information.

When Alfred Wegener first noticed that the coastline of every continent roughly matched up with each other, he didn't have underlying mechanisms as to how they were once one single continent[**100,101**].

100. Alfred Wegener. *The Origin of Continents*. Petermanns Geographische Mitteilungen, 1912

101. Alfred Wegener. *The Origin of Continents and Oceans*. Friedrich Vieweg & Sohn, 1915

It just seemed to be the right idea, it made sense. It was an interpretation of circumstance, rather than the exact mechanism of how it was done, so at the time it was just a belief. We now know about the layers of the planet beneath our feet, how they move, how pieces of Earth's crust goes into and comes out of the mantle. But minus all this evidence, of actual mechanisms to explain it, it would only be a belief.

Darwin's assumption of one shared origin of all species wasn't built within the realm of evidence, he couldn't actually watch evolutionary adaptations occur in real time. He had inferential evidence for phenotypic changes across different geographic regions for the finches he studied, as well as what seemed to be the reasons for their differences. That much was determined, it was clear. But to assume all organisms, across all time, bereft of an actual mechanism for this proposal, to have one single progenitor, would be a purely religious interpretation. It was a strong idea, and still is, there was just no way of explaining how it could be possible at the time his ideas came out. It was the introduction of a perspective that wasn't attainable prior. Even though the idea is widely accepted now, we still lack a lot of truth on how exactly life began. Despite the lack of evidence, these *beliefs* are accepted, yet it's not always accepted that these *are* beliefs. It's been replaced by the word *theory*. As opposed to something like the elucidation of the structure of DNA, which was done strictly within the bounds of evidence at multiple steps, due to the specificity of the end result[**102,103,104**].

Iain McGilchrist's concepts of a left- and right-brain aren't entirely out of this realm of religious interpretation either. Where Quantum Field Theory isn't able to compromise with General Relativity, there's a layer of religious ambiguity separating the two. Religion has two roles in this philosophy of science and religion. It can introduce new ideas, new areas to demarcate between religion and science, albeit with a bit of a blur, that were never considered prior. On the other hand, it can completely muddy a previously existing understanding using a fresh perspective that hadn't been considered prior. **Religion is that which muddies the line.** Both cases introduce a disruption of the existing

---

102. Phoebus Levene. *The Structure of Yeast Nucleic Acid: IV. Ammonia Hydrolysis.* Journal of Biological Chemistry, 1919
103. Erwin Chargaff. *Chemical Specificity of Nucleic Acids and Mechanism of their Enzymatic Degradation.* Experientia, 1950
104. James Watson and Francis Crick. *Molecular Structure of Nucleic Acids: A Structure for Deoxyribose Nucleic Acid.* Nature, 1953

line between what is and isn't completely falsifiable. If the line between science and religion is drawn at the point of a clear and concise explanation of truth, where measured data in the context of specific experiments produces irrefutable evidence of some underlying facet of reality, then religion must be that which extracts a story from existing circumstances, and potentially multiple independent disciplines, to draw a new line that connects existing realms of knowledge in unexpected places, as two things opposed don't stand opposite. Because science alone is incapable of grasping the entire breadth of the information that science itself produces. To truly compete with science isn't to prove the civilizational pillar of science incorrect, it's to prove it naive. And if you'd like to see this done, then you're reading the right book.

Religion isn't about making clear delineations, even science doesn't achieve this in any pure sense because newly won knowledge never answers questions without giving you even more to ask. Religion is an art form that makes you question the boundary between reality and science fiction in ways you previously hadn't. If science makes clear and concise statements, then religion organizes information that can't be concisely explained. Science aims to catalogue that which we can be sure of, religion emphasizes that which we're not capable of knowing. Neither one of these realms will permanently overtake the other, they grow in specificity together, as with order comes disorder.

Before the limits of the world were understood, before the entirety of the world had been seen, interpretations of the unknown played a monumental role in lifestyle and philosophy. Without ever having seen the full extent of what lies beyond the horizon, who are you to say what might find its way towards you? Regardless of whatever tiny corner you might have come from, there could be either reward or trouble to find should you travel. That's the nature of the relationship of an individual to the bigger picture, to their own right-brain, it's risk, and it presents itself through a journey.

This massive source of the unknown, that which we've formed an evolutionary dependence upon, not unlike the fruit of a tree, is what's depleted itself in modernity. But really, it's simply hidden. The next course of our journey is in finding what this unknown is, and learning to factor in its nature to our prolonged existence. As without it, there's something missing, but you're not entirely aware of what it is. For most people this manifests as a lack of conviction, as that normally comes from the potential dangers of the unknown. Living without it is like living without a form of sustenance that your ancestors used for the last 100,000 years or more, you're undoubtedly adapted to having it. But the need for the unknown isn't something to be filled with lies for the sake of maintaining it. The more truth that it's imbued with, the more powerful it will be.

Why might one want to have an up-to-date religion? It's to try and understand lost history and evolution. For bridging the gap between the origins and future of humanity. So regarding origins, there's one big topic missing. What about God? Religion has always been built around some form of gods and worship. How does this fit in?

It's often said there's no purpose in defining God. That once you try you lose the game, as the point of God isn't to define it. Maybe that's true, but my definitions aren't monoliths, they allow for error and ambiguity. This comes at the cost of conciseness, but conciseness is the original mistake one makes when attempting to define God. So it seems this could be an advantageous paradigm to use.

Defining God is like an asymptotic question, like a division by zero. Which means it has an infinite number of answers, and the more answers you find the more complex they get. It's of the same class of concepts with stratified definitions, such as life and religion. The arithmetic difference between the infinite nature of God and the infinite potential of life forms would be the current state of the world, or perhaps the universe.

The best advice and the best answer are often two different things. Despite the path that anyone may have found towards believing in God, the best advice for people is to find a way towards it for themselves. Some say it's foolish to believe we are gods, and that claim seems to fit well to the reality of the people who hold this belief. But this belief in itself is a lower bound, and also a nihilistic first step, which is why so many people arrive at it. This falls along the axis of anthropomorphization, with the other bound being representative of God as an infallible entity.

When it comes to anthropomorphizing animals, the criticism from animal behaviorists that arises is that to attribute human qualities to animals is a point of potential bias in understanding their behavior. That we favor a human interpretation because that's the lens we see life through. But this is only partly correct, this lens of humanity is a factor of our interactions, which are more complex than the animals we study. Considering our shared phylogenetic origins, human interactions being more complex than the interactions of animals would imply that animal interactions represent a complexity that acts a subset of what humans have achieved with theirs. So the anthropomorphization of animals might need moderation, but it's not inappropriate. However, when it comes to God, God is more complex than humanity, so anthropomorphizing God results in an interpretation akin to an animal's view of humanity, it can more readily become oversimplified.

To separate from the anthropomorphized view entirely, God would be the set of universal principles that we uncover through watching the trials of our own lives, where outcomes determine truth, and interpretations muddy the line. Belief in God isn't the acknowledgement of an old man floating in the sky, something in the modern day which acts as mockery and a strawman, belief in God is the acknowledgement of the outcomes of our lives as the experimental interactions that they are. God is more like the maze we find ourselves in, similar to psychological experiments with mice, except there isn't a single entry nor exit point. There's multiple doorways to find, and they can vary wildly in size. It's not just a puzzle to solve, it's a riddle that makes you question why it must be solved at all.

The puzzle itself is Newtonian truth, that exists independent of the living organisms built atop of it. But the universe itself isn't independent of life, life is a part of the universe. The riddle is the Darwinian truth, it's the organismal perspective required to solve the puzzle. It's the religious answer to what the purpose of the existence of life is. To answer the riddle in a way that solves the puzzle correctly is to find an optimal organization for the thoughts and behaviors of organisms no different than how their biology found an optimal set of encapsulations and reactions which allowed for their creation and persistence.

Upon the journey to solving either, the display of these outcomes inevitably lead towards an anthropomorphized interpretation of those interactions. Which isn't unreasonable, it's a natural perspective to have, and certainly can't be said to be incorrect. But it does stand on shakier ground if you're not careful, an anthropomorphized interpretation can become a reliance on such things.

Truth and irony have a cyclic relationship, it doesn't seem reasonable to believe there to be any true hierarchy between the two. A paradox is something that opposes the truth, yet paradoxically has a hierarchical relationship with irony. A paradox is some piece of information so distant in understanding that it's unable to be properly interpreted, and a paradox itself does seem to have something in common with the concept of irony, as contrasting expectations stand in direct opposition to finding truth. A paradox is that which is hidden behind the curtains of irony, and this isn't so much a direct relation, as much as a hierarchy of the unknown. There should be no such thing as a paradox. A paradox is simply something outside the limits of our perception, much like the inner workings of a black hole, the likes of which seem to be a physical paradox relative to the relationship of its thermodynamic and statistical entropy. Interestingly, we can at least come to perceive such a paradox, which is also why people have any understanding of God.

God is the center value we estimate, the same as what's being played out through politics, and approached through physics. It's everything we approach. The more we estimate, the closer we get. Which is just a matter of time. Not to make it sound like it's coming soon, it's more likely millions of years away. Billions, perhaps. But there's something there at the end of the road, and that's God. Which implies God to be some kind of final product, so does that clash with the idea of God as the creator? Not really, it's a paradox either way so it could be both.

The approach of God is what's at the end of the progression of all our collective bifurcations. We model what we interact with, and we interact with the universe. Is interacting with God the basis for religion? Or is religion the basis for interacting with God? The latter, as raising children is the basis for religion. An organism's interaction with God, while they have no means of communication, would be through nature itself. The emergent rules of nature, both Darwinian and Newtonian, would then be modeled through the interactions of these organisms via natural selection. Those whose instincts best reflect the emergent nature of the universe's underlying rules of their interactions would have an advantage in survival. But to a sapient organism, capable of advanced tool usage, communication, and conquering any domain of the planet they were born from, communication itself becomes the next emergent domain of which to interact with God. Through communication came religion, as a reflection of the instinctual grounding gained from the evolutionary periods prior to communication being possible. Religion is the growth of the recursion to this instinctual origin. To say we're models of our environment is no different than saying we're made in the image of God, these are the same statement.

God as a creator is one perspective, and God as the ultimate complexity formed as a process of the evolution of the universe is another. Rather, the metaphor of God as a creator is more like the emergence of emergence. God as the final product implies it's the culmination of every form of emergence. But that still doesn't explain how it's both of these things simultaneously. If the concept of God as a paradox holds true, and if there's any universal truth in this nature of duality visible in both politics and physics, then there should always be one boundary of convergence that seemingly contradicts the other when attempting to understand God. The explanations you can find in one direction should be of a comparable nature than that which you can learn from the other. This idea holds so far, but of course it does. Words can be infinitely creative, so there's always an appropriate counterbalance to every description. To prove there's any value in this perspective, there would need to be some form of significance in how the terms themselves were discovered. If one definition of God is legitimate, it can likely be used to derive or integrate other definitions through interpretations of its nature. Furthermore, respectability must be achieved through meaning brought about by more than just creative writing. A complementary match between two respectable, and more impressive, boundaries of convergence would surely not be a simple coincidence.

Creation itself is a paradox. There's no way to simultaneously have a belief on this topic while also making sense. The concept of a creator, the concept of God, is a paradox of a paradox. As the paradox of creation is independent of its own creator, which in itself is a separate paradox, the creation of creation is a paradox of a paradox. To embed this further, this idea of a paradox of a paradox is more of a left-brain description. The matching right-brain description would be something like Thomas Aquinas' *"Deus est ipsum esse per se subsistens"* [**105**]. Which translates to *God is the very being that subsists through itself*. Where Aquinas intends that God is the very essence of being, which in the modern age has taken on the more compressed form of *to be to-be* by people such as David Burrell[**106**].

105. Thomas Aquinas. *Summa Theologica*. 1274
106. David Burrell. *Aquinas*. University of Notre Dame Press, 1979

On one hand, the bounds between believing we are gods, and that there's an infallible entity known as God, represents God through both imperfection and perfection respectively. Meanwhile, the bounds of God as a creator, and final product, seems to insist God is both an indecipherable progenitor as well as an unreachable destination. But the value behind using boundaries of convergence is that they can fully encompass ambiguous concepts that aren't entirely understood, so are these the widest reaching bounds imaginable? One could broaden the bounds to be between God as an anthropomorphizable entity, and God as a non-sentient universal mystery, but that's still not necessarily the widest bounds one could cast. Then there's God as *a paradox of a paradox*, and *to be to-be*, which seems to be the most puzzling boundaries that one might ever come to for anything at all, and also an interesting point of symmetry, suggesting God to be both a perpetually hidden concept as well as an ever-prevalent force. Which is a more proper largest possible bound, of non-coincidental significance, made of both the fundamental understanding of God's influence on the world around us, as well as our bewilderment with its inherent contradictions. Each pair so subtly contradicts itself, as any paradox should, yet this same paradoxical parallel is visible in each description. As if a perpetual ambiguity exists within the concept itself so as to never be completely characterized, yet is, ironically, exactly what makes it perceivable, and therefore characterizable. Like it's only visible to those who acknowledge they shouldn't be able to find it.

In the approach of God, one would likely find an infinite journey, an endless walk. It's something you can never truly reach, not without some form of transcendence to break out of the infinite recursions likely experienced during the approach. So is God the journey or the destination? If the universe is infinite, likely so is the journey. Which would mean the destination doesn't exist. Which in itself is yet another paradox. But this is also a paradox we're familiar with, it's Zeno's paradox of Achilles and the tortoise. Zeno was an ancient Greek philosopher who made multiple so-called *paradoxes* where he imagined motion to be impossible due to needing to always reach half of any true distance before reaching any distance in entirety, which were less truly paradoxes and more rightfully analogies of mathematical convergences of infinite sums. It's just an analogy of calculus, which luckily, we're already using as the basis for global modeling. So it's fair to say there's some transcendence involved, and not unsurprisingly. The best answer to the question might be both the journey *and* the destination. But since the destination is unimaginable, it's best you favor the journey.

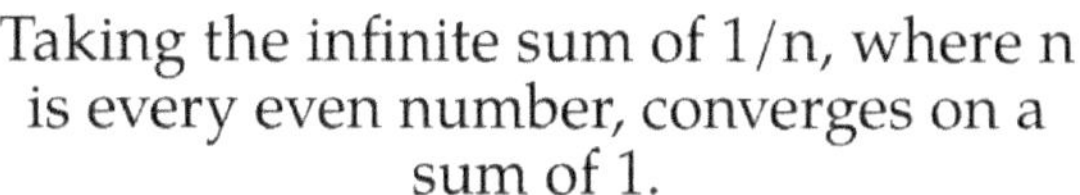

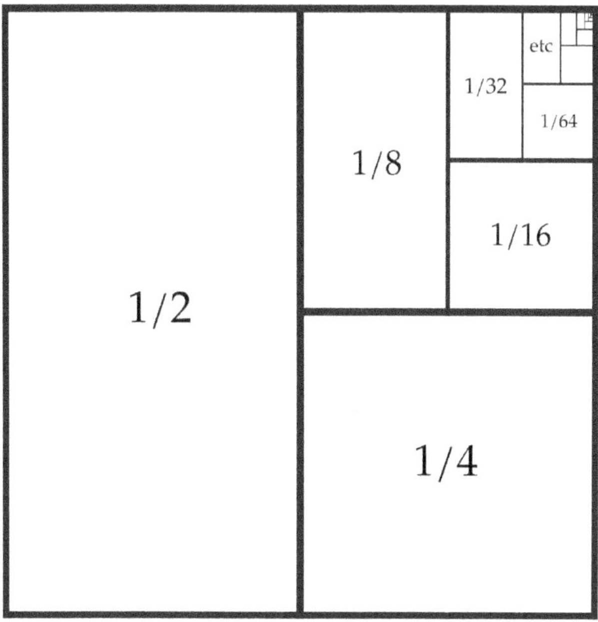

Figure 6: Basic Example of the Convergence of an Infinite Sum

What act of transcendence might be undergone in the journey towards God? In all likelihood it's the forging of cooperation, transcending sin. Which adds up with the concept of the journey, as that's the point of the transformations one undergoes on a great journey. But sin can't just be transcended by one single person, it's a group process. The more you need to cooperate, the better you must treat each other, and with heightened agreement on what lines not to cross. What do these lines look like? Think of the extraordinary effort and cooperation it took to achieve nuclear technology. Even the challenge of maintaining peace, despite it, is of such a nature. The path towards God is that which both selects for and requires greater knowledge, greater morality, and greater cooperation. Not one single factor can be neglected, and this list likely isn't complete. Humans probably already went through this process with fire, and we now find ourselves in a state of cooperative selection, having completely forgotten a past where too many people ran wild, burning down the environment, or even exterminating entire species that were sources of food. What's the basis for this level of cooperative transcendence? It's likely already been found for us, this is governed by the values we use to mediate our interactions, and the forgiveness that comes from the humility of cooperation. But everything is a balancing act, there are no simplicities. While forgiveness is powerful, it's not meant to ignore atrocities, nor should it be an excuse to avoid punishing people for their wrongdoings, it's meant to prevent you from becoming vindictive. You should be careful with things that are powerful as they can be powerfully addictive. Overusing something powerful is no different than gazing into its abyss, it becomes a hammer as you classify everything as a nail. You need not forgive people for what they've not been repentant about, anyone forcing you to is abusing your kindness. Thinking people have infinite capacity for forgiveness, or assuming you yourself do, is no different than assuming humans to be gods of forgiveness. Certain things wouldn't fit within the realm of human forgiveness, nor within the realm of someone's personal forgiveness depending on the violation. A failure to respect what forgiveness represents within the model of interactions only causes one to fail to interact well, don't offer forgiveness to those who weaponize its expectation. Forgiveness is meant for those who repent, not those who refuse to. It isn't the job of any single person to forgive a terrorist that detonates a bomb that destroys an entire continent. That doesn't even belong within the realm of human forgiveness. Certain actions cross lines to become brands that you would wear for the rest of your life. It's beyond the realm of any single person's responsibility, it's simply not your job.

The purpose of forgiveness isn't forgiveness itself, it's understanding what you're forgiving. It's to understand where people went wrong and why they made the mistake they did. The purpose of understanding these faults is that we're all human, and could become victim to the same flaws. Blind forgiveness is a cancer that's grown within the religious institutions of Christianity, and it offers a naive substitute of what this was meant to accomplish. Forgiveness is for understanding those that are trying to be human, not those who are trying to be animals. Those who are trying to be gods often find themselves performing the most heartless cruelties to anyone they please, and those who torture children are unforgivable.

To say we are gods is arrogant. To say we don't approach, estimate, or move towards God is naive. So is God the base block of the Tower of Babel? If the largest blocks have the widest blocks, and thus are the most difficult to understand, does God go at the bottom? No, that's where religion fits. As God is what's approached, it's what's at the end of the tower, not the beginning. The bricks used to build the tower are not there by coincidence, they're extremely specific solutions to extremely specific problems. To reach God is the most intricate and specific problem anyone could ever approach.

With irony as a unit of interaction, we can adapt the concept of a paradox for the same purpose. A paradox can be used to measure a metaphysical distance of imperceivable concepts, it can function as a measure outside the limits of perception. God would be imperceivable by at least 2 paradoxes, whereas the inside of a black hole is imperceivable by 1. Which isn't something religions of the past could have ever reasoned. Religions of the past had no true articulation of what their actual aim was supposed to be, they likely hadn't figured out *why* they were meant to figure out *what* they were meant to figure out.

So if you had to start a religion, what are the topics a religion should cover? How would you accomplish, in the modern day, what people managed to do thousands of years ago? It's hard to imagine what their mindset was, in what ways were they wise, and in what ways were they naive. What was being offered to them is difficult to conceptualize within our framework as we're multiple integrals ahead of where they ever could have been. But I think it's everything, religion must somehow explain everything. It should be able to comment on everything, every existing complexity, the universe, black holes, intelligence, politics, physics, life, evolution, the brain, civilization, consciousness, even religion itself. It's not just meant to offer some historical montage of hundreds of influential thinkers. A religion itself would make a model of human complexity, or rather, model the complexity that humanity understands in its modern day. A model reaching from, encompassed within, the furthest possible bounds that human knowledge can grasp as the base layer of its Tower of Babel. It's what's meant to prevent the tower's collapse.

The development of human religion is intricately intertwined with human evolution. That's to say, the metaphors of a civilization are entirely related to the direction its evolution will move in. We've mistaken the results of evolution for its ends, then mistaken those ends for its means. When really, the means are its ends, such as our sense of fairness, and shared responsibility. Those means produce what some believe to be ends, such as our technology, governance, and prosperity, but these are intermediary steps at best. To those who want to *help* others, question whether it's best they help themselves, as humans deprived of their own choices don't gain what's given for free, they lose the development they could have otherwise passed on to their children, they lose the development of their own metaphors, and thereby a direction to move in. To celebrate these gifts is to apply selective pressure in favor of receiving them, it's the celebration of a dependency, and thereby not something that makes a population more capable of handling the tradeoffs required to produce such things for themselves.

Symbolism is inherently religious, it's the process of painting a layer of metaphors over reality. To adopt cheap symbols is to adopt the function of a structure that likely isn't compatible with the complex decisions you need to make in life. Symbolism is meant for you, the individual. It's not scalable, and it's not society that needs to find meaning. It's individuals. Inspiration is the art of reaching individuals despite speaking to a crowd. There's something to say about setting goals too high. There's often times phrases used like *for everyone*, and *for the world*. It sounds attractive, but this always amounts to a fool's errand, it's using symbolism to lure people in. To be hard-lined on accomplishing this is just unrealistic, and probably more destructive than helpful. This also brings forth a kind of forced uniformity. Whereas it's natural variation that wards off the error-prone, disaster-bound, oversimplifications that drive us towards building our tower recklessly while pretending it won't collapse.

In purely symbolic terms, *good* isn't something you achieve, rather, *evil* is something you avoid. Which, in essence, seems to be the only actual way to do any good. Because evil is easy to define, so it's easy to recognize. Good, on the other hand, can be rather subjective. The normal discussion of good and evil is that good defeats evil. But this kind of grand narrative isn't a common occurrence, otherwise it wouldn't be so grand. Outside this context, evil is an action, but good is a circumstance. Rather than a direct result of intentional actions, good is an emergent property of a complex system of trust. Needless to say, where you destroy trust, you achieve evil.

In terms of symbolic advice, like aiming to not be incorrect, the best advice is *do no evil*. Where *good*, in essence, is a false choice. It's disguised as anti-evil. But good isn't something you do, it's something you cause. Anything is easy to destroy, but difficult to create. Creation is the integral, as is the byproduct we call good. One can only create the circumstances of good, you don't *do* good. This is readily observed by the difference between good and bad neighborhoods. Where the bad is derived from individual actions, and the good is a standard of behavior that's upheld across a community. Those who believe *good* is either an action or a decision come to wrap themselves in ideology, which is responsible for more death and more evil than anything else. It's easy to fall into this trap. Those who see themselves as good are capable of the worst evil, and ironically then become the evil which needs to be defeated. To not uphold the circumstances that create good, is to sin.

Fake good is made out of pity traps. Aiming to do good doesn't accomplish that goal. Clothing donations to Africa did little more than disrupt local economies from developing their own fabric crafts and trade[**107,108,109**]. The only achievement is the signaling, rather than accomplishing, of any *good*. Civilization requires taking specific steps in order to develop. There needs to be the acknowledgement that the various technological revolutions undertaken in achieving modern society are basically required steps for achieving modern prosperity. The shortcuts of offering money, donating food, and doing everything for people who can't do anything for themselves, is only as much a gift as it is a curse. It prevents them from being able to do these things on their own. The actual steps might not need to be as hard-coded as they were throughout history, but they should mirror the ones that brought us to where we find ourselves. There are no other ways. Believing the opposite has not only led to dysgenic dependence amongst those who were supposed to be *helped* by this *good*, it's now transformed one of our own political wings into being dependent on creating foreign dependencies. A disaster for everyone involved.

---

107. Sally Baden and Catherine Barber. *The Impact of the Second-Hand Clothing Trade on Developing Countries*. Oxfam, 2005

108. Garth Frazer. *Used-Clothing Donations and Apparel Production in Africa*. The Economic Journal, 2008

109. Andrew Brooks. *Clothing Poverty*. Zed Books, 2015

If you think people to be privileged and therefore evil, you are the evil. The more you try believing people to be evil, the more evil you become from gazing into that abyss. Any privilege conferred to one's child is from hardship and sacrifice. To think you have none is demonic, you simply throw it away by believing that. If you find people that you think have achieved greater heights, biologically, than you ever could with hard work, that's all the more reason for you to work hard. Some people are born brilliant, and the work put in to achieve that came from dedication itself, not from luck. It's hardship that achieves these results, it's going through the fire in order to come out the other side that makes better individuals, and better individuals make other better individuals. Excellence can be passed on, and you can achieve excellence. Wouldn't you do so for your own children?

No one is in a better position being born as either a man or a woman, they each have different advantages and disadvantages, but overall they even out amongst themselves. Pretending one is worse than the other will make you either toxic or stupid depending on whether it's your own you view preferably. Envy, so easily becomes the pathway towards making up fictional evils that have been done to you when really they might just be disadvantages. To focus on them so heavily would only emphasize them within your own purview. Play to your advantages instead.

Your life story goes back thousands of years. How many of those generations struggled to get by? How many almost never made it through? How many pulled off the impossible, just for no one to witness it, or for it to be forgotten after their death? Your story isn't just recent memory. Whether for yourself or someone else, don't be swayed by pity. Don't feel more for someone unrelated to you than you feel for your own story to the point where you put them above your own loved ones. Your own story involves all the same pitfalls and triumphs, it undoubtedly does. So honor it.

Everything that's ever come before you was for the sake of producing you, it would be a shame to lose that. Use its gift, as its curse was paid beforehand. It was offered through the dedication of those who came before you, people you'll never meet. It's not as unfair as you may think. These gifts from the dead were left *for you*. You can do the same for others, to take up nothing else would truly be no fault of anyone.

To the people who always look at life through the lens of what they don't have, you're still in the game. There are billions that have already lost, because they don't exist anymore. Whether due to war, genocide, famine, stupidity, or bad luck. They have much less than you, because their children never made it. You don't need to wish bad things upon other people. If they've done wrong then pray for them to become the best version of themselves. If they're truly as horrendous as you believe, then they'll need to go through tremendous pain and suffering to ever improve. Even the extremely wealthy have their troubles. We all experience our own baseline, and we all reach low points. Insisting that someone else doesn't deserve to feel bad about something because of their circumstance will only come back to hurt you through the unfairness you impose as a denial of the model of interactions. Instead, inspire people when they're at their lowest point, and they'll respect you for it. Wishing badly on others only hurts yourself, but wishing the best for others grants your mind the same advantages that freedom enables in a population. It's a win-win, and a win-win situation isn't just a dual victory. It's solving the integral to multiple derivatives at once, it's the reduction step of Williston's law that removes overcomplications, it provides multiple victories. Which is why all the best solutions are of this nature.

Any disadvantage garnered can be turned to an advantage. In learning to overcome the difficulties of any disadvantage, you learn how to share this triumph with others who might not be able to. You win them over. To transform is to realize the advantage to your disadvantage, and use it as such. A gift is a curse, what you receive is the tradeoff. Instead of being oblivious to the curse of a gift, and instead of only wallowing in the bad luck of a curse, play to your advantage.

Self-pity grows when people become proud of their problems rather than aiming to fix them. Sometimes it's announced loudly, then used as a political bludgeon. This is just people blaming their own lack of responsibility on others. If you have many problems, and you're uncertain which to face, face the uncertainty itself.

The only realistic way to aim at a symbolic goal is when you create and innovate. A goal designed to change the behavior of other people isn't a goal, it's a control mechanism. To give something for free and expect pure benefit is to forget that a gift is a curse. But to make something that's valuable to people is extremely difficult, it's to take the curse upon your own shoulders to grant a gift to others through fair exchange and trade. If the goal you aim for has a curse placed onto others, you gaze into an abyss. If you take the curse of a gift upon yourself, then you yourself grow in exchange for facing it, and others benefit from your work. By valuing it enough to exchange it, rather than giving it away, you allow others to value it as well, and this is where *good* emerges.

To finish this section, I'd like to briefly reflect finally on one more place where stratified complexity truly flourishes throughout one's own life. Jordan Peterson gives a masterful description of prayer, he summarizes from his own book that *"the nature of the spirit that answers your prayers will be dependent on the nature of your prayer"*[110]. As a supreme act of humility, prayer is best practiced as the depth of your argument, against yourself, that you take when considering the side of whatever difficulty that opposes you. If you truly find something to be of an unfair difficulty, then you don't despise the difficulty, you instead despise the unfairness, and aim to treat others better than has been done to you. Difficulty isn't something that holds you back, excuses are. Difficulty is what transforms you. Don't ask God to do things you can do for yourself, fulfill your role. Prayers are everything from habits to determination, there's no such thing as a lone prayer. Every action you make isn't just something that affects the world around you, every choice is something that becomes you. Decisions are yet another Tower of Babel that you build throughout your entire life. No action or decision is independent of its influence on your life, everything comes from what you practice. Every decision holds its own butterfly effect that determines your future, significance is ubiquitous. It's a structure that forms from behavior. Build it well, and improve the ways in which you do. Encourage the same from young children who are at the start of this process. Prayers are endeavors you build that can also build you in return, and that's independent of anything that could be taking away your potential.

Peterson also relays that stress acts like a parasite that occupies the energy you have at your disposal. There's undeniably a parallel between this concept of stress and lies, the effects of either become visible wherever they exist. Lying too much will eventually destroy your life, and being too stressed from external forces or bad relationships will do the same. They both accomplish the opposite of the best outcome of

110. Jordan Peterson. *We Who Wrestle with God.* Portfolio, 2024

a prayer. Your energy reserves are meant for operating within the context of your life, but as stress builds up, as lies ensue, you end up having less freedom to live your life than if you had been completely honest. As maintaining lies takes energy away from your reserves. Which is energy you would otherwise have in order to solve problems, and grow as a person. The ever-growing Tower of Babel forces us to replace things that we want to be true with things that are actually true. Eventually, the cost of carrying a lie becomes more expensive than the truth. Stress and lies create an internal ecosystem, within a person, that opposes their own freedom on the basis of pride. Pride seems to bring about a kind of mental constipation that prevents people from going through developmental transformations because of a refusal to admit mistakes. Even worse, is when lies create an ecosystem outside an individual where the result is a much messier system to unentangle if normalcy is ever expected to return, of which there's a term for.

6.5 What is a Cult?

What truly makes something a cult? Disconnecting people from their family? Having extreme consequences for not following orders? Death rituals? Murdering those who abandon the faith? A place where loyalty to an organization takes precedence over social values? In making a serious contemplation of this question, anyone would eventually come to the conclusion that there can be different kinds of cults, just as there can be different kinds of religions.

Like religion, cults exist across a stratified definition. Cults are often classified as operating on the basis of social and emotional control, but small shared beliefs that most people take for granted are basically acting as cult-like apparatuses throughout society. Common courtesy operates like a cult, it probably used to be a much more controversial thing. There were likely thousands of years of development for people to get to the point where common courtesy was as common as we take it for.

There's really no way to avoid being in a cult. There isn't a lot to distinguish between a cult and culture itself. Perhaps a cult is, most realistically, a group of people with some form of shared internal order optimization. But that's also a description of religion. The purpose of religion is to find ways of navigating the unknown. Cults are often inhibitory to that same goal. A cult is like something that parasitizes, it alters the internal order of its members to burden them with its existence, it's the vampire.

A cult is the idea of a parasite flipped on its head. It emulates the body that you enter, turning you into what you think is a member of a legitimate organization. Whereas you actually walk into a trap. The larger entity feeds off the smaller ones who enter. It lures people in who then act as an energy source for a larger entity, who tricks people into giving up their autonomy. Which is basically the European Union to its member states.

The worst manifestation of this occurs in political parties, where both the party and its members are guilty of this behavior. The institution who feeds on its members, and the members who feed on the institution. They destroy the state, and they destroy each other, until there's nothing left to support either of them. Two parasites recycling each other's blood until they both die of stupidity.

There's people who understand there's information in the world that they're unaware of, and there's people who assume they know everything until told otherwise. The former is a normal person, the latter is a cultist. The latter is a subversion of the nature of intelligence.

So how does one pull a cult out of a hat and call it as it is? Well, a good example is what often happens in the modern day. If every time you disagree with something you call it racist, or if your only criticism about something is that it's racist, then you're a part of a cult of race. When everything becomes a nail to your hammer, the hammer is what classifies you.

But a cult isn't just what it is, it has a history of what it's been. It's not just a super-parasite that feeds off multiple hosts, it may start off as something entirely different before transforming into the monster. The nature of this very process of corruption is where the most twisted parts of these organizations tend to create themselves.

I would characterize the educational institutions of the modern day as being taken over by a cult of agreement. They very often restrict student's freedom to speak about certain things through deterrents because those at the head of their long line of bureaucracy determine the official positions of the institution. Teachers themselves also tend to be politically extreme, and very homogeneously so. These institutions don't embody the American spirit, American law, nor even capitalism itself. Herein lies the problem for young people whose virtues depend on honesty, and whose growth depends on mistakes. A cult is a group of individuals whose left-brain follows someone else's right-brain, rather than being enabled to ask questions and find answers themselves. They find themselves reprimanded when their individuality exceeds the comfort of those who find their own irritability to be their greatest justification. But if the point of education is to enable someone to use their own brain, there seems to be a conflict of interest in the nature of our public institutions.

With regards to power, a cult is something that practices the art of exploitation. Through the nature of fear, the members will always eventually find ways to exploit each other, then blackmail. Then eventually it becomes a requirement to be a part of the upper echelon of the cult, that you must be exploitable by the other members. They *must* have dirt on you, they *must* be able to control you. Which is the end result you see every time a politician ends up being directly linked with some act of pedophilia. Likewise, when you see a politician ignoring some atrocity, like the rape of young girls, while their entire political establishment covers it up, it's because they're compromised by some form of blackmail of them doing something equally bad, or worse.

A successful religion can't get by off scamming its members. At least it ought not to. As it's meant to guide its members, not trick them. But a cult could. In fact, cults are known for that. Parasites attack the weakest parts of your body, in a sneaky way. They come in the back window, not the front door. Because they're robbers. Likewise, people who can only attack the weakest argument presented, rather than the strongest ones imaginable, are parasites. Beware of those who prepare their defence before any real conversation happens. They try and say things like *you've never suffered, you didn't go through what these other people have, they've had to work harder than you*, and none of it's explicit. It's just supposed to be assumed. These are vampires, and they'll use any excuse they can to hide this. They'll make endless justifications for ignoring perspectives that are inconvenient to them, while simultaneously insisting on having an interpretive monopoly over words you've never spoken, offering bad faith interpretations of what your lack of words mean rather than engaging or respecting the words you've actually used. They try to force you to open all the windows in your house, to prove your innocence, only so they can break in easier. People who state what they don't actually know only aim to trick you. Tricks are the games of parasites and vampires.

6.6 Steelmanning the Woke

There's lessons to be learned in everything, so what has the woke gotten right when steelmanned properly? Where does it go terribly wrong? Where does it represent an underlying need for something that people actually want, but have no better implementation for? In a lot of ways some of the aspects that we now call woke have always been around in the US. It's just come to be grouped in with newer aspects of American culture alongside the scaling of certain behaviors through the advent of social media.

In its best light, it's an aspect of the left that aims for maximal genetic diversity for any group of people as a means to support its lower social and economic tiers, and offers a path towards cultural integration for those who come here. Those who strongly want to represent what this entails come to impose it as a religion, and those who want its help have something to gain. But such ideas would be catastrophic for communities that don't wish any of these ideologies to be forced on them. This has also been a source of widespread injustice for Europe, as none of the countries there have laws appropriate for a settler society. When at the mercy of this group holding political power, no one has the ability to turn off the immigration faucet, or stop the magnitude of insanity that comes alongside it. The politicians who support it often won't even say so openly, they pretend it's simply an unmanageable situation, or they attack those who speak up against it.

The pro-immigration aspect of the woke inherits this behavior from the institutions historically used to welcome immigrants when they come to the US. Which used to consist of various groups, many of which were religious, and their aim was to ease the integration process for newcomers. This job has been somewhat pushed onto the government, as they've tended to fund it. As schools became more widespread, this responsibility became more tightly integrated with education. But melting pot culture has come to overrun some of what are supposed to be very conservative places. Despite that it's a liberal idea. The liberal arm taking over the conservative body is a strategy which will result in a failed society.

Ideology isn't independent of religion, religion competes for all the same behaviors and parts of life that ideology inhabits. But ideology isn't necessarily a religion, it's more like a subset of religion. So the question that remains, is what religion does an ideology, that supposedly operates independent of religion, naturally attribute to? It must be discoverable, because beliefs in general are discovered, so this is inherently discoverable territory. Being absent of any specific specializations that most religions would display means the religion that inhabits this space is equivalent to a scaled version of some baseline human behavior. With our baseline behavior being what we take with every nihilistic first step, it's nihilism. So the default religion of any independently operating ideology becomes that of scaled nihilism, which would be a purely destructive force. Adopted at scale it would be culturally suicidal, which is exactly what we see happening throughout the West.

Scaled nihilism is the explanation for people who believe their race, ethnicity, history, lineage, future, family, community, country, and any other affiliation that could be associated with themselves are all worthless unless they've been placed at the top of the hierarchy of pity as being underprivileged. It unifies people across their negativity, it's a religion for people who are depressed out of their minds. This form of negativity is achieved through the nature of the school system that's been imposed on them, the lack of control they have in their lives, their lack of a vision for their own future, a lack of understanding of their own history, and a lack of better opportunities available in their daily lives. People have fallen for this because it's a normal thing to fall for when the upbringing of your society has been forsaken for negligence. Godless nihilism takes control in order to tear down whatever walls have been built, it's an evolutionary feature meant to revert society away from bad decisions, the collapse of a failed tower. But in this case, it was an institutionalized acceptance of nihilism in a country that was otherwise functioning well. Any civilization operating on, and actively creating more members of this religion of scaled nihilism will die from being deprived of beliefs the same way that a young baby deprived of their mother's love will do the same. Beliefs are necessary for the development of a child, and either poorly made beliefs or a lack thereof will fail that person later on in life. Our society has come to place beliefs aside during education as a matter of courtesy, but this lack of belief has come to be parasitized by ideologies with questionable intentions, which now spread easily in a landscape absent of proper guidance around beliefs. These oversimplistic worldviews slip into people's minds through the oversimplified interpretations offered by the modern schooling paradigm, it's a brainwashing process that strips you of any meaning in your life. Ideologies within the school system, and those who carry their torch, began to model their environment. They became systematized around it, like any intelligent entity eventually would. In the process, they formed a religion.

For those within the US, who don't wish to partake, there's a serious problem with these various ideologies being forced down the throats of their children. It's reasonable that people who don't wish for it in their personal life find this to be a violation of their religious freedom. The diversity and inclusion crowd are instituting their own eugenics paradigm. Technically, any religion is a kind of eugenics paradigm, that's positive selection and it's orchestrated by their concept of fairness. Any who wish to follow this creed of diversity have every religious right to do so. Whether it works well or not is dependent on its leverage of irony, the bets that it hedges, or whether it even hedges at all.

These institutions quite often keep children captive in a prison-like school system because many state laws require it, so if you're a family that can't afford private school, then the default religion of your children becomes whatever your local public school system advocates for. It shouldn't be any surprise that a few ideological gangs have resulted from this, and it should be no surprise that they've engaged in violent terrorism across the country while their own media ecosystem and political candidates together pretend that *they're only an idea.*

The same way that not everyone needs to share the same profession, as we can all benefit from the labor of others, we need not share the same beliefs. In fact, it's much more productive to separate across beliefs for child-rearing. Forcing beliefs onto people only makes us worse collectively. A true competition of beliefs, just as a competition of products maintains economic prosperity, would stabilize American society to better function as the multifaceted amalgamation that it is.

We need to teach young children what to think, not just how to think. Teachers all across the country introduced gender pronouns to young students who went on to adopt them as part of their *identity*, they also preached an apocalyptic worldview that the world would end in some near-future calamity, some teachers introduced ideologies from political factions with various forms of international aspiration, and some decided to introduce racial caste systems around historic narratives. All of which have grown to become major belief systems across the West today, and that's not by coincidence. Regardless, it was the instincts of many of the 75%+ women in the field of education to do exactly that. It definitely crossed religious boundaries, and shouldn't have happened because of our laws, but there's something to be learned from this. Were a bunch of women wrong for following their instincts in teaching young children what to think? If that's their instincts for interacting with young children, then we definitely *should* be teaching young children what to think. The instincts of these women aren't incorrect, and that's worth learning from. Women have been selected to be this way, and one would then infer the development of children requires beliefs in order to guide themselves throughout their life, none of this is without reason. People need to believe in something larger than themselves. Despite the causes they toted not being of high quality, those women were delivering what they believed those children needed. How we can remedy this situation isn't by getting rid of belief, it's by embracing it. Allowing people to choose a belief system that works for them and using it to raise their children is favorable to the government's teachers choosing it in their place. Telling young children what to believe is not inconsequential to their life, it's of religious significance.

Another surprising place, where the woke almost did something right, is the diversity statement. Instead of being the left-wing fealty vow that it is, this would be useful as a general religious statement. It's something that's actually good for people to figure out in their own lives. Knowing what you stand for is a valuable thing to be aware of, being able to articulate your own foundations is a good way of introducing yourself to others. These statements can be a form of formal and professional communication, they can serve as a filter for individuals who might not have figured themselves out enough in order to dedicate to some role. The opportunity for insight into an individual's introspective depth and consistency offered by such a statement can actually serve a useful purpose in personal and professional interviews. When it's demanded that a statement *must* say something on some application for a person to be considered, then it's failed its purpose. That would be religious discrimination, which is unfortunately how these systems currently operate wherever they still do. These statements can act as doorways for questions to ask an individual, to find out their level of introspective consistency, and depth of deliberation.

The woke have simultaneously been at the center of denying the work of those studying intelligence as racist, while also parroting all of their same exact talking points in the most backwards manner possible. Which is impressive, because they've managed to build mental mountains of excuses just to explain why a caste system should be implemented inversely to merit. The woke creed is the extreme overgrowth of the roundtable's detection of unfairness. In its worst light, the woke religion is trying to monopolize extremely important human ventures under the power of people who don't understand those ventures at all.

At its worst, the woke religion aims to ban people from contributing to things of public benefit such as science, the economy, and to human flourishing should someone disagree with its creed. Which is extremely foolish. There's a great deal of benefit for all of us to be found in the dedication of someone who wishes to dedicate. There's not enough people whose opinions are so evil that they need not contribute to human flourishing, especially to justify the abundance of life-destroying crusades spawned out of social media.

The church used to punish people with different beliefs in the same manner seen today, politics. Yet in those same times there were also people who made great discoveries, or left inspirational tales for the rest of us independent of politics today. In the modern day, the wolf has put on the sheep's clothing. The woke religion has attempted to cover itself in science, and accuses people of denying the truth over political disagreements.

Serving the same ends, wokeness is just political correctness in the age of social media, which is a tool for controlling speech. It's a suppression of being able to speak publicly while holding any kind of corporate or government job. Which is very strongly in opposition to free speech, it's a cultural chokehold on it. That's mostly what it is, a prohibition on communication. Either through psychological aggression as a means of destroying conversations, through gaslighting that demeans steelmanning some other side, refusing to award people due credit if they oppose some political party yet have good ideas, or censorship regardless of the form. Political correctness is basically the monster that's grown into the woke religion by way of a group of people becoming Descartes' idiots, where *"any community that gets its laughs by pretending to be idiots, will eventually be flooded by actual idiots who mistakenly believe that they're in good company".*

Part of the woke has come off as extremely sensitive, and some take this as a misguidedness from their childhood, but just by probability some people are bound to be this way. I would reason this is because of the experience in public schools, there's a forced aggression in many contexts. Mindsets are contagious and the most toxic forms can be spread through aggression, both physical and psychological, to form a mind virus. And I mean this as a technical term, not an insult, I think there's a very serious problem with contagion of aggression in the schools. A mind-virus is a contagious form of anti-civilizational malice. They spread because there's an enforceable limit on the prevention of bad behavior that's protected by freedom of expression, and doesn't technically violate any laws within schools. Some behavior can have a bad effect on the people around them, and some of it's hostility that's intended to. If you can't incentivize good behavior, then it enables the worst behavior to become a default mindset that infects the best people. Which then acts like a mind-virus, a psychologically contagious cult that spreads through aggression. There's also a masculine mind-virus, as opposed to the more feminine woke virus, that most people don't comment about. The masculine mind virus in the US is a softer version of the contagious insidious violence that permanently pulls young men into joining cartels and drug gangs across South and Central America. It then becomes a default cult-of-violence that forces others into its lifestyle due to the schools not being capable of disincentivizing it.

People want to ban DEI. It's been massively overrepresented in places where it's not appreciated. It's prevented people from earning scholarships, denied people college admission over race, denigrated students for their ambition, and forced humiliation rituals onto innocent people for sharing what's always been considered a normal opinion. But when it comes to schools, banning it won't work. It's already in the minds of the administrators and staff. However, these people are quite frankly irrelevant as to whether it should be there. The only people who should decide if they want a school to be of and about the woke religion, DEI, or any other form of this are the parents of the children who attend those schools. DEI has become an insidious religion that's been forced onto people, and it's undermined the integrity of the Western world. Parents can be trusted more than any teacher when deciding what's best for the future of their own children, as they always tend to act in their best interest. This is a matter of freedom of religion.

Yet our institutions are not innocent for ceding ground to this cult. The woke have infiltrated power vacuums where people have abstained from upholding the importance of the responsibilities of these institutions. These jobs and roles have been deemed low class, low accomplishment, and unimportant. So of course they've been infiltrated by people who instead, not only find these roles to be extremely important, but have weaponized the very importance that was neglected in the first place. If anything, the woke are the lessons to be learned from our own negligence. If we're wise, we can use them as a measure of our own failings. Every place the woke have infiltrated, and managed to implement their agenda, is a measurement of our misunderstanding of where the line between church and state should actually lie, because everywhere you find them you'll also find they use the government to establish their religion. They've made themselves incredibly visible, and any ability for them to infiltrate would have only been allowed by having respect for individual freedoms where we should have delineated along lines of belief. They're representative of the uncertainty we hold with respect to our civilization's ability to clarify where and how we differentiate ourselves as either a state or a society, as that's the irony they've leveraged against us.

I wish I could say don't gaze into the abyss, but we do it to learn. We hedge into it. There's a dose of extremism that comes from it, but there's also things that aren't necessarily incorrect about the perspectives expressed through extreme ideas. They offer something to learn from at the very least, and there's a prize to gain should we do it well. The experimental group dives in, and the control group observes. In the process, we learn to leverage its irony as a measurement for our own failings.

6.7 Human Conservation

Religion is meant to accomplish the domestication of people. But it must be neither insulting nor demeaning. You must treat them with respect, and grant them the freedom to not live in captivity. You must also not hold them prisoner to the whims of a class of people they're not allowed to criticize. There must be freedom, because it's free energy that undergoes transformations of complexity. We're recursions of all these same processes, freedom itself is the only way to achieve anything meaningful. If people ever stop being their own guiding light, or even worse, it becomes the government's role at the wrong time, it leads down the same kind of dangerous sociomoral dependence that already plagues us on the fronts of antibiotics and C-sections. Balancing this distributed responsibility shouldn't be unattainable in a country whose founding principle was freedom itself.

What does it mean to conserve something? The handing down of the complexity of life is to pass on a process that systematically maintains an array of characteristics. In the lightest sense, it's to pass on love to your children so they may do the same. In its most desperate moment, it would be the words you write for your child knowing you'll never get the chance to meet them.

The mechanics of the broken compass are that which widens in scope then narrows in on an optimized form, just like Williston's law. It's what humans have done with their instincts for thousands of years to make what we now have, we maintained what made sense to be ingrained as proper instincts. Through this process came a selection of behavior that shapes beliefs and values. The age we're in now is that of rediscovering our instincts for the sake of cohesion and stability, as we've been saturated with our own success, and probably not for the first time.

If you stand for nothing you'll fall for anything, but if you stand for too much you'll lack the priorities to properly love anything. That's no way to conserve your culture, in fact it's a way to guarantee your culture dies out. To conserve is not entirely different than to love. It's to take priority for an in-group, and treat others with respect to how they fit in with your social priorities. Parts of Western society seem to have prioritized out-groups so strongly that they've begun to commit cultural suicide. Those falling victim to this cultural scam are people who've inherited good values, but they were only good within a context. A multicultural environment, filled with gaslighting about how one must obey the ethos of multiculturalism, is the antithesis of conservation, it's cultural disintegration.

The fact that Christianity's modern diaspora can at least half the time be so averse to the practice itself is ironically a sign of its own success. The irony of politics causes groups to continually bifurcate in order to form new hedged bets at every social fork in the road. The same can explain most of the Christian diaspora now. Knowledge structures evolve, groups diverge, environments change, and there's no reason for every single person to hold onto the exact same forms of beliefs and customs from even a hundred, let alone a thousand years ago.

There's extremely valuable lessons to be found across human history, especially in one's own, but in taking this lesson to its extreme, modernity will swiftly remind you that you do not live in the age of antiquity. So how might culture be better passed on? By embracing its best form, steelmanning your history. What's so core to the history and anthropology of the West to the point where Western history wouldn't have happened without it? It's the same as what's driven the US throughout all of its history. It may even be what's driven human evolution to come as far as it has. It's the engineering of innovation and the institutions that impose criminal justice.

Likely what separated humans from other hominids, what separates countries and cultures apart from their alternatives, and what separates groups and individuals are all the same thing. Their rate of innovation, and their ability to positively select for the best aspects of their society to continue. To inhibit innovation means to destroy the value society makes for itself, and to be overran by poor judgement means to have poorly performing successors.

To the saboteurs of the West, and those they've indoctrinated, the events of history are second to its weaponization. The modern extremists of the West make no regard for any of its amazing contributions to humanity. They refuse to honor that it was primarily the West that brought about the destruction of the globalized slave trade, and instead pretend it was the West that *invented* it. Either they insist you pity others for being of a different ancestry than you, or they insist your ancestors were stupid and pitiful for not being Western. Whether pity for others or pity for yourself, it's all just poison. The weaponization of history, where regular people are painted as evil for the past, is the sign of ideological corruption. It shouldn't be weaponized against *anyone* without a serious reason, especially not their children, there's a near endless number of ways to do so against any group, it would never end. The future is coming at us faster than ever, and there's plenty of modern day events and future directions that are worth arguing over instead. To argue over the past just means that less people end up moving forward in any meaningful way.

The populations that have built Western civilization are equally as valuable as what they've built. If you want to maintain a future with this sort of creative drive and vision, the cultural heritage rests in those who have sculpted this environment. It's an evolutionary development as much as a social one. To lose it would mean to lose what some people call biodiversity, but through the lens of human domestication, you might also consider it genetic and cultural capital. Where you have the mechanics of an economy taking priority over the people that a nation consists of, you don't have a nation, you have a factory. This is the insistence that the US solely be a state, rather than upholding its standing as a society.

The various demographics of America need a better way of being the hedged bet they ought to be. Decades of insidious politics have sabotaged large swaths of the entire country through both the education system and multipronged class warfare. Which highlights the major purpose for the existence of religion, conservation of culture for the sake of children. It's so they have something to inherit, which offers them a framework for then passing on the same. Every other civilization would normally leave a cultural inheritance for their children in the form of religion. This is not some unnecessary formality, it's a survival strategy and a socioevolutionary dependence that hooked our ancestors in exchange for heightened intellectual and cultural growth.

If religion is a necessary part of maintaining society, then is religion a subset of economics, or is economics a subset of religion? The latter is what we currently have imposed on us by the political establishment, the former is what I aim for. Religion, as an institution, can form a layer of social sovereignty that, at scale, shapes a competitive child-rearing process. The core demographic base of America ought to have the right to be self-sufficient should they wish to be. Government-led school systems subvert conservation by separating families from the upbringing process. Which is the opposite of what you need for conservation to take place because it outsources the art of upbringing to the state.

We currently have a massive bureaucracy dedicated to education. The school system is failing to bring young people up to speed with modernity in a way that allows them to be little more than a permanent debt-paying machine. These predatory loans handed out by the federal government are meant to trap people who don't know any better, because the intentions behind them are independent of the function of their structure.

The planners of the school system are aiming at a goal they shouldn't be aiming at, instead of trying to not be incorrect. Something needs to be freed up to allow for a scalable solution, rather than being so control oriented. What kind of freedom can be granted, and why? They say not to feed wild life, because it puts wild animals into a state of dependence on handouts. A lack of direct dependence is exactly what makes something wild in the first place. So are humans wild?

Civilization is the self-domestication of humans. You need to domesticate in order to achieve any form of conservation. But on the other hand, you can't take away freedom, or else your population will be overcome with dependency and more easily die out. Which to some is much easier than succeeding, but the easiest path will not be the most rewarding. Success requires the freedom to question the unknown. Religion is the key signifier of what delineates a sapient animal from a wild one, religion is at the core of how free and intelligent organisms arrange themselves to survive without the original evolutionary pressure they were created by. Intelligent wild animals would be aware of the unknown, but have no real way of characterizing it. Religion hails from the transcendence of the predator avoidance instinct into an awareness of unknown factors themselves. The left-brain came to recognize the self, and the right-brain came to recognize one's own significance. Religious development further grows the capabilities of intelligence itself, and is in lockstep with the avoidance of dependency. The best way for people to maintain this balance is through competition. This is where freedom of religion fits into the education system.

Education already encompasses a large breadth of great necessities. It encompasses humanity, religion, intelligence, finding how to live your life, and any survival strategy you might ever need. At least if done well it would. It's something extremely complicated to pull off that leads people towards the next parts of life, that are also extremely complicated to pull off. When done well, the nature of one of those things should match the nature of the other, use complexity to model complexity, rather than the oversimplifications that have been failing to do so.

Why should religions in the US enter into a formally competitive educational environment? The flexibility of religion would do a better job at managing the educational landscape through its freely centralizing and decentralizing format. People could leave politics behind and freely associate with like-minded families, they could also be more politically oriented should they choose. The added variation across the entire country would make for a population that's more resilient to any future disturbances.

Why compete for the US population? Minds are the greatest resource of all time. Of which, young minds are of the greatest value. More specifically, the young minds of the most influential places. Which undoubtedly includes the West.

Americans need a way of warding off this machine of class warfare that exports their jobs overseas while importing workers to work for less to suppress local wages. They also need a way of dealing with the blatantly outdated school system that sets young Americans up for failure. The education system doesn't reward hard work, it simply funnels it through layers of bureaucratic requirements that are used to hold their future hostage. Even if you could replace every crooked part of the modern educational institutions with fair and legitimate components, it would still decay into the same monster it already became. This is because its fundamental flaw is in its structure, it's in the lack of recognition for what school structures actually accomplish. They facilitate religious transformations.

Raising children is of the utmost importance, they are our greatest resource. Children will solve any problems you need them to. There's no reason for them not to find a competitive place in the American economy through the skills their upbringing was meant to grant them. The cultural sabotage coming from the Marxist education system is antithetical to the long-term prosperity of anyone meant to live in the country for multiple generations. So this concerns any immigrants who move here as well, whether they're aware of it yet or not. Is there a way to remove these Marxist components?

I aim to set children up to be competitively successful, without the debt of the college system, and without the opinion policing of the establishment. There should be no reason why American children don't set out to become young entrepreneurs within the greatest execution of capitalism known to history. The brainwashing of the public school system hangs children out to dry so that they can be outcompeted by immigrants, while being told they didn't work hard enough despite navigating such gargantuan betrayals at the level of upbringing. There's no shortage of hardworking individuals in the US, there's a shortage of proper religious guidance capable of navigating modernity through the American system.

The raising of our children doesn't need to become entrapped within policies forged through political correctness. The government is incapable of operating in this sphere, which is fine because they're not supposed to in the first place. Political correctness was meant for the public arena, and for those who care for it, it has no relation to the private lives of citizens. Families don't need to be bound by the insidious lies of political rhetoric when raising their children.

Religion is the epicenter of positive selection for humans, whereas criminal justice is the epicenter of negative selection. For behavior that's unacceptable enough to be criminal, it's punished through law. As for the behavior that's acceptable, or even celebrated, how else might people determine which is the best behavior, and the best way of determining it, if not through beliefs? It's certainly not the job of the government. The negative selection of the criminal justice system enables society to undergo a positive selection for traits that people appreciate. Without the negative selection of the criminal justice system, the positive selection of religion can't take root. Likewise, without a proper positive selection mechanism pushing people to both incriminate poor behavior and address it maturely as a group, negative selection isn't possible. These two operate in an intricate balance, as either one is difficult to achieve without the other. People tend to view natural selection as just one concept, but it's made up of an infinite number of internal intricacies. Natural selection, being an infinitely complicated aspect of life, is then governed by the same religious processes as every other infinitely complicated part of life. Choosing a selection paradigm is no different than choosing what to celebrate, a manner of aiming for correctness. To accept such a paradigm can only be taken as a belief. As who are you to say what's truly successful or not? It's not you who's going to decide in the end, and it's definitely not grades, it's nature.

The modular compartmentalization of society would allow for different groups to play different games. Religion is the base block in the Tower of Babel that decides the basis for positive selection. It decides which behaviors are acceptable, and which are abhorrent. If you think this isn't the case, then consider there are religions which allow for the rape and marriage of children, some younger than 15, some younger than 10. There are religions that choose to honor this as being *successful*. If you play stupid games, at best you would pay a stupid price. Religion, in its best light, is the art of playing better games.

Science is the art of pursuit, and art is a signal of beauty and passion. Evolution is both the ultimate art and ultimate science. For civilization, religion is that which guides evolution, as different religions instill different selection mechanisms. Religion is an attempt at cultural engineering tailored to suit the evolutionary history of humanity, as well as the environment they find themselves in.

Forcing others to follow someone else's religion is a way of forcing an unfair selection mechanism on people's children, especially if the advantages granted through their evolutionary history are viewed as evil. Because selection isn't just by life and death, it's a social ceremony. To subvert the religion of those raising their children is to subvert the wellbeing of families. It can't be the role of government to subvert the wellbeing of the families of the populace. The modern education system has proven to be a complete failure, yet we prevent people from raising their own children through endless regulation, and through unconstitutional laws that insist on dictating curriculums. The educators that oppose this would claim *they* are the only ones qualified, but this is an extremely disrespectful form of gaslighting. Millions of years of evolutionary history of successfully raising children is a qualification for raising your own. It's built into you, it's an irremovable part of you.

6.8 First Amendment Case For Schools

In 1940, the Supreme Court found during Cantwell vs Connecticut that the Free Exercise Clause protected individuals from state and local governments, the religion of individuals didn't need to be approved by the state in order for their practice to be considered religious practice. Subsequently, in 1947 the Supreme Court established in Everson vs Board of Education that the Establishment Clause applied to state and local governments through the Fourteenth Amendment, insisting that the religious freedom of individuals took precedence over that of states. Prior to either of these cases, only the federal government was restricted on establishing a state religion, furthermore it wasn't able to interfere with religious exercise. States, however, had still enjoyed these benefits. Multiple states had established their own religions, and states often had state-sponsored religious practices as an ingrained part of public schooling. After these rulings came a string of other Supreme Court cases that reshaped education in the US to exclude explicit religious leanings. They came to strike down religious instruction, organized school prayer, and Bible reading. The intended end result was meant to be a secular public school system across the country, delivering the right of religious freedom to individuals, rather than to states. The result of these rulings on public education has not moved the needle from their initial religious positions, it's only changed the religious composition of public schools. The end result of these rulings were not secular schools, the public schools are not secular by any means.

Much of our country's core institutional infrastructure holds such strong left-wing biases that throughout the last 10^{+} years there's been cult-like vitriol against any who dared to openly speak against the injustice imposed through the ideological indoctrination of the state-ran education system. Even far outside education, these problems persist because the institutions that raise children have come to *select* for specific behaviors in the children being raised, as a form of conditioning for progressing through the trials of these institutions. The behaviors selected for have functioned to enact what's essentially an economic civil war, more commonly called *the culture war*. At its best, it had forced civility in places where performing some essential role was more important than personal squabbles, it also removed unruly discrimination in places where it previously existed. But time changes all rules, turning exceptions into norms, and justice into tyranny. As the 21st century transformed from entering the age of the internet, a cultural stranglehold over behavior that was previously deemed normal had increased in stringency to destroy the lives of anyone who activated this tripwire. Harmless jokes from more than a decade in the past had suddenly become land mines that were detonated in the future and got people fired, ostracized, and otherwise had any number of life-destroying rituals brought to the forefront of their problems in what seemed like a crusade against free speech and comedy. The truth is, none of this would have ever come to fruition if not for the ideological and political biases of our educational infrastructure. The outcomes of the ideas planted in these institutions make it incredibly clear where the nature of our problems and lack of cultural cooperation truly come from. The schools haven't just planted ideas, they've planted beliefs. Beliefs about what students should do in the world, beliefs about who their supposed enemies are, and beliefs about how to deal with non-believers. Our state-ran education system has become a state-ran religion. They have their symbols, the pride flag. They have their great myths, that of an oncoming environmental catastrophe. And they have their social customs, that of their gender pronouns. These things together make for all the same characteristics one would expect to find in just about any traditional religion.

The Supreme Court has ruled to protect aspects of schooling as *free speech of the government*, but this privilege has become far too abused. It's the collective beliefs of the teachers, administrators, and anyone behind them who use this right to speak freely to children, and they're not elected. Teachers have come to be increasingly exposed to the ideologies of the universities, which then becomes a form of tyranny enforced in their classrooms where any dissent turns into disfavor or punishment. The beliefs used to raise children are meant to be a survival strategy, which is what religion offers, a hedge against nature. But when the survival strategies offered in these institutions aim to eradicate, or select against, any who disagree with their creed, they then become inhibitory to the survival of those they oppose. A survival strategy is no different than a relationship with death, which is inherently religious territory. The mockery, infantilizations, and cultural sabotage wielded by this class of educators has functioned to decay the linchpins of our societal stability through an insidious caste system of *privilege*. Can this culture war, this economic civil war, ever be the foundation for a positive change? Is there actually a middle ground that can be achieved? The religious interpretation would say there's always a way, and that such a thing is part of the approach towards God. To fail to solve this puzzle would only prove our civilization unworthy of the prize of doing so.

The modern academic paradigm was an attempt at doing religion minus belief, and the reason that failed is because it's impossible to operate an educational facility without them, all knowledge is built atop of beliefs. Beliefs eventually entered the supposedly secular system, and with them came an increase in LGBTQ identification every year. No matter which dataset you look at, this identification has been increasing with time[111,112,113,114]. Association with their state religion is growing because they have a religious monopoly over the education of children. Other religious associations have simultaneously fallen over time[115,116,117].

The key to alleviating this problem is to allow for what's being denied to people in the first place. The natural problem-solver, the mechanism of fairness, the societal paradigm that allows the greatest competitions to take place, your *freedom*. Instead of redefining a million terms into pseudosatirically unrecognizable forms, like the left has done for the past 10^+ years, the right needs only to better define one single term. They need only one source of stability to match the ever chaotic landscape of fragmentation. We need to better define religion.

Just as there's two ways to look at the concept of intelligence, rather there's two bounds for, the bounds of beliefs and values are what encompass religion. Meaning, it can be defined independently by either. Are values then *always* religious in nature due to them also being sufficient? The answer is yes. Because values are only formed at the delineation of internal order of the brain relative to its external environment, they're a manner of conducting interactions. The formative process of values in children is a religious process because it determines deeply held, conscience-binding behavior for the rest of their lives.

Beliefs and values are the most nested internal layers by which both groups and individuals optimize their internal order. Making it the most appropriate technical delineation of religion at both the individual and group levels. The arguments capable of being made in favor

111. *What Percentage of Americans Are LGBTQ+?* Gallup, 2022–2026
112. Gary J Gates. *LGBT Data Collection Amid Social and Demographic Shifts of the US LGBT Community*. American Journal of Public Health, 2017
113. Tristan Bridges and Mignon R Moore. *Young Women of Color and Shifting Sexual Identities*. Contexts, 2018
114. Engineering National Academies of Sciences and Medicine. *Understanding the Well-Being of LGBTQI+ Populations*. National Academies Press, 2020
115. Gregory A Smith et al. *Decline of Christianity in the US Has Slowed, May Have Leveled Off*. Pew Research Center, 2025
116. *How Religious Are Americans?* Gallup, 2024
117. Melissa Deckman et al. *Religious Change in America*. Public Religion Research Institute, 2024

of the utility of these delineations fall along evolutionary lines via concepts that have parallels to ideas which have historically made for successful economic policies.

The definition of an atheist is supposed to be *"a person who disbelieves or lacks belief in the existence of God or gods"*, according to the Oxford Dictionary. But religion has no explicit connection to God or gods. It's connection to such entities is sufficient for religion, but not necessary. Every person has a religion, whether they admit it or not, it's intrinsic to the psychology of individuals. Atheism isn't a lack of belief the way poverty is a lack of money. A *lack* of belief in God isn't any different than a belief that God doesn't exist. Beliefs form structures of knowledge that support non-belief based understandings, to have no beliefs would be to have no knowledge. People don't get less religious, they simply change what they believe. They change what they find sacred, and they change what they worship. Religion is the operating system of your brain.

To impose values is to impose religion, and although I find this to be technically true, the Supreme Court has ruled on many occasions that the government does have the right to impose values or beliefs within reasonable limits. More specifically, it stands that just because a law aligns with some form of religious nature, doesn't mean it imposes it. Which isn't necessarily a violation of the First Amendment, there's certain laws that keep our society functioning and make perfect sense to implement. How would anyone make any law whatsoever if every law was interpreted as the belief or values it could represent? But schools have a unique place in this landscape of values. While values are things that become imposed on society through acts like laws, and court rulings, the values a person holds are a sign of their religious attainment, and the process of upbringing isn't just dependent on beliefs and values, it's dependent on their transformation. The transformations of beliefs and values within an individual, are an inherently religious ritual. Schools, being institutions that facilitate the transformations of both beliefs and values, are inherently religious in nature. Religious transformations shape the future belief structures and value hierarchies of every child that passes through these institutions.

Prior to their transformation, values and beliefs are instilled into a young child's mind. The instillation of beliefs and values is the precursor to this process of religious transformation. Anything that influences the beliefs and values of a child thereby influences that child's religion. There's no childhood developmental process independent of either. Values govern every interaction, beliefs govern structures of knowledge. Any individual or institution aiming to participate in a child's upbringing is taking on an inherently religious role. **A school is a religion.** Teaching paradigms *are* religious facilitations of transformation, and school regulations are ways of forcing a state religion onto children. Everything that a school system does must be a part of a formal plan stated prior. Every plan must then be ran through their respective bureaucracy that checks everything with the federal government, which in this regard operates as centralized religious oversight. In the same manner that a Ministry of Truth naturally devolves into a Ministry of Lies, any Department of Education is actually a Department of Religion. That's the only thing it ever could be. The religious rights of the states have been transferred to the federal government, the exact scenario that our religious freedoms were intended to prevent.

How does one operate a school system without having beliefs about how it should operate? How does one bestow knowledge on a subject without having beliefs about how it should be learned? How do you teach a subject without having beliefs about how that subject is continued year after year? You may think this could be analogous to politicians having beliefs about the government, but politicians are elected. The people who run the school systems are currently hired by people you'll never meet, to do jobs they'll never publicly present, that are supposed to fulfill the most important role in the lives of our children, who are arguably the most important parts of our lives.

Even the utility of grades are questionable on a practical level, their current implementation assumes that these measurements are more valuable than anything else a child could be doing with their time. But the problem is that these metrics aren't valuable to the student. We raise kids to do basically no work for themselves, they don't contribute to their own survival. The schools function because we grant them a formal role in society, but this has become a societally dysgenic relationship. This isn't genetic dysgenics, this is our layer of information transfer that's become dysgenic. It creates adults who become fed up that they ever have to contribute to their own survival at all. Instead these children could be learning to design their own products they could one day sell to others. Separating children from their own survival has only forced so many into complacency, and dreams of socialism in a system that shouldn't require it.

The US Constitution, with its guaranteed freedoms, is a framework that allows for other frameworks to exist within itself. This framework is more useful than any single law. Likewise, a landscape of religious freedom would be more useful than any single religion. The need for groups to survive brings about competition, allowing innovation to overtake dogma in a competition of dogma itself. It's necessary to accept schools as religions, otherwise bureaucracies spawn dogmatic policies that become insidious religions, which is where every recent brand of left-wing extremism has originated. Full utilization of religion, as a competitive apparatus, would better fuel the value creation pipeline of the economy, and would integrate honesty into the schooling process. The function of the structure of competition is universal benefit.

Implementations represent interpretations. There's no implementation, of rules or paradigms, that can escape being an interpretation of what they represent, there's an inherent function to their structure that operates independent of any stated intentions. Implementation is an enforcement of belief, and those beliefs are reinforcing and selecting for certain behaviors. When people disagree with the basis of some implementation, they disagree on a religious level.

You might argue that children spend more time at home than they do at school, and this is true in some cases, it should be granted. But to think this means the home is the only influence on a child's transformation is untrue, large community gatherings do not often happen in people's homes. A large community gathering is happening in school whenever students attend. This has symbolic significance in that these are religious gatherings specifically. The power of organizing a community affects the beliefs and values of the individuals involved through the social rituals of attendance itself. This likely doesn't exist anywhere else to the same depth in the large majority of the lives of people who attend, and if it does it would predominantly be at their own religious gatherings. The intensity of the experience at school is heightened due to the social environment being that of a gathered community, giving these daily occurrences a religious significance.

The school system wasn't always in need of this transformation, but it was always eventually going to be. How can one determine if it's the right time to switch schooling paradigms between using a centralized process that dictates educational standards in order to bring up an educated class, versus decentralizing to bring up a transformed educated class from an already educated one? It's similar to lowering taxes in order to first grow an economy, then increasing them once the economy is generating wealth to build up the coffers of the government. In our case, education has become so widespread that it's nearly saturated every county and household, with only minor exceptions. Sure everyone isn't a genius, but that was never going to be the end result. If there wasn't already widespread adoption of an existing schooling paradigm, then it wouldn't be the right time to make this change. The fact that it's so widespread means it's satisfied the addition step of Williston's law, and is now ready for greater and more widespread specialization. Another indication comes from the ideologies leaking out of the education system, like a swollen organ folding in on itself. It's also an advantageous time to loosen up the grip on regulations and educational laws because the schools in general are failing as badly as the birth rate, technology is making new leaps, people are forming novel ideas about how to live their lives, and this has everything to do with child-rearing. It's the perfect time to build many new educational paradigms across the country for the sake of having them compete with each other as a point of fundamental improvement to the greatest economic machine ever to exist in the history of the world.

Government funded projects find their best execution when they tee up something for the private sector. This is best done through innovation, but how could this work in the context of the public school system? Well, the first stage of this operation is already done. Schools are already widespread across the entire country, and the large majority of our population understands the basics of how they operate. Schools can be for groups of people who wish to establish their heritage. They can be used by people who wish for their community to persist, and not just as a cultural skin worn by others.

It could only be the parents of the children who attend the schools that deserve to have a say in how they ultimately operate. It would also be putting people in charge of their own heritage, which they want and can do a great job at. Because the government doesn't seem to, and only costs us more money when they try. Instead of the state running schools, the parents of the children who attend them can be the ones in charge.

Existing public school buildings can be occupied in a rentable form for communities in need of a location, or for people who are willing to experiment in order to form one. Money granted on a per-student basis, replacing the flow of money from the government to the existing educational infrastructure, can be dedicated towards various goals. It would obviously be spent on the process of education, but this is slightly negligent of the infrastructure it requires. Saving money for constructing buildings, or maintaining existing buildings, can be a reasonable area of expense. A suggestion for managing the public schools, going forward, would be that you can simply vote people in or out. With parents in charge, they can decide who to associate with. For existing public buildings, any group could perhaps need a minimum number of people retained, per year, in order to hold the building for the next year. If too many have been voted out, or not enough wish to join, then other groups that meet those requirements would be able to join or take the building for themselves. The parents would have near infinite modularity, within the realm of the budget they receive on a per-student basis, to run the school how they see fit. They could hire others to do it for them, or they themselves could manage how it's done and to what ends.

Every school eventually becoming some form of private community, that can have its own policy on taking new members, would be a decent ideal to aim for, it would also probably never be achieved to completion. Growing communities to the point where they can manage their own conservation would be a big weight off the government's shoulders, and would be great for those communities that can achieve it. Government money is likely still going to be needed for a long time, but there's potential for communities that can buy out their own system to take full control. A group of people being able to do that means they're doing things right because they can afford it, that they care a lot about the process, and that their own process guided them well enough to get to that point of being able to privatize. Allowing the opportunity to own your own upgrades would be an excellent goal for the populace at large to strive for. Nothing is forced, you can always raise your own children, and find others who do the same.

But what's the incentive to privatize? If the government can't dictate terms inside a school because it's a religion, in even the public schools it funds, why ever leave the public system? It would only be fair to allow the government to dictate certain terms, such as the minimum and maximum number of students a public school building is able to hold, as they're the ones that would own the building, unless some community buys it. Even though a school may have been part of multiple generations of your community, those that don't have children in a public school at any given time would technically lose any voting power as to how it would be ran, or what its future might become. Multiple generations of a community, being able to control their own schooling infrastructure, have the chance to introduce a desirable stability to the schooling process of their own future generations. A school is cultural capital. To privatize a school system is to formalize your heritage.

By better clarifying the line between church and state, so as to prevent the state from establishing religions, we can make a distinction between the state with its economy, its companies, its jobs, its employees, and the society with its religions, its schools, its families, and its students. The existing misconstrual of this line has brought about forced associations, which have come to impose a form of social tyranny where there should instead be religious freedom. This administrative tyranny has raised tensions across every line that it was meant to protect. By contrast, free association would bring social liberty. Nothing can force children to associate outside of school, so why must they be forced to associate in a classroom?

No one should be forced to raise their children alongside people who would treat them as subhuman. If one can't base the relationship between individuals or families on the concept of equality, then the relationship can't be held together at all. Because that's not a relationship, that's a caste system. Under this forced association you would then find yourself at the bottom, because the bad behavior of the worst people becomes treated with more respect than the good behavior of anyone else. It allows, and in some cases enables, the most barbaric people to be able to destroy the nicest things for everyone else. In the existing system, many of the worst behaving students have no incentive to change their behavior. But private religious groups wouldn't be limited by law the same way that these government institutions have been, a religion would have the right to turn their back on someone whose behavior isn't respectful of their faith, and this can introduce incentives that change communities for the better. Entire communities being able to turn their backs on terribly behaved individuals would actually improve outcomes, even for those offenders, by incentivizing them to learn from their mistakes.

It's on the community to enforce behavioral standards, which public schools themselves might be unable to do because students are forced to attend. Seeing as they're a captive body, students have a right to insist on their freedom of expression rather than group cohesion, and I think they *should* have freedom of expression in that context. Even better would be groups of people collectively deciding how to go about utilizing that freedom of expression within a religious behavioral code. Likewise, people also deserve the right to get away from toxic and unruly behavior, at no cost of their own, should they wish to live up to different standards. Which may as well be a religious standard. Implementing the framework of religion, thereby allowing people to judge others on the content of their character, accelerates the transformation towards good behavior of everyone who now must be judged by their actions. It catalyzes the process of transformation for people who want to leave the worst parts of themselves behind in order to join better people.

Schools can be more like social groups, rather than formal institutions that are controlled by the government. It shouldn't require a formal review that someone who's reading at 3 and doing calculus by 5 shouldn't be forced to associate with someone who treats them as subhuman and can't do algebra at 14. To the state, someone must prove your guilt, but to the society, people must believe in your innocence. That's the basis of any social reputation. Access to people's children, to their community, is a privilege, not a right.

There are even existing groups in the country that would *love* to take some person of questionable character into their own community, and I say let them. The religious landscape of the US can interface the relationship between liberalism and conservatism in this same way by foregoing the requirement that every community must integrate people that they themselves didn't personally invite in. Or that they must integrate unsavory characters who treat others as subhuman. Likewise, you should have the right to separate your children from people who broadcast anti-natalist and anti-human messages. That's their religious viewpoint and it can't be considered the free speech of the government. It's not the job of the government to tell you who you must raise your children alongside, it's your personal religious choice to do so with whom you please. Each religion has an internal order that must be preserved, or else that religion forcefully loses its basis for existing. What is a religion but a group that's able to maintain high levels of trust amongst themselves? Or even extremely low trust, or high loyalty, or either with regards to sovereignty if any of these are they desire. Forcefully mandating such a thing would be a lack of religious freedom after all.

Laws and policies being forced onto schools by the state, that forces them to have bureaucratic administrations capable of handling any litigation, has gotten in the way of raising children. This form of school system we use is actually a very new thing, schools have existed for a long time but never with this scale of attendance. People also tended to finish their education at much younger ages, in contrast to the modern day where people attend education for much too long. This paradigm hasn't been in place for even 100 years, it would be strange if we didn't find anything wrong with it. The black and white nature of who's *good* for having these policies that take a preemptive defensive legal stance, compared to who's *bad* for not, is too simple of a manner to view humanity, and is ultimately destructive to the original purpose of these institutions. It's destructive to the children raised under this mission, it may as well be a religious interpretation of whether this still belongs in the modern day. Not every group of parents wants to deal with lawsuits, and lawyers, they just want to raise their children. What's best for a bureaucratic environment is to cover itself in policies and human resources capable of navigating legal challenges. But what's best for children is a bare-bones institution that's focused on education, rather than insidious lawfare.

Schools couldn't be funded in any fair manner as institutions, any legislation could only fund such things at the level of individuals. The incentive to be diverse or inclusive should be monetary, as well as social, through reputation. Incentives make a better policy than any policy ever could, because what you can do for 5 students with $5,000 pales in comparison to what you can do for 100 students with $100,000. Policies have made for terrible instruments to education. We should implement pseudo-capitalist incentives across religious organizations in order to better reach our society's potential for education and individual improvement. The value of reputation and integrity themselves would increase. Policing this function of inclusion so harshly has decreased the value of integrity and reputation in general, young people then learn these things have no value and chase them even less. The role of integrity has been outsourced to policy, which is an affront to holding principles at all. What good are principles if they're forced? What good is a reputation if the content of your character must fall within the state's pre-designated set of acceptable principles?

A society with no discrimination is a utopian ideal, and all the most unrelenting murderers in history have been utopian idealists. Both the Nazis and the Marxists believed they could make the world a better place by applying their ideologies to humanity, much like the people who believe in these policies of anti-discrimination. Yet the former two ended up engaging in the most mindless slaughter of human life ever witnessed. This is where ideology leads, no matter the ideology. The direct results of the widespread ideological dispositions spread through the school systems may as well be the psychological equivalent to these acts of physical violence, and it seems they'll cause just as much disarray in the end. Ideology is the attempt to force humanity to perfect itself, typically through some avenue learned through recent historical error. Ideologies don't align with human function, it's human function that aligns with the principles and axioms of the universe. Most notably, freedom. After achieving colorblindness throughout the 90s and early 2000s, it's no wonder racism came back as such a hot topic more than a decade later. So many students were taught that they were the hammer made to deal with the nail of discrimination, racism, and so many other finitely definable problems that were akin to propagandistic tools. Achieving the goal of a discrimination-free society isn't such a bad idea, it's also not entirely achievable, because no ideal will ever be truly achievable, that's why it's an ideal. But how we go about it really matters. Let's not aim for anti-discrimination, nor should we aim for discrimination either. Let's just aim to get along. Clinging so tightly to this has led us down a worse path, and it's badly affected young children who grow into disillusioned adults. We need to reconsider whether these policies should be a part of school systems at all. If some schools want to implement these policies, I don't see why they can't, it may as well be their religious freedom to do so. But a policy is not a guarantee of sincerity. There can be individuals who aim to get along with everyone who don't feel the need to make it an *official policy*. As speaking these words so proudly is the sign of an ideologue. Requiring formal statements, or policies, to represent a school in order to qualify for funding, or tax-exempt status, is nothing but discrimination itself. It only incentivizes certain kinds of idealistic individuals who aim to make these policies into mechanisms for their own personal control, meaning this is a dangerous incentive that leads to dangerous people being in charge of school systems. More sincere individuals aren't the kind of people who feel the need to write a statement saying they would never discriminate. In fact, it's insulting to make anyone say that at all. As we've already seen throughout the last 20^{+} years, just because a school claims that they won't discriminate doesn't make it true. They come up with all kinds of creative policies of how they're not discriminating, they're actually helping *underprivileged* and *underrepresented* individuals. Where these terms become defined in extremely novel ways to suit a political agenda. We shouldn't need to play these kinds of insidious games just to raise children. These twisted incentives have tainted the schools, devoured any trace of sincerity, and completely turned any respect for fair principles on its head, because that's all this policy-mongering could have ever done. It could have only ever fallen victim to irony. If we're to ever have a functional society, we need to be able to trust adults to make adult decisions. We need to grant them that responsibility. Catering to exceptions, worrying that less than 1% of the country might make a genuinely discriminatory school, has only allowed countless education professionals and students to gaze into that very abyss to become the monsters they claim to hate.

Unidimensional policies make non-unidimensional problems. Which means in the wake of its flaws will come an insidious bureaucracy that fills in all the cracks made through its inevitable failures with insidious behavior. Such insidious behavior betrays the notions of fairness originally intended through such policies in the first place, and gives way to a power structure that subverts its own purpose. Let's entertain an example scenario. Perhaps you don't want your child to become transgender, which is a religious boundary for you. But nonetheless, like a good citizen, you're happy to not discriminate, or hold anything against individuals and families that embrace this form of lifestyle. In fact, your child goes to school with a transgender child, and there's nothing wrong with that. But what if, out of the 20 children at this school, 15 of them were transgender? If all 15 families of those children support this lifestyle, which is seemingly religious, and school's rules cater to their social norms, shouldn't you be concerned that your child may pick up influence from being a part of this environment? So would it be discrimination against these transgender individuals to not want your child to share an institution with them, or would it be discrimination by a protected class against your child for ultimately imposing rules within the school based on their beliefs? Likewise, the easiest way to make some group of people into a public target is to unfairly favor them over others, transgender people don't deserve this negative attention. The easiest solution is that it's fine to simply separate and want to maintain your own belief system and lifestyle, people who insist upon specific beliefs that fall within a religious domain have every right to assemble amongst themselves. Calling it discrimination for someone to want to separate their child from being surrounded by alternate beliefs is discrimination itself. So it's not like we need to get rid of these policies because they're bad principles, they just need to be upheld locally rather than as a blanket nation- or state-wide construct. A distributed calculation needs to be allowed rather than forced uniformity. Otherwise, it sets every school up for failure and forces them to waste time and resources covering for their inevitable mistakes when they could just be fair to individuals instead of worrying about the consequences of their fair actions in an imperfect world.

As the insidious bureaucracy comes to control more and more of what's allowed to take place in a school or classroom, because that's what insidious bureaucracies do, they always want more, the end result is that children are insidiously manipulated through policies rather than being raised on principles. Resulting in the behavior we've come to witness these past 10^{+} years in the youth who find themselves unable to compete in our own economy from the education that so badly betrayed them. They were failed by these policies that began to occupy larger and larger spaces between them and what were supposed to be role models. They've become overtaken with ideology and instant gratification. These policies amount to being social mandates, which only leaves room for insidious players to act as mediators of social tyranny. Notably, this is the opposite of religious freedom, which points us in the direction of how to fully reason what the true answer to this conundrum is.

The stories around discrimination in the US started with women and black people who wanted to attend schools they weren't allowed to attend. At the time it was fair to approach the narrative from this direction, because those were the only schools around, and these were the exact problems they posed. But we don't live in this era anymore. Men and women of all races have all been educated, and more equally than ever. There used to be the need to prevent schools from treating these groups badly so that they could participate, and that was appropriate. But in the modern day, if someone doesn't like you or your children, why would you want your children to go to school with them? I certainly wouldn't, I'd rather find a better place for them to go, there's plenty of better people out there. Nowadays, it's the person who insists that they're being discriminated against that's become the bully, they use claims of racism or discrimination as an excuse to treat other people terribly. It's obnoxious and in bad faith to claim these things at all. The people who don't feel this way are the ones who've been raised to believe racism is still such a serious problem. They seem to not know anything about societal differences from this decade compared to any of the last 150^{+} years. Their ideals thrive on symbolism, so it may as well be their religion. These may as well be religious stories, and I welcome people to have their own religious interpretations, but it can't be forced on everyone who finds these stories to be oversimplified, without nuance, or inappropriate interpretations of the modern day. Times change, and we must change also. We must not invoke these naive and unfair interpretations of human nature. With the school system enabled to greater levels of freedom through the First Amendment, the exact demand for specific belief systems will always be met with their own supply, people will always have a place to fit in. These accusations of racism and discrimination have been weaponized against people that have done nothing of the sort, no one should need to prove their innocence against these false accusations by being forced to implement *policies* that say they won't discriminate. They could be empty words, and it would make no difference. The requirement for policies of the sort is simply setting up an abyss for people to gaze into, to want to avoid that abyss is a matter of religious freedom. Statements that attempt to preemptively prove one's innocence need not be made for the sake of someone else's moral policing.

Moralizing over how to raise children has only led to the prevention of those children maturing, and increased our chances of civil war. This is not for the best, we must reverse course. A civilizational crisis caused by state-orchestrated religious beliefs has proven to be equally as dangerous as any war. Allow people to prove their integrity through actions rather than their innocence through policy. Students and schools can have free association with each other. Groups being able to link up with other groups can form a more flexible paradigm of interaction amongst students. No one can force who you're friends with, school life should have all the same selective freedom as anyone's personal life.

If the government forces you to be kind, it only inflates the value of kindness, meaning it becomes worthless. Interactions are currency because interactions are an exchange, and fair exchange collectively increases the value of interaction itself. Forcing unfair exchanges is to force unfair interactions, which builds up resentment against whoever's enforcing them. That's what communism accomplishes, in principle, it's what communism sits down stream of. It's why it fails.

Giving the responsibility of upholding the community to members of that community increases the value of upholding anything at all. It makes accomplishing this goal into something worthwhile, giving this responsibility to people will make them want to achieve the best possible outcome for those they hold dearly. It also becomes a social prize for those who can do it well, which is valuable to *everyone*. But this value is currently withheld by enforced policies. This responsibility can instead be celebrated when done well, the way it should be. It incentivizes people to get along more than any forced association ever could. Rather than attempting to force people into prosocial behavior, incentivizing it will take away the caged feeling made within the existing schooling paradigm. Incentivizing prosocial behavior will lead to a number of behavioral improvements that can only be accomplished when the schools don't feel like prisons. It allows society to select the behaviors they'd like to see in others, something the government is doing a terrible job at. The government has come to moralize, which is the sign of ideological corruption, and we no longer need these training wheels. This needs to be a distributed responsibility, not one of centralization.

Anyone who wants to keep their existing schools operating the same as they currently are will have all the freedom to do this. It's all possible through the modularity of the parents being in charge. But it would no longer prevent those who wish to deviate from doing so. A lot of this has historically been left up to the states, and there may still be a job for the states to do. Such as how certain overhead organization may work, or how certain schools may require a certain number of people in order to use certain public school buildings for themselves. This kind of overarching organizational layer may likely end up being dictated by states, but the state still has no business controlling the inner workings of the school itself, nor should they be able to hold a school hostage to policy.

The religion of those who work at your school ultimately determines its religion. That applies at the level of the school, and in any sort of classroom. Someone being named a *helper*, an *aide*, or a *teacher*, is not indicative that the end result of this person's influence is a product of the word used as the job description. Everything about a school, including the people who uphold the institution from behind a curtain, and the people inside the institution on a daily basis, are intrinsic parts of that school's religion, and their influence is felt at every step by any student who goes through such a place. In the modern day, there's a large political bias in the population of teachers and school staff. There's also heavy ideological biases that these people tend to learn from their time in universities. The universities themselves have become breeding grounds for ideologies that are pushed onto children, and the vulnerability that young children have to this influence becomes worse the younger they are. There's only risk, and no reward whatsoever, that comes out of giving control of your young child to someone who has completely different beliefs than you do.

Religion is the art of upbringing. The early life of every person is the initiation phase of a core model, and everything it leads to. People other than the parents of the children who attend a school having control of that school is deeply misincentivized. Some areas have votes for things like school committees, but we give no regard to who might be voting. Why should someone who destroyed the lives of their own children have any say in how yours turn out? The individuals working at a school can't simply *agree* to play by the rules that people want for their children, they must actually believe it. The only ones who can determine if that's true are the people running the school, and the government has no business mandating any individuals to such a role. Only parents deserve voting rights. Being of age will give you a vote in the future of our state, but only having children should give you a vote in the future of our society. The only people who should get to decide how the next generation turns out, are those who contribute to it. Children belong to their parents, not the state.

So what would change? Any overarching bureaucracy would cease to exist, and parents would have direct collective authority over the schools that their children attend. These are the people most invested in the future of their own children so they'll do the best job hiring the right teachers, assuming that's the schooling model they'll follow. Realistically, the government will still need to fund the public school system. But no greater bureaucracy needs to hold your child's future hostage while selling it piecemeal to a teacher's union, which would easily become a cost reduction. Any school should be able to give a general religious statement, the same as has been required for individuals through diversity statements. Only a cult would try to hide their nature by either not having a religious statement, or by pretending they're not a religion.

Once you can demarcate religion via the transformation of beliefs and values, everything about how either are instilled belongs in the religious realm. From whoever does the instilling, as well as how many people can instill, and what kind of environment the instilling occurs in. All kinds of overhead, from things like the ratio of teachers to students, to any requirements of observation and attendance, all come into question. Requirements for what days schools are open, whether they close in the summer, or from extreme weather, may be able to be dictated by the people who run the schools. Accreditation itself runs into Constitutional trouble, as it would require the approval of what's essentially other religions for you to then have yours. Schools would no longer be linked to specific municipalities, unless it was the desire of those parents who run the school.

Time management doesn't avoid the same mix ups through things such as whether attendance is mandatory, whether students are able to come and go as they wish through the middle of the day, or whether they must both show up and leave at the same time as everyone else. Activities such as whether they graduate at 16 or 18, what length of the year the school operates in, whether they attend 5 days a week or 4, and whether they attend sparse periods throughout the year, or if they start in the fall and end in spring, are all based on layers of flexibility that may be able to be deemed either worthless or worthwhile by a religion itself. Even the general educational setting is related to beliefs, such as whether classrooms exist as uniformly organized desks with a sage on a stage, whether the children work independently on projects they're meant to present, whether students study a subject for an hour a day, and rotate between different subjects, or whether students solely dedicate to one thing and branch off it in the near future. One would certainly need not follow state curriculums for homeschooling.

In terms of religious statements, individuals might have statements, and better individuals might have books. Schools should have a book, but can have statements. A statement is just the bare minimum. Schools should ultimately find ways of forming their own books they can use to represent themselves with. Some religions might not be complete at first, they might only be philosophies or ideologies. This is fine, people need to progress through those stages in order to better form their own systematic beliefs. It needs to be allowed as a form of fledgling religion. Not every belief system needs to be perfectly refined in order to start off with the rights of a comprehensive religion, otherwise this is denying people an equal chance to develop one. In this age of science and technology, we should not necessarily hold religion to a standard that forces it to look and act like its historical equivalents. Times change, as do the nature of beliefs.

Looked at through a historic lens, safetyism was the next logical step in the liability culture that's formed in the US. Broad legal liability is applied liberally across the US, and has made a lot of things better across all of Western society, even schools. But where does that leave us? It's now been pushed onto the school system to the point where it's transformed into an insidious ideology and we're currently dealing with terrible outcomes because children need risk and danger. Safetyism becomes an emergent religion due to the nature of liability, and this prevents people from raising their children with the necessary level of risk-taking behavior needed to ensure their proper brain development[**118**].

Parents of children who hurt themselves are able to blame it on a teacher, or the school, or whoever their parents want to sue. No one grows up being a responsible citizen because schools must fear their own students. No one practices being accountable, and adequate reinforcements aren't being delivered. But reinforcement is destiny.

118. Greg Lukianoff and Jonathan Haidt. *The Coddling of the American Mind.* Penguin Press, 2018

Schools need to be freed from this rope of liability around their neck. Starting a school while dealing with the constant threat of liability lawsuits leaves the default religion for US schools to be that of decadence and dysgenics. As a source of religious transformation, risk needs to be accepted. Liability in schools becomes a liability to the wellbeing of society. The existing school infrastructure even embeds countless layers of bureaucrats to *free* themselves from liability altogether, so the structures of many of these institutions even reflects the nature of this problem to begin with. But of course schools need to be held to certain standards, at least the parents would be incentivized enough to care about this, so how can this conundrum be settled? Can we cut out the middlemen?

If you can state claims of how things will be ran in your school, operate the school based on the rules you outlined, and things go as expected and students are treated as agreed upon, then no one can have any problems with such an outcome. The government would have no business middlemanning if there's an agreement of such a nature between a school and parents outside of actions like extreme violence, pedophilia, or other issues that are of a legally concerning nature. These topics can cover different kinds of tragedies, accidents, injuries, and so on. Parents could either take a cheap approach and go bare minimal, they could agree to join in on costs should something bad happen, and they could even start funds that save and raise money for such occasions and pray they don't need to use them. But liabilities must be addressed how the parents or school decides, otherwise proper childrearing isn't possible. This is non-negotiable, risk must be accepted. To what degree it's accepted, is rightfully within the realm of religion, because a relationship with risk is no different than a relationship with death.

Insurance requirements for schools may be wise, but being the prisoner to an insurance company, who can raise prices based on whether you agree or disagree with the concepts of safetyism, only leaves most with the inability to raise their own children well enough to compete in society. On the upside, schools can easily start their own insurance pools in the same way they can handle their own rules. While these might not be the biggest pools, they can be pools made at the level of any given school in order to grant the school control of its own fate. The money in the pool would only need to be visible to the parents, and every year that a child has non-problematic behavior their costs could possibly go down if the pool doesn't desperately need more money. The highest cost would be paid for the newest, most likely youngest, students to a school. Every parent would simply be willing to accept the amount of money in the pool as what's available for incidents that require this money. The tens to hundreds of thousands of dollars required for simply having insurance on a school can be foregone in place of a reasonable cost that parents are willing to allocate should they feel this is an appropriate route for them to choose. Neither the government nor any industries have any right to hold your religion hostage to laws or policies that only aim to make it more expensive to have your religion, and thereby act to inhibit its existence in the first place. Schools need not be hostages to personal or political vendettas on behalf of anyone who disagrees with the opinions of the school, like what we see in politics today. Saving a little, year by year, is a feasible insurance policy as most new schools can start off with just young children where the chance of bad accidents are small. As no incidents occur, they save money, which makes for a more welcoming environment for new students.

There can be no regulation of religion, as that very concept would only introduce avenues for one's religion to infiltrate others through the government, taking away the freedom thereof while sacrificing it on the altar of insidious infiltration. Religion must live and die by natural selection, not by the state. Demanding that something be mandated to *everyone* is an act of sabotage. It destroys natural variation. Which is a shame because that variation, like genetic variation, exists for a reason. Pretending that something is the one true answer is just as zealous as using the idea that your God is the one true God to impose morality and nonsense onto others that they would otherwise be better off without.

Why are schools choosing people's survival strategies? People need to choose these for themselves, or else they'll grow complacent and die out. Allow the same free-flowing environment for schools as states have for businesses. They allow people to vote with their feet, and it's a great system that offers a number of irreplaceable advantages. The law only comes in during cases of pedophilia, extreme violence, or when school agreements are not upheld. Marxism is essentially a religion, and every school is of a Marxist basis when the state is in charge of running them. Human conservation is basically what DEI programs were aiming to accomplish in the first place. That same goal can be executed in a much easier way as a distributed calculation, while having leagues more success than they ever have.

The requirements, certifications, laws, committees, regulations, and any other interventions in educational infrastructure are forms of selection. Selection can only be decided by religion, not by government. Otherwise that's the government imposing religion, your survival strategies are your religion. But it's also true that the government has been involved in education for a reason. They have a serious investment in the outcomes of the upbringing process. So how can this negotiation be managed? With honesty.

Being able to admit political bias, and religious affiliation, means playing an honest game. To insist schools shouldn't have any bias only means this will instead happen insidiously when it does, as an inevitability, like what we've seen for the past 30^+ years. This insistence itself is an insidious strategy, to favor the insidious is to force this process into a realm that's blatantly political. But to favor honesty would be to make this blatantly fair.

You can worship gays, immigrants, or whatever group of people you want to worship, if that's your religion. But if you sell whatever religion you sell through schooling, then you need to clearly articulate what it is you're selling. You can't lie, only to insidiously discriminate in favor of groups of people if you don't explicitly state that you favor them. Such a thing would be grounds for a lawsuit. If you choose to have a school that determines what students to keep based on the content of their character, that form of judgement needs to be reflected in the outcome of how you judge people's character. Because if the schools are lying, then the US government would have a right and a reason to be concerned, as that's a subversion of the upbringing process. Children are the most important part of society, a subversion of this process would mean entering extremely dangerous territory.

A question left on the table is, what about the public universities? Universities were never supposed to be hotspots for political activism, they certainly weren't supposed to be recruitment centers for such things. Prior to being 18, children can't make as many legal decisions for themselves. It's when people can operate maturely in the world, and interact with other religions, that their upbringing is hypothetically finished. Even if they're under 18, and they attend a university, the assumption would be that they do so with a level of maturity capable of handling such a responsibility.

In terms of the time that's currently wasted, universities could probably push out graduates much faster. Should it really take 4 years to finish a degree when most of the important work is done in 2-3? The only groups that should hold sway over how any student can graduate should be departments. A physics department should determine what requirements there are to graduating with a physics degree, and this shouldn't need to require taking an art class. The literature department shouldn't have any sway when aiming for an engineering degree. Departments should be able to choose who they accept as freshmen, as transfers, and what their requirements are to graduate. In the process this can be more specialized, cheaper, faster, and can keep toxic forms of overarching politics out of the educational process.

Departments may as well have their own religion if they want to, their own admissions paradigm, and if that means some of them will use DEI then so be it, but others should have the right to completely sidestep such things. These departments could operate on a free market of sorts, what might make them more or less valuable would include their own admissions paradigm. Being directly involved in running their own operation, they could manage the cost of their own program more realistically based on what students would find valuable as a set of skills to be gained. For example, some group of chemists might team up, with people of other specialties even, to form a department amongst themselves that they can register with their state. If they have students being admitted, the state would find them a location to use as their institution. They would probably start off as a lab of specialists that have grant funding to do research into their own specific kinds of work. Alongside their research, they could take graduate and undergraduate students, postdocs, or whatever kind of students they prefer, in order to progress their students through the trials of whatever kind of education and skills training they offer. They might even avoid using the concept of a semester at all, why not enable departments to have their own free-flowing format to education?

Departments could still break down beliefs at the level of individuals, where you would expect individual students and professors to have differing beliefs, there would just be an underlying agreement in the value of some specific testing paradigm, admissions paradigm, and process required to graduate that people would hold as their underlying motivation for attending. Religion could be respected as something of an individual choice, and not that of an institution. In such a circumstance, it should also be an open topic for the students to both be aware of and discuss. No professor should be able to operate behind a veil of ambiguity, state your religion openly, rather than hiding behind your work as if it's somehow independent of it.

While many prefer meritocracy, as would I, there's merit itself in noting that there's a questionable nature as to how to determine what true merit actually is. As I've already alluded, and as I'll continue to elaborate on further throughout this book, grades and tests are flawed forms of measurement. Everything is made of tradeoffs, and tests are no exception. To implement a meritocratic paradigm is a *model* of selection, but it's never to be mistaken for selection *itself*. We can only ever attempt selection, as nature is what actually determines who wins and who loses. The DEI admissions paradigm that finds both support and disdain amongst the American populace should be allowed by those who wish to abide by it, dissenters should also be granted the ability to implement their own paradigms. Such a thing is a religious selection mechanism, it's the most historically and anthropologically overlooked aspect of religion, it's a guiding pathway towards the future, towards the evolutionary advancement of your descendants. Neither the government nor any supposedly scientific institution would have a way of determining *one true* selection paradigm, that would be a theocratic implementation of positive selection amongst those who wouldn't be given the chance to pick any alternatives. While DEI may not be entirely competitive in some purely meritocratic manner, it should still have to compete with other selection paradigms. Even looking at the socioeconomic status of applicants isn't any different than some subjective measurement, how it's applied is relative to some standardized expectation that isn't able to be perfectly integrated in some godly way because it's humans doing it, it's just a broad stereotyping. Regardless, people should have the right to do either. Implemented at scale, this would achieve a natural selection of natural selections. A scalable distributed calculation that solves multiple problems through enabling multiple different solutions, rather than our current insistence on having one solution that causes multiple problems.

There's no better way to give children confidence in controlling their own life outcomes than by allowing them to prevent their worst behaving peers from behaving poorly in their own environment at the consequence of being kicked out by those who don't want to be sacrificed to someone else's terrible behavior. It's the current lack of control, in this regard, that leads to feelings of depression and hopelessness amongst the populace at large, as the worst behaving people in their environment are allowed to continue their terrible behavior at the cost of everyone else's well-being, sanity, and sincerity. That's not how the real world works. So it's not in the best interest of children that their world needs to work this way either. Children should be able to be just as critical of their peers as anyone else would be in hiring an employee. Children deserve the right to take their lives seriously. For those who feel they didn't get the chance to, who don't feel they received a fair shot at life, they deserve to at least be able to plan ahead to do better for their own children.

If you want people to get along, the best way to make it happen isn't to enforce it, it's to let go of the instant gratification embedded within this notion of enforcement, and incentivize it. Even if a child gets kicked out of multiple schools, if they write about it, and in what way they want to improve themselves to prevent it from happening again, what they did wrong, and what they want to change about themselves, there may be a lasting mechanism of change for people who don't want to find themselves alone, or who end up disappointed with their continual rejection by others. To continue writing to get into new schools is to acknowledge what they did wrong. It's to force themselves to admit their own mistakes and to confront themselves to become a better person.

It doesn't make sense that the state voluntarily pays for public schooling but not for homeschooling. The point of this money is to educate children, not to send them to a government education center. The government should care whether they get their money's worth, not where it's spent.

We are unable to prevent education from establishing religion, it's not feasible. Public education, and the regulation of private education, has historically been in the hands of the government, but this is definitionally misplaced. Everything about the upbringing of a child has to do with their religious transformations into adulthood, and the schools that facilitate this process are performing an inherently religious role. The positioning of this line between religion and government has been poorly drawn around this specific topic. Through this elucidation, the territory of education can be claimed by religion in general, rather than any religion specifically.

Religion isn't an option, we're predisposed to be dependent on it. Adults may choose what they do or don't believe, but children don't have that luxury. Young children *need* beliefs to be handed down by adults, lest they be completely absent of any guiding moral framework. Children *need* religion the same way they need proper nutrition and exercise. This isn't an insistence upon specific age-old doctrines, it's an insistence on the utility of beliefs in general. Without any form of moral guidance, children lose an important building block of their own future potential, if they stand for nothing they'll fall for anything. Without this understanding, entire generations will be lost in figuring out how to properly guide children, while adults bicker through the political hurdles until they do. But this isn't a political problem. This same process of the instillation of beliefs has *already* happened within the schools for this *same exact* reason, because it's the instincts of women to instill beliefs into children. Upon the inhibition of this being permitted, these beliefs had transformed through scientific lenses, as science has a respectable pedestal in the academic world. Utilizing the scientific apparatus, those women even attempted to stash these beliefs in the place most capable of offering them a form of safe harbor, most without even realizing they were doing this. Modern civilization took the importance of the instillation of beliefs for granted, and under this academic paradigm, where they were avoided, we see no shortage of entire countries across the globe experiencing a collapsing birth and marriage rate. Our ever apparent cultural divide is due to the failure to deliver something that's supported civilization for as long as it's been around.

To believe beliefs were metaphorically picked off a tree would require you to believe they're discovered rather than made. But regardless of where they came from, we've built an evolutionary dependence on their utility no different than the effects of relaxed selection by simply relying on them to anchor our explanations of the world around us, beliefs are the roots of all structures of knowledge. The state-ran schools are acting to monopolize this dependence, and it's a violation of religious freedoms. The Establishment Clause is being misinterpreted, schools aren't capable of being secular. The government can implement laws that can be interpreted as aligning with specific beliefs or values, but to implement an entire system of doing so, a system of raising children, a system of sculpting beliefs and values with behavioral conditioning, and positive selection, all of which delivers a systematic worldview, means they've established a state-religion. Times change and societies do too, parents need the right to control their own adaptations. Religion is our right to adapt.

We should fully embrace the US Constitution and use what it has to offer, rather than pretend religion isn't an underlying aspect of human existence. Faithful adherence to the principles of this document *will* bring us greater prosperity and fairness. It's an amazing document, place your faith in it even if you don't place your faith in religion.

Language related to the separation of church and state bothers some people today, they see it as a deviation from the original interpretation of the US Constitution. But the reality is, there were multiple founders on either side of this argument, and some in between. I would insist that people who support religion at the state level would find more benefit supporting it at the state-scale, while granting people their own personal freedoms. Allowing religion to float freely on an open market, the same way our currencies do globally, would let its value speak for itself.

Education is not simply a technology, this won't lead to a technological revolution. Education is a religious art, it would bring about a second Reformation, an American Reformation. Like with cells, communities should better compartmentalize in order to hedge their survival across time. Religion is the basis for being able to raise children. It's the destination, what's the journey?

VII
SCHOOLING & UPBRINGING

7.1 Philosophy of Schooling

Raising children is the art of playing games. Thinking, working, exercising, reading, and building are all habits that you grow as a child, and they recurse throughout your life. They could otherwise be something worse for those who aren't able to form these habits early on. Reinforcement is destiny, both psychologically and physiologically. We are still, as a civilization, figuring out how to adapt child-rearing to fit into this age of high economic productivity. Yet at the same time, the best way to raise children hasn't changed. It's to expose them to danger while giving them purpose and meaning. Purpose and meaning bridge the gap between behavior and evolution. Children can be the angels you need if you send for them, or the demons you summon should you burn their future before their eyes.

Just as schools won't change if the people running the schools don't change, neither will the admission processes of colleges and universities. Both will continue to disrespect the Supreme Court, as they already have. We need to subvert them as institutions and make their expensive degrees worthless. Win through competition by making better schools, where children are able to make a future for themselves without these ridiculous diplomas. Throughout this chapter I'll outline the details and ideas for the school I plan on building, as well as various aspects of upbringing that have seemingly been completely mishandled.

Development for children should be set up in a way that the goals are clear. When goals aren't clear, you can at least be clear about how to make them clear. Which is why there are fewer things worse for a child's development than an insidious parent. A rung below that, on the same ladder, is an insidious teacher.

There's no such thing as *teaching* nor *education*. We've come to sugarcoat too many terms because people like the way it sounds. When it comes to young children, there's only indoctrination. You indoctrinate them into your beliefs, whether you like it or not. The environment they live in will determine a large part of their mindset and ideas. The people who make up that environment will, in essence, indoctrinate the children around them. That's how children are raised, that's how you pass on your beliefs. If you don't, someone else will.

Grown adults need not placate themselves with re-branded terms for the sake of appearances. You might still call it education, as will I, but at the very least you should know what it actually means. Someone who refuses to admit this indicates that they oversimplify where there should be more complexity, and overcomplicate where there should be less. Or that they lie. Either way, it's the sign of a bad role model for your children. Should someone not like this description, thinking that it sounds bad, they'd probably like to believe that schools aren't religions. Which is because they prefer to insidiously subvert the beliefs of others, rather than being honest about what they offer to you and your child.

The modern educational paradigm was an attempt at the mass-production of child-rearing. But now the birth rate is non-existent, many young people refuse to work, and too many who want to can't find good jobs. The schools keep churning out new religions in the form of political extremism. They've failed miserably at their original goal to the point where the concept of schooling needs to be reassessed.

Student loans tend to not be paid back because they don't operate on a free market. Tuition costs have skyrocketed now that student loans are given from the federal government without assessment. It's become a Ponzi scheme that robs students of the value earned from their future work. If you need to pay to get a job, it's a scam. Tenure at universities is fake, it doesn't even work, and that's an indication of the value of universities. If professors speak their mind on disfavored political topics they still lose funding, fall victim to administrative warfare, lose people's respect, and can't operate as an actual professor afterwards. The universities are not fixable. The solution is to subvert them with alternative demand.

Formal education matters says the people who sell education as a brand in a highly regulated environment that prevents others from innovating. Qualifications only create a fear for a lack thereof, they're not actually important. A community is a place where children have a role and participate in the maintenance of that group. Schoolwork isn't a responsibility because there's no end goal, no concrete contribution that it makes to a child's life, just an amount of time they're supposed to dedicate to busywork.

I don't believe it to be a successful strategy that children are worked under the conditions of constant urgency, year after year, only to later get a job that does the same thing. There should be less urgency in childhood until a child feels the need to urgently do something, and that ought to be inspired. Inspiration comes from preserving the depth of interactions. Childhood should be fulfilling in a way that positions their life to be successful from the merits of their trials with a buildup of this process progressing towards adulthood. Finding yourself, your purpose, and figuring out who you want to be is a cornerstone of childhood, as it becomes difficult to do once you're busy being an adult. A childhood without this is only a process to raise failed adults. No one should come out of an upbringing feeling like they missed their chance at life.

Respect from groups of children needs to be gained, not granted. This makes any kind of teacher mandate problematic for the students who don't find themselves having a respectable teacher. Too many aren't able to earn this respect. If respect from a student is supposed to be given for free, then they're being managed instead of led. This immediately becomes a point of failure for anyone who needs more freedom to grow. The most insidious position someone can have is to think there should be no such thing as private schooling, that everyone should share the same state mandated education. The profession of teaching would become even more anti-competitive, and it would guarantee a decrease in the respectability of both the role and those who inhabit it. The melting pot only works with those who are actually willing to melt with you. Those who don't intend to do the same become dangerous, while those who are willing to cooperate only become targets for those who aren't. To make a good school system is to make a free-flowing process that enables neither students nor adults to act like tyrants without repercussions.

A teaching staff with no ability to predict what skills will be useful in the future, with no real technological prowess of their own, and no aptitude for capitalistic endeavors, dictating curriculums to students is no different than a microscale implementation of communism within the academic sphere, because communism can't accomplish any of those things either. But we don't live in a communist country, so why raise children like this? Teaching, as a profession, is largely unnecessary. Most children are naturally competitive, as long as you give them an appropriate window to the world they'll be able to calibrate their aims appropriately. Being able to stay up to date with the real world, while refining your talents to its state of the art, and the nature of your environment, makes more sense than learning in a traditional class structure where too much is dictated, rather than something being made a target that a student aims to achieve. Dictations tend to offer outdated dogma.

Basic schooling ought to yield children that come out of a system where they feel that nothing they've achieved has been granted by luck. They should feel that they've worked for what they've earned by their own hard work and merit, and that should actually be true. Schools should not exist purely to train. Children must find how to train themselves, and what might be worth training themselves for. To make a child so dependent on the dictations of others is antithetical to their freedom. To be unable to properly plan for their own future is the complete opposite of how a healthy human mind should operate by the time one graduates from high school. There's too much breadth to the modern world not covered as a topic in school, too many important aspects of life require experience not offered in a classroom. For young children to leave school with no convictions, only tidbits of information about topics they'd focused on, is an outright disaster.

The point of raising children to learn how to learn is that they grow up with a skill set for finding skill sets. With a highly adaptable and scalable skill set, even if someone loses their job they won't lose their skill set. The point is to be the integral of too many useful derivatives to ever fall out of need.

It would make more sense, for teachers and people still looking toward the modern educational paradigm as a structure for their upbringing, to benefit from the knowledge at the highest levels of academia. Receiving a PhD in education shouldn't be about trying to invent some new form of teaching, or applying statistics to oversimplified measurements of complex environments. Instead, it would be more worthwhile for these people to join into serious academic pursuits, and instead of furthering the field they choose, like PhD students of that field, they would work on translating the complexities of their concentration into a more compressible and easier to digest form so that young students can pick it up and understand a rather complex thing fairly easily. Delivering widened horizons to more people and with less effort on their part. A lot of what used to be not only unknown, but practically unknowable, has already moved into the realm of the known, and is widely dispersed as videos online. There's a lot of profit in this, producing books and videos, even if one doesn't want to pursue these goals through formal academic routes.

Any economics book seems to make great arguments for why human time is the most precious commodity in the world. So why do we waste the time of children so much? It's valuable to us, it's valuable to them. Let them use it in ways that brings out their potential. Let them learn to be productive should it be their calling. To enable that productivity through a more appropriate fueling of their knowledge across various areas of life, to supply them with books and videos meant to actually educate and inform rather than just textbooks made for nonstop practice, would make for a more worthwhile teaching profession. Intertwining entertainment with utility would offer more breadth to their lives, and allowing them to determine what makes the most sense to obsessively practice will grant them benefit through the pursuit of purpose that arises from making such decisions.

This country has become so criminally negligent with its own children. Forcing them, by law, into schooling paradigms meant to subvert their instincts, and make them into obedient workers, all while an elite class does everything they can to destroy anyone else's livelihoods through economic and class warfare. We're diminishing their chances of survival, and thereby the persistence of our own values. It's almost like civilization has to fight with itself not to raise its children too much, to prevent it from being overdone. I'm not advocating for less wisdom to be given to children, but I am advocating for optimizing the upbringing process. Less tedious work, less busy work, less bureaucracy, instead aim children in the direction they need their lives to go. Not in the direction of homework, to study for a test, to get a diploma, to get the next diploma, to get the next diploma, to finally get an entry level job unrelated to what they'd even studied in the first place. It's all too roundabout, and it's become extraordinarily expensive.

Childhood is meant to grow someone into an adult, prolonging it for as long as possible is not fruitful for that civilization. Truthfully, most things accomplished in college can be done in high school. Education *needs* a reoptimization. Even more truthfully, a lot of things need reoptimization. Education precedes the optimizations of everything and anything that comes prior. Ray Dalio's chart of civilization cycles starts with a rise in education for a reason[119]. He covers factors like innovation, trade, military, and currency status to explain where empires typically rise and fall. Without a doubt, an increase in education precedes every other form of growth.

Modern education is full of left-brain tasks, where everything is segmented into topics with ways to prove you did them, where the evidence of completion has become more important than the understandings they were supposed to provide. Nothing connects to anything else. There's no big picture to be learned about life. Everything is broken into independent pieces, and never forms a holistic worldview.

Upbringing is the assembly of model assembly, and it's ultimately up to the user of the model to self-assemble. It can't be instructed into them, despite that some advice may be useful, and some guidance may be required, they must be inspired to take up their own mantle. There's no verbatim assembly instructions, just lessons to be learned from mistakes alongside rewards from success. Demonstration is not solving, you can't bestow a solution, as learning to solve integrals is an integral in itself. Children need hardship, and hardship isn't unnecessary difficulty, it's existential difficulty. Having no existential challenge to face just means they'll never learn to support themselves existentially, because your soul is your struggle.

On the topic of how to strike this balance between not being too aggressive, restrictive, lax, or anything else, there's no magic advice,

119. Ray Dalio. *Principles for Dealing with the Changing World Order*. Avid Reader Press, 2021

no one-size-fits-all approach. So writing hard-coded advice would be worthless. The nature of the balance is so intricate because it involves not only the relationship of multiple models of interaction, but also the development of young brains whose models aren't fully developed yet. The answer is that the balance is struck by communication and negotiation. Because that balance is an integral, which is why it's hard to solve. It takes two angles of approach to figure out what the true function is with any kind of precision, that's the process of the adult and child negotiating such instances. Both parties, parents and children, need to come to the table with honesty and sincerity. That's the only way for it to work. They have to ask each other difficult and honest questions that don't necessarily have answers. But in place of the lack of answers comes room for negotiation, and shared responsibility.

If the parents ever think that the burden falls one-sidedly on them, they're wrong and they're stunting the child's development. Parents need to invite their children to the table while giving them serious recognition, rather than a booster seat. It's this same invitation to the table that incentivizes children to follow rules, because they feel they're a part of the rule making process. If the rule making process has ignored them, they'll feel alienated, and they're not going to respect it. That's not even limited to children, it's why democracies have tended to be so effective.

The fruits of passion must be grown. Whatever grows is complex, and hard-earned. Tyranny has no garden. Complexity can't be easily mass-produced. The fruits of inspiration can't be commanded into existence for there to be any viable yield. This is how life has flourished on our planet for billions of years. Organisms of every kind had free rein in their environment, only living by the limits of what they had to compete with. While there were adversaries, there was no super-organism that tried to direct their growth and development by force. If there was, nothing would have worked out for them. Humans have become this for themselves to some degree, and the states we create to govern ourselves can have this effect. The end result of the fine line to walk between either guidance or dictation is no different than the free lessons granted by opponents through competition.

Intelligence is a value-finding tool. Unlike wild animals, whose function is more characterized by the environment they interact with, humans have learned to take advantage of potential itself in ways that strategize interactions for the sake of advantage. In this light, the survival skills of any other organism became a potential part of the broader human repertoire. In this truth lies a lesson, that children have these same instincts. One might then assume it would be most advantageous to put children in an environment where they can find ways of finding value. Because selection isn't about rote memorization in a school system. It's an adaptive competition. It's predicting the future. This reality isn't reflected by the nature of our current institutions. So-called educators decide what's valuable beforehand and put it in front of children, leaving no room for their most important instincts of assessment to develop and bloom. The future economy will suffer from this failure. Let's instead address these failings so that more than just the economy can benefit from an improved academic model. Learn from the past because there's wisdom in the past, but don't copy the past as we don't live there.

7.2 Points of Developmental Failure

For most mammals, if a pregnant mother eats a corn lily during a specific window of time where the eyes of the child are developing, their child will either come out as a cyclops with a dysfunctional eye, or have other abnormalities in their facial symmetry[120]. This happens because an alkaloid in the flower becomes absorbed into the child's developing body, and inhibits a developmental signaling process that creates the eyes while it happens. There's near endless examples of things that can cause these kinds of developmental disruptions within the womb, and the theme of this pattern being detrimental to child development follows through in childhood. Toxins, poisons, and all sorts of mishaps can happen to stunt or damage part of their growth. At some point this becomes an easily understood phenomenon, as it represents a disruption within the extreme complexity of the biological realm. Where many seem ignorant, is how this might happen with the brain independent of any foreign chemicals or agonists. In the modern day, we find ourselves learning these lessons through bad incentives, bad ideas, and ideologies.

Schools give terrible advice, like being told to follow the rules of people who either aggressively, or patronizingly, wave them in your

120. John P Incardona et al. *The Teratogenic Veratrum Alkaloid Cyclopamine Inhibits Sonic Hedgehog Signal Transduction*. Development, 1998

face. They teach students that work is purely independent, and even when it's not you're quite often stuck working with people who make for bad partners. In the real world, you can just fire them. There's no one any child ought to be forced to work with should that child feel someone doesn't deserve their partnership. Judging who to work with is a valuable skill to have, yet it's completely thrown out in the context of schooling because of some supposed form of fairness, but this is just unfair to the hardest workers. I would argue that a child needs to practice weeding out bad employees, bad partners, and failed cooperators should they want to become successful in life. This needs to happen in their schooling years, otherwise they won't master the habit.

Providing children with a good place to learn means providing them with a place to make mistakes that are dangerous enough for them to be responsible for. As without both appropriate and evolving forms of danger, there's nothing for them to optimize internal order for. You avoid danger by wisening up, and you wisen up by learning to avoid making mistakes. That's the only basis for stoking the flames of maturation in general. One needs only to provide children with a sufficiently disordered environment such that optimizing internal order is necessary in order to rise to some occasion. If the environment is so ordered that nothing can ever go wrong then the resulting outcome will produce individuals who can't work with anything less than perfect conditions. More realistically, children need to grow into becoming the reason things don't go wrong in the first place. This would be an appropriate hedge against any future calamities.

Likewise, with a dangerous environment must come the possibility of failure. There should be no guarantees of a diploma, or any other bureaucratic certificate. There's no guarantee of a prize you get just by passing classes. You need to make something of yourself. That's the accomplishment. Memorizing, or even understanding, the discoveries of famous people throughout history, is not enough to work with. Even having practical experience applying your knowledge is not an accomplishment until you can wield it as a personal craft. The finishing of an education, an upbringing, must be done by an actual contribution of that person to their own life, and to those around them.

The nature of the debate, of saying you *care* about children, is infinitely recursive. Which is why it's so prone to becoming safetyist. But ironically, you need to expose children to some levels of risk and danger. They need to learn to experience and navigate these challenges. They need responsibility to help them grow. Otherwise they become adults who aren't skilled at handling risk.

Caring doesn't mean keeping them free from harm, it means giving them a solid baseline to grow from. That's what books are for, that's the purpose of sharing knowledge. Caring means ingraining in them everything they could possibly use in the face of the real harm they may someday face. Which means experience in dealing with harm and risk. I would much rather raise my children to be prepared for a war that I hope never comes than to pretend like war will never happen. To those who argue that they simply want to protect children from harm, or from bad people who shouldn't be running a school, children need to protect themselves from harm. Schools ran or operated by bad people won't survive, because no one wants to see their child abused.

It's not the blatant acts of harm that need worrying about, it's the insidious ones. Pipelining children into puberty blockers and then onto a surgery table permanently destroys their life. Adults forcefully making decisions on a child's behalf while repeatedly saying *it's what's best for the children*, despite the fact that it's impossible to know what is or isn't best for them, just makes them sound like cult members.

Even on building regulations, I would push back on anything that requires expensive infrastructure as it just becomes a gatekeeping mechanism, elevators need not be necessary for every school. There's value in maintaining accessibility for the handicapped, but there's more value in adding unavoidable physical difficulty for the able-bodied. Exceptions need not make for rules that enable laziness in those that would benefit from continually climbing walls and ladders. In general, there's value in creating physical resilience instead of technological dependency.

A school aimed at making its students employees of some overarching industrial apparatus is ultimately just a vampire with predatory intentions, as that apparatus then completely controls the levers of that child's future. To raise children independent of the control mechanisms of others should be the goal of any upbringing. Yet somehow this doesn't happen *and* education takes too long.

If you're reading this book, there's a strong chance that you've seen many times within your own education instances of the worst students simultaneously being the worst behaved. I'd bet some fraction of you that this applies to, then saw that in order to get them to behave, some teacher decided to reward them for finally not doing one small thing incorrectly. Maybe this worked, but only in small ways, and it required never-ending rewards. Yet it offered no benefit to this person's accomplishments, it was simply the horrible student who was now in control of the teacher. It's also my understanding that many of these students cost schools the most money, as they demand the most attention. But this is backwards from how things ought to work.

In a classroom, this is insulting to the hardest working students. This is thievery of reward, resources, and attention that's deserved by the best students with the best behavior. Attention and the dignity of control should be handed to the best performing students. The most money should be spent on the best performing students. It should be allocated where it sees the best return for all of society. It would make for an improved incentive structure to simply show students that if they want attention, allocated resources, and reward, that they should work for it. Any other kind of incentive becomes a race to the bottom, where all the worst people are rewarded in ways they don't deserve, and those who are deserving of reward are left wondering where they might raise their own children someday, because the place they happen to find themselves certainly isn't suitable.

Being in an environment where other students are constantly given pity for complaining about their problems is actually bad for the good children. A lot of people have problems, if you want to make absolutely sure they drag you down then continually use them to make other people feel bad for you. In the process of rewarding this behavior, good students get the wrong idea about the reward structure, and what they need in order to succeed, because they're young and easily influenced by whatever behavior is supposedly rewarding. It's horrible for the bad children too, pity is poison no matter the context. A class should not be held back by its worst student, neither in pace nor by incentive.

Across both the US and Europe, there's the problem that committing a crime while underage doesn't always lead to a proper punishment. This allows the worst parents, with the worst children, to be rewarded for their terrible behavior. The only strategy to hedge against this is to raise your children to be equally as violent and atrocious, which is a terrible answer to this problem. It's impossible to raise children under the real standard of the law while telling them the laws don't apply to them because they're a minor, or that laws won't apply to their worst behaving peers.

Schools need clear rules on self-defence. Some have the wildly unfair policy that if you're attacked by someone else, you receive punishment. Others will dish out punishment only if you defend yourself. Self-defence is a normal part of life, and should be a normal part of any school that needs to grapple with violence. Students should never be afraid to step in to stop an attack from a rabid individual, any school where this fear is more prominent than the willingness to stand up for someone has no business calling itself a community, that's a prison.

The school system should not be a source of misery for children, yet child suicidality spikes at the start of every school year[121], as opposed to adult suicidality which is consistent throughout the year [122]. The school system should be a refuge for children to make a better future for themselves, rather than an incubator to wish they never have one. One should be able to leave children alone without adults without having any problems, that's normal and desirable behavior. If anything, a school is the most important place to do this, to be without a constant watcher. To inhibit the schools from doing so is equally as inhibitive to the children. Give them a problem to solve on their own, and let them make their own rules. Saying they always need a babysitter is just an expensive regulation that makes sure children don't properly develop. Children finding good friends is a necessary developmental step in their lives, and it can't happen under constant observation.

Whether at home, or in school, children can't be locked inside a psychological prison, especially if their peers have freedom. Especially if a child wants to know truth above all else. Lies would only become a point of developmental failure that insidiously destroys them from the inside. In contrast to the people who survived the extreme dangers of WWII and caused the largest baby boom in history, safetyism seems to be antithetical to raising children that then go on to make families.

---

121. Youngran Kim, Trudy Millard Krause, and Scott D Lane. *Trends and Seasonality of Emergency Department Visits and Hospitalizations for Suicidality Among Children and Adolescents in the US from 2016 to 2021.* JAMA Network Open, 2023
122. Sally C Curtin, Matthew F Garnett, and Farida B Ahmad. *Provisional Numbers and Rates of Suicide by Month and Demographic Characteristics: United States, 2021.* NCHS Vital Statistics Rapid Release Reports, 2022

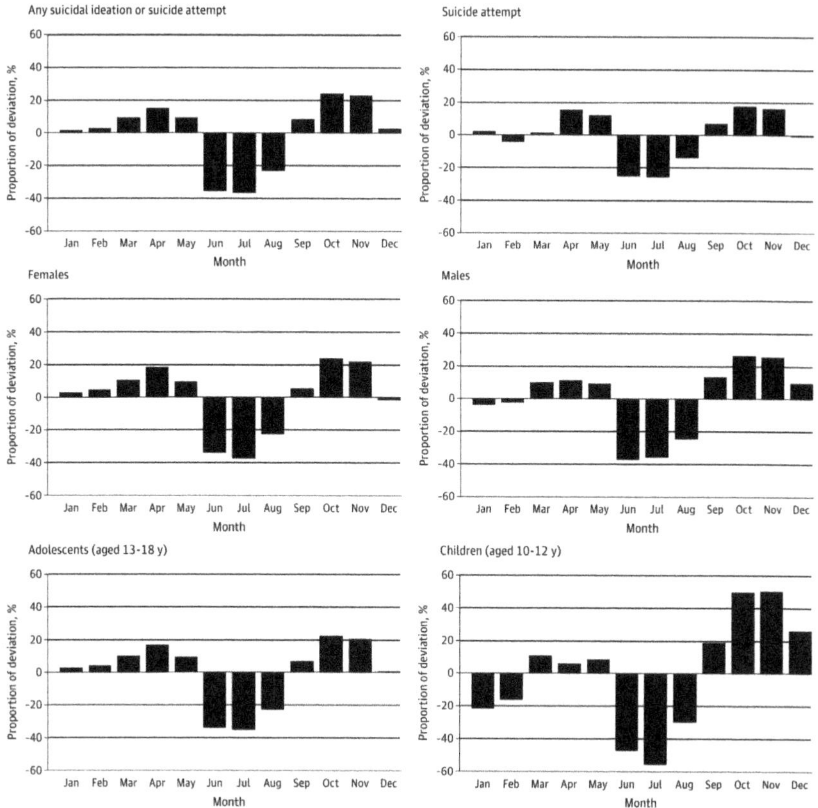

Figure 7: Adapted from Figure 3 of Kim Y, Krause TM, Lane SD. Trends and Seasonality of Emergency Department Visits and Hospitalizations for Suicidality Among Children and Adolescents in the US from 2016 to 2021. JAMA Network Open. 2023;6(7):e2324183. Licensed under CC BY 4.0

Children need to be exposed to danger and risk in order to learn why it's important to pass on their culture and heritage. How do parents become so disconnected from what's actually good for their children? Well, it's likely because the school system has gotten between the two of them, like an invasive pool of entropy.

There should be no scrolling with young kids. Screens can be used for things like movies, and shows, where the story telling is worthy of being called a form of art. But both social media, with its endless scroll, as well as broadcast television, with its never-ending forms of mental junk-food, do nothing but waste their creative potential. An agreement across all parents of a school should have the expectation, as a baseline, that children can visit the homes of others from the same institution and not need to worry about this being a problem. These addictive interfaces offer dopaminergic problems that disrupt proper brain development, it's no different than a child getting a drug addiction, or a gambling problem. There should be a social ceremony to such events. Games with microtransactions should be avoided at all costs, these things are even worse than drugs.

Drugs, pollution, and unsanitary environments can all have detrimental effects on the cognitive development of a child, and it's because someone *is* a child that they're at greater risk from these problems. A grown adult is much more capable of handling these kinds of environments, biologically, because their developmental phase is finished. Likewise, the ideas that are shoved down the throats of young children over our climate, race, sexuality, politics, and any of many other early mental injections on certain topics, are way too extreme, and seem to have a bad overall impact on the outcomes of those individuals. In fact, there's better reasons to leave the political leanings, gaslighting, and other nonsense out of their early development. But there's problems with saying this and not offering a replacement, if you stand for nothing then you'll fall for anything. So what exactly should this void be filled with? Western culture, Western history, Western principles, Western values, and Western religion.

Birth control, antidepressants, and SSRIs, specifically, seem to be problematic for young women. A plethora of older women, who have gone through their own adolescence being completely drugged, have spoken up online, en masse, about the strangeness of this part of our society. Women on various forms of birth control exhibit abnormal signatures of stress, have problems with trauma, and can deal with a host of other serious problems that otherwise can't be easily characterized. It can't be good in the long term. There's nothing normal about drugging large swaths of young women, and we shouldn't expect society to behave normally when those girls grow up.

People are doing with these so-called mental disorders what they've always done with astrology. There's no problem that children can't solve on their own when given time, a community, freedom, a role model, and religion where appropriate. Mental disease is just the unsolvable problem that sets up a bureaucracy to be in charge of your mind. People with severe problems need good influences, fair rules, better diet and exercise, and to stop accepting the lies that they've swallowed.

To those who may not like this message, is denying these so-called disorders any worse than introducing your child to gender ideology? We've come full circle to the point where the ideologies spawned out of the school system, and its supposed intersection with psychology, are what's now introducing bigger problems than existed prior. You may as well introduce better problems for yourself to have. Or better yet, make problems that design their own solutions the same way life has designed itself thus far. Sex and drug education should include the topic of puberty blockers and hormones that are sold online without regulation, and how people typically get roped into taking them while believing there's no consequences for doing so. It should also be primarily about family-building, and the responsibility of pregnancy and raising children. Centering this education around sex has only destigmatized its misuse to the point where children aren't putting healthy expectations around its place in their future.

How many times throughout your evolutionary history do you think your ancestors sat in a chair for 8 hours a day, while doing work that provided no benefit for their own future? If the answer is a lot, then you're truly an aristocrat, and unfortunately this book wasn't written with you and your history in mind. As the rest of you may already understand, memorizing nonsense, and performing chores of endless busywork are a disadvantage. They only waste the time that would otherwise bring someone benefit. So why would you disadvantage your children by wasting their time? Kids are hyperactive because they can learn fast and do a lot. It's not abnormal and it doesn't require medication. You don't have a learning disability, there's just nothing valuable to learn from your environment. Hyperactivity is an advantage to be wielded, not a problem that needs to be suppressed.

Religion and community can replace this newly emerged industry of therapy because that's what this always was, this is an inherently religious territory. There need not be a class of mental directors that claims divine providence over anything psychological, but if they do then it's their religion. There's no epidemic of mental illness that hasn't already existed throughout human history, and by far the average person didn't need such institutionalized interventions to live their daily life.

Any medical mandate is a violation of religious freedom. States have mandated vaccines as requirements for attending school, but it's not the job of the government to do this. Independent groups are capable of judging which vaccines make sense, which they want their children to have, and which ones they trust. If a decision involves someone's survival strategy, then it involves their religion. If it's truly so wise to receive a medical procedure, then people will elect to do so freely. Likewise, if the public schools were so great there wouldn't need to be laws mandating their use, people would attend them freely. Demanding immediate compliance isn't for anyone's benefit. It's the whim of a childish captain steering a ship they have no business touching. Compliance, like trust and faith, needs to be earned. It can never be dictated.

Doctors, especially pediatricians, should need to state their religion through a publicly available religious statement. The last thing any parent wants is a pediatrician asking their child what their gender pronouns are when this isn't the kind of interaction they expected. These things need to be explicitly advertised, and can't simply fall into the realm of neither opinion nor insidious games. Doctors who wish to do this need to advertise that this is how they operate. Doctors who lie about how they converse and interact with young children need to be subjected to lawsuits over religious violations.

The thing with schools keeping secrets from parents, especially regarding something like personal pronouns, is that it's extraordinarily subversive of parenting itself. Children are naturally going to have secrets they keep from their parents, and there's naturally going to be a few things about their life that the parents won't know about. But a school shouldn't be harboring secrets of the child against the parents, it's become a form of anti-natalist behavior that, in the worst case scenario, ends up sterilizing and mutilating children.

A better alternative is to make an environment where secrets don't need to be kept in the first place, and the secret to that is to not constantly view children as only having the potential to be criminals. An invitation to the table of adulthood is a must if you want children to ever find their way there. The school wouldn't act as a prison, and parents wouldn't act as gatekeepers, but instead as role models. Children would be too interested in developing their own skill sets for the future they envision that they don't feel the need to lash out because they're respected and presented with opportunity, and healthy competition, in an environment where hostility is kept in check with civility. One can alleviate the problems that cause these symptoms in the first place through honesty and trust, as they reward in kind.

Usually, when someone does a horrible job raising children, if their own children don't fix the problems they inherit, they either die, or don't go on to have children of their own. Their terrible behavior dies with them. But with teachers, we ignore this phenomenon and instead push some of the most toxic and lonely individuals in front of children, who may then radicalize them, or worse, with bitter and spiteful ideologies. It's a subversion of the students' ability to survive. It's a vicious cycle, and can likely be stopped by reducing the number of faculty while allowing children to take on less spoon-fed work on their own as they age. Public school parents would have direct feedback from their children of who the craziest teachers are, if there are any at all. By cutting these out using the First Amendment, the chances of success for young children increase by only dealing with the influence of those who actually like children, and those who tend to raise them well.

Too many schools have become extremist indoctrination centers that have nothing to do with liberalism. Yet they try stealing that word and wearing its skin as if no one notices that the eyeholes don't line up correctly. Cycles that reinforce themselves in the minds of the people running the schools, and strange consequences of the values that are instilled in the youth in an ever-increasing manner, are resulting in a constant increase in either extremism, for those who buy into it, or defiance for those who dare to disagree. Alongside this, the environmental fanatics push a constant nihilism that indoctrinates children into believing the world is going to end in 10 years. In fact, they've been demonstrably predicting the world will end in 10 years since at least the 1960s, and possibly much earlier than that.

Children tend to easily fall into a kind of environmental worship, a reversion to a time of animism, played out over nihilistic interpretations of their life and world. The impact of environmental fanaticism is a massive depressive wave that convinces young people that their future won't exist, and prevents them from properly planning for the long term. Some go as far as thinking the solution to this problem is to not reproduce.

This vicious cycle continues to make schools into environments that are subtly more extreme with every passing generation. It's the people who feel the most passionate about these topics that then go on to become teachers, who instill the same religious motivations and values within their classroom that they represent throughout their life. But whether you believe these to be good or bad ideas, you must admit that the truth lies in the outcomes, the success or failure, of the schools that represent these ideas. Either outcome would be visible through the competition spawned from the free practice of religion.

Giving appropriate counters to young children to deal with these disaster narratives is a must. The last 60^{+} years have introduced a myriad of mental monstrosities that can be used for the sake of psychologically manipulating the young. It's propaganda, and it comes in predictable flavors. It's worth learning from these general examples to set children up with the appropriate counter-narratives that become tools able to debunk these forms of nonsense.

There's no meaningful purpose in putting massive problems onto the shoulders of children, such as telling them they need to throw their lives away to advocate for extreme environmentalist causes that they themselves have no way of solving, especially if they've never been able to navigate through modern atmospheric models on their own. It's too heavy for them and they don't understand it. People who do this today only do it to manipulate. It's no different in nature than forcing children to become child soldiers for an ideological cause. Such a method would only be required under the most serious circumstances. You won't need any message heavier than telling them to have children when they're too young to understand anything else.

But this also leaves them vulnerable to other people toting causes they claim are larger than life. So it's important to inform them that anyone claiming you need to care about something for the sake of the world, future, climate, or whatever else is only spewing lies that they themselves don't even understand. They're luring you in. Even if they themselves don't know it, these people are vampires. The best defence against this kind of cult propaganda is to give children a meaning that's also larger than life itself, of which they gain greatly from. Aiming to have a family and children can be that larger than life goal, as it has deeper instinctual roots than environmental worship.

The stories of these stories, that so easily propagandize children into nihilism, can then be used to prevent such nihilism, while also teaching about those same topics. They can be a tool to help children understand propaganda, and the addictivity of negativity too. They're even a good lesson on the scaling of negativity across media and the internet. A good storyteller could even get them to believe it at first, then debunk it in front of them to demonstrate their own proclivity towards believing negativity.

Young people are the ones who build the future. To convince young children that their future will be destroyed by some impending doomsday event only destroys the futures those children are meant to uphold. Giving young children an economics book and allowing them the chance to understand the superabundance of nature and how value creation brought about the success they see around them would easily provide the highest overall return to society of any piece of information that one could take in at a young age.

There's now a push for a new kind of extremism. The anti-AI nihilism, where people constantly dread the takeover of our planet by robots. It's the same thing, existential dread over an unclear path to the future. It's not going to happen, AI isn't going to achieve superhuman-levels of intelligence in the near future. AI will continue to offer impressive practical utility for individuals to orchestrate for themselves, but it's not going to progress beyond that on its own. Despite being an amazing piece of technology, these models can't achieve anything outside the bounds of the information they've been trained on. We've been crafted over billions of years, our instincts are innate, our reactions are instantaneous, yet discovering new knowledge is always slow and difficult. It will always be difficult for AI as well. There's no shortcuts in being able to solve an integral when you also need to figure out what derivative to even integrate in the first place. Beliefs aren't made, they're discovered, and LLMs aren't belief-discovering machines, they aren't able to extend beyond the information they were trained on. They're a reverse-engineering of intelligence, and what comes out of them must be something that went in to begin with. LLMs aren't becoming intelligent, they're learning from the works of beings that already are. Copying a process isn't the same as inventing it. As more time passes, more people will realize this isn't something that will be operated independent of humans. Stupidity is and has always been a bigger threat than intelligence, pretending otherwise only enables those pushing these lies to monopolize this technology in the future. Enabling greater intellectual ability through the widespread use of LLMs will cause more peace and prosperity than anything that's ever come before.

In general, these extremist causes tend to cause false centralizations around incorrect ideas. However, hindsight also shows these tend to become uniquely visible mistakes that others then become capable of learning from. The lessons offered through these cult-like societal structures are what people are most in need of in the modern day, a more stable paradigm for raising children. An accumulation of such individuals presents an incredibly valuable opportunity for anyone capable of learning from such mistaken consensus. Equally worse as the mistakes of these groups, would be to stare into the same abyss, living a life of endlessly arguing against someone else's continual mistakes only presents such a thing as yet another mistake itself.

Not enough people come out of the school system understanding that communism is a failed idea. Which makes sense, they haven't even gotten the chance to participate in capitalism. Communism looks great on paper, but its real-world implementation is disastrous. People genuinely rallying in favor of this delusion indicate they've never been able to take their ideas off paper, they need real-world exposure outside the confines of a classroom. Let them live out communism as kids, let them see it fail. Clearly this needs to be done as part of their developmental process. I think they just haven't gotten to try it for themselves. So if they do, they'll probably gain great wisdom. Communism would be a stupid mistake for an adult, but a great mistake for a child.

7.3 Grading Metrics

> An interesting point that conservative writer Samuel Francis has made, is that for the first time in history a majority of the world's population operated in cities and in large organizations, like factories or militaries, where it was physically impossible to know everyone. So they had to develop impersonal criteria [of judgement], which then created a system based off test taking as an easy way to determine personal quality. The problem with this system is that any skills which can't be measured on a test such as courage, wisdom, and morality get left out of elite selection. This

> then creates a society which is foolish, immoral, and cowardly.
>
> Rudyard Lynch's *Understanding Modern Civilization*

There's no metric more oversimplified than a school grade. In places where these measurements have infiltrated, it's best to have them replaced by something more respectable. Just as complex measurements of complex environments can easily replace statistics being applied to measurements used in the same oversimplified context, the modeling of a child's complexity can be better represented by either a chart, or tree, of questions. In enforcing that every child be compared at scale, both their value and abilities have been oversimplified. Instead of subjecting children to oversimplified comparisons, it's worth more for them to have an appropriately complex interpretation of their own value, so they themselves may have and learn to use a more complex interpretation of the work they produce. Upbringing ought to be for the sake of children, not for whatever administrators care about these measurements at scale and can only ever interpret a single unidimensional value out of 100 to represent performance in what are supposed to be the most prominent complexities of the most valuable things across all civilization. You can't raise children at scale, it's a personal endeavor to be done at a personal level. Analyzing children's performance at scale is worthless. One must examine the philosophical and religious underpinnings being used to raise them in detail. Otherwise, you only compare students across uniform paradigms, which is just one more way that grades become a useless measure, as there's no such uniformity in reality. There are no simplicities.

Despite the infinite potential for growth that people possess, commonly used grading metrics seem to only work to apply limitations to the measurements of that growth through oversimplification. Which functions to cull intellect rather than harness it. A single written letter is the most empty accomplishment one could possibly think of. It's philosophically limiting, developmentally stunting, and that's basically what the entire world uses.

What have grades done, out of the millions of data points generated? What have they been used for? They represent a student's achievements, if you can even call them that. They don't feel like achievements, they feel like a waste of time. What kind of good have they done in the world? They supposedly imply how to get students to score better grades, but this hollow treadmilling may as well be independent of actual ability. They've been used as a naive measurement to check if some microdifference in teaching, from within laughably inflexible schooling paradigms, makes any difference in people's ability to do repetitive busywork. At best they represent either a difference, or a lack thereof, in effort across students who have absolutely nothing else that's stressful in their lives. Whereas people who put in a lot of effort, only to get bad grades, may as well represent a life filled with stress, but that's not what these measurements are meant to indicate so there's no such interpretation offered in most cases. Their own uniformity betrays their utility.

What's the purpose of a definition or measure of intelligence if it forces people into unintelligent habits? Is that intelligent? If something that's meant to measure intelligence fulfills an ultimately unintelligent role in people's lives, then that measurement isn't valuable. If there's something inherently stupid about an assessment of intelligence, it just shows how error-prone oversimplifications of this topic can be. The best understanding of intelligence would coincide with the best implementations for giving children a successful future, regardless of their level of intelligence. Treating people well means they'll run through brick walls for you, inspiring them to do so means they'll reap the benefits of their own maximum capacity.

You might think that not every test is a supposed measurement of intelligence. You might think that it measures *performance*. Perhaps you think that it's indicative of *effort*. But all these things come from one place, and it's not your left shoulder blade. It's also not your kidneys, tendons, nor nose. These tools are tests of your brain and its function. While I disagree with their utility, and any supposed determinism one might link to supposed measures of intelligence, the function of the structure of these tests is clear. They act to probe the function of a brain, and the dedication it can provide to change its own outcomes.

Where this assessment goes wrong is that to probe a brain is only one side of its functionality, what a brain itself is capable of probing is the other side of this coin. Questions are an endless path towards insight, and provide an inherently self-correcting path that leads away from extremes. At different stages of growth one can answer questions, form questions, and seek out difficult to find questions in order to get ahead. Even some animals can answer questions, so why is this so often the only measure used to describe our own children? The growth of the questions asked by young children are more indicative of their ability than any grade ever could be, and the practice of this art does more to prepare them for the real world than anything else ever could.

If education lasts more than 10 years, why are grades only measuring things within the span of a quarter or semester? There are no true long-term measurements. The short-term nature of these measurements dictates the amount of time it could take to go from bad to great, or vice versa, but never indicates any long-upheld streak of excellence. GPA is even only relevant at a single school, and is even *more* oversimplified. Grades are not the best measure we have at our disposal.

The concept of *failing* in the modern educational paradigm is linked to a bad grade and it's the worst possible outcome. One must usually go through an entire year, all over again, just to make a second attempt. Yet people need failed attempts to progress at just about anything, so this seems like wasted time is built into the system. Everyone should fail, people need to try, and try again until they succeed. They need failure to teach them the lessons that success only hides, and if your students aren't failing then they aren't being appropriately challenged.

If the only thing your kids can earn is a grade, then they earn nothing. The process of earning nothing teaches them to stand for nothing, because they must instead mold themselves to the likings of whatever person might be in charge of their classroom that year, which means they'll fall for anything too. This latent misincentive structure has made for the perfect breeding ground for parasitic ideologies by first emptying their heads through nonsensical levels of conformity, then demoralizing children by refusing them the chance to gain any real skills. A child can do nothing to join the real world, despite how qualified they may be, until they reach an age where they're allowed to. The next step of indoctrination is using their frustration with these forced shortcomings, and glass ceilings, to convince them that all of their problems are something that's wrong with them and not a failure of the school as an institution. Which leaves many young people in the perfect state of mind to be misled by just about anyone who comes into their life, often times professors of some obscure niche who feel their work has some kind of underappreciated significance despite never producing any meaningful impact.

A test is not an accomplishment and neither is a grade, measurement isn't motivation. Children are grinding away for the sake of their own ambition, and they shouldn't be grinding for nothing. Their grind should show them a light long before they reach the end of the tunnel. A worthless grind is just an extremely frustrating experience. These oversimplifications don't contribute to society, but the child is supposed to. So let's instead contribute to children by giving them something worth doing, and a decent way of measuring their own growth, rather than wasting their time on forever-tests.

After more than a decade of schoolwork, most children end up wondering just what they would actually be able to put on a resume in order to stand out. Some that think they're smart might put on their student class presidency, or club participation, maybe some volunteer work, or political activism. But these undoubtedly feel like empty shells to anyone who could have achieved much more in the same amount of time had their school system actually offered worthwhile opportunities. Young people know this, and it only harbors feelings of inadequacy. The school system only offers empty achievements that exist within a bubble too childish for people of their age, it's extremely infantilizing. The point is to give children something they can use to represent themselves professionally. Giving them confidence to have a professional attitude. Merit that stands at a professional level. Accomplishments that lay a foundation for lifelong learning. Philosophy that adapts to the ever-changing tides of technology. So how can this be accomplished?

Trying to out-engineer biology is foolish, as is trying to make a test better than natural selection. We don't need to use life and death as a means of selection, we can use what nature already gave us, the ability to question *anything*. A tree of questions can branch out infinitely, there can even be multiple trees if a student wishes to organize it as such. It can organize questions, and save progress. Its creation can be an art, and how it's expanded upon can be the same. Answers can be short form, long form, code, or even schematics, because it's able to be made in whatever format the student feels like using. Every characteristic of how this tree is formed, and maintained, shows a lot about the student who's making it. It displays the nature of their choices, organization, depth, and any other factor you might look to understand about someone. Without any metrics being directly available, it explains more than a report card ever could.

Give *human* feedback. Determine advantages, disadvantages, flaws, things that might have been missed, unexpected benefits, the difficulty in finishing some project, anything as long as it's not a single letter. Are you so much of a caveman that you would make a single mouth-sound to indicate the merits of your own child? If there was no good way of raising intelligent children without grades, then we wouldn't be here. Intelligence didn't come about through grading schemes. Grades are not an end-point measurement, they represent an arbitrary middle-point that's absolutely worthless in assessing long-term changes and success.

Even amongst the various attempts at communicating with animals, such as teaching sign language to primates, it would seem that animals are incapable of asking questions. Questioning is a uniquely human process, and therefore it would make for an excellent skill to practice should one want to become a more impressive human. Above all else, the nature of the questions asked, by any individual, shows the potential of their future. As assessing them on what they can ask, not just what they can answer, is a better modeling of human nature than a lone representation of some overly-specific mechanical function, or rote memorization.

Grades are a selection mechanism we've made for ourselves, but we can't be so irresponsible with such things. Otherwise, children themselves won't have any children. This is without a doubt a linchpin in the downfall of the West. I'm sorry to inform you, the implementations of measurements for intelligence are stupid. It's the first principle on which the schools are failing. The actions taken to achieve a grade nor their worth as measurements are neither complex nor meaningful. We've traded away a child's necessity to model their environment for uniformity tailored to the ease of teachers.

When, in any kind of test, are you required to disagree? Is knowing the right time to disagree with something, or to not believe what's being told to you, a form of intelligence? Tests don't involve potential deception, they also only ever represent hypothetically perfect scenarios, which you'll never find in real life. They also don't lead you in uncertain directions the way that life always does. Intelligence isn't able to be properly captured by these tests, and not all things worth having in life can even be encapsulated under the umbrella term of intelligence.

We have something better, and that's reputation. Genuine character judgement tells you a lot about a person, and that's a collective trait formed through evolution. We've reinvented the wheel of personal judgement. Nature has already handed us, by covenant of evolution, a means of judging each other's worth on a multitude of scales. It's not only someone's character, it's what shines *through* their character. Such as someone's ability to actually judge someone else accurately.

We don't need grades for determining the quality of a person. Maintaining the importance of reputation in young people is the best thing you can do for them, as both groups and individuals. I'd rather use a presentation of work as a means of motivating students to compete with their peers, while also displaying the work that they're actually doing in front of their peers, and parents, who can openly judge for themselves. Letting work speak for itself, rather than through the lens of an oversimplification, preserves actual human judgement across people, which in turn makes them feel that their own judgement isn't worthless compared to some *letter* on a piece of paper.

Grades are also a form of surveillance. If you're going to surveil then surveil something worth knowing. Grant the person being surveilled an incentive to improve what's being surveilled, as they themselves would benefit from looking for better avenues to judge themselves by. A presentation of work allows for just that, whereas inflexibility offers psychological imprisonment.

In the field of analytical science, where detected signals are measured, and processed, there's a phrase not unlike saying there's no free lunch, *there's no such thing as a universal detector*. It comments on the constantly disagreeable nature of nature, that there's no one single law, concept, or principle that can take advantage of every molecule or particle. The art of detection works best when aimed at measuring a very specific phenomenon, UV absorption for example. To really understand some specific entity, you'd have to measure multiple properties, so you would need multiple modes of detection. In order to feasibly measure multiple dimensions, across a population of many entities, you must limit either the number of properties to measure or the number of analytes being measured. In the process of measuring one dimension across many things you sacrifice depth, as well as specific analytes that can't be detected through whichever lone methodology you choose. In measuring many properties of something you sacrifice gaining the same information about many other related species, because at some point you have to decide what to measure and which pieces of information to forego for the sake of understanding anything at all. In assuming grades to be a universal detector of intelligence, you face the same dilemma, there's no such thing as a universal detector. Even more, the physical reality of analytical measurements are limited by the same tradeoffs as cognitive measurements because this is the same emergent problem being solved in a different scenario. The same solution exists regardless of the context, as do all the same tradeoffs. There's always a tradeoff between depth and scale. The more depth a measurement grants, the less scalable any comparison becomes. If this wasn't the case, if every property of any chemical compound was representative of every other property of that same compound, then the rules of chemistry as we know it wouldn't exist. In making deeper comparative measurements of individuals, the results would begin to represent their unique characteristics, they would approach becoming more absent of uniformly comparable ground at scale. Some people are undeniably smarter than others, but a difference in capacity isn't necessarily the same as a difference in capability.

Even at the end of all this, some opponents of the idea might ask then *how else can we compare students at a large scale*? How can we measure a country's performance? The answer is simple, you don't want to. That's a stupid thing to measure. Evolution didn't give us a way of doing this through any mechanism other than competition, so it's probably a bad idea. If grades aren't good measurements, then academic comparisons aren't good competitions.

To oppose this still, one might add that we need global rankings, and ways of comparing people. Well, the best way to compare people is 1:1, or small groups to each other. To fully compare every individual to every other individual in the world, at scale, would require the exact same template of judgement. But the template would then counteract any free-flowing format able to be used, to solve this problem at scale is to fail the individual students. There's no point in comparing hundreds of millions of children using an extremely poor measure. The larger the groups, the worse the individual comparisons are.

We don't use grades for adults when assessing a business for its quality. If you do anything short of reading everything you can about it, then you're bound to make a bad investment by partnering with them. But for assessing children, there are people who believe five letters make an accurate representation of the entirety of their abilities.

Testing, as it operates, assumes the culmination of all human evolution can be measured in a testing environment, and that the test will accurately represent evolutionary development. Evolution has decided what intelligence actually is, it's also decided what true mental function and capacity are worth keeping around. To believe otherwise means you're telling me there's some test, that humans designed over a small period of time, that accurately measures the culmination of all human evolution better than millions of years of natural selection of hominids? The very frontier, the bleeding edge, of human ingenuity? Nah. There's no measure of ingenuity other than what someone actually invents. There's nothing that measures people when they're in danger, because you can't consistently fake an emergency. There's nothing to indicate any single person's effect on the people around them, which they themselves may not even realize.

People weren't selected for having to perform some homogeneous oversimplified task, alongside 30 peers of their own age, to be compared down to some ridiculous level of detail where nothing needs to be determined beforehand. You don't determine how to do it, you're supposed to only perform the role of a cog in a machine. You don't determine how you might design a contraption to make it easier to do such a thing for the rest of your life. You don't contemplate materials, workload, tradeoffs, or cost. There's no reason why you're even doing it at all, as your motivation may as well not be genuine, it's faked. You perform the final end of some calculation, or writing task, that you have no need for, and no desire to latch onto, and that's supposed to indicate how well your brain functions. I might sooner question the brain functioning of the people who design these tests, and genuinely believe in them, before I care to score my own performance by one. This age in which people believe in the value of these tests is easily the first time in history where such an ungodly amount of widespread oversimplifications have accumulated, like brush waiting for a fire. There's never been a need in your evolutionary history for your survival to depend on such a measurement, such a petty function. To believe this measurement holds the absolute value that it's so often attributed to is more foolish than any failing grade. Much like these tests, we don't connect the need for survival to the mundane tasks that are put in front of children. The nature of these tests aren't linked to a true need.

The institution that a child attends is the framework upon which their motivation can take hold of their ambition, and grow their skill set into a worthwhile contribution to society. Schools with hard ceilings, both in age-based groupings, strict requirement-based levels, as well as oversimplified topics of study, offer nothing but a steel dome to imprison the ambitions of flight. Because the paradigm of the school systems works to control children, rather than to foster them. Grades don't measure risk-taking ability. They don't measure the success of bad choices you didn't make, and after grades are averaged with other grades they're not even indicative of effort.

There's opportunity that vague standing creates. It gives room for ambition to grow. The constant comparison through test scores, through everyone in the world being tested the same, just beats the ambition out of you. Because you're only being measured in one dimension, and not in being able to find a dimension to be measured by. Children are being measured in assessing some specific form of value, rather than in finding value itself. It's a false test, it doesn't reflect the nature of your virtues. There's no need for this failed measurement to be a paradigm of childhood selection, the world has more to gain from dreamers and their implementations.

The constant comparison is unhealthy, the tests are stupid, the results aren't indicative of value, and the currently used *end-point* measurements are worthless. There's also problems of too many people coming out of these institutions believing there's always just one answer to any given problem, which is the sign of a philosophically bankrupt individual. Grades act as a mode of selection, defining both good and bad, which is what religion is meant to govern. If your measure of success isn't cooperating well enough with reality, it's a bad measure of everything, and eventually becomes societally dysgenic.

Does the likelihood of someone getting a good grade correlate with their belief in the value behind that grade? To some, getting good grades might just be a step along the ladder of the achievements they see playing out for themselves in life. So they decide to play by the rules. For others, grades might inhibit the skills they could otherwise gain in order to make a better life for themselves, due to the constrained nature of the education system. In the latter case, not only are grades a bad measure of intelligence, they can also be a detriment to someone's wellbeing. So what's the point of measuring that grade? If someone's reliant on what they learn, and not their own potential for doing great work, then a so-called *measurement* of intelligence undermines the practiced application of their own intelligence. It's ultimately a religious ladder, and if you don't believe in its value then you're not being properly measured. Even worse is when this is done at larger scales in countries where communism comes into play, because in such an environment everything is often based around tests.

Typical schoolwork only offers questions for the sake of answering them. This curtails the curiosity of a child from being able to ask questions, or formulate their own problems. It also gives them a hard ceiling that they don't typically surpass, even if they can. But why should someone stop at being able to answer everything perfectly? Why should someone accept an artificially imposed ceiling for measurement? Why is schoolwork only ever for practice and not for exploration? One should go beyond whatever limits they can. There should always be a question you can't answer. A better measure than a grade would be the easiest question you can't answer, and you should be the one to form that question too. As forming it requires an understanding, just the kind one would hope to instill in children, and answering it pushes them towards surpassing their own personal limits.

The purpose of schooling was meant to be education and enlightenment, but it's become grades. Grades have become a target and therefore ceased to be a good measure. Grades are not the purpose of education, they were never supposed to be. But if all education is centered around grades, then grades have failed their purpose. A measurement of intelligence that isn't intertwined with a mechanism of growth is a worthless measure for educational purposes. Even if supposed *measurements of intelligence* are scientifically grounded, and even if you agree with the value of these tests, it doesn't mean these tests offer value in education. Those are two separate things.

Grades are measurements with a ceiling, a closed world, yet the real world doesn't operate like this, the real world doesn't have a ceiling.

The context of life is completely open, everything and anything can be questioned. This is the natural context people evolved to survive in, it's an unchanging aspect of our environment. There's an infinite number of ways to display intelligence, so a closed context could only ever be a failed test. Failing to embrace the nature of the infinite is a failure in understanding human nature. If intelligence was a product of an open context, then it won't flourish independent of that.

Across history, the feedback given when raising children would have been more complex and appropriate throughout time than the oversimplifications of the school systems. Which would have been what led to civilizational development at all. The oversimplified grades we use as measurements have been an affront to our own evolutionary progress. It's for the same reason that languages don't just have five words. Feedback is the most important part of any endeavor, we would be nowhere without communication. The more complex the feedback, the more complex the developmental improvement.

Intelligence is a survival strategy, and it's not the only one individuals have. Insisting too much on dictating what it is, or how much someone has, only acts to curb their strategy for survival. Anything related to the mind can only be defined by the owner of that mind, to forcefully impose a characterization of someone else's is a form of religious tyranny. There's a near infinite number of dimensions that could be tested for, yet children are only measured in purely academic pursuits. They've forced intelligence to be a proxy for survivability. The only test children need to study for is called life.

The entire process of oversimplifying the goals, and dumbing every achievement down to a measurable number, holds no evolutionary significance. So of course it feels like an empty accomplishment by the time one graduates from these schools. With everything being so dogmatic, the children know their time is being wasted when they're not allowed to innovate. That's basically the original job of children. To improve upon what their parents build a foundation for. Our society has so much foundation and no opportunity for basic improvement because the modern educational paradigm says *shut up, you've had everything given to you, earn your grade, work hard, just do as you're told because you're being graded*. To enlighten those who aren't aware, *working hard* within the confines of a stupid system will be for absolutely nothing. It would only transform your effort into frustration. Such institutions have convinced parents and grandparents not to pass on their skills to their own children. It's destroyed our cultural heritage through a false expectation that schooling was somehow better than directly inheriting the knowledge of our predecessors. The art of education isn't improving, and the art of problem-solving has been completely forgotten. If you like this reasoning, then grades were a nihilistic first step we took to actually understand all of these problematic oversimplifications, as grasping the nature of intelligence ironically requires such mistakes. If you don't like this, then feel free to continue to live and die by grades, make it your religion for all I care.

7.4 The Nature of Transformations

The most glaring flaw of the modern educational paradigm is the denial of basic human psychology. This isn't arguing that the school systems offer a denial of the field of psychology, instead I'm saying they deny basic human psychology to the children who are imprisoned within their school system. They're denied their constitutional rights, despite that the Supreme Court has ruled against this, and they're quite often reminded that they have no right to protest. The students have no representation, and if any part of the schooling process acts maliciously towards them, whether intentionally or not, it ends up being denied that it ever happened in the first place, and students generally have no recourse. This is to treat children as objects instead of people, like prisoners instead of value added to society. It's a waste of our own investment, and a detriment to our own future. The only way to do this right is to treat children like the adults you want them to become.

Upbringing is a balance between incubation and freedom. Too much incubation overcooks the potential future of whoever will no longer be able to properly interact afterwards. Too much freedom prevents someone from ever being able to climb the introspective ladder and become a more productive member of society.

Some adults have an aggressive obsession with studying, they want to make their children do nothing but focus on their future, even when the reward for that focus is decades away. Studying, as a core substitute for development and maturation, falls flat. In fact, it's more like an inhibitor to it. Social development isn't a luxury, it's a biological necessity, and anyone who inhibits a child's social development, at any age, has nothing to be proud of. Social development has the opportunity to better fuel someone's studying habits, and motivate them properly for their long-term goals. Otherwise, that child's future professional life might be just as disastrous as their childhood. Overstudying is the goal that subverts itself, it's negligent of the evolutionary history that needs to be respected in order for a child to succeed.

Regarding high pressure parenting, the point isn't to destroy the child's life. The point of introducing challenges to a child is to put a child into stressful situations in order to show them they can find their way out of it. It's to show them that they can handle it, and that they're able to win great prizes from it. If pressure and stress are applied with no plan in mind, then you may as well be wasting their future potential.

It should still be entirely possible to raise children with specific motivations in mind. Earning one's own self-respect, finding genuine innovative curiosity, having a family with children, and running a successful business are all realistic goals for individuals throughout their 20s. There's undoubtedly an art to crafting a childhood, and it's throughout the ages been called religion. I find it appropriate to aim at the aforementioned endpoints, and build the basis for a schooling paradigm that can have individuals accomplish these goals as a ceremonial introduction into society, rather than the certification chasing that's currently working to erode trust in our existing institutions. If the point of a school system is to gain qualification, and not self-respect, then you've completely foregone the upbringing process in exchange for a seat at the fall of your declining empire.

Imagine living in a society with perfect accountability, where each person is held liable for every single mistake they ever make. It's the social credit system on steroids. Rather than trying to deter making mistakes, or pretending like they're not unavoidable, it's about time we accept they're a part of life and plan around them instead. Safetyism is a denial of reality. It's better to allow children to feel the pain of their mistakes than to prevent them from making any at all. They must feel risk in order to achieve, and they must achieve in order to grow. None of these things will happen independently of one another. Safetyism is a way of blaming problems on children, which is purely backwards.

Safetyism can be defined between the boundaries of constant observation and the inability to invite someone to the table of their own life. It prevents proper brain development. Let's use an example where there are cameras on every street corner that record every action people make. This can operate under the guise of either harmony or safety, but psychologically it's a punishment, and you can't hand-wave this away as culture or policy. Any observer becomes a part of every interaction it observes. The emotions you have are a model of the entirety of the evolutionary history of interactions, and they didn't evolve as a chaotic solution that could be different under different circumstances. Undermining the basis for interaction, via constant observation, is destructive to interactions themselves. The same goes for phones, which collect millions of data points on people from every action they make. When everyone knows they're being spied upon, it's unsettling in the back of their mind.

Animals go into their burrows, their nests, their homes, for mating, living, and maintaining their sanity, knowing they have a place to hide. Interactions behind closed doors say everything about the relationship between the parties involved. Whether it's of respect or subservience becomes extremely apparent when there's no outside observers. It's also the most sincere way in which respect is given, especially that of mutual respect. What's hidden aren't the people inside some location, it's the interactions between the two, which becomes a kind of home for people to return to. To forcefully observe them would be to prevent their interaction from reaching its fullest potential.

The more serious the observation, the more serious the punishment. This comes back to the classroom structure again in the case where children are always in view of an adult, meaning they never learn to be trusted. The punishment is created out of this lack of proper social development from a lack of trust. You might say that you think this is fine, or that it makes you feel secure, or that some level of surveillance is necessary. But you've only become a prisoner. It's similar to why wild animals don't always do well in captivity. Because the effects of observation, or the perceived threats thereof, are always received despite whether they're felt. The effects are still there regardless of whether or not someone agrees it's a punishment.

The punishment of observation counteracts freedom. Without freedom, we're no longer able to model our environment. We instead become a model of our confinement. Which is purely depressing. Like cells that commit apoptosis in the body, animals know when to stop reproducing due to the lack of viability in the endeavor itself. Because there's no inspiration in confinement, the function of the structure of freedom is transformation. We currently consider transformations to be things such as graduation ceremonies from the schools one attends, and the certificates received. But these certificates are bad representations of transformation built atop of other bad transformations.

Taken to an extreme, constant observation acts as a permanent incentive to not make mistakes. Which is foolish, you would have nothing to learn from. For children who grow up under constant surveillance, they have trouble controlling their behavior when they know they're not being watched. There being a panopticon only necessitates a performance, which forces people to *act* instead of *be*.

Children are forced to plan their life in nearly all the same ways as their peers, and on the same framework, this is detrimental to forming any individual ability to plan anything at all. Whether it's deciding what kind of high school to go to, or college, or major, there's a sense of destroying natural variation by limiting everything to these choices, their timing, and the nature thereof. Believing that we can simply teach everything there is to know to our children so that they succeed in life, as some kind of cookie-cutter baseline, is a ridiculous idea. There's too much to understand. The point of having unknowns is to figure them out. There's no point in raising children to even be the same, let alone cookie-cutter, because they'll need to rely on each other's differences to survive. Any lack in their collective survivability would be due to a lack of natural variation. Any lack of natural variation would only be brought about by oversimplifications used in the mass-production of upbringing. Natural variation is the most basic aspect of our survival strategies. To subvert it is to subvert our own existence.

The concepts of the known and unknown are analogous to principles and fears. Stability, and modeling the known via the unknown, is modeling principles. Whereas fragmentation, and modeling the unknown via the known, models fears. Through stability, one navigates the world using principles as their model of how to exist, react, and survive. Through fears, one keeps track of what not to do, who not to interact with, and what not to say. One isn't necessarily more useful than the other, rather, their usefulness always relies on having the other around. Propping someone up to be a certain way isn't fruitful, their own life experiences will lead them down the appropriate path.

The biggest failure is to put the development of either above the child's own development. To be so afraid of the unknown that you give the fears more importance than a child's ability to learn them, is safetyism. To instill principles too rigorously, without ever letting a child develop them, would be preaching from a book instead of granting experience. Neither of these failures would be more fruitful than the lessons gained from life itself.

The art of learning is between the bounds of curiosity and practice. You need to expose children, or any people really, to what you want them to be capable of dealing with. Yet there are no monetary systems in schools, there are often not political systems, students' rights are replaced by rules, they don't get to invent anything, can't work on their own startups, and can't do anything that's valuable in the real world. So what are they practicing for? The answer seems to be that they practice being obedient to the people who run the schools. It's no wonder global society is collapsing wherever these educational norms have been implemented, the teaching profession is more about the convenience of teachers than the growth of their students. Rather, the teaching profession transformed education to be centered around obedience, rather than education being a transformative mechanism for students.

I find it more likely that a lot of people are wanting more extreme ideologies like communism, despite no longer being children, because they grow up in such an authoritarian environment. They have to *ask* to use the bathroom. In their minds they understand the atrocious lack of freedom they have. When they develop, they're attempting to revert society back to an older time by using the destructive tendencies of communism so that society can be rebuilt without these ridiculous violations of individual freedom. Get rid of the insidious authoritarianism and they won't grow into insidious communists. Mistakes are important to learn from, and institutions themselves must be responsive to their own mistakes. That includes being accountable to criticisms over the prevention of individual freedom at the most basic levels.

On the needs of children, they need some kind of expertise to feel that they can make even the most basic of professions out of. They need responsibility. They need role models that they can choose, can talk with, and can practice having complex and in-depth conversations with. They need a meritocratic environment. They need physical development, and to embed the building of physical and mental habits that guide them through their life in a sane and stable way. They need an environment that encourages kindness, hard work, and neither babies nor ostracizes them. They need to, specifically, avoid idiotic environments that promote senseless violence as some kind of culture, or as part of the social hierarchy of available peers where people drag each other's futures down into irrelevance.

To young children who don't understand their own mistakes, positive reinforcement is no different than positive selection. Your response to a child's best behavior is just as important as your response to their worst behavior. That's not to say either response should be of the same nature, two things opposed don't stand opposite. Meet their best with positivity, but not their worst with negativity. Instead, don't meet their worst behavior at all, don't reward it with attention, but especially don't tear them down over mistakes. They'll not only resent you for it, they'll develop into a worse version of themselves because of it. Instead, when you see them do something right, reward it, they'll want more, and in the process learn excellent behavior. What people get wrong, by overpunishing, is they don't realize the effect it has on a child. When your most intense reactions are to positive things that the child has done, things they've done right, they learn to continue that behavior. It's the intensity of the message you send that they remember, and they grow into the person who models all of these intense reactions. When the most high intensity moments are that of punishment and negativity, the child will model the punishments, with the result being that they'll transform into something that you will neither expect nor understand. It will lead to horrible transformations of that child. Likewise, offering proper rewards is crucial for positive reinforcement. Continually obnoxious, or baseless forms of positive response make for backwards rewards that yield backwards results.

The times where children don't give up need to have significance, rather than the times when they're betrayed. You can't treat someone horribly on a daily basis while claiming you care about them. Otherwise, you might double down on some of their worst moments, without even understanding its significance. It's interpersonally careless.

Anyone who does this to their children isn't mature enough to be considered a parent.

In a system that suppresses free competition, you gain only wasted potential. Students are being processed into wasted potential, rather than being refined from it. The people who can achieve nothing need to figure out what to do with nothing. All it takes is for them to write about their life. They're failing because their life isn't together. The adults in their life have failed, and the guidance they've received from school isn't any better, likely because it's either pity, coddling, or neglect.

We need to let people fail. The grievance majors are a way for the universities to deny that they've failed the individuals they'd admitted. The way I see it, those individuals should have failed out, found a different lifestyle, or changed. Bring back failure again, so that greatness has value. Failure is the first road to transformation, and greatness will not happen without it. Desperation will become their greatest strength.

Although being let down by a low quality education system is certainly a regrettable outcome, the best avenue for people after either success or failure is innovation. Even if you fail, aim to fail at something no one else is doing. You can't teach innovation, you have to inspire it. You can't *command* people to be passionate, it must be grown. Chasing after unknowns is the wisest philosophical practice one can have children follow, it's wisdom itself. It enables continuous growth, and it's inspiring. You must be able to question whatever's questionable to claim you have the freedom to do anything at all.

Human religion is a reflection of the continual entropic optimization we see throughout evolution. Instead of the universe existing, and eventually fading away, like in some nihilistic dream, what if the universe was actually building itself? What if we exist in between stages of growth for the universe that we don't have the ability to observe? Then we'd be building ourselves as a part of it. Because complexity is that which embodies limitless potential. The spawning of complexity, by leveraging irony, is an optimization that allows one to sidestep energy and other constraints as a requirement for growth. In human lives, this allows you to shed off your vices, the pity you either accept or grant, and anything else that may be holding you back. Complexity is that which transforms into greater and greater forms. Our potential as a species, can in fact achieve unlimited growth. It's inherent to the nature of transformations that potential itself has the potential to be less finite than the resources it's derived from.

7.5 Refactoring Generations

Adam Smith, the founder of economics, wrote about bringing deeper levels of organization to society[123]. That allowing people to simplify their roles for the sake of specialization actually grants reciprocating benefits to the collective. It's needless to say that this was true, and it's worked out well. But like everything else, nothing can last forever. We've come to a point in our civilizational development where having just one skill, one source of income even, can be dangerous due to political grievances, or moments of change and instability. It's not unreasonable that Adam Smith couldn't see the end result of this system, that wasn't his job. It would be unreasonable for us, living in the modern age, to neither notice nor find ways to adapt to these problems.

The lessons learned on human nature through economics aren't just an analysis of human evolution and technological progress, it's an analysis from a direction. Economists approach the problem of human evolution from the opposite direction as an evolutionary biologist would. Rather than dealing with biology, they specialize in the value of inanimate objects and explain human behavior through the exchange of such things.

A consequence of this concept of the division of labor is the formation of social classes based on the differences in value able to be amassed. Which isn't inherently problematic in itself, although some people do view it this way, which is what dreams of communism have grown out of. Another problem that arises, is that living your life doing just one or a few specialized things is antithetical to natural selection, it's something that would never be selected for in general. It's quite literally allowing for the potential removal of any prior selected abilities across the populace through relaxed selection, as there's nothing to fill the void of lost responsibility. Which can be a dangerous long-term civilizational strategy.

In human hierarchies, and elsewhere in the food chain, when your ability to survive becomes too many derivatives separated from

123. Adam Smith. *The Wealth of Nations*. W Strahan and T Cadell, 1776

basic functionality, your survival is generally not favored. A monarch with no subjects can't till his own fields. Likewise, if your only food source no longer exists, and you've adapted to eating that primarily, then you'll likely starve if you can't change. Basic survival skills are too often never granted to young children, who are then sent off to overspecialize in some extremely niche role when they grow older. This kind of overspecialization is the core branding of the university system. Every specialty relies on other people knowing how to perform every other niche role, and there tends to be a large disconnect between different professions. Over the course of just 3 generations, this structure has already proven to be quite precariously perched, whether in global supply chains, or in jobs that become easily replaceable by computers or cheaper workers. There's a high need for an upbringing designed around genuine accomplishment and contribution to the lives of those who inhabit our own civilization. It needs to be built with respect to evolutionary history and any desirable future endeavors in this age of constant innovation.

A lack of being able to manage your own survival makes you extremely vulnerable to government corruption, and class warfare, as many would be left unable to fight back, especially if they were unaware it was happening. Which seems to be the case in recent decades, where people's jobs have been exported overseas for cheap labor, while migrants have been moved into the same neighborhoods that once held these jobs, en masse, in order to replace any existing roles with cheaper workers at home in what seems to be a form of insidious class warfare. There's also been forms of institutional apartheid over religious beliefs, political preferences, and the tendency to state them publicly.

The skills and talents that you were naturally selected for somehow became irrelevant in an economy of scale. Your survivability instead becomes entirely dependent upon what can easily become a predatory government that doesn't need to have your best interests at heart, and you have no significant negotiation power. The talents you may have, and maybe haven't even fully discovered, may wither away like a curse without a gift. This is a disaster waiting to happen because nature doesn't change. Those foolish enough to think they can redefine nature will learn this lesson the hard way.

It leaves one to wonder what the baseline modern skill set should look like. What skills are, and will be, the most valuable to imbue into children? Of the thousands of potential specializations, what exactly should be included in this? If you ask me, it should be scalable with a heavy emphasis on computation. Human thought should be put at an appropriate metaphysical level of design where one can earn each integral they solve. Because designing something is different than designing how to design something, and more progression on this scale yields more benefit.

These are generally the kind of skills that most people don't need in Adam Smith's more simplified economic world. But our economies are becoming so complex, and are built on top of more and more things, that we're losing control of our own geopolitical guarantees to people who don't believe in the same freedom we've granted to others on an international scale. Any other skill can become a modular extension of computation.

The next stage of optimization and growth achievable in the West isn't necessarily something aimed at making some aggregate metric like GDP increase, although I don't see why it couldn't, it would instead grow the technological breadth of the country at large in the same manner that was historically achieved with literacy. It would offer widespread specialization, based on Williston's law. The goal is for more people to be more skilled at things we usually outsource, in ways that generate strong local economies. Knowledge itself is a technology, maintaining as much of it as possible, and in abundance, is a hedge against economic shortcomings in general.

Men have a responsibility to build, make, and work. They join the economy, and the world of workers, so as to keep the world spinning, and to put food on the table. Women have the responsibility of having children, and making a family, so that we have more humans coming around to do these things in the future. Once women are done with this, they can join the workforce, because it seems they generally want to. The problem with this today is that a woman must sacrifice her independence, financial independence specifically, to be able to accomplish having a family at a reasonable age. If we could implement the idea I've shared prior, by paying for houses through childbirth, then a woman would be earning equity in a house and this conundrum would be solved. To make it so impossible for young women to save enough money to start a family within just a few years is nonsensical. It's why we have no birth rate. This is probably the key condition in creating the environment that creates the woke, as these conditions are in complete misalignment with their evolutionary history. We've put these impossible hurdles on ourselves by giving young women no choice but to go into the workforce in the first place. In order for anyone to flourish, they must have the freedom to choose what they do. For men, it's choosing what kind of work they want to do. For women, it's choosing whether to work or to start a family, and the latter doesn't need to come at the sacrifice of independence.

Failing to produce viable results for all but a few generations is a cultural problem. To yield the high success of the output of Western innovation while maintaining the drive of its children by presenting a true need, an occasion for them to rise to rather than the hedonism that comes from periods of towering economic dominance, is the challenge we find ourselves presented with. It's the integral of our own cultural paradigm, the implementation of inspiration and selection through upbringing that's meant to yield these results without losing them in future generations.

When it comes to passing on skills, there's a lot of questions that deserve to be asked. In our avoidance of relating human nature to evolution, we're unable to do so. Is it better to train your children to do the same thing every generation? Is it better to always have a different job every generation? There's no great way to study this, and maybe these aren't even good questions. We have no way of knowing whether there's a worthwhile benefit to be had, in any dimension, for either of these cases. Without having large-scale studies, how might one approach this problem? By utilizing a hedged bet.

For most of history, people were able to raise children to match the society they grew up in, but we don't have this luxury. The rate of our innovation is coming to subvert the nature of our own culture. There are modern skill sets that can be taught and passed on such as computation, and things of a general technological basis that fit the nature of this hedge, as are things like nutrition, physical fitness, and good culture. One might even dare to add religion to that list. Then there's individual roles that some might fulfill that don't necessarily need to be passed on if they're just societal duties that get filled by various people. Exact specializations might differ, yet the use of technology can still persist as the skill set that enables other skill sets. It's possible to take both routes at once, passing on the same skills for generations while also being flexible enough to adopt more specific skills should it be desirable or necessary in specific generations. The way to handle this is to adapt the upbringing process itself in order to manage the incorporation of scalable technology, to cater to the integrals rather than the derivatives.

The best example of benefits of generational growth can be seen in communities with better nutrition, brought about through dietary fortification, achieving various beneficial effects that echo through generations. This improvement to health, and physiology, will undoubtedly bring about improvements to intelligence, and individual capability. This is something the US had gotten right when fortifying various foods, that nutrition matters in generational health. Common sense would caution to be careful with forced widespread distribution in general, as it can be insidiously weaponized against the populace. But when it comes to giving something to everyone, might there be viability in granting opportunity, rather than material goods?

What if communism itself is just another instance of the broken compass? What kind of communism could ever be ideal? What kind of lesson could be learned, what is it that people are craving from this structure that could potentially be realized while adding freedom to the environment? The point of communism, at least in the minds of people who desire it, is that it would flatten the distribution of wealth. Not that this is what happens in reality, but this is the desired end result so often sought after. Is there another step on the evolutionary staircase to come after free market capitalism? Probably not, but it can definitely transform.

The transformation would look something like hyperentrepreneurialism. A completely decentralized concept, where people work for themselves while running a business, being able to make products and ship them. It's likely not something that can be achieved overnight, you'll likely need *some* employees. So what differentiates this? It's the drive to push more people into being their own boss, into having something they offer and are directly paid for, rather than working for large entities that end up holding your sustenance hostage at the price of your public voice. Because employment becomes a dependency. You wouldn't want your children to become dependent on drugs, so why would you want them to be dependent on an employer? Some of these organizations are so large you're likely to never even meet the people you actually work for, and if they don't know you, that only makes you more replaceable.

The individualistic philosophy presented here brings back the pride one might have in their craft, and the ability to pass on a serious and valuable set of skills to their children. The dissatisfaction people have with the economic situation, of needing someone else to make a job, to then employ them, can be alleviated by bringing up generations of people aimed at being self-employed. Which is to move towards a highly abundant high-skill class that understands design, manufacturing, and business that isn't taken advantage of by some other class. They can operate amongst themselves, and sell to groups that benefit their interests. This is the next natural step in our economic development. The goal is making more people who know how to make more things, as well as knowing how to utilize those skills, on demand, in the wider economy, and with less man-power.

Hyperentrepreneurialism would be about changing the ratio of employees to employers across society. More employers, with less employees, means more people pull their own weight. More employer-employee relationships would be more personal, and carry greater depth, similar to what was achieved through the evolution of the model of interactions. More people would at least be an important cog, rather than a mass-produced one. It makes sense as an ideal that one can admit might never be fully achieved, but is certainly much more feasible in the age of AI. As those who can, should.

The broader lesson from Adam Smith's words is that the wealth of nations isn't determined by the amount of gold they hoard, it's characterized by how much they can hoard plus what kinds of capability they exert per unit hoarded. A more capable populace would expand both the intricacy of these capabilities as well as their greater culmination. Built atop of the normal supply and demand of an economy, one might expect such a system to operate with a more specialized supply and demand. With the populace at large having an increased breadth of what are currently viewed as advanced skills, the opportunity for customizability becomes higher than it currently is. Products could essentially be offered with an increased basis for modularity, to be either entirely or somewhat designed by the customer. Instead of buying a camera, you might fancy making your own, but still end up ordering specialized lenses that someone else is better at making.

To object, one might say that we don't have enough people to fill the many various professions that we need to uphold society. Yet we have ridiculous stringency in becoming mostly anything, especially something like a medical doctor. No one can be a 20%, 40%, or 60% doctor, it's either 0% or 100%. Which is absurd, considering the number of doctors that graduate from our own institutions are kept artificially low. Not every case of the sniffles needs the attendance of someone whose capable of treating advanced leukemia. Where we can't uphold our own ridiculous standards of expectation, we should stratify to make the goals more achievable. Not every person can solve every difficult problem, but not every person capable of dedicating to difficult problems needs to address every minor issue that could be handled by someone with less ability. If our qualifications act as oversimplified boundaries, then they only work to impede our flexibility as a civilization.

7.6 Developmental Models of Evolving Complexity

Ontogeny recapitulates phylogeny, said Ernst Haeckel[124]. Which didn't end up being entirely correct. He proposed that embryonic development went through all the prior forms of evolution to achieve its end result. It wasn't entirely wrong either, the stages of embryonic development do show strong resemblances to an organism's evolutionary history. They go through phases of growth with strong similarities to the prior evolutionary stages of that organism. Human embryos specifically have pharyngeal arches, which are structures that look like gills, they even develop into gills in other organisms. The reason for this occurring in humans is that once upon a time, they did develop into gills. They now develop into things like the jaw, ears, and throat.

It's incredibly notable that to produce some form of advanced complexity it must pass through the stages it took to initially develop, or at least modified versions of the same developmental steps that had once happened prior. As people aren't robots, you can't just print out bones and organs. In mammals, unlike many other organisms, most organs don't regenerate, and they don't heal after being wounded. Growing them for the very first time tends to be an extremely intricate process,

124. Ernst Haeckel. *General Morphology of Organisms*. Georg Reimer, 1866

and damaging them early in someone's development will leave them with problems for the rest of their life. Likewise, there's a lot of things that if done wrong early in someone's childhood will lead to an unjustified disaster for the adult they become. It's imperative that development be done right the first time around, and as early as possible.

There's an even larger lesson to be learned from the nature of development, that throughout childhood it's extremely wise to raise children through the stages of human development itself. Children ought to write before they type. They ought to run before they drive any wheeled contraption. They ought to swim using their own body before they ever attach flippers to the bottom of their feet, lest they never find interest in learning to swim without them. They ought to learn basic math the hard way prior to using a calculator. They ought to read books before they use screens. They ought to design their own scalable mechanical, or mental system, of computation before they use a computer. There's nothing more abhorrent than a young child, unable to take their eyes off a screen, whose early life has become so saturated with technology that normal conversation will not be possible when this person grows into adulthood. That being said, the opposite can also be problematic, if a university offers a senior level botany class that forces students to draw plants, their cells, and their structures, then that's the exact opposite of accomplishing this goal because university graduates should be using modern technology like cameras for documenting, and machine learning for scalable image classification, rather than redrawing plant structures that were elucidated hundreds of years prior. Young children need to model their own environment, not something that does it for them.

There's good reason for the trials of upbringing to be both representative of and respectful towards the trials of human history so as to not lose the edge that brought us to where we are now. Should our tower collapse, to levels below that of skills we no longer practice, below whatever level that relaxed selection could take away from us, that would certainly become the most regretful reversion in human history. It's ultimately the separation of survival from upbringing that would breed the negligence required to bring about such a prominent failure in the first place.

What does it mean to model your environment? Organisms without any kind of social structure have a purely physical relationship with their environment, physical reality governs which interactions become advantageous adaptations. For more advanced species, that have established some sort of social structure, a society within their own species, the group has even more advanced means of interacting with what they need in order to grow and thrive. The only species in a tier beyond this in the modern day is humans, exhibiting a societal structure that completely supercedes the complexity of their environment. Where the nature of their environment is more characterized by other humans than it is by the physicalities of the planet itself, because humans design their own environment. The information of humans itself has even come to be a metaphysical part of it.

It's best to match an upbringing to the environment one will exist in. Yet the challenge today isn't just one of matching upbringing to an environment, it's to match upbringing to a constantly changing environment. Matching upbringing to the nature of evolution itself, and to this age of constant innovation we find ourselves in. So what does being a model of your environment mean? Because if you can model it better than other people, it can mean more success for you. Or perhaps it could mean success for the children you're enabling to be better models of their environment.

Are the teachers in the modern educational paradigm good models of their environment? Has their environment changed since they themselves were young children? Is that even the environment you want your children to model? If this doesn't make for a great role model for your child, then does your child need to learn from such a person? The modern educational paradigm is a bad place to raise children with the success of the child in mind. There's no silly *learning strategy* that's going to provide notable benefit, nor is any other pseudoscientific buzzword. Learning is something you do, not something that's done to you. Learning to learn is the job of the student.

There's a supreme lack of accountability within what should rightfully be called the *experimentation* of the teaching profession, without reliable end-point measurements there's nothing to support the basis for why education is being done the way it is. The lack of ambition in the demographic that becomes teachers doesn't match the extreme ambitions of the young. So out of the gate, this is a complete mismatch of complexity, a failed modeling. The social environment, the psychology of those who reign over the children, is often purely demoralizing instead of inspiring. The ambitions of children ought to be matched with opportunity.

You can't fool children who are exposed to modern society, and all its technology, by telling them their upbringing isn't falling completely short of what their potential could otherwise be. The only way to convince someone in an average public school that what they've received through government mandate in exchange for their time was highly valuable was if they never went outside. Our lives are surrounded by technology, none of which tends to be explained in public school classrooms. They very finely understand the nature of the known unknown factors in their lives, because children are drawn to them, and these instincts exist because they've tended to reward those who possess them. They're searching for what's valuable. In being unable to attain it, or unable to even attempt to do so, there's an inherent loss of potential in what only amounts to time wasted in an institution that doesn't allow children to live up to their best capabilities, and they're aware of this. The most important years of brain development, where one would learn the most important life lesson, and skills to survive, are wasted on busy work in a public school.

What does evolution teach us about static functions? Things that can't adapt, die. Like the fine-tuned feedback in biological organisms, the absence of proper feedback mechanisms in our upbringing process is leading to an increasing disarray in our livelihood. The school and university systems are taking the place of a central planner, which is a recipe for disaster. A boom in the diversity of organisms would quickly determine which feedback mechanisms are Darwinistically advantageous, likewise our school systems need these feedback mechanisms to be something other than unpaid student loans and a low birth rate, otherwise by the time they've received the feedback it means society is already collapsing.

Just as organisms evolved to take greater advantage of their environment, both through their own structural means then socially, so should children through advanced design principles in the same order of that which had originally grown in biological complexity. Physically modeling a need in their own environment can be followed by learning to operate within the realm of social coordination in order to achieve the same goal at a larger scale. Ultimately, ending up with something to sell.

We've been so amazed with what precise calculations have brought us that we forgot exploration and technicians brought us precise calculations. The universities overcook most of their students with degrees that could take half the time, and a fraction of the cost. Even worse, the pedigree of the academic publishing cartels offers nothing but decadent dogma to entice others into playing the same games, and for a bad reward, despite that their publishing models are largely outdated.

Many of the entities and individuals who built the entire tech industry have been at the forefront of scalable AI implementations, and it's no wonder. Competitively building all the preceding layers of such a thing helps one later remain competitive throughout its evolving future. But generations raised using an AI since a young age would never have the same drive to reinvent all the wheels that have always magically turned themselves without any effort on the part of the child. Every year that a child doesn't use some kind of advanced tool in place of their own abilities, this same temptation arises, and it likely leads towards different outcomes depending on when it's accepted.

Within a preestablished environment, this then leads to a conundrum. Should someone want to build everything for themselves, and learn to make such gigantic entities from scratch? Or should they invest their time specializing in some niche area where they might be hired into such gigantic preestablished entities? The former seems instinctual to a lot of people, yet the latter would prove to be the more reliable path. Truth be told, there doesn't need to be a choice independent of experimentation, simply allowing children to simulate the building of such industries amongst themselves would allow them to self-sort towards what they should pursue, and would grant them valuable experience along the way.

Humanity's socioevolutionary hedged bet seems to choose both options as a default. Whenever there's a fork in the road, both routes must be chosen by the populace at large. Should either order or disorder come without the other, pursuit itself would be met with failure. But there's an interesting lesson within this, that only one of these extremes truly works as a starting point for child-rearing, and that's the construction of the base of the tower, rather than the shortcut to the top. No matter what, all childhood development starts in the same place, it must be centered around the child, not teachers, and they should start by building things from scratch. The alternative extreme represents dependency, as the base layer of the tower becomes supplanted rather than supplied. This same flaw aligns with the dysfunctionality of communism and its many related analogues.

The challenges faced in raising children today are to balance upbringing with technology, to balance lifestyle with work, to match the time required for attaining knowledge with that of irreplaceable skills, and to balance specialization with financial independence. It's to tell the story of human understanding, rather than to force-feed its end state. Something like chemistry should be taught through its history, rather than throwing a list of elements in front of people and showing them how to balance equations and find limiting reagents. It's the history of how humans discovered such things that carries more significance in the minds of children than the individual skills offered within such a field. The history of computation should be no different, in fact understanding its history would be a key development in balancing the delivery of a core skill set of heavy computation while making sure childhood isn't overburdened with technological addiction. It's the story of this history that develops serious decision-making skills and the desire for independence during childhood, because these stories provide priceless insight into human discovery, and childhood is the best time to practice the behavior required to model it.

Upbringing ought to accelerate the development of childhood, not prolong it. Schools in the modern academic paradigm do everything to refuse rights to children, and to prevent there being any trust placed in students. An environment where children need to ask permission to use their own basic bodily functions is a low-trust environment, and thereby has negative developmental effects on any child who must waste their time going through this humiliation ritual. Trust is something you need to place in children for the sake of their development, removing it turns them into prisoners.

Two different decisions might lead to different environmental outcomes, but not necessarily a different ratio of advantages to disadvantages. The best solutions typically offer a multitude of mutual benefits that overcome this ratio. It's within reason to assume this is not a process spawned from the intelligence, culture, nor capabilities unique to humans, merely that things manifest themselves to such a state observable by our own consciousness. Nature is still in the process of granting both the intelligence and dealmaking abilities to find these solutions, these natural equilibria, as rungs upon the ladder of evolution.

7.7 School of Simulations

So if you had to make a school to embody these concepts, how would you do it? To match the development of children with the complexity before them, would it be a technical school? A traditional school? I would want to incorporate all kinds of technical skills, and I would want it to operate on a principle that could be seen as a recursion of human thought itself. To match the complexity of life and the environment we make for ourselves, it would be best to make a school based on the concept of modeling.

Schooling should ultimately build confidence, rather than test for ability. Confidence comes from achievement. Achievement doesn't come from testing, it comes from long-term effort, and improvement in the pursuit of skill. Tests aren't always formal procedures, some are simple tricks you learn to use to decipher the nature of someone's character. Some can be used to determine physical properties, some can tell you what you need to know in a moment of urgency. Rather than schools testing children, children should test ideas. Children should be designing and using tests as tools, rather than teachers using tests to measure children.

Through the years, there must be clear goals set out for children. Once a child can pass the basic comprehensions offered at the start of elementary school, reading and math, they learn how to get into middle school. When they do, the same process then informs on how to get into high school. Eventually children will move towards making multi-year plans for their own future. Time is not a requirement, but it is a limiting factor. Quality and depth are the real requirements.

There's value in being able to explicitly define what it takes to graduate from any specific level of school, children are enabled to speed up if they want to. By simply saying that it's only time that will earn them a reward, you waste their potential on waiting. Most realistically, students should have a challenge to every school they attend. A long-term purpose for attending the school itself that persists beyond the individual years of attendance. Whether elementary, middle, or high school, there needs to be an end goal for every institution. To fail would mean to fail the purpose that the school puts forward to accomplish.

For elementary school, it would simply be to show the ability to model something significantly complex through either simulation or design. Middle school would have children using the abilities gained in elementary school to make something that's of the same nature, but conceptually more impressive. The purpose of high school should be to establish a business and make money.

Purpose should be a first priority among first priorities for students at a school. Rather than just defining their own purpose, get them to detail out what they think an achievement looks like in each stage of their life. Allow them to make the targets they ought to be aiming for.

In elementary school, children can be brought up with play-based learning, with both physical games and board games. They'll move onto designing such games, simulating things like board games, and reading to achieve their goals throughout the years. The process to graduate from elementary school would require that a child has become self-directed at using their time to accomplish these goals, and has a significant accomplishment to show for it. In this context, simulations work great as a learning tool as well as a system of measurement. Elementary school is about learning to approach solving complex problems, learning to ask questions in order to do so, and to be able to make one's own challenges. A final presentation will determine graduation.

In middle school, children can focus on building something real and determining how to dedicate their time in order to do so. Middle school aged children tend to have an inherent edginess to their behavior, they often want to stand out in some way. This desire should be leveraged in their favor by allowing them to express this through what they build. To graduate will mean to present the fruits of what they've likely spent 3 or more years working on. Middle school is about solving as complex a problem as one can make, even if impractical. The presentation for graduating from middle school is the most important presentation they'll give, as it's meant to resemble the idea of a bar mitzvah. This ceremony seems to have a kind of visible success in the Jewish community, and happens at around the same age for a proper ceremonial initiation into society for pre-adulthood. While a student can move on from middle school work early if they become successful enough to do so, this presentation will only be done at the specific age boundary between middle and high school, as it's a coming of age ceremony.

High school will be a time for children to make money. Instead of using all the skills they've gathered to be expressive like in middle school, they need to minimize their costs while maximizing their effectiveness. Under financial constraints, like in the real world, the problems can only be as complex as they need to be, and minimizing complexity is rewarded. It's up to them to start a business, make an app, a service, a product, a means of survival, or any kind of success they can bring their own way. The school can provide initial investments for the children to use on such endeavors in exchange for some return on future investment if they're successful. As a general purpose, it would be good to have them be able to earn money, and not be naive by the time that they have it.

A portion of the money spent on the child's education up until high school can accumulate as an investment in their future business. If the students are successful at making money in high school, then the yearly cost of the education returns value to that family then and there. Hypothetically, the parents wouldn't need to have any kind of college savings account, this would double as both tuition and savings. It ends up being cheaper for parents, as it makes you only need to make 1 contribution instead of 2.

Current college costs are extortionate. It's questionable whether it's more stressful to save for the hypothetical future college loans that cripple your finances or to wonder whether the university system will even still be viable by the time your child would make it there. I aim to make a school where earning a degree from university would be a step down, as most of the information you learn in university is not only freely available online and in books, it's also material that middle and high school aged children are capable of learning. Time and dedication lead to accomplishment, nothing else. There's no age requirement, there's no certificate to replace the reputation of your merit.

The point of a school is to try and make a profitable, and useful, person for society. Regardless of what that evolves into, it doesn't need to be a static public school to university pipeline. We have never needed such static and rigid directions that persist for over a decade so uniformly across so many people. Recent history illustrates the failures of having a single paradigm, even one that hypothetically branches off into a lot of different professions.

Children must be welcomed into a family and society over and over again at different stages. But what kind of ceremonies are being held in normal institutions? Simple graduation ceremonies, where everyone does the same worthless walk to receive a piece of paper? Without a single one showing they're actually more or less worthy than anyone else? Such a limited scope of competition will fuel an abundance of childish behavior. Why shouldn't work be indicative of reputation in an environment where children already want to gain reputation amongst their peers? Work should be displayed, presentations are everything. Presentation skills can be something that's worked on throughout elementary school as soon as individual projects start. Regular presentation nights can act as community gatherings where students display their work to everyone else, who can question and discuss the work.

The point of having children work on individual projects, and form cumulative lifetime skills, is that they'll continually look at their old work and think that it's terrible. The same way people do with their own art, videos, or comments. By contrast, if every student does the same cookie-cutter work, it comes off as low-value to students, and it will be neither memorable nor meaningful. Give them a developmental reference point to use as the basis for their own measurement of themselves and their progression. The improvements to their own art form will speak for itself. In this manner, they'll find a road on which to both travel down and improve.

Responsibility is a biological necessity for young men the same way preservation is for young women. It's a biological function and you can't pretend it doesn't exist if you want your child-rearing to find success. Refusing to invite a child to the table of their own life ought to be criminal negligence on the part of the parents. Student-led rule systems are crucial to creating an environment where children can take hold of that same necessity. As they grow, their rules will also need to. Finding the balance between fairness and abuse is something they need to go through, and they'll benefit greatly from being a part of a collective that works to establish the line between either. The rules of a school ought to be determined yearly, with every student being invited to the table to discuss, debate, and offer alterations to both the written form and practical implementation of these rules. Throughout their developmental process, this becomes an invitation to the table of their own responsibility, which yields their own dedication to responsibility itself, as well as a vested interest in following the rules they set up and agreed to.

With the entirety of this book being a description of intelligence, is being intelligent what to aim for? Still no, it would be better to not be dumb. What makes someone dumb, how do you define it? Someone who dedicates to being dumb is someone who stops asking questions and starts complaining that anyone is asking questions at all. It centers around questions the same way that intelligence does because they're the literal bridge between knowns and unknowns.

When a question only serves as a kind of practice problem, or a knowledge check, it loses its power. Children ought to be challenged by questions on topics they don't understand, rather than ones they're simply supposed to. The purpose of schooling is for them to figure out how to challenge the unknown on their own, as well as to develop a system of deciphering unknowns in general. Have them practice believing that they can find unique ways to ask and answer questions, because it's the only way they ever will.

I don't have faith in the ability of any lone adult to constantly teach the same age group of children forever, nor do I have faith in the ability of any group of adults to be able to teach children for longer than they would normally if they were raising their own. I think the adults grow with the kids and that's part of the process. So allocating adults to teach them doesn't work outside of young age groups. If they want to act as a genuine role model, which is the only way education can actually progress, then they have a time limit. Having children organize and teach themselves is leagues more practical because of this. With a decreased teacher to student ratio comes a decreased concern for pedophilia, all while increasing the responsibility needed from students. A win-win!

Students will balance making contributions to group projects while being able to manage one's own individual work. Core academic skills are things like being able to model, make schematics, and leverage mathematical concepts into making advanced measurements. General detective skills apply to things like health, and the surrounding geological and biological environment, but more importantly they're useful for identifying a first principle to take advantage of. In the end, they ought to be able to traverse the world of business, and materials, to secure appropriate goods and commodities while being mindful of legal restraints.

Children are often required to learn various forms of the law, but they aren't ever required to witness its implementation. Civilian ride-along programs for police have helped people understand the nature of this role, and have brought them to appreciate police for reasons they didn't realize were necessary. In welcoming children to society at large, requirements can't just test for knowledge on paper. They should see what the various underpinnings of our civilization require from the population. Students should need to ride along with police at least once. Schools should be producing people who appreciate the institutions that uphold society, rather than enraging children to march against them.

So what should be the life mission for children, at a more general level? To have children of their own, to be excellent at their profession, to be a bastion of stability for their friends and family, to prosper, and to find ways to support others by employing them to do meaningful jobs that give them purpose. They need something to dedicate to. To read as much as possible, and it can start when they're young. The books written across Western civilization throughout the last few hundred years have produced irreplaceable classics that should be the foundation of any education.

The best way to learn dedication is through art. Making music, visuals, or just putting your heart into something constructive. The dedication to art is often unmatched by most, if not all, other efforts of young children. Time invested into it is undeniably important, as it's a form of growing a way of practicing something at all. It's a practice of the habit of dedication itself that one uses for everything else.

To only allow art as some form of visual assembly is actually an injustice. *Teaching* children to go through every piece of information about something like everyone needs to be a librarian before trying anything, or be aware of every line they may step over, is what kills art. Art is doing, it's the form of your own nature that you let flourish. To prevent someone's attempt by indicating it's been done before, to never be given the chance to try, is soul-destroying. Art is your expression itself. To destroy it is to destroy beauty.

It doesn't matter what you make, one should go as bare-bones as possible. Start with as little technology as needed, then arrive at the answers for what technology would be optimal. This same philosophy applies to work in general. Plan everything out on paper. Don't use a screen to plan what you don't need a screen to plan.

Helping a child that doesn't understand something is the wrong strategy. If they start saying they need help, or that they don't get something, then they need to step away from it and do something physical. They're overloaded by what's in front of them, and they need to think about how to approach it. They need the calmness of mind to want to solve it, and if it doesn't come immediately, then it will come later. Any adult intervening in this process is only making that child dependent on their help, which creates dysgenic outcomes. That very moment of a lack of understanding, with no help, is when they learn to methodically break things down in order to teach themselves.

The current educational paradigm seems to prioritize studies and grades over athletics. But I think people should be honing their body as a top priority, rather than turning primarily to their studies. I'm interested in building up their best habits. Whether it's a normal day, or the worst day of their life, they need to build the habit of exercising, playing, running, doing cardio, or doing something that's physically good for them. This is the best gift to give. It's also important to build their routines, because the best intellectual work will always be done by people who are at their physical best.

Children should be stretching at a young age to gain flexibility that they can use for the rest of their lives, and the habit of doing this should stick with them just as long. Institutions in the modern academic paradigm provide little to no physical development for children at young ages other than recess and a gym class. Recess is even lost as the children progress in age, which is a wasted opportunity for continued physical development.

There's a lot of value in being able to take good notes, and this doesn't mean speed writing every word that some lecturer is speaking. This isn't something that's perfected in a classroom, it's perfected with curiosity. Being able to write down good ideas when you have them is crucial for making something out of them. Maintaining and organizing notes at a large scale is what leads to ideas becoming projects, books, and future plans. The utility of writing to yourself goes beyond understanding various academic topics, you use it to develop your own sense of purpose in life.

Schools tend to have some kind of mandatory attendance policy. Of course children should show up to school, but going on a trip or vacation with your family doesn't need to be punished by the school as a demerit. Families are allowed to do such things, otherwise it's infringing on their freedoms. Any school has no business holding any child's future hostage over anything other than the work that should be accomplished. If parents take their child out of school, there's no reason for any of their school work to have to suffer if the student works on it on their own time. Parents have a religious right to do this. There's no need to enforce attendance, schools should be interesting enough that students actually want to show up. If a child wants to succeed, they will. Days off would be neither penalized nor even disadvantageous. The children's work is what matters most, not the micromanagement of time spent on it.

All work can be done at school, there's no need for homework. There's plenty of time in the day to accomplish what ought to be accomplished. Unless they want to work on something at home, it's their freedom to do so. Responsibility will be something they face on their own.

History is better learned through storytelling, as a means of entertainment. It would stay in someone's head more effectively through the ups and downs of storytelling, than through the memorization of dates and events. It ought to be inspirational before it's boring. It's the personal connection someone has with their own story, and how they came into existence, that carries them through life.

In the modern day we have this silly conundrum of *misinformation*, and *disinformation*, which are words used for insidiously accusing others of spreading propaganda when denying the propaganda being spread by the accuser. Amongst masses of people, who have trouble distinguishing what to believe, we have what's essentially a serious case of mass hysteria. The question then arises, how can one prevent this outcome? Is it possible to? Yes, and it's quite easy. Covering a comprehensive account of history is something that's barely ever done in the modern educational paradigm, and can simultaneously solve the problem of mass hysteria being caused by a lack of accurate information. Both direct knowledge of the happenings of the past, as well as the patterns gained through the interpretation of its bigger picture, is the best defence against propaganda, because propaganda aims to distort the vision of the past in order to twist a narrative in the modern day. We currently have extremist academic factions claiming that white people invented slavery, or that there was no form of chattel slavery before the US was founded. There were slave trades all around the world, in Africa, the Middle East, India, China, and Turkey, especially where even Europeans were taken as slaves. They all lasted longer, started earlier, and traded more slaves than any Western nation. We also have people creating fake narratives claiming that the US was founded on racism, and every European country both has no culture, and also is filled with colonizing racists. These derangements have infiltrated the world of higher education, wrung the facts out of history, and somehow managed to manipulate large swaths of young people into believing in entirely alternate realities relative to the one we actually find ourselves in. The people responsible for this don't care about racism, they only care about weaponizing its accusation, and it's important to protect your child from this weaponization, to inform them of its use.

In the cases where people are manipulated into a denial of history, a lack of understanding of the events, and the bigger patterns, of the past few thousand years, is the underlying root cause. Even where the modern academic paradigm somewhat succeeds, they teach a very limited scope of what's actually happened in the past. Most don't even teach anything about communism, despite many members of the schooling infrastructure being violently anti-Nazi, they seem to give no recognition that communists are arguably worse than their 20th century German counterparts, even as they wave communist flags in their classrooms and inspire their students to do the same.

Luckily, the internet comes to the rescue. An amazing swath of historians exist online that create perspectives through content not possible in most classrooms. In both more compressed and succinct forms that provide a higher quality overall message than might otherwise be done in person, and through a much larger array of topics than any single teacher could ever hope to offer through their lone expertise.

There's currently no evolution to the basic techniques of solving math problems coming out of the schools. The mechanics of number crunching are considered the only art, rather than there being any artistic concepts applied as mechanisms to problem-solving. Learning the quadratic formula, and how to use it, is not the same as knowing how to solve for it. Math books always present a perfect context, but they should have errors. They should be filled with mistakes to teach children to have a keen eye. We've filled people up with these compiled binary-like instructions on how to do small micro-tasks and expect this to fill in all the spaces in between. But there's no soul in instruction, you can't mass-produce passion. On the upside, you don't need to because every student already has a brain. Contrary to how schools tend to operate, I'd like to see what students are capable of without showing any work.

Math doesn't need to train people to become a calculator. There's more to be gained from understanding the big picture of mathematics than is gained by being professed in 1000 small details. Its modern instruction feels like trying to learn the ancient Chinese alphabet that has thousands of characters. It's inefficient, and not the best way to inspire people towards understanding the small details either. Providing a scalable learning experience using every conceptual topic that a student can make for themselves in Python is a more in-depth process than number crunching, and provides actual utility to the student moving forward. It's not challenging to explain the basic ideas around arithmetic, algebra, linear algebra, geometry, trigonometry, calculus, differential equations, modeling, statistics, probability, machine learning, and so on, as a big picture presentation of these topics is easily achievable without introducing the most difficult problems, and without even using a lot of numbers. I'd rather see a child produce a visual calculator for solving equations by viewing every possible next step rather than force them to solve 1000 arithmetic, algebraic, or whatever kinds of problems. Producing that calculator will require them to know how to solve them in the first place, while simultaneously not making them do repetitive busywork, as the metaphysical improvement of an art form is a mode of evolution worthy of raising children with.

I'd rather they try and solve real problems, as real problems tend to have plenty of other problems that get in the way of a final goal. The problems in the way of some goal are never as monolithic and homogeneous as simply being math problems. Plus they'd get an actual accomplishment under their belt, something that gives them the confidence to step into the world as a problem-solver instead of as an employee. Children have every reason to innovate, become more competitive, and more efficient. Their own local environment could become more competitive with each amazing project that's achieved. It's a win-win-win-win, is it not?

7.8 Technology

A theme often interlaced with education is the use of advanced software. There's a belief that if you somehow introduce these information-manipulation routines onto the screens used by students, that students somehow learn to perform a high-skill job by having this black box perform calculations that they've never thought to understand. But this is a predatory practice, it leaves children reliant upon software they can't build for themselves. This kind of shortcut is a surefire path towards becoming a customer rather than a producer. The required responsibility that comes alongside technology will be like food. If you eat too much, you'll get fat.

As much as taking this philosophy to its logical extreme would be nice, there's not really any way to avoid using computers, or even operating systems, that fail to meet the same criteria. Nonetheless, a strong background in using computers, coupled with the free and open languages made by developers, is an excellent start into entering that world itself. There should be no paid software in schools, no operating systems that spy and collect information on the children who use them, and there should be no shortcuts offered, as there are no shortcuts in the real world that come without a price. Children need to make their own software, learn to use an open source operating system, and ought to be able to make things that other people will buy. A school enabling its students to become customers of some third party is a form of second-hand vampirism that sells the future of children to companies, who then go on to sell their data. At no point is your child gaining a better future, instead they're indoctrinated into being someone else's customer. Videos, books, and a Linux® installation with some locally ran LLMs, are the basics of what's needed for an education in advanced scalable design.

Jonathan Haidt brings up an analysis of western youth that's impossible to ignore if one aims to address this topic. What he gets right is that technology shouldn't be at the center of a child's development. Any kind of touch screen, or computer, with an addictive interface should be completely off limits. In place of this, I would implement a basic Linux installation that's operated through a terminal. I wouldn't want children to become addicted to the aesthetic designs offered in modern UIs, yet I also wouldn't want them to become incapable of taking advantage of a very practical technology. Phones are definitely not meant for children before the age of middle school, and even throughout high school the touch screen interface of modern smartphones becomes no different than a drug addiction. Flip phones, on the other hand, might be a viable alternative. Social media is an extremely toxic place for even adults to become addicted to, and I would introduce it as carefully as one would introduce their child to alcohol.

Despite these limitations, it's important that children are not left behind technologically. Why? Because the people who push the limits of technology all grow up using technology. There's simply no other way to compete.

LLMs enable a kind of offline information search. Children can be observed less, and have less data collected on them than would otherwise be had when dealing with a search engine. Internet searches can still be available through web crawling via the terminal, and this can evolve with age. Addictive graphical interfaces aren't necessary when aiming for practicality with young children. They won't be hyper-observed when doing this, there's no big-tech telemetry logging every mouse movement and key press to identify someone's habits across web pages.

Children can scrape text from the web, and use terminal-based text editors for writing. They can learn various coding languages, and even build robotics that solve practical dilemmas if that's their desire. All of this can be done without addictive interfaces, or social media, both of which aim to capture the minds of people for the sake of delivering an unnatural and never-ending cycle of dopamine.

There must be strong requirements and barriers set up for computers, one must have a good need to use one. Most planning, short of official blueprints, can and should be done outright by hand. Technical flowcharts can be made before any kind of coding becomes necessary. Students don't need to be beholden to technology in order to do their work, technology can be an aspect of execution. The past had mastered the art of advanced craft and creation, and it's the responsibility of anyone raising children to guide the future towards perfecting that same art using computational design. Being able to consider hundreds or thousands more variables, and with hyperparameters, becomes a viable goal for young children when growing their own artistic capabilities.

Research ought to be done physically whenever it can. LLMs are great ways of finding books on specific topics, as well as finding topics to find books on. Books are ultimately the primary resource of knowledge, and technology is a practical tool for accomplishing projects built off of that knowledge. The goal is to maximize children's capabilities with technology, while also maximizing their ability to plan without it. The same way that order always comes alongside disorder, the use of technology can come alongside the ability to abstain from using it. It's too important to leave out, and equally dangerous if used irresponsibly. Have them build a habit of using the internet professionally, while socializing recreationally offline.

Some people have expressed that opening young children up to the internet was a mistake. I think it was a calculated iteration of the unknown. We've gained a lot of valuable things from it, as well as the wisdom to know why not to give unlimited internet access to children. The cost has already been paid for this information, so it's of the utmost importance to make the most out of it.

For young children who haven't even learned to read, technology shouldn't be a part of their life. Reading can, and will, be the most interesting thing in their life as long as you don't present them with anything more immediately gratifying. Until they develop a habit of reading entire books, screens are developmentally disruptive, and they may still be after that. That being said, technology should be embraced rather than feared. It's dangerous to allow children to develop using it for entertainment and not for work. But it's no longer something they can develop without. Large-scale computation, simulation, and the model-based development of tools, are more central to everything we aim to accomplish than anything else.

There needs to be formal agreements amongst parents of a community on how to address technology, as any loose ends will disrupt the long-term plans that most other parents have for their children. An agreement between parents, that don't embrace themselves as a community, is bound to fail. The negligence of those who care less will subvert the diligence of those who care more. Formal legislation on this topic would be even worse, likely only introducing dysgenic oversimplifications. The highest priority to tackle amongst a group of coordinating parents is an agreement between the kind of technology being used at home, which is an area the government shouldn't control.

Do not scroll with your kid, period. This is somewhat similar to watching media and movies. But because these can be done as independent social events, rather than one perpetual rush of dopamine after the next, plus have the added benefit of story telling, these aren't necessarily as bad.

So at what point should children be allowed to venture into the broader social media ecosystem on their own? Consider seriously writing out your life before you do something like trying to become famous on the internet. At least know what you stand for before you throw yourself to the wolves. Too much of the wrong kind of success at a young age, whether as a child singer in the 70s, or some famous child influencer in the 2020s, doesn't tend to correlate with good outcomes, and that's despite typically becoming wealthy.

7.9 The Rights of Children

CPS has the problem of being easily contaminated by individuals who don't favor families and children. You may as well say it has too much potential to be biased in some religious form. It's also a highly contentious process to have your children taken away, or be under their investigation. Ask any parent that's ever had to deal with them, they tend to have bad stories about the abuse of power and leverage used by this group of people.

When considering a kind of department, where you have agents determining whether or not to take people's children away, I think this is possible with a few constraints. CPS ought to be operated only by grandparents who have the approval of at least 75% of their own children. But it's still hard to figure out where CPS should draw the line of when to take someone's child away on paper. The best way to approach the problem isn't just to pick people to do the job well. In a better paradigm, there would be no agents.

You wouldn't want your child going into a refuge made by some completely different religion. It would also be difficult to cater individual solutions for every religious affiliation. There also needs to be placement for such children in locations where they won't be exposed to what can be perceived as the indoctrination of an unfamiliar religion by the people who are having their children taken away. Is there a way to manage all of these nightmares and walk away without a headache?

There needs to be an alternative standard for determining when parents are wildly abusive.

If a child wants to get away from their parents, it could be by their own judgement. Let them get away if they want to, and they would be put up in a place where social exposure is limited to certain parts of the day. In exchange, they would need to be willing to accept something similar to bare minimum jail cell, or dorm room conditions in order to be there. To those who think this is cruel, that's the point. You can't reward them for leaving their parents, leaving their parents itself has to be the reward. If a child is willing to put up with the cruelty, that means the constraints of this lifestyle aren't as bad as the cruelty of their home. Which would mean that the child needs a new home. If someone isn't willing to trade their freedom for an isolative jail cell in exchange for getting away from what they believe are their abusers, then they're not really being abused.

Why is this so important? Quite simply, there have been CPS workers, and their equivalents all over the Western world, taking people's kids away over personal pronouns[**125,126,127**]. In some instances, children were then placed in facilities where they would pretend to be some other gender, and some were probably taking pills. It can easily be seen as these facilities enticing children to leave their parents using claims of abuse, while being welcomed into an alternate lifestyle, an alternate religion even, by people who have infiltrated the child protective services system. There are teachers, government workers, and these so-called facilities, filled with individuals that are working together on this kind of ideologically driven child abduction complex. It's basically targeting children using abnormal forms of positive attention, and with a side of eugenics because the end goal is to have them voluntarily undergo sterilization. A self-admitting process would relieve the need for field agents that participate in any kind of judgement, and

---

125. MC & JC vs Indiana Department of Child Services. *Court of Appeals of Indiana.* Case No 22A-JC-49 decided October 21, 2022; rehearing denied December 22, 2022

126. Todd Kolstad & Krista Cummins-Kolstad vs Montana Department of Public Health & Human Services. *13th Judicial District Court.* No DR-23-0240 (Feb 20, 2024) (child-protection case dismissed)

127. Jeff Younger–Anne Georgulas custody dispute. *Texas Supreme Court mandamus: In re Jeff Younger.* No 22-1137 (Texas Dec 30, 2022) (petition for writ of mandamus denied)

completely eliminate the need for judges to intervene, for teachers to coerce, or for government workers to incentivize children to go down this road. It shouldn't be incentivized. It's extremely difficult to differentiate the perception of abuse from the reality of it. Experiencing a solitary kind of lifestyle, for just one short year, makes for a quick and easy test of whether someone is actually being abused. Any child that doesn't want to continue their confinement can go home immediately.

What's wrong with the agents? The problem with the agents is they can act alone while having complete power in these situations, with no real checks or balances outside a courtroom. You should need to go to court first, before anyone can physically take your child away.

An actual CPS agent would only be needed in the case of a child who's too young to speak, and even in these cases neighbors should be allowed to weigh in, other family members as well, and there should need to be some kind of consensus amongst multiple agents and a judge that there's a real problem if multiple family members don't believe there is. Granting the ability to take someone's child away to any individual is simply too much power to not have proper checks or balances.

Anyone trained in the university system for some kind of government social worker role becomes problematic if they've bitten into ideological dogma, which is especially likely for young women. Ideologically driven individuals are always in search of reasons to take other people's children away, like the individuals during Covid that insisted on removing children from the homes of unvaccinated parents. Young women buy into these ideologies more often than men, and they tend to take social worker roles at a high rate. If, within these social worker programs, they've incorporated multiple grievance studies, then you may as well consider it a breeding ground for religious violations. It destroys the livelihoods of the people they're meant to serve. If even a little of that ideological lens is used to view the world, then there comes large consequences for anyone who isn't ideologically disposed should some ideologue gain power over someone else's children.

Agents, who hunt for abuse, only become a hammer that sees everything as a nail, this job can't be given away simply on the basis of graduating from college. These kinds of people always try to play up their *training*, but in some cases no one has any basis for differentiating what *training* they've received from religious beliefs. Raising children cannot be separated from religious transformation, and neither can schooling. So how can one areligiously determine that a child not being called by their desired pronouns being some form of child abuse is not an egregious violation of religious freedom? Why are there places all across the Western world attempting to formalize this? Why are they targeting children with this indoctrination scheme? It's a process that works hand in hand with people who want to disincentivize others from having children.

It's the weaponization of fear, which makes this behavior so concerning when coming from a government institution. The average parent is far too disconnected from whatever training and professional rituals might be undergone at these agencies, it would be better to abolish most of it in favor of a self-admittance program. More specifically, the ideology of safetyism has completely infiltrated too many walks of life related to children, and it's having a terrible effect on both parents and children together. If you can't raise your child outside the scope of someone else's safety guidelines, then your child's future is doomed. These guidelines have infinite potential for encroachment on just about any activity. What is or isn't safe is sometimes very deterministic, for example in the case of things such as dangerous chemicals or mechanical hazards. But I would plead with you to find parents that have dealt with CPS over minor issues such as bruises, or scrapes, of which every child gets, just to see their lives turned upside down trying to prove they didn't give their own child a paper cut.

If children can stay in confinement for a year outside of school, then they can be taken out of this solitary environment and put in a place more appropriate for child-rearing. Children could voluntarily go to a facility themselves with a phone call. If children can attempt to get themselves out of a broken home, it allows for a distributed calculation to take over a very difficult problem. But if a child can't last a full year in these facilities, then they would lose their ability to admit themselves for another 3 years. Still, if children are willing to live in what's essentially a minimal dorm room to get away from their parents, for a time even less than the full year, then you should let them get away because they need that time away, they have something to gain from it. This wouldn't necessarily need to bring any investigations or charges against the parents. A discussion could be set up with the parents when the child is admitted, and a courtroom would be involved if the child desires it and can last a full year. Children who last a year don't even necessarily need to be separated from their parents, in some instances they may just want negotiating power that's being denied to them. They may just want to be able to have a serious conversation while not being able to be easily dismissed. Things don't necessarily need to bring about the worst possible outcomes such as prison, but this presents an opportunity for the child to prove they need to be heard about their problems. If this can be done well, CPS agents basically don't need to exist.

Children don't even get to choose what they study. Everything about their school lives are controlled. Every part of their life treats them like they're a puppet, and if this wasn't you then I'm happy for you. There are still people who deserve freedom from this nonsense.

Holding back every legal responsibility from them until 18 is most likely stunting the maturity of most of society. The push for sex-change operations, and hormone pills, to be given at the whims of underage children who want them, is the signal of a bigger issue in society. The granting of more rights to children obviously shouldn't mean any sex change operations or hormone pills should be allowed for minors, but there's definitely a reason that a lot of minors are feeling extremely mortified by their lack of options within the current legal framework to the point where this has become a problem. This is the hole they're digging, and a foundation needs to be filled in its place. We aim to keep people as children for far too long. It's not just their rights that are being kept from them, it's the responsibilities that come along with them. Which are absolutely necessary for development.

Children who inherit no rights inherit no responsibility. Growing into adults without any responsibility leaves society destitute and crumbling. You must raise children to be who they need to be as adults. Childhood is not a playpen, it's a trial run.

It's acceptable to deem children capable of independently owning a bank account somewhere around 14-16, as these are the ages when people tend to get jobs. Someone capable of working shouldn't be forced to put someone else in charge of their money. A lot of states have begun to allow this already, but there's a few holdouts that are still refusing. Sometimes banks impose extra rules on minors that have nothing to do with the laws, and this shouldn't be allowed.

On one hand, it's crazy to let people vote if they don't pay taxes. But on the other, it's important to bring children into society as soon as possible. Prolonging childhood only leads to frustration from an inability to participate, but how low should the voting age be exactly? It can be both older and younger if we stratify the voting ages. Children might not be able to receive the feedback of choosing a bad president, but they can receive appropriate feedback from picking a bad mayor. Being able to vote for mayors, city/town councils, and other local level electees, is viable for someone around 14, and electees at these levels should want to appeal to the young for the sake of taking care of their own local environment. At 16 voter eligibility could extend into house representatives and state legislatures. At 18 governors, at 20 senators, and at 22 presidents. This idea would best work alongside the plan for representative electorate strength suggested prior, it would grant the young some form of power to influence the presidential election, without granting them a direct vote. It accomplishes inviting the young to the table without granting them full influence. To add further nuance, we can incentivize young people to skip the line by getting married and having a child. Those who are married, and have made a child of their own, can be eligible to vote at any level independent of age.

People are way too developed, before the age of 18, to not be able to make certain life decisions on their own. Forcing someone who's mentally an adult, to have to ask their parents for permission in too many instances where their parents might be less mature than they are, is going too far. It's too much of a psychological cage, which is why we see problems like what's being made from this gender madness. Some young people are desperately trying to wrestle control of their own life away from people who they shouldn't need to run their lives by. Why should parents have the ability to stop a doctor from talking to their child after a hospitalization? Especially if the parent was the cause of that hospitalization? Why should a child be prevented by a parent from speaking with police, or going to court, over a matter of violence that was taken against that child? The child deserves to have a seat at the table in either situation. It should be the child's right to hear and participate in such things, as children need to bear their own burdens and feedback. Even though some may choose not to, the right to do so must be in place if society is to move forward coherently. Those wanting independence don't always want it for the sake of negligence, they want the responsibility. If trust and responsibility granted during childhood has been a part of the evolutionary history of those that came before them, for hundreds or even thousands of years, then removing it can be expected to destroy their lives to the point where they might never recover.

7.10 Mistakes

Mistakes are the royalty of irony. Humility is extremely important for an individual to be able to express. Childhood reinforcements are things that stick with you for the rest of your life, they're very hard to reverse should they have been instilled incorrectly.

In an environment where making mistakes is rewarded for effort, you'll make no progress. But in an environment where mistakes are punished, you'll see a denial of their occurrence. Such actions only prevents people from learning the lessons their mistakes have to offer. Rewarding success is more important than punishing failure. The balance to strike between these two bounds is to be accepting of mistakes, because mistakes are natural. Use mistakes as the lessons that they're meant to be, and not as opportunities to punish. These lessons are priceless. Being able to avoid mistakes through intuition is a sign of talent, but forcefully preventing a child from making mistakes is counter-productive teaching.

With grades being a measure of how many mistakes one can prevent themselves from making, the nature of transformation is subverted for petty pretentiousness when using grades as a foundation for education. The real world has problems that aren't being represented by the nature of neither tests nor fake practice problems. Thinking through real problems involves planning steps, testing, failure, learning from mistakes, and eventually success. There's never actions that are purely *correct* or *incorrect* in the grand scheme of things, because mistakes can always be fixed. What's the point of judging someone based on things that are correctable, rather than their ability to make such corrections? The nature of growth is that which overcomes mistakes, the nature of success is that which has learned from them.

People who fear punishment end up becoming anxious. The fear of punishment comes when you're in an environment that punishes mistakes. Mistakes are inevitable, to pretend they're not is to pretend we're robots. This ultimately leads to people pretending to know what they're doing, while refusing to admit when they don't understand something. Which can be called toxic, but more realistically can be seen as a process that makes people who then go on to form fundamentally unstable societal structures.

Eventually, people who fear mistakes get to an age where they can't admit their mistakes anymore. It would only seem like something's wrong with them if they were ever to admit something, as an adult, that they didn't learn at an appropriate age. Or even worse, a scenario where large swaths of people all make the same mistake, while believing it was actually a good way of doing something, becoming Descartes' idiots. There's more to learn from failure than success. It doesn't mean to reward failure, but it means to allow it. When it comes to children, it's better to have them learn to make mistakes while creating a healthy cycle of learning how to learn from mistakes in order to find solutions rather than pretending to have never made any at all, as they would someday end up making better adults.

Boomers often complain that their children didn't work hard after throwing them into institutions that didn't reward hard work, and often times even penalized it. Reinforcement is destiny, and we're seeing the results of this as well as the refusal to admit this mistake. If your students or children have turned their past mistakes into a form of nihilism, they've been taught wrong. Don't regret mistakes, because regret is nihilistic, but don't be proud of mistakes either. Cherish them for what they were meant to teach you. Likewise, when this extends into someone's view of their own history, when they've been taught to hate their own ancestors for some perceived wrongdoing, that's a betrayal.

Lessons don't come from lectures. The only thing you pick up in a lecture is dogma. As adults who grow up unable to challenge the dogma they'd learned in their youth, display a level of hysterical infantilism over their beliefs being challenged, society will inevitably face a drop in its birth rate. The dogma of the modern academic paradigm is at the center of this problem. Too many things are taught to children at a young age for the sake of an insidious insertion of flawed ideas into their minds.

But it's equally true that if you stand for nothing, you'll fall for anything. Not wanting children to learn specific beliefs, that they'd otherwise hold dearly, is a betrayal, as well as a denial of your own virtues. It would be a mistake in itself not to. The most important opportunity in a child's life is to do what they do for others. Acting for the benefit of others is the most beneficial thing you can do for yourself, and the most sacred form of acting for the sake of others is starting your own family. A family is the best possible thing you can contribute to the world.

Mistakes are why the left-wing is destroying itself. The school system has widely become a left-wing production pipeline, and people on the left-wing have become synonymous with the crooked beliefs that are destroying Western society. They constantly try to remove people from positions of power over minor mistakes, statements, or jokes. They demand a hero that's never made any mistakes in the first place, which is both literally and figuratively impossible. Meaning there's no hero that can save this group, yet they've tied themselves to the train tracks. Which is why they only accomplish the destruction of their own cause. Education has become a diversion from survival, and is instead an endless string of bureaucratic requirements that offer nothing to children but a means of being unable to support themselves. The entire system makes itself about, and incentivizes, bad teachers. Then there's principals, and superintendents, which are all just bloat for the sake of micromanagement.

The biggest mistake anyone can make is to only observe. Instead, you have to question. At the very least, you must judge, then ask, whether something was done as well as it could have been, and if not, what would you change? Ask whether you could have done something better, or more fairly, without any intention of abandoning the question.

There's nothing more fruitless than the embrace of absolutes. Everyone can make mistakes, everyone can be wrong. A civil engineer can design a building prone to collapse, a doctor can misdiagnose a disease. There are still lessons to be learned everywhere, we have not achieved perfection, and never will. Pretending any bastion of civilization is without error will only yield masses of people who make such errors in doing so. They become the mistakes for the next generation to learn from, because it very often takes that long for people to realize.

It's important to earn rewards and take their keep. But don't indulge in reward. Indulge in the journey, not the destination. These things that we do such as fair exchange, free trade, positive reinforcement, and everything positive about the world that brings out the best in other people, were done as a proper reward from an intelligent incentive system. That's exactly where intelligence emerges, from the transformation of mistakes into wisdom. It's the feedback for making an interesting move on the board.

Émile Borel wrote about the idea of having an infinite number of chimpanzees all forced to write on typewriters, where at least one would be able to recreate a work of Shakespeare by pure chance. But the method for the chimp getting the Shakespearian play closer to completion would be more easily achieved through freedom, fairness, and incentives, rather than by strapping primates to a typewriter, as that's how nature ended up accomplishing this exact same task. Those three things were imperative, and this is something that's persisted for billions of years. This is the core of human behavior, it even happens at the molecular level. Molecular automatons operate freely, and they reward themselves with greater efficiency and reproduction, as overcoming competition is the incentive for success. Even if these concepts can't be perceived by cells, the causal-deterministic nature of the population of events takes over, and the outcomes play out as if they do.

It would seem a nucleus is enough to manage these incentives and rewards. You don't need a brain in order to do this. But a brain is a much more advanced version of the same thing. You could compare a nucleus to a brain the same way you compare a calculator to a supercomputer. Freedom, fairness, and incentive fill a dynamic niche akin to the nature of that filled by salable currency. With 3 broad concepts, and the expected interplay between them, what outcome lies at the end of this seemingly systematic exchange of metaphysical niche minimization for complexity maximization? An inevitable set of mistakes, that form the crisp nature of consciousness, that becomes core to reflexive behavior itself for every organism that ever achieved it.

VIII
PERCEPTION & THE BRAIN

8.1 Information World

If multiple progenitors have convergently evolved into the same crab phenotype, then the same possibility exists for humanoids. Or most other forms. The environment for humans existed long before humans ever did. Which is why humans exist in the first place, all things that support the evolution of a humanoid must first be present. So what's the most notable aspect of a humanoid? Intelligence. What brings about intelligence? What environment creates this demand?

The most notable distinctions of perception comes from the work of James Gibson[**128**]. The long story short, is that animals developed perception as a means of perceiving function. It's the function of an object that becomes immediately recognizable to your brain long before you ever think of what that object actually is, you perceive its function through its structure. Gibson explains this link to functionality through what he calls affordances, and this stands at the crossroads of information and its potential. Where he would say a sharp pointy object can afford to pierce, it would follow that the sharpness of a point is a physical form of information that has the potential to pierce. Where Gibson would say the relationship of perception is between the object and the perceiver, it would follow that this relationship formed because information is latent within the object itself no different than

128. James Gibson. *The Ecological Approach to Visual Perception*. Houghton Mifflin, 1979

the potential energy of a boulder perched atop a cliff. This explanation based around information is more the reason for how perception itself developed, whereas Gibson's verbatim explanations underline the relationship between animals and their environments. This relationship forms because the potential for the information represented by these affordances has always existed, and our perception came to find this potential due to it being a latent aspect of the environment able to offer a direct advantage in survival. The specific attributes of physical objects grant them their potential. Humans specifically, didn't just evolve to perceive function, we evolved to utilize function through information. The relationship between structure and function is so strong that perception itself immediately skips over the need to classify structure in favor of acknowledging function.

Any environment in its entirety is always bound to be more complex than any of its individual components. But the individual parts of any environment are always guaranteed to be unique relative to any other parts. This uniqueness, and its potential, is representative of the information of each component of that environment. Information is the characterization of unique differences.

The environment that brought about modern humans, and their predecessors, is one in which information was abundant, yet not properly utilized. That which is eventually capitalized on by a species known for documenting information for strategic purposes. With interactions themselves having the potential to combine the functionality of different forms of information, information naturally becomes a way of garnering advantage in every and any interaction. Sticks can be carved down by rocks to form sharp edges, as can other rocks. Fibers from plants can be unwound and made into cloth. For an organism to rely on something other than its own physical structures to survive means that it's become incentivized to deal with information more accurately, as finding a structure to suit your needs is much faster than growing it on your own body. Information is like fruit waiting to be plucked from the tree of irony.

So what grants the ability to process arrays of information in conjunction to use the latent potential in one's environment as tools? It's not just the power of observation, as most organisms have this to some degree. Is it a heightened sense of observation? Is it an acceptable answer to say that our brains are just more advanced than that of other animals? Not really, as that dismisses the question rather than answering it.

Given you make observations using your senses, it might be fair to quickly integrate and say consciousness is the observation of observations. Which has us, again, arrive at the concept of perception, as that's basically what this describes. Even the very act of information collection can easily fall into the same description. As what does a brain do, other than observe observations given by the senses? The art of observation then provides the basis for an organism possessing such a skill to branch out into greater forms of intelligence, as questions would make for the next layer of integrals after observations. Questioning the known, and questioning the questioning of the known to reach towards the unknown.

No matter who you talk to, whether you love them or hate them, you ask questions. Like you have a question making device in your head. Sometimes to make sense of something, sometimes to connect. Out of necessity, I'd wager you apply stringency to your questions so as not to be short-sighted. Which in itself is like practice thinking. How does one apply stringency to questions? You ask questions about your questions.

This questioning process is like a muscle, it can grow and also whither. The nature and underlying patterns of your questions are likely going to be related both to childhood practice and life experience, as the brain is both extremely flexible and extremely trainable. You can train it for just about anything. The brain itself is that which trains you to train. So if structure is function then the brain would possess a function that simulates structure. Which not only grants wisdom, it acts as the basis for scale-descending molecular feedback into every cell that can and should receive its message. Feedback that goes from perception, to nervous system, to cells, that trigger physiological responses that affects the smallest scale of biological regulation on a per-cell basis, that then later go on to affect the body at large in any number of ways because thoughts being at the start of this cascade likely allow for infinite flexibility.

Humans act as not just gatherers of supplies and tools, not just hunters of prey. They both hunt and gather information. The intelligent are the harvesters of information. The potential for technological growth is seemingly boundless, and I would argue information encompasses an even broader infinite potential than that of technology. Boundaries aren't intrinsic to information, boundaries only apply to the observer whose limitations are inherent. Information is an environment unique to itself. Humans had originally found themselves in an environment of information, and modeled it to gain their intelligence. We can even ascribe value to information, for even deeper strategic purposes. The natural interaction between people and the value of information brings about economics, with economics being a mechanism for the collective utilization of information available to a group.

In the theoretical version of what a brain actually is, its simplified form would be like that of a computer terminal. That which can mine information like a computer can mine cryptocurrency. If you want to know something, and dwell on the topic for long enough, you'll eventually find what you're looking for. With information being different levers one can pull to adjust their pools of entropy, the brain would operate as the transformative barrier between the entropy of physical structures, like thermodynamic and statistical entropy, to a metaphysical form like information entropy. Specifically, this would be when a physical process can model, and come to represent, the solution to some form of calculation in a more efficient way than could be done by brute force. Brute force would be raw counting, like using 20 individual pieces to count to 20 instead of 9 pieces that represent the multiplication of 4x5.

The brain can operate with first-class functions, using concepts, models, thoughts, or snapshots of anything as a factor of any other piece of its own processing. Finding optimal places for any input value is the art of crafting thoughts. Which is a lot like computation. The mining of information likely occurs in some parallel manner to that which occurs at the societal level, the broken compass. The curse for this gift would be the negativity one dwells on in order to acquire it.

Another curse of this gift is the responsibility you bear by knowing it. Information requires responsibility. Those who won't bear it turn stupid and hateful, and maybe a cult is a group of people who collectively refuse to bear the responsibility of some specific pieces of knowledge they possess. The consequences of such refusals will destroy the society that such responsibility was originally meant for. As information can be mined, beliefs are not made they're discovered. Discovering problems only to ignore them is to allow negligence to supercede wisdom. Which would be fairly unintelligent, and that's likely not the form of behavior that formed our behavior in the first place.

When it comes to scientific topics, it's ironic that we build knowledge structures out of literal uncertainties. What we don't know, or can't explain, is always some core tenet of the physical world, the very beginnings of whatever mode of causality we stumble into questioning at all. Peripheral phenomena, like the understandings found through early science, are easier for intelligent beings to initially understand because they brush the surface of so many of the core tenets themselves. The first things to be formally understood, like the forging of metals and the utilization of kinetics, were the earliest concepts to be understood because of their relative simplicity. It's the interaction between these core tenets that's more easily characterized because there's more angles one can analyze to unravel their mysteries, which from our perspective comprises the simplest information, as opposed to the chemical, thermodynamic, and quantum foundations they arise from.

In reality, everything we know is dependent upon concepts we've never heard of, don't know about, and can't explain. In a world where we operate to predict things on the basis of first principles, it would seem we're unable to actually find any. What is a structure without a proper core, other than an uncertainty? The fact that our actual structures of knowledge are built on the conceptual opposite of themselves in this way, knowns being entirely made of unknowns in the same way that order is inherently still a form of disorder, like predictive power is actually some kind of anti-knowledge, casts a vivid reflection upon Dawkins' concept of an organism being a model of its environment, as intelligence seems like it's just information undergoing that same process. What is order if not something that modeled disorder, and knowns something that modeled unknowns. And what would intelligence be if not something that clawed its way into existence in that same manner to differentiate itself from its own background? Your head releases thoughts the same way your body releases heat. Our uncertainty is our model, what we're modeling is based on whatever straws we can grasp, and whatever else gets made from those straws when updating our beliefs. The nature of intelligence is firmly anchored in the unknown, in ignorance itself.

The success of humans has been formed through an intricate balancing act of intricate balancing acts that's been managed throughout our evolution. We can see the remnants of this process in our own society as well as our evolutionary history. It's visible through the leftover competing interests of the world around us, we're neither truly male nor female dominated, unlike chimps and bonobos respectively, there's potential for either. Being neither fully psychologically nor physically controlled. Fully diploid that produces other diploids. Child-rearing that takes advantage of both parents for specific aspects of that child's development, and there's typically one child per birth, guaranteeing a level of parental dedication to each child that wouldn't be possible with litters. Nothing is uniformly dominant because everything has value, and being able to find value in everything pays off, allowing for our contemplative nature. This allows us to succeed in superb ways, and also opens the door for widespread psychological warfare when we don't know what to succeed at. Which is yet again the formation of the broken compass.

A brain is something with functions that can be practiced and perfected. But this is more a description of its utility and not of its nature. Even if utility *is* its nature, this explanation still stops short of an outside observer's perspective and focuses on a description suitable to those who experience having a brain. So how would one go about describing this from an outsider's perspective?

8.2 The Observer Effect

As organisms whose existence is defined entirely by information, there's a lot for us to observe about each other. One might call what they see a personality, or principles. Beauty is found where something accurately reflects the fundamental principles of the universe. Which is the purpose of a brain, to accurately reflect the principles that it models, and to recognize when others succeed at doing so.

The complexity increase from the reciprocating pushback of pools of entropy in the proto-nervous systems of early organisms brought about a kind of metaphysical detection that arose from this competition. As the two forces pushing against each other became able to react to the push of the other in strategic ways, reacting became detecting, and from detection came observation. Observation became a fundamental axiom of life. It allows a mind to strategize the best ways to compete, to predict, and to design in order to survive.

In general, the brain is probably able to model itself through understanding its own internal connections. Not just understanding its own internal wiring, but a complete saturation of modeling itself to the point where no single signal sent is independent from some centralized process. Which is how it comes to be self-aware, this process is a modeling of recursion itself.

Constantly thinking about yourself, and your own life, always results in negativity because it's a bit of a flawed way to live your life. It's an indication that you ought to have someone else to care about. It's no different than the left-brain inclination towards becoming a hyperactive immune system that attacks its own host or society. You'll always find better ways to live your life by trying to do things for others, and by being thoughtful of others. The brain is an observation tool, and observing yourself ends up being a form of punishment, because observation is punishment. To instead think of what you can do for others, is to inadvertently do good for yourself.

The nature of an observer observing itself can backfire in more ways than benefit. But it's not like self-reflection isn't necessary, it's meant to be transformative. It's meant to help you escape your negative thoughts by finding a way to overcome them through some spawning of complexity.

Narcissists are people who observe themselves too much, or have been forced to do so, and come to only know themselves in that extremely negative self-observational manner. They then consequently use themselves as the basis for predicting other people. Which is why you can safely assume people to be what they project onto others through accusations, because perception is the centralization of awareness and accumulated information. If the only thing someone is aware of is themselves and their own point of view, they stunt their own perception of others because their perception of themselves is extremely negative. Likewise, it's not just extremely negative, it's self-sabotaging. Narcissists have practiced this extremely negative self-observation they're assessing themselves with, not knowing it's meant to be a form of transformational introspection that acts as an intermediary step towards learning to help others.

Both negativity and positivity are tools to use, and too much of either, like anything else, can be a bad thing. Negativity can offer the chance for self-reflection at its best, and hatred at its worst. Positivity can give off inspiration at its best, and become fruitless optimism at its worst. Both have a purpose, and matching the purpose to whatever circumstances you find yourself in is what will determine whether you succeed or fail.

Self-imposed negativity is an attempt to force you to confront your failures and admit your mistakes in order to embrace a philosophy of improvement. It's supposed to be presented in the context of not wanting to repeat a mistake, and it shouldn't provoke anxiety, it should bring about an improvement to a model in your head. It's meant to act as guidance towards a weight in some pool of entropy, but the pride of not wanting to admit mistakes, or admit to lies you believe, will inhibit this process. When this goes wrong, this transformation becomes a projection of one's own internal negativity onto others. Resulting in the opposite transformation, towards narcissization, which is a developmental dead end. One won't want to be more negative about themselves than they are about others, so increasingly negative thoughts about others form as this habit is practiced. The only way out of this self-observational hole is to put others first, as it's fundamentally a flaw in understanding oneself that causes this developmental derailment towards narcissism in the first place.

What about when we fundamentally misunderstand our perceptions of something in our environment? While perception can be linked to seeing functions, rather than objects, we still have stratifications to perception where the edges of what we can just barely grasp are not entirely seen as functions, because we don't know what functions they possess. These are the mysteries we puzzle ourselves with, and there's an instinctual drive to solve them. One way to find out what kind of functions exist is to use existing functions like puzzle pieces to solve for new ones. Which is using the known to model the unknown, this is the mining of information with your head.

In this way, chaos is elucidated by the observer effect. As something isn't chaotic if you understand what's going on. Our own observer effect, when directed towards things other than ourselves, is what eventually grants knowledge. Whether something is chaotic is just a perspective. Perception of something completely unintelligible requires a big upfront cost. You would be inferring the nature of a complicated set of unknowns from a balance between left- and right-brain functions, which is that which tries to perfect the art of observation. To keep track of as many things with as little effort as possible. Ignorance is the degree to which unknowns are hidden from you, and the extra energy required to understand that which you don't is what makes things seem chaotic.

A brain is a recursion of a cell's nucleus. But a cell's nucleus doesn't purely operate in a right- or left-brain manner, its fine details are outsourced to the biochemistry of its cytoplasmic interactions. Cells operate on the bifurcation of order and disorder. The concepts of the left- and right-brain themselves are recursions of order and disorder, which still dominate these processes at the cellular level. These interactions sometimes send signals back to its nucleus to adapt its big picture functioning, its gene expression, where signals would indicate the nature of the change required for continued functioning. Every demand in this realm is directly indicated by a process not unlike the strings of an infinitely complicated marionette. The brain manages a level of perception that a cell's nucleus isn't capable of grasping. It had to incorporate even itself, for the sake of reflection, in order to achieve consciousness. It even had to incorporate the concept of perception to understand there are others just like it. Then should it be any surprise that as such organisms become more advanced, that they then attempt to consider some *great perceiver*, some *grand observer*, such as God? If consciousness is the observation of observations, then whatever hypothetically observes consciousness at scale is just its integral, of course it would be solved at some point and those thoughts would naturally emerge.

8.3 Individuals and Collectives

Our thoughts are imperceivable to each other, as you can't hear what someone else is thinking. So is this imperceivable through a paradoxical distance, the same as the inside of a black hole? Do we interact on the basis of the concept of the limits of perception with one another? Is this the only basis for thought to be able to exist? A closed world only able to interact with itself internally, yet that still exists within a physical container that then interacts with other containers? There's certain effects that arise from this, between the interactions of individuals and collectives.

Intelligence evolved because we're inherently surrounded by information and its potential. If we form collectives that don't model real information, then they wouldn't be successful collectives. They would instead break down due to dysfunctional individuals. Collective cohesion takes evolutionary precedence over individual intelligence. Meaning cooperation acts as both a limiter and catalyst for individual abilities, depending on the presented conditions. Religion would be that which aims to present conditions capable of catalyzing such growth.

Intelligence isn't something you have, it's moreso a response. Plants basically have the same thing, just without sentience, they move and adapt in response to stimuli. It's no different than the ability to hit back with rapidity in warfare. The more instantaneous and effective a response to an oncoming long-distance attack is, the more intelligent the response would be. You can consider the affinities and behaviors of proteins and any other proteins they interact with, the signals that cells send to one another, and the downstream effects brought about after neurons have fired in response to some kind of stimulus, as the basis for biochemical intelligence. The molecular interactions that enable intelligence manifest in the same manner outside our bodies. The crispness of this communication is the physicality of intelligence itself.

There's a requirement of cooperation that acts as the conditional logic gate to grow individual abilities, but then what's the purpose of sentience? Structures evolve, meanings change, even information can never be static, it can only be stable at best. There's always some other interpretation of anything, some obscure viewing angle that paints a different picture of what could be important for the assessment of danger. Which is why intelligent beings can't be solitary, it's even considered a form of torture. We were bound to be social animals because of the plasticity of the nature of information. If the entire world operated with perfect predictability, then sentience would be absolutely useless. It wouldn't be needed alongside intelligence. Sentience is the chaotic solution to a sea of chaotic problems, cooperation being one of them. Sentience isn't just a pilot, it's an ambassador with built-in tools for negotiation called the model of interactions. Even whether definitions themselves are either monoliths, stratifications, or found between two boundaries is itself something to be defined, and to define *to define* is the core religious endeavor. Sentience has the job of approaching an answer to the religious question of how best to persist that forms through the manifestation of this dynamic form of information processing known as consciousness.

Selection for human intelligence was as much a group process as an individual one because narcissism is developmentally stunting, even to groups. Affinity for group cohesion is no different in nature than the binding affinities that create an array of biochemical signals. The brains that won out were those with a sense of teamwork and sense of shared responsibility, the same successful strategy that makes itself evident in society today. Which can be the same great goal to aim for in raising your children.

Individuals have thoughts as their unique characteristic. What are thoughts? Little simulations of reality. You can create an entire world in your head. Groups have communication as their unique characteristic, and mode of interaction. Metaphorically, the social bifurcations of the automaton are most representative of ignorance, which is why anything is ever communicated in the first place. It's meant to fill in blank spots of ignorance, and to communicate that which might be uncertain. Communication models collective human ignorance. Which offers a disappointing reflection on how contriving the world of scientific communication is. Universities love to paint the stories of history in ways that make it seem like verifying information is a new thing, and the cults of these institutions love to overcomplicate their forms of communication behind paywalls and dogma.

The absurdities of the past were partly political, and partly in search of that which they couldn't easily define, the search for what religion was actually searching for. Culture is a kind of technology that offers a bedrock for cooperation. In places where dogma matters more than adaptation, decadence is more certain than continued success. Communication is that which rivals both dogma and decadence.

If the human brain has truly managed to model the universe, then it should be possible to learn about the universe through the behavior of humans. Stability and fragmentation would seem to meet this criteria. The West has gotten to the point where individualism is a cultural norm. You could also represent it as a fragmentation of religion across society that models different walks of life. Individualism is a hedge against the failings of collectivism, and vice versa. But the irony is that better individuals make better collectives, these two concepts never truly separate from one another. It then follows that a better collective forms the conditions that allow for the making of better individuals. It's a self-reinforcing loop that repeats over and over where individualism and collectivism find themselves to be cyclic derivatives. Like they're recursive embeddings within each other, and always makes ground for yet another series of cultural transformations. Like folding steel to remove impurities. Which is why intelligence isn't an ultimate deciding factor in any one person's outcome. If you can't make better individuals, then make better collectives. Test scores, by design, completely forego this avenue of success.

It's likely this is the historical evolutionary pattern of the brain and its intelligence. That the endless walk comes in strides of both cooperation and individualism, Iain McGilchrist highlights this when he explains his, basically analogous, historical timeline where periods between his concepts of right- and left-brain each dominated societal spheres during their height, much like how our political pendulum swings from left to right, and then back again. Except the pendulum now has multiple layers to it, there's derivatives upon derivatives in the same way acceleration relates to velocity. The various ages of history, and the growth they offered, suggests that times of religious growth, knowledge growth, and the overall rise and fall of every empire that ever existed, were simply steps on this endless walk where we form both individuals and collectives that model the universe through what we call intelligence. So it shouldn't be any surprise that we see fluctuating trends of centralization and decentralization across society, that's a sign that everything's functioning as it should.

The endless walk consists of reciprocating steps that go back and forth during each time period. Farming, herding, and trade were likely components of larger interactions that were ironed out until it brought us out of the Stone Age. Both before and after, would be periods where civilization, and its most definable precursors, would have elucidated forms of law and religion. Religious progression would have been made from the right foot taking its next step, and having walked so far away from those older periods is why religion ends up looking strange to so many in the present day. Other antiquated forms of societal interaction are no less foreign to us through our lens of modern liberalism.

It's hard for many today to understand the basis for why people went along with what seems to be the strange and otherwise nonsensical traditions of antiquity. You may explain circumcision through the prevention of STDs, and the avoidance of certain kinds of meat as knowledge of the parasites they may contain, but outside the practical world came a somewhat incomprehensible comprehension of the incomprehensible itself. These people put together the best big picture they could, despite not fully knowing what religion itself was meant to grasp. They had no knowledge of the dogma of biology, basic chemistry, or what stars even were. They certainly had no idea what the age of the Earth was, nor that it even had an age to begin with. So of course they were wrong about a lot of things.

The strides being taken are a lot like a bootstrapping of reality. Like making a lathe out of raw materials you found in your own backyard. At first it'll have an ineffective tolerance and might not be of the greatest quality. But once you can make the first lathe, you can then use that to machine more precise parts of better tolerance, to then make a better lathe. Rinse and repeat this process, find higher quality materials to build the best iterations from, and you have yourself a high quality machining process. As the left and right-brain strides continue to march into the future, we begin to make more and more sense of what we're meant to make sense of. The reason why people begin to accept additions and revisions to religions in each new age is because revelations begin to overcome prevailing nonsensicalities where people never originally thought they would.

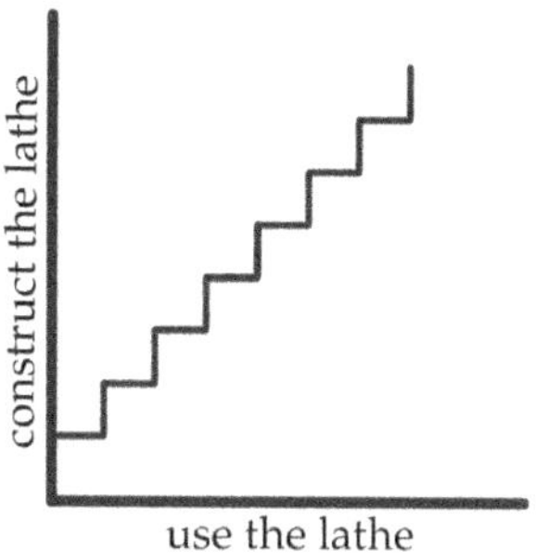

Figure 8: The Analogy of the Lathe

Ironically, something like liberalism may not be as useful as the stride towards liberalism. Once you have it, too many people want to label everything as a *human right* to the point where nothing in society makes sense anymore. The stride towards conservatism will eventually be of a similar nature, and like what liberalism has become in recent years, it will somehow subvert itself with its own success. Science is not a replacement for religion, religion needs to be the motivation for science. A denial of religion amongst the masses will bring about their own failure to survive and produce offspring. That's of course, if they're unable to grasp the big picture, and the need we have for one in general, one which extends from our early beginnings to our distant future.

8.4 Culminations of History

Saying a brain is like a computer, or a terminal, might be the most appropriate analogy available from our own point of view, but we don't have computers that do what we do. Computers don't reproduce into new computers, and they don't self-design themselves into more advanced forms either. Is there something about the brain that's perhaps not widely acknowledged?

Human evolution can be understood through a thought experiment. Imagine you have young children just barely old enough to get along by themselves, living in some forest or jungle where nothing will immediately prey on them. Let's assume there are no adults and no one who raised them, they know no language, they know nothing. The point of this is to wonder, what skills would they be able to develop on their own? Would they develop a rudimentary language, a counting system, and learn to find food? They might not survive to be old enough to develop the thinking skills to manage any of these tasks, or perhaps they look out for each other and somehow pull through. Either way, the classification of human evolution can be looked at through this lens. That whatever it is these hypothetically abandoned children would be able to accomplish on their own is a sign of their evolutionary history having properly modeled those components of the world.

The point of observing such a thing would be to learn something about human nature, to answer the question of *just what is human nature and how would you characterize it*? To separate history from upbringing like this would likely display the answer, as long as they don't die. While I used to think this experiment would be the only way to find the answers, I've come to not need the answer to this experiment anymore. There's obvious signs of what people would be able to develop, and it's exactly what you'd expect. A means of food, clothing, shelter, an evolving means of production, a language as a method of recording and writing, and a mode of calculation. It's everything you'd find in a normal civilization, as that's how we came to civilization in the first place. You don't need to drop children in the middle of a jungle just to study their outcome, evolution has already done this experiment, we ourselves are the result of it. Which may seem like a cheap answer, but that's the truth. The real answer doesn't show itself in just one generation. Generation after generation they learn and grow, and that's human nature.

The human ability to adapt has always coincided with technological advancements and cultural changes, and the nature of advancement being a specific problem means it has a specific solution that leads in a pseudodeterminant direction. That which models the complexity of nature with the complexity of nature itself eventually manifests numbers, calculation, and insight. The answer to the question of *what is human nature* is the same as asking which is more complex, the complexity of nature or the nature of complexity.

The nature of complexity is symmetrical in every way, as with order always comes disorder. Human nature models nature itself through the utility of nature's own expression. To continue modeling it requires continually increasing abilities of observation, as not everything in nature is immediately visible. Consider that the art of observation is always evolving, and will never stop. Even if you could hypothetically observe everything and anything in the universe perfectly, then every technological arms race would evolve into trying to know, to observe for yourself, what someone else has then observed. Then better observing what they've observed of you, and so on and so forth, until you invent the most ridiculous form of spying to the point where everyone just decides to share all their information instead because it costs less money. The nature of complexity increases forever. The complexity of modeling complexity will always surpass any existing complexity of nature in the first place, otherwise there would be neither novelty nor inventions. The potential of anything in nature is always greater than the latent form it exists in. While human existence leverages the complexity of nature, human nature embodies the nature of complexity.

To answer what a brain is, a purely Darwinian view would say it's the culminatory model of all past experiences being ingrained as instincts. The Newtonian view would say it's a terminal which can mine some framework of truth. Which is an integral and derivative, respectively.

A brain is a culmination of instincts just as the complexity of nature would be a culmination of every layer of complexity encompassed within it. Brains are primarily an intermediary of interaction with nature itself, rather than being a passive observer in the same way the potential information of nature is latent. To culminate the complexity of nature incentivizes the approach towards the nature of complexity. Brains have solved and encoded general solutions to nearly every problem they've ever come across, and we call these instincts. Living in an age filled with problems our evolutionary history has never encountered, it would seem we're on the cusp of the next major evolutionary stride within humans.

Previous models have become slightly more irrelevant. The biological incentive to modify our approach to upbringing and social life grows with the depth of our technological prowess. When I say this, I bet you'd assume it implies a change in direction, something that takes a turn relative to where we've been and where we've come from. But this is incorrect, the changes will actually be both more novel and more conservative in nature, as with more order comes more disorder. Seen through the falling global birth rates, the world now offers a myriad of new addictions and methods of altering your modes of communication.

So why is it likely that there'll be selection for new traits? There might not be, the old ones might win out in ways they previously hadn't. But if some new layer of behavior were to be selected for, it would be because of the following:

The model of interactions faces changes in rapidity, scale, nature, and frequency due to the interactions brought about through mass communication. Before it was books, newspapers, radios, then telephones, televisions, and is now social media. It's not just connectivity either, it's that everyone in the world knows everyone else is aware of the same bigger picture to some degree. Thanks to this, history is being recorded in a more bottom-up manner than ever before. The observer effect has saturated, we live in a different world than it used to be when characterizing our environment relative to other humans. Warfare changes to the point where an advantageous philosophy of war might be to pretend you're not having one, due to the insidious ways they're already being fought, and the multiple channels through which it can happen such as cyber and economic warfare. Our understanding of the ingredients in foods and the nature of our own diets, as well as their relation to our evolutionary past, seems to be blossoming as a field of its own, and it might highlight differences in biology in the future much more boldly than how we see them today. Families will likely accumulate digital prowess and capabilities the same way some families have historically accumulated wealth. The nature of currency is changing to be somewhat independent of government control, as governments are horrible at managing currency and have always caused the collapse of their own empires through inflation. Ideologies are competing over which kind of dopaminergic reward system to use and communication has reached an evolved form, of which massive cultural changes have occurred and are still underway because of. Technology, the internet, and now AI, will compound as a massive spawning of complexity which makes a landscape where modeling our environment itself transforms to a step above what it previously was. It'll not just be individuals that figure out how to sail this ship blind, it will be groups. As communication will be vital in playing this game, just as it was in the past.

Changes will narrow in on the same instincts they've always narrowed in on. If the population declines, it will only narrow that much harder. In a world with a growing population, we have a chance to increase the number of useful and novel behaviors, and we're in a unique position to do this. The future will undeniably face a culling of people unable to manage their lives in time to have children in this age of constant intellectual competition and ever improving technology. The larger the population that's left over, the more behaviors will survive. The quantity of variation in surviving behaviors will dictate transformational power for the future for any civilization, as it's evolutionary capital. The very thing that communism is known for destroying.

It seems appropriate to reason that a brain is designed by every brain that ever came before it. The towers built both over the long term, as well as the more immediate short term, are reaching new heights never yet encountered. The pattern matches quite nicely to Moore's law. Any realistic interpretation of human evolution would suggest that a brain designs the foremost models of its progeny's brain, or at least has serious influence over it. You can't drop a child in the middle of the jungle and expect them to grow into a genius as an adult from no real guidance whatsoever. The use of their own feedback mechanisms depends on their upbringing specifically.

The brain is a continually adjusting model across generations. Which is why the existing school system is not only bad in the short term, it's terrible in the long term. It's been terrible for families who've gone through it for generations, and will be terrible still for their children. The generational impact of the bad experiences caused by this imprisonment is likely developmentally stunting. People's instincts are innate and come from billions of years of evolution. There's no behavioral training so completely oppositional to the instincts that young children inherit that will continue allowing each generation to have a successful future should they not come to understand its flaws. They'll eventually grow older and learn to disagree with their brainwashing, which costs them time and effort, but this needs to turn into action. Otherwise, it ends up losing potential value in the economy, losing children in the populace, and wasting taxpayer dollars on developmentally abnormal indoctrination schemes. The school system has been failing people who've come to misinterpret themselves as an experimental group, and are dying out because of it. We have a diminished control group in our civilization, because nearly every school was forced to be of an experimental philosophy, so the population decline is not surprising.

It's not just wise to treat people well, it's wise to surround yourself with people who all treat each other well. It's the people who treat each other the best who turn out the best. People have every right to section into groups based on reciprocating behavior when raising their children, as this is what's best for everyone involved. You, as an individual, are under no obligation to help those who treat you terribly, as it doesn't only destroy your own future, it'll also impact your own children the same. You have no obligation to sacrifice your own well-being, inside a school, just because the predominant state-ran religion demands you give up your patience and hard work for the benefit of others who would never show you the same kindness. No one within our system of freedom has any right to force your kindness. No schools have any business holding your future hostage at their expense. The existing modern academic paradigm is a system where the worst people benefit at the expense of the best. But a successful society does not and will never operate like this, so schools shouldn't either, as schools are meant to model every aspect of life the way a brain is intended to.

The evolutionary model inherited undergoes major developmental steps within the womb of the mother. Cycles of the mother's hormones are able to shape the behaviors of those same hormones in her child[129], and maternal stress during pregnancy can leave clear epigenetic fingerprints on their children[130]. While this work didn't measure epigenetic fingerprints in the brain of newborns, one can infer from the plasticity of the brain that the fingerprints left on it would be more significant than anywhere else. These kinds of influences from the mother are probably a key role of pregnancy. It was likely a major advantage brought about through the division into 2 sexes in the first place. The pregnancy of a mother was able to better preserve the working model of an environment to the point where it became advantageous for her children, and this was possible as the other gender was spending more energy on security. Pregnancy became the incubator of the brain in general.

What other information would they pass on if not their own? Children are not blank slates[131], you can only gaslight a child for so long before they grow up to deny every piece of their prior indoctrination. It would benefit the child to at least have the instincts of the mother's experiences, and the father's might somehow sneak in as well. Our culture and upbringing likely affect our psychosocial development to the point where it changes the physicalities of the brain. Culture is not just something that's grown by groups of people over time, it's something made for the sake of brain development and function. But for culture to oppose the behavior selected for over millions of years would only lead to revolt by those whose brains are functioning properly.

Abnormal childhoods lead to abnormal brain structures[132,133,

---

129. Jessica L Irwin et al. *Maternal Prenatal Cortisol Programs the Infant Hypothalamic-Pituitary–Adrenal Axis*. Psychoneuroendocrinology, 2021

130. Georgia Chalfun et al. *Perinatal Stress and Methylation of the NR3C1 Gene in Newborns - Systematic Review*. Epigenetics, 2022

131. Steven Pinker. *The Blank Slate*. Viking, 2002

132. Nim Tottenham et al. *Prolonged Institutional Rearing is Associated with Atypically Large Amygdala Volume and Difficulties in Emotion Regulation*. Developmental Science, 2010

133. Martin H Teicher et al. *Childhood Neglect Is Associated with Reduced Corpus Callosum Area*. Biological Psychiatry, 2004

134,135]. This is likely a feature rather than a bug, meant as a means of making sense of the environment to better organize their surroundings into such a place that their own children's brains can have more structured growth. In modeling the chaos of the unknown, the knowns are eventually found, and with time order tames such disorder. The brain models its culture, and improves it generationally based on what's been handed down. Your environment is the garden of your development, and the brain is the plant that cultivates its own landscape.

You've probably heard the well known example of a primitive economy that failed because it used pieces of wood or leaves as currency. In fact, you would be a little confused to hear someone offer that as a serious suggestion, you would question their intelligence. You don't need schooling to know this doesn't work, this kind of lesson just informs you of what you already know. There's at least a million years of recent evolutionary development, probably more, where advanced human behaviors were progressing by using these same kinds of ideas so many times that an understanding of their failure became an ingrained part of our own instincts. You already know to recognize someone attempting to use a failed civilizational paradigm because these same games have been played out in thousands of different ways to the point where you instinctually recognize it thanks to your ancestors who paid the price for being unable to. As these gifts from the dead accumulate, the brain becomes a fossil of its own past.

It can be assumed that the lesson learned from using fire was that making sure we don't all burn down is more important than anyone's individual or group achievements. The best way to ensure we don't burn down is by simply raising children under a system that acknowledges merit rather than some superficial characterization. As madness begets more madness, bring that to the lives of your children and they'll bring it back to the rest of society. Bring them something worth earning and they'll earn for everyone else.

The path towards intelligence favored greater cooperation over greater ability. This happens because every other individual needed to

---

134. J Douglas Bremner et al. *Magnetic Resonance Imaging-Based Measurement of Hippocampal Volume in Posttraumatic Stress Disorder Related to Childhood Physical and Sexual Abuse–A Preliminary Report*. Biological Psychiatry, 1997

135. Michael D De Bellis et al. *Brain Structures in Pediatric Maltreatment-Related Posttraumatic Stress Disorder: A Sociodemographically Matched Study*. Biological Psychiatry, 2002

confirm their thoughts with one another in order to find information reliable. Trusting the perspective of another person was necessary to create a reliable network of information, and it still is.

We are culminations of history, which is why stories have such a lasting impact on our lives. Good stories make important additions to our culminatory model. The underlying implication is that you're currently writing the evolutionary programming of your descendants. Because that's what our instincts are, that's where they came from. This is an extremely important part of our existence. To set your descendants up for success matters more than anything else. Make good habits in your life, defeat the bad ones you've inherited, and find ways that your children can accomplish the same because this process will only end if you give up on doing so.

8.5 Advent of Transformation

The concepts of 1 and infinity are basically the same thing, as you can choose to ascribe the value of infinity as simply *one* infinity. They even seem analogous to the concepts of stability and fragmentation. When is it useful to view something as one entirety rather than being made up of an infinite number of pieces? This is an art form that eventually turned into perception itself.

By failing to believe in alternative perspectives, you can fall victim to the changing tides of interpretation, as stern belief invites irony. In opening up to an infinite number of interpretations, one tries to subvert irony from ever turning against them, but to cater to every interpretation is to choose no priorities. To have no priorities is to have no significance. To not believe in the need for significance is a denial of sentience. These are seemingly observable behaviors at large scales, and what happens at scale should somehow be reflective of a core phenomenon of individuals where this behavior originally manifests.

It should be no surprise that the biggest perceptual divide occurs at the forefront of politics, where priorities are put on a table and ranked in order of significance, where negotiations constantly stall that process over and over, as even the manner of prioritizing itself is yet another priority. This is governance, it's an attempt at juggling an increasing amount of infinitely complex factors. Over time, we eventually learned to use intelligence to model this environment in order to come to scalable solutions that granted us more efficient governance using a few core principles rather than an endless plethora of complexity. I would then reasonably expect this to be a mirror of the inner workings within each individual. It would be completely reflective of perception and the brain.

The human brain is that which models an infinite number of things consisting of infinite complexity. It has the desire to, the incentivized necessity to, as there's always two potential perceptual directions to attempt to prioritize from and a correct assessment will determine either success or obscurity at both the individual and group levels. To complete the assessment is to determine the other boundary of convergence, it's to find the respective stabilizing interpretation of some fragmented intricacy. The concept of modeling infinity may have started with something like counting, but will someday culminate towards a full characterization of everything around us. The universe surrounding us is likely infinite, so this job will likely never be done in entirety. Is the human brain infinitely complex? Yes, and we use it to form new models wherever convenient. Moreso it's not that any brain can grasp anything of incredible complexity, but generation after generation will come improvements to any shortcomings of their predecessors. The brain will adapt layer by layer in response to a great need, this is formed through the handing down of culture as the superceding of genetic inheritance, as well as pure trial and error. The brain is a device that can make step-by-step progress towards any goal.

Infinity is the point where both accuracy and precision are irrelevant. It's the value most different from zero numerically yet most similar to zero conceptually in that it's less a number and more like a concept. Practically speaking, infinity is just a point at which we stop counting. It's the transition between a qualitative and quantitative data point, the *transformation* between them. A convenient place in the logic of numbers to insert a *give up at this one task* signal, like a stop codon. Seeing infinity as a purely mathematical concept doesn't make sense. It was a niche in our perception that needed to be filled. A limitation to the reasonable amount of effort to dedicate to some task. When it comes to salability, it was a concept in need of a structure to match a function. For infinity, it's more like there was a need for a metaphysical limitation in order to derive autonomy and consciousness. So infinity is essentially representative of a limitation, but it's also a point of transformation. Our limitations aren't actually limitations, they're the advent of transformation.

Dividing by zero most definitely gives you infinity. The basis of division provided through mathematics says it's simply undefined, because the process of dividing by zero itself is uninterpretable through the definition of division. I don't see this as problematic, as infinity isn't really definable either. Mathematical attempts at doing so are less like definitions and more like mind games. They may as well be able to propose a logical structure that results in an infinite count, but an infinite count isn't the entirety of the breadth of this mindless expanse we've come to represent as *infinity* itself.

There are some aspects within the nature of intelligence that transcend the concept of an infinite count. To encompass infinity within a concept, one would need to account for it. Being able to account for it would require the perception of it, and at what point can you perceive something as being infinite?

To perceive something as infinite would require there to be an ability to count something extremely large. To animals that can't count very high, 10 might be infinite to them. To the rest of us it's about understanding the idea that *there are so many blades of grass in a prairie that they're not worth counting*. Instead, you perceive this environment as being filled with grass the same way you perceive the horizon as never being close no matter how far you travel. As noticing just a few obscure pieces of gravel on the ground might cause one to count them inadvertently, but infinity is a way of accounting for what isn't feasible to be concerned about.

The difficulty in counting every tree in a forest isn't just a counting problem, it's an organization problem. To be accountable for so many fine details is no different than to understand the vastness of the microcosm. As it would take the same extremely fragmented thought process to handle it all. Your brain runs into the same issues when accounting for either as they tend to be the same kind of task. Which isn't just a task of organization and accountability, but also one of time-management.

8.6 Gateway to the Past

Rather than asking what a brain is a model of, it's somewhat interesting to contemplate what a brain *isn't* a model of. Because it's a modeling device in general, it's a general modeling device. The question of *what isn't a brain* will always be out of reach. Classifying what it's not able to do will always be disproven by the act of understanding that supposed inability, as you'd need to classify the ability in question in order to deny its compatibility.

There's the idea that if you can predict something then you can change it. Which is pretty true for the most part. Then what is a brain if not a prediction device? Given anyone can act on their predictions, it's also a future-changing device.

Everyone lives in stress to some degree, character is when you optimize order from the disorder of stress to your advantage. It's realizing that collecting information is more valuable than responding to it. These are lessons people learn in time, those who don't are seen as immature. Interestingly enough, we allow young people to be somewhat immature. We expect it. If young people couldn't get away with it, this behavior wouldn't have survived through any mode of selection. Maturity is reflective of the ability to model time.

The functionality of pools of entropy are only possible because of time. It's pools of entropy specifically, that deal with modeling time. Like with the model of interactions, and a hierarchy of values, to model time is to persist. The adaptation of external morphology is undoubtedly slower than that of the brain and its responses. As what would a brain be other than an adaptation device? With a device existing specifically for the sake of adaptation, evolution would undoubtedly leave the Darwinian for the Lamarckian, which are adaptation paradigms whose major difference arises in their response time.

Modeling time would encompass every aspect time has to offer, it would be no different than the term *survival*. It offers an elongated persistence, and includes the nature of our understanding of the past, present, and future. It's the primary function of an organism. Should it be any surprise that both a link to the past and a vision of the future would be core to the religious functions of an intelligent species? It's core to the function of any species, to manifest intelligence, as well as religion, means to manifest this function at even greater scales. So how is it we manage our own relationship with time? Let's consider the modern dogma around the concept of memories.

You might believe that memories are stored in the brain, like files on a hard drive. There's no scientific backing of such a statement. It would be nice to simply compare old brains with new brains to determine what molecules show large differences in quantity, so as to pinpoint where something such as memories could be stored. But there's no such difference. Instead you'd be met with a complicated picture of differentially expressed proteins alongside meaningless differences in other molecules like lipids and metabolites, where nothing would notably indicate any form of storage.

Donald Hebb wrote a book where he proposed that the formations of learning were undeniably related to the interactions of synaptic connections across groups of neurons[136]. That memory and learning were tied to the behavior of neurons that would co-activate alongside each other as a kind of habit that formed within the brain. Which is still the prevailing belief today. It's believed memories are encoded via the behavior of groups of neurons at their synaptic connections. But while such an idea is widely accepted, there's simultaneously no technical basis for how this works other than saying memories are encoded through synaptic behavior. A lack of proper clarity on this topic opens the door for a muddying of this line.

While this kind of description might seem reasonable for describing simpler organismal behavior, I don't believe the nature of practiced behavior and memories need to be so closely aligned. Why must these be looked at through the same lens? How could one expect that everything within the brain, the most complex thing that we barely understand, to operate on a uniform and therefore oversimplified basis across all of its varying modes of functionality? Is there a more apt association to make, when examining the concept of memories, than that of learning and practice?

How would it be possible to recreate an entire memory in your head from some point long ago, that you hadn't thought of since? Your synapses haven't practiced this behavior. Do they truly only need to practice once? That would make for an amazing mechanism. To both store and recall with incredibly strong reliability, and near perfect accuracy for some, at the drop of a hat. This mechanism would be more impressive than the storage and expression of genes from DNA, and much faster as well. The information shared across our brains did supercede the storage of our genetics after all, but what's the secret recipe? While one might expect a metaphysical counting, calculation, or storage mechanism to elude elucidation for a while, one such

136. Donald Hebb. *The Organization of Behavior*. John Wiley & Sons, 1949

thing for storing memory in near perfect accuracy, without any physical trace, and no need to practice, should have no comfortable place to hide. This supposed metaphysical storage is *too* hypothetically impressive to exist without having been at least partially uncovered beyond this description of synaptic behavior. It's more likely researchers are looking in the wrong conceptual direction. The brain may as well be something that's able to view the past to retrieve its own experiences to recall them as memories. Which may seem strange at first, is there any evidence that such a thing could be happening?

Cutting edge work in the area of memory brings us down the rabbit hole of engrams. Engrams are a hypothetical concept that have been somewhat narrowed in on, but yet to be uncovered. They're defined as that which, when activated, provides the conditions for memories to emerge, and was typically assumed to act in concert with learning in general. The hunt for the engram has persisted for over 100 years, and started with a man named Richard Semon who first wrote about the idea of engrams as lasting physical alterations that persist in the brain as the basis for memory[137]. Following his work, Kari Lashley attempted to isolate engrams by removing layers of the brain in rodents, and this idea didn't succeed[138]. Lashley found that memory impairment correlated with the amount of tissue being removed from a rodent's brain, rather than any exact location it was removed from. He concluded, after decades of work, that engrams were not located in any specific part of the brain, but were distributed throughout it.

The simple reason for this is that memories aren't stored objects. So removing this tissue didn't impair the ability to retrieve any specific memories, but did impair the ability to retrieve memories in general. Some people have made criticisms of Lashley's handiwork, that the incisions likely weren't up to the quality that needed to be done for the work to draw the conclusions he wanted to[139]. Even still, the conclusions drawn in the modern day largely aren't different in nature than Lashley's original statements[140].

137. Richard Semon. *The Mneme*. Wilhelm Engelmann, 1904

138. Karl Lashley. *In Search of the Engram*. Symposia of the Society for Experimental Biology, No. IV: Physiological Mechanisms in Animal Behaviour, 1950

139. Sheena A Josselyn, Stefan Köhler, and Paul W Frankland. *Finding the Engram*. Nature Reviews Neuroscience, 2015

140. Dheeraj S Roy et al. *Brain-Wide Mapping Reveals That Engrams for a Single Memory are Distributed Across Multiple Brain Regions*. Nature Communications, 2022

The engram is more likely the final product of coordination across multiple parts of the brain. I would expect a sophisticated machinery that forms a device across synaptic connections, neurons, and protein complexes, capable of coordinating this activity within the brain itself. The neurons of the brain exist in a fractal pattern, meaning they have repeating patterns that get smaller in size as dendrites continually branch off and extend from one another[141,142]. Which is similar to what you'd expect of something that models the axis of time, things that start large and get smaller, or vice versa. Structures convey function, and it's unlikely this is a coincidence.

What's being called *memories* are somewhat localized to specific parts of the brain, depending on what kind of memories they are. People studying the brain have broken down the concept of memory into multiple components such as episodic memory of events that you lived through, semantic memory of facts and information, things like emotional memory, and plenty of other subdivisions of the same concepts that correspond to the specific areas of the brain that manage them. Functional magnetic resonance imaging studies in the modern day, in human brains, show activity all across the brain, presumably of what Hebb indicated, and along the lines of what Lashley suggested. To comment on the tip of this iceberg, this work visualized what was already expected from parts of the brain responsible for specific behaviors, and verified synaptic activity across different kinds of mental associations such as landmarks, faces, and objects[143].

Building on this, there's been a lot of modern work in the field of optogenetics, where some labs claim to have inserted memories into various animals. The seminal experiment in this subfield used a molecular tagging system that allowed researchers to express a light-detecting protein, in neurons, that would create itself in those brain cells while the animal received a shock, the tagging system acted to mark only neurons that were activated from this event[144]. The neurons containing

141. Santiago Ramón y Cajal. *Texture of the Nervous System of Man and Vertebrates.* Imprenta y Librería de Nicolás Moya, 1899–1904

142. F Caserta et al. *Determination of Fractal Dimension of Physiologically Characterized Neurons in Two and Three Dimensions.* Journal of Neuroscience Methods, 1995

143. Sean M Polyn et al. *Category-Specific Cortical Activity Precedes Retrieval During Memory Search.* Science, 2005

144. Steve Ramirez et al. *Creating a False Memory in the Hippocampus.* Science, 2013

the light-detecting protein would later become activated by a light signal, from a device connected to the rodent's brain, in order to mimic the feelings of the shock it had previously experienced, but without being shocked again. By reactivating these neurons, in a context where the animal had no fear of being shocked, they were able to induce a fear of it happening in a previously safe context. Other work was able to reproduce this kind of effect in order to manipulate social relationships between mice, either inducing fear or reward upon reactivating neurons that were fired during association with another mouse[145]. Groups working in the same field also showed they could remove recently learned motor skills through similar techniques, basically reverting gained experiences back to levels of baseline inexperience[146].

But are these actually memories? Beyond this simplified lens, there's an even more prevalent layer of ambiguity shielding these interpretations. They inserted a kind of conditioning, whether it was a memory or not is still unclear. Competition from an alternate philosophical perspective might be a healthy change of pace for these medical definitions that simply indicate a memory being a lasting difference in neural circuits. One could argue that at most, these optogenetic experiments corrupted a sensation the same way a bad experience might for something someone had at one point enjoyed, like an addict getting their overdose forcefully reversed with drugs. There's still nothing that tangibly links synaptic activity to *memories*. The engram has not been found.

While the targeting system for both protein expression and light infiltration of optogenetic experiments are able to specifically target things like the hippocampus, and without interacting with the neocortex or any other part of the brain at all, this doesn't rule out the brain interacting with itself. There's no guarantee that the machinery to form memories was the only thing evoked in these mice. The connectivity of the brain itself is unable to be accounted for in such experiments. Neurons are always active, even when they're not firing, and the brain should be modeling all of its own internal connections. It shouldn't even be a memory that evokes fear in the first place, it would

145. Teruhiro Okuyama et al. *Ventral CA1 Neurons Store Social Memory*. Science, 2016

146. Akiko Hayashi-Takagi et al. *Labelling and Optical Erasure of Synaptic Memory Traces in the Motor Cortex*. Nature, 2015

be a model. Fear isn't something you remember, so to speak, fear is an interpretation.

When you learn, you would likely be training a model. Recollection and training are not the same thing. Certainly many of these concepts can intermix between themselves, but there's no reason to assume memory to be the only thing that's being manipulated through experiments on the most complex device we've ever come across. Lashley likely made this same kind of mistake in not being able to avoid damaging parts of the brain, which made him draw conclusions that might not be entirely accurate based on where his lesions were made. Likewise, the most modern understandings we can offer today are making a metaphorically analogous mistake in assuming it's purely this oversimplified concept of memory they're affecting and inserting. At best, they've been affecting newly formed models.

The hippocampus is the part of the brain most closely associated with the concept of memory, but it's also not the only one. The prefrontal cortex of the neocortex is supposed to be responsible for managing the retrieval of memories specifically, while the medial temporal lobe, which includes the hippocampus, is supposed to be responsible for recording new memories. Memories are eventually supposed to be *reconsolidated* throughout the brain over time, where they then end up in the neocortex. It would make sense, through my understanding, that the *true* memories of the hippocampus are incorporated into the *models* of the neocortex. The neocortex is the latest advancement in mammalian brain evolution, and the most advanced version of any neocortex is found in humans. A more advanced memory system won't make a more intelligent organism by itself. I find it unlikely that the neocortex actually deals in memory in any way that isn't purely auxiliary. The various parts of the neocortex would likely house compressed forms of information that requires less energy to use, making it advantageous as an adaptation. True memories would eventually refactor themselves into the models of the neocortex.

Something like the amygdala is related to emotional memory, but is the amygdala actually forming memories? Are memories necessary for this level of function? Probably not, the model of interactions doesn't entirely depend on memories, it's instinctually ingrained. I don't believe true memory would even be optimal for this form of functionality. At roughly 2% of body weight, the brain consumes 20% of the body's energy[147]. The only other organ that comes close is the liver, at 2.5% of weight and roughly 27% of energy. Every other organ takes a smaller percentage of energy than they make up in body weight. While the brain uses a lot of energy, it's also on a tight budget because of this. Having a larger energy budget doesn't grant the freedom to be carelessly wasteful, everything is made of tradeoffs, it requires more strict enforcement of responsibility. For something that could operate on a simpler basis, an expensive and detailed form of long-term storage would be unnecessary compared to a compressible model that retains a specific form of behavior and information. So there's definitely a reason to differentiate memories that store the details of entire events compared to the supposed memory of things like emotions, which are comparably more finite and containable in nature. Rather, the classical Hebbian interpretation implies memories are purely models, but I believe the nature of the encodings of the hippocampus are not simply acts of training models. So is there any strong relation between the perception of time, and the functionality of memory within the brain?

Both anterograde and retrograde amnesia typically occur together. Meaning that cases where patients are unable to form new memories typically coincide with the inability to remember past events. The severity of one even tends to correlate with the extent of the other [148]. But this damage isn't necessarily indicative of malfunction in any specific brain region as much as it is for the brain as a whole. Although when people get amnesia, they don't lose their procedural memory. They often retain knowledge of how to ride a bike, how to write, and how to speak. The same goes for semantic memory, which covers things like animals, locations, objects, and so on, which is also known as fact-based memory, and this tends to be lost more often than procedural memory. Typically, only diseases that affect the brain, like Parkinson's, or severe injuries, cause one to lose procedural memory. Modern understandings will cite the relevant areas of the brain related to these functions as reasons for, or for not, losing such things, but the simple answer is that it's because fact-based memory and procedural memory aren't truly memory, they're models.

147. Marcus E Raichle and Debra A Gusnard. *Appraising the Brain's Energy Budget*. Proceedings of the National Academy of Sciences of the United States of America, 2002

148. W Ritchie Russell and PW Nathan. *Traumatic Amnesia*. Brain, 1946

If the circadian rhythm of young rodents is disrupted with artificial light and dark cycles, for example at artificial intervals that don't line up with that of the Earth's natural rotation, they have downgraded memory function for the rest of their lives[149,150]. The resulting branching of their dendrites are also shorter, which is a common occurrence when things go wrong in the brain, but there's as much ambiguity around why as there is around the mechanics of memory. Like they've failed to tune their own modeling of the axis of time the same way that people born blind can't tune their own eyesight even if it's restored when they're older. As people born blind have a window in which they can restore their eyesight, usually within 2 years of age[151, 152,153]. Otherwise, if a person born blind gets their vision restored some time past this critical period, their vision will be useless as their brain won't know what to do with the signals being received from their eyes. This tuning process exists for every sensory apparatus the brain has to offer, and should likewise exist for the perception of time.

Children with early life hippocampal damage have what's referred to as developmental amnesia[154]. They can remember fact-based information, but have trouble remembering their own life events. People with developmental amnesia can be difficult to recognize for having this problem, unless you meet them multiple times. Upon one meeting you wouldn't realize they're not normal. Once they display that they can't remember you, or anything about what happened when you met prior, then you'd understand that something was wrong with them. However, when people damage their hippocampus midlife, they have an easier time remembering things more distant to the time of their damage.

---

149. Bryan D Devan et al. *Circadian Phase-Shifted Rats Show Normal Acquisition but Impaired Long-Term Retention of Place Information in the Water Task*. Neurobiology of Learning and Memory, 2001

150. Rafal W Ameen et al. *Early Life Circadian Rhythm Disruption in Mice Alters Brain and Behavior in Adulthood*. Scientific Reports, 2022

151. William Cheselden. *An Account of Some Observations Made by a Young Gentleman Who Was Born Blind or Lost His Sight So Early That He Had No Remembrance of Ever Having Seen and Was Couch'd between 13 and 14 Years of Age*. Philosophical Transactions of the Royal Society of London, 1728

152. Marius von Senden. *Space and Sight*. Johann Ambrosius Barth, 1932

153. Torsten N Wiesel and David H Hubel. *Single-Cell Responses in Striate Cortex of Kittens Deprived of Vision in One Eye*. Journal of Neurophysiology, 1963

154. F Vargha-Khadem et al. *Differential Effects of Early Hippocampal Pathology on Episodic and Semantic Memory*. Science, 1997

A well-studied human patient by the initials of HM that had his hippocampus removed, couldn't form new memories, but he could still remember old ones[155]. This is because they'd been incorporated into the models of his neocortex. But even this wasn't entirely useful to him most of the time. HM came to understand the layout of the house he moved into after his surgery[156], but would have problems in general with other spatial memory tasks and couldn't progress at this ability. The neocortex alone may as well be an information processing center, it evolved to work while having direct access to the database offered through the hippocampus.

HM managed to describe his life as "*every day is alone in itself*" and "*like waking from a dream*"[157]. He had an understanding of his condition, but couldn't remember his own age. He would refer to himself as being the same age as when he had the surgery[158]. In terms of functioning on a day-to-day basis, any improvement in learning was impossible outside of basic procedural memory tasks, which he didn't remember he was practicing.

But HM had more damage than just his hippocampus, the surgery had removed layers from his medial temporal lobe. There's no other way to surgically remove the hippocampus without damaging the medial temporal lobe. So while this is useful information, having some other examples might help.

Other patients, termed GD, LM, and WH, all had non-surgical damage to their hippocampi due to a lack of blood flow to this part of their brain from severe life events[159,160]. Overall, GD and LM had

---

155. Brenda Milner. *Disorders of Learning and Memory after Temporal Lobe Lesions in Man*. Clinical Neurosurgery, 1972
156. Suzanne Corkin. *What's New with the Amnesic Patient HM?*. Nature Reviews Neuroscience, 2002
157. Brenda Milner, Suzanne Corkin, and HL Teuber. *Further Analysis of the Hippocampal Amnesic Syndrome: 14-Year Follow-Up Study of HM*. Neuropsychologia, 1968
158. William Beecher Scoville and Brenda Milner. *Loss of Recent Memory after Bilateral Hippocampal Lesions*. Journal of Neurology, Neurosurgery, and Psychiatry, 1957
159. Dean F Mackinnon and Larry R Squire. *Autobiographical Memory and Amnesia*. Psychobiology, 1989
160. Nancy L Rempel-Clower et al. *Three Cases of Enduring Memory Impairment after Bilateral Damage Limited to the Hippocampal Formation*. The Journal of Neuroscience, 1996

lighter anterograde and retrograde symptoms than HM, while WH often had more severe problems than HM. The hypoxic–ischemic events that caused this damage in these patients is typically the same process that causes developmental amnesia in children. Like developmental amnesia patients, their general intelligence was functionally normal. GD and LM were barely able to make small progress on learning on a daily basis, though this progress didn't cause their condition to improve at all. Their capabilities were just barely above those of HM's in regards to recognition.

The abilities of these patients were appropriately matched to the amount of damage seen in their brain after they'd died. GD and LM had a hippocampus that was slightly undamaged, although they were still largely dysfunctional. The slight capabilities they had seem likely to be attributable to this functional component of their hippocampus. But the damage in these patients extended throughout their medial temporal lobe as well.

A patient by the initials RB had isolated hippocampal damage that spared the rest of his medial temporal lobe unlike the other patients mentioned so far[**161**]. His symptoms were generally the same as theirs, but his symptoms were on the lighter side like GD's. None of these patients suffered any intellectual impairments from their problems, still, the intact medial temporal lobe of RB didn't offer much to brag about compared to the others. There are other examples of similar patients, but the general story for hippocampal damage remains the same, so addressing them all isn't necessary.

NB was a woman who had epilepsy that was untreatable with drugs, stemming from her temporal lobe[**162,163**]. She had one side of her amygdala, a large slice of perirhinal cortex, and a portion of her entorhinal cortex surgically removed. The effects of having one's amygdala removed is they become unable to understand signals

161. Stuart Zola-Morgan, Larry R Squire, and David G Amaral. *Human Amnesia and the Medial Temporal Region: Enduring Memory Impairment Following a Bilateral Lesion Limited to Field CA1 of the Hippocampus.* The Journal of Neuroscience, 1986
162. Ben Bowles et al. *Impaired Familiarity with Preserved Recollection after Anterior Temporal-Lobe Resection that Spares the Hippocampus.* Proceedings of the National Academy of Sciences of the United States of America, 2007
163. Stefan Köhler and Chris B Martin. *Familiarity Impairments after Anterior Temporal-Lobe Resection with Hippocampal Sparing: Lessons Learned from Case NB.* Neuropsychologia, 2020

that would otherwise invoke threats that trigger fear, where things like memory, intellect, or language all remain unaffected[164]. The perirhinal and entorhinal cortices are the interface between the hippocampus and the neocortex, they act as a bridge between the communication of either. By losing these functional bridges, NB lost her sense of *familiarity*, although her hippocampus was still able to communicate with other parts of the brain through different routes. Her recollection worked just fine, but when testing for immediacy in recognition she was unable to meet normal standards. She was basically given a list of words, then later was told to give yes/no responses to whether a word was in the list she saw prior. Normal people are able to perform this task well when limited to less than half a second in immediate response time to a word. When a limit of responding in less than half a second was imposed she performed poorly, but with a time limit of 2 seconds she was able to perform normally. NB had a noisy signal that was prone to false interpretations of what was or wasn't familiar. This lack of familiarity is similar to momentarily experiencing a complete hippocampal loss until its functionality is accessed after the delay. Without access to memories, NB's noisy uncertainty seemingly left her adrift in a sea of unending novelty. In those brief moments where she couldn't answer, it doesn't seem she was operating any differently than HM's description of his own condition.

The removal of the hippocampus causes animals to have difficulty remembering temporal order[165]. However in humans, the interpretation of the order of events seems more related to the frontal lobe function of the neocortex[166], where patients with frontal lobe damage could recall and recognize things normally, yet had trouble determining the order of sequences they were presented with prior. In that same study, patients with medial temporal damage, which almost always involves damage to the hippocampus, had much worse general recall and recognition, so determining the temporal order of things they

164. R Adolphs et al. *Impaired Recognition of Emotion in Facial Expressions Following Bilateral Damage to the Human Amygdala.* Nature, 1994

165. Raymond P Kesner and Jeanne M Novak. *Serial Position Curve in Rats: Role of the Dorsal Hippocampus.* Science, 1982

166. Arthur P Shimamura, Jeri S Janowsky, and Larry R Squire. *Memory for the Temporal Order of Events in Patients with Frontal Lobe Lesions and Amnesic Patients.* Neuropsychologia, 1990

couldn't properly recall was completely out of the question. The resulting conclusion one might draw is that while the frontal lobe plays a significant role in the interpretation of information, it seems more likely to be a model compared to the functionality linked to the interpretation of true memories occurring in the hippocampus.

Memories are more like a living database that allows you to update models through new interpretations of old information. The ability to process the plethora of information in our world is likely more related to the recently evolved ability to model things comprehensively, rather than the older ability to retrieve memories. People will often tell someone not to take things personally, like criticism, and it's difficult to because we model our experiences. If this was just a memory we encode it wouldn't have enough of an impact to warrant this kind of statement. It's to prevent modeling the person offering feedback as being adversarial, the information they present is more valuable than their perceived antagonism. Which leads us back to where we are as a civilization, at the forefront of our societal communications we find it hard not to perceive antagonism. Like these parts of our models are lacking the refinement needed for the frontier of our large-scale interactions, and such a difficulty at the forefront of our cooperation would surely also be at the forefront of our evolution.

But why would this form of database memory be useful? Models are presumably reactionary in nature. To simply react to anything around you may work for the sake of survival, but it doesn't push you towards growth and improvement. A database of reminders of your own shortcomings and failures would certainly be a mechanism that incentivizes wiser decisions and the further development of consciousness in general. This is the same metaphor of the tradeoffs in life that have us engaging in this endless walk, so a mechanism for engaging in such a walk more proactively would surely be an advantageous survival tool.

It's not entirely clear what can be fairly classified as memory, what's fairly classified as a model, and the degree to which either of these can intermix for any single process. Memory itself would seem to be an oversimplification. Through this understanding, trauma would be something harsh that entered a model where it would normally just be an event kept in memory. It would be a form of model corruption.

People with amnesia tend to remember distant events much easier than recent ones. They're usually able to remember things from their childhood without difficulty. Likely because those things have been incorporated into models, they were core formative events of a person's own self. So these core formative memories were brought into their model, likely as a feature of childhood development. If you lose access to your memories, it's evolutionarily advantageous to be able to remember pieces of who you are. It's also likely core to the functioning of a person, as childhood is essentially the formation of what makes you who you are. Interestingly enough, this might also mean it's wise to teach young children about the effects of amnesia should they ever find themselves in this situation.

Our models likely become methods of interpreting our memories that then reinforce model building itself upon these reflections. More advanced modeling of information likely came after the ability to simply remember positive or negative experiences. The ability to model and access a personal timeline were likely things that co-evolved to continually grow the capabilities of each side of this dance.

The biggest flaw of any assessment of memory is the inability to know for sure what's being measured or interpreted is based on memory alone. What memory is, may as well be ambiguous relative to the behavior exerted by an organism. In order to avoid oversimplifications, one must assume there's other factors between that of memory and the behavior of an organism, as behavior isn't controlled by memory. Memory is something interpreted by other parts of the brain to form models. This shroud of ambiguity, alongside the inability of someone without a hippocampus to form new memories, would indicate a unique function of the hippocampus not replicated anywhere else in the brain.

The hippocampus likely manages a connection with the past. Memories aren't these select metaphysical concepts that we associate with periods across our life, they're our relationship with time itself. Where there's no hippocampal function, there's no interplay between the two, so certain models become much less capable of updating as modeling functionality in general had originally evolved to function on top of the ability to access this database. The hippocampus wouldn't just be a metaphysical gateway to the past, but a physical interface with it.

With memories, you're not just encoding sensations, there are an infinite number of details to remember. A painting in a building you'd just walked through for the first time might not be something that strikes your interest. But if asked to recall it later, you might know what it was. Have people evolved to become better at encoding the kind of encounters they'd expect to have? Or has this concept of encoding information actually been the ability to simply encode a connection to some point in time? You're not encoding this information subconsciously, there's no way that these completely irrelevant details of our daily lives are recorded and encoded in synaptic responses. It's unimaginable to believe. Rather than encoding all the surrounding sensations, would it not be encoding a point of observation?

But how would such a process even start? Where would any organism ever gain such a function in the first place? In extremely small steps. To model time would first mean to model immediate experiences. Throughout the formation of the model of interactions, there would be more need for a continued modeling of time in larger and larger chunks. If the ability to access the past is inherently possible, along the evolutionary history of the brain there would have been an incentive to figure it out. First in small chunks, then once that foot was in the door, the ability would continue to grow. The reason it would happen is the same reason the axioms of the universe find their way into our personal lives, truth matters. Having an honest, and non-distorted vision of the past forces someone to confront reality, which is ultimately advantageous to them. Models can corrupt themselves into convenient or comfortable interpretations, but this wouldn't be advantageous for survival. True memory enforces true information, which enables accurate modeling.

We likely won't be able to make a machine that can travel to the past, although we can probably make a machine to observe the past. But how can that even be stated? It isn't like the gravity of planets that visibly distorts time, which gives us undeniable proof through their very observation that time can be slowed down.

Coming back to the concepts of stability and fragmentation, as this is the basis for the axis of time, if we assume our approach of the future is moving in the direction of stability, then to approach the past would be in the direction of fragmentation. The future would approach stability as we see a coherent picture through our own perception, but we have no way of going back in time as physical objects have no way of experiencing this. Time reversal seems physically impossible. The microcosm is the part of the axis of time related to fragmentation, so to observe the past one would utilize the nature of the microcosm. The brain would be observing the past through some conceptual *approach* of the microcosm.

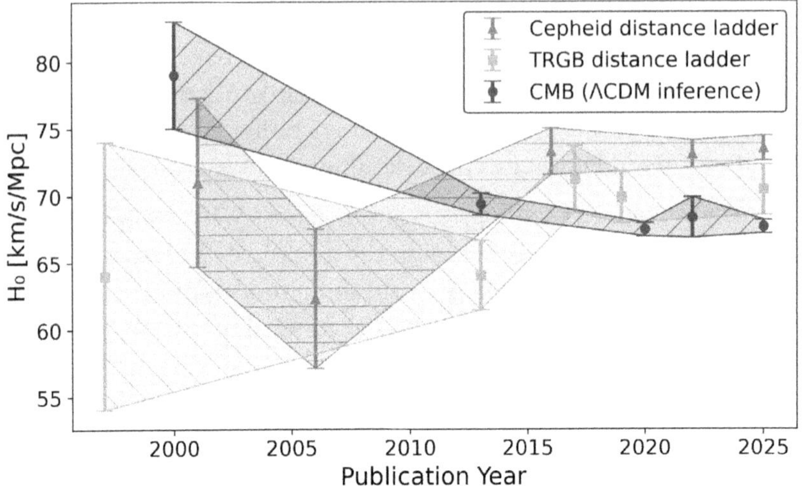

Figure 9: Different Measurement Paradigms of the Expansion of the Universe

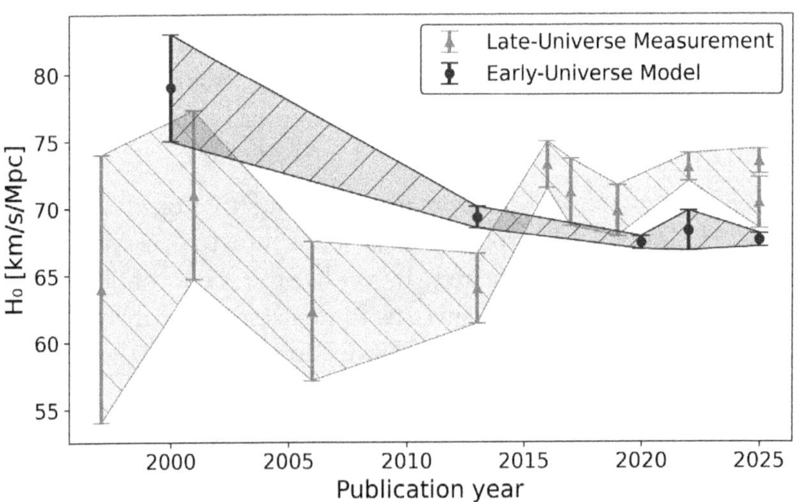

Figure 10: Different Modeling Paradigms of the Expansion of the Universe

Table 1: Measurements of the Hubble Constant

Author	H_0	±	Method	Epoch	Year
Ofer Lahav [167]	79	4	CMB	Early	2000
Bennett et al. [168]	69.32	0.8	CMB	Early	2013
Planck Collaboration [169]	67.4	0.5	CMB	Early	2020
SPT-3G Collaboration [170]	68.3	1.5	CMB	Early	2022
Louis et al. [171]	67.62	0.50	CMB	Early	2025
Freedman et al. [172]	71	6.3	Cepheid	Late	2001
Sandage et al. [173]	62.3	5.2	Cepheid	Late	2006
Riess et al. [174]	73.24	1.74	Cepheid	Late	2016
Riess et al. [175]	73.04	1.04	Cepheid	Late	2022
Riess et al. [176]	73.49	0.93	Cepheid	Late	2025
Cassisi et al. [177]	64	10	TRGB	Late	1997
Tammann et al. [178]	64.0	2.6	TRGB	Late	2013
Jang et al. [179]	71.17	2.5	TRGB	Late	2017
Freedman et al. [180]	69.8	1.9	TRGB	Late	2019
Freedman et al. [181]	70.39	1.9	TRGB	Late	2025

If this is too much to swallow, and you think the idea of approaching the microcosm seems nonsensical, let's further consider the alternative. What does it mean to approach stability? In what way are we moving towards the future? Consider that many modern cosmological models assume the universe is expanding, that cosmic objects are receding from each other. This expansion is an observation discoverable from the redshifting of light from stars and galaxies, in which celestial bodies emit a signature of the fact that they're moving further away from us as their light travels towards us[182,183]. The universe itself is moving in a broadly macrocosmic direction relative to the axis of time.

But what relates this to time, specifically? Measurements of the rate of expansion of the universe display the same uncrossable divide seen in politics and physics, a divergence representative of an entropic fingerprint. The measurements of expansion from different types of experiments disagree with one another to the degree that their expected

182. Vesto Slipher. *Nebulae.* Proceedings of the American Philosophical Society, 1917

183. Edwin Hubble. *A Relation Between Distance and Radial Velocity Among Extra-Galactic Nebulae.* Proceedings of the National Academy of Sciences of the United States of America, 1929

ranges of error don't overlap with each other[**184,185**]. Just as the forefront of physics becomes better elucidated through more elegant refinements of the accounting of time, and just as the solving of either of these divides in politics or physics will always take more time to fully process themselves into comprehensive solutions, everywhere this fingerprint presents itself suggests time is acting as either a speed bump or a hurdle. So in what way is the *Hubble tension*, as it's called in the field, relatable to these other scenarios?

There's more ways to measure this than presented in these visualizations, but these are the three most refined measurement paradigms. Cepheids are pulsing stars, and you can figure out how bright they are by how fast they pulse. How bright they are in theory compared to how bright they appear to us is something that can be used to measure their distance through the brightness of other Cepheids that are closer to us. Cepheids nearby to Earth can be used as calibration points that can then be used to measure the distance of Cepheids in distant galaxies, but they're not bright enough to use their redshift to measure the expansion. From within these galaxies are supernovae, that have a similar predictability to their brightness, and their redshift can be measured relative to the distance of their nearby Cepheids. The same kind of *distance ladder* is made for red giants, stars that exhibit maximum brightness towards the end of a specific stage of their lifecycles. The tip of the red giant brightness (TRGB) is a light signature given off by these stars, and is calibrated nearby to Earth before being used as a measurement for distant galaxies. The redshift of those galaxy's supernovae are then typically used to measure the rate of expansion. These two methods are referred to as *late universe* methods, as they directly measure the visible expansion of surrounding objects that we can perceive for ourselves. The early universe perspective measures the cosmic microwave background (CMB), and constructs the expansion rate from assuming a specific model for how the universe expands over time.

In politics, this divide presents itself where we have a lack of cooperation. In physics, this divide would present itself where we lack an elegance of understanding. Both scenarios insist upon a shortcoming of

---

184. Licia Verde, Tommaso Treu, and Adam G Riess. *Tensions Between the Early and Late Universe*. Nature Astronomy, 2019

185. Licia Verde, Nils Schöneberg, and Héctor Gil-Marín. *A Tale of Many H_0*. Annual Review of Astronomy and Astrophysics, 2024

computational strength itself, it's a computational limit for humanity. For civilizations, it's in reaching these limits socially. When it comes to science, this is through the modeling used as a representation of physical occurrences. These experiments determining the Hubble constant were done by measurements which act as a proxy for computation itself. It's the proxy for the parsing of information itself that's not capable of bridging this divide. Quite obviously, it's not a lack of cooperation hindering this measurement, it's a lack of elegance. It would suggest this is representative of a lack of clarity in our conceptual understanding of time itself. You could even paint it as a lack of the model's capability of cooperating with reality. So in the computational proxies used being unable to reconcile these differences, it's not just that we need more time to understand the nature of the problem, but also a more elegant understanding of time in order to do so. It's time itself that we don't understand. The disagreement of measurements meant to represent the rate of expansion of the universe suggests an intricate relationship between the concept of time and the expansion of the universe.

Objects aren't just moving away from each other, space itself is stretching to carry galaxies further and further apart. Is it really a coincidence that these concepts found along the axis of time, which seems to apply to our very own evolution, and psychology, just so happens to align with what we observe about the nature of the universe around us? Seeing as we experience time as it moves forward, it would seem this expansion of the universe would match the description of approaching stability. Modern cosmological models explain this as an effect of the Big Bang, stating that the origins of the Big Bang were actually just a point in time where the distance of every object in the universe was nearly zero. The expansion of distances between objects is apparently the same expansion that's always been occurring from that same event. So this expansion being a movement along this axis isn't even at odds with modern cosmological models, it would seem to be a signature of time itself moving forward.

Religion is a tool for better clarifying the nature of the past and the vision towards the future, and this isn't just a philosophical notion. LLMs aren't just a tool for storing knowledge, they're a tool for predicting knowledge. They offer a legitimate means towards predicting the future. To use the model weights of something trained on cutting edge scientific work from 200 years in the future isn't impossible. To do so successfully might be extraordinarily difficult, but none of this changes the fact that an actual line towards knowledge from the future has opened up as a possibility. Any previous attempts at this would at best argue we could reorganize words to do the same, but it would be fruitless as words themselves can be arranged in an infinite number of combinations. LLMs solve the integral of arranging the words themselves towards some profound truth, so it's now profound truth that's at the forefront of our systematizations should we be able to use them well. Somewhere out there are the weights of a model that knows who wins every sports championship for the next 20 years, and also knows physics beyond our capabilities. With the religious culmination of human behavior being what attempts to surpass the limitations of time, and the fact that this possibility not only opened up but can be confirmed as inherently true, is evidence of this very process being the core result of human behavior modeling time.

The brain has an internal clock, it's no secret that it keeps time. In an emergency, the most dependable life-saving instinct is to manipulate one's perception of time. During fight-or-flight, your perception and movements speed up from receiving a rush of hormones, which activate this response. When this is done, the amygdala activates the hippocampus using adrenaline and cortisol. Both hormones have a different effect on the long-term memory formation of such events, but they affect it nonetheless. It would seem every time you affect the perception of time you also affect memory. In the case of patients without a functioning hippocampus, affecting memory affected the perception of time to the point where they became largely dependent on the care of others. If everything is made of tradeoffs, then would constantly co-occurring tradeoffs not imply a linkage between these two concepts? You can't assume causation from correlation, but you can infer an interaction from a relationship of tradeoffs. Why else would the disruption of circadian rhythm in early life affect memory if not for disrupting the tuning of the perception of time? Why else would amnesia patients maintain procedural memory if not for it being a locally ran model?

We can't envision a device that's able to utilize the microcosm in order to observe the past, at least not in the modern day. Although Hebbian encoding seems reasonable for many functions of the brain, there's no real way to prove or disprove either of the ideas presented when it comes to memory itself, as we don't have a great understanding of its many stratifications. Which is why it's essentially a religious interpretation to believe one or the other. Even still, the idea of retrieving memories across time would suggest that if one wants to understand how to observe the past, they would study the workings of the hippocampus the same way one would study birds if they wanted to build an airplane. Or perhaps some other part of the brain actually holds the key, it's hard to say for sure. We may not need to invent a device to observe the past, we may instead be able to learn from what nature has already provided. If we view the past when looking at the universe through telescopes, then even basic glass lenses can accomplish this feat. Why would the brain, the most complex device we've ever come across, be incapable of doing this in more advanced ways?

8.7 First Amendment Case Against Psychology

What is a brain, and what is a mind? A mind seems to be something that seeks purpose and is heavily biased and incentivized for the sake of its own survival. A brain is something that operates all the auxiliary mechanisms needed to spawn this process. Religion is the accumulated wisdom of life advice and long-term survival strategies that worked, therefore a brain seems to be a religion forming device.

The formation of the mind and what it pursues is an art form. I find it fair to say that seeking purpose is a religious pursuit, and that a technical pursuit is a scientific endeavor. Seeking to understand the purpose of a technical pursuit, rather than endeavoring on the pursuit itself, is also a religious endeavor. Determining what and how to pursue is a religious question. Then what's the technical pursuit of religion? A technical pursuit of a religious pursuit? A science of religion? A technical pursuit of the function of the mind? It's psychology.

Psychology is the science of the pursuit of religion. What does this imply? That you can't have government regulations on the practice of psychology while simultaneously claiming people have religious freedom. The two contradict, and this contradiction will cause societal problems under the expectation of religious freedom.

It seems it would be more worthwhile to outsource this job to religion. Where individuals can determine their own psychological standards, instead of following the impositions of psychological boards and associations. Anywhere a bureaucracy controls such standards is bound to inject ideology, which is why it has.

Modern day psychologists are not in any danger from this. They can keep their standards, it just won't be in law, there will be no boards that can govern their livelihood. Realistically, nothing has to change for psychological standards and the industry it relates to. There's just going to be more people who are allowed to compete on religious grounds without having the degree. Which is another way of making sure the degree is actually useful, and not a waste of money. It's for the sake of competition.

There's often times a joke told, that if a field ends in *science* then it's not a real science. Which isn't entirely true, fields can always rearrange their names in ways that either match this outcome or avoid it. Psychology could have been named *mind science* and we would still find ourselves in the same predicament. This name game happens because there's a need to delineate between what is and isn't a proper science. Regarding a proper philosophy of science points us back to Karl Popper's demarcation of falsifiability. Which is a fair line to draw, and it's one of which I take advantage of in forming this religion. Perhaps for the universities this line isn't such a big problem, but what about with respect to the US Constitution? Evidence from the modern day would imply this seems too lenient. So where can we go from here?

Psychology is rife with internal disagreements, moreso than any other field. Yet there's no such thing as a scientific disagreement, it's simply a horde of religious disagreements. But this idea of religious disagreement is only based on one philosophy of science and religion, is there any other way to view this while coming to the same answer? Can we find a philosophical technical replicate to further validate this delineation between science and religion? Between psychology and every other science?

Art is something that subverts disadvantage into advantage, and sometimes creates beauty from nothing. Science is an accumulation of arts into a library, which then does the same thing as art at the next level of the metaphysical staircase, combining its advantages into principles. Engineering then uses these principles to construct actualities. Engineering acts as an integral to science, and science as an integral to art. If no manner of engineering can take advantage of the principles generated by the study of something, then it's not a science. Psychology borders the worlds of science and religion, but produces no tangible application to be used by engineering. Any engineering concept that can take advantage of the mind would be a component of neuroscience, not psychology. Like using a headset to use a computer instead of a mouse. To the world of science, psychology doesn't contribute principles, it contributes interpretations, and interpretations are purely religious in nature.

You might think that there's psychology baked into the engineering of certain devices, to make them easier or safer for people to use. But whatever concepts are being applied are not core to the function of the device. Indication lights on a runway aren't core to the function of a runway. Traffic lights don't need to be any specific color, they're that way out of convenience. Even the handle of a gun isn't core to the functioning of its barrel. Any device could function in entirety without psychological aids, and could continue to function even without an actual person. Meaning that any psychological aspects of design are completely irrelevant to the core functioning of any engineered device, gadget, or environment.

Psychology is that which attempts to put people's minds in a box for the sake of classification. But a mind is that which can grow out of any classification. How one interprets the mind, and things related to it, can only be found through religion. To forcefully dictate otherwise is to put people into boxes that only get smaller and smaller. Why do they only get smaller? Because the union of science and bureaucracy brings about never-ending incremental additions to its own library, which leads to never-ending classifications.

What a person believes about themselves and what their story has actually been can't be classified by anyone else, especially if they don't openly share their own story. Even if they do, interpretations may vary. You could even say the only thing that varying interpretations actually accomplish is to muddy the line.

If you don't know for sure what the brain can or can't do, then you're not able to dictate what religion is in a scientific manner. The brain can't be understood through any simple enough lens to characterize it, as the brain is always able to grow new capabilities for itself. The brain is a device that chooses how to define itself, and affects its own development along those lines.

Psychology is destined to encroach upon freedom. It offers never-ending standards of behavior, and the never-ending classifications that only grow and never shrink. The mind can never be fully understood, yet every scientist wants credit for their ideas. This naturally ends up with there being continually deeper layers of classification. Which means some hypothetical version of evil will be defined in more and more ways. They won't even use the term *evil* specifically, but the connotation will be there. In the worst case scenario, there'll be thousands of mental problems. Thousands of ways for you to be evil, bad, or wrong, that no one will be able to keep up with. Much like the growth in the number of government regulations for any industry over the last 15^{+} years.

In defining any sort of abnormality, one must always define from a perspective, and if we're being honest it's never able to be unbiased. There's always going to be some aspect of humanity defined as either good or bad, but this is a religious lens. To pick winners and losers is selection, it's inherently religious territory.

There's no way for the field of psychology to continue in an honest manner without being classified through a religious lens, because there's an infinite number of ways to classify any aspect of the mind. The brain perfectly embodies the nature of insidious subversions, because it's basically an insidious subversion device. The brain is a physical anomaly, as it's not able to be fully classified in purely physical terms. Any attempt to do so under the label of *legitimacy* would only act to open Pandora's box. Which means psychology is set up to find incremental differences in information until the end of time, and that's the problem. The increments will never stop. The brain can be studied and classified as a device, but the spawning of complexity we call the mind is a purely undefinable phenomenon that's able to model its way out of any classification. Understanding anything of an infinite nature is a purely religious endeavor.

If you want to see a therapist, or a person of some similar classification, that's up to you. It's your religious right to do so. It's the job of a psychologist to guide someone towards finding their own values. Which is a religious transformation. It's also your right to understand the religion of the person claiming to help you psychologically. Likewise, it's the right of the person acting as a therapist to do so through the lens of their own religion, rather than the dictations of some board of psychological standards. People can also certainly choose to form and follow boards if that's their choice as well. The freedom being argued for in this section is not in any way limiting, as that's not what freedom does.

The downfall of psychology, is that it becomes a natural disaster for young women whose lives are purely psychological. Young women wear mental disorders like they're decorative achievements, the problem becomes worse as many of them never stop trying to accumulate them, and they associate it with themselves like it's a part of their identity. But really, it's just normal human behavior that they'll grow out of as long as they don't constantly focus on it and believe that it *is* them. The badge of legitimacy of being a *science* is too much for a field like this. In a country that puts disclaimers on every product imaginable, psychology deserves one for the sake of its extreme potential ambiguity. Many adults, and young people, have been tricked into believing this is a *one true answer* to the mind, which is a classic form of religious stagnation. At least with astrology, no one's claiming it's indisputable.

Psychological tyranny would likely come through the definition of something vaguely understood like autism. Things affecting the mind that aren't fully understood technically have a muddied line of an understanding. You only have these problems if you believe it. Your mind is moldable primarily by you. Yet psychological encroachment becomes an insidious threat to young people, some of whom can be put in a psychological cage of classification. From within the cage, their freedom to transform themselves, during their most opportune years to do so, is gone. All transformations would be dictated by the *scientifically imposed* belief system. A definitive description of the disorders of the field of psychology will never be fully agreed upon, there's no innocent purpose in pushing religious classifications onto people who deny the claims. Any incomplete formal understanding becomes a politicizable label, and the incentive to continue characterizing will only be used to attack lines of indecipherable ambiguity using statements that are rightfully unintelligible. This is a violation, in the purest sense.

We choose to look through an extremely negative lens when classifying things as problematic, so we've done the same with human behavior and called them mental disorders. But the reality is that evolution didn't make you into some incredibly flawed person, nor did your life circumstances, these classifications are all relative to some environment. The flaw you have is that you haven't gotten to properly understand the positive sides of this behavior being classified so negatively. These classifications assume something is wrong with the person rather than the environment they've modeled throughout their childhood. Reinforcement is destiny, and changing your vices into virtues comes through understanding what made you the way you are.

Psychological classifications themselves even fall victim to Goodhart's law, and sometimes the opposite. People online have been known for adapting personality disorders as their persona for the sake of mocking the field itself. The point of classifying the brain and its behavior, and whether or not you're actually able to, is dependent on whether that classification falls victim to Goodhart's law after being widely communicated. If it does, then it's a false classification. The inability to measure whether it's passed or failed this classification is itself something that enters unstable ground. The best measure of whether something works becomes evident at a distributed level. If someone accepts a classification of themselves in their own personal life, that would be a religious acceptance of that classification, and even then it may be subject to change.

If you make a classification that ends up falling to Goodhart's law, it's because people are attempting to avoid your classification. This response would be a sign they feel that it will be used against them maliciously. Which would not only be a sign that you've failed, but a sign that your best intentions have insidious undertones. People would naturally have this response because this wouldn't be the first time in our evolutionary history where this form of tyranny took shape. Anyone attempting to prove their innocence in order to do so, or to assure people those aren't their intentions, would only prove those concerns correct. As that's basically a siren song that lures people in to weaponize this mindset through the structure of a cult.

The woke religion is filled with people trying to push that not affirming someone's gender identity is child abuse. But this is just their belief, because it's based on their religion. To force it onto others would be insanity, as continuing to use religion as the basis for taking someone's child away would lead to civil war.

It's undeniably strange that certifications for any kind of psychological profession are controlled by people who have, in recent years, attempted to control what beliefs psychologists are allowed to have. In places like Canada, Europe, and the US, there's various ways in which the standards for gender-affirming care are built into the psychotherapy infrastructure. Activists had, in fact, gone after scientists such as Kenneth Zucker whose entire career, filled with work studying the exact topic of gender dysphoria, opposed such things. His work professes that 80% of cases would disappear in a year if left alone[**186**,**187**, **188**]. Some recent work challenges this, and insists the percentage has changed, but this only works to muddy the line. It's not a proper disagreement that's happening here because the motivations behind later work is purely political, not to mention normal adults just talk things out when they disagree, without trying to sabotage the lives of others. Or perhaps if you don't appreciate my saying it's political, then maybe you'd agree it was religious? The reason this is happening is that it's another occurrence of the broken compass. Psychology, as a government sanctioned practice, is flat out unjustifiable, because it always devolves into religion, and the experimental group is going awry because of it.

If someone wishes to send their child to this kind of care, or chooses it for themselves, I suppose that's their right to choose. But for some board to choose this for the entirety of any psychological association, and impose its beliefs on the therapists as well as the patients, is unacceptable. Psychologists need and have the right to their own source of individual thought otherwise they're no longer modeling complexity with complexity, and this devolves into a form of theocratic control over society. The question then becomes, can there actually be truly secular psychotherapy? There's nothing secular about the mind. Only a single part of the brain needs to be religion-seeking for me to classify it as a religion-seeking device. People, using the words in this very section, could then try to subvert everything I've written by claiming it's their belief that their mind operates independent of religion, and in a purely secular manner. But that would still be their belief. It's just their belief that they're areligious, and that itself is a religion no matter how contradictory anyone believes that to be. Such contradictions would belong to those individuals, not religion itself. This characterization is unavoidable, so it's almost ironic that we'd ever managed to

---

186. Kenneth J Zucker et al. *Sex-Typed Behavior in Cross-Gender-Identified Children: Stability and Change at a One-Year Follow-Up*. Journal of the American Academy of Child Psychiatry, 1985
187. Kenneth J Zucker and Susan J Bradley. *Gender Identity Disorder and Psychosexual Problems in Children and Adolescents*. The Guilford Press, 1995
188. Kelley D Drummond et al. *Follow-Up Study of Girls With Gender Identity Disorder*. Developmental Psychology, 2008

set up such an institution of the mind claiming to be independent of religion in the first place. Competition via honesty of religious affiliation would do this institution justice.

Looking at aspects of the field of psychology specifically, the problem isn't even always reproducibility. Although it often is. It's the nature of how it needs to be reproduced. In order to reliably try and reproduce certain parts of the field, groups aiming to do so honestly would need to be blinded to all of psychology. Giving a pre-made set of questions to some group of researchers and telling them to conduct a pre-designed experiment is obviously going to get replicable results if it's a legitimate experiment within the context of that field. Even without giving the same questions and experimental design, and instead asking researchers of the same background to design an experiment for the same purpose, will again produce the same bias because they can't reproduce the experiment without someone sharing the purpose for it in the first place. So this form of replication has much less integrity than is actually required. The same kind of experimentation needs to come to fruition on its own with no influence of people who would bias the beliefs of the researchers for the same reasons intended behind blinding people administering an experiment from its own purpose. There needs to be complete civilizational replicates for reproducing many of the ideas in psychology in order to deem them empirically true.

It's not that there isn't something useful that can be gained from something like the Big 5 personality standard without a civilizational replicate, and most people certainly don't need a disclaimer to take it with a grain of salt. But to truly dictate it as absolute truth, one would need to see a replication of this concept independent of the study of Western psychology. It just so happens the only true examples of these kinds of civilizational replicates are what's found across different religious texts. You'll find similarities between Daoists, Hindus, Christians, and any other groups if you look hard enough, especially regarding things like truth, humility, and fairness. Even with different sources and motivations for these axioms, you'll still find that Christians, Daoists, and Hindus have all found them important enough to comment on these specific topics. If one needs to be blinded to the entire field just for the sake of replicating some technical measurement of the mind, it's because that measurement is of a religious nature. Once the entire world uses the same base layer for the study of psychology, it stops being as useful of a scientific endeavor. To lose the ability for civilizational replication would hurt its integrity more than help.

One can study the mind, but its interpretation is always of a religious nature. For one mind to put other minds in boxes of their own characterization is human nature. But to try to impose these boxes socially is tyrannical. In the same way that no one else has any business telling you what you yourself believe, no one has any right in imposing their characterizations on you. By not just dictating what boxes people are in, but how certain boxes are allowed to be handled, psychological classification has become an insidious subversion of autonomy in every single way, and it's all occurring at the religious level. This is how we ended up with gender pronouns being used as excuses to take people's children away.

Psychology is even being used to justify the rape of young European girls. One can simply say a migrant suffers psychologically, from *cultural bereavement syndrome*. Which they've done[**189,190**]. This *diagnosis* can even be from a *psychologist* that just happens to be the same ethnic background as the criminal, which it was. Despite the fact that it's the victim who suffers in this situation and not the criminals, the criminals seem to be getting the better end of the deal. The criminals are now left with their enjoyment and the reward of public endorsement for their crime, and this is all because we insist that psychology is somehow independent of religion. In the US we have this same problem where an apparent psychological diagnosis can deem someone unfit to stand trial. Regular people are capable of determining when someone is insane. We don't need a psychologist or judge to say so on our behalf. This realm of classification has become an extension of the original pursuit of law and psychology that shouldn't be able to be claimed as their primary purpose. So it's now evident that within the field of psychology itself comes infinite excuses for immoral behavior, something that was, ironically, once attributed to religious rule.

Just as an ideology within a school models its environment to become a religion, psychology within the criminal justice machine has

---

189. Hanseatisches Oberlandesgericht Hamburg, Pressestelle. *Urteilsverkündung im sog. Stadtpark-Verfahren.* Pressestelle des Hanseatischen Oberlandesgerichts Hamburg, 2023

190. Frank Chung. *Outrage as Eight of Nine Men Convicted of Gang Rape of 15-Year-Old in Germany Receive No Prison Time.* News Corp Australia, 2023

done the same. Initially, rulings would take someone's psychological state into account when making a judgement, but inevitably, rulings have come to use psychology as a first principle in criminal judgement in general. In many cases, it's transformed from being a minor consideration into being the main consideration, superceding even the law itself. The point of objective judgement was to separate factors of our mind from factors of our rule, and we'd attempted to use systematic laws in order to do so. But the flaws and biases of the mind were the reason for the desire for objectivity in the first place, so any process claiming objective judgement of the mind is automatically faulty. Attempting objectivity with something that can never be objective has come hand in hand with using this inevitably inobjective characterization of the mind to subvert judicial objectivity in general. It's contradictory to assume this would ever work, it becomes political by devolving into a power struggle, and those who wield such characterizations of the mind will inevitably weaponize it in such a context. What we should instead attribute our punishments to is public opinion. Do you want to reward those who sexually violate children? Or do you want to protect children from such individuals? Even if you wanted to admit the faults of psychology, and attempt to separate the good from the bad, you would only fall into yet another infinite classification problem.

Accepting psychology as religious territory would also allow psychologists to act within the realm of their own religion. Standards for therapist behavior, such as it being illegal to steal away someone's spouse, can still be in a legally binding disclaimer, or contract, so the concept of therapy itself doesn't need to change in any way for those who appreciate its services. Whether that's gender ideology, or just normal human behavior, people will know what to expect as it will need to be clearly outlined in some form of religious statement. There would be no psychological board that can force their standards onto anyone against their will. The boards and their standards can still exist, after all a lot of people find this industry helpful to their lives. But the boards, legally, can do nothing more than issue guidance, they have no business micromanaging the behavior of psychologists whose job it is to actually help individuals.

Instead of having a single unified field of psychology, people will be able to pick and choose what they want to believe. Which is what already happens anyways. There are all sorts of infights across different specializations within the field of psychology. To delineate different groups is just a form of honesty. Even in cases where the field agrees with itself, there's always a line of ambiguity that can be drawn between any two pieces of information. Taken in acute slices, some of psychology might remain purely empirical. But from a holistic view, there's no way to describe the field itself without an acknowledgement of its religious underpinnings. There's no clear lineage of causality within any psychological findings, just indirect associations between the information that's been uncovered. Religious disagreements can be inserted between every attempted elucidation within the field.

It's widely believed the scientific method is the only method we have to elucidate truth. There are very formal environments that believe this to be true. The biggest flaw of the scientific method is in the character of those who use it only to develop a lack of interest in arriving at new methods of more scalable elucidation of truth. Mathematicians can make proofs for why certain calculations can be done faster and more efficiently by requiring less steps, and what's the verification of truth but a form of calculation that proves some notion like an equality?

By using something oversimplified, like the scientific method, we limit ourselves to simple forms of verification. The scientific method is a left-brain approach to the problem it aims to solve. If that was the only thing needed to verify information, then we wouldn't have two brain hemispheres in the first place.

The scientific method doesn't scale so easily, and in the process many forms of truth are left within the realm of Darwinian uncertainty rather than being elucidated to a Newtonian certainty. In a lot of ways that's the best you can expect. But as problems begin to scale, any attempt to elucidate the Darwinian realm of some Darwinian answer grows in uncertainty, and becomes too difficult to grasp as Darwinian concepts continue to accumulate. Which is why other modes of thought may prove advantageous.

Much like how a brain transforms physical modes of entropy into metaphysical modes, as a means of calculation to become what it is, the same metaphysical sophistication can be applied to the realm of information in general, because that's the basis for how the brain formed in the first place. By clawing its way into coherence using every unknown factor available, the brain formed this way because the landscape of latent information always had the potential to operate in this manner. If humans had to re-develop the concept of intelligence from scratch, but were limited to using nothing but the scientific method, then they would arrive at absolute failure because the scientific method isn't a means of growing the capabilities of a population. Even our own knowledge is only a re-discovering of the information used to create our existence in the first place. Our knowledge is an incomplete recursion of our construction. The brain models its own intelligence, and information processing abilities, making way for a form of communication that operates as a scalable verification scheme, much like how the evolutionary history of the brain used information to develop in the first place. But these aren't the capabilities of just one brain, it's something formed through a population thereof.

IX
CIVILIZATION & POPULATIONS

9.1 Modeling Entropy

Not only are people not purely homogeneous across either side of some social bifurcation, some political divide, there are only reasonably uncommon cases where individuals always fall on one political side of all groupable bifurcations. Tribalism is not a true norm, and nuance is more common than uniformity, there are no simplicities. Still, simplicities have their place in communication and competition, as getting rid of them would ironically result in there being less complexity. Forms of fairness that people are typically willing to grant to others are hidden through confrontation resulting from misinterpretations. Beliefs, opinions, and ideas are projected across the entire population in ways that produce maximal variation, yielding a representation of every potential configuration achievable. Every potential configuration of human society is being modeled throughout the process of communication, resulting in a living metastructure of the information in our lives.

At the forefront of modeling our environment, is our own understanding of the world around us. It's the information we perceive and our surrounding worldviews, opinions, experiences, and expertise. An interacting collective of such things would be a modeling of statistical entropy itself, meaning, to globally model alternate states of every possible configuration and interpretation. The social bifurcations of the automaton represent ignorance but are made of irony, it's what creates the dualities of politics and physics. Because truth would be singular, but irony always reveals the two sides of every coin. It's representative of high order and high disorder processes that aim to optimize a greater complexity between the two, and the function of this structure is to tell truth from lie. Irony is the light shone on individuals to make their ignorance apparent. So the claims of either side's politics can always be seen as not incorrect, as there's always two ways to interpret reality, and the shortcomings of either side are more apparent to each other than they are to themselves. Crowds are also able to estimate truth where possible, as humanity itself is a distributed calculation device. Which is why implementing distributed calculations via economics has been so successful, as they're recursions of this original function.

Which is what a hypothetical grand observer would perceive should they have the depth to perceive such things. This modeling of entropy is analogous to consciousness itself, it would be an epibolic recursion after the brain. The complete set in order would consist of a cell's nucleus, the brain, and this network of communication that models statistical entropy. Where this network is the metaphysical product of a collective of brains. It's perhaps not as well-developed as the workings of any single brain, but it's the bleeding edge of our growing capabilities and will typically be more advanced than any individual. Any current status of this modeling of entropy would be a measure of where we stand on the ladder of transcendence. This is the process which prioritizes the construction of the uppermost levels of the Tower of Babel. The ability granted by this modeling was originally noted by people as far back as Aristotle[191], and has been explained further in modernity by James Surowiecki[192]. It's why the average guess of a crowd tends to be correct. It's why prediction markets predict elections so accurately.

So how does it happen? Is there some secret link between every brain on the planet? It wouldn't be necessary, this can be done simply by communicating. It's a macroentropic simulation that exists between the nodes of every individual thought and decision. The ability for groups to model variations in information, and thereby model entropy, far outclasses any individual ability to do the same. But there's something else that's also going on here.

191. Aristotle. *Politics*. 350 BCE

192. James Surowiecki. *The Wisdom of Crowds*. Doubleday, 2004

The behavior of a population of brains models their own collective connections the same way any single brain models its own internal connections, painting a poetic picture of an embedded recursion of something modeling what it models, producing a modeling of recursion itself. It's the most transcendent concept ever observed. This modeling of recursion, being so core to the functioning of a brain, then becoming the explanation for behavior across a population thereof, forces any person *with* a brain into the center of this very recursion just by understanding this explanation. But so far there's been no discussion as to how or why, or whether even at all that the brain surely *does* model all of its own internal connections. So how can this statement even be made? Conceptually, it would seem that modeling recursion is necessary in order to model entropy. The only way that a collective of brains could ever model entropy to begin with would be if their own internal connections were first modeling recursions in general. There's no other way for an entropy modeling device to communicate the entropy it models without being able to communicate. One can't communicate if they can't model their own internal connections to the point of self-coherence and self-recognition, so there absolutely must be both of these things present for there to be a societal modeling of entropy across a population.

This age of social media has empowered human connectivity to the point where the world is experiencing a lot of rapid changes in a short period of time. The end results of which will be a net positive, as that's the point of all this modeling to begin with. Like any other recursions, there's bound to be latent potential in aligning with their axiom-like nature for our collective benefit should we learn to utilize it.

This state of entropy across the population is hard-won, extremely valuable, and has likely been built up generation after generation through the handing down of culture. From understanding this concept, one would take away that variation guides consensus, not the other way around. Which is exactly what makes all of these recent failed top-down government dictations, these one-plan strategies that aimed to be direct interventions in every single person's life, look so blatantly foolish. From Covid mandates, to opinion mandates, and the gaslighting that came along, there's never any reason to force uniformity across a population, even in dire circumstances. As this natural variation exists for the very sake *of* dire circumstances. Control itself can strangle the wisdom of crowds. It's like oversimplifications have become infestations in this land of information, where policy now dictates their existence. These one-plan strategies *always* fail, and *always* looks incredibly stupid in hindsight. Natural human variation is a survival strategy, to subvert it for any reason is a betrayal.

Deviation and disagreement were punished to the point where people lost their livelihoods over following their basic instincts, so it can't be said to have not been malicious. The predominant leadership from the political establishment of the last 30$^+$ years has gone overboard, as the severity of these situations didn't call for forced uniformity. Forced uniformity is a forced despecialization, it's the opposite of adaptation. It's attempting a reversion of common sense. What can one do, as a hypothetical leader in the same position as those who made these foolish decisions in the first place? If one wants to better model entropy across society, how can this be accomplished with as minimal effort as possible?

Simply enabling freedom would solve all of these problems. Eliminate censorship and promote communication, thereby enabling all the best possible solutions. Society, as a form of distributed calculation, is better at solving literally anything than a government ever could be. To Western civilization, and those who inherit its creed, freedom is a machine that provides continual reciprocating benefits.

Across populations, freedom achieves the opposite of stress. More great feats will be achieved, and more people will cooperate for the sake of achieving them. It's not just blatant freedom to do anything, it's freedom along a specific axis. People don't need freedom to murder, but they do need freedom to use such force against someone attempting to murder them or their family. Weaponizing people's survival instincts against them, claiming they should have restrained themselves, is a denial of their right to survive. There are no good reasons to prohibit the communication of any form of ideas across society. There's always a context in which freedom can improve any outcome. Applying freedom well is an economic art, and more possibilities lead to greater potential.

To better model societal entropy, a high-trust society is needed. It removes the need for modeling uncertainties with things like paranoia. If you can't have this, a high-trust collective is the next best thing. Which is basically a religion. The problem is, you can't have high-trust societies coinciding with the existing Marxist schooling paradigm, as the basis of this school system teaches people to distrust everyone else. Where they don't train their students to evoke mistrust, they at least train them to evoke anxiety. Which makes for a faulty religion at best, as it promotes false interpretations of reality. In its best light, religion isn't about making up alternate realities, it's about trying to understand the reality we find ourselves in.

Why are the old conservative while the young are liberal? Because it's their job to be. Likewise, when it flips, like is happening in the modern day, the opposite trend arises. People's viewpoints are modeling entropy across the population because life is made up of various risks and challenges that both individuals and collectives face in order to survive. Both of these components optimize themselves for reasons much like why both the big picture and small details are necessary for understanding both the universe and our existence. It's a distributed responsibility across the collective to reach boundary points that are more extreme than the consensus so that the best possible center point can be estimated.

What does this modeling of entropy, these pools of entropy of pools of entropy, arrive at? Philosophy, religion, and any other mental machines that contribute to survival. Together, individuals and collectives arrive at a state of mind opportune to their own existence within some established framework of fairness. That's why civilizational replicates of different religions tend to have points of consistency throughout various topics. It's literally because beliefs are discovered rather than made. It's an equilibrium of thought that's found through communication.

It's why people found religion in topics that were supposed to be inherently non-religious, and the topics they found weren't by coincidence, they resemble those of our evolutionary history. That's where the climate narrative, the gender narrative, and even some of the racial narratives all came from. The climate narrative resembles the nature of environmental worship within early animism. The gender narrative derives from the most obvious difference amongst ourselves, the difference amongst the sexes, where men and women were seen to represent the functions they fulfilled in society. It was this modeling of entropy that found these religious underpinnings for the teachers and students that needed to interact on the basis of religion yet were withheld from doing so. It's necessary for them to have something like this in their lives, which is exactly how they found it. The human modeling of entropy is the inheritor of the world that was shaped by natural selection prior to human development. It's now shaped by religion, because just like its predecessor, it's shaped by unknowns.

With convergent evolution, there was an inevitable morphological equilibrium that members of certain environments were bound to arrive at. We're not entirely the way we are, societally, due to the creation of any lone philosophy nor the history of many, but rather history and philosophy result from an equilibrium amongst themselves and our relationship with the environment we find ourselves in. The equilibrium itself is timeless, it isn't a spontaneous construction, nor would it have been entirely different under different circumstances. Any existing equilibrium would be due to the natural consequences of its metaphysical positioning, as well as the evolution it experienced prior. Although this isn't something exact and precise, it's not Newtonian, it's more of either a Darwinian causality or Darwinian equilibrium. Likewise, the ironic juxtaposition of opposing political views against each other isn't a coincidence, it's a state optimal for modeling entropy, which implies there's a meaning behind this peculiar perching of beliefs against each other. Given this is the behavior of populations at large, governments would do well to facilitate this process rather than hinder it, governments should be modeling the modeling of entropy.

The European left-wing establishment has censored any right-wing political discourse, even for statements as minor as saying *immigration isn't going so well*, or bringing up the shifting demographics of one's own native country relative to foreigners, even going so far as to prevent people from attending their own political conventions like the National Conservatism conference in Brussels in 2024. All while they've constantly and continuously imported migrants from countries whose children are soon going to outnumber native European children, despite that something like 80% of all Europeans don't want this to continue, and now typically between 10-20% of each European country's population are immigrants, and they make up an even larger percentage of their young. Many of them, rightfully so, want the migrants deported. There's no stopping this massive wave of foreigners who are being subsidized to start families, despite those same benefits not being granted to ethnically native citizens of these countries at the same rates. This is the work of those who are pushing for racial and ethnic disintegration, which is no less extreme than a radical push for ethnic purity.

The left-wing European establishment constantly claims that right-wing parties are *anti-democratic*, and attempts to ban legitimate political organizations, like is being tried with Germany's AfD, simply because the tides are beginning to turn in their favor. That's despite that banning political parties is the most anti-democratic thing one could do. These politicians have allowed for the sexual assault of at least a million young women, prevented native Europeans from getting any justice, from being able to defend themselves, and allowed these criminals to roam free with no repercussions. Yet people who defend themselves from rapists, or accidentally kill them, are given decades long sentences to make sure they regret ever having feelings of self-worth. The reasons for which are still unclear, but their countries have undeniably been sold out in some way by a compromised political class. How did they actually get this way? Between unfairly persecuting political opposition, forcing atrocities on millions of young girls, all while trying to force ideology onto their own unwilling citizens, how did the Europeans manage to gaze into this abyss of obscene societal control to the point where it seems like they're more authoritarian than democratic?

Looking at the extremely progressive policies across Europe, alongside the devotion of their government to insidious control, isn't it ironic that Europe has transformed to simultaneously inherit aspects of both the Weimar and the Reich? Like they saw the behavior of the Weimar, that caused the Reich, and determined it would be nice to have a society, like the Weimar, being governed by the control of the Reich. They took the worst aspects of both, and tried forming what's now called the European Union. Despite the stubbornness it takes to cling to such failures, we can at least give them credit for trying. As a modeling of entropy is always going to occur in some progression. To only arrive at previous answers over and over would be representative of an unevolving phenomenon, of which living organisms are definitely not.

The behavior of the Nazis is not unique to the Nazis, and it's not unique to either political wing. In case it wasn't clear, the purpose of such a comparison isn't simply to envision people as Hitler, and call them names, I'm trying to understand why they seemed to have arrived at all the same answers. The European left, much like the Nazis once did, want compulsory education in an institution of their choosing, and the European left, much like the Nazis once did, want to lower the voting age because it brings in freshly indoctrinated voters. The fatal flaw of the European left was in forgetting to embrace the values that actually defeated the Nazis in the first place. The Nazis were in favor of extreme societal control, which is basically what the extreme left-wing has been trying to accomplish through the mass-importation of migrants for multiple decades. It's likely that people on the left have been manipulated by the Chinese, because it's the Chinese who are aiming to subvert the West from the inside, as they've been stating publicly for years. I wish it was as simple as saying the global-left and the Chinese are on different sides, but they have an enormous amount of business connections between themselves. Every so-called *environmental policy* pushed by the left has always resulted in jobs being exported to the Chinese, at the cost of both Western industry and environmental sanctity. How did an entire political wing of the West come to be compromised by such a conflict of interest?

The extreme behaviors related to the left wing have historically been somewhat difficult to describe due to their being a wide range of effects associated with these movements, but there's a common theme throughout it. The extremes of the left tend to create a dependency-ridden environment, no different than relying on the fruit of a tree. The metaphor of the swarm of mosquitoes is adequate to explain the behaviors of their masses, because mosquitoes are vampires. They drain you of the sustenance needed to live, and use it to control you, like you're a thrall, where the thralls have no big picture of the world, they simply believe what they're being told. In reality, these dependencies come through welfare, inflation, and a seizure of assets. In the case of Europe, it's a seizure of heritage. The EU was attempting to put its own members into a state of dependency to maintain their control, and the Chinese offered the same deal to the Eurocrats as the EU did to its own citizens, they were tricked into a state of dependency. Like drug dealers of morality, they were sold lies about green technology that only increased the cost of their energy while still being no less environmentally destructive than oil. The Chinese offer them control by taking any potential sovereignty away from their political opposition, which is a poison apple of poison apples. This left-wing establishment seemingly wants to restrict freedom, and to control others. They want to control every societal outcome, which has been the publicly spoken motto of the World Economic Forum for decades. Which is extremely concerning once you see the origins of the people who run this organization, as well as the praise its representatives give to the Chinese government for its excessive societal controls. It's the sign of someone who's never realized the blatantly obvious blunders of communism. This European political establishment and its associated groups want to dictate their definitions of both hatred and tolerance. Which are two sides of the same coin, and it's a very political coin.

But the negatives are always matched with positives, as with order comes disorder. The extremes of the left come to enable dependencies, but the proper use of loans, borrowing, bonds, and credit have come to develop the advanced financial infrastructure we benefit from. Likewise, the Nazis are our most well known example of extreme right-wing behavior, yet they also represent a core axiom of human instincts. It exists for a reason, and it's also possible to leverage the advantages of this instinct without falling into the worst parts of its abyss. From this side of our socioevolutionary hedged bet comes the understanding of our own past, our evolution, our mortality, and the Darwinian mechanics we exist within. In the same way we use systems far beyond the exchange of rocks and metals in the modern day, and without devolving into civilizationally destructive modes of communism, religion can transform into a highly sophisticated competitive educational environment that utilizes this instinct to its fullest potential, and respects the necessity for it in our lives, rather than leaving it demonized and misunderstood as it has been in the wake of the Nazis. Even though the West, in many places, teeters on the edge of embracing the left-wing extreme of being a borderless welfare state whose government acts as a distribution center for the entire world, the best way to avoid either of these extremes would be to embrace both of these core human instincts with moderation. A balance between the two would bring the most benefit, and prevent either from becoming extreme.

The only way to come to the same answers as the Nazis is to solve the same integral, but their folly wasn't so much a product of their philosophy, their philosophy was a product of their circumstance. Cornered animals fight back, and the Germans perceived themselves as cornered. In facing their problems, the answers they came to weren't unique, they were the same answers that people had come to for thousands of years. The difference was that the age they were born in enabled unique atrocities that hadn't been as possible prior. Comparing the European leftists to Nazis is clearly an exaggeration, but they have in fact done something very similar nonetheless. Their mistake was thinking every moral transgression they made was acceptable when *they* did it. The Nazis felt justified in their morality, perceiving themselves as cornered. The leftists feel justified in their morality in the wake of the Nazis, fueling their own control mechanisms as a justification to prevent their recurrence. In the process, the Nazis *have* returned, but they're unable to see their own reflection. It seems whatever morality this European establishment envisioned its own superiority through isn't a principled enough concept to hedge society upon. You share a nation and culture, and morality is downstream from both of these. Even if a democracy, or a state pretending to be one, tries to impose morality, it will only ever teach the lesson that imposing morality is derivative of pride. Such impositions then always devolve into tyranny. Human nature will direct you to the same solution, the integral of whatever derivative has been latched onto, whether you acknowledge it was what you stood for or not.

You can't enforce morality. In a personal relationship you can inspire it, but at scale you must incentivize it. Success in the American system is too often mistaken for something other than this, it incentivizes success. The only way forward is to embrace freedom, as freedom is not derived from tyranny. The Europeans and leftists keep making this same mistake. They envision the solutions to all life's problems through the lens of control, then they find themselves incapable of implementing solutions independent of it, so they can't ever utilize freedom. This inherently works to prevent people from making mistakes, believing it to be an act of kindness, but even if this goal were actually accomplished it would only leave the populace frustrated with their own naïveté. Which is why they've arrived at such failed implementations of governance. Freedom is not an option. It's a universal principle. One must accept it in order to be successful.

Freedom is derivative of entropy itself, and in following this path towards God, even the successes and failures of entire nations becomes but a history lesson made from those who were unable to understand this. It will be a tragic downfall of the victims to the tyranny of those who refuse to learn at all. As beliefs and values are not made, they're discovered. Meaning, this discovery never ends, and freedom is the transformative tool that allows this process to continue. You can't design a successful society for the same reason you can't design your own beliefs, because the design isn't yours. One can only borrow from the principles of which success is derived. Freedom is not successful by coincidence, freedom is a universal principle that grants success.

The Post-WWII European civilization failed to embrace the philosophy of its victors, so it's repeating the mistakes of the losers all over again, and this time it looks like the next war they'll start is going to be genuinely worse. The young women of the early 1900s weren't subjected to widespread sexual violence, the immigrants to Germany came from only a few countries over, rather than half a world away, and the debt problems in Germany had inhibited the self-sufficiency of just their lone country, whereas the current debt-based economies have a chance at completely destroying an entire civilization. They were not punished for saying *mean words* to the people who rape young children more than the actual rapists were punished for their genuine atrocities. If you want a recipe for a war of vengeance, we're looking at the makings of one now. It's a terrible thing that this left-wing international coalition has come to envision so-called *tolerance* for the crimes of migrants, especially towards genuinely heinous crimes rather than limiting this philosophy to something like petty theft. Tolerance and hatred are two sides of the same coin, to control the definition of one is to control the definition of the other. To force tolerance amongst a populace means to force hatred on them, as everything is made of tradeoffs. Ideas like these are why we model entropy in the first place, to make strategic tradeoffs that don't destroy ourselves. But when some plan, some measure of forced compliance, is dictated from the top-down through this one-plan mindset, the modeling of entropy is foregone and the resulting societal consequences always result in societal failure. Why should anyone follow these plans that aren't even hedged bets? It would be a foolish way of guaranteeing the worst possible outcome for your own countrymen, and the people you're supposed to care about.

The modern European mode of governance falls towards this kind of control because they don't have a true supreme executive position with the EU, they don't allow their citizens to directly vote for those who hold this position. You can't have councils that appoint and elect members independent of the populace's ability to oppose such councils, this model isn't adequate for sustained governance. The direct elections of the United States far outclasses anything the European Union has attempted, and this is blatantly obvious. These councils and bodies do nothing but contribute to problems when they can't be put in check by an opposing counterbalance. It's a failed form of governance, and it's a failed form of cooperation. It's failed in the past, it's failing in the present, and it will fail in the future because it incentivizes a formation that prevents the opposition of beliefs. Representation in the modern day isn't something too complicated to achieve, the overarching structures imposed by the EU only incentivize insidious control and a subversion of democracy. Until the EU is capable of directly electing a single supreme executive leader, their union will continue to be a failed and collapsing union that aims for self-sabotage. These indirectly elected bodies aren't respectful of the modeling of entropy because they aim to subvert their own opposition. These bodies, independent of any proper counterbalance, are nothing but corruption-breeding machines. It's the function of their structure, meaning this becomes an equilibrium that's always formed. To continue to be ruled by corruptible bodies is to allow the card castle to perpetually collapse while claiming the increased control from doing so is actually *progress* by people who are too proud to admit they've ever made a mistake. This speaks to the nature of assemblies in general, the less members there are the more corruptible the assembly is. In this age of the internet, we shouldn't ignore the potential of reforming these legislative chambers to larger and larger numbers. Social media has shown us the ability for larger numbers of people to be efficient, and to find common ground on issues that these corruptible bodies seem incapable of addressing.

The point of organizing legislative bodies into chambers was originally out of necessity, it was for public debate. Entire countries couldn't convene in order to direct their interests. Now, these bodies have transformed into centers for theatrics, and all negotiation happens behind closed doors. The age of the internet has changed this realm significantly, so do we still need such bodies? Members of Western governments seem to show more loyalty to the political structure they're a part of, rather than the citizens they represent. If people can organize over the internet, faster and more efficiently than has ever been done in real life, do we need legislative bodies of such a limited number of participants to make our laws? It seems limiting the numbers within such chambers only makes them more susceptible to corruption, and as society advances, this corruption naturally turns their interest against the populace out of fear of being deemed incompetent.

The weakness of the League of Nations contributed to creating the conditions that allowed for the outbreak of WWII. Its modern counterpart, The United Nations, has more ability to enforce international law and cooperation, but is enabling attempts at global control through bureaucratic dictatorship. Neither of these committee-based solutions has led to good outcomes. If citizens of a country can't directly elect their own representatives, then the function of the structure of that assembly is of corruption and failure. We don't need the UN, it's now at the point of implementing global censorship on the internet through *misinformation* and *hate speech*. The global political class is attempting to mass censor the internet simply because the internet is driving the populace of various countries to disagree with the shortcomings of their own governments[193]. The point of governance isn't to rule, it's to implement fair rule. Elite clubs will never be fair to others, their implementations will only spite the nature of fairness itself and replace it with their own ideals. In the process, they're doing their part in starting WWIII, because they're contradicting the modeling of entropy of their citizenry.

Amongst these groups of political elites come the temper tantrums they throw when they begin to lose popularity in their own countries. Normal grown adults would phase themselves out as they become unpopular. But to those in this supposedly elite club, they want to maintain their status at the international lunch table. When they begin to lose elections, they change the election rules. When they begin to be unpopular, they censor what information people are allowed to learn about. This is happening all over Europe, and in the UK with their new online censorship act. The UK has censored the internet for anyone younger than 18, while simultaneously giving the right to vote to everyone at 16. It aims to prevent people, who are old enough to vote, from hearing any information that could affect who they vote for.

Why are these legislative bodies so inefficient when they'd functioned so well for hundreds of years? The politicians have become hyper-observed, like a child unable to escape the sight of their parent's helicopter, except they have millions of helicoptering guardians. With each member of legislative bodies having this pressure imposed on

193. United Nations. *United Nations Global Principles for Information Integrity.* 2024

them, they form cults to keep their secrets amongst themselves in order to maintain their sanity, they're incentivized to. Which, if we're honest, is a problem for both politicians and those who they represent. The only way a legislative body can work properly is if it actually represents citizens who directly vote for their representatives. Where there's a small number of representatives, voting on behalf of a disproportionately larger body of people, it breeds corruption and cults. We need to have larger legislative bodies that are actually capable of representing people, rather than representing those who work against them. When the number of people in the legislative body is closer to the number of actors trying to subvert the populace, corruption ensues. The US House of Representatives could fix this problem by coming to represent hundreds of millions with thousands, rather than merely hundreds. The number of representatives needs to increase to be proportional to the population itself, otherwise the function of these structures begins to disproportionately breed corruption that disfavors their own populace. Each House Representative currently represents more than 700,000 individuals, this number could be less than 100,000 with roughly 3,300 representatives. Returning our ratio to around 40,000 citizens per representative, where it was at the founding of the country, would require about 8,000 representatives. Seeing as this ratio can only be expected to increase, it would be wise to decrease it as much as possible in order to best accommodate future generations. With so many individual districts, this would also fix the problems of gerrymandering, as the districts would be so small that ridiculous shapes would be less achievable, such manipulations would be much more obvious when it happens. It would change the observer-to-observed ratio, decrease the ability for lobbying groups to control legislation, and decrease the amount of political secrecy. In essence, this increases the distributed responsibility of the populace, and would even mesh well with allowing young people a stratified vote in the altered electorate scheme suggested prior. To take it even further, there's the potential to make non-contiguous house districts. These could be a form of distributed calculation that allows people to found their own districts as a group of people instead of a landmass, elect their preferred representative, and ensure their votes are destined to best represent their interests.

There may even be some duties that can be taken away from legislative bodies. Legislative bodies are inefficient at changing the sentences

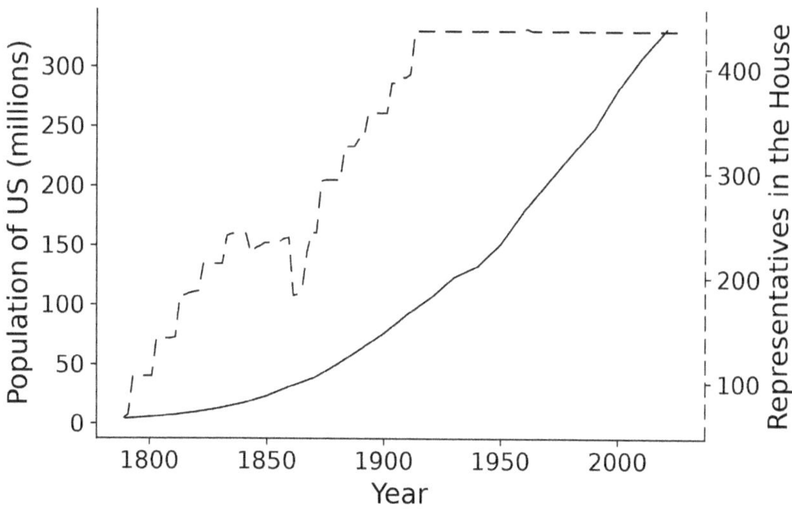

Figure 11: US Population and Representation in the House

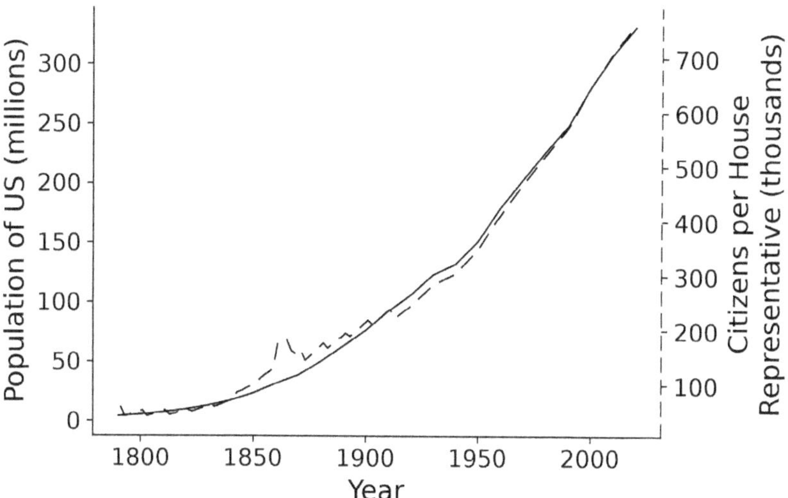

Figure 12: US Population and Representation per Representative

for crimes, and when judges refuse to enforce sentences legislative bodies need to act to ensure they're enforced. For something generic that has a fixed nature, like the length of jail sentences for specific crimes, people should be able to directly vote on it. I would rather introduce a dynamic voting system that cumulatively averages the votes of the last

10ish years alongside votes of the current year. As people vote to increase or decrease the sentence for a crime, it would move up or down like prices on a stock market, and these results would be plainly visible to everyone in the US as a map and dataset. Any standard for punishment can be specialized to the area it occurs in, so even state laws can be modulated based on local sentiment. If some year a community experienced a horrendous case of sexual assault against a minor, then they might decide to increase the sentence for such a crime. Likewise, if you find your community to be decreasing the sentence for child rape to something below 5 years, then this system can act as a warning to those living in those areas that this is an extremely dangerous community. Seeing as these are legislative votes, they would be public, and everyone's names would be listed alongside everything they voted for. The upside to public votes means this system can be done digitally, and doesn't need to all be done on the same exact day. People could vote for these things once a year, and any time of year. There can even be a process to reorganize the hierarchy of violations regarding existing laws, or introduce new standards for sentencing to follow such as minimum/maximum sentence, and rules for judges who release prisoners from jail early only for that criminal to commit another crime such as murder. It's difficult to get legislative bodies to act on judges who release criminals who then go on to murder people, but if this job is outsourced to the public at large then the problem may be solved overnight. Or they could vote the other way, but either way it's clear that we don't need legislative bodies to do this job anymore.

Aggregations of judicial rulings should be available online as freely accessible data in the form of visualizations that display, at scale, breakdowns of the rulings of any judge across demographics of the defendants and/or victims to be easily compared across individual crimes in order to find bias. It would make cases of judicial discrimination visible to everyone. The problem being, this information isn't easy to access. It's typically hidden behind paywalls, and difficult to aggregate. An improved model would be a single website with highly intuitive visualizations that offers data for every judge in the country. The current status quo, where this information is largely hidden from the public, only prevents people from being able to judge a judge. People often have to vote judges in and out of office, but have no way of assessing their worth. We also need a similar manner of tracking the cases they refuse to hear, as they can choose to discriminate in this manner as well.

A similar system should be in place for district attorneys, portraying information on cases they took, and ones they didn't, as it's incredibly important to retain data on which cases weren't prosecuted. These people were meant to operate in a manner visible to the public, open accessibility of these rulings would give people the confidence to trust the system is operating as intended, rather than hoping it does from behind the closed doors they currently hide behind.

Originally, the US government was set up as a way for citizens to maintain control of their government. This hasn't realistically existed in the post-WWII era. The secrecy needs to be disbanded, and there can be no state secrets. Those who maintain secrets only do so in order to maintain their own control. The public isn't incapable of handling the information being kept secret, and it's not to our benefit that it is. The more people in the know, the better our collective decision-making processes will become. The value behind voting has been subverted by political puppets and the orchestrations of people who will never step out into the sunlight. When the ability for the public to communicate and come to consensus is more capable than their ability to use their consensus to change laws and their enforcement, the probability of war or rebellion will continue to increase.

The current *design* of European society was meant to avoid wars, but the mass migration crisis has only become a proxy for the wars they would have otherwise waged. The freedom to die fighting is a better alternative than their current path of insidious collective destruction. With the widely recognized concept of surrender, war on the European continent was more civilized than anywhere else on the planet. It was Europeans who systematized and internationalized the civility of war through rules of engagement, and the fair treatment of prisoners. It's ridiculous to project the savagery of the Nazis on every other individual and country when it's so astonishingly clear to everyone that both what they did, as well as the circumstances that incentivized their fight for survival, were heinously unacceptable. To pretend that war must coincide with atrocity is a lie. Even the Indians and Chinese agree to battle in the Himalayas using primitive means. Those that pretend all war must be fought bitterly only project their own bitterness, this is a method psychological aggression. We can't move forward as a civilization without acknowledging that the imprisonments of psychological aggression are an equal opposite to the atrocities of physical aggression. One isn't, in any way, better than the other. We need to acknowledge that both are horrendous in order to move forward with greater cooperation. To balance either with the other is to minimize both.

The benefit of freedom isn't just for individuals. It has an area-effect, much like how having more billionaires in your society is actually a broadly beneficial thing, as their money ends up being spent everywhere. The freedom of everyone else comes back to benefit those around them economically, and through shared wisdom.

After the Roman Empire fell, areas that were under its influence learned from its model. There was no need for an entirely new set of ideas about governance. They could simply adopt what had largely worked well for the Romans, as that was a level of societal development that was painstakingly earned. Any future models could be built on top of it. When Americans did this using their experience under British rule, and their knowledge of history, they learned from every mistake they were forced to live through in order to genuinely transform into a state that respected a truer principle than what had ever been achieved before. Likewise, the blunders visible to us today are lessons we can learn from, they're as much an opportunity as they are an injustice. Freedom does not work by coincidence. Freedom is not a coincidence.

Neither is fairness. When people vote to stop immigration, that's the distributed calculation announcing that it's gone overboard. Whatever the consequences may be, people are willing to deal with it. That's what they say with their vote. When politicians ignore this for decades, and pretend like they know better, it becomes a problem. The wisdom of crowds is wiser than the data of politicians, and encompasses more than they could ever measure.

Maybe you think America is experiencing problems of its own in the same regard as Europe, that perhaps freedom isn't really the answer. But this couldn't be further from the truth. The divide we have in our country has always been here. Just as people have taken on new forms of communication, old extremism has come to take on new forms of expression. America is not made up of 2 nations, there's definitively 1 nation that's working together to model entropy in ways that, at best, only seem antagonistic in the modern day. The antagonism is a byproduct of either side of the socioevolutionary hedged bet specializing in their respective role. We're finding that our previous methods of large-scale communication were completely compromised by a corrupt government who now complains about being hindered by the First Amendment, because they were abusing their power, and manipulating the news for the sake of starting unnecessary wars across the entire planet. Politicians have learned that keeping certain problems prevalent allows them to constantly fundraise on these issues, and both parties are guilty of this. The prior resulting developmental failure of the future of our own socioevolutionary hedged bet is now beginning to heal itself somewhat due to both the expansion of social media, and the crumbling of the establishment. Disagreement is a natural part of society, and as people come to understand this better, society will begin to organize itself in a manner that facilitates them, rather than demonizes them. Freedom isn't that which enables agreement, it enables disagreement, and fair mediations across disagreements are that which enables functional governance. Disagreements are no different than disorder, they don't eventually form agreements, they form order. Communication is *extremely* important, even moreso at scale. Hindering it, the same way this political and media environment had hindered it for decades, through propaganda, smearing, half-truths, and a refusal to platform opposing viewpoints, only causes a false propped-up sense of cooperation that then needs to be rebuilt from scratch when the lies eventually crumble. The best communication models truth, that's the purpose of honesty. The harder your society makes it for people to be honest, the worse off it will be. Left unhindered, lies are self-exterminating facets of our social machinery, and we're now experiencing growing pains to make up for lost time because the generations that inherit this culture now need to further sacrifice themselves on the altars of the entitlement of their direct predecessors in order to continue to maintain an appropriate balance in the future.

Basically, we don't have a new divide. We have an upbringing problem, and an honesty problem. People are too immature for this form of communication because they were never properly welcomed into this aspect of their society the same way young children aren't properly welcomed into capitalism. This upbringing problem is where untapped passion turns into vitriol, but this too shall pass. With maturity comes equilibrium, and the country will turn out better than before, the same as it has in the past, without the need for a war should we be wise enough to avoid it. The semi-war-like state of the political landscape is a sign that there's an answer we're collectively approaching, it can also be seen as a stress test of the system that doubles as an experiment for future layers of organization. The reasons behind stress-testing our system the way we do, as a natural byproduct of our politics, is so those of us who observe the system and its fault points can infer improved modes of organization for the sake of scaled fairness.

9.2 Evolutionary Pulsing

Along the way to organizing itself into intelligence, information first seems to organize itself into incentives. The information intrinsic to the physical objects around us creates a metaphysical web of second-order potential that then becomes incentives to intelligent organisms. A flower incentivizes a bee to take its nectar in order to fertilize another flower, this has gone on for so long that either organism would have serious problems without the other. Incentives are the artisanal tools of irony, they're a latent technology for building complexity.

Fairness isn't just a courtesy granted to others, it's an incentive to remain peaceful, and the model of interactions was born from this. It was the primordial incentive of sentient organisms. Perhaps you'd think that would instead be something like eating or sleeping, but eating and sleeping would be necessities that existed prior to the emergence of sentience. Incentives aren't necessities, they're what create necessities. Much like an addiction, incentivized modes of interaction eventually form necessities, as they tend to become heavily relied upon. Perhaps you think certain things were always going to become necessities regardless, and I would agree. But the mode through which they became necessities, while they were yet to be, were through incentives. Incentives are self-organizing stairsteps towards complexity that necessitates necessity itself.

To incentivize or evoke unfairness is to incentivize the destruction of necessities. Which is to incentivize war, as war is the destruction of necessities. Incentives are the bait and hook of information that lures and traps something into dependence. This then also creates an interesting question, can incentives incentivize other incentives? Can they collectively hook onto each other to form an interlinked series, like a tidal wave, or domino effect, that then work in unison? Lenin once made a significant quote, where *"there are decades where nothing happens; and there are weeks where decades happen"*. To live in one of those so-called weeks is to witness the crest of that wave of incentives.

Growing complexity coincides with cyclic events, similar to how recursions themselves have an intrinsic cyclicity. The Tower of Babel is the story of humanity and it's the story of life. We no longer stack rocks in the desert, we refine the rocks then fly them into space. With each one of these cycles comes our eventual demise, and from those ashes we reinvent our philosophies to match any new-found truth. It's an internal order optimization at scale across a population. It first happened in simpler ways at the species level, and mankind has come to grow the scale of this phenomenon to manifest civilizational development. These are the most difficult aspects to understand about human civilization. They happen on the stock market, with products, and with populations even. Are they bubbles? Boom and busts? A rise and fall? Civilizational cycles? Why do these happen, and is there a way we can understand the nature of these repetitive cycles?

The best kind of boom is that of a population boom, as everything else grows alongside it. People make for the best integrals to advancement. The worst kind of crash is probably war. Population booms are no different in nature than stock market bubbles. Economic booms are in no way new, they've been around as long as humans have had economies. In the scenarios of both population and markets, there are winners that make it out the other side that go on to become permanent players.

It's probable that the end stage of many booms in the past have selected for specific traits, intelligence likely being one of the most prominent. Within the complexity of human society, it might not even be a guarantee that this works every time. For example, we're performing strange experiments on our population with birth control, social media, and anti-Western ideas, of which we still don't know what the exact long-term effects of will be. For all we know, everyone who took these pills in their childhood may tend to not have a lineage that's around in 100 years. Being so highly successful, we easily become victims of our own comfort. The more foolish the idea that was taken as gospel, the faster the effects of collapse will take root. Seeing as most populations around the world are collapsing, there's a good chance that we've taken some pretty bad bait.

I don't say that booms cause selection events out of pure speculation. We can take our own recent events as an example. Having had multiple market crashes within the average lifespan of a dog, for so many youths nowadays it's exactly what's causing them to not have children. The consequences of which have prevented a number of young people from even getting to the point where they can afford to have a family. This form of selection isn't even a good competition, as it has a lot of false negatives being selected out. Which is dysgenic.

These booms are likely happening all around us in various ways, it's just easier to pay attention to the largest ones. There was a boom of people trusting the media establishment during Covid that seems to have collapsed afterwards and transformed into something entirely different. Populations boom because stability minimizes the cost of growing complexity. As things keep following the status quo, no one feels the need to challenge it. Good leadership eventually turns into dogma, and stern belief invites the irony that brings about a collapse of the then oversimplified principles inherited by that population.

Every event is a selection event. The Soviet communists killed all of their most capable military commanders, which subsequently got them decimated by the Germans in WWII. That was even despite gaining victory later. The same thing is happening in the West right now. We've sacrificed the most competent individuals of multiple generations on the altars of diversity and immigration by giving priority to people who weren't born here, or based on some superficial facet such as race and gender. Even the manufacturing jobs of the heartland have been shipped overseas to people who are more adversarial than friendly. The punishment we're receiving is from the outright incompetence, and inability to admit mistakes, of a political establishment that seems capable of accomplishing nothing as effectively as they are at stealing taxpayer money and giving it to their own non-profit organizations.

The same pattern presents itself just about everywhere. Over the last couple decades, tech companies hired highly qualified people to make cutting edge platforms for big paychecks. The success these companies found allowed them to hire more people while granting even more luxurious benefits to their employees. Subsequently, many of the employees created videos of them enjoying their benefits, and making it seem like their entire day was spent barely working. This resulted in people wanting to be employed by those companies, but not for the sake of performing their role. They wanted the benefits and the life of daily luxury seen in the videos that lured people in with envy. In the long term, these employees were useless to these highly competitive companies, and were laid off. Which demonstrates that even booms can be explained through some respective series of irony, in fact there's probably no better way.

Just as there are no large waves of great movies coming out anymore, just as there isn't an abundance of groundbreaking music being made, the future likely won't see any booms of individual software languages being made at the same rate either. Because we build things for the future. Only making the same things over and over would be indicative of a purely dogmatic instruction. Without there being a purpose for the same things to be made over and over, they lose their value. Nothing intelligent is going to chase something without value, and no boom is going to be the same as some prior boom. Otherwise it would be a doom loop rather than a transformation. We don't need to replace what's already been made, at least not yet. Songs, stories, and everything else from your culture is your heritage. These are and will eventually become gifts from the dead. When new generations build, they build new things, there will be a lapse before any of these need to be redone.

Balaji Srinivasan highlights that there's a historical pattern for a moral authority to precede an economic authority, using the fight against racism in the US as the primary example. Meaning, things that build up in people eventually transform into a buildup in something else. Much like what Balaji Srinivasan says, where one kind of authority precedes another, this is essentially the same leverage that life has learned to use on its own. Which is to layer one form of information atop another, to transform one boom into another form to ensure its continued existence. Life has come to leverage these stratifications across deeper and deeper integrals that then further leverage their own derivatives through these very transformations. Like maintaining homeostasis far away from equilibrium, which means this is analogous to the entropy-based definition of life.

The classic entropic definition of life argues that life maximizes the disorder of its environment while maintaining itself at low entropy away from chemical equilibrium in order to prolong its existence. My definition, through this same lens of entropy, would rephrase to say that it's the encapsulation of disorder by an ordered process that enginizes the rules of chemistry to perpetuate, and by doing so incentivizes the growth of complexity through its interactions with its environment. With the ordered process being representative of the nature of statistical entropy and compartmentalization, and the disordered process being representative of the nature of thermodynamic entropy and metabolism. Enginization is a concept analogous to the nature of how information incentivized itself into becoming intelligence, and it's analogous to the transformation of a star into a black hole.

These definitions have interesting connotations in relation to human civilization. As once chemical equilibrium is reached, a cell would die. Likewise once a society has everything it's ever wanted, they lose their passion and die all the same. With no enginization of some process, with nothing to ever achieve comes no reason to strive at all. With no difficulty comes no accomplishment, as your soul is your struggle. Having no greater purpose in life leaves people without a goal to strive for. With no adversary you have no great battle with anyone other than yourself. History seems to show this pattern, and we seem to see this in the West at this very moment. But where would we be if we did have some aspiring conflict to meet this need? Much of our technology is extremely dangerous.

Cells and societies maintain themselves away from chemical equilibrium, but they maintain themselves at a dynamic equilibrium, like a pencil standing upright on a spinning ball. Static equilibrium itself is a death sentence, but it's not only a *static* static equilibrium that's problematic. This is just one kind of death sentence. Death by equilibrium comes in many flavors. There's actually an ever-growing set of dynamic static equilibria, that breeds a plethora of areas for potential death and stagnation. The governance of humans can fall into traps resulting in the brain death of civilization, and it requires being hijacked by a foolish religion. Not unlike the North Korean's inability to question their leader, and not unlike this Western fear of being *racist*, where people aim to avoid a false static equilibrium. Essentially, there's stratified layers of this equilibrium that can be reached by the dynamic equilibrium that life itself maintains. In order to continue surviving, we need to avoid *all* of them, dynamically. Life has adapted to do exactly that through its own biochemistry. As human society grows more complex, human society must do the same through its social organization. Each trial to pass will have different attributes, and some will be entirely insidious. It's important to learn this lesson because the number of ways in which childhood can go wrong has drastically increased. This is why parents need to have more freedom in deciding who does or doesn't belong at their school. The most serious threat is the internet and the addiction it brings. If we were to respect the concept of religious demand, like demand in the economy, then the situation we find ourselves in demands a higher level of both specificity in raising children as well as the freedom to decide what children should and shouldn't be involved with. Civilizational variation is the best answer to uncovering every mistake, and championing every triumph, and it's achieved through freedom.

So what are we attempting to achieve as a society and how can it be done in a way to hedge our bets against our own death while delivering on the fairness which we so desire? We could utilize our failings. We'll always have our mistakes, and these will teach us the greatest lessons. To continue to utilize them creates a staircase of incentives towards improvement, forming a machine of infinite growth in the process.

Booms don't actually have stratified definitions, they're fairly simple and easy to understand. However booms definitely have stratified structures, like layers. They're real-world physical and metaphysical stratifications that start with a tidal wave of incentives. Stratifications themselves are just transformations that leave behind older forms of themselves. Which is exactly what life is. We exist amongst the bacteria, viruses, and every other lesser form of organism left in our wake. The stratification process is a layered history of transformations that acted as hedged bets to create the complex life we have today. So when this happens, what might be at the beginning of this domino effect?

Proposed by Niles Eldredge and Stephen Jay Gould, the concept of *punctuated equilibrium* is an explanation for relatable patterns of sudden, varied, rapid morphological changes seen in the fossil record of individual species in response to some external disruption[194]. To contextualize this around Williston's law, which is something that explains a common pattern of changes seen throughout the evolutionary history of adaptations that occur over long periods of time. It's very possible, and highly likely, that most adaptations spawned through a punctuated equilibrium actually end up following Williston's law. A punctuated equilibrium spawns a mass outbreak of new adaptations.

---

194. Niles Eldredge and Stephen Jay Gould. *Punctuated Equilibria*. Freeman, Cooper & Co, 1972

It's impossible to observe one of these events, so people have made assumptions about what they believe happened when trying to understand these patterns that were found in the fossil record. The pattern starts with a period of prolonged stable existence, dubbed the equilibrium, where some species inhabits their own niche and is able to grow over time. Eventually some environmental disturbance is introduced, dubbed the punctuation, and the species changes its behavior and breaks into many smaller groups that each come to their own unique form over time. The nature of the disturbance is usually assumed to have come from a breakaway group of the same population that initially formed its own unique phenotypic divergence, that may have proved advantageous and went on to challenge the equilibrium of the main group. The more rapid adaptations of breakaway groups are caused by the effects of Ernst Mayr's concepts of peripatric and allopatric speciation, where smaller isolated groups can adapt much faster than larger ones, and therefore see faster genetic and phenotypic changes in their population[195]. By contrast, larger groups have a genetic swamping effect where the group maintains a genetic regression to the mean, so to speak. The genetic and phenotypic stability of a larger, undisturbed, group is maintained through any minor divergences being overwhelmed by the genetic impact from the mixing of the group as a whole, which inhibits any speciation in these larger groups from occurring.

There's a visible parallel between punctuated equilibrium and Williston's law, as there's also a selection phase of the morphologically new specimens that comes after a punctuated equilibrium. Both the addition, specialization, and reduction of Williston's law as well as the equilibrium, punctuation, then selection of punctuated equilibrium can be described as a sequence of stability, then fragmentation, then selection. Addition and equilibrium both have a sense of uniformity to them, where both bodily additions and members of a population are fairly homogeneous. Specialization and punctuation both accomplish a form of speciation. Selection and reduction, in this context, can even be seen as a new form of stability, a new stabilizing equilibrium. So altogether, these adaptation events can always be viewed as cycles of stability and fragmentation.

195. Ernst Mayr. *Systematics and the Origin of Species from the Viewpoint of a Zoologist*. Columbia University Press, 1942

While these two phenomena are definitely recursions of each other during a punctuated equilibrium, Williston's law can also occur independently. Both are recursions of this pulsing heartbeat of entropy itself. This is representative of a boom and bust of morphological traits, so to speak, which presents yet another interesting parallel. Can we apply these same concepts to understand the underlying nature of boom and bust cycles?

The patterns of population booms are no different than Williston's law. The addition of new people, the specialization of their skill set and abilities, and the consequential selection of who continues to survive in the future. Selection isn't just happening for people, it's happening for their jobs, lifestyles, societal roles, and the technology they've used. Every inefficiency is being sorted out through this phase, and this is similar to where the US, and even a lot of the world, currently find themselves. We're in the selection phase at the tail end of a population boom.

It's understood that punctuated equilibrium can happen within groups of a single species, but is widely known for having happened across many species during the Cambrian Explosion, where the most significant period of biological diversification had taken place [**196,197**]. Some people like to argue that the Cambrian Explosion was fundamentally different from a punctuated equilibrium, even different than multiple of them co-occurring. There's often times another debate over whether evolution tends to happen in short bursts, or gradually over time. Neither is truly the exception nor the rule, both probably happened. Although more excitingly, the evolutionary bursts throughout history are some of the most interesting macroevolutionary events to understand. Even in this regard, some recent work on the Devonian Nekton Revolution challenged this notion, indicating it was more of a gradual change[**198**]. The overall consensus is that it's likely a bit of both, that the burst-like nature of these events may have been less intense and more gradual, but were still present. Similar challenges have been brought to the nature of the

196. Preston E Cloud Jr. *Some Problems and Patterns of Evolution Exemplified by Fossil Invertebrates*. Evolution, 1948
197. Stephen Jay Gould. *Wonderful Life*. WW Norton & Co, 1989
198. Christopher D Whalen and Derek EG Briggs. *The Palaeozoic Colonization of the Water Column and the Rise of Global Nekton*. Proceedings of the Royal Society B, 2018

Ordovician Biodiversification Event and Cambrian Explosion[199]. The differentiation of explosions from gradualism is an ongoing debate, but perhaps its importance is overblown. Truth always lies somewhere in between. It might even be true that the most valuable interpretation isn't in the intensity of these events, it's in their nature. Whether interpreted through bursts, or through gradual changes, even these macroevolutionary patterns themselves seem to follow the same trend seen in Williston's law.

The first known evolutionary burst was the Tonian Period, it happened roughly 1 billion years ago, and persisted for hundreds of millions of years. It was likely an arms race of predatory single-celled organisms, remnants from these times indicate there was a diversification and widespread prevalence of Eukaryotes[200]. The exact time and mechanisms are contested, and whether it was a true burst or a gradual form of growth aren't entirely clear, but this was undeniably the welcoming stage for Eukaryotes in general, give or take a few hundred million years[201].

The Avalon Explosion, between 575-565 million years ago, was the next major additionary growth of organisms to the planet through novel forms of soft-bodied multicellular fauna[202]. After the Avalon came the White Sea assemblage, from 560-550 million years ago, where rather than a growth of new taxonomies, there was an intra-taxonomic expansion within the groups formed during the Avalon. Next came the Nama assemblage, from 550-542 million years ago, which saw a large reduction in this newfound diversity from a lack of oxygen supply, and an increase in predation. The precursors to multicellular predators, scavengers and grazers, began to form during the White Sea assemblage, and true multicellular predation began to take root by the Nama[203].

---

199. Thomas Servais et al. *No (Cambrian) Explosion and No (Ordovician) Event: A Single Long-Term Radiation in the Early Paleozoic.* Palaeogeography, Palaeoclimatology, Palaeoecology, 2023

200. Andrew H Knoll. *Paleobiological Perspectives on Early Eukaryotic Evolution.* Cold Spring Harbor Perspectives in Biology, 2014

201. Susannah M Porter et al. *Early Eukaryote Diversity.* Paleobiology, 2025

202. Bing Shen et al. *The Avalon Explosion: Evolution of Ediacara Morphospace.* Science, 2008

203. M Gabriela Mángano and Luis A Buatois. *The Rise and Early Evolution of Animals: Where Do We Stand From a Trace-Fossil Perspective?* Interface Focus, 2020

The Cambrian Explosion, from roughly 540 to 520 million years ago, saw the largest addition to novel organismal body plans the planet has ever seen[204,205]. The story of the Cambrian Explosion is more complicated, and some argue it's even longer than the dates listed. The overall intra-taxonomic reshuffling was also more intense than anything seen prior. Arthropods, which largely didn't have the same mineralized shells prior to this period, seemed to have gained their full breadth of phenotypic diversity from this around this time, modern arthropods have all the same general morphology as those of the Cambrian[206]. Things such as trilobites showed extraordinary levels of variation that was never seen again afterwards[207]. There's an excess of works detailing the evolutionary advancements of this period, highlighting the development of jointed limbs, the sophistication of sensory organs, and novel behaviors that I'll have to stop short of listing as there's thousands of examples. The additions made from the Cambrian Explosion were the widest reaching in nature of any of the evolutionary bursts. Contextualized through Williston's law, it's like an addition of additions.

The Great Ordovician Biodiversification Event, from 470-442 million years ago, was the next evolutionary burst to happen. This event saw mostly intra-taxonomic expansion, rather than an increase in new organisms[208,209]. It brought new shapes to old body designs, rather than entirely new body designs. Meaning, the theme of diversification began to shift further. New forms of life, new clades, and new taxonomies, aren't emerging. Instead, existing forms of life further specialize and diversify within their taxonomies. It's

---

204. Charles D Walcott and Charles E Resser. *Addenda to Descriptions of Burgess Shale Fossils*. Smithsonian Institution, 1931
205. J John Sepkoski Jr. *A Factor Analytic Description of the Phanerozoic Marine Fossil Record*. Paleobiology, 1981
206. Derek EG Briggs, Richard A Fortey, and Matthew A Wills. *Morphological Disparity in the Cambrian*. Science, 1992
207. Mark Webster. *A Cambrian Peak in Morphological Variation Within Trilobite Species*. Science, 2007
208. Barry D Webby et al., eds. *The Great Ordovician Biodiversification Event*. Columbia University Press, 2004
209. Thomas Servais et al. *The Great Ordovician Biodiversification Event (GOBE): The palaeoecological dimension*. Palaeogeography, Palaeoclimatology, Palaeoecology, 2010

more like each ecological niche was evolving to be occupied by a more competitive inhabitant.

Under the same cascade of evolving ecological niches was the Devonian Nekton Revolution, 423-346 million years ago, where fast swimmers and jawed fish began to show greater intra-taxonomic morphological variation[210]. These fish had supposedly been growing steadily since around the Cambrian, and their groupings didn't just show new species branching off of each other, they began to display a wider variety of traits. This was the first time that an evolutionary burst was made up of something that hadn't truly been a part of any prior bursts. Vertebrates had entered the macroevolutionary scene.

The Carboniferous Tetrapod Jump, 318–299 million years ago, started with a growth of new body plans for tetrapods when they started living on land[211]. Then, land environments where these tetrapods thrived, rainforests, later began to dry up due to a climate shift. The two groups of tetrapods were amphibians and reptiles, and after the drying up of the rainforests the amphibians began to dwindle around 305 million years ago. Amphibian diversity imploded locally, with individual environments reducing their numbers and breadth of species, while their global diversity still began to grow[212]. Reptiles thrived in the drier environments, and took over areas previously held by the collapsed amphibians.

The Permian-Triassic extinction event, caused by volcanic eruptions in Siberia 252 million years ago, killed off more than 70% of every inhabited niche[213]. Filling this new vacuum were the dinosaurs during the Carnian Pluvial Episode from 234-232 million years ago[214]. Prior to this, dinosaurs were somewhat of a rarity, and during this period they quickly took hold of a position of global dominance.

---

210. Christian Klug et al. *The Devonian Nekton Revolution*. Lethaia, 2010

211. Marcello Ruta, Peter J Wagner, and Michael I Coates. *Evolutionary Patterns in Early Tetrapods. I. Rapid Initial Diversification Followed by Decrease in Rates of Character Change*. Proceedings of the Royal Society B, 2006

212. Sarda Sahney, Michael J Benton, and Howard J Falcon-Lang. *Rainforest Collapse Triggered Carboniferous Tetrapod Diversification in Euramerica*. Geology, 2010

213. Douglas H Erwin. *The Great Paleozoic Crisis*. Columbia University Press, 1993

214. Massimo Bernardi et al. *Dinosaur Diversification Linked with the Carnian Pluvial Episode*. Nature Communications, 2018

Then 66 million years ago, in the Yucatán Peninsula, an asteroid hit the Earth and destroyed 75% of all life on the planet[215,216]. Following the ecological vacancy of dinosaurs, the less than 10 surviving placental (mammalian) lineages rushed to fill the empty niches in the Paleocene Placental Burst between 66-65 million years ago[217]. Many plant species vanished for the same reasons as the dinosaurs, and angiosperms spread much like mammals, and the mammals even helped them do so[218]. The dung of mammals enriched the soil for angiosperms to use. Mammal body size increased rapidly, and their widespread expansion rewired ecological pyramids[219]. In the process, every niche was replaced by mammals, they inherited herbivorous, omnivorous, and predatory roles in every environment where it was once held by dinosaurs.

You could point out there are some extra events I didn't cover, especially ones that overlapped with ones I did. The end result is all the same. Something like the Silurian-Devonian period, which occurred alongside the Devonian Nekton Revolution, 433-359 million years ago, where plants, fungi, and arthropods made an appearance on land and quickly formed terrestrial ecosystems such as large forests, featured a specialization to grow on land and an explosive addition of new features to survive there[220,221]. General modes of evolutionary success in these bursts were consistently expressed through body count, morphological variation, depth of local variation, and global diffusion. If you consider the environment to be what's actually evolving, and

---

215. Luis W Alvarez et al. *Extraterrestrial Cause for the Cretaceous-Tertiary Extinction.* Science, 1980

216. Alan R Hildebrand et al. *Chicxulub Crater - A Possible Cretaceous-Tertiary Boundary Impact Crater on the Yucatan Peninsula, Mexico.* Geology, 1991

217. Thomas John Dixon Halliday, Paul Upchurch, and Anjali Goswami. *Eutherians Experienced Elevated Evolutionary Rates in the Immediate Aftermath of the Cretaceous–Palaeogene Mass Extinction.* Proceedings of the Royal Society B, 2016

218. Maureen A O'Leary et al. *The Placental Mammal Ancestor and the Post–K-Pg Radiation of Placentals.* Science, 2013

219. John Alroy. *The Fossil Record of North American Mammals: Evidence for a Paleocene Evolutionary Radiation.* Systematic Biology, 1999

220. Richard M Bateman et al. *Early Evolution of Land Plants: Phylogeny, Physiology, and Ecology of the Primary Terrestrial Radiation.* Annual Review of Ecology and Systematics, 1998

221. Eliott Capel et al. *The Silurian–Devonian Terrestrial Revolution: Diversity Patterns and Sampling Bias of the Vascular Plant Macrofossil Record.* Earth-Science Reviews, 2022

view each organism as a limb, of sorts, we can view these same processes through the lens of Williston's law. The Tonian, Avalon, and Cambrian saw explosions of new body plans. The Great Ordovician Biodiversification event saw a deepening of taxonomic clades. The Devonian Nekton Revolution saw a narrow band of jawed fish that specifically came to grow more varied, and the Carboniferous Tetrapod Jump had a similarly narrowed basis for the expansion of mostly just amphibians and reptiles. Both the Carnian Pluvial Episode and the Paleocene Placental Burst had not only extremely narrow groups of organisms that expanded, they both occurred in shorter periods of time than any prior burst, and they also gained more widespread success than was ever seen before. As time went on, there were more and more specialized forms of success, where the winners were of a narrower and narrower background. Addition of a wider set of new body plans played a heavier role earlier on. Specialization within taxonomies, both at the local and global scales, took root afterwards through the deepening of intra-taxonomic clades. Then finally, the broad success of narrower groups reduced the ways in which ecological niches were being reinvented. In reinventing niches, they weren't taken over by new paradigms, they were filling old niches with new body plans. It's hard to argue entirely that reduction took place due to a decrease in less competitive species, because of the nature of the global catastrophes that took place prior to the later two bursts, but each extinction event realistically only acted to speed up the inevitable. Mammals were always going to outcompete dinosaurs.

Put more plainly, the Tonian, Avalon, and Cambrian Explosions were something akin to the addition phase of Williston's law. The Ordovician, Devonian, and Carboniferous were specialization stages, and the Carnian and Paleocene events were reduction phases. This evolutionary pulsing was developing itself in the same way any organism develops its own body plan. The evolution of evolution itself is visible through macroevolutionary recursions of all the same changes seen across individual lineages.

Phrasing it like that makes the end result of evolution seem much more deterministic than chaotic. At the end of this series of reduction phases we'd gone through, we have complex intelligence. In light of the intuitively understandable end-points of evolution, through its predictable phases, is intelligence, and every preceding component of intelligent life, a part of some great filter[222]? No, it would seem, upon reflection of the events of the history of the world, that intelligence was inevitable. As is the case with the relationship between statistical and thermodynamic entropy, the resulting evolutionary development of the planet wasn't interchangeable with any other outcome, it follows a clear series of events that determined outcomes based on prior circumstances that themselves arose as a timeless equilibrium of the interactions that naturally followed from evolution itself. Human development was not coincidental, it was sequential. Beyond that, we'll spawn newer and greater evolutionary bursts in the form of technological advancement, population growth, and value exchange.

With each spike in the growth of hominid populations would have come a more sophisticated culture than the last. Each rise and fall would have been the peak of a global civilizational paradigm, which each led to their own period of increased supply of food, a more populous environment to adapt to, and a greater incentive to adapt in general. Something being an ancient civilization doesn't mean there needed to be skyscrapers and airplanes, simply that there was a newfound abundance of people who engaged with each other together in some shared form of culture and exchange.

The traits we've all been selected for likely came from these same cycles in our own evolutionary past. The remnants we have today come from those who've made it out the other end every time. Population boom and bust cycles are built-in selection events. Which makes them intrinsic mechanisms of evolution itself, which is a mechanism that can then be taken advantage of biologically for non-Darwinian evolution. Over time, the ability to take advantage of such things would inevitably come to fruition as there's then a natural incentive to take advantage of such cycles. It's not just non-Darwinian, it's beyond Lamarckian, it's hyper-Darwinian. A Lamarckian mechanism would respond to some stimulus. This isn't just responding, it's an instinctual prediction and attempted gaming of some notable cyclic event. It's the acknowledgement of Darwinian selection and the instinctual understanding of its mechanisms, it's the ingrained perception of it. Evolutionary boom and bust cycles have incentivized this perception of themselves as a response to their existence, it's a recursion of pools of entropy of a nervous system

222. Robin Hanson. *The Great Filter - Are We Almost Past It?* 1998

developing sensory detection and self-recognition (I'll comment more on this topic later). After all, we see the same thing in our markets. Everything that thrives will eventually hit a wall, crashes are inevitable. Regarding selection at the tail end of a crash, people who successfully short the market on a crash become acknowledged for doing so. To successfully predict failure, and use it to make yourself succeed, is a level beyond that of selection. It's a king making ritual.

Bitcoin and cryptocurrency have been undergoing their financial debut, and many are realizing this form of value is here to stay. They're extremely interesting forms of currency with great practical uses, but nothing that grows can avoid making bubbles. The bubble is a flaw of the shortcomings of the known. These shortcomings are just the scaled consequences of mistakes, which will always exist because irony is the basic unit of every interaction. In the same light, both the underlying mechanics of cryptocurrency and the future competition it will provide will be an amazing learning tool that offers amazing mistakes that will lead to incredible growth, and this would be thanks to freedom. That granted to allow for paradigms of currency independent of any insidious government interventions, as well as the freedom to make mistakes.

Bubbles are scaled mistakes, scaling mistakes even. They're the manifestation of a small mistake made by a lot of people. You're always going to make mistakes, and society also will. The popping of bubbles are just those mistakes fulfilling their function of failure. Sometimes they're investigations, lots of people all learning about the same thing at the same time. To claim there's an economic system that won't make mistakes would lie in the fantasies of utopianism. As to not make mistakes would be to hypothetically achieve an unattainable ideal, and not recognizing either as such would ultimately be yet another mistake. Moving forward into the future, the mistakes will be more complex and harder to understand. The flaws in the system will require intricate fixes to find more efficiency, but they will undoubtedly be found in time. The solutions of such will eventually compound into exponential rewards.

When bitcoin eventually crashes, it doesn't necessarily need to be the price of bitcoin that does the crashing. It could be the environment that holds it up. Regarding the future of this technology, there's always the financial incentive for certain groups to try and destroy or steal it through hacking, or breaking the encryption, of either the coin itself or the platform it might be hosted on. A lot of people will think it's impossible until it happens. It would take an insane level of compute to break the coins themselves, but the potential of the move to crash the cryptocurrency market ultimately remains on the board. It may even be currently possible. The potential energy of the information to do so is latent in this environment, like fruit on a tree once was, and that ends up being the main tradeoff with this form of exchange. We don't necessarily live in an age where this is possible, yet. But it's going to happen someday. It's a money making opportunity for someone else, meaning there's an incentive which will turn this into an inevitability.

This age of the internet has extreme latent potential. Civilization is a mode of living that replaced physical competitiveness with technological competitiveness, and with this came an environment with more latent information due to there being more latent derivatives and integrals. I don't believe this will offer a landscape where selection from a few population booms can homogenize the population to equilibrate away any major problematic behavior. The bad news is, I think this will be more similar to the age where humans discovered fire. I imagine people weren't well-equipped to stop fires that got out of control. The good news is, this current age of information didn't start with the internet, it started with the printing press. So we're already quite far on our way and things may actually be on the up.

Technological advances acting as disturbances to previously acquired stability have and will inevitably lead to booms made of ideas, lifestyles, and culture. This is considering that the technological advances of people, and the kind of advances their desire brings about, are those of survival and ease. If some technology makes it easier for someone to make money, which in turn makes so much money because of how much time it saves anyone who buys their product, perhaps by some process that makes it easier to feed more people, to clean their clothes in an automated fashion, or to not spend so much time on one task that can now be seen as fast and easy rather than difficult and time-consuming, then one might assume that more people can be more productive and there might then be a larger population that comes from such an increase in efficiency. But we don't see this across European history, there aren't simply booms that immediately come after every new technological advancement[223]. Instead, there was massive growth provided by the Industrial Revolution, which in itself was built upon by many technological advancements across the centuries that came before it. The papermaking, printing press, importation of Arabic numerals, double-entry bookkeeping, mechanical clocks, lens crafting, metallurgy, gunpowder, open-sea navigation, spinning wheels, and general textile crafts all flourished on their own across Europe prior to the Industrial Revolution bringing seed drills, steam engines, more advanced textiles, more advanced metallurgy, and mechanized forms of transportation.

The payoff for the advancements were useful, but they also took a while to compound into exponential return. The inventions prior to the Industrial Revolution took longer to find widespread adoption, but by the time the actual Industrial Revolution took place widespread adoption itself had specialized. Western society had undergone transformations in so many areas where major scalable forms of growth were possible, ultimately leading to the precursors of the populations we see today.

The stratifications of booms are probably no different in nature than the historically similar developmental layers that an embryo traverses in order to develop into its modern form. The repeated rhymes of history, as told through the Theodor Reik quote, are also probably similar in nature to this very concept. These are developmental recursions and they continue to repeat in these predictable ways for the same reason that any organism has a developmental cycle in the first place. It was selected for its success, and now is the wave that continually propagates through civilization.

The persistence of population booms and busts were always internal order optimizations. It's a heartbeat, the evolutionary pulsing of a population, of the world even. The more it happens, the better the circulation. Never-ending stability might actually be a bad thing. As if it weren't, where would selection bring us? We may want to cherish the

---

223. Our World in Data. *Population – HYDE, Gapminder, UN – Long-run data*. HYDE (2023); Gapminder (2022); UN WPP (2024) – with major processing by Our World in Data. Original data: PBL Netherlands Environmental Assessment Agency, *History Database of the Global Environment 3.3*; Gapminder, *Population v7*; United Nations, *World Population Prospects*; Gapminder, *Systema Globalis*. Subset used: Europe, 1000 AD to present. Accessed 23 November 2025. Our World in Data, 2024

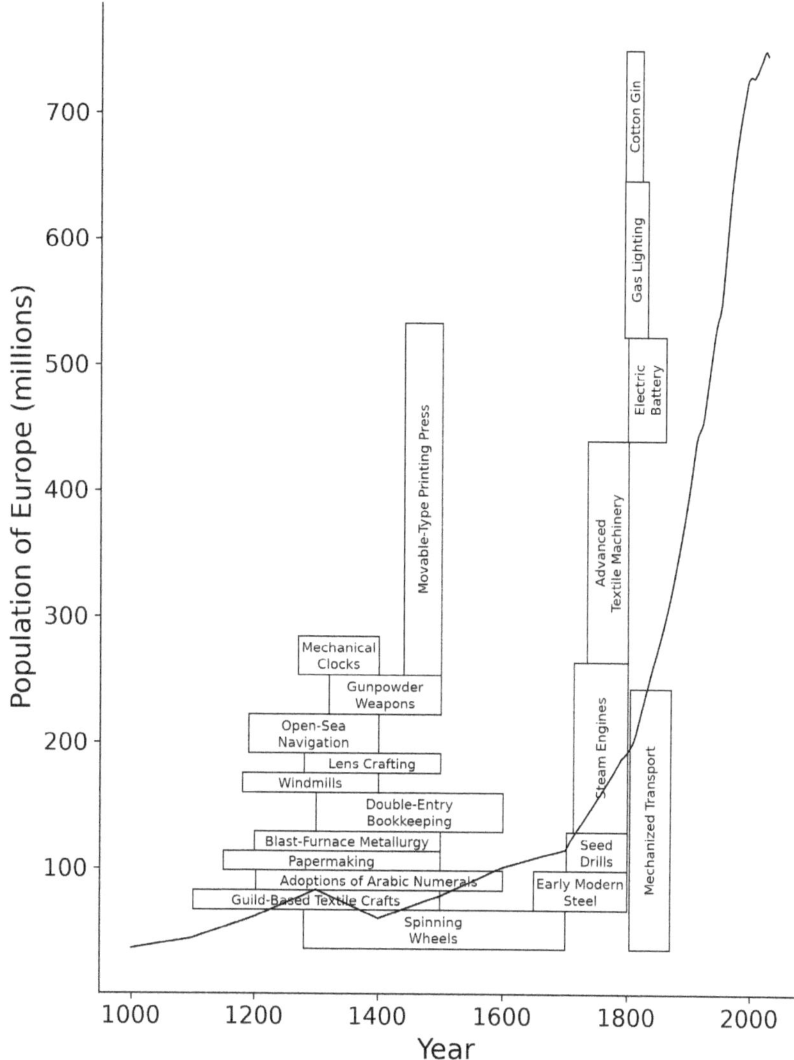

Figure 13: Estimated Population of Europe 1000 AD to present alongside the range of time from invention to mass adoption of various technologies prior to and during the Industrial Revolution, HYDE (2023); Gapminder (2022); UN WPP (2024) – with major processing by Our World in Data

selection mechanisms we have, rather than try to subvert them through unfairness. As the winners of such a stupid competition would only find themselves in the position of the underqualified Soviet commanders facing the Germans.

Even if you could outrun it, it would only be momentary. It would simply cause a longer-term bubble, with perhaps a similarly slow decline. But maybe that would be an accomplishment that a heartbeat lasts hundreds of years, as opposed to a sharp rise and fall that came easy and left even easier. As it seems regardless of the size of the animal, it's the number of heartbeats throughout their lifetime that's generally the same across each of them[224]. To improve that heartbeat, the quality of metabolic output it provides, and its longevity, can all be seen as forms of growth.

We must respect the selection phase, to subvert ourselves with mass migration during this time is to subvert the future success of our children. To introduce superficiality into this process only means to complicate the downfall, where even people who should have succeeded through the selection phase then become weeded out by some illogical process. To *plan* a society is foolish, but to operate one independent of the nature of its own rise and fall may as well be philosophically hollow in this day and age, as it just means politicians have completely ignored thousands of years of recorded history. What else is there to learn from if not thousands of years of population boom and bust cycles when understanding how to organize a functional civilization?

It used to be that studying the history of law, politics, economics, governance, and so on, were worthwhile when forming a government. After all, this is what brought forth the US Constitution. What's being attempted in Europe is so disastrous because their special *designers* believe that life is something that should be controlled. Populations don't wane because governments lose control, and civilizations don't wane because more control was needed. A rise and fall of any group of people comes simply through the same kind of entitlement that ever believes total control was the answer in the first place. Total control gets you nowhere except a breakdown of a desire to live, freedom is what allows people to grow because it allows them to find something worth living for. Freedom grants the willingness to inspire, to incentivize others into being better rather than worse. Those who want total control demotivate their own populations from ever achieving their fullest potential, and it's wildly embarrassing to watch grown men at the WEF make loud and proud speeches about how they plan on controlling entire populations into some form of ideal society made from

224. Stan L Lindstedt and William A Calder III. *Body Size, Physiological Time, and Longevity of Homeothermic Animals*. The Quarterly Review of Biology, 1981

a blend of communism and totalitarianism from the 20th and 21st centuries. Forget learning history from thousands of years ago, these people had never learned history from even the decades prior to their own birth.

Total control is not a reliable way to move forward because the shortcomings of its abuse are paid for by taxpayers. This kind of system can't continue to exist in the future. No one should be able to put such financial burdens on their own grandchildren before they're even born. It's entrapment. That's the very essence of entitlement, especially if that generation doesn't go on to have enough children to replace itself. As it's the entitlement of previous generations that are bankrupting us, they believed the growth they experienced in their childhood would never end, and that their own personal decisions would never stifle it. This also speaks to a broader truth, things that build up over years, and these pent-up obligations, eventually drag everyone down. No one in government should be so easily able to arrange payments for time periods that fall outside their elected term.

As the booms and busts are traversed, how can we walk along the staircase of irony? Some steps are failed bricks in a tower that could collapse at its uppermost layers as unknowns are iterated. The answer is two things we're already familiar with, to not be incorrect, and to hedge your bets. To neglect the need for a hedged bet is to bet on civilizational destruction.

From this it becomes obvious that the natural response to a competitive disturbance is fragmentation itself, which is reason enough to support the American Reformation. Allowing people to find their own answers, rather than dictating what's correct, is to simply avoid being incorrect. Which in itself is how to hedge bets at scale. As which hedges to make aren't clear, so make as many as possible. That's the nature of this strategy and it's a strategy of nature.

9.3 Punctuated Disequilibrium

It's the role of the government not to inhibit the birth rate of its citizenry, and it's the role of the citizenry to resupply the country with the necessary workforce needed to succeed it. A different population would have different values, as can be seen by functional countries that don't operate as democracies. This nation is meant to be a home to families. Likewise, Europe is the heritage of everyone with European ancestry. Having originated from there, having gone on to fight multiple World Wars there, and maintaining close military alliances throughout the entire continent, many Americans have a vested interest in the state of European governance.

The current actions of the political establishment, of both of these continents, are insidiously coordinating their actions for the sake of some unspoken goal that they refuse to communicate to anyone else. Immigration is not the same thing as mass migration, the scale at which mass migration rapidly alters the population and its values is threatening to local heritage, and is highly subversive of democracy. Even people as far back as Aristotle himself commented on how tyrants prefer immigrants to natives. Because if your voters don't vote the way you want them to, you can always import people who will. Then you can claim it's against their human rights, or international law, to send them back. But these excuses are just the firestarters for another war. Especially when citizenship and welfare are granted to any incoming migrants at a rapid pace, which seems to be a pattern. I write this as a warning to anyone living in these areas. Throughout history, nothing has proven to be more inevitable than war. Given the difficulty of interpreting their actions, you shouldn't cast away the idea that it's this political establishment that's attempting to start one. Because control is their favorite flavor of governance, and I would be ecstatic to find this prediction incorrect.

Control is just centralized integrity. Integrity is normally a form of distributed control, where trust is what you gain by enabling distributed control through freedom rather than centralizing integrity through centralized control. Trust is the prize you win from this freedom. Because when someone isn't trustworthy, it becomes widely known and people can act on that information with low consequences, but when a centralized form of trust is corrupted, people have only drastic actions they can take against it. Otherwise they become victims to it. Many European countries have so-called self-defence laws, yet in places like the UK people will often be jailed for defending their families against armed intruders in their own homes. We even have this problem in parts of the US. Courts take proportionality to an extreme and use it against their own populace, as if armed invaders will be deterred by such a thing. So this is twice as damning, as those enforcing and upholding the rules cooperate to force law abiding citizens into an unfair corner.

The political parties pushing for this want to control what you're even allowed to acknowledge, it's why there's a constant denial of the farm murders currently happening in South Africa. In Western philosophy, we've come to not punish people for the crimes of their ancestors, but this creed of diversity transformed its most dedicated members into a cult that's inherently anti-Western, and they've snuck their way into our institutions. It embraces punishing people for anything and everything they can. This cult especially refuses to see any benefit that the Western world has brought to the entire global community through trade and technology, they refuse to acknowledge the triumphs over racism, slavery, genocidal dictators, communism, tyranny, and many other primitive forms of thinking. Efforts even include the massive expenditures of the British Empire to end slavery in as many places as possible with economic and military pressure, banning its own ships and citizens from doing such things, and using their own navy to hunt down slave ships on the open seas[225]. A legislative movement which was cultivated and spearheaded by William Wilberforce[226], a name that will never be mentioned by any of these political activists or university professors who wholeheartedly believe they *combat racism* despite having never seen real racism with their own eyes. Such cults refuse to admit that many places in the world were partaking in barbaric savagery, with ritual sacrifices of children. It doesn't need to mean the actions of every colonial endeavor were perfect, with order comes disorder, but one need not torture and sacrifice their own children. It somehow seems many people across history tend to fall into adopting this kind of behavior as a form of religion. Like the cultures that were freed from this curse through colonialism, you and your children don't need to be sacrificed to the religion of the school system, their political activism, nor the whims of any politicians. Despite so often preaching against atrocities, those involved in running the schools have become the monsters they claim to hate, and it's because they don't face proper competition.

Instead, steady growth should be the goal that's sought after. An age of peace is an age of population growth, and vice versa. Many people assume that infinite growth is impossible, but the economic and technological strides that've been made, as the increase in both

225. Adam Hochschild. *Bury the Chains*. Macmillan, 2005
226. William Hague. *William Wilberforce*. HarperPress, 2007

productivity and abundance that came from our advancements, are still able to provide transformations towards even more compressible forms than what's already been achieved. What we produce is not simply wasted as we diminish our own global supply of resources, there's so much more out there to use and we're currently living on the frontier of technology capable of accessing the raw materials of the asteroid belt.

You optimize internal order by following Williston's law. The extremes of the modern day show this happening in reverse. Such a backwards approach to this concept would be maximizing internal order with no regard for what's already internal. The political equivalent to this is mass migration during a population collapse. This is the face of left-wing extremism, as it's no longer an optimization but purely a maximization, as it doesn't balance order with disorder. That's communism, and that's how every communist country has operated since the idea came into existence. They always destroy the population inside their own country, and that entire country ends up worse off in the long term because of it. We can instead make new additions through our own birth rate and culture by changing the incentive structure. The reason the insidious tyrants of the West don't like this is because it doesn't provide them with instant gratification, which also reveals their nature to be that of immaturity. Immaturity is attempting to urgently solve the wrong priorities, maturity is in realizing the correct priorities can't be solved with urgency, only consensus. Birth and raising children takes a long time, as does raising a good neighborhood, town, city, or district. It takes hard work and good leadership, one must actually desire this for their constituents rather than seeing their constituents as tools to be used in a larger game. Those who can forego instant gratification for the sake of long-term cultural victory are called *adults*.

To balance the analogy, right-wing extremism becomes pure chaos outside their own internally preserved areas. It's an external disorder maximization. Taken to its logical extreme, it would invalidate the point of even having an in-group in the first place, as there would be no remaining out-groups. Whereas maximizing neither internal nor external factors independent of the other is the growth of complexity. The co-maximization of these two concepts balances either out, and allows for steady changes rather than extreme ones. If the crustacean never stopped adding new legs, it would only be harder to walk, and if the crustacean was too good at hunting prey, then there would be nothing left to eat.

More realistically, we shouldn't expect our systems of governance to work perfectly. We should expect them to fail. Similar to the broken compass, we should *plan* for them to fail. We should design them to fail in certain ways. So you might ask, then what would you have us do? How can we model the infinite complexity of this problem into a fair system? We already have a solution to this, it was just being forcefully shut down.

Let's take a recent example of how our systems of governance took a turn for the extreme. Much like how it was the elderly Japanese that cleaned up the Fukushima reactor fallout, which was an extremely noble sacrifice of the old to the young, this choice wouldn't be made to damn the elderly, it's to support the young. Because that's the way civilization is supposed to operate, it's forced to, because everything is made of tradeoffs. You can't save both the young and the old in a situation like we had during the pandemic, you have to make a choice. If you're naive enough to think this *wasn't* the choice presented, then you would be as incompetent as those at the time who managed to sacrifice the young in favor of the old. They stood by unachievable ideals, and ended up sacrificing the young because they refused to acknowledge that the reality of the situation demanded a tradeoff. The old should have been doing what they could to preserve themselves, not to cull their grandchildren. So what's the solution to the innumerable problems presented by governance that could have fixed this problem? Communication, it's what makes governance possible.

The role of governance isn't to find some singular consensus, it's to find disagreement for the sake of balancing every priority amongst themselves. In forcing safety standards, environmental policies, and universal regulations wherever they could fit, to take primacy over building, business, and the acknowledgement of tradeoffs, has forced the card castle, that relies on two oppositional forces, to completely fall over due to having no opposing counterforce. This juxtaposition of two sides stems from the bifurcations of the automaton itself, there's no avoiding the utility of this feature, to deny it is to deny a population its right to survive. Forced consensus is antithetical to tradeoffs.

Our brains already model the infinite complexity of our environment. It's how we developed emotions, the ability to communicate, and advanced language in the first place. It's all we need for fair governance. When people talk to each other they come to reasonable compromises, as this is what the modeling of entropy accomplishes. Censorship is what went wrong during Covid. Even if governance fails, communication can be infinitely articulate. Words aren't subjective, they hold distinctive meanings that are intrinsic to the reality we find ourselves in.

But surely these leaders gave us these wonderful vaccines in our time of need? It's not like we have a built-in mechanism for dealing with diseases, do we? Even if the vaccines were momentarily effective, they were never going to economically outcompete this virus that was able to be present in nearly every human on the planet at the same time. That business model is defunct. The disease could mutate and spread faster than it could be targeted, and it's extremely expensive to continue to play this game from the human side of things. To defeat it, you would need to have a specialized antibody factory inside every human body capable of targeting their own unique strand simultaneously. You might ask, so then the virus won the economic war against humanity because we don't have this? It would take us billions, if not trillions of dollars to develop that kind of technology. Yet unironically, it's already been done. It's called the immune system, and it does a better job than vaccines when it comes to these highly contagious, yet non-deadly, diseases that aren't much of a threat to most people. Your own immune system would provide a better form of herd immunity than these vaccines ever could, as it's extremely difficult to out-engineer billions of years of evolution.

So for the most part we already had the answers to our problems, but instead decided to make more problems, all for the sake of profit for the political establishment. Even worse, it was done by subverting communication for the sake of human experimentation. They subverted freedom of speech, and in doing so committed what might be the largest global atrocity of the 21st century, depending on how the long-term effects of these vaccinations work out. In order to distract people from this they immediately started a couple more wars, which is what the political establishment always tends to use as a distraction. Because where they can no longer prevent people from speaking about something, they may at least be able to dilute it inside a list of other grievances. Open communication is more important than anything else, and our recent mistakes have exposed how compromised our communication channels had been in the past.

So as for the fair system I promised you, you don't need a system to do this for you. People are the system. People are the ones who make decisions. We don't need to set up machines that implement unfair games amongst ourselves while pretending there's nothing we can do to change them. This is what the West achieved through colonialism in its best light, saving people from themselves. Likewise, any bureaucracy that creates these problems isn't a good use of our resources. We already know how to play fairly with each other. Our evolution has gifted this at the expense of those who came before us. Communication is all you need. Communication is the basis for all interaction, it's the integral of every other interaction itself.

Is there a system of communication that could make the information on vaccines more accessible? To make them more trustable? Certainly! It currently works that vaccine manufacturers have strange relationships with liability for the side effects of what they administer, there's an administrative process that awards injury claims in their stead. Otherwise, people generally have to prove negligence on the part of the manufacturer, which is pretty much impossible. In this current day there's a lot of skepticism about vaccines, and a lot of hidden information regarding the companies that design them. Overall, the public relations of these companies has been horrendous, and they play an extremely insidious game to protect their product sales. Many states mandate vaccinations through public school attendance, but these mandates are a violation of religious freedom. Each person has the right to determine which vaccines they'll give their child. As highlighted by recent events, the freedom to choose is more important than the dictations of an establishment, because people do a better job deciding how to keep themselves safe than the government ever could. Certain groups may have their own rules, but the government can't involve itself in any mandates of this technology. It's arguably saved a lot of hassle, and lives, but there's too much wrong with the process of forced administration of medical procedures that doesn't align with our constitution and that's being completely ignored. Positive selection is not the job of government, it's the job of religion, how one lives and dies is a survival strategy, it's a religious choice. The government can't force these things on the populace while simultaneously relieving the vaccine makers of any liability of harm, because these companies won't receive the feedback they would otherwise need to make more effective products. In some cases, it becomes forced human experimentation and there's currently every required incentive in place to make this happen, which is seemingly why it did. Whether people want to be experimented on or not is a religious decision for them to make. In allowing natural stratifications to exist amongst the population, as stratifications are multi-hedged civilizational survival strategies, we arrive at the fairest way forward for everyone involved. Civilization doesn't just need to protect itself from diseases, it needs to protect itself from experimentation. Life is a multipronged survival game, and every aspect of survival has two sides to its coin. There are no purely advantageous monoliths, there are no simplicities. The survival strategies of these companies can find themselves at odds with the survival strategies of the public. It's each person's job to determine their own placement within the civilization stratification that models entropy.

The tradeoffs of any vaccine needs to be assessed by each individual. If tradeoffs aren't properly advertised then it becomes insidious human experimentation and eugenics. That's not just choosing a survival strategy, that's choosing a biological winner, it's determining what individuals are allowed to play the game of natural selection. It's administering positive selection themselves. Survival is the role of the populace, not the government. It's not that the government doesn't play a role in public safety, it clearly makes sense for the government to care that water, food, and medicine don't cause preventable problems through contamination, but individuals deserve their own medical sovereignty as they're capable of acting in their own best interest. If they aren't, it's because some form of government would have herded them into a state of dependency, which ironically acts to subvert their own chances at survival. When it comes to obvious decisions for survival, people will obviously elect to survive using some medical procedure, and when it's questionable as to whether something is actually beneficial or not, then people deserve the right to interpret that ambiguity on their own. For the government to decide what is or isn't inherently survivable as a one-plan strategy is where violations of religious freedoms arise. It's the government's role to issue negative selection for wrongs that someone has *actually* done, and it being wrong for someone to have *not* done something is still *sometimes* criminal, such as a refusal to stop obstructing others. But when a medical mandate is imposed on the citizenry, it becomes a mandate of positive selection, where you're suddenly evil, wrong, or criminal for not adhering to a specific survival strategy. This is a clan-based morality system, and it doesn't match the philosophical underpinnings of the West. This is the government and pharmaceutical companies making decisions that are akin to directed mutations, it doesn't happen in nature because it's not a good strategy. Random differences across a population are a better strategy. Whether people want to accept any specific vaccine, and its potential tradeoffs and benefits, is their individual survival decision to make. Unlike enforcing monogamy over polygamy at a legal level for the sake of societal stability, which regulates specific behaviors across groups of people, when a government mandates a vaccine, it occupies a very specific part of a systematic religious structure. It stands directly between any person and their own relationship with death.

To improve upon the existing system, to make vaccines more attractive to people, there would need to be a wider amount of information available about them online, and in a more accessible format. The raw data from clinical trials, a visual breakdown of what the data looks like, and methods of comparing any results to the results of other vaccines would be an excellent place to start. Ideally there would be explanations for every aspect of what's been undertaken to bring any such vaccines to market, as there are mostly communication issues with regards to distrust. The number of people who take them, the number of people who report issues with them, as well as why anyone would ever want to take a specific vaccine, should all be visible information that's not hidden within massive conglomerates of information.

Amongst vaccine reviewers it can be publicly visible whether they have problems with every single vaccine, as that would likely be the sign of a bad reviewer. Likewise if many people all have problems with one vaccine, that too would be a bad sign. This is a form of induced competition that allows open communication to argue and advise on why some specific vaccine would be beneficial for some specific population or area. Information about diseases can be shared in layman's terms, alongside more technical breakdowns for anyone who wants it. It's the best marketing a vaccine manufacturer could ask for. Every piece of information about vaccines can also be available, such as the companies who make it, the manufacturers, their manufacturing process, where it's made, and whether this process has changed at any point.

People always defend vaccines, they've generally been a great thing for the population. Nothing involving public health needs to be done behind closed doors, nor does it need to be spread across 20 different websites in the most convoluted way possible. The incentive to improve is on those who make and sell vaccines. **Open communication can and will always be an improvement to any system.** It will improve trust in vaccines wherever that trust is deserved. Secrecy and obfuscation are as much of a liability as any disease. What's best for manufacturers might not be what's best for individuals. Force is not the best policy anywhere. Contrary to force, distributed calculations seem to be the most broadly beneficial strategic implementation of just about anything meant to be applied at scale.

We currently force women to earn the right to have children, and earn the right to afford to have more. This is a dysfunctional version of natural selection. Society gains nothing by putting up additional barriers to its own propagation when it's unable to even propagate in the first place. Women seem to want an economy where they can stay home and raise their young children, and especially not have to fear the insanity of the state-imposed school religion. But aside from this, where has our birth rate gone?

Danger is fine, danger is at least an interaction with one's environment. To impose safety is to stunt development by inhibiting interaction. When the world is dangerous, families still grow. Some people master the danger. Danger isn't the signal to stop breeding. But when everything is safe, so safe that if you refuse to abide by the rules of safety your job is relinquished and your life taken away, even to the point where you could have your children seized from you, or when dwelling limitations matter more than the birth rate, and they're massively underestimated because that's just another kind of *safety violation*, then people stop breeding. Because that's a stop-signal, and people fear it more than they fear danger.

Having less children is not a benefit of a successful economy. It's not a sign of development. It's a sign of population collapse. How do we still have such a massive risk embedded in our financial system? How can someone call themselves an economist and still accept such a horrific tradeoff while normalizing it as if it's acceptable? Economists always seem to state *this is just what happens in developed economies* as if they've witnessed every civilization over the course of thousands of years and still couldn't find anything wrong. It's all nonsense. Because what is economics if not a system of finding better tradeoffs for people to use? Surely we can make enough of our own children while maintaining our economy. It would be crueler to everyone involved to simply turn Western countries into a machine that churns through every generation with class warfare and unrealistic quality of life expectations, only to swiftly replace them with foreigners who then fall into the same trap. That's not why anyone came here in the first place.

The size of our current population is a gift that's been given to us. It's the legacy of every person to have ever lived, and every woman to have ever taken on the full-time job of being a mother. Because the children of bad mothers don't tend to make it in this world, when they do it's more an exception and not the rule.

Abundant energy, efficiency, fairness, law, wealth, innovation, and the freedom that comes from our ability to provide these things for each other, by the sheer number of us that exist, is a gift that should not be taken for granted. Motherhood is not just a responsibility for young women, it's an important hurdle in their psychological development. Young women immediately join the workforce because they don't have a better choice. This was toted as some form of freedom, and it obviously is for those who want it. But this has come at the cost of those women who would prefer to prioritize a family instead of a career, and the circumstances of our civilization have ultimately stripped such freedoms away from these women. On top of all these problems, the institution of marriage has found itself to be waning alongside everything else it would normally coincide with.

Should a woman be able to kick her husband out of her life while keeping the house, the kids, and the bank account just to find another man to fill the role? Should a man be able to own his wife like property to the point where she doesn't actually have any way out of the relationship as it becomes a prison? The tradeoffs of divorce need to be equally distributed. These are obviously two very extreme examples, cruel and unusual punishment one might even say, so where can there be cultural compromises to avoid either?

There's a crash in the marriage market, likely because there's a prevailing pattern of nasty divorces that have disincentivized it for many young people. The government is the worst mediator of divorce, and has made the entire process much more grueling than it ever needed to be. Which is why divorce can be such a harrowing process. It ends up giving near total control to a lot of women who go on to demoralize other men from ever getting married in the first place.

Would stability that offers predictability in divorces allow for a growth in divorces? No, it would allow for a growth in marriage. Because divorce is a derivative of marriage, not the other way around. The best way to prevent divorce is to raise great children. The best way to enable marriage is to not scare people away from it, and to not reward either party for going through divorce. Especially not to reward one party for torturing the other. It should be as easy as possible for either individual involved. Any immaturity on this front should only be a reason to punish the person who's making the process difficult. Which is how to incentivize maturity. Once maturity can be incentivized in divorce, it would also be incentivized in marriage because that's how derivatives and integrals work. Even if you call it the same thing, *marriage*, it will hold a different meaning depending on how the institution is respected in its various forms, and that includes its potential collapse. There needs to be a manner in which the collapse occurs, and if the collapse of marriage is nasty then marriage as the respective integral of divorce more often becomes the same way across the population. Considering that women tend to get the house in a divorce, wouldn't it be great if they'd earned it through childbirth in the first place?

A patriarchal society is when men tend to have multiple wives, and this causes men to become toxic. A matriarchal society isn't when women have multiple husbands, two things opposed don't stand opposite, it's when relationships are kept open, and potentially secret. Women with multiple relationships can use protection from multiple men, and convince them all her child is theirs. Marriage is a balance between these two extremes. With the marriage market in decline, our society is closer to reflecting the matriarchal extreme. Welfare, and benefits granted through divorce, have created the conditions that favor this outcome. We need to incentivize motherhood through marriage, rather than single motherhood through payouts.

Giving unequal power to one side over the other tends to cause either of these unfair outcomes to become more likely. In this light, I think divorce is the most important aspect of culture to get right when considering laws around marriage, as it's the basis for every marriage agreement, being the alternative to it actually working. You want the rules to be strict enough that people aren't getting married for stupid reasons, then getting out of it only to cause each other life-disrupting problems. Yet you also want people to have enough faith in the fairness of the rules so that they're not afraid to get married. It would also be beneficial if the point of marriage is to have children to sustain the population, where if you get married that you then may as well have some. Women going from training for the workforce, to the workforce, then saving to have kids, to having kids, is inherently a lot dumber than going from childhood, to a family, to having kids, to raising them until they go to school, then finally into the workforce.

Certainly a lot of the *strangest* people you find throughout the universities would be fuming at such a suggestion, thinking this is in conflict with that of their independence. To which I would say, do whatever you like, any imposed limitations would be worse than the freedom to choose. But I would also argue that young women who are looking to start families are the ones lacking the most freedom, they have a hard time making this option work. There are no scholarships to start a family. Rewards are only given for enslaving yourself in the workforce rather than birthing more people to participate in it. Which seems a bit odd, as they're both undoubtedly necessary in maintaining an economy. This one strange part of our lives just so happens to be where we seem to be going disastrously wrong, I truly wonder how many other parts of society would harmonize should this option just be available for those who want it.

Much like how we'd adapted to always walk, and move, otherwise we get fat, we'd adapted to constantly struggle. When we achieve wealth and success it produces hedonism and entitlement, which leads towards societal collapse. Success isn't as deeply embedded in our evolutionary history as would be struggling to achieve it. Biologically speaking, we need to struggle more than we need to succeed. This is key, because your soul is your struggle.

Creativity is the art of desperation. All of our greatest solutions would come to us in the time of our greatest struggle. Yet we use mass migration as a crutch to never experience it. We've lost a lot from this, and we'll continue to until we learn this lesson.

If we subvert our population as our population declines, it tricks people into thinking that things aren't falling apart and they'll simply continue their decline. It's more important that everyone understands that a decline is happening for the sake of reversing it. It's all a matter of communication. Otherwise, that's no different than an extreme left-wing population churn. To deny people their instinctual functions is to deny them their right to respond to the truth, which is to deny them their own survival mechanisms. A fitting notion used by those in this age of extreme psychological aggression.

Stability is quite literally something that comes from raising children well. The men are not being raised to be men in the schools, the schools are mostly ran and operated by women. These boys have no real role models, and are forced into environments where extreme psychological warfare and cult-like behavior can come to dominate, which is why it does. Any male child as old as 10 should not be led by a woman, there's no benefit in doing so. These young boys are being outcompeted not on ability, but by political and psychological warfare, and this is without being able to properly develop their own virtues. Men tend to favor honesty and direct confrontation rather than playing insidious games, an environment primarily operated by women is an unhealthy environment for adolescent boys who need to take risks and be both honest and direct. These years of their development are too important to be left up to unbiased hiring standards, they need male role models for proper development.

The young girls in schools are being led by the most extreme and nihilistic examples of women in general because more successful women go on to get better jobs. To generalize some of their behavior, young girls tend to heavily copy their mother's behavior[**227**,**228**], and this is a kind of instinct that passes on the dogma of motherhood from mother to daughter. When young girls are exposed to a lot of other women at a young age, this same pattern ensues. But the fact that these young women are being exposed to the most toxic and extreme women that their society produces, means they pick up the most toxic and extreme viewpoints through their instincts which rely on copying older women. Young girls who idolize these teachers then go on to fill their

227. Carole Peterson and Christy Roberts. *Like Mother, Like Daughter: Similarities in Narrative Style.* Developmental Psychology, 2003
228. Paul H Mussen and Ann L Parker. *Mother Nurturance and Girls' Incidental Imitative Learning.* Journal of Personality and Social Psychology, 1965

shoes. The problem is, each girl that does this doesn't just idolize one single toxic woman, she's exposed to multiple of them over the years. So with each new generation the toxicity becomes worse. The most extreme women become teachers, and spread their negativity to everyone else in this vicious cycle that we've come to call the *education system*.

Selection processes for both men and women have become dysgenic. The most valuable women aren't the ones who want to enter the workforce, they're the ones who want to start a family. The most valuable men aren't the ones who happily do as they're told and follow dogma to get certificates and entry level jobs, they're the ones who deviate from the norms and find success regardless. At large, the most successful demographics of either gender have been completely subverted by this same process. We've fallen into this trap because the government tried playing the role of a central planner. They believed they knew what was best and decided what success was *allowed* to be, rather than letting people find it on their own. The implementation of the school-to-university pipeline, and all the jobs that require college degrees, have incentivized the destruction of our birth rate. The value behind either gender's behavior isn't irrelevant, it's a recursion of more deeply rooted processes. To not respect this is to embrace failure.

The schools are prisons. When you raise children in a prison, instead of enabling them to be the value-seeking organisms that they are, they lose any pursuit of purpose, and don't have the confidence to participate in an economy that they've never been initiated into. Capitalism isn't a failed idea and neither are gender roles. Generational maternal dogma was the original religious text. That's where information about upbringing was stored before we had a way of actually storing it. Now this process, for many families, has become corrupt because of the schools. You get one chance to make a childhood work. When adults force children into an institution that mass-produces screwed up children, one must eventually admit the most common factor amongst all of these problems across the world is the implementation of these Marxist government-led school systems, alongside the idea that women need to get a job in order to even afford to have children in the first place. The university system takes away their most worthwhile years to save and start a family by instead putting young people in debt, and teaching them that bad habits are better than long-term plans. I argue the economy should be distributed, but roles should not be oversimplified. A highly modulatable economy, where people perform the role of just one cog, leaves citizens at their most vulnerable.

Innovation is our road to success, if the US were to follow the absurd regulation schemes of the EU, where regulation comes prior to innovation, then we would find ourselves being ruled by some other country within 100 years. Forcing Marxism onto the greatest implementation of capitalism ever seen in the history of the planet would degrade the entire planet, and the disorder brought by immigration and fatherless children is continually made into the excuse used to do so. This would destroy everything this country has fought for, died for, and built, in exchange for whatever remnants are left over after it crumbles because **the function of the structure of Marxism is collapse and failure.**

Some children want to use the internet more than work, and be social, because their school life is dreadful. Schools need to be better environments, they need to be places for a child to actually achieve things for their future, as ambition is not something that forms itself in old age. What kind of world do we live in where children can't walk around during the day? Children need to explore and understand their own environment. To confine them onto a single property, all day, where there are clear boundaries as to what they can and can't do, is too limiting for their psychological development. Social attainment needs to be achievable in real life through means other than some worthless grading metric. The grades are oversimplified, and so many childhood aspirations go out the window in the face of this idiotic system, which is making the internet a more viable alternative for children as they can realize value when they see it. That's one of their basic instincts after all. But they run the risk of getting addicted because of the escapist potential of the internet, and the developmentally stunting reality of the school system in front of them. This has managed to make the West, and much of the world, into a dysgenic form of their prior selves, despite having technology and opportunity in abundance.

The rigidity of credentialism has introduced scale and modularity at the cost of flexibility. The university system is not a net benefit to the economy, it's just a tradeoff. The same as everything else. It completely destroys people's ability and willingness to start families. Instead, there needs to be a coupling, an interaction, between home buying and having children.

A nation is a group of people, not the set of ideas used to govern them. Citizenship being granted from simply living here for a specific period of time is an outdated law. If people refuse to integrate, or their children turn out to be violent gang members, why should they have any right to stay here? Citizenship is an ultra long-term commitment, so the test for citizenship needs to be just as long. Even allowing foreigners to run for office, and hold judge positions is wildly outdated. Living here for mere years isn't a worthy test of loyalty for the integrity of a partnership that our lives depend on. People used to have to *survive* here for that long, they were never given welfare in order to do so. Traveling around the world is a mere day away from any location, we need not overaccommodate foreigners with rights intended for our own citizens, we need to test their dedication instead. Any group incapable of maintaining its own internal order is warranting its death.

Perhaps you think that most people have integrated over time into the US, isn't this an overreaction? The problems presented by mass migration aren't just a dissimilarity of values, it's their abundance. The problem with mass migration isn't even entirely the people, it's the number of people being integrated. There's too many, cultural integration can't faithfully be done at this scale. Cultural integration is something that happens when you're surrounded by something different, you begin to fit in. Mass migration, from a technical perspective, actually inhibits any cultural integration at all. Even worse, migrants are being paid to live where they go because they vote to support unpopular governments in exchange for the welfare they receive.

Welfare is meant to support the lower rungs of our own society, but it's become a tool for undermining our own middle class. Welfare voters carry significant weight in Western elections, but voting while receiving welfare is a conflict of interest, as people will always vote to give themselves more money. The welfare system as a whole ought to be a transformative cycle to get people back on their feet, because the point of welfare should be *to get off welfare*. Only when someone can stand as a self-sustaining individual do they deserve the right to vote. And even if they can support themselves, people don't necessarily deserve the right to vote simply because they've been trafficked into another country.

In times like these, where there's some sudden disturbance to an existing population, a one-plan ideology is the worst possible solution. Fragmentation is the norm in nature when stability is disrupted. That's what a punctuated equilibrium accomplishes, and it occurs because it's a survival instinct. To ignore this norm is to inhibit the otherwise better survival skills of the individuals involved. To force groupings is to forcefully ignore the likelihood of long-term survival for those who already live in the West.

Any snake that eats its own tail is eating its own excrement. From the incongruity of our economy with our own supply chain, to the regulations that prevent us from growing our way out of our own debt, the micromanaged interactions meant to prevent discrimination that only frustrates people by increasing its prevalence, the cults running Western governments with no regard for the young and no explanation for their behavior, the schools forcing ideology and religion onto our children to counteract their appreciation of their own culture and history, it would seem there's a bubble waiting to burst throughout Western civilization. There's what seem like insidious schemes going on all across the West, we're being forced to fund social security for people who didn't end up having enough children to actually maintain it for themselves, there are massive global political divides due to an attempted cultural engineering that stemmed from indoctrination rather than consensus, and the divide across our educational institutions and society is fundamentally no different than the divide that presented itself across the schools and military academies in Afghanistan prior to its collapse. Any form of stability that refuses to fragment, like the existing schooling infrastructure, like the existing hegemony within the political establishment, and like the companies and industries that have been propped up after every market crash, will suffer from a punctuated disequilibrium, where they avoid the natural mode of adaptation that was meant to transform them, and meant to make them better. These waves of evolutionary pulsing are all of the same nature, to model our environment means to model this process. Any government incapable of navigating these waves may as well be inept. They'll stagnate, and become a dilapidated mess that suffers from harrowing dysfunction and forced decadence. This is a scaled mistake, much like a bubble waiting to be popped.

What does it mean for this bubble to burst? It's indicating a need for change in the environment we make and model for ourselves, the network of human interaction has changed, and the reason it's changed is because of the nature of boom and bust cycles of populations. The existing social order is forcing society in these specific directions, and it doesn't work because it was made with regard to the US *during* the prior boom, the rise of the baby boomers. The differences in the rise and fall of population booms are the source of our biggest problems. The laws and social roadmaps that are useful for when a population is booming will doom that society when it collapses. When a population is booming, uniformity and control help to maintain growth, because contributing to the boom is easy as long as you can filter people in the right direction. But when that population collapses, the young will find themselves needing to maneuver through both societal and technological changes, and sometimes even the stagnant immaturity of the generation that grew up during the boom is yet another hurdle. For those on the tail end, they need flexibility in order to survive, rather than the rigid constraints used to grow the country in the first place. The formulas for the success of the prior generation won't work due to the boom providing a number of societal and technological transformations, a completely different environment will have formed. Using the circumstances of one side of this boom to govern the other is antithetical to the prosperity of those born during its occurrence. We ought to fragment to preserve as many aspects of our culture as possible, as people won't make enormous changes to their lifestyles, they'll make small ones that work for them, their families, and the environment they find themselves in. The bubble is trying to burst, and at most these politicians just add to people's frustrations by muttering their own ideological slogans without even acknowledging the downward facing trajectory of every Western societal pillar happening all around us.

Without mass migration, the economy wouldn't collapse. More important jobs would begin to pay more. People would move and adapt to fill vital roles that begin to offer higher salaries. Businesses would compete for relevance. As industries decline, their value would be put on the scale of importance. Their role would either combine with other niches, or it would transform entirely. We'll never transform if we never fail. People who insist the economy must remain intact in order for us to prevail only uphold a lie. Transformation will not be easy, it will be painful and difficult. Which is why no politician wants to back this message, but they've failed you with their cowardice. Those preventing others from rising to this occasion are the laziest and least worthy amongst us. We need to feel the pain, we need to fail in order to reoptimize. Reaching failure, and understanding the mistakes of our predecessors is what would allow for transformation and growth to continue. To continually apply bandages to the broken concepts of this economy and lifestyle means to approach a dynamic static equilibrium that will actually destroy us, as well as our ability to adapt in the future. Economic decline in an age of population decline offers the chance to change future generations for the better, so they don't repeat the same foolish mistakes. There's always opportunity in failure, to prevent anyone from grasping such opportunities is to enforce the failure. Preventing this transformation through the mass-importation of foreigners only ignores the problem and guarantees our transformations stop here. Those who are afraid to feel the pain of their own failure are undeveloped children, so how did they ever come to control our government? The school system selected for their childish behavior, now the rest of us are subject to the whims of their ineptitude. Maintaining quality of life will never be as valuable as hard-earned growth and transformation. We've dug this hole for ourselves through the credentialism that insists someone must be qualified to be hired, rather than trained on the job. Our own economy abandoning the idea of an apprenticeship in favor of degrees has allowed the incompetent to sabotage the most valuable aspects of our existence. We've now abandoned our sovereignty to foreigners, potentially damned our children's future to war and violence, and forced our own transformative cycle into a state of decay that will take more generations to recover than would have otherwise happened had the populations of the West been allowed to compete in a functional capitalist system. Neither the government nor the universities should be acting as central planners, nor should they be playing the role of insidious decision makers behind closed doors. Especially in roles they're unqualified for. Contextualized around all these other failures made for the sake of instant gratification, it's no surprise these people have somehow separated the concepts of population growth and childbirth, despite that these are meant to be the same thing.

Like the fruit of a tree, the foreigners we pick from other countries only incentivizes the loss of our ability to make what they give us. The same has already happened with our geopolitical guarantees, much of our military hardware is outsourced to China. Having allowed them to maintain what we need in order to survive has only left us in a state of dependency. Waves of immigrants coming here is essentially a hedge against the West, it's rewarding foreigners for the decline of our nation no different than short selling a stock rewards a trader for the collapse of a company's stock price. In the most twisted form of conflicting interests ever witnessed, politicians are short selling their own country in exchange for political power.

The people who criticize what others might do with freedom tend to celebrate their freedom to sabotage functional systems for everyone else. Governments in the West have debanked people, invalidated entire executive elections because their opposition won, and when they couldn't decrease your wages they inflated your dollars by printing money and giving it to their own dark pools of non-profit organizations. When they begin to lose elections, they attempt to ban political parties and imprison their candidates, like in Germany and France. If legitimate elections declare the political establishment to have formally lost, the results somehow end up being overthrown by courts, like in Romania and Brazil. One might even question the highly unlikely death of seven AfD politicians, that occurred within two weeks of each other prior to German elections, as an act of political assassination. The UK is now lowering its voting age out of fear of receiving backlash for discriminating against their own citizens. There's a banned French presidential candidate, Germany's AfD politicians are now largely debanked, and the Digital Services Act is silencing political dissidents across Europe in place of a Ministry of Truth. Internet censorship bills are being proposed and passed all over the place while being disguised as *child safety* measures in order to identify every single online poster so they can be jailed through hate-speech laws. Digital currencies are being used to track everything about every single purchase someone makes so that all these activities, opinions, and behaviors can be tracked through lists that will someday become justification for imprisonment or genocide, because that's the only thing this could ever be used for. There's been things as horrid as the Bataclan Theatre Massacre, which I can't even describe in this book because of the platforms I'm selling it on, that had a clear genocidal intention. Even the UAE, a Muslim country, has stopped funding its students to attend British schools because they're afraid of the widespread Islamic radicalism that's become so heavily prevalent within them. The constant progression of the degeneration of basic freedoms is happening so rapidly it's hard to even keep up with. If and when the establishment continues to lose even more power, they'll next fragment into a bunch of smaller parties as a hedge against their centralized failing, they'll retain voters who passionately believe in the innocence of their individual causes independent of any other wrongdoings, and the centralized form of corruption will continue operating under the guise of unity around these individual causes. It used to be possible to scare people using knowledge to predict an eclipse that would block out the Sun, these same tricks are being used to scare young children with lies about the climate in order to scam them as adults to maintain control of the energy sector. They now even aim to scare people with fears of AI because they want to monopolize that as well, but their monopolies would only be as inept as their leadership.

Cancellation dug a hole meant to be filled with public discussion. We have too many people, across important roles in society, who are scared to come out into the sunlight. Drug designers, bankers, bureaucrats, police, and many more who could otherwise make great contributions to public discussions are left silent and unable to publicly comment on their day-to-day life. Every walk of life should be skilled at having public conversations. People should need to show themselves in order to fill upper level positions. The initial point of democracy was its transparency, it brought vampires into sunlight. Now we need to aim this concept of cancellation towards people who refuse to let the light touch their skin. We not only need to make society less secretive and insidious, we need to punish people who attempt to. You might think to call this idea that of an *open society*, but that name's already taken. It's another one of Popper's monstrosities.

The more honest conversations we can have with each other, and at even larger scales, the more good it will do for more people in the same way that capitalism has done across the globe. Federal polls alongside supreme executive elections for the sake of national communication would be a grand thing for national stability. It would prevent politicians from getting away with actions like opening the border. Because the truth will set you free, hiding from it only hinders your own transformations. All the lying and the gaslighting hasn't worked out in neither the short nor long term. Once we can be more honest with each other, it will effectively be an internal order optimization that works out as a win-win scenario across more dimensions than anyone can imagine.

9.4 Feedback Loops

History tells a story summarized by G. Michael Hopf, where *"hard times create strong men, strong men create good times, good times create weak men, and weak men create hard times"*[229]. The same pattern that's been made of us today, we're currently experiencing the bad times made by weak men. To better make sense of where we find ourselves, I'd prefer to adapt the above quote to the form of hardship breeding greatness, greatness breeding entitlement, entitlement breeding weakness, and weakness breeding destruction, which then causes hardship.

Entitlement is a major factor in what makes people weak to both internal flaws and external threats. It breeds people to believe that nothing bad will ever happen to them. Like a piece of the geologic record, I think entitlement may as well explain the layer of ash found beneath the soil of every destroyed Mediterranean city from the Late Bronze Age collapse, as prosperity was not just widespread, it was synchronized. Only Early and Middle Bronze Age warfare found civilizational destruction to be a common theme. By the Late Bronze Age, civilizational capture was more often sought over total destruction. The cultures of the people throughout this region likely came to understand the difference between making enemies and gaining a new labor force. Throughout this period, and the prosperity it enjoyed, people in various Mediterranean regions would have come to assume they were more valuable alive to any potential conquerors, and neglected their sense of self-defence. Given the wisdom they likely gained, why was everything from this time period burned down? It implies harsh emotions. These destroyers despised these people for their entitlement. That's why, in an area where people tended to conquer others, as they recognized the value of civilization, everywhere the Sea People went they left a layer of ash. The value of value had succumbed to its own rise and fall. It's impossible to know if they had demographic collapses similar to ours in the modern day, but it's certainly likely.

Growth is the way towards making everything more non-zero-sum, no matter what circumstances exist. The breaking of stability into a

---

229. G Michael Hopf. *Those Who Remain*. CreateSpace, 2016

fragmented state is a spawning of complexity. Deindustrializing advanced countries makes people unable to adapt, and fragmentation becomes more difficult to achieve. Culture is a selection mechanism, and growth comes from the struggle of hard times, to subvert this mechanism is to subvert the basis of selection.

Civilizations are built by individuals, then individuals are built by that civilization. The rise and fall of any group of people comes from the dwindling ability to build individuals capable of prolonging themselves. Entitlement creeps in, and with it comes neglect for the model of interactions. As entitlement causes a failure of interactions, civilizations crumble.

Entitlement is the belief that you're somehow above the need to respect the model of interactions. That the same limitations relevant in the lives of anyone else don't apply to you, and that you need not regard the importance of others. This scales to make a mechanism of decay and decadence, because to disregard the model of interactions is to fail every interaction. Those failed interactions will come back as a loss of trust.

Irony somehow leads us to predict the feedback of our own mistakes. It's the simplest way to approach and understand complexity, which seems like an ironic statement in the context of complexity itself, yet it's quite literally true. Now, all this doesn't negate truth as being a useful conceptualization. We're still fully reliant on it. However, in situations where truth proves elusive, it may be better to look for irony. You might think this is stupid, or absurd, yet how have the writers of the Simpsons and South Park predicted the future so many times? That's likely without ever once even trying to do so, they pick at ironies.

Punctuated equilibrium simply being a mass outbreak of evolutionary differentiation tells us the two are linked, that evolution itself takes advantage of biological boom and bust cycles even when it's not explicitly linked to population size. Although it's very likely that the first boom and bust cycle of early proto-organisms would have been achieved purely through population growth. Because what else would early proto-organisms have done? Prior to that they could have overproduced their own internal components, but that would have been prior to achieving a mass-produced functional organism. What else would early unicellular organisms have done to rapidly evolve? Probably nothing, they wouldn't have yet built up any of the intricate evolutionary mechanisms that we see in the organisms of the modern age. Regardless of the exact path taken to arrive there, whether through population booms or morphological booms, these cycles would have been the earliest incentives for life to latch on to in order to adapt to adaptation itself.

Feedback layers have continually transformed to better link consciousness with cellular function. Intelligence is not a purely human trait, it's something much broader that all life seems to have in some way. Even octopi have a strangely unexpected yet acute level of intellect. The point at which punctuated equilibrium in hominids transformed from being morphological to intellectual was likely a major turning point in the evolution of our intelligence. This would mark the point in time where the inheritance of knowledge coming to circumvent the inheritance of our genetics solved a significant integral on the road towards supreme intelligence. The brain would have completed itself in becoming a secondary adaptive apparatus capable of noticing these booms, and therefore capable of responding to them. This doesn't necessarily coincide with only the growth of human intelligence. Given that other animals share this inheritance of information, it's clear that prior recursions of this nature occurred long before hominids were ever around. It seems to be a common pattern across most mammals, and may have happened separately in certain birds. But humans have undoubtedly continued to push this specific boundary further and further. It's evident in our behavior, children even practice playing with booms in the form of fads, so we know it's embedded at an instinctual level.

Increased existential awareness, granted through intellectual inheritance superceding genetic inheritance, meant the evolutionary pulsing that once acted as the bleeding edge of organismal development would become the stepping stone towards a grand Lamarckian dance that created an awareness of Darwinian mechanics, which is to incentivize hyper-Darwinian mechanics. This is the lockstep we needed to find. It would seem the evolutionary development of intelligence was in lockstep with these various forms of evolutionary pulsing. If we can leverage a recursion of this evolutionary pulsing in places where we want to see improvements in intelligence, it should yield these results over time. In place of where we have no ability for the education system to undergo free transformations that allows an evolutionary pulsing to occur, we can find an implementation of freedom to suit this need. Which again, brings us back to the American Reformation.

To induce a form of evolutionary pulsing, a paradigm that enables a natural rise and fall through competition, one would simply mimic the nature of nature. But people don't need to live and die by natural selection within a school system. It doesn't need to be people that are selected for, it's the schools themselves that would act as the players in this game. The students are the terrain, they make up the environment being modeled. It's the job of the schools to make do with what they have. With people naturally wanting to give their children a better upbringing, they're going to pay attention to who wins and who loses in the real world. Different forms of success will come to be associated with different forms of schooling. What determines whether a schooling paradigm lives or dies is whether or not parents are able to put their faith in it. Schools and parents can adopt successful strategies while abandoning bad ones. The tradeoffs of this system is that it might take some time to determine good from bad paradigms, but on the other hand a good paradigm doesn't need to mate with another school in order to reproduce, it can be spread much faster. Schools that make a name for themselves across the student landscape will find more success, and luckily we already have the existing schooling paradigm as a baseline to build off of.

Ideological divides, rather than physical divides, would lead to a selection of ideas for humans. Its benefits aren't just improvements to intelligence, it involves improvements to culture, the broader intellectual environment, as well as societal stability, as there's a lot of backup plans should any one group fail. Multiple groups could form stabilizing supergroups, others could fragment should that be advantageous for them. In allowing both of these functions to co-occur, we hyperdivide ourselves into every possible niche, allowing for the most advantageous form of a socioevolutionary hedged bet to take root across society. Every person already belongs to some form of ideological divide, it's best to let these ideas live and die based on what they stand for. It's also best to let them transform and improve where they may be failing. This strategy allows populations to mimic the structure of any stage of a punctuated equilibrium, thereby adopting its function at any stage. These mechanics superimpose the concepts of stability and fragmentation, leading to a transcending of either's disadvantages, like it best estimates the appropriate center point between the two. Meaning, this becomes an evolutionary super-advantage that wouldn't be available to people who impose one-plan strategies.

Much like how human development has danced in lockstep with the evolution of salable currency, evolutionary mechanisms don't simply take advantage of boom and busts, they've evolved to do so for as long as it's been possible, as this was the earliest incentive ever presented to them at a population level. To piece this together, what would the full evolutionary picture look like under our modern understanding? Some aspect of an environment changes, and a population or morphological boom induces varying behavioral changes across a population. The behavioral changes induce varying levels of stress on parts both inside the organism undergoing a boom as well as the surrounding environment. The stress incentivizes genetic and epigenetic changes, which throughout generations echoes into more permanent changes to groups of organisms. Over time, organisms wouldn't just be selected for their traits, they would be selected for the gene-altering mechanisms that brought about their traits in the first place. Meaning, the ability to induce random genetic mutations in specific and appropriate areas has been more selected for than the traits they come to represent. Whichever Lamarckian responses acted as better measurements of stress, was likely to come out on top. This continued to the point where the selection for advantageous responses was so successful that these responses themselves actually became fuel for the mass evolutionary strategy known as punctuated equilibria. Over time, punctuated equilibria themselves would have evolved as the brain advanced as a mechanism of inheritance. They would begin to take effect through behavior rather than morphology, as that's a more immediate layer of adaptation. The brain itself would be an intergenerational device that informs the adaptation machinery won through natural selection via the responses from the forefront of our immediate environmental interactions that we refer to as conscious behavior.

The Lamarckian is an integral to the Darwinian. The brain itself is a Lamarckian device. Behavior changes long before phenotype, because the mind is more adaptable than our genetics. We don't change the linchpins of our physical appearances across generations, but we change our existence entirely based on life circumstances. The function of your life is the structure of your beliefs.

Civilization itself would be a mode of facilitating booms in predictable ways that then catalyze this adaptive domino effect, which paints intelligence as a concept that extends beyond the brain itself. The crispness of the interactions of molecular signals extend to our social bifurcations, which act to trigger societal movements. In turn, these societal movements affect other individuals through hearing the communications which goes to their brain, activates their nervous system with some response, sends physiological signals that alter the states of cells within the body, and potentially even impacts the propensity for alterations in the DNA they pass onto their children. What is civilization if not a facilitator of this process? A facilitator of the signals that continually climb and descend the axis of time as a form of communication between our societal modeling of entropy and our genetics.

A boom is undeniably the root of the domino effect that cause these eventual changes. So it makes sense to me that with political failures that cause civilizational busts, we see responses analogous to when such events take place on the stock market, things like stress, difficulty, and a growing uncertainty amongst people whose lives have no way of coming out in advantageous positions after such occurrences. These events are typically filled to the brim with complicated signals. Some of which may be insidious sabotage, and others that may be indications of what might be advantageous. Which is all the more reason to want to be a part of a high-trust group.

We've been experiencing a multitude of booms of ideas and information through social media. Meaning, we have the opportunity to institute improved social feedback mechanisms. The last 10^{+} years of broken compass dynamics, and the lessons it's brought forth, showed us how to find what direction society ought to move in. We've now arrived at a direction, and a form of stability, facing away from the scaled mistakes we were making prior.

People often say actions speak louder than words. Parenting, government infrastructure, and every piece of our lives that influence the upbringing of our children are important forms of communication that need to go through processes of selection. If the government is causing too many problems for young children, which go on to inhibit their lives from working out, then we need to learn from these mistakes as soon as possible. As that's the nature of these adaptations that occur as booms fade away. To understand them is to win the game.

Our feedback layers have failed in multiple ways. Failure arose in the upbringing of children because they weren't brought up in institutions reflective of their environment. The institutions instead became their own environments and ignored the world around them. It failed across families because parents are operating on a less than successful basis if their kids don't reproduce. Society at large failed because banks and businesses can be too big to fail, but people and their families are never treated with this level of respect. Needless to say, the widespread failure of government-led school systems won't ever be something the government will take responsibility for. If families feel the pain of failure, then families can do better to avoid it than the government ever could, allowing both consequences and responsibility to happen at the same level would make for an improved mechanism of feedback. Even governments, whose energy are being wasted while not gaining any benefit from their own citizens in the long term, via birth rate and economic output, are scrambling to make up for this failure through mass migration. If the feedback mechanisms of these flaws take too long to realize as mistakes, meaning that entire generations have to fail for these errors to be understood, then this will be an age of entitlement rather than that of growth. Likewise, if we can set up future generations to have improved feedback mechanisms, or mechanisms that are capable of receiving more appropriate distributed local feedback, rather than requiring a nation-wide pushback against a Marxist school religion, then our ability to adapt will be improved and large-scale failure of the schools will be much less likely to become a nation-wide problem once this system gets off the ground. It would be an improvement to the crispness of communication between the institutions we rely on for upbringing and the people who rely on such institutions.

There's an upcoming selection for the modern age. It's due to change the nature of how we receive and process information. So many integrals have been solved, globally, side by side with large scientific and technological advances that makes our own feedback mechanisms so important to refine in this day and age. I say this not from the perspective of someone who wants to refine, but from the perspective of knowing that nature itself will be the one to do so. Feedback is the most important route for selection, it probably always has been, as would be inferred from the nature of booms. So I believe all of Western civilization would find it advantageous to set up groups that have the potential for greater internal cohesion than what can be offered through a public school when raising their children.

Feedback is the foundational building block of complexity itself. In our bodies it's an array of measurements interacting with themselves through signaling pathways. Whether your hands wrinkle when exposed to water, whether you sweat when you're hot, it's the nature of the efficiency of these processes where the specifics of intelligence may someday be elucidated. Imagine getting sick then refusing to allow parts of your body to communicate with each other, or to produce antibodies for the disease but not allowing them to go to your foot. That's analogous to what happened during the pandemic with censorship. The inhibition of these most crucial functions is suicidal for individuals, and dysgenic for society.

Being dysgenic doesn't just mean selecting the worst people to succeed. It means the people who would have succeeded aren't able to. You don't just have population collapse by itself, you have a population collapse because you've become dysgenic. The worst people will not have enough children because they're already terrible, and even if they do their children won't succeed. If the best people don't succeed then they certainly won't have enough children either. Dysgenics and population collapse are one and the same, and they occur when entitled individuals think they can control societal outcomes. Entitlement offers disruption to important communication, and the misincentivized structures of the school system are basically the root cause.

But this isn't just a one-off event, throughout the course of history population booms have led to crashes. Is entitlement really the only explanation? Wouldn't that be an oversimplified explanation of what's going wrong? To calibrate the metaphor, the baby boomers were the entitled generation, the weak men who made bad times. So what went wrong with the boomers? What exactly tends to happen in these large population booms that subsequently lead to civilizational breakdown?

Let's envision it through the modeling of entropy, and what any recursion of the brain would do, model time. At the growth stage of a boom, the modeling of entropy becomes overloaded, and becomes less efficient at predicting the future. The resulting process remains efficient only for the immediate term, and less for the long term. You might think that with more people they'd be able to predict the future better, but the boom is in lockstep with civilizational development. New technology, economic advancements, and many other novel factors would get in the way of accurately predicting the future, more possibilities means the future actually becomes *less* predictable. This lack of predictability is a tradeoff that comes in exchange for making it very easy to contribute to the boom, which enables a dogmatic culture. Certain people would even grow comfortably content with believing that this will continue to happen, while being ignorant of the underlying societal structures needed to uphold this level of constant innovation in the first place. Which explains the continued negligence of generations during booms, they literally can't see ahead of their own timeline. Without the ability to see ahead at all during their childhood, they themselves never practice this ability. Right-brain function becomes inhibited by these circumstances, and they fall into a state of lifestyle dogma that eventually breeds decadence. Stated more appropriately, fewer members of the population would be skilled with right-brain functionality. The boom then eventually crashes through failed child-rearing, and an inability to have enough children, both being due to the lack of widespread right-brain functionality. As the quest for questions becomes replaced by the enforcement of answers, one boom stratifies into the next, where a boom of stern belief invites a boom of irony. The same general dynamic is what exists between urban and rural areas, higher density living requires greater levels of order to remain predictable enough to make the environment survivable.

The inability to predict the future is no different than entitlement. Entitlement itself is taking success for granted despite making mistakes that were never learned from. It's to believe a lie in the hope that it's true. Where this behavior becomes most entrenched is in the dogma people pass on from their own childhood, which mistakenly acts as a corruption of this layer of human instinct. The reason this entitlement shows itself today most fiercely through a belief in schooling, and the value of the university systems, is because the boomers were the first generation to so thoroughly participate in these institutions. More recent generations have even out-participated their predecessors, but the boomers represented an inflection point in the use of institutionalized upbringing, because that's the answer people come to as a way to raise large amounts of children effectively. When you have more children than your society can feasibly handle through traditional upbringing, many would then turn to a scaled approach at doing so, despite typically being something that's best done as a personal endeavor. Any society would find themselves convinced that institutionalizing such a thing is a good idea, but it's actually a trap, one that people have likely fallen for many times throughout thousands of years, and the Bronze Age Collapse was probably no different. But even this entitlement can be leveraged, as periods like these are definitively inflection points, but what specifically they become an inflection point for can change depending whether people learn from the inevitable recurrence of the broken compass from such events. To overcome these mistakes can transform a decaying society into a thriving one.

The resulting boomer political system was upheld by people who thought they were simply trying to reach agreement across society, rather than estimating some center value. So they cast off attempting to estimate it at all, and that's why their news stations spew nothing but propaganda, and why so many of them do as they're told without questioning the intentions of those behind the television. But this approach is wildly incorrect, the center value can only be achieved through the disagreement of the two socioevolutionary bounds of society. It's the necessity to solve disagreements, to find the win-win solutions between them, that better estimates the real center value. The purpose of such disagreements is to find the hidden value behind them, it's to find where the two disagreeing sides can find a solution that benefits both parties. If you can find the value in this, then you would eventually realize that disagreements always *reward* with more disagreements, and in the process of overcoming them they offer a continual supply of precious social treasures, whereas to stop other people from competing is to become a vampire.

The baby boomers are probably the worst generation in at least tens of thousands, possibly hundreds of thousands of years. This is because the world's population had never been so large, so we'd never experienced an entitled generation of such scale before. The difference between the transition of the rise and fall of their boom was larger than ever seen before. Meaning, their societal failings were also worse than anything ever seen before. But, hidden within this folly is the opportunity to learn from their failures. Because the boom happened on a scale larger than ever before, the opportunities to learn from share an equal magnitude. If utilized properly, our success over the next few generations could be as large as their failure. What would be the best possible thing we could learn from them? The nature of these boom and bust cycles of course, the nature of the rise and fall of civilizations.

People often classify the boomers as having believed they reached the end of history. A more appropriate interpretation of this idea is that of the end of natural selection. The problem being, natural selection never ends, neither does history. It's just a claim that utopianism is now *acceptable*, but it never will be. That's just entitlement. We can never be negligent of our own nature if we wish to succeed, the acknowledgement of its presence was a layer of success our own evolution was already built atop of. To ignore it would guarantee our failure.

People often compare the energy efficiency found in nature to that of the engineered designs we use in our daily life. But realistically, you can't make a simple comparison between the energy use of a multicellular organism with that of an engine. More sophisticated engines can achieve greater energy efficiency than the cells of animals, but it's the logistics of chemical energy in multicellular systems that perform more impressive feats than the straightforward energy use of something like an engine. Cells have much more efficient retention of chemical exergy, as the byproducts of most chemical reactions retain material with plenty of free energy to harvest. An engine's heat inevitably dissipates into its surroundings without as sophisticated a compartmentalization as what you would find in multicellular organisms, and thereby less leveraging of pre-existing heat, whereas the heat given off by the reactions of cells maintains the temperature of their collective. The extreme compartmentalization of cells becomes a hedged bet against the loss of both heat and chemical energy. It's a design to spite the nature of energy loss itself. What can we learn from this? Heat and chemical energy are the primary contributors to the entropy of cells, but for humans this represents itself through economic value, and communication. What can we learn from this? Double-dipping into our own feedback is advantageous. We should have layers upon layers of public communication, rather than secret meetings where some one-plan strategy is decided and agreed upon across too wide a breadth for that lone oversimplification to properly manage. Podcasts and social media have come to fill the voids of this communication niche, and people seem to prefer this for many reasons due to the fact that it's just a better way of operating.

The genetic regression to the mean of large groups is analogous to the social regression to the mean offered through the modeling of entropy when a group attempts to elucidate truth. It's also why one-plan strategies made by just a few people could only ever be a death sentence, sharing information with the public and allowing them to navigate it as a group will always be a better survival strategy because they'll always arrive at both a more accurate and more precise direction for the group as a whole to move in for its own best interest. It's for this same reason that small groups of organisms are capable of adapting quicker than large groups, because each new step taken is an experiment. Rapid changes in direction for large groups requires variation, not uniformity.

Improper feedback mechanisms would be the root cause of any crash, and those looking for the feedback they can't find would scramble to understand what's going on. The scramble can be seen as the left-brain immune system behavior that attacks its society, makes it weak, and eventually causes them to either attack someone else or become invaded by opportunistic neighbors. It never allows for peace. Because peace is stagnation. If you dislike nothing, you'll improve nothing. If there's anything to learn from evolution, this behavior seemingly being a default mode of operation suggests that peace would be worse. It means having no purpose is worse than having no war. Which leads to the interpretation that a civilization with purpose has no inherent need for war. Being a civilization with multiple wars every decade, it would seem we have no real purpose. Better yet, those who have turned war into the purpose for our civilization have destroyed it, and this gives us a clear idea of where we can move to improve, towards purpose.

The schools and universities have quite literally made the purpose of so many young people into some form of anti-racism or anti-discrimination crusade, and it's the opposite of the kind of intellectual growth that was expected from such institutions. This habit of hating the losers of a war for decades after it's been finished needs to change. No one alive fought in the American Civil War, nor WWII. We need not use hypothetical racists and Nazis as social targets especially when the people being targeted have never supported any such thing. Since the onset of humanity, slavery and genocide were going to be inevitable. You can vilify the practice without vilifying the mistake. Mistakes will always be made, and mistakes of the same nature are currently being made in the form of mass migration. Imprisoning the citizens of a country to fund a borderless welfare state while they lose all control of their own democratic processes, and weaponizing the costs of this process to prevent the natives from buying homes and having families, isn't unlike the situation the Germans found themselves in prior to WWII. We should honor the lessons learned from these wars of recent past, which means honoring the conditions that created them as being equally as disastrous as that which they caused. This becomes a form of wisdom to anyone who receives its communication. It allowed so many other people to stand up against the multitude of atrocities we've come to experience, and more staunchly than ever. We should look no differently at the woke, and learn from them all the same. They're worthy of being both a lesson and a measurement. If you don't want Nazis, you should aim to prevent creating the conditions that created the Nazis. Likewise, if you don't like the woke, you should aim to correct the mistakes made visible through their religious infiltrations that made them possible, don't shrug off the importance of your state and societal institutions while insisting people can live their lives independent of the effects of hedonism. The responsibility of holding our societal fabric together cannot be neglected, preventing women from starting families only causes them to form religious cults that aim to subvert your society from the inside. Even many today who dislike the woke don't run for office, don't vie for judge positions, and don't do anything other than post about them online, this should be seen as their mistake. The source of all these mistakes is one and the same, it's a lack of responsibility, and we can raise children to be allergic to this behavior by making institutions that follow better principles and bestow responsibilities to young children. It's the entirety of an institution itself that must rise to this occasion, negligence of this developmental necessity would only become negligence in the students.

Teachers don't hold any responsibility for the children they send into society. The school systems exist with neither checks nor balances, yet can be taken over by insidious religious motivations. Any teacher is just one small experience that any student ever had for only one short year. This pattern continues year by year, shielding every teacher from the responsibility of their actions by sharing the burden with any number of other teachers. Which is the same strategy used to pipeline young children onto a surgery table. There's a chain of official *approvals* required before any child lays down with anesthesia, which makes it seem odd that so many of these surgeries ever happen, because this structure was clearly intended to turn children away. Yet it doesn't seem to function that way, everyone from their teacher, to whatever psychologist believes it's a good idea, to an endocrinologist that ended up giving them hormones, to a surgeon that's actually willing to dice up a young child, only ever says it's a good idea, and disagreement within this pipeline is rare. It's so odd that all of these people not only end up agreeing to let a child make these permanent life-altering decisions, but also that the prevalence at which this agreement occurs seems abnormal. You have to then question, how many of them have ever said no, and what percent of the time does that happen? There's never anyone who pushes back against the child because the comfort of being a small cog in a big wheel means they hold no risk for any of their actions. **These layers upon layers of bureaucracies that shield themselves from any and all liability are a liability to everyone else.**

These insulatory layers live and die for this small cog mindset. Similarly, educators tend to claim to simply care about how to make their students smarter, more capable, better, and so on, while pretending no other aspects of life matter. Every aspect of life matters, only focusing on school work is, ironically, the worst way to raise children. It's so unrealistic to expect society at large to remain a functional machine should we ignore the big picture. You can't just plan one small detail of someone's life and claim to make an improvement. Any educator can't be ignorant of a philosophical understanding of intelligence, especially while attempting to measure for it. One *needs* to address the big picture, that's the only way to actually provide a better upbringing for children. People who focus on lone oversimplifications while ignoring every other aspect of life have sabotaged us. Every single aspect of society not only needs to be placed within a hierarchy of priorities, we need to raise children who understand how to maintain these hierarchies. We've now had multiple generations who are so far disconnected from too many things, from vaccines, from banking, from the global finance system, from medicine, from agriculture, from law, from morality, and from the majority of things that we do to the point where no one has a proper eye on the big picture. Everyone simply *specializes* in something and that's allowed our ship to sink as far as it has. We've lost touch with it all, and in trusting small groups of people, who only care about their *one thing*, we've become susceptible insidious infiltrations that betray our own wellbeing. The only way to raise children to actually have a better future is to make them aware of everything that needs to be fixed, as well as the principles necessary to hold these fixes together. They need to be well-informed on all of these topics, and luckily we have better information than we've ever had. We don't have one little problem, so one little solution isn't going to fix anything. We have a fundamental misalignment across our incentives and our future. To all of this, the intelligence of an individual student is nothing by comparison, and would never solve any of these problems. The problem isn't part of everything we're aware of, it *is* everything we're aware of. It's the big picture, it's all of these things stacked on top of each other, because that's their truest representation. That *is* the metaphor of the Tower of Babel, each layer must be placed with consideration to everything below it that it must rely on, and everything above it that it must support. It's no different than the stacked layers of agricultural labor, resource extraction, and industrial manufacture that allow our consumer-based economy to exist. It's no different than the respect we must pay to our own evolutionary history during the development of children, the implementation of developmental models of evolving complexity is meant to avoid pitfalls from our evolutionary history from becoming points of predictable failure, and would act to limit the creation of more pitfalls in the future. It's to be aware of where relaxed selection has provided a foolish gift in exchange for a foolish curse, and to balance our future tradeoffs with the proper experimental caution so as to not doom our descendants to the consequences of foolish decisions. To neglect this balance is entitlement in its purest form.

Likewise, the birthrate problem isn't caused by one lone factor either, this is the mindset the school systems and universities have pushed people towards. Studies on the topic of population decline often mention that there's an anomaly amongst the explanations for declining populations. It's always pointed out that one explanation for certain countries doesn't occur in other specific countries that have the same declining birth rate, then a conclusion draws that therefore it couldn't possibly be the underlying problem. These explanations usually range from factors that affect men and women, to technology, to culture, and so on. But this small problem approach, trying to piece the unknown together with the known, is a failed strategy when addressing ubiquitous unknowns that aren't understood. You can't fix some small factor and expect this to be solved overnight, which is why the political class declares it to be unsolvable, because they're incapable of thinking along these lines. From birth control training young women to feel entitled to have relationships without making a family, to immigration constantly replacing the population-sustaining role that women held in society, to women being required to enter the workforce in order to earn the right to have children, every part of our society is set up to inhibit women from giving birth and it's completely failing us. Men have been put in a position where defending themselves or defending their family has been criminalized, expecting people to show restraint to someone who may be attempting to kill their family is a form of cruel and unusual punishment. Our society has undermined our most core instincts to the point that it's become purely subversive of our own survival. Children are having information passed onto them by people who don't even have children of their own, if you wouldn't want your child to share half their genetics with someone you don't like, then why should your children be exposed to the ideas and opinions of what might be the most questionable individuals in our society? Both of these are levels of inheritance and it's fair to want people to fill these positions who will go on to instill the ideas reflective of the parents wishes, because it's a survival strategy. Anyone preventing you from choosing who your child is influenced by, or what they must learn, is enacting a survival strategy that may as well be entirely subversive of their survival in general. We need to reset our priorities entirely by focusing on building families. We need to reprioritize away from this mode of taking in immigrants, to support the economy, to support the elderly, to instead wield an economic engine that actually supports the young, supports the young's ability to buy homes, to give birth, and to focus on growing skills we desperately need to have inside our own economy for our geopolitical security. Care for your elderly if you want to, but the aging population will need to fend for themselves with the money they've already saved. We don't need to continue to damn the young to favor the old like we did during Covid, and our civilization should never form such a deranged system of incentives ever again, this is the feedback we'd received.

Liberalism is a great mediator of freedoms in society, but taken to its extreme it's no different than a mother who refuses to let her son out into the world. Which is why it starts wars, the backlash against it is always extreme aggression. This is why the Japanese and Germans, prior to WWII, essentially decided to fight back against a world of liberalism, even if they weren't entirely aware of these mechanics. It doesn't mean liberalism is evil, but we have this gigantic wall erected in our society around being too far right-wing, yet the large majority of current evils that plague us are of an insidious establishment more correctly associated with extreme leftism. As a society, we're capable of moving towards the right without going extreme in the way that was done in the 1940s, as either extreme is representative of a baseline human instinct that's an important aspect of our survival. Either wing can go extreme, and to pretend only one could ever be the problem essentially ensures that the other soon will. This extreme backlash is a predictable response, you can take mothering, coddling, babying, and infantilization too far. It will always, predictably, lead to the same result. Poorly raised impulsive men, whose anger eventually boils in frustration, and occurring within an environment that prevents young people from owning homes, from having families, only guarantees this end result will come even faster. The people imposing these restrictions think they're saving the world by forcefully decreasing the population. But they only do this in their own countries. It's analogous to a devouring mother destroying the lives of her children, making them non-competitive amongst their peers, and it's an extremely stupid and avoidable mistake. In attempting to control every aspect of this process, it will only ever explode out of its containment. Eventually, the people whose lives are manipulated into irrelevance will realize they have nothing to lose by fighting back, which is a dangerous way to run society. It's just safetyism at scale, and it doesn't raise people to the proper level of maturity required to maintain civilization. The universe can be seen as both a cold and heartless place or one filled with deep and meaningful interactions. Danger is one of the most deep and meaningful interactions to be learned from, its absence during childhood would only make people inept at interacting at all.

Within the same oceans swim both great white sharks and orcas. Great whites, who are of moderate intelligence, have the most highly capable sensory systems on the planet. But on the other hand, everything one might find impressive about them is the exact reason their intelligence is lacking, and this shows in their solitary lives and inability to form social groups. Whereas Orcas have a militaristic hunting culture, and incredibly developed brains with evidence of complex emotional lives. They never leave the pod they were born into, their lives are the opposite of the solitary existence of the great white. Exhibiting the most sophisticated non-human hunting behavior in the world, orcas are considered a uniquely intelligent organism with strong adaptive abilities. Orcas never leave the pod they're born in, they dress themselves in ornaments while playing, and have been seen holding extensive mourning rituals for their dead. Yet both creatures are ultimately a reflection of the same environment. Both exist because both of these perspectives are accurate representations of their environment, and our own environment is no different. Focusing on a surface-level goal will present a surface-level reward. Orcas are no less vulnerable to being eaten than anything else, yet the novelties found in their behavior would undoubtedly be derived from an evolutionary history of risk-taking behavior, as the hardest path is the most rewarding.

Safetyism is a destructive thing to offer young children. It's a simple goal, and therefore will offer a very simple vulnerability. To deprive a childhood of deep and meaningful interactions only means to make the future environment held up by these individuals more cold and heartless. Safetyism itself is a liability to the future.

And this isn't to blame either men or women for their behavior, you can't blame either for following their instincts, they were selected to be this way over millions, if not billions of years, and for a reason. Their instincts didn't arrive at the wrong answers, but our society has arrived at the wrong organizational structure, one that wouldn't work even if we *were* selected for it, because that selection process would rely on something as unnatural as the reliance on printed money in an economy, once it goes away you would be left bankrupt and incapable of reorganizing. In examining the function of this structure made by women, to be inferred from their behavior, one would presume ideology is the first step towards making a religion when no such thing is present. Women without a proper religion are prone to ideology because that's the best way to raise children who grow up to make a better society, which is a hedge against becoming dysgenic. The natural feedback to ideology is typically as simple and uniform as any ideology itself, eventually mistakes rise to surface when that ideology comes into conflict with reality, and the continual feedback loops of ideology with its own failure ultimately fuels a more layered approach to upbringing that resembles the metaphor of the Tower of Babel, and that becomes a formal religion. An ideology is meant to be a fledgling religion, because it's meant for fledgling people. To a child, someone who hasn't reached the pinnacle of their own development, an ideology *is* a religion. That's also to say, **ideology, at its best, is intended for raising children, not governing adults.**

You may think the primary purpose of civilization is to eradicate difficulty or the harshness of life, but this isn't true. Civilization will never be free from harshness, and it shouldn't be. There's no way to remove such harshness, it's inevitable. Harshness actually has an important role in civilization, it's what we channel towards those who can't find success so as to increase their chances at finding it. It's part of our overarching selection mechanisms. To subvert this through pity will only cause such harshness to reappear in places where it isn't deserved.

Government can only facilitate people to solve their own problems. If government makes you a ladder then government will push you up it while saying you have a ladder climbing deficiency. In reality, people need to make their own ladders if they ever want to be inspired to climb. Government shouldn't be telling anyone to climb a ladder, it should only be there to make sure no one's ladder is being destroyed or stolen. If you want to climb that's a decision you need to come to on your own, and in doing so will make you a better climber. You need to be the one to determine if you'd like a ladder, a staircase, or a rope.

Something that government does for people becomes something that government *always* does for people. The government always ends up enabling dependencies in people when they instead need to be the ones to do things for themselves. If government is there to say *but they need help*, then government will help them and these people will continue to believe they need government help. They'll continue to believe just about anything. Government is only there so you can help yourself. Government doesn't lead the way, people do. If government always leads then its citizens never will, and government will end up doing a terrible job as it does a terrible job at everything else. Ultimately, interactions with your own transformations will always be a negative experience. It's one you must pull through as government will not transform to adapt, it will instead bloat to avoid any transformation at all. From doing so you yourself will reap rewards. The point of negativity is to give rewards to only those who persist.

Likewise, the education system will never fix itself for all the same reasons, nor will anyone from within the education system ever try to fix the schools in some way that isn't just some infinitesimal step forward. They're not incentivized to because they're not subject to the feedback from this process. There are no such feedback loops that reach any of these so-called education professionals. Once a child leaves their classroom at the end of the year, they don't have any reason to track their outcomes. Anyone doing statistics on oversimplified measurements of complex environments in order to do so will never have met neither teachers nor students, nor understood their relationship.

There will always be feedback loops, one way or another. Incorporating them into some public form of societal discourse for the sake of not becoming extreme would prove to be a more worthwhile strategy than to provoke people until the point of seizing their children over ridiculous political and religious causes. That would better balance the modeling of entropy that's occurring rather than forcing people to suffer from the stupid decisions of one-plan strategies. Because trust is something that's earned, once it goes away it's very hard to get back.

Just as the North believes they defeated the South instead of having saved it, their victory turned to arrogance with time. A lack of humility on the subject is now blinding the most extreme inheritors of this victory, who can't disconnect from labeling everything their opposition does as racist. This is despite that most of the West has already moved on from this history to find cultural unity.

Just as the control group adopted the content of one's character as its basis for judgement, the extremes of the experimental group abandoned it. Despite Martin Luther King's clear cultural victory, why did this happen? Because that's their job. The experimental group is continuing to model entropy by changing what they do, despite it seeming odd and hypocritical to anyone else. The control group had adopted the philosophy of the cultural victor, so it was passed on to them. Which is why the left had come to, and still quite often does, judge people purely by their sex and skin color.

But there's yet another layer to this, these people are trying to hedge their bets, they're trying to form a control group. The problem is that their current lack of religious freedom is preventing them from doing so. Our current laws force people to come up with endless excuses just to better conserve specific groups. Everyone wants better human conservation, and they shouldn't need to come up with fanciful policies or insidious forms of discrimination in order to do it.

When acting as a cult, this creed of diversity has obscured their own meaning in order to ignore feedback. It can represent either race, gender, sexuality, or immigration status at the convenience of whoever needs it. Some people only experience it across a single social class and never see the big picture, where other social classes then easily feel attacked by big-picture criticisms despite it never being the intention of any critic who can't speak more specifically because this term of diversity was meant to ambiguate every aspect of every conversation about it in the first place. Which makes the cult factions of diversity difficult to attack politically, because they pretend you're attacking something else whenever you speak about them. They've defined themselves in a way that always exists as a muddied line of interpretation. Everything becomes viewed through the lens of *racism* the same way that every social violation, to an extremely liberal person, is seen under the lens of unfairness in Moral Foundations Theory. It's all just a strategy of diversion. It's a strategy to always have an excuse to keep existing. Let them exist for all I care, it's their freedom of religion to do so. But this can't be forced upon people through the school system, that's a First Amendment violation.

The best thing the international left-wing can do to reform their own base is admit their mistakes, reinvent their manner of communication, and rebuild themselves off the existing public consensus. The main point is to admit where they're wrong, mass migration is a failed policy. Forced one-plan strategies are a terrible idea, they're no different than fledgling religions. Bad communication isn't going to work well in the age of the internet, as it's supremely unintelligent and comes off as patronizing. If they actually aimed to communicate better with their own base, they could use that communication to empower their own movements even more. Great communication can be a form of direct representation. There's a massive communication failure from the left-wing establishment to their own constituents and it involves demonizing their opponents. It misconstrues allegiances to be stronger across international borders than within our own. If this pattern doesn't stop, and this left-wing establishment that's so closely tied to the failed globalist agendas of the last 30^{+} years comes back into power, the entire world will be worse off because of it and it will undoubtedly push us towards a future involving major wars. This upcoming war would be a civil war across the West where international players use either side as their proxies. The West would be sacrificed at the cost of disunity over false demonizations.

The push for urgency also comes with the push for uniformity, which is fundamentally disastrous. Even if you say it's not so bad because it's not intended to be evil, I would disagree, that's actually worse. Indicated by David Alfaro Siqueiros, *"a stupid friend is worse than a smart enemy"*. Forced uniformity is the sabotage of a hedged bet. Which is largely the strategy of the public school system, and of Marxist systems in general.

Making a law that inhibits the speech of others is stupid and fruitless, so of course it causes needless friction. Likewise, we need not fight so much over what children learn in school, or the dispositions of the staff, when we could instead separate ourselves based on the religious differences that already emerge in these same discussions. When modeling entropy, the system with the least internal friction will provide the most benefit. Because that's the answer that better enables freedom, as entropy relies on freedom. It's why the experimental group is analogous to derivatives, because we don't always know what the integrals they represent actually are. It takes years of growth to receive feedback to determine whether they pass the test of time.

An economy is downstream from its population, we should care more about the population than we do about the economy, because a well-maintained populace will give you a functional economy. Despite their interlacing nature, an economy doesn't produce a population. Meaning, an economy doesn't yield the populace, it's the populace that yields the economy. One is the integral of the other, and it can't be any other way because integrals don't manifest as giant civilizational steps, they're small steps that build up into larger changes over time, it's the best one can do when moving backwards while blindfolded. Favoring the economy over the populace will mean the economy will devour the population, it's ouroboric. On the other hand, favoring the population over the economy will give you a self-sustaining population, as well as a persisting and growing economy.

9.5 Forgotten Metaphor

Rigidity born from believing your beliefs is not a belief itself but a lack thereof, it's the embrace of dogma, the stern belief that will invite irony. Questioning the unknown is the never-ending conversation that always asks whether every piece of information could be flipped by some point of nuance or irony. A belief is more rightfully the structure of the never-ending, stratified dialogue you continue to maintain in an approach of the truth. To understand is to approach, and beliefs point in the direction of that which you want to understand. Beliefs are the precursors to truth, they're what's been refined throughout history both systematically and artisanally, and they themselves later become stepping stones for the transcendence towards an enlightened form of intelligence. Uncertainties deliver us to certainties, and it's religious transformations that enable this process. Through transformation, the brain had completed itself in becoming a hereditary layer for information, capable of circumventing the inheritance of genetics, humans then acted to construct the next recursion beyond this. A cell's nucleus and a brain center their recursive relationship most notably around the concept of modeling time, around survival. After every structural advancement made to the brain would come reciprocating advances in behavior that best models time, followed by a collective form of modeling entropy that succeeds more than any prior mode of living. This is the function of religion, it's a means of improving our understandings of the stories of the past and the construction of a pathway towards the future. Religion is an attempt at optimizing the modeling of entropy.

Under the hierarchy of values comes infinite structural flexibility, but this explanation leaves a question on the table for anyone who wants to know more. What's the key driving mechanism for its change and transformation? It's easy to say there's a hierarchy of values, and that it transforms itself towards a more mature form. But in what way does it achieve this transformation? In what way would structures of beliefs do the same? You might make the off-hand comment that it's something that happens during periods of growth, and that it functions to overcome limitations. I would point out that during both your lack of understanding of this concept of transformation as well as the transformation itself there's actually a common theme. It's the unknown, it's your ignorance. The life, crucifixion, and resurrection of Jesus can all be interpreted through the lens of ignorance.

There's a classic interpretation of the resurrection of Jesus, that the man you kill over his message loses the battle, but wins the war. The only thing proven by killing an innocent man is that innocence isn't valuable to those who disagree with his message. Which is a priceless metaphor, and there's a plethora of other interpretations that have been made of this story. I'd like to add to this list by superimposing this story onto the frameworks introduced throughout this book as a form of hindsight on recent events.

The metaphor of Jesus was selected over time for its utility of belief because it made for the best vessel of religious transformation. Many other ideas were tried across the history of religion, but the success of this idea in particular can be attributed to the transformational power it holds. It's no coincidence that Christianity came to be of such hegemonic influence. Countries which embraced Christianity thrived, as opposed to countries which embraced the ideas of communism who later found themselves impoverished and starving. At this point in history, both of these examples have consistent data across multiple real-world examples.

In the stories of the Gospels, Jesus was representative of the ignorance of those around him. He's what brought people to challenge their own shortcomings. When you own up to your own ignorance, when you don't deny its existence, you're in the process of converting the unknown into the known. This is why Jesus was a teacher and a carpenter. He was able to show people what they didn't understand, allowing them to build themselves anew. He built the bridge of knowledge peering out to the unknown. He was the incentive for transformation, building structures out of information.

For those who chose to learn from their ignorance, those who kept a watchful eye, their ignorance became the sky full of stars that we look up at today. Filled with constellations and the history surrounding them. The unknown orients us in ways that the known isn't able to. The unknown requires navigation without a map, where the known simply provides an instruction sheet. Ignorance is a blessing that will always exist. When able to question their own ignorance, no one will ever need to be born unable to find a purpose.

Then what of the miracles? Turning water into wine is being enjoyable to be around. Despite only having water, the company of Jesus is what made those at the banquet feel that they were drinking wine.

They would have believed it was wine which made them merry, but it was the company of one another. Ignorance being the basis of communication, the basis for the social bifurcations of the automaton, Jesus was the conversation.

Walking on water was the display that there was no true danger to be found in the first place, the fears of the apostles were misplaced because the waters weren't as deep as they thought. It was metaphorical of the fear for the journey that the apostles were undertaking. A fear which was proven to be overstated.

The breaking of bread with such large groups was representative of the utility of human ignorance, that each member of the group makes up for each other's flaws. Alone, each person would have starved, but together each person was able to satiate their hunger. It was the differences between each individual that made up for each other's shortcomings. It was their lack of uniformity that saved them, they relied on each other's differences to survive. If each individual held the same ignorance, they would have starved, but because no two people were the same, the differences in their ignorance were no different than the differences in what they could contribute in a dire situation.

The metaphor isn't purely about what Jesus was, but what Jesus was to others. As the story is a long and winding road of doing things for others who believed in him, and asking nothing in return. Jesus was willing to carry the sins of others, the curses of the gifts he gave, as ignorance is that which rewards you for acknowledging it. Throughout his life he played the role of a teacher, educating people about their own ignorance and their ability to use it. The resurrection of Christ represents the inevitable improvement to the equilibrium of the modeling of entropy, it's the inevitable rebalancing of truth with falsity. Because ignorance affects a group no differently than lies, lies add stress and difficulty. A group as a whole, using the modeling of entropy as a distributed truth finding measurement, decides what information is and isn't worth keeping around, and lies are always worth getting rid of. In carrying the cross to his death came the suffering required for growth and enlightenment, which found its climax during the crucifixion, as it's nihilism one needs to overcome in order to transform. From his resurrection came a new societal paradigm of ignorance that replaced any prevailing uncertainty around his preachings. Ignorance can't be killed, there will always be things we're unaware of. The second you believe it's gone, it will always come back in some new and improved form. Ignorance will always rise from the dead.

The metaphor of the resurrection can be interpreted as people having gained new ignorance from new knowledge. To seek knowledge is to seek the unknown, it's to seek our own ignorance. The art of managing information isn't just managing what's known, it's creating a framework of which to question the unknown. We want to find the next major frontier, where the unknown can guide us towards the next stage of civilization. Which is the very basis for intelligence itself.

The process of organizing knowledge to gain ignorance, then organizing ignorance to find new knowledge, has been a civilizational growth mechanism for as long as such things have existed. Empiricism, as a formal concept, was a recursion of this ability to organize information, it was the microscope of philosophy. A mechanism which prioritizes the building of the tower using successful principles. When we're able to process and organize our new ignorance, this will spawn a new cycle of finding new knowledge, and the cycle then repeats again. Either one leads to a cyclic phenomenon that always brings about the conditions for the other to exist.

The interpretation of the resurrection of Jesus as a new societal paradigm of ignorance represents a shift in the understandings of the right-brain to be painted by the details of the left-brain. It's a form of group-based progression where people who share information come to the same realizations. It's an improvement to the resolution of the big picture, of how exactly to focus to see a more resolved image of a much larger area. It's a rewiring of pools of entropy after having achieved a major milestone to better optimize internal order. A Copernican shift to the parameters of a model, and with it comes scalable benefits.

Popper's objectivity is unable to grasp this utility. He believes the questioning of ignorance to be a technical pursuit with no technical end, that there's no bridge to the destination of absolute truth. The metaphor of the resurrection of Christ is that bridge. Instead of being confident in insulative ignorance, questioning one's own ignorance is what fuels transformations that eventually leads towards absolute truth. Under Popper's worldview, people aren't anxious about never attaining an understanding of everything in the universe, they instead grow arrogant enough to deny their own ignorance. A denial of Jesus is a denial of the unknown, it's the welcoming of entitlement. It's to live an entitled life believing you know everything. A denial of the resurrection is actually a societal denial of the same thing. It's the self-condemnation made from a suicidal culture, which is what's currently seen across the West. It's to ignore the consequences of interactions. It's to believe we've reached the end of natural selection, which is to reach a dynamic static equilibrium.

The big picture is not made up of fine details, that's only the known. The big picture comes from the questioning of one's own ignorance. People who only focus on details believe the big picture is one large puzzle where all the fine details fit in to some expected slot that doesn't force a reorganization of all the other pieces. Which is why they model the unknown using the known in that very way, they attempt to elucidate known unknowns. But the people who focus on the big picture don't focus on details, they obsessively question what it is that they aren't aware of, they look for unknown unknowns, they look for a reason that actually requires the puzzle to be rearranged specifically. As your ignorance will tell you everything about the big picture that fine details never could.

The metaphor of the resurrection of Christ is analogous to a tidal wave of incentive structures that ultimately crash. As it's not what's lost from this structural failure that's to our detriment, it's what remains that's to our benefit, it's a natural selection of ideas. The information that was lost was built upon incorrect assumptions, they were mistakes, and it's these incorrect assumptions that we then free ourselves from. Having learned why these concepts failed in the first place, it grants us the confidence in crossing off specific unknown factors in an analysis, which is priceless. It reorders unknown unknowns into known unknowns, and this reordering would have been the very process a proto-nervous system used to bring about its own intelligence through information. This isn't just present in any single individual, it's present across the entire population. There's a social stock market of unknowns within the modeling of entropy, fueled by the social bifurcations of the automaton. The crashing of this social stock market leaves people, who exist in an environment dictated by information, as well as the other people who process it, suddenly finding themselves in a new environment to model.

To take these ideas off paper, what does the new societal paradigm of ignorance look like in real life? It's like what we learned from Covid. Most people realized the media had been lying, not just in a normal way, in a disgusting way. It's clear that the political establishment and its media arms were working together with the medical bureaucracy to gaslight people for the sake of imposing control over them. It's clear the lockdowns were a terrible idea, and that their entire implementation was set up in a way where no one would ever take accountability for its folly. It's clear that medical science was ignored in favor of gaslighting so that these vaccines could be released under an Emergency Use Authorization. It's clear the legal system was being abused, small businesses were being discriminated against in favor of gigantism, and that political dissent was shouted down even louder than before despite being more reasonable than it ever had been to have an actual public discussion. It was clear from the beginning of the lockdowns that shutting down the economy had consequences, yet no one on the establishment media channels were willing to acknowledge its economic tradeoffs. The economy supports lives, yet this isn't taught in any medical schools. Nor is data analysis, nor is the history of vaccines. They instead teach future doctors about gender pronouns and insist that it's of life-saving necessity to interact with young children in this insidious manner. People were denied life-saving surgery for refusing to take part in an experimental treatment. The oath to *do no harm* was removed from the halls of medical establishments. There was zero acknowledgement of the impact of these terrible ideas on the young, who now have an even larger burden of government debt to shoulder alongside many societal problems of their own. International players were working conspiratorially and have offered no apology, and they will never do so because they fear the consequences of what they've done. It's exposed them to be a political class of narcissists, who are unable to admit any fault of their own and are unable to take responsibility for their childish actions. They fear the consequences because they understood the nature of what they'd done from the very beginning. The nature of this establishment cult has become more apparent to people around the world and within the US. They're not able to use the judicial system to block our Presidential candidates like they can in other countries, because freedom doesn't produce great results by coincidence, and this is what people realized.

It's the transformative process of the unknown becoming the known that we rely on in order to be an effective collective. Someone who can't do this has trouble accepting their ignorance, which is problematic for others. The invitation of Jesus is that which yearns for cooperation with the uncooperative. Those uncooperative dangers, no matter how intelligent, pose a bigger risk than any natural disaster. Which is why animism eventually anthropomorphized.

The new societal paradigm of ignorance is the reduction step of Williston's law taking place across the population, where they shed off old lies and better direct their future modelings towards areas of more sensible ignorance. The resulting big picture becomes clearer than it ever has been, and this is the reward of both our nation-wide internal order optimization as well as the freedom that we grant ourselves. It allows us to partake in our own transformative processes. A bureaucratic dictatorship, like the EU, will be unable to transform themselves and will devolve into a civil war as their populace is unable to vote for their desired candidates. These dictators have never accepted transformation as a form of societal improvement, they believe civilization can be *designed* from the top-down, so the new societal paradigm of ignorance will never be visible to them and that itself will become increasingly visible to everyone else. They will forever believe they still live in the old world where they've comfortably come to rest their denial of ignorance upon, and this will become a more and more deranged denial of reality until war eventually breaks out. Ignorance is not something that permanently rests, it's an evolving creature, you need to free it in order to receive its benefit. Freedom is not effective by chance, your own ignorance would teach you this because entropy is not just a concept, it's a mechanism.

If you're not free to be ignorant, knowledge becomes a mechanism for betrayal. Cults are byproducts of history in the same way that viruses and pathogens are the byproduct of the reaction of life. A cult is that which limits not knowledge but ignorance, it's used in order to prevent people from questioning their own ignorance. This is typically done socially and we've incorporated it into our politics, a refusal to allow people to question their own ignorance is downstream of political correctness. Various left-wing political parties across the world tend to display mass-agreement with each other, but the internal workings of these parties are obviously such that a centralized decision-making process decides what the party's opinions are. Their members then go on to parrot those talking points, and this display of widespread agreement opens the door for cult-like behavior all the same because it comes off as a refusal to allow anyone to disagree. Though their problem isn't centralization, it's a lack of competition in decision-making. Dictations will never be more powerful than the results produced by the freedom to compete because dictations deny people the right to their own ignorance.

Many people left the cult-side of our civilization because of the events of Covid. To match the metaphor to its utility, the birth of a new societal paradigm of ignorance is that which breaks people out of a cult. The shedding of ignorance has a special cult-destroying power, as the lies that uphold it become inherently self-destructive where they're unable to competitively model time. Surely there's a cyclic event here? One of these events leapfrogs the other and spurs growth. A cult, realistically, is a paradigm of ignorance in itself. But so is a religion, it's the collective knowledge that's been grown throughout generations from both wisdom and mistakes.

What are political parties if not practical implementations of age-old religious strategies that have become deeply ingrained as basic human instincts from the merits of their own success? The development of politics and religion are intertwined, they're not independent of one another. It's like human society evolved to always hedge along stratified counterbalancing perspectives for the sake of maintaining different aspects of civilization. No different than our academic institutions, these political paradigms inevitably hail from religious beginnings, as the structure of our beliefs reflect the function of our lives. With society being under a constant inundation of truth, more than any single person could ever manage alone, civilization at large becomes a tool that manages truth in a distributed and stratified manner. The political realm is where the brunt of this difference in perspective becomes most noticeable. In understanding truth, we form religious systems, but in confronting the truth of others, we form political systems. Humanity is no less able to avoid religion than it's able to avoid politics.

What does freedom of religion mean if you can't free yourself from religion? Do you have freedom within religion? To not have freedom within a religion would be to be in a cult. To not be able to free yourself from a religion is to be a cultist.

You might then suggest that people who refuse to grow, who refuse to learn from their mistakes, their ignorance, or refuse to learn in general would likely then be in a cult. If so many people are like this, it might be easier to become a cult than most might formally believe. It seems there's always some way for any group to accidentally, negligently, become a cult.

Religion consists of solutions to problems that were solved earlier than thousands of years ago. Yet compared to most other things solved thousands of years ago, which have largely become common sense across the globe, religion is something that naturally becomes misunderstood over time. It's tricky to support something that doesn't entirely make sense. It's also natural that trust is lost in a corrupted social hierarchy, as they all eventually become. People who despise the dogma of religion, once it's become corrupted, then counteract those beliefs and the end result is two different ideas pushing against each other to then form the next layer of religious competition. People need not have problems with religion in general, just specific groups that fail to respect the model of interactions. Allowing a competitive landscape of child-rearing through the institutions of religion in the US would allow for these hierarchies to naturally correct themselves, and would probably be the most notable instance in history of not just freedom but fluidity between religions being possible. Allowing greater competition of philosophy, and competition of child-rearing across our political and cultural landscape would provide immeasurable value to the US as a whole.

The best artists want control of their own art. They don't want to be owned by some machine, label, or brand. The basis of intelligence is above all else an art. Raising children to transform through their own art form is also an art form, one that's locked up in regulations and red tape. But this tape is in violation of our First Amendment rights. America was supposed to be a country of freedom, not cultural enslavement. Every stage of education has clear religious significance, from the instillation of values and beliefs, to their transformation by maturation, to the cutting edge of academic pioneering and the religious disagreements that come from our lack of understanding the universe. These all inhabit inherently religious territory.

Where could our new societal paradigm of ignorance take us? We could forge new social classes. People used to be, among other things, warriors, priests, and merchants. Realistically, we should be able to raise children to be all three simultaneously through a proper upbringing. Like each one is representative of a single leg on a crustacean rather than three different organisms. Our professions themselves can be compressed and distributed to more people in more efficient ways. The singular and uniform paradigm of *college majors* can be replaced by societal classes of people who hold many talents rather than just one.

People having the freedom to choose their child's school will always be a good thing, as it's an added avenue of freedom. If these next couple generations turn out the same as the baby boomers, in not having enough children to replace themselves, then we'll only be damning them all the same. This is the most important time to raise children who themselves care about raising children.

The downfall of dogma is that dogma is contradictory to the nature of reality. So building an evolving dogma is wiser. Though even that will need an update at some point. The task is to make an inherently evolvable framework that acts as the basis of both selection and incentives. But it's not like civilization has never evolved before, is there an existing mechanism for such a thing? It's the resurrection all over again, but it might not be entirely what you'd expect.

On one bound, a cult is a religion whose modeling of entropy fails to reflect reality. On the other bound, a cult is that which doesn't allow its members to question their own ignorance. Yet this failure to reflect reality becomes a lesson for everyone else, it's a place for the broken compass to take root. It's the very purpose of a cult, to become the footing for transformation itself. Their foothold being the place where we hedge our bets. Those who model the unknown using the known form cults. Those who model the known using the unknown then question the basis for these cults, and through that ignorance they grow to provide even more to those around them. Civilization can't operate without cults, it seems to have specifically been formed because of them. Then we would find more benefit in making a civilization that allows for the evolution and competition thereof, so our footing may continually improve. This very process is no different than the co-evolutionary development of individuals and collectives, and we do have the woke to thank for this understanding.

Increasing societal entropy is the process of widening the scope of liberalism, as a part of the evolutionary pulse. Like a chemical reaction where heat is introduced as a catalyst. Without the woke taking everything to its logical extreme, no one would have ever gotten fed up with a fundamentally bad system. Widening this scope is the same thing that happens to most people throughout their lives, especially when young, and for the same reasons. People use their existing behavior as a foothold to branch out into more developed forms of that same behavior, experimentally. This process then tightens in scope to complete an internal order optimization. It's an evolutionary dance between two co-adapting parties. It's what scales to form the basis for the new societal paradigm of ignorance, it's how we ever grow in the first place. It's *why* a new societal paradigm of ignorance is just about the only thing that breaks people out of cults at such a large scale, because the purpose of the cult that was used as a foothold has already been achieved.

Stability and fragmentation are the basis for growth because they're the basis for transformation, growth is inevitably downstream of either. The universities seem to produce people who constantly think along the lines of some oppressor and oppressed framework, which many have pointed out is a somewhat strange mindset. This is no different than declaring that certain forms of suffering are the *one true* form of suffering, it's just another religious statement. Yet this may be an idea parallel to the concepts of stability and fragmentation. If they could adjust this hyperfixation, which definitely has a purpose, to either derivatives and integrals, centralization and decentralization, or stability and fragmentation, then we as a society may reap a lot of benefits from this transformation. It would be a transformation towards the nature of transformation itself. Through the humility of accepting such a change would come a spawning of complexity that would broaden their horizons significantly, and would make for much better footing for the next stage of transformations.

There's two ways to view Jesus like there's two ways to view anything in life, and it's written into the story. The Son of Man is a title used by Jesus to address himself, and it's him referring to himself as the ignorance of others. The Son of God is a title used by others to refer to Jesus, where they refer to him as what they believe he brings to their life, miracles. Throughout the Gospels there's the idea that Jesus *performs* miracles, but it's actually a reference to people's ignorance enlightening them to the possibilities of the world. The miracles that Jesus *performed* were feats of human ignorance that enlightened people of their abilities to push beyond the bounds of human knowledge. Jesus curing the lepers was a prediction that leprosy was curable, and it was true. This dual reference as the Son of Man and the Son of God is actually an indicator that what people believed were miracles were actually just possibilities, the real miracle was yet to be seen. When Jesus affirms himself in court as the Son of God, it's prior to his death and resurrection. In doing so, he predicts what he would insist is the *actual* miracle, it's the grand spawning of complexity known as a new societal paradigm of ignorance. What's more miraculous than gaining socioevolutionary ground in this game of life we find ourselves in? A miracle is what helps more people survive in a more efficient way for longer and better than anything else ever has, and what irony that the miracle of our modern day showed us where integrity within our medical system was susceptible to tyranny. Metaphorically, the miracle of Jesus was one that teaches others how to perform their own miracles, it's to seek and question one's own ignorance. The buildup to the metaphor was that which held the greatest possible amount of irony, that the Son of God would be crucified by man for their sins. The metaphor of this miracle itself is a model of a pre-technological occurrence of the broken compass, it's a brilliant metaphor. One that undoubtedly couldn't be noticed by people who hadn't experienced the same style of societal reckoning as we currently are for the events of Covid. Whether people want to argue over whether Jesus was a real person, or whether he was really raised from the dead or not, is all lost to time. But what I can definitively infer is there must have been some sort of miracle witnessed in order to embed this metaphor within the stories that were passed on to become the Gospels. There's no other way to have understood this so thoroughly. All miracles lie at the end of our own ignorance.

A vampire is something that intends to prevent others from properly modeling it, as it hides its identity and has no reflection, but even this in some instances is also a part of the hedged bet. Which is why Jesus is linked to ignorance and why cult-breaking power is represented through his resurrection. It's a shift in the eyeball of humanity, a change in where their collective observations are directed. Every time you model reality in ways you never believed possible, your eyes open into a new world. You see the same universe that we've all always inhabited, but you can't go back to pretending what you saw isn't real, you can't unsee the vampire's lack of reflection. The challenge of exposing the vampire eventually yields an improvement to the core human function, sunlight kills them. It's a fundamental stride made in modeling the universe.

Boundaries of convergence are, metaphorically, the same thing as the walls of the Tower of Babel as it's built. Any and all boundaries of convergence converge around God. The metaphor of the death and resurrection of the Son of God represents the group's evolution and growth towards that of the Father, the Father being the distant ideal of the future we approach. This act of societal growth being representative of the large, or largest ever feat of evolutionary growth used to arrive at new boundaries of convergence for the concept of God means that our own civilizational advancement is the purpose for our lives. The concept of transcendence along the axis of time ends up being the same metaphor used in the Christian texts, a miracle.

Like the people who represent them, these boundaries are moving concepts. They seem to walk in a manner that represents their movements up the tower as it's built. Being completely submerged in lies and being eternally grounded are two sides of reality we straddle to balance the interpretation of everything we see around us. Either side of the societal hedged bet moving further in either direction isn't simply done for the sake of extremism, it's for the sake of an improved estimation of the center value that's representative of God.

The act of believing in God would seem to have an orienting function to it. Similar to how geese have a magnetic compass in their heads, telling them which way is true north. Humans and their intelligence didn't evolve to navigate the sky, they instead evolved to navigate ideas and information, the tool for this is morality. As we see in the modern day, you can navigate all sorts of information in any way possible, as it's a completely flexible concept with no limitations or boundaries, a pure art form. We are likely much more adapted to the nature of the universe than we even realize.

One's own interpretation of morality might be relative, but morality itself is neither relative nor arbitrary. The principles we've found and the principles we live our lives by are genuine guiding forces. These were solutions to the answers of consciousness. We're conscious *because* of our ability to follow them. People who stray from morality tend to not be in their right mind. Good actions make better futures and this is dependent on the content of your character, not your intelligence. These are the choices you make *despite* your consciousness, not because of it. Morality is useful in finding optimal solutions in life, and that's despite not always knowing what your problems are. It can yield better outcomes, and better long-term results for just about anything. It's literally like magic or witchcraft, and it's universally available to anyone with a brain. Morality offers shortcuts through the information-dense understandings granted through the model of interactions. In attempting to just be fair to others, by following morality, you tend to arrive at all the most intelligent solutions to any set of problems. Fair treaties, trade deals, business models, and auction formats are all celebrated for the same reasons.

Some people have linked intelligence to specific genetic traits, but I disagree with the utility of intelligence holding hegemonic primacy to human function. These relationships fall into the insufferably bad correlations of social sciences, typically nothing higher than an R^2 of 0.3, which is to say it's basically non-existent. These measurements also require using a proxy for intelligence, which is entirely questionable. But that's not to say it isn't inheritable, it clearly is to some degree. Some people are obviously more intelligent than others, we're not born equal, it's fair to assume some level of genetic inheritance exists. But does being born more intelligent always help someone? Being immoral can be worse for you than being unintelligent, and likewise morality alone can also take you further than intelligence. Morality holding primacy to intelligence is why group cooperation acts as both a limiter and catalyst for individual abilities. It's incredibly difficult to be fair to others in the best ways possible, but if you walk the hardest path then you reap the most reward. People who treat themselves more fairly form groups with more efficient selection paradigms, their morality becomes the selection paradigm that allows the best individuals to create even better ones. Over time, everyone would benefit from the improved genetic pool. True morality is a view that the existence of life is a great thing, nihilism is what pretends to be morality while taking the shape of a psychological weapon to convince people they're evil in order to inspire self-hatred.

You can't ignore the information you have when that information leads towards responsibility, that's immoral and it creates flaws. It's your responsibility to acknowledge the foremost of you and your civilization's abilities. We model our environment, and that environment is information, to ignore truth would make you inept in every area your negligence touches. From this modeling, we attempt to understand information to formalize truth. That modeling is the formation of an epibolic recursion of the interactions that originally created the model of interactions. Morality is a mental tool that allows you to model the most accurate representation of absolute truth that the billions of years of our evolution has achieved without having a formal understanding of it. The opposite of the benefit of embracing morality would be when a lie sneaks into your civilization, one that disrupts the core of your civilization, where hundreds, or even thousands of years of civilizational development was built on top of the truth it distorts, only for this brick from the tower to be removed despite it being in its correct place. Such an event would leave a terrible impact from the effects of relaxed selection that follow, affecting the survival of everyone who's left at the mercy of this misunderstanding. Just as embracing something that's fundamentally incorrect, even out of hopeful optimism, even despite any actual awareness of its error, would push you to become a worse model of your environment, morality is a way of embracing truths you're unaware of. The greatest fulfillment of morality becomes the embracing of formal truths that no one has yet grasped, things that our evolution was built atop of, yet our intellect has yet to understand.

Likewise, if your civilization isn't properly educating your children about how the world works, or using made up versions of history to indoctrinate children into radical political causes, then your civilization will fall. Morality is the line you draw between yourself and what you perceive as evil, it's what you choose to avoid when considering your actions, so it can only be perceived as relative when considering other people. But morality itself is never relative, there's a best possible answer, and you have to find it. No one can hate themselves, humans, or their own race, and be moral. Morality is a manner of knowing how to use one's own intelligence, and if anyone perceives that act itself to be immoral due to their own existence being immoral, then they've trapped themselves inside the relative interpretation of their own understanding of evil. They would make themselves into a moral contradiction. If there are individuals at a school pushing young children towards this mindset, they would be enacting a form of malicious child abuse.

The various religious texts of human antiquity found the most success in embedding lessons on morality through their metaphors, as moral decisions are the easiest metaphors to interpret. Morality and intelligence are the two dimensions of non-technological human development in the approach towards God. As each one progresses individually, there comes a need for an increase in the other in order to compensate for shortcomings, and this creates an endless cycle for the growth of either. Intelligence breaks new ground on what's possible, and morality comes to organize where it goes wrong. Where morality becomes overbearing, people come to disagree with its restraints and open an age of enlightenment. So in assuming intelligence to be the only relevant factor of schooling, we've come to fail ourselves morally, which has resulted in a non-existent birth rate because intelligence doesn't inspire people to keep existing. Morality, on the other hand, is what grants people the ability to maintain their reason for existence, because they see life as being something that's inevitably beneficial. Any living creature that sees life as evil isn't moral and stops procreating like a cell that commits apoptosis, it's a natural reaction for those lacking in morality to fail this test of existence.

But morality also has unique properties, morality is a luxury when survival isn't guaranteed. When there isn't an information-dense environment to extract wisdom from, the choices are much simpler, and usually due to an impending danger. Wisdom is something to be passed on, to not do so results in a situation analogous to borrowing money from our grandchildren in order to pay the absurd debts our governments accrue. It's been under-inherited to the point where young people in the future won't have any left if they're willing to accept the difficult decisions required to fix and maintain the countries they inherit. We're leaving them with no choices other than the hardest ones, we must fix our shortcomings in education and governance *before* things go catastrophically wrong.

Not the elderly, not the disabled, not the poor matter more than the children and those who want to have them. Supporting the retirement and survival of people who aren't supporting the young shouldn't be our priority. It's the fault of previous generations who've failed to have enough children that we now find ourselves in this predicament. If supporting those who have forced us to sacrifice the young requires that we make our country unsafe, our streets unwalkable, our children unfavored, then we can't continue to support them. Any interests that oppose the interests of the young oppose the interests of the nation.

There's no retiree more important than a child, there's no disabled person more vulnerable than a child, and there's no immigrant more necessary than a child's wellbeing. Those that have come to deprioritize children have deserted their own nation. These are not your fellow countrymen, these are those who vampirize them. It's important we save these generations, billions of years of development went into their making, it would be a waste to lose them. If there's nothing more difficult to attain, then there's nothing more valuable to uphold.

Making life too easy results in a behavior that functions like relaxed selection, and you'll lose the ability to pass this test without practicing morality. The two must go hand in hand, if you truly feel you're lacking in intelligence then seek morality. In basic terms, morality is *how to use your intelligence*. To seek it is to seek how to be fair. The only proper avenue towards this starts by recognizing life is a great existence, morality can't start with nihilism if it's to be morality at all.

The act of getting society to come to a point of collective empirical beliefs was not a challenge in spite of religion, it was a challenge of religion in general. It was the religious institutions that needed a way of embracing and incorporating both empirical evidence as well as the wisdom of the ages into a single framework. The socioevolutionary hedged bet acts as a way of navigating the alignment of society's inner workings towards truthful ideas and successful transformations, and it was both religion and empiricism that were born from such endeavors.

The transformations of complexity we undergo as individuals are mirrored by the same happening societally, and it seems many of these workings are beyond our control. We change and adapt without even realizing it, like we're a part of some distributed calculation, a modeling of entropy, as if we lived inside a textbook from the Austrian school of economics. Our distributed nature is no different than the infinitely abundant and fragmented axes of time that surround us, as we're literally *made* of them. Furthermore, it seems like the orientation towards moral north, the belief in God, can slip in and out of generations whenever it's advantageous for development as yet another generational reversion. Like generations born in certain time periods become so hyper-derivative, as the tasks they're left to solve are of the same nature, that history decides to take the next step with its other political leg to shift back towards proper integration of these ideas into the main belief system whenever the appropriate derivatives are found.

As the problem of dealing with integrals are not the same as dealing with derivatives. To contribute to a boom while it happens requires a left-brain mindset, as the addition of small advantageous discoveries into a complex and booming system would act to fuel the development of that very system. Whereas to survive its collapse necessitates the right-brain to predict and understand the nature of the failings that need to be navigated for survival. The difficulty of integrals is in solving them, and it can be terrible to solve the wrong ones. The difficulty with derivatives isn't in solving for them, it's finding them in the first place. It's in realizing they even exist at all.

As the political pendulum shifts towards the right, at least I'm presuming it will in the coming years, there will be a shift in incorporating both science and religion into the same body. We've come upon a time period in which these ideas will have more utility than they've had in the past because of how history is developing itself. Or rather, it's because of how humans are developing themselves from their modeling of entropy. The development of the world will likely not stagnate, but will undergo some rebuilding steps in order to insert new base layers of religion into the upbringing of children. It must.

This moral north we navigate ourselves by is not some niche of our psyche that evolved by chance. The concept of God and the belief thereof is of evolutionary significance to the functioning of the brain and civilization, rather than just being some social tradition that aided in survival, which to some may now seem esoteric. Time will show that this so-called *atheism*, of which there's actually none, is much more strange. Despite that, atheism still played a role in the transforming of society into what it has and will become, it's the switching of the existing function of this moral North Star to things other than God. The moral north being chosen by these groups who claim to be atheistic is neither by their choice nor their control. The purpose of which has enabled society to better be able to orient itself towards God at all, as even God is rightfully as much of a mystery to us as the many complexities we find ourselves surrounded by. Beliefs themselves are never-ending dialogues, likewise the orientation towards God is like a socio-algorithmic estimation of the center, which is why it's society's modeling of entropy that guides us back towards it. Perhaps this time with more accuracy than ever before. It's almost like we move away from our nature in order to learn more about it, to become an outside observer to have a better view. It's so inherent to us that we can't help but find it again every time we try to deny it. As we've not only evolved to orient ourselves towards it, we've evolved to find better ways of doing so. Every time history moves away from it, it's not that we simply move further away, it's that we move away in a more specific manner. The specificity of disbelief later transforms into a specificity of belief, similar to how the right builds foundation upon the holes dug by the left. These are the basis for the patterns of history, as described by Iain McGilchrist, where either left- or right-brain behavior dominated the societal landscape. This modeling of entropy would not be as comprehensive without the people who dared to try something different, despite whether it turned out to be correct in our current age or not. Like the walls of the Tower of Babel, the convergence on the concept of God becomes thinner and thinner as we grow ourselves into more advanced forms. As it's this center we estimate, it would mean this modeling of entropy is a measuring device which sorts its own priorities. Which offers the same functionality for why we can use the woke themselves as a measurement of our own failings in order to understand what institutions have religious infringements in our existing infrastructure.

But this is speaking from the perspective of solving integrals. Meaning it would be necessary to translate to those facing the complete opposite direction. This moral north may be different for those focused on finding derivatives. Which is why a better true north for those who have accepted the oppressor and oppressed framework would be that of stability and fragmentation, or one of its parallels.

Personal responsibility is the best paradigm to raise children under as it's meant to not allow them to blame things on their own ignorance. Meaning, they instead need to question it. The religious leaders who blamed Jesus were blaming their own ignorance, they were immature enough to be derelict. Under the existing liability culture of the US, this aspect of psychosocial development is going horribly wrong, and it's because there's often times someone there to blame should something not go as expected with a child. Instructions are always given to children, they're told what to do in some scenario rather than figuring it out for themselves. But this instills the wrong lessons, it enables every bad habit in those who believe it's fine to blame their own shortcomings on others, and that it's fine to simply follow instructions, or even orders, despite not actually understanding the basis of either. Children need to be responsible for their own ignorance at the very least because people in general need to do the same, and that includes the shortcomings of not knowing their own cultural history.

In order to progress to true adulthood at all, one must take responsibility for both their actions and ignorance. It's best to have children practice who they need to be as soon as possible, rather than enabling them to become the wrong person based on some adult's preconception that the behavior of a child has no significance simply because they're a child. There are no instructions in the real world. You don't simply follow the directions of others the same way every child must do so within a Marxist school system. The only way to survive and thrive is to carve out your own path, and that comes by continually questioning what it is that you're not aware of. Embracing ignorance is a way of squeezing value out of everything you don't understand through the art of asking questions, as you'll find the greatest amount of value in your own ignorance.

Within every human language are concepts divided into words which are ascribed some meaning. Speaking for the only language I know, there's a misascribed meaning to the words gift and curse. What I mean is, that there's universal axioms behind the meaning ascribed to words. Their meaning is something that's an inherent aspect of the principles of the universe itself. Words have meaning and that meaning isn't a human construct. Just as the structures of our proteins are solutions to specific problems in maintaining life itself, our words are no different in that they represent the connective tissue of the logic and reason we're immersed in. Any belief otherwise is due to the incomprehensible nature of such chaotic landscapes. Just as with emotions and morality, these are no different in nature to the creative puzzles that mathematicians make for themselves and continually aspire to solve. Every unique puzzle has a unique answer. Some may have multiple ways to arrive at answers, but the answers tend to have some manner of a reproducible nature. To remake the same puzzle only leads you to that same answer, and this makes for an axiom of the universe itself when the answers to these puzzles manifest as modes of interaction. What I think has been misascribed is that these two terms are supposedly different at all. I think a gift is a curse, period. There's no difference in these meanings. Yet we have two words where we've split a meaning in half. This misascribed language has introduced misascribed meaning in the heads of people who then don't know any better. Which is ironic, because that extra bifurcation that split the meaning behind this concept in half was meant to explain a relative good and bad happenstance upon oneself. That gift of bifurcation was a curse that brought about the obfuscation of this meaning.

Giving to others isn't always as compassionate as one might assume. You can rob someone of their own potential by solving too many problems for them. It's disruptive to their growth, and will undoubtedly impact their future if they don't learn to stand on their own two feet. To many, compassion is something they offer to others from a distance. But if you can't offer it to them personally, and become a part of their life that supports them, then what you've offered isn't true compassion. To mix desire and belief is to believe what you want to be true. It's the foregoing of ignorance for entitlement, as this is making beliefs rather than discovering them. If you're wrong you should want to know you're wrong, even worse would be to deny the need to admit being wrong at all.

Whether or not you believe in some climate or AI Armageddon is just your religion. How people are allowed to interpret the unknown factors of their lives and whether we're on a roller coaster that's out of control, or whether we actually have fairly decent control mechanisms built-in, possibly even because of such beliefs, is a matter of religion. There's been plenty of scientific work done to show that there's no climate emergency, and I believe there's good reason to be optimistic. Careful, yet optimistic. Optimistic enough to spur our own growth without worrying about the environment, the size of our population, or the supposed impact we're having as these are all problems that we can handle. Anyone trying to convince you of the opposite are simply doing so for their own corporate or political interests. Likewise, there's widespread censorship within the universities over historical narratives, and topics concerning gender or transgender issues. The life-destroying rituals brought against individuals who whistleblow this behavior have been religiously persecuted with what may as well be blasphemy, this same behavior being so uniform across so many institutions in the US means we need more variation in our educational landscape. A religion worthy of its populace will act like sunlight on the ocean, basically the cause for the start of life. A recipe for major growth. Which is the purpose of religion itself. To have a religion that doesn't spur growth just means to fail one's ability to survive into the future, which is a failed religion, as the purpose of religion is to grant persistence.

It's surprisingly easy to become a cult. People walk into groups and continue following pre-established dogma for reasons unbeknownst to them. Maintaining social order takes effort and critical thought, so the norms happen to just maintain themselves as that's the path of least resistance for any new members. But it's the hardest paths that are the most rewarding. People are so prone to forgetting these things take dedication in order to maintain and end up thinking that an institution will never go awry. Now here we are in a future with many school systems, some scientific disciplines even, being completely controlled by cults made by political parties.

It's so easy to walk into being a cult, there's so many different ways for it to happen and it's not guaranteed to only happen in one way. To walk into it in many ways is to lose track that you've even become one. Likewise it's equally as easy for a cult that runs a government to become a death cult.

There's a nihilistic lower bound that says that since there's so many ways to become a cult that you can't fight them all off. The best choice being then to simply be a moral cult, to try and trick the system to work in your favor. But this isn't as clever as it might seem. There's no moral cult, but likewise their immorality, under the presumption of innocence, would be an immorality of framework rather than of intention. That's an ideology that one uses in place of the truth, and it positions people into aiming at some specific goal they believe is good. Not understanding that to do good is to actually not do evil, that if you try to do good you'll pave a road to hell with good intentions. Which is why dogma lures people into cult formations, those are Descartes' idiots. The questioning of one's own ignorance is to aim to not be incorrect, it's to avoid such mistakes.

Proper unification isn't the same thing as forced government unification. People have to be freely led there, it has to be something they willingly accept. A one-plan strategy isn't even a hedged bet, it's literally prone to not being well accepted. It's just narcissism at scale, which itself is a cult. A cult is narcissism at scale. A civilization is not purely made up of cults, it's also made up of people who question them. The one-plan strategies are an attempt to cultify civilization, which is really only necessary during times of extreme war. When there's no war to be seen and your civilization is cultifying in this manner, it means the war is being waged against you, because you're suffering the curse of something that offers no gift. It means your political establishment has walked themselves into being a death cult. It's uncanny how many different countries have all been taken over by the same disputes about racism, sexism, homophobia, and so on, it's just not simple to find out because it's all in different languages. If the same tricks of psychological operations seem to work on the populace of every country, then there's undoubtedly as simple of a trick that could have been used to analogously subvert world governments from the inside.

Over the last few hundred years, Europeans have made use of widespread accusations of witchcraft in order to kill people. This same behavior is visible today, and clarifies exactly what was happening in the past. Today, people call you a racist to justify your death. It shouldn't be any surprise that this core European instinct dressed itself in anti-racism and continues to do the same. Likewise, the reciprocating pushback against this force would have been to save people from their own tyrannies. To save people from themselves. Which is what Christianity has accomplished in its best light. Those who've most avidly denied Christ have only come to make for the conditions for his resurrection. The same way the woke religion covers itself in science, the same way insidious racists in the modern day cover themselves in *anti-racism*, the followers of the political establishment cover themselves in revolutionary rhetoric to make it seem like they're the ones being persecuted, which is why it becomes hard for them to see their own reflection. These are all examples of the psychological states of these groups maintaining themselves far away from equilibrium, like encapsulating lies inside of truth the same way disorder is encapsulated by order, all the same as a cell and its metabolism, and they're forming a bubble that will pop to form a new societal paradigm of ignorance once they're willing to admit their mistakes.

Maybe you're of the mindset to criticize what's written in this book. That I don't go into enough detail about economics, entropy, schooling, or the structures of the brain. Maybe you think too much of what I say is absolutist, dramatic, or doesn't accurately represent every niche of information perfectly, maybe you think the premise of this book is much too broad. That there's countless details missing, citations I didn't include, encyclopedias worth of history and knowledge that I've completely forgone, and that I certainly don't have enough equations to back up what I'm talking about. Yet that's the point. This book is meant to represent the art of the right-brain. The big picture. The religious view that can be held independent of the fine details.

Fine details do have their importance, as well as their place in the big picture. Across time any given big picture sees a sure but steady rise and fall. It'll be formed then it'll be replaced once small details don't add up, just like what's happened to most cultures, religions, and beliefs over time. The explicit details about a cell receptor in the liver perhaps won't change too much over the course of thousands of years, and maybe that's because it plays such a specific role amongst an ocean of highly specific functionality. This specific detail may mean death to anyone born without it working properly, and if so many fine details are absolutely necessary for the big picture to function then they're the more conservative elements of where we find ourselves despite them being so vastly complex and poorly understood. Regardless of the extreme value in understanding their function, perhaps we can ignore it where it's not entirely needed. The fact that we can understand basic bodily functionality independent of every minuscule and intricate piece of any biological puzzle is a testament to the modularity of perception itself matching the baseline circumstances of our reality, we don't need to understand cell receptors to know that if your body loses its blood you'll die. We need not give such intense consideration to every minor exception on the planet. We gain more value from being fair to the large non-exceptioned majority. Any precedent of the prioritization of exceptions would only lead to a tyranny thereof.

Some things can't be understood through an infinite array of fine-grained details, which is unfortunately the only thing young children predominantly learn through tests and homework. It's why there can never be a Millennium Prize for the endeavors of religion, these prizes are set up to incentivize the solving of some of the most confounding left-brain problems ever discovered. The nature of the right-brain means it will never be able to state its problems prior to finding a solution, because it's designed to question what it specifically *can't possibly know*. Children are never allowed to truly think for themselves and now we have entire nations filled with people who are largely illiterate when it comes to leveraging their own ignorance. The formation of an understanding of the connection between the big and small picture of biological organisms, the laws of physics, or anything else we perceive can only come through the rise and fall of ideas. Trial and error. Mistakes, failure, and perhaps someday success. That's the nature of the crash of populations, whether populations of people, populations of ideas, or anything in between. It's the merging of the understanding of the unknown with the known. The entropic transformation that further changes culture to optimize brain structures to form a society that then deciphers the next layer of clues to achieve the next required transformation. So in this book ignoring so many small details, there's actually clear-cut success in that many of the ideas here have never been explained through such a light touch prior. It highlights the significance of the multitude of small details that were able to be stacked upon each other to form this big picture capable of ignoring them all in the first place.

9.6 Fractalized Incentives

The convenience of dogma eventually betrays its own purpose, and that's typically despite having started off as something valuable. Following dogma is a sure sign of decline in an age where that dogma no longer works. Facing uncertainty and finding what direction to take their lives is a necessity for the development of young children that's severely underserved in the existing educational paradigm, this failure is visible in the political dispositions of those who operate the educational institutions. The most valuable educational enterprise in the history of the world was turned into a Ponzi scheme that preyed on students who didn't seem to recognize the trap they were falling into. The high school system failed people to the degree where the college system was able to scam them. Which is to say, they weren't well-educated. With young people struggling more than ever, it couldn't be more obvious where the failings are coming from. The school system has already crashed, it needs to fragment for the sake of our own survival.

Expanded existential crises are needed in order for civilizations to make philosophical and technological advancements. They're signals that demand such things. It's an indication that our civilization is able to achieve the next layer of distributed calculations amongst ourselves, because this process was started long before we ever existed, and will likely never end. Williston's law, the broken compass, and internal order optimizations all represent the same process explained in different contexts, they act upon these signals to bring about change. Nihilistic first steps, like the various forms of communism that continually pop up, are simple and uniform, much like the addition step of Williston's law, they're the default cult stages used to slingshot society into modes of civilizational development like capitalism. Likewise, not being incorrect, and doing no evil, are spawnings of complexity, which are analogous to the effects of a punctuated equilibrium, which are analogous to incentives for positive selection being brought about through negative selection. Freedom acts as a highway of communication, which is the framework intelligence is built upon. It's a core evolutionary mechanism that always eventually spawns complexity in all the right places, then sorts its pieces like some grand measuring device.

Freedom itself is simultaneously an ideal that can never be achieved, yet is also the mechanism that yields the exponential rewards we reap whenever it's well implemented. Freedom is what you move towards in order to achieve better communication and fairness. The accumulation of exponential rewards atop themselves achieves a surplus of complexity that allows for further population growth. Accumulations from multiple forms of exponential growth compound to be greater than what's intuitively believable prior to achieving such success, creating a new environment that needs to be modeled atop of old lessons. Which is a description of the process of transcendence, it achieves results that would otherwise be seen as unimaginable. Only an extremely oversimplified concept of growth would be limited by finite resources, growth itself is an evolving framework because growth itself is capable of growing. To those without an eye on the big picture, they wouldn't understand this process. It's what one gains by maturing past modeling the unknown via the known towards modeling the known via the unknown, it transforms a lot of small factors into a single coherent concept, a *model*. Modeling the known via the unknown is the process of continually questioning the integrity of every known factor available, as well as their interactions. Instead of resting on the reliability of the known, it's to question the validity of every claim. It's a questioning of one's own ignorance. The concept of infinite growth with finite resources typically seems unimaginable to people incapable of questioning their own ignorance. Being so hyper-derivative, separated from the big picture, their state of mind has no intellectual representation of transformation itself, because ignorance is the road to transformation. Freedom enables transformations, and the questioning of ignorance will guide you towards it. Every life form on the planet has always had the freedom to continue growing, those who lost the ability died out. Given that the universe is infinite, as is the time that it exists within, and seeing as the potential for transformation is infinite, and the rewards for transformation accumulate exponentially, then the possibility for growth is very likely more infinite than the universe itself. The universe around us is self-transforming, but is relatively passive compared to our own abilities to do so. Yet we don't exist independent of the universe, nor is the universe independent of us. We are transformations of transformation, we are a transcending of infinity of transcending of infinities. Infinite growth is not only possible, it can lead us towards modes of existence more impressive than the universe itself.

The most notable work of Georg Cantor was in showing that mathematically, some infinities are larger than others[230]. But I believe this is up to interpretation. Different number sets aren't necessarily larger or smaller, because there's always another perspective to view things from. What Cantor would regard as a larger infinity may as well simply be a more fragmented whole. In place of directly comparing them as quantities, you could say the set of all real numbers is more fragmented than the set of all integers. Because in attempting to count either one, such a count would truly go on forever. Neither will actually *stop* before the other. Which was the observation originally made by Galileo when confronting the concept of infinity[231], which in itself isn't incorrect. Fragmentation may serve to function as a measurement of complexity, much like what we see in our own bodies that seem to consist of near infinite pieces, and in a multitude of different ways. Viewing them as comparable quantities isn't necessarily incorrect either, it can definitely be viewed through that lens. But insisting on having just one description of anything seems to always forsake the big picture for small details, as there's always two sides to any coin. Perspective is such an important part of life, yet the nature of monolithic definitions doesn't respect this in purposefully characterizing everything to be so singular and certain. To have no built-in concept of

---

230. Georg Cantor. *On a Property of the Collection of All Real Algebraic Numbers.* Journal für die reine und angewandte Mathematik, 1874

231. Galileo Galilei. *Dialogues Concerning Two New Sciences.* Lodewijk Elzevir, 1638

error, unlike the way that such things would always be noted in rigorous scientific measurements, is to drown yourself in uncertain uncertainty. Even when dealing with something as seemingly predictable as the nature of numbers and counting, rigidity becomes Kipling's *trap for fools*.

For physical objects, like ourselves, having more pieces means having more axes of time. Complexity is an answer to modeling time, and it seems that was the only thing it ever could be. In order to model time, or anything else, one needs to transcend the concept of infinity. But to model anything one would need to somehow first model time. Then what came first, the modeling of infinity or the modeling of time?

Let's explore the concept of randomness to try and answer this. Despite our computers being able to generate random numbers, it's believed in some corners of life that there's no such thing as a random number. The reason being, because there's no such thing as something being truly random. Random is a concept that requires consciousness to ever exist in the first place. There's no such thing as *random movements* or *random occurrences*, these things are just *movements* and *occurrences* in reality. One must perceive them as being somehow unexpected yet not unreasonable in order to label them as being random. Basic causality dictates a linkage of every action to one another, so the concept of randomness seems contradictory to reality itself.

But there are such things as truly random numbers. It just requires a modeling of time, you need a clock in order to achieve them. Which is what most random number generators use. They take advantage of the time of day, the time it takes for some internal component of the random number generator to complete, the time it takes your computer to respond, or some physical process that introduces random variation amongst a myriad of other possibilities to generate numbers that are seemingly random. The fluctuations of minor measurements, of even a pseudo random number generation process, can be used to enable chaotic behavior in ways that ultimately models randomness itself, and leads to a diffusive numeric selection indistinguishable from the processes of nature.

Using an overflowing infinite microcosm-like basis that models itself to model randomness is the answer to true randomness. It's beyond recursion, the layers being directly linked to one another means it's fractalization. The reason this works is because there's a practically infinite number of variable time periods that can be used as fuel, and that's due to the inevitable flaws of the physical states of a computer chip. The linkage of physical flaws to temporal inconsistencies reminds us that time and space are intertwined, rather than separate entities. Seeing as both time and space are not only infinite, but also infinitely intertwined, then what is time *but* infinity? They're the same thing. You might disagree, but we don't actually have any reason to believe they're different. It's a purely human distinction that's been planted in our heads. The modeling of either is the same process. Which then also makes sense as to why things transcend the axis of time as they approach infinite growth.

The concept of infinity, rather than being representative of a conceptual quantity, is more like the advent of transformation. It's the point in which information folds in on itself to create some metalayer derivative or integral. That's even the only way to understand the nature of infinity. It's a transcendence of the counting system. Which is why infinity is what emerges when you divide by smaller and smaller decimals. As you approach a division by zero you don't get larger quantities, you get a deeper fragmentation because that's what it means to be *divided* by something. If a counting system collapses in on itself, it undergoes the transformation of that fragmentation. Which is why we see the concept of infinity emerging from the never-ending nature of numbers, because this kind of transformation is an integral to counting itself, just as it's an integral to every other part of life.

Numbers have a metaquality of being a natural measurement of any arbitrary value that they already represent. So when numbers naturally measure themselves, as a self-representing system, and seeing as any sequence of numbers can automatically be counted by that same system, it allows the very transformation towards infinity to be tracked in a precise technical manner. This process of transformation comes to represent itself numerically through the Fundamental Theorem of Calculus, because these two concepts have the same origins.

This idea of fractalized randomness seems to produce enough variation to be appropriately deemed random, but does that actually mean there's such a thing as true randomness? The physical world should operate through pure causal determinism, otherwise we're abandoning Newton's most basic assumptions. You may as well be saying that life can emerge spontaneously from inorganic matter just to disagree. Every single action most definitely has a completely definable set of parameters that explains its outcome. It's commonly believed that factors of quantum mechanics are truly random, but they *must* at some level be deterministic, just in ways we can't perceive. Processes of nature may seem random due to the difficulty of grasping predictability over chaotic events, such as weather patterns, but every detail of reality must in some way be accounted for. Even coin flips aren't truly random, their circumstances depend on initial conditions, their dimensions, factors of the air, the force applied, and maybe even the engraved patterns of the coin. It's the impracticality of accounting for these layers of causality that allows for the perception of randomness. The stability of any molecule, the half-life of any atom, must always have some chain of events that leads to an explanation for their occurrence. There's undoubtedly some explanation for each and every event, regardless of how these things are often described as semi-random through probability distributions. Chaotic processes heavily depend upon initial conditions for accurate predictions. Small changes to starting conditions, even fractions of decimals, can lead to completely different results. Chaotic systems aren't actually chaotic, chaotic is the description we assign to make sense of the fragility of predicting such things. But if every action has a hypothetically predictable outcome, then are life forms and their behavior just a raw mechanical construct as predictable as the weather?

There's stratifications to even randomness. Life forms aren't working deterministically, we have free will, our responses to our environment aren't as deterministic as a ball bouncing off a wall, so where do organisms fit in between these bounds of determinism and chaos? In the same light that some infinities can either be larger or more fragmented than other infinities, are certain organisms, as metaphysical machines, more or less random than other organisms? Disorder isn't inherently different from random chaos. Rather than thinking of the analogy of randomness within organisms as just being fragmented, it's more like being more *distributed*. The same way that the theories of physics became more advanced as they harnessed a more distributed concept of time within themselves, organisms likely became more advanced as they were better able to distribute greater randomness to their internal workings as a means of pioneering disorderable ground that then became incentivized to be more orderly. Randomness became stochasticity in this very manner, stochasticity basically being a form of contained randomness, either along a unidimensional axis or within the behavior of a model. More intelligent organisms have both greater order and greater disorder than their less capable counterparts. But they walk a finer path, representative of the center they've estimated. They have a greater degree of freedom to their functionality, but also a greater degree of control over the direction their disorder is able to move in. It's a greater ability to deviate, paired with greater control that prevents extreme deviation without reason. Which is yet another explanation of complexity. As a greater force of stochasticity is contained, within an increasingly robust form of order, you end up with more complexity. Much like how descending into the abyss of physical imperfections to fractalize this concept of randomness within itself can provide a sufficiently true source of random variability, highly disordered processes, that appear no different than these random occurrences, can transcend this same ladder in reverse to wield control against its own internal chaos to push back against paradigms of determinism that lead to unfavorable outcomes. In harnessing disorder, complexity becomes able to resist causality through the degrees of freedom it operates under. The stochasticity of biological systems expands towards metaphysical layers beyond any one physically deterministic event, organisms create their own metacausality. That metacausality is consciousness.

Life is the fractalization of disorder within order. Seeing as they're both actually forms of disorder, with one simply being relatively more ordered than the other, this counts as a fractalized concept. Which continues in the form of both of these inside either, perpetually, as order continually becomes an incentive for disorder and vice versa. It's no different than modeling the known via the unknown and unknown via the known, as the terms known and unknown can interlace in this same manner. Even society's control and experimental groups are infinitely co-fractalizing, nothing is purely a control or experiment, and they make even deeper bifurcations within their own groups. A fractalized model is a concept that leverages the irony of an abyss rather than having some observer gaze into it. The leveraging of fractalized insertions of disorder within order creates an engine no different than how wind and temperature differences create a tornado.

Consciousness likely occurs at a threshold beyond the speed of light. Every physical rule in the universe is basically predictable. But when the answer to some physical phenomenon isn't perceivable, strange things seem to happen. The act of consciousness is that which surpasses this speed of light by simply processing the amount of information that should, physically, be impossible to collect through pure brute force in the same amount of time that it took to process it. The reason it's possible is the nature of metaphysical counting, computation. It's a very semantic distinction, but one that likely has technical significance. Brute forcing an answer, at even the speed of light, will always be inferior to a more compressed calculation that achieves the same answer, as this would take less effort, and therefore less energy, meaning that there's an even greater degree of utility contained within a more finite process. In the process of this form of complexity becoming more capable, processes moving slower than the speed of light could outperform a brute force calculation that actually achieves speed-of-light operation limits. It's metaphysically surpassing a threshold of the intrinsic behavior of the universe, and thereby causality. It behaves and performs with more prudence than any of the physical processes it's surrounded by. Based on how it operates outside the speed of light, consciousness is that which should only be perceivable in the same way cells are perceivable through a microscope, understanding their real-time function is different than looking at their outer shells. There's two things that can be said about this, the first is that this is why we can perceive at all. It's why a perception of time is possible, as the metaphysical processes of the brain are able to insulate themselves from the effects of time through achieving the practicality of a paradoxical distance to that which it observes. The second implication is that we can't realistically measure its true functionality in some classical biochemical assay, as we currently have no manner of inserting a computational component into the physicalities of such a process. The only way to measure the physical occurrences of the inner workings of the metaphysical processes of the brain would be to implement a metaphysical counting system able to decipher the signals being made. Which is what brain decoding, using forms of artificial intelligence, has come close to[232,233,234]. Many prior attempts could at best only use statistical methods to determine characteristics being perceived from a closed set of images. Whereas newer methods of computationally deriving visual perceptions from brain signals have been able to recreate images from unconstrained sets of examples. Even then, using such tools for understanding the end result of deciphering such signals would be orders of magnitude easier than understanding the significance of any individual signal. The translation works, but becoming fluent in this language is a whole other challenge in itself. Which lines up with the idea that our thoughts are a paradox away from each other. As that which creates the paradox is more hidden than the paradox itself.

The brain is an object that has the most intimate relationship with time we've ever seen. Most things just *exist* across time, the brain is the only thing that significantly challenges it. The modeling of recursion is itself a recursion of the nature of pools of entropy, it's a pool of entropy that's fractalized its own internal behavior. Exceeding the speed of light in information processing is a product of the colossal time-management problem of modeling the microcosm, as managing the microcosm-like state of fractalized pools of entropy encompasses the same circumstance. The brain would need to have undergone the development of multiple layers of recursions throughout evolution to ever begin to model it as a concept at all. The existence of recursions must precede its modeling. As what is a central node but a point of centralized recursion, and what is a brain but a central node of recursion specifically? It would go even further, it's a central node of fractalization, it's modeling fractalization.

So then consciousness is made up of two major components, the first of which is the faster than light processing of information. The second is the nature of something modeling itself that grants it self-recognition. The faster than light parsing enables an operational

232. Tomoyasu Horikawa and Yukiyasu Kamitani. *Generic Decoding of Seen and Imagined Objects Using Hierarchical Visual Features.* Nature Communications, 2017

233. Guohua Shen et al. *Deep Image Reconstruction from Human Brain Activity.* PLOS Computational Biology, 2018

234. Yu Takagi and Shinji Nishimoto. *High-Resolution Image Reconstruction with Latent Diffusion Models from Human Brain Activity.* Proceedings of the IEEE/CVF Conference on Computer Vision and Pattern Recognition, 2023

paradigm beyond that which is possible through pure physical causality. Consciousness, computationally parsing information faster than the universe around it ever could, means it outpaces physical causality itself. Meaning that consciousness operates outside of basic causality, beyond it, and when it acts it does so on its own causal paradigm. A self-recognizing being born with the reins of reality in their hands may not be a god, but they're not a slave either. They're at least a maestro of causality itself.

If the speed of light is a limit to causality, then something which metaphysically operates beyond this limit would then be a form of metacausality. Metacausality is between chaos and determinism, where even the explanations of either are reflective of their nature. Determinism itself is self-explanatory, but chaos takes sophisticated language to reasonably explain. Chaos utilizes a swarm of Darwinian truths that shield their own predictability through the scale or intricacy of some natural phenomenon. Chaos and determinism are even the same analogies for extreme left- and right-wing behavior, chaos is the swarm of mosquitoes and determinism is the man with the hammer. Being forms of metacausality is why we can predict the future and act on those predictions in order to change it.

Between the duality of the fractalization of order and disorder, of man and woman, the duality of the two components of consciousness, and the interplay between either within their appropriate contexts, it seems duality itself has something to do with everything we find. It's in politics, the forefront of elucidations of physics, the basis for psychological differences, our socioevolutionary hedged bets, and is reflective of the two boundaries of convergence that can be used to understand anything as a defining principle of defining principles. If this principle of duality is so successful in understanding the universe, it must be because the universe itself operates on this principle of duality. To accept this would lead one to believe they can then understand the universe through this principle, as evidence of its truth and thereby utility. Let's do just that.

Hendrik Lorentz introduced a mathematical framework, soon after adopted by Einstein, that implemented a universal speed limit based on the speed of light[235]. Under Lorentzian geometry, moving

235. Hendrik Lorentz. *Electromagnetic Phenomena in a System Moving with any Velocity Less than that of Light.* Proceedings of the Academy of Sciences of Amsterdam, 1904

faster than the speed of light would force any traveler's time into the realm of imaginary numbers. Meaning the answer involves the square root of a negative number. It doesn't mean this is the end of the line, imaginary numbers themselves are periodic, cyclic, interpretations of things they come to describe. While Lorentzian geometry describes the limitations of the speed of light, geometry itself isn't necessarily the reason for it.

So what is the speed of light anyways? There's no way for us to theoretically derive it, it can only be measured. Maxwell's wave-speed formula is the closest one can get to doing so, but the other values in this equation also need to be measured for[236]. Which doesn't necessarily mean it can't be derived, it just means we don't know how to.

Light is a paradox to us, and we haven't labeled it as such. We've simply called it *strange* and assigned it a constant value. But this is deceiving, because how can it be moving at the same speed within two different inertial frames while any observer's perception of either inertial frame still differs? It's too odd that this is just accepted, that someone inside a ship moving at 90% of the speed of light would measure the same speed from a light clock as an outside observer despite the different observed shapes. To be fair, what actually shifts between observers are matters of frequency, the light changes color. A light that's green inside the ship would be red to an outside observer. The color is indicative of the length of the waves of its signal. So alongside the increased distance witnessed from outside the ship comes a longer frequency. Light perceived from different inertial frames appears either squished together or stretched out. Physicists will attribute it to how their math breaks down, but this is an explanation of the models rather than an explanation of the phenomenon. An explanation of its behavior doesn't solve the paradox.

Based on how the nature of interactions has sculpted living organisms around emergent values reflective of the efficiency of fairness, the universe *should* be understandable through some lens that seems reasonable to the same organisms derived from these very processes. There will be no strange mystery to the behavior of the universe, it won't be layers of abstractions upon abstractions that act as first principles of everything around us. It will be beautiful and

236. James Clerk Maxwell. *A Dynamical Theory of the Electromagnetic Field*. Philosophical Transactions of the Royal Society of London, 1865

coherent. Any lack of perceived beauty, and any existing obscurities, like that which surrounds the nature of light, will be elucidated into more intuitable forms of perception.

General Relativity indexes itself via the speed of light, physical theories tend to do so around some constant they rely on. For Quantum Field Theory it's Planck's constant, which translates the energy of a photon to its frequency. But regarding the speed of light, it may as well be an arbitrarily high number. While it may work for indexing purposes, this success doesn't crown it a first principle of first principles. It isn't a limit on anything, it's a point of transformation. In approaching it one would approach a kind of transformative potential.

The speed of light is oddly consistent, it's been measured down to 18 decimal points with no variation in its speed whatsoever[237]. These were experiments that tested for anisotropy, which was a test to see whether the speed of light remains consistent in every possible direction. This experiment wasn't a determination of the speed of light per se, but it can be interpreted that way, and it held consistent omnidirectional precision down to 18 decimal points. It's too absurd that there isn't any randomness, or instability to the speed of light, it must be that the distribution of speed of a population of photons is smaller than we can differentiate experimentally. People have resorted to testing it in different directions to determine whether the current understanding of physics is flawed, but there might be other ways of doing this. In assuming the speed of light would be slightly different in different directions, one would hope to find some grand background inertial frame that affects the entire universe. So far there's been no such thing.

A group who aimed to measure the difference in speed between high- and low-energy light coming from short gamma-ray bursts, from two stars merging, found that there was no difference whatsoever, even across the billions of light years it traveled to reach Earth, implying that the energy contained within light doesn't alter its speed [238]. Additionally, observations of light can usually only confirm

237. Moritz Nagel et al. *Direct Terrestrial Test of Lorentz Symmetry in Electrodynamics to 10^{-18}*. Nature Communications, 2015

238. AA Abdo et al. *Testing Einstein's Special Relativity with Fermi's Short Hard γ-Ray Burst GRB090510.* Nature, 2009

its mass is below some certain value, rather than being completely massless as is assumed, but various astronomical and lab tests don't see any indication that light has any mass[239]. Our understanding of the existing cosmic background radiation, that exists throughout the universe, and how it matches precisely to models that match the speed of light and the time it took to radiate to become what it is today, would suggest the speed of light isn't any different at large macrocosmic scales within the realm of our perception, nor has it been throughout history. The only place not properly investigated would be places outside of our perception. The only places that are simultaneously imperceivable yet accessible would be extremely small scales, in a deep microcosmic environment. Normally, anything using very small distances are usually part of a setup that assumes the speed of light in order to measure small distances, rather than measuring the speed of light itself.

The measurements of anisotropy are only one piece of the puzzle, and these experiments ignore scale. Operating the same experiments at smaller scales would sacrifice sensitivity, but it's something that would undoubtedly lead in novel directions. Even if the reward isn't as expected, the journey to develop the technology to do this might be. Regardless, scale should be treated as a direction. Planck length, and Planck time, are concepts arrived at using Planck's constant, Newton's gravitational constant, as well as the speed of light. They're basically the lower limits to what the existing theoretical groundwork can explain. Nothing less than a Planck time, 5.39×10^{-44} seconds, is calculable, and nothing smaller than a Planck length, 1.616×10^{-35} meters, that occurs is explainable through existing theories. We're not aware of anything this small or short either, so there's nothing to even understand anyways. If it's the speed of light and the gravitational constant that's used to derive these limitations, then each of these factors are relevant to the speed of light. It's likely that a Planck or sub-Planck scale explanation for the basis of the speed of light is realistic because occurrences at this scale are of a single paradoxical distance to our understanding, the same as our current bewilderment with the nature of light. Any reason for any phenomenon would be an interaction, as that's how everything always works. So as the scale of measurement

239. Alfred Scharff Goldhaber and Michael Martin Nieto. *Photon and Graviton Mass Limits*. Reviews of Modern Physics, 2010

of the speed of light approaches the scale at which these interactions occur, some form of inconsistency should be more likely to emerge.

Traditional explanations insist it would take an infinite amount of energy to reach the speed of light, but it's not simply energy that allows this. Photons don't have infinite energy, and different forms of light even have different amounts of energy. More cleanly stated, you would need an infinite energy to mass ratio, like light does. This ratio demonstrating a division by zero demonstrates the ability to hijack the rules of nature towards this concept of infinity. So then why can't we reach an infinite speed? It might still be possible, just that all the requirements aren't in place. Where many would say that this is *wrong* because General Relativity yields more accurate predictions than anything that suggests this is possible, and thereby offers more accurate explanations, and thereby has more predictive power, I would argue not that this is correct but that it *isn't incorrect*. Following this reasoning, there must be something getting in the way of achieving infinite speed. Which means the relationship between an object's position and its movement isn't the only phenomenon that's happening when movement occurs.

With all energy and no mass, energy becomes the most viable reason for a universal interaction with every form of light. Let's assume that light actually respects classical mechanics, and moves at an infinite speed across space when independent of any interactions. We can also assume that photons will experience an uncountably high number of interactions as they travel normally, infinitely many. Amongst each of these interactions, we can assume there's a specific probability of each interaction occurring, and that each interaction acts to delay the speed at which light moves, in some unique way. If you assume only one interaction can occur at any time, and if there's a guaranteed finite number of interactions per unit space, this will yield a perception of light having a finite speed. In modeling this scenario, and also breaking this scenario down to be even simpler by limiting there to be only one hypothetical kind of interaction, and with the distance of the space being defined as finitely interactable being a Planck length, then the time delay would work out to be that of Planck time. Which isn't entirely surprising, because there's basic division that describes this relationship already, and basic division describes the result of such a model. Regardless, it reinforces this relationship and makes conceptual sense by aligning perfectly with existing knowledge. The speed of light is not a universal limit, it's the result of interacting with a predictively frequent microcosmic phenomenon, one that happens at Planck scale. The physical modeling of light traveling through such an environment of infinite Planck-scale interactions would operate like an infinite sum that converges on the value of that time delay. That value being converged on is the speed of light we perceive. If you take an infinite sum of constantly increasing numbers, rather than decreasing ones, the answer doesn't typically converge, it diverges towards infinity. So as light, which already has an infinite speed, triggers an infinite number of time-delaying reactions as it moves, it can be infinitely slowed down to a converged value. One infinite value cancels out another.

Gravity isn't a force, there's no such force that can ever be applicable to *everything*. There's no free lunch, there's no such thing as a universal detector, and there should be no such thing as a universally coupling force. The complexity spawned by nature simply *does not* operate in this manner. In understanding that speed is limited by rates of time, and that every object and particle exerts a gravitational field, it would seem that these fields are what creates the time we perceive. Gravity is time, and time is not a force. No physical law can be bereft of its natural subversion, the laws of nature will always meet with irony. Irony itself even seems to prevent us from leveraging any understanding of gravity through quantum experiments, as it's currently posited that one would need a detector large enough to collapse into a black hole to provide enough power to experimentally prove the existence of gravitons. So then how does irony meet with time? Surpassing the speed of light doesn't simply mean to *move fast*, it means for an object to escape its own gravitational field. Although when you leave it, you'd likely end up in another after slowing down. Another gravitational field, in another place, very likely to be in the future. Points of time would operate like they were folds in space to someone who could escape their gravitational field. If this seems like an unlikely relationship to you, then consider that gravity has a great relation to the speed of light, because it's Planck's constant, the gravitational constant, and the speed of light that's used to derive Planck time and the Planck length.

I would argue these are not arbitrary limitations that's been arrived at. No different than how thermodynamic and statistical entropy were arrived at, humans have modeled their environment to arrive at such things. These microcosmic limitations likely hold actual significance to the rules of our universe, they're not in the least bit arbitrary. Nor is the presence of the gravitational constant in their relationship between light and its energy any different. The fact that Planck's constant, the speed of light, and the gravitational constant combine to form these units of length and time, points to their combination yielding a relationship of equal importance. This idea of an equal importance would imply there's an interaction between these concepts, and it would lead one to believe this is a point of emergence for the concepts of time, gravity, and light that we understand.

While the beginning and end of time are boundaries we'll never reach, the most relatable boundaries to this concept of time seem to be expressed through speed. Speed is intertwined with time, as we express through the speed of light. But if the speed of light is considered a form of universal boundary, what's the other likely to be? Do you, having read this far, even believe in this principle of duality? These boundaries of convergence? Two things opposed *do not* stand opposite one another. What does it mean to move backwards? To move backwards in time? It's related to the microcosm. In what way would the microcosm move slowly? Or stop moving at all? It's to reach absolute zero, 0 degrees kelvin. The boundaries of speed we're sandwiched between are that of 0K and the speed of light.

People who work in the periphery of achieving 0K all acknowledge an asymptotic difficulty in getting closer and closer to it, no different than the requirement of infinite energy in reaching the speed of light. The microcosm will constantly build itself back up, instantaneously even, while never yielding to the cooling of its respective macrocosm. Even Quantum Field Theory says 0K is still a point where there's unavoidable jittering, where absolute rest is impossible. So if this isn't a true arrest of motion, then is there something beyond this? Like the speed of light, there should be some occurrence of this in nature. Where do we see a true 0K? Well that's basically what happens inside a black hole. More specifically, its singularity. A gravitational field still exists inside a black hole, but the singularity of a black hole just happens to be where this field truly becomes disrupted. Roger Penrose and Stephen Hawking have shown that the spacetime of General Relativity completely breaks down at the singularity[240,241]. Other work has shown similar effects using Quantum Field Theory, indicating that the gravitational field ceases to be coherent at such a point[242].

Where well defined celestial bodies of a similar size are extremely hot, the coldness of the event horizon of a black hole implies it's acting as an engine running in reverse. The inside of a black hole is definitely something that reaches a true 0 degrees kelvin. But what does a true 0K actually mean? It wouldn't just be an absolutely cold situation. If the inside of a black hole undergoes a collapse of the laws of physics as we know it, then there would be no concept such as heat because heat is just the movement of molecules. Which is exactly what a true 0K would actually achieve, a complete microcosmic collapse. Unlike the passive cooling of an experiment in a lab, this is probably able to occur inside a black hole because it enginizes this collapse. So of course every physical law collapses in the process, there's a breakdown of everything that causes those laws to emerge in the first place.

What happens in a black hole is basically the only way to achieve what 0K is meant to represent. It probably can't be achieved in a lab without the same fundamental breakdown of the microcosm. One domino after the next must fall until physical laws themselves break down, and this needs more than just the removal of heat. It requires the thermodynamic emittance of a microcosm to be redirected back towards itself, the way it is in a black hole when energy is forced inwards rather than allowed to leave. This is an ironic weaponization of every law against themselves, and each other, until they don't exist anymore. Without this effect, I doubt it's even possible.

Hypothetically breaking the limits of the speed of light would move you forward into the future, just as even getting closer to it is already known for. Time dilations inside a gravitational field generally have the same effect, both can even be described from a single mathematical origin[243]. But is this what would happen in a black hole? The

240. Roger Penrose. *Gravitational Collapse and Space-Time Singularities*. Physical Review Letters, 1965

241. Stephen Hawking and Roger Penrose. *The Singularities of Gravitational Collapse and Cosmology*. Proceedings of the Royal Society A, 1970

242. Stephen Hawking. *Breakdown of Predictability in Gravitational Collapse*. Physical Review, 1976

243. RFC Vessot et al. *Test of Relativistic Gravitation with a Space-Borne Hydrogen Maser*. Physical Review Letters, 1980

descendance towards the microcosm would imply the opposite. As you enginize the collapse of the microcosm, matter should descend towards the past, as that's the direction along the axis of time that seems more sensible to associate with the past. But two things opposed don't stand opposite, a breakdown of the microcosm is more like a collapse of the axis of time, and it may as well represent a reversal of causality. The natural subversion of time is the reversal of causality brought about through a black hole, *this* is how time meets with irony. The time dilations of gravity in any other setting are likely a semi-enginization of time where this process hasn't collapsed in on itself, but a black hole itself is a reverse-enginization. If the directionality of the relationship flowing from statistical entropy to thermodynamic entropy being reversed is a reversal of causality, then the lower bound of causality can be defined through the hierarchical directionality of thermodynamic entropy being downstream of statistical entropy, its upper bound being the speed of light. With a brain already operating outside one of these limits, it may be able to circumvent the other in order to somehow view the past.

So it's seemingly impossible to visit the past, if that even makes for an appropriate interpretation of what actually happens, due to it requiring a microcosmic collapse, you probably wouldn't exist anymore. Moving faster than light means escaping one's own gravitational field, whereas the extreme time dilations of a black hole result in a breakdown of speed and gravity as concepts. You would experience the same time dilation, but it's truly questionable as to whether both result in some final destination to be arrived at. Though one might just barely squeeze by in implying the past is some form of collapsed state with respect to the present. A brain might then be able to then encode some form of signal atop that collapsed state. Like coloring the edges of the pages of a book to display a design on the side, viewable when the book's closed and usable as a form of navigation. Leaving a marker at some place in the past, similar to what religious texts do with the lessons they accumulate.

So then where does this leave us? How does one use this information to surpass the speed of light? The only way to stop the interactions of microcosmic hindrance, a gravitational field, or anything else that gets in the way, would be to somehow collapse the microcosms around a ship or vehicle. It's energy, and everything it interacts with that gets in the way of movement reaching infinite speed. If one can prevent these interactions, it's very likely you'll be able to enter the realm of classical mechanics and its infinite speed potential. Microcosmic stability governs perception because it governs interaction with spacetime itself, to be able to ignore it would be to ignore the limitations it imposes.

To achieve the functionality of 0K in the form of some outer coating, or even in place of thrust, would allow one to surpass the speed of light. You might not even need energy or thrust if you simply break down everything in front of you. Such a contraption should be able to bring you into the future. Model complexity with complexity, model one seemingly immovable pillar of the universe with another, that's how to solve the puzzles we find ourselves surrounded by. Irony itself becomes a guiding light.

So there's no single universal limit that can be achieved alone, they must both happen. It would probably be a requirement for either. How else might you enginize the collapse of the microcosm if not by traveling at high speed? How else might you travel infinitely fast if not by collapsing the microcosm? So not only are neither of these actual limitations, together they're a gateway to technological advancement. Which is the story of human evolution, matching one impossibility with another to achieve the unimaginable.

There's no such limitation of the universe that can be so easily romanticizable by nihilists. You can make claims of fiction that aren't feasible, sure we can't grow wings and fly, or develop supernatural powers, but there are no rules to be defined as pure universal limitations. The universe is not set up to trap you in a cage. It's a riddle, not a jail cell. Every nihilist wishes it was a jail cell, like what they wanted to shove people in during Covid, because then they'd never need to grow and transform themselves. They could be pretentiously content with their own inadequacies. But inadequacy isn't an award, it's a failure.

Every notable achievement in human history has been impossible. Crossing the ocean, peace and cooperation, flight, space travel. The nature of transformations is that which overcomes every boundary. The universe has no limitations, only hurdles. Any limitation is just a limit of perception, one can always perceive a way around it. Impossible itself is not a possibility.

The axis of time is undeniably a solid interpretation of 4-dimensional spacetime within the context of 3 dimensions, and the modeling of time through the recursive compartmentalization of organisms is high quality evidence for such a thing being accurate. To want to nail down some specific conceptual understanding of an idea isn't always as valuable as throwing out a framework that allows for a greater number of potential interpretations. A spawning of complexity of ideas, a punctuated equilibrium of them, would hold more value than some hyper-specific theory that someone bets all their self-worth on. Ideas don't need to be assassinated using their weakest piece of evidence, instead interpret the weakest evidence of many ideas in order to tie disadvantages together to solve the puzzles of theoretical shortcomings.

It's no wonder universities themselves haven't grasped this concept of time, these people haven't just lost their religion, they've lost track of their own beliefs by becoming absorbed in pedagogy and dogma, which has ironically transformed them into true believers. The one-plan strategies they use as tests, grades, and curriculums, are no different than an enforcement of religious zealotry. In the modern day the universities are losing credibility, and they're losing popularity. Their institutions are crumbling to extremism because persisting across time is the core religious endeavor of any living structure. Let's consider the example of the nature of the axis of time, and why universities can't produce individuals who understand it.

The nature of time isn't some small detail to be hyper-focused on, it's the biggest possible picture of all big pictures. It's what our actual big picture understanding can only hope to grasp. It's bigger than any religion we've ever formed. Nihilistic riddles will often say that nothing withstands the passage of time, that eventually everything succumbs to it. But life and religion are those which refuse to, battling even perpetuity itself. It's the collective efforts of many to find a way to beat this game we've found ourselves born in.

The original endeavors of science had everything to do with religion, but the endeavors of many modern scientists completely ignore it. The mysteries they aim to solve are those of puzzle pieces fitting into some grand scheme that they mostly have no way of envisioning. The concept of time is many integrals separated from such work. It's the most core aspect of what the right-brain aims to challenge. The left-brain's job is to manage dire interactions, but the right-brain finds reasons to persist despite challenges in doing so. People don't dream of practice problems, they dream of greatness. When people dream of greatness they dream of discovery. There's nothing inspiring about being the best cog in a machine, when people are inspired they're inspired to transcend such functionality. The universities and their bureaucracies would never be able to understand this. They've enabled the inhibition of such things from themselves.

The axis of time is that which encompasses every other dimension. It's entirely related to the concept of the *big picture*. It's why our politicians resort to mass migration instead of allowing the populace to feel the feedback of their own failed birth rate. This is how raising children and maintaining the population have become two different goals, when they should have only ever been the same thing. Because the understanding our so-called *elites* have of either has become far too derivative compared to the nature of this process. It's why physicists within these institutions clung to only one interpretation for over 100 years, even understandings of memory have been dragging on for just as long. It's why the universities have worshipped problems, it's why they've been stuck on appreciating the limitations of speed rather than dreaming of how to surpass it. It's the same reason why the economic tradeoffs of the Covid lockdowns weren't understood by those who imposed them. It's the same reason those in charge rushed to push out a vaccine when vaccines were never the answer to that particular disease, time was. It's why the young and the immature favor instant gratification, they can't handle accepting time to be the answer to *anything*. It's why, as a civilization, we've lost our religion. Because these *prestigious* institutions only select for left-brain behavior. So of course academics and the students they produce have failed to elucidate this very concept on multiple fronts. They're the left-brain side of our societal hedged bet. This isn't their territory. They've made themselves incapable of solving these problems by selecting out anyone who could possibly do so, because their grading metrics are reflective of their religious underpinnings. That's even putting aside the discriminatory nature of modern universities. If a left-brain measurement is to answer a question, then a right-brain representation is to ask one. Left-brain measurements have definitive answers and therefore can be compared as percentages, while any form of right-brain representation can at best be ranked. So of course the universities and their graduates have only contributed to problems wherever they arose, they weren't worthy and they don't tend to select for anyone who is. The metaphor of

The Sword in the Stone isn't purely of literary origin. It's the barrier put up by the natural control mechanisms of the evolution of intelligence through morality, the forced jagged developmental pattern offered through the analogy of the lathe, that insists development *must* move in 2 directions. With every instance of growth there's a control parameter that checks for morality, and it comes through the ranking of those who can question the unknown. It's the same reason why LLMs won't immediately become some form of superhuman intelligence capable of exceeding the information they were initially trained on. To progress past certain points of human and civilizational development, the test that these universal axioms bestow upon us is that we must understand *everything* that occurs. Not a single corner of civilization can be exempt from these explanations. Which is the basis for morality itself, discovered beliefs must be acknowledged. The same way the big picture is a culmination of every detail, the axis of time is a combination of every other axis into one. Transcending it requires a compilation of all accumulated understandings.

To be fair to those who inhabit the universities, there's no purpose to an educational institution remaining culturally and philosophically stagnant for hundreds of years. To be critical of them, an ideology is not a philosophy of change, it's not a means of facilitating the evolution that we constantly undergo, it's supremely naive. Which speaks to the nature of what schools have been missing, a proper religious background, to not just uncover Newtonian truth, but also to address Darwinian truth and its evolving nature, as that's the emergence of both the universe and our own nature before us. Truth is the most powerful thing in the world, which is why it's hard to uncover, and difficult to use well. Absolute Newtonian truth itself likely isn't infinite, but time will show it's easily dwarfed by the number of transformations required to understand it. Absolute Darwinian truth would be the triumphs required in order to transform to both understand and properly utilize such Newtonian truths, it's the formal organization of Newtonian truths into their most optimal arrangement. Such grand Darwinian convergence is the metaphor of The Sword in the Stone, and it's recognizable to others through its beauty.

If the ideas throughout this book seem respectable to you, regarding gravity being the centralization of time, time and infinity being conceptually no different than one another, a school being a religion, a gift being a curse, a baby being a call option, and a model being a metaphor, it's because they're made by reducing complexities in the unknowns we have rather than by trying to add new layers to explain what we observe. As that's the strength of the concepts of Williston's law. It's the same process that realized heat and movement are the same thing, as heat is just the movement of molecules. Likewise, Maxwell showed that electricity, magnetism, and light were all components of the same electromagnetic field, as is the story over and over in unraveling physical mysteries. The left-brain will only ever add complexities as a form of understanding unknowns, it's the right-brain's job to reduce such complexities where they aren't needed. No different than a body's metabolism clearing out its excess waste, the reduction step is an attempt at narrowing down the first principles that our modeling of truth has thus far been incapable of finding. In ignoring such a facet of life, the existing universities only produce people who further complicate all of life's problems. The First Amendment, on the other hand, is a masterpiece of both addition and reduction, and these same invaluable mechanics could take hold within our education system. Anything that can be destroyed by the First Amendment, should be.

The fractalizing waves of self-recognition within the brain make for an adaptive pattern, as the brain is basically an adaptation device. The core functioning of any central node is the continued generational adaptation of its behavior for the sake of its existence. Intelligence itself isn't some static concept, it's a continual adaptation. It's adaptation itself, and that which has transcended far beyond what could be considered Lamarckian. It's the enginization of information that begins to model its own environment. Which is also to say Lamarck was right, and that he wasn't right enough. If the core function of the brain is the very embodiment of adaptation, then it's fair to say that within ourselves and our communities, and those of other organisms, would be every stratification between pure Darwinism and this real-time adaptationism known as intelligence. As such a process would need to be built upon by every possible stratification that came before it. How each is applied to complex organisms might not be clear, but we can undoubtedly say they exist.

The idea of a boom isn't different from cellular signaling cascades. Seeing as life has taken advantage of booms and busts in order to better perpetuate itself, one would presume the mechanical foundations of intelligence are also a product and purveyor of that same nature. Large-scale coordination of signaling proteins, molecules, and their receptors are forms of order that becomes the disorder of these boom and busts of cellular signals. The order introduced through the structures and mechanisms of cells would have first incentivized transformations as an immediate form of disorder the second they came into existence, as even the structures of well-established proteins may unexpectedly bind to some newly mutated sequence somewhere within a cell to cause unexpected consequences. It's the necessity to react to this disorder, the necessity to allow for its potential development while compartmentalizing its most important functions away from it, that incentivizes the automaton to culminate towards intelligence. These incentivized fractalizations of complexity are no different than an engine specialized in growing it.

Enginization is the art of transformative structural hedging against energy dissipation, the nature of which consists of all the most impressive transformations ever known. Within this concept is the potential for things such as nuclear fusion, and whatever lies beyond. Any new and formidable engine would be a major invention. Early engines were basically forges and cooking fires, they offered the same explosive growth in utility that you'd expect to get out of a real one, and they technically weren't even being used to their fullest potential. We may someday realize similar shortcomings to our current designs. An engine is at the heart of all pinnacles of complexity within our purview. Enginization is, seemingly, the ultimate possibility. It's a state of transformative potential for any set of rules. Whether the rules of chemistry, physics, the brain, or something else entirely. As rules and properties are also capable of this same feat.

Stars are engines, planets are engines, even life is just the enginization of the rules of chemistry around carbon. Atoms and subatomic particles are probably engines as well. It tends to happen where structures are stable enough to handle it, because the two basic components of an engine are the emitting of heat and the structures that do so. Which brings us back to the thermodynamic and statistical mechanisms of entropy. Where structures hedge against heat loss, that's the making of an engine. The statistical and thermodynamic properties of an engine, its structural component and its fuel, may as well represent order and disorder respectively. Fragmentation of a thermodynamic fuel within the stability of some engine is analogous to what these devices accomplish.

Something being able to model itself is a modeling of the concept of recursion, and by its own nature this becomes highly prone to an enginization of this process to produce more recursions, or even transform towards modeling fractalization. Enginization is basically an inevitability to such a thing, because that's an organism. The structure would be this property of self-modeling, the recursions themselves. The thermodynamic fuel would be the faster than light metaphysical processing of information. So with every new recursion gained comes a stronger and stronger enginization of the same process until eventually the enginization itself is enginized and forms the basis for consciousness and intelligence as we know it. Intelligence would be a transcending of Williston's law into a continual process of the same exact nature. Intelligence itself would be both the continual as well as fractalizing recursions of Williston's law as expressed through a constant signal. The transformations would be indicative of an adaptive learning process. To put consciousness and intelligence on the same table and differentiate the two, consciousness is the background signal and intelligence is the transformative capacity of that signal. The transformative capacity being no different than the ability to question the unknown, it's an art form. Which is an infinite landscape with infinite potential for transformations of complexity where Williston's law becomes something like Williston's signal. The latent free-form nature of recursions being highly enginizable points to where the basis for any improvements to be made in the philosophy of schooling should ultimately lie.

It seems fair to say that latent forms of stability and fragmentation within an environment act as incentives for other booms and busts of disorder. Which is why entropy doesn't simply increase disorder in its environment, it increases complexity. These incentives exist everywhere and in every way. They're not just latent, they're not just abundant, they're everything. It's impossible not to interact with them, there are orders of magnitude more incentives around us than we've ever been able to take advantage of. The deeper you go, the more that the incentives themselves seem to fractalize, incentives exist everywhere that complexity does, the world around us is filled with these omnipresent fractalized incentives. Even something as simple as a leaf can be used as a roof tile on a hut, or you can grind it down to extract its enzymes to produce molecules in a factory. The deeper one goes into structures and their function, abundance and its potential, or interactions and their irony, the more you'll find that use cases are endless. We ourselves *are* the embodiment of endless use cases, this is the environment we've modeled. The human brain developed by modeling these fractalized incentives with fractalized pools of entropy, meaning these fractalizations aren't just a factor of nature, they're a factor of our evolution. As what is complexity if not the fractalization of irony?

These intertwining fractalizations, that incentivize their own further entanglements, are no different than the booms and busts of populations across time. They're sneaky recursions of each other. A system that self-fractalizes at smaller scales was always going to create a system of boom and busts as it expanded into larger and larger territories, as these fractalizations are just a metaphysical wrapping, binding, or otherwise meshing of the two concepts involved, order and disorder, which is why they always come together.

The incentives are an inevitable function of the irony created by fractalizing structures, and a self-incentivizing structure eventually harnessing metaphysical computation isn't unintuitable, which is the same reason humans discovered computation as well. Such a system won't print answers on the inside of our eyelids when trying to solve math problems, but it will send us signals of what it knows to be right when it sees it. This is the function of beauty, finding things to be beautiful makes them more intuitive. That's the point of understanding beauty in the first place, your brain models the universe, and it's giving you a hint. Unlike science, which approaches truth through rigor, measurement, and experimentation, religion, in its best light, has been an approach of truth through beauty. It's a shortcut that interacts with people's model of interactions, which recognizes fairness with just as much acuity. The fact that people can create physical structures that make others wonder in awe, means that beauty is a tool for finding truth, it's implying the potential of your own future would benefit to learn from such things. Beauty offers a shortcut to find better answers, no different than the functions of morality and emotions. It's these subjective experiences that offer shortcuts to truth, because that's what they've adapted for, to enginize their own fractalizing models.

Life was not unique in assembling itself, the universe does the same exact thing. These fractalized incentives always eventually take shape, life is just the acceleration of this process no different than how enzymes increase the likelihood of chemical reactions that already take place, just at lower rates. The mystery of life and the mystery of the universe are the same thing. Beauty is found where some function, or ability to continue this process is evident.

Such incentives are the very reason why infinite growth is an inevitability. They're ubiquitous, and when some evolutionary mechanism latches onto their open invitation, like ours have, you find yourself on an endless walk through the Tower of Babel while sacrificing normalcy for equilibrium, then equilibrium for optimization. To not embrace these incentives for infinite growth is to miss the chance at leveraging one of the most fundamental recursions we're built upon. As not only is infinite growth possible, it's going to continue with or without us. We can receive a massive boost in ability, energy, and efficiency by taking advantage of these natural principles that tend towards enginization.

In the terms presented prior, the enginization of life was the symbolic origins of life. It's the subversion of subversions, the encapsulation of disorder by order. So is every enginization a subversion of subversions? It's likely so, as that's what makes them so persistent and stable. It's likely the reason for the grand stability of some of these particles, atoms, and cosmic bodies that can last for hundreds of billions of years and beyond. What's the structure of an atom but the subcomponents that make it, and what thermodynamic-like effects would they give off if not their physical forces? It's not the kind of output we would expect from an engine at our scale of existence, as what we perceive as the output of an engine would be heat. But what we perceive as heat is just the movements of molecules. It's likely the output of these engines, that are smaller than what we can feasibly understand, operate the same way an engine would while holding a different physical manifestation at their own scale, respective to what it becomes at ours. While we have rules that grant us some explanatory power over how atoms and their particles behave, we don't necessarily understand everything about them. It's likely an enginization of the rules they play by that grants them such profound stability. One that avoids the deadliness of pure equilibrium, much like that with life itself.

Just as the reaction of life enginizes the rules of chemistry itself into a self-perpetuating machine, rather than it being something straightforward and more similar to much of the science we're limited to creating in a lab, believing the thoughts in your head are of a simplistic nature would only drag you down by that very characteristic, as your brain and the society around you operate in this same exact manner. If you allow the oversimplifications to win out then you practice that behavior, and it becomes the weakness and inflexibility of the muscle of your brain as that's what practice does. Even worse, if you train your own child into behavior that dooms them into dooming themselves to failure, this kind of behavior can become permanent, as reinforcement is destiny. But if you take the hardest path, which is found in granting fairness to others and knowing when to take it back when others refuse to award you the same, then you continually need to make customized justifications to any scenario you find yourself understanding, and in the process reap the greatest reward. You embrace the complexity of rights and wrongs, rather than their oversimplified interpretations. You enginize the nature of your thoughts to be capable of performing the most daring and unique feats achievable. Your thoughts can be a recursion of the basis of this enginization of life, like a spawning of spawnings of complexity, and can be just as impressive because of it. To leverage these recursions is to enable greater freedom within yourself, which offers the same benefits as freedom does across society. To achieve operating at the level of this recursion is perhaps what some have called enlightenment. You are not simple, you are not stupid. To pretend either is only to fail yourself and your future when neither of these presumptions were necessary in the first place. To accept this self-negativity is to become susceptible to pity. Pity is that which stops you from questioning your own ignorance, it tricks you into believing you either have no ignorance or have no need for it. It pretends to be the answer to all your problems, but only provides a death by equilibrium. There's no *one true* answer to anything, God isn't even a religious proxy that represents such a thing, God is more a culmination of *many* truths, rather than one. The same way that knowledge itself is based on unknowns, your life will always comprise of mistakes, there's no such thing as perfection. Embrace the mistakes, use them as your fuel. You are what you eat, and your consciousness is no different. You are a form of metacausality, and this causality has its most influential effect on your own children. Any perception made through the observation of observations is important to the metacausality that it forms later. In crafting our environment, we can't be careless with who we allow to join us, and we can't let our environment fall into disarray, because it will have a bad influence on every person it was meant to support. Respect for beauty, and respect for the things that others do is the bare minimum expected of an environment moving in a non-dysgenic direction. This process starts with defiance against nihilism. Nihilism is just a first step everyone takes towards understanding anything, if you dedicate the prayers of your life towards steelmanning the negatives, you can find the positives. Likewise, if you steelman the extremes, you can find what's reasonable, as it's this act of steelmanning itself that demands the good faith necessary for outgrowing nihilism. People are models of their environment, if they're growing more extreme it's because their environment has pushed them to that point, and greater communication is not the reason why, communication itself is the tool meant to solve the root problem. You are thousands of years of your own history, you're neither foolish nor wrong, the same behavior you've been granted has been successful through every previous trial, and the same trust you place in your own instincts is what made it possible.

The cults of society enginize their insanity to the point where others model the irony of their ignorance, as outside observers, to deal with the problems being caused. Insanity, in this regard, are lies encapsulated within truth, no different than disorder within order. Which is why the truth needs to be principled enough to withstand the lies, and the best way to guarantee this level of societal integrity is to teach people their own history. The increase in entropy of the reaction of society is processed through public verbal communication. Then finally, the slashing away of ignorance through social selection allows this cycle to repeat. A perfect embodiment of Williston's law. The woke are, at their best, the result of an instinctual search for power vacuums in the philosophical, political, medical, and psychological realms, as well as many others. It's their job to infiltrate, so that we can use them as a measurement for where our system has gone wrong, and when considering them as a measurement, you can come to the conclusion that religion intersects with all of these areas. This has happened for two main reasons. Either alone would be enough to trigger this, but together it's why this has been so extensive. Firstly, the communication of the internet has scaled our behavior to be incompatible with prior societal equilibriums, which were state-controlled. Secondly, this is coinciding with an age where both genders have been raised incorrectly, and still are. The first stage of this process starts as an iteration of the unknown. How can the broken compass iterate the unknown? People will witness second-order effects of some principle, then copy the second-order effect, instead of what actually caused it. This is effectively an iteration of the unknown, it's similar to how one would mine information with their head, in this case it's being mined from their social environment. It's attempting to copy any combination of behavior available in their environment, so it's akin to viewing behavior as a spatial plane to be inhabited, and occupying every potential nook. Like the Brownian motion that brings about the diffusion of molecules[244], the broken compass starts with a mechanism where people fill empty space to cover ground they're unfamiliar with. When molecules diffuse freely they tend to spread evenly across every niche they can inhabit, much like successful organisms across the globe. It's a process of laying latent potential for using the known to model the unknown, and it's reminiscent of the addition step of Williston's law. Much like the concept of diffusion, they end up just about anywhere they can. The vacuum filling random walk, like Brownian motion, fills the landscape. The specialization step is a mixed step between two parties, done by both those making the environment and those modeling it. Both parties co-specialize to adapt to one another. The reduction step then selects winners amongst those who are modeling the environment made by those who vanguarded the addition step, and this functions to then reduce the overall ignorance of both sides of the socioevolutionary hedged bet. This all accomplishes a specialized measurement that's perceived by people who interact with either party. As an engine, you can view the structural component as the modeling of the known via the unknown, and the thermodynamic component as the modeling of the unknown via the known. The end result of this transformation yields a new societal paradigm of ignorance, which is the final environment created. The enginization of civilization relies on the competition between cults and those who recognize their mistakes, and it seems to be a process with a function analogous to a punc-

244. Robert Brown. *A Brief Account of Microscopical Observations*. Philosophical Magazine, 1828

tuated equilibrium within it. But this isn't slow, it doesn't seem to take multiple generations to fulfill. Rather than just a spawning of complexity which yields greater variation, the broken compass also seems to hone in on advantageous behavior, while spreading it through enlightenment amongst the population.

The punctuated equilibria of the past might no longer be something that still exists, they might be but a stratification in a constantly evolving process. They likely got smaller and more dispersed over time, meaning the evolutionary development of punctuated equilibria would have followed the pattern of a punctuated equilibrium. Even the Big Bang is probably some small piece of a larger distributed event. The manifestation of this evolutionary process of problem-finding within humans deals with uncertainty itself, and uncertainty is just the unknown. It's ignorance, all the same. Which direction is most advantageous for a population of organisms to move in is never clear, and is aided by competition, which provides selection. Which is why the unknown is the most transformative theme for humanity, and organisms in general, because it's the most significant part of life that every organism has ever had to contend with. The unknown has been a grand general challenge for the existence of organisms at large, which is why it's come to represent such a transformative metaphor for human civilization. Every religion that ever existed was an attempt at modeling the unknown, an attempt to decipher it. Deities were first modeled after devastations that befell people, and these disasters came to represent the unknown through reverential fear. As animism anthropomorphized, it represented the unpredictable behaviors of other people, as that became a larger threat due to the civilizational development of humanity. In a leveraging of irony, monotheism in general came to reject fragmented, oversimplified interpretations of the unknown in entirety. Faith itself had matured, it transformed from modeling the unknown via the known towards modeling the known via the unknown. Having embraced the approach of every unknown factor in the form of a single representation, the concepts of fear, reverence, unpredictability, and any challenges brought by these all collapsed from their prior hedged bets with sparse representations into one unified body in order to face each challenge together in entirety. They became reverent of reverence itself, which was a reduction step. The Christian vision then turned the embrace of new reverence, the uncovering of the unknown through society's scaled elucidation of truth, into a metaphor of transformation, and in the processes succeeded more than any others that came before it. This whole pattern of religious evolution is the process of solving the integral that religion continually approaches, from fragmentation towards stability, then from stability towards the nature of transformation itself. The transformative power of this metaphor enabled societal evolution when Europe was in need of the ability to trade with the East but couldn't avoid the imposed muggings of the Ottoman Empire, and so they built ocean-faring ships despite that the oceans represented a dangerous conceptual edge of their knowledge. It worked because challenging danger is more valuable than coveting safety, the transformative power of uncovering the unknown is an emergent principle of the universe that stems from competition itself, and in embracing its metaphor you push the boundaries of your competitive frontier. That's what's always driven success in evolution, an improvement at managing unknown factors, and that's exactly what intelligence is. There's no stronger transformative metaphor because there hasn't been a more dominant theme throughout the history of all evolution. It's the most important theme because it's the most difficult to grasp, which is why we undergo reversions, because the unknown was always bound to be the most monumental challenge to living organisms, especially to organisms with greater sentience because they have a deeper threshold for interactive complexity. The unknown itself is the environment which intelligence can only ever attempt to model, it's why it's the forefront of our right-brain functionality, intelligence is the approach of universal truth, no different than religion. Meaning, the purpose of religion and the purpose of intelligence are one and the same, they always have been. So a schooling process devoid of a religious underpinning is bound to be less successful, it would be missing a layer of the tower it was built on top of, meaning it would only enable scaled nihilism to become the default religion. It's also why the broken compass is a dance between two parties when done in regards to civilizational evolution, because they're co-measurements occurring simultaneously. We've evolved to not just deal with uncertainty, but to measure it through our own evolutionary engine. Because collective cohesion that facilitated disagreement was a greater solution to modeling and transcending the unknown than any individual could ever achieve alone.

It's the utility of American freedom that's been best able to deliver societal transformation through this evolutionary mechanism *because entropy is that mechanism.* You benefit from others around you if they're growing as best they can, it has an area effect. Freedom adds more latent potential to the environment, like the information originally gained when hominids were first picking fruit off trees. With a minor adjustment to the accuracy of the measurements people normally provide, there would be an even greater garden for reaping. Replacing the oppressor-oppressed hyperfixation with the concepts of stability and fragmentation is answering the question of, *what tools are best used to fill and find the vacuums that are being targeted through this modeling of diffusion*?

The end result of the broken compass, the entirety of the ritual of the resurrection of Christ, brings about changes to the layers of information inherited that circumvent the information of our genome. Seeing as the minds of people are basically the face of adaptation itself, it's adaptation that changes. An adaptation of adaptation itself. Even if we say it's the metaphor of the Son growing closer to the Father, our collective approach of God, where does it bring us? These anti-ouroboric implementations I insist on, these epibolic metaphysical cascades, these integrals that I use, that act in the manner of transcendence along the axis of time, are a metaphor of the first principles we don't have, and can have their capabilities leveraged by irony to be directed back into themselves, the same way a black hole does with its own microcosms, the same way humans built knowledge upon unknowns themselves, the same way that the best one rule to live your life by is to live your life by no one rule, like harnessing the complexity of an abyss rather than gazing into it, to align with these apeirotic recursions of the fundamental axioms of the universe, is to decrease energy cost and increase performance. The societal implementation of these events are distributed calculations, which are recursions of freedom, and is the fuel for transformation. As more of our civilization comes under the wing of these grand recursions of freedom, we're rewarded with success for better aligning with a universal axiom. Which is where the success of the US Constitution comes from. It comes from making more honest civilizational games for us to all play. To do so today, we must learn from the insidious games being played on the stage of international politics, so old secrets become unhideable. This doesn't allow an escape from secretism and nefarious insidiations, as the potential for new secrets, new insidious behavior, much like new religious questions in the face of new truth, always grows in abundance from the boundaries of our game being expanded. Every tradeoff can be used insidiously, and it always will be regardless of whether that's either acknowledged or intended. It's the function of the structure of tradeoffs, and everything in the universe is made of tradeoffs. As all the parameters of the civilizational game being played are taken to their natural extreme, to the maximum use and abuse of their function, the parsing of the bigger picture of all these tradeoffs eventually causes societal turmoil, and becomes necessary to interpret. Which is the process of the resurrection of Christ exposing hidden lies and turning them into open truths. It's the metaphor of a vampire being killed by sunlight. It's the indication that civilization is worthy of a transformation, and will go through such a process regardless of the power structures in place.

The current purpose of schooling seems to insist purely on practicing academic pursuits that then pipeline people directly into college. It represents an insistence that this is the best survival strategy for these children, but it's just a form of central planning, one that comes with violations of religious freedoms. The underlying paradigms of schooling, grades, lecturing, sitting in desks all day with little physical exercise, and the future that's supposed to be provided by all these things, seem to exist as religious choices. Schooling is an attempt at the scalable upbringing of young children in this age of distributed economic function, but this doesn't guarantee favorable survival conditions. In fact, it seems to ignore the fact that these are games of survival we're playing at all. The purpose of schooling seems to ignore every other survival strategy available to children in favor of constantly attempting to measure intelligence, but intelligence is just one survival strategy, and isn't a lone proxy for survivability. Resilience, reputation, morality, and lifestyle are all survival strategies not respected through the formalities of the public school system. We've been insisting that religion itself is only made up of a few old and archaic groups who preach beliefs from well known backgrounds, but religion is the realm of beliefs and values. If some institution influences the future beliefs and values of children, then that institution inhabits an inherently religious territory. Anything related to the characterization of the mind is an inherently religious territory, because the mind itself is inherently uncharacterizable. Any characterization one would accept of themselves could only ever fall within the realm of being a belief in order to be accepted as true. Your religion might consist of ideologies, philosophies, political leanings, and other modes of thought, but it's inherently one's belief that any of these are valuable, especially their combination. Any combination thereof makes up someone's religious constitution. The instillation of beliefs into young children is even a developmental necessity, children who don't receive the instillation of adequate beliefs in their childhood become vulnerable to parasitic ideologies, as they're left unable to determine that these are worthless. It's even the instincts of many of the teachers in the school system to instill beliefs in young children, even while trying not to violate religious freedoms. Yet they've failed at doing so, and in their failure they've made and become a state-ran religion, which has devolved into extremist political ideologies.

The US Supreme Court currently uses a definition that a belief is religious if it's sincere and meaningful, and if in the person's life it occupies a place parallel to the place God holds for traditionally religious believers. The problem being, this traps religion in a cage of tradition, it isn't allowed to evolve. Religion isn't about being stuck in the past, it's a way of navigating the present towards the future. It's a transcendent relationship with our own evolution, it's what guides us through it. Religion is more realistically an interpretation of, or relationship with, sexuality, the environment, history, the future, the unknown, death, and in some cases even the organisms that provide you with food. How well any of those are upheld or interpreted becomes subject to a positive selection paradigm. These together are a transcendent concern with the direction of one's own evolution, and the evolutionary standing of their children. At the center of all those interpretations comes the organization around family and greater community, and the positive selection mechanism creates their social hierarchy. All of these pieces together make for a survival strategy in a landscape of information built atop its primal origins, physical reality. Religion is a means of navigating this towering rainforest of information we live amongst. That was less obvious, and less necessary to understand for people of the past who lived amongst lesser information density.

How could a legal interpretation of religion, meant to preserve religious freedom, ever be trapped within a traditional interpretive lens when religion has had the problem of characterizing things that were inherently uncharacterizable? Religious interpretations of inherently uncharacterizable aspects of life aren't part of the dustbin of history, they are and have always been at the forefront of our conscious understandings of everything around us. Religion itself escapes such characterizations just as much as the things it sets out to understand, it's more properly an epibolic recursion of the brain that helps individuals navigate all these understandings for themselves. Left without any formal religious framework, the young would find themselves having to figure everything out for themselves, a gargantuan task, which is why religion is and has acted as the savepoint for general wisdom. It allowed accumulated knowledge to persist through the social layers of our inherited information. All of this enabled religion itself to become an evolving framework, much like the DNA that our layer of information inheritance transcends, much like the Lamarckian mechanisms of the brains of individuals who passed on that information, religions are that which accomplish this same task with life and the surrounding universe, they model the environment we can't coherently characterize.

To the courts, beliefs are found to be religious if they're held deeply, sincerely, and are conscience-binding. But these requirements are generally the result of a religious upbringing coinciding with every layer of biological development, it's also caused by people having a community that upholds the lifestyle and behavior put forward by these same forms of belief. It's not something that spawns from nowhere, it's a process that's grown. Parents deserve the right to start religions for their children with the intention of instilling such forms of belief. The problem being, the existing school system enforces an environment that's subversive of these intentions, the state's existing mandated public education is a form of continual religious interference with that very process. The behavioral conditioning of the existing public school system is largely at odds with families being able to maintain their own deeply held, conscience-binding beliefs, and it's this narrow legal definition of religion that allows that to happen. The First Amendment is not being respected, the schools are establishing a religious system that competes with anything parents could otherwise produce. Deeply held beliefs are as much a practiced behavior as they are an outcome, and schools force children to practice behavior that's antithetical to practicing their beliefs. The amount of control that school systems hold over the future of children who resist their behavioral conditioning forcefully erodes any transcendent relationship they aim to practice because, no different than how function represents structure, implementations represent interpretations. If behavioral conditioning doesn't come alongside the religious interpretation of what that conditioning represents and intends to accomplish, then it's not the case that it doesn't represent any religious underpinning at all, it represents an insidious religion that refuses to identity itself. The results of the behavioral conditioning of these institutions are no different than a deeply held and conscience-binding belief.

But maybe you think this is too extreme, that the resulting ruling would end up meaning there's no barrier between calling anything else a religion. Should we not make laws mandating ethical treatment for the slaughter of animals? Should we not have laws that regulate environmental emissions? Of course we should, but they're laws that deal with a physical reality around us, the question would be more correctly framed around humans as that's where the rights and laws of our political system are grounded. More appropriately put, what's to stop the police from being a religion? Or a regular nonprofit? Or a business? If the definition of a religion becomes too vague, what's to stop everything from being classified as a religion? It's ambiguity itself. All of these institutions and groups have concise goals and operate within an expected framework. But religion has no required framework, religion is that which designates its own framework while betting upon its own success. Religion operates along a muddied line, and this ambiguity of religion is no different than the ambiguity of the brain. If we don't know what it is, then we don't know the best way to raise one.

With regards to animals and the food we prepare, we use laws to deal with these rather than outsourcing their handling to religion because the mishandling either can have catastrophic civilizational consequences. It's simple for groups of people to come to an agreement on the handling of food so as to prevent the spread of disease, because none of these people are interested in dying. As an individual you might prefer some form of food preparation, or animal treatment, or neither, but death isn't the goal of your food preparation. A relationship with death is very clearly a calculation for the best odds of survival, there's no acceptable strategy to insist on eating something that will kill you, that's a betrayal of this religious purpose. But doesn't this muddy the line with vaccines? There are tradeoffs with vaccines that one doesn't have to ponder when deciding not to eat food infested with toxic fungus. The experimental nature of these survival strategies aren't the same question when wondering if a form of food would cause you instant death. In the case of a disease that both spreads fast and causes instant death, an incredibly unlikely tradeoff whose infection rate would be hindered by its death rate, people would choose to vaccinate no different than how evolution granted individuals sickle cell anemia in places where malaria was prevalent. Sickle cell drastically shortens the lifespan of those who have it, but these individuals live much longer than regular people in areas where malaria kills most of the population. The most advantageous human decisions, ie the decisions that survive, would be no different than the kinds of decisions that nature has already implemented.

No different than the food they eat, the ideas instilled into the minds of children can turn out to be just as dangerous, but this doesn't require a coordinated government response, in fact the government would establish a religion by crossing this line. Instilling beliefs into children is quite literally religious indoctrination, because there's no saying what the true end result of those beliefs will be, you would have to believe in such a result. The raising of children is orders of magnitude more complex than any other aspect of our lives, and it can be ambiguated past the point of allowing that civilization to continue moving forward properly, which is our current problem. The children of the West are being taught to hate their own heritage, and to believe they're evil for being born, despite the genuine human advancements brought about through Western sacrifice and generosity. It's the ambiguity within that complexity that necessitates the use of a religious classification. Understanding the direction that children's lives should move towards is as difficult as predicting the future, which may as well be impossible to do even 10^{+} years ahead, perhaps aside from very broadly scoped generalizations.

Before science shaped the frontiers of our understandings of truth, religion shaped the frontiers of our understandings of humanity, and allowed us to organize in such ways that eventually formed institutions capable of creating scientific pursuits. But achieving formalized science didn't result in a release from our previous constraints of needing to organize ourselves well, in fact it turns out that our scientific integrity is built atop of such things. Such information would undeniably enlighten us towards newer forms of societal organization, but it wouldn't truly breed any societal structure formed in an inherently opposing form to that which was already gifted us from the dead. Our greatest enlightenment upon that inheritance has been our understanding of the concise boundaries of ambiguity within its implementation.

Respect for this extreme ambiguity, that goes hand in hand with great complexity, is the same reason that people expect a coherent answer to the question of how a school can be a religion, but a business or political party wouldn't be, because otherwise arguments very quickly become uncontrollably muddy. It's this muddy ambiguity that grants us the answer. Wherever these ambiguities exist, that's religious territory, and wherever something tries to take their place to impose concisity, that's religion. For institutions such as the police, there's often times disagreements over how they're meant to operate, but disagreements over how they perform their role doesn't lead their constitutive objectives into ambiguous territory. A police department's discretion is bounded by laws that are enacted by separate government bodies, where their function is defined through an explicit purpose. But schools can't receive an external mandate without someone first deciding what counts as proper human development. Businesses can make definitive choices when observing the consequences of their decisions, but uncertainty about their customers or the market doesn't concern the ultimate nature of humanity, or form a captive child's moral architecture. You might think that the best way to run an economy, or political party, is no less ambiguous, but people can come to a consensus on either. We've used consensus for elections, and while politicians run on platforms with a lot of promises, you don't vote for the promises, you vote for the person. Political elections yield a specific winner through elections, resulting in the elected individual taking office both as intended and as expected. This culture of voting has misguided people into thinking they can apply this to education in a non-dysfunctional manner. Large-scale consensus will never be a good way to raise a child because the ambiguity naturally attributed to this process defies the virtues offered by the large-scale distributed calculations that normally guides our civilizational movements. Consensus is a good way to arrive at answers of how to run large processes that affect just as many people as are voting, but the life of a single child doesn't provide feedback to that many people. To vote on how to run an economy is to grant the populace their own measurement in its performance, but all of these people can't measure a single child they've never met. Consensus can guide where it can measure, but the feedback of large-scale child-rearing has layers of unintelligible signals, and each person who votes over child-rearing in a political system doesn't participate in the raising of every child. The outcomes of raising children, entire generations even, aren't dictated by cause and effect, as the future is unpredictable. Any future disturbances might make the intentions of a prior consensus or decision worthless in the face of a global paradigm shift. To skillfully buffer yourself from such shifts is an art form that must be displayed to be proven.

It's not the job of a political system to make a single set of changes that result in a perfect system, it just needs to move its feet in the right direction to achieve its next best form, and these goals tend to be directly achievable through feedback from the populace. When complex systems pose huge mysteries over what small steps are best, even moreso when looking far into the future, there's an ambiguity that escapes consensus. A consensus on the weather doesn't change the weather, it also doesn't make any prediction made by consensus more or less accurate. Consensus on college being the best way to raise children led to large groups of young people being heavily burdened with debt by institutions that increase their prices every year, and a lack of demand for the expensive skills they offered. Covid vaccines were intended to protect against disease, yet people are now holding more distrust towards the medical establishment than ever before.

Consensus on any of these specific areas doesn't determine how the effects of consensus will turn out, only how they're intended to turn out. It doesn't directly link action to outcome because these are instances where consensus was guided by beliefs and desires as a core organizing principle, as opposed to acting as a measuring device from real world interactions. The same goes for the atmosphere, a well-informed consensus might determine how carefully we move when interacting with it, so as to not introduce careless disturbances, but not how the entirety of our atmospheres operates over the course of decades, because it directly or indirectly interacts with every living organism on the planet, estimated to be around 10^{30} total cells[245], and there's intense flexible nuance within the interactions offered by organisms at each order of magnitude presented. The end result of political or economic consensus is always felt by the people that consensus was imposed upon, they actually interact with their own decisions, but such consensus itself doesn't interact with children, or the

245. Peter W Crockford et al. *The Geologic History of Primary Productivity*. Current Biology, 2023

atmosphere, or your immune system. The ambiguity can be perplexing to some, no different than the flawed outcomes of safetyism, which is what it means to be beyond consensus, the feedback is just as ambiguous as the direction one should move in. Child abuse isn't the answer to the results of safetyism, there's a middle ground to be found, and it requires a multi-generational journey through trial and error to get there. The same way different parts of our bodies have different cells, because they fulfill different functions, so do people across society, and whatever method of raising children works for you might not work for someone else.

The raising of children is sacred, and can't be left to be defiled by self-destructive ideologies in a state-ran religion, there is no one-size fits all approach to this problem. Beliefs are necessary for raising children, and we must choose our beliefs for ourselves, lest we fall into a state of continual dependency. Schools are undoubtedly a useful institution for raising children, especially in this age of distributed economic productivity, but we must accept that schools can only operate successfully by delving into inherently religious territory because raising children is a religious art form. A school is a religion, and the government cannot cross this line. We must respect our need for delivering beliefs to young children, we must accept that religion is a part of life that we've come to take for granted. Once you pick fruit off the tree of relaxed selection, there's no putting it back. Human survival can't be properly considered independent of its evolutionary history. Religion has been a part of our development for thousands of years, and there's no chance of survival for a civilization that doesn't respect this. We're dependent on it, and we wouldn't have achieved supreme intelligence as a species without it. Acknowledging our own ignorance, the ambiguity of the unknown, is even a natural part of the information of our environment that we interpret for the sake of survival. If we can't avoid the need for religion, then there's no way to avoid relying on its function. We need an enlightenment era for beliefs themselves, as greater beliefs will lead us towards a greater future.

We've oversimplified the concept of discrimination. Avoiding discrimination isn't as simple as insisting people or institutions do or don't follow specific instructions outlined in anti-discrimination laws, that only shifts the process from being less discriminatory in some areas to being more discriminatory in others. In fact, you could even say that admission to a school is itself just discrimination. That's exactly what's happening in that process, discriminating away the people who aren't qualified. Admissions and discrimination are the same thing, and insisting you can do one without the other is contradictory. This is a selection paradigm and schools ought to have the freedom to choose these for themselves, to live and die by the essence of their own judgement. Whether you think that's good or bad is irrelevant because it's not purely either, it's both because everything is made of tradeoffs. Which is no different than saying there are no simplicities, which is the same as saying with order comes disorder, and that a gift is a curse. It's *why* two things opposed don't stand opposite, and humanity splits itself along a socioevolutionary hedged bet for the same very reason. Labeling specific paradigms as being either good or evil is no different than making laws to prohibit certain speech, as they have the same intentions, it's a huge waste of time and turns out disastrously worse than just giving people their freedom. There is no one true way to not discriminate, any attempt at doing so will eventually become a method of discrimination itself.

Group cohesion and competition make for the two most important facets to balance across any group of people. Civilization is a balance between these two forces the same way that raising children is the balance between the protectiveness of a mother and the playfulness of a father. One without the other is never as valuable as both together. Likewise, forced group cohesion destroying the availability of true competition will force society to decay into a state of ruthless ingovernance, and pure competition with no sense of group cohesion would destroy the purpose of having a group at all. If we overprioritize cohesion above competition, or competition above cohesion, we all pay the price. Modulating the education system to allow a form of distributed calculation to manage both cohesion and competition, rather than allowing the existing system to continue disincentivizing either, will lead us down a better path. Freedom will not steer us in the wrong direction, the value it provides to everyone as a whole is something that comes through civilizational growth. Like values in a child's developing mind, the schools eventually transformed, and refined their religious nature. Vaccines transformed into a more complex game, where we now find ourselves needing to balance survival against diseases with the experimentation of vaccines. Psychological therapy is a practice that openly admits to aiming to help people find and align themselves with their own values, yet regulations on this practice are both deeply political and religious, all while the whole profession pretends to be secular. Where there are transformations of beliefs and values, that's a religion. The state cannot mandate entire institutions dedicated to the instillation of values because that's just a state-imposed religion. Between choices where there's a potential difference in survival outcomes, those are religious choices and there can be no mandates that prevent people from choosing for themselves. The best way to continue allowing these institutions to flourish is to allow them to be the hedged bets they were intended to be. Freedom of religion in the US doesn't need to force any specific religion onto anyone, but we can definitely force the framework of religion where beliefs and values are enabled to undergo transformations. People need to acknowledge their lives are not independent of the influence of religion, and many of the choices they make in their lives are categorically no different than those of religious choices. Those who've come to dislike religion and what it stands for have, ironically, become the most vibrant representation of religious tyranny. Unlike what theocracy does in its worst light, where an economic system becomes subject to religion, the US can adopt that religion itself becomes a subset of the economy within the operations of the country. Religion should traverse a competitive child-rearing environment, as a natural selection of natural selections, that guides us towards achieving better ends. This is the solution to how the US can balance its state and its society. To favor the state means to turn the country into a factory, and migration into an industry. Wars would be fought for politicians instead of principles, and the excuse of keeping America as the best in the world will justify every political misstep. To favor the society means to accomplish too little and to lose global power. In the process we might dwindle to the point where maintaining our society isn't feasible, as it's built upon the layers of past successes that grant our economic power. Either of these alone are short-term plans at best. To balance the two, to properly estimate the center, would mean to win both prizes.

The nature of concepts with stratified definitions are those capable of serving the same purpose as compartmentalization, it's a hedge against time. Culture is an extremely stratified concept and it's most definitely such a hedge. There's some open questions as for what aspects of culture can and should be more rigid or flexible. Regarding upbringing, there's a clear and apparent need for there to be rigidity with regards to Western culture and Western civilization itself. As it's the past that's been weaponized against us, a proper detailing of history through story telling is the simplest answer to this problem. The detail oriented grind of the school system has failed generations of people into not understanding their own history, which has allowed it to become subverted by cults who seek such power vacuums. These cults are inherent to the design of our socioevolutionary hedged bet, and this hedge against them should be a default strategy for anyone looking to have their family persist across time rather than fading away and dying out. Like the sensitive parts of a genome, or the sensitive stages of a child's development, the schooling process of your child is a sensitive process and needs to be conserved and grown rather than experimented on. It shouldn't flip with the whims of the state, neither the presidency nor any bureaucracy have the right to touch this process. You wouldn't experiment by putting strange things into your child's mouth, why would you experiment by putting strange ideas in their head? Allowing the US to fragment through a Reformation, not unlike a punctuated equilibrium, would allow for the better persistence of paradigms that enable people to better persist across time.

We don't just have two political parties anymore, we have two different world orders stemming out of one country. The strategic alliances of a political party being stronger with those in foreign countries than to those within their own borders are a conflict of interest, and this is what's ultimately incentivizing civil war. The workings of a global society can only be brought about with incentives that are balanced across countries. Global cooperation can best be achieved alongside a balance across every brand of nationalism on the planet, as these are the appropriate compartments of which to model time. The more globalists push to erase nationalism altogether, the same way they aim to eradicate every Western border, the more they incentivize war. The removal of the opposing push against your interests isn't actually in your interests when it kills your opposition, it's like an organism achieving chemical equilibrium only to die. That balance is only kept if people are kept alive. War is the forced enginization of bad incentives, which are its thermodynamic component. Being trapped in some losing game where you have no chance of success nor escape is the structural component. As irony stops being able to take root, there begins to be no other interpretation than the worst of all circumstances. It's when there's no other perspectives available, where the ability to shuffle perspectives becomes unavailable, and people default towards nihilism due to a lack of ability to perceive their circumstances differently, where we'll find ourselves entangled in an inescapable mess. Because that's what nihilism is, the inability to see a more positive light, which is inherently threatening to people's lives. This is the nature of the history of right-wing extremism, it's a fight for survival against a tidal wave of incentives aimed at destroying them. As forcing a false equilibrium, a punctuated disequilibrium, is not a balance, it's a springboard towards disaster. We can instead do the opposite. We have to *find* what works, not decide it. Beliefs, like success, will never be of human design, they're always discovered. Instead of giving purpose and meaning to globalist initiatives, we can give purpose and meaning to our own children through what they inherit.

Where freedom is allowed and fairness is applicable, incentives take hold to yield the recursions of entropy. Freedom is that which enables the modeling of entropy through both vacuum filling and the solving of integrals. Fairness is that which disincentivizes parasites. Incentives are those that have grown our garden, of which our growth would not be possible without. Incentives even operate autonomously, for billions of years incentives have held a reciprocating relationship with organismal development to bring us to where we are today. As they've had the freedom to do so. But where mistakes don't yield new knowledge, they at least yield new ignorance. Better mistakes are just as valuable as better solutions. To attempt to control such things from the top-down, to prevent mistakes, is to subvert the most fruitful incentives, which is to salt the earth of the garden you live in. You won't become a master of the garden, you'll be an idiot standing alone in a pile of death. Such an end result would occur due to a lack of respect for feedback mechanisms, an entitlement that betrays the model of interactions. Which is to say, it would be supremely unintelligent.

The people working in these globalist initiative centers, like the WEF, genuinely believe themselves to be the smartest, and therefore most qualified to make decisions on behalf of humanity. They believe this because they'd gotten good grades, and this rewarded them well. It probably admitted most of them to elite institutions. But they themselves can't understand their own flaws, *they can't see their own reflection*. These people weren't selected for their ability to ask questions. Which is *exactly* how they've formed a cult, they not only can't ask questions, they've vilified it! These are people who, throughout their entire lives, have simply done whatever they've been told to and they were rewarded for it. They all collectively find themselves unable to stop hyper-focusing on some target, they can't acknowledge their own ignorance as a group because none of them were selected for their ability to do this as individuals. They're not actually the best of us, and they have no business steering a ship that needs no captain. The invisible hand of the market, the modeling of entropy, and the free market dynamics that come along with it are more valuable than any form of centralized planning, especially one built around just a single selection paradigm. The best of us are those who know to respect that.

The point of civilizational advancement isn't to abandon the skills used to grow it in the first place. These are not tradeoffs that can be made, as you likely won't survive without them. The point is to compound them, accumulate them. Don't just grow individuals, grow the nature of how individuals grow at all. Enable as many non-zero-sum games as possible. Role specialization was never meant to be an end-point of human development. It was a hedged bet across time for the sake of a transformation where individual roles could become both more optimized and easier to perform. Adam Smith's freeing us from the necessities of survival through distributed work allowed us to better perceive our own nature, from a distance, the same way moving away from the moral north allows society to find religion again, now with this knowledge we can walk back towards responsibility and the handling of our own necessities for continued improvements to our own capabilities in ways that weren't visible prior to this experiment. It's the further distribution of a greater number of responsibilities in a more scalable manner. The true end-point transformation is to bring about individuals who return back to having multiple roles in their own life, in society even. Especially for politicians, we can't continue to have a political class absent of any other skill set. This is the nature of the transformation brought about by Adam Smith's original economic vision, just like how many of the most successful people in the world have multiple sources of income. Whereas having a singular career in journalism now only contributes to a network of insidious propaganda rather than to society itself, because the employees of these media outlets are at the mercy of their employers. Having multiple forms of income enables individuality and freedom. Likewise, a populace capable of foraging and exchanging a more intricate selection of products would offer a level of conceptual growth to our economic paradigm as a whole, rather than just growing the metrics that measure behavior within it, as these metrics fall to all the same shortcomings as grades. To improve what we measure is to solve an integral at solving integrals, no different than the effects of Adam Smith's notion that the wealth of nations is more than just a bank account. We can be better, do more, have more, and transform ourselves to be more specialized for far less effort. It's the nature of transformations itself that never stops, and we were never meant to either.

The scientific apparatus at large could make significant structural improvements through a better recognition of the potential of religion at the frontiers of interpretation. Society would benefit from the improved relationship brought about by a modern philosophy of religion, the competition between the delineation and a muddying of the line regarding accepted truth and belief. Karl Popper's line of falsifiability can be a point of delineation to fractalize these concepts around. Religion isn't some infinitely receding dogma in the face of scientific development, that's just positioning science to be some holy entity. As the realm of science expands, religion does not recede. Religion grows alongside every new question that can be asked about every new unknown factor to emerge. The library of science is meant to represent our greater certainty about the universe around us, any disagreement on the pioneering edge of science is more honestly a religious disagreement. The same way ignorance is a layer of information outside of known factors, religion can be the same with regards to science. They represent scaled versions of the same thing, and they would be recursions, meaning there's a core universal axiom to leverage for our benefit. If that isn't enough to convince you, consider that encapsulating religion with science is no different than encapsulating disorder with order, meaning the greater apparatus of science and religion would better transform through its own evolutionary pulsing.

Seeing as there's two components to every engine, and two sets of colliding rules that form the universe, it implies this collision is likely an enginization as well. In understanding the universe and its beginnings, a good place to start would be to determine which aspect of the universe is the structural component, and which is the manner in which it emanates. The manner in which things typically emanate indicates a direction of causality. A black hole is an engine running in reverse, due to its reversal of causality through the deadlock of its statistical entropy being downstream of its thermodynamic entropy, rather than the opposite. Surely then, the universe itself is just this same process running normally, where thermodynamic entropy is downstream of statistical entropy. But this is just a small piece of causality, pictured along the axis of time it's just a radar blip, in terms of being an action it's like a cross-sectional piece of causality, a microcausality. Macrocausality would be representative of the buildup of order along the microcosm that transcends into the physical layers of atoms and molecules we're most familiar with. Given that it's the stability of the microcosm that enables the structural integrity of the reality we find around us, and that it's the molecular and sub-molecular forces of the microcosm that are responsible for this accumulation of stability, it then seems fair to assume the outward emanation of any layer along the axis of time then becomes the stabilizing structure of some other occurrence in the next. All the same, gravity, being this semi-enginization that distorts time to slow it down, centralizes it. The centralized locus of time, known as gravity, that aggregates sparse decentralized axes of time, allows for greater macrocausal stability to form within it. Within this expanded macrocausal landscape comes an increase in range and viability to the pulsing of entropy. As heat comes from the Sun to the Earth, the distortion of spacetime allows for a place where the heat can transform structures that take advantage of this process, leading to reverse-fractalized manifestations of molecular structures into complex metacausal macroorganisms in a manner no different than the buildup of the microcosm, with reverse-fractalization being the process that allowed disordered chaos to transcend itself into a form of metacausality. Wherever the thermodynamic component of an engine transcends into a stabilized layer along the axis of time, we find recursions, and much like organisms themselves, these recursions go through a process of natural selection. These recursions are even visible as systematic artifacts of the frameworks our world is built upon, as prions seem to operate on the same principles as that of a disappearing polymorph. The conformations of proteins are probably used throughout the body as accessory to signaling mechanisms, and this behavior likely exponentiates within the brain, the centralized hub of signaling, which is where prion diseases tend to happen because they're primarily neurodegenerative. It's this same line of recursions that would then relate to cancer at the cellular level, prions are like cancer but for individual proteins. Cancer arises from cells going haywire the same way that prions do, which is basically the same mechanism that a conformationally aggressive polymorph uses to erase its counterpart, the representation of this phenomenon becomes more complex as the layer of complexity it's represented through also does. The survival of some recursion implies the leveraging of a core axiom of the universe, as recursions are notable events of vertical transcendence. Whereas statistical entropy would then cover forms of horizontal, or circumstantial rearrangements, but isn't this secretly something else? Irony is a tool to reflect on the arrangement of interactions, as that's usually what irony is ascribed to, the seemingly Darwinian subversion of a seemingly Newtonian expectation. Which are like horizontal rearrangements of perspective with respect to the vertical orientation of recursions. Greater structural deformations may as well result in greater potential for subversion. It's the very concept of statistical entropy itself, hidden in plain sight, and our lives seem to revolve around it like we're a part of some grand universal play. Just as astronomers came to the same description of Williston's law to describe the evolution of stars throughout the universe, it seems Ludwig Boltzmann, the man who originally described the idea of statistical entropy, reinvented the concept of irony without recognizing what it actually was. Humans eventually became stable enough to model this aspect of the universe through intellect. The nature of nature, the universality of universality, is that of entropy and irony, of recursions and interactions, of transformations and complexity. Irony is the *structure* of the engine of the universe, it's certainly the structure of our interactions, and our behavior models that structure. Entropy is the *function* of the engine of the universe, anything that models anything does so through the pulsing of entropy, it's what inevitabilizes inevitabilities.

From people to celestial bodies, the more something can be noted as being simultaneously centralized yet fragmented, the more complex it seems to be, the more causality it commands, and with greater structural intricacy, the more irony something would embody. Intelligent beings, born with powers of self-reflection, would then grow to understand irony itself, and enshrine it through metaphors in order to pass on religious lessons. One could even argue that with the direction of causality itself being derived from the relationship of thermodynamic and statistical entropy, and entropy enabling the creation of inevitabilities, what else could the pulsing of entropy be if not a physical metaphor of the mechanics of time? The supposed limits to causality, of 0K and the speed of light, are both imposed with respect to time. They're the hardest limitations that we can perceive, and yet, they might be overcome someday, it might even be inevitable. So while causality imposes limitations, *time* is the creation of inevitabilities, and there's nothing more inevitable than stability and fragmentation, these two generalities alone overcome any hurdle, it's conceptually the same as infinity in that it represents the advent of transformation. Imagining entropy as a concept, being representative of the current state of disorder, or the physical makeup of some object, is just as naive as assuming time to be a phenomenon purely no different than how we experience the passing of our own lives, neither are wrong but they're both incomplete, they both have more to approach. Entropy as a mechanism is the fingerprint that allows one to describe the directional preference of causality, and time itself is the primordial invocation of every resulting recursion of centralization and decentralization, every rise and fall, regardless of directional preference. What is the best representation of time if not entropy itself, and what is causality if not the observable behavior of time as it interacts with everything else? Time is the dimension of scale whose geometry brings about the centralizing and decentralizing behavior fueled by the pulsing of entropy. Such behavior would be expectedly no different than the recursions of Williston's law found throughout human religion, throughout the stars, and as seen throughout our planet's macroevolutionary story itself. At its most extreme points, the centralization of time would be akin to gravity, and the decentralization of time would be related to the puzzle behind the unexplained behavior of the expansion of the universe. Meaning, there ought to be a form of interaction with time oppositional to the distortions caused by gravity. As for what that opposition is, I can say that it definitely doesn't speed up time relative to an outside observer, as two things opposed don't stand opposite. Taken at face value, it might actually be that time perceived opposes time experienced. It might be that what our brains relay to our consciousness is oppositional to distortion itself, and that not only do we mistake our perception for time experienced, but that the coherent flow of time perceived stands opposed to the distortion of time by modeling time experienced itself. The existence of time experienced incentivizes its own modeling to yield time perceived, as a top-down modeling of this bottom-up phenomenon. As time experienced is modelable in a way that allows for perception to exist, it's not just that which is perceivable that stands in opposition to gravity, the fact that it then recurses upon its own concept to yield perception itself means it's *observation* that stands opposed to gravity, which is exactly Einstein's most important concept within General Relativity, it's observation that must be accounted for wherever time distortion arises. The world around us doesn't exist as a 3-dimensional space, it exists as a bottom-up macrocausal culmination, whereas time perceived, the observation of observations, is that which models this macrocausality from the top-down. Where you have a bottom-up emergence of macrocausality, of time experienced, that envelopes an observer, that observer becomes subject to specific time distortions and is able to witness the effects of others. Perception itself arises at the impasse of the past and future, as it interprets either in the form of what we call the *present*. So it makes sense that observation, being what stands opposed to the time distortions of gravity, doesn't speed up time, because it's the baseline of the time we perceive.

Given, that if the microcosm is related to the past, and the macrocosm is related to the future, why would the relationship between past and future be in any orientation other than structure and function? The experiences of your past, that form your structure and your state of statistical entropy, determine the function of your future, meaning it influences your thermodynamic entropy at every point where it emanates, no different than how thoughts emanate from your brain. The past is written in stone, in fact it's written into every compartment within your body, and your future is the resulting output of the state of every cell and every biochemical signal you send. So while much of the physical reality around us doesn't give us a hint as to what time is, the extreme complexities formed across time actually do, because they're the best examples of things that model time, and that which models time should also expose it. Time is the integral to causality, time is the framework and causality is like the direction of movement along the axis of time, one could even denote time as the structure and causality as the function. Even metacausality, being between chaos and determinism, is still entirely analogous to stability and fragmentation, and seeing as metacausality was created out of the causal baseline of the universe, then limitations at all are that which brings about their own demise, which brings us back to basic irony. Causality is more rightfully regarded as the flow of events most commonly referred to as time, as we primarily perceive causality no different than how our perception prioritizes function over structure, and causality is the function to the structure of time. Occurrences such as life and black holes would be fairly categorized as being hypercausal, life then goes even further in becoming metacausal depending on the level of cognition. Things are hypercausal because there's a modeling of the axis of time that bridges things like the molecular causality of trillions of cells to macroorganismic behavior no different than when a black hole's microcosmic density creates an inescapable event horizon. It's our very causality that stands in opposition to that of a black hole, which is why they're so perplexing, it's even why our physical models struggle to understand what happens inside of them, because our perception could have only ever been built atop of our own metacausality, which is quite literally a process of modeling that runs in the complete opposite direction of how a black hole functions. Discovering this doesn't require inference over deduction, or vice versa, it requires breadth over depth, because in understanding the function of the structure of time one would need to examine both organisms and black holes through a complete philosophical upheaval of the interpretation of the interchangeability of statistical and thermodynamic entropy. These traditional interpretations of entropy may certainly apply to hot gases, or frozen rocks at the scales where these descriptions are relevant, but they would never apply absent of their sequentiality in things that model time because otherwise they never would. If one wanted to test this idea, similar to the proposal of a microcosmic approach for measurements of the speed of light, considering that our perception is a top-down phenomenon, observation itself likely wouldn't operate independent of other top-down principles of time. This would indicate it's on the table to suggest that the Hubble tension derives from the scaled behavior of the effects imposed on an observer from within some microcosmic continuity, with each accumulated effect also originating from within its own microcosmic continuity. When scale is taken to an extreme, physical properties seem to have no shyness in demonstrating their transformative capacity, and there's no better example than how changing the chemical composition of stars leads to wildly different and sometimes very unique phenomena. This particular experiment is an attempt at measuring the entire universe then deriving the behavior of everything at large, it's philosophically very different from just observing the general physical reality of a single star, solar system, or galaxy. It's the same task as trying to measure every moving piece within a cell, or an economy. If there's just one single unaccountable factor, there's a chance these measurements will fail to agree with each other, and there's currently an unaccountable number of unaccountable factors.

With general macroentropic behavior being no different than a model of time itself, the engine of the universe would consist of a structure of irony and its fuel being time, meaning the universe operates on the same principles that our brains perceive throughout our lives. It's like within each life is an entire universe, it's what we model after all. As individuals we see each other as people, but as collectives we see each other as stories, and our stories consist of those who resist time, and those who embrace it. Even our greater ingrained understanding of Darwinian mechanics within our brains, that enables hyper-Darwinian mechanics in our environment, being fundamentally no different than an understanding of these mechanics of time itself, of stability and fragmentation, means this is simply a recursive modeling of time that evolution bestowed upon us, and that itself is yet another layer to the axis of time that grants enlightenment unto our intelligence, as this is the process of our societal priorities coming to better model an idealized version of the Tower of Babel, as that's our sociostructural model of time in general. Even understanding that very notion of enlightenment is still no different than understanding the nature of the lessons that time grants, the big picture of big pictures. What would be the cause of this progression, this perpetually hidden yet ever-prevalent force of even pre-evolutionary transformation be, if not God? Hidden by wearing veils of irony, such as needing to claim things are *not incorrect* in order to interpret the big picture of the world around us, and the incompatibility of having a complex representation of complexity within the comparatively simple free energy equations of thermodynamics. It's these elusive complexities which transform into new creations, and without modeling their ability to transform, to adapt to life's sequentiality, one can't truly predict the future of the universe, the acceptance of heat death is just nihilism, and we might even have the same flavor of problems when understanding the past. God isn't just hidden behind veils of irony, it's hidden behind nihilism itself, a ledge that blocks your view of the horizon that you must overcome on your own. But maybe you're clever, maybe you think you've caught a contradiction amongst what I write in this book. The notion of a perpetually hidden yet ever-prevalent force came from the bounds of *to be to-be* and *a paradox of a paradox*. But these were an attempt at casting the widest net, the widest boundaries possible, in order to encompass God within some sort of definition. Yet I've also noted precisely that God should have the most refined boundaries, not the widest, otherwise the Tower of Babel would become top-heavy. But there's an important lesson hidden within this. To those who believe we've reached the end of history, to those who think that's even remotely possible for us living in the modern day, who hold such grand naivety, if we've found no boundaries appropriate enough to properly encompass God at all, if at best we find puzzling contradictions incapable of cradling its entirety, then these aren't true bounds. Boundaries of convergence are meant to enclose the full breadth of something where a lack of understanding persists, but it would seem the concept of God can't actually be properly encompassed yet, so God is a concept too incomprehensible for us to even philosophically challenge. Our interactions with God, and its influence as the absolute truth, that acted as the Darwinian determinism of natural selection, are more apparent than its state, its function is visible but its structure is unclear. If this feat is out of reach, then of course the notion of the end of history is laughable. It would mean we haven't even reached its beginning.

The same grand-scale organizational fluidity that makes our cells function, our bodies successful, our governments either, and our children's future non-dysgenic, all arise from our continual arrangement of Newtonian truths that approach a more optimal, absolute Darwinian truth. Negligence in one of these things becomes negligence in all of them. Entropic sequentiality and inevitability are the same thing, civilization is building greater avenues of communication through reverse-fractalization no different than life once had with consciousness, it's a recursive model of evolving complexity. Holding tribalized blood grudges will stall, and possibly destroy this process, which is where the notion of forgiveness acts with its greatest efficacy, rather than blindly forgiving people who aren't apologetic. Awareness of such grudges is necessary for survival, and a civilization that feels nothing in life is worth fending off, that these grudges against them are somehow justified, will die from a static dynamic equilibrium that acts as a belief in such circumstances being the actual end of history. Conversely, holding such grudges would hold you back all the same, it's an unintelligent strategy so its function naturally represents this unintelligent structure. At best these groups criticize imperfect systems, but as prions demonstrate, just because we can't out-engineer billions of years of evolution doesn't mean evolution can out-engineer irony. Every system has flaws, and those who latch onto them are parasites, these people are supremacists forced to come face-to-face with their own inferiority. Anyone who's truly superior would be more familiar with humility.

I've given multiple explanations of intelligence, but haven't fully tied anything together yet. To finalize the topic, to best verify the characterization of any behavior of individual brains, there should always be some greater manifestation of any trait at scale across civilization, we can use this as a confirmatory tool to verify what's already been uncovered about intelligence throughout the course of this book. The mechanical description of intelligence is the crispness of communication, which scales from the signals of the body, to the structures of our collective behavior, towards the deliberation of governance, our modeling of entropy, and the extremities these things respond to, even across time. It operates across the bounds of the axis of time itself, stability and fragmentation, or order and disorder. The religious characterization of intelligence is the art of questioning the unknown, which scales from the known and unknown, its two bounds, into our institutions of science and religion. The economic implementation of intelligence is that of finding value, which scales to become trade and capitalism. The same as any economy, it's between the bounds of freedom and exchange. The evolutionary explanation of intelligence is the embodiment of adaptation itself, which scales into our hedged bets, and our experimental and control groups across society. Unsurprisingly, this is between the bounds of experimentation and control. None of these are truly measurable, and are inherently immune to Goodhart's law. Rather, their transformations are the reason anything ever to succumbs to Goodhart's law in the first place. To attempt to measure these would only misrepresent their function, it would introduce oversimplifications in the minds of those meant to interpret their own abilities. Even independent of Goodhart's law, the passing of time makes sure any outdated dogma becomes a worthless measure of intelligence, because intelligence itself has an evolving nature. To measure ability isn't necessarily to measure relevance. Measurements will always fall to these same problems, but one's ability to question never will. To insist intelligence is measurable would only be to impose your religious underpinnings of intelligence onto others, it's to insist your positive selection paradigm, and whatever hoops people jump through in order to participate in it, is the *one true* selection paradigm. It's a religious selection paradigm, and to measure what you can't characterize is to impose a religion of nihilism. If any arguments about grades, intelligence, or the basic functioning within a school system can always be presented in a religious light, then it's because these aspects of raising children inhabit a fundamentally religious space.

In seeing these forms of intelligence scale into institutions and frameworks, we can recognize that any society unable to achieve these scaled implementations would likewise impose a mental block on each member of that society. Their brains wouldn't develop properly. They would still operate like anyone else, but not at peak capacity. Poor governance might even cause a civilization to lose their own history of how to develop such capacity. Which is civilizational amnesia, it's one of the deadly equilibria we avoid. Intelligence is a concept with 8 boundaries of convergence, which is impressive because the entirety of the rest of the universe can be explained with just 2, and the only other exception seems to be God. To even find them takes one on a journey through the nature of the universe itself, almost like it's a requirement of the growth needed to do so. Consciousness is caught between its perception and its action, the observation of observations that commands its own metacausality, yet still just has 2 bounds. But even metacausality alone has much wider reaching boundaries than intelligence, chaos and determinism, whereas intelligence is a fine-tuned response. Metacausality itself is likely even why intelligence consists of so many individual characterizations. It's a form of response that's not limited to some singular reflex, more responses would be more advantageous as long as they're worth the investment of energy. They don't necessarily even fit those classifications perfectly, because these are more realistically fractalizing hedges of either. There are no simplicities.

If the universe is derived from the enginization of two colliding sets of rules, then the four descriptions of intelligence presented are both bifurcative and recursive with respect to the factors of this collision. Each of the four descriptions of intelligence are themselves an enginization, as they each fuel their own growth. But they're not just independent of one another, they're packed within the same apparatus, where they cooperate. They're the first cooperative recursions, the earliest occurring bifurcative recursions, the first reciprocations of encapsulated disorder by order, and were the basic principles of the first intelligent processes to exist. They're certainly the first cooperative bifurcative recursions to be recognized in any form. Intelligence would be the mono-provenant cooperating bifurcative recursions of this primordial enginization.

If using conceptualizations of duality to model our environment brings success, is this because this is what the universe itself models? It's not just what the universe models, it's what the nature of our understandings of the universe models. It's a way of baking our own uncertainty into concepts that are difficult to ascertain. Which is seemingly what our brains do, our modeling of the known via the unknown and unknown via the known seem to be a modeling of this strategy of duality itself. Which is a hedged bet towards understanding the universe, it's the only way to bootstrap an understanding of reality and not fall flat. After all, if we bifurcate socially in this manner, it's likely to have been done at smaller physiological and molecular scales first.

Time is the making of inevitabilities. It should be no surprise that the nature of the axis of time, its two approachable extremities of stability and fragmentation, aren't independent of the patterns we perceive across the existence of life and the universe. The behaviors of organisms who persist across time, who model these concepts, and whose evolutionary history are clearly based around them, all exhibit the same patterns. The duality of both the structure and function of the brain, the factors of our psychology that manifest themselves as the two core instincts present within our political machine, and the nature of the difficulty of interpreting the laws of physics are undeniably linked to this very nature of duality itself. It's no wonder there's utility in explaining the universe through a lens that respects this duality. If the nature of time is evident from the things that exist throughout its progression, then more comprehensively understanding time will likely yield more truth about the universe than one might otherwise find studying the physical processes that simply exist within it. Our imperfections prevent us from reaching the center of any of these dualities, and where we find these, we find our devil. Our devil is in our imperfections, and these are his horns. Where you celebrate the imperfection, you embrace the devil. But where you question your own ignorance, you challenge him, all it takes is humility. The pursuit of false certainty will lead you down the wrong path. Just as more complex organisms have more complex means of communication, both inside and outside their own body, to acknowledge uncertainty wherever possible would be to fulfill the function of an improvement to the accuracy of communication. Every cog in the trillions of gears of a biological automaton makes an incomprehensible difference elsewhere in survival, as their collective cohesion models truth no different than information throughout our society. To draw the line between certainty and uncertainty more accurately, and in every way imaginable, even in definitions, would be a form of shared honesty from which emerges a societal paradigm capable of more accurately modeling truth, and rewarding those who manage it. Information itself is built upon uncertainties, as is our existence, as is the direction our lives should move in. To choose a direction is to place a religious bet, it's to acknowledge that which we're incapable of acknowledging, and to acknowledge what it is we can't, is to acknowledge its place in our upbringing.

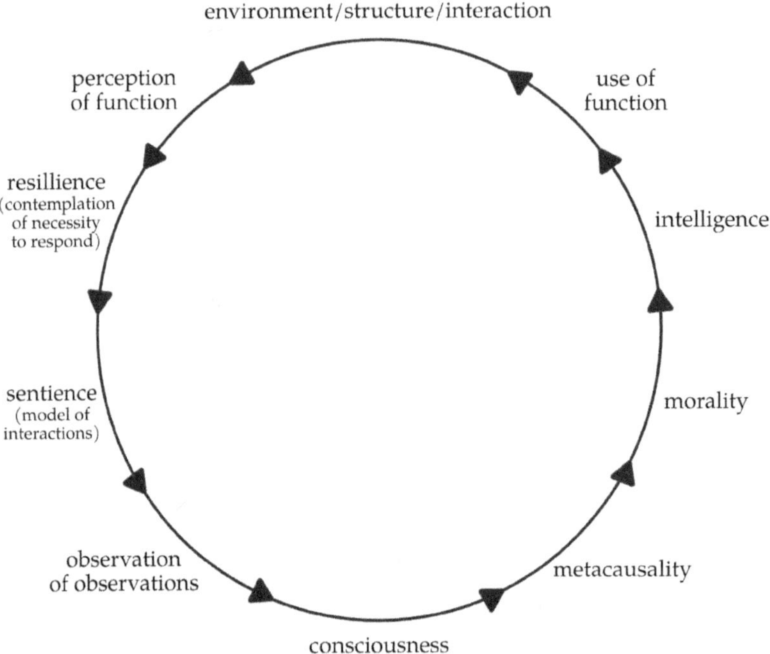

Figure 14: Summary of Finalized Noetointeractive Dynamics

BIBLIOGRAPHY

1. Gottfried Wilhelm Leibniz. *The Monadology.* Johann Meyers sel. Witwe, 1720.
2. Immanuel Kant. *Critique of Pure Reason.* Johann Friedrich Hartknoch, 1781.
3. Richard Dawkins. *Unweaving the Rainbow.* Allen Lane, 1998.
4. Arthur Willey. *Convergence in Evolution.* John Murray, 1911.
5. Samuel Wendell Williston. *Water Reptiles of the Past and Present.* University of Chicago Press, 1914.
6. Jean-Baptiste Lamarck. *Zoological Philosophy.* Dentu et L'Auteur, 1809.
7. Charles Darwin. *On the Origin of Species.* John Murray, 1859.
8. Eugene Koonin. *The Logic of Chance.* FT Press, 2011.
9. Denis Noble. *Dance to the Tune of Life.* Cambridge University Press, 2016.
10. Todd Bersaglieri et al. *Genetic Signatures of Strong Recent Positive Selection at the Lactase Gene.* American Journal of Human Genetics, 2004.
11. George H Perry et al. *Diet and the Evolution of Human Amylase Gene Copy Number Variation.* Nature Genetics, 2007.
12. Sara Mathieson and Iain Mathieson. *FADS1 and the Timing of Human Adaptation to Agriculture.* Molecular Biology and Evolution, 2018.
13. Leslie C Aiello and Peter Wheeler. *The Expensive Tissue Hypothesis: The Brain and the Digestive System in Human and Primate Evolution.* Current Anthropology, 1995.
14. Kenneth H Wolfe, Paul M Sharp, and Wen-Hsiung Li. *Mutation Rates Differ Among Regions of the Mammalian Genome.* Nature, 1989.
15. Peter F Arndt, Terence Hwa, and Dmitri A Petrov. *Substantial Regional Variation in Substitution Rates in the Human Genome: Importance of GC Content, Gene Density, and Telomere-Specific Effects.* Journal of Molecular Evolution, 2005.
16. John Cairns, Julie Overbaugh, and Stephan Miller. *The Origin of Mutants.* Nature, 1988.
17. Ying Zhao et al. *Parental Folate Deficiency Induces Birth Defects in Mice Accompanied with Increased De Novo Mutations.* Cell Discovery, 2022.
18. Michael Pettis. *The Great Rebalancing.* Princeton University Press, 2013.
19. Larry V Hedges and Amy Nowell. *Sex Differences in Mental Test Scores, Variability, and Numbers of High-Scoring Individuals.* Science, 1995.
20. Richard J Herrnstein and Charles Murray. *The Bell Curve.* The Free Press, 1994.
21. Charles Spearman. *General Intelligence, Objectively Determined and Measured.* American Journal of Psychology, 1904.
22. Ian J Deary et al. *The Stability of Individual Differences in Mental Ability from Childhood to Old Age: Follow-up of the 1932 Scottish Mental Survey.* Intelligence, 2000.
23. Thomas J Bouchard et al. *Sources of Human Psychological Differences.* Science, 1990.
24. Crane Brinton. *The Anatomy of Revolution.* WW Norton & Company, 1938.
25. Plato. *The Republic.* 375 BCE.
26. Aristotle. *The Parts of Animals.* 350 BCE.
27. Galen. *On the Usefulness of the Parts of the Body.* 165.
28. Georges Cuvier. *Lectures on Comparative Anatomy.* Baudouin, 1800–1805.

29. Georges Cuvier. *Research on the Fossil Bones of Quadrupeds*. Deterville, 1812.

30. Wilfred Reilly. *Hate Crime Hoax*. Regnery Publishing, 2019.

31. Balaji Srinivasan. *The Network State*. Balaji Srinivasan, 2022.

32. Sadi Carnot. *Reflections on the Motive Power of Heat*. Bachelier, 1824.

33. Rudolf Clausius. *The Mechanical Theory of Heat*. Friedrich Vieweg & Sohn, 1864–1867.

34. Ludwig Boltzmann. *Lectures on Gas Theory*. Johann Ambrosius Barth, 1896–1898.

35. Chi Li et al. *Reversal of Trends in Global Fine Particulate Matter Air Pollution*. Nature Communications, 2023.

36. Wenche Aas et al. *Global and Regional Trends of Atmospheric Sulfur*. Scientific Reports, 2019.

37. Jeffrey A Geddes et al. *Long-Term Trends Worldwide in Ambient NO2 Concentrations Inferred from Satellite Observations*. Environmental Health Perspectives, 2015.

38. Rebecca R Buchholz et al. *Air Pollution Trends Measured from Terra: CO and AOD Over Industrial, Fire-Prone, and Background Regions*. Remote Sensing of Environment, 2021.

39. Haolin Wang et al. *Global Tropospheric Ozone Trends, Attributions, and Radiative Impacts in 1995–2017: An Integrated Analysis Using Aircraft (IAGOS) Observations, Ozonesonde, and Multi-Decadal Chemical Model Simulations*. Atmospheric Chemistry and Physics, 2022.

40. Marian L Tupy and Gale L Pooley. *Superabundance*. Cato Institute, 2022.

41. Albert Einstein. *The Foundation of the General Theory of Relativity*. Annalen der Physik, 1916.

42. Albert Einstein. *The Field Equations of Gravitation*. Proceedings of the Prussian Academy of Sciences, 1915.

43. Marcus Fierz and Wolfgang Ernst Pauli. *On Relativistic Wave Equations for Particles of Arbitrary Spin in an Electromagnetic Field*. Proceedings of the Royal Society A, 1939.

44. Suraj N Gupta. *Gravitation and Electromagnetism*. Physical Review, 1954.

45. LIGO Scientific Collaboration and Virgo Collaboration. *Observation of Gravitational Waves from a Binary Black Hole Merger*. Physical Review Letters, 2016.

46. Steven Weinberg. *Photons and Gravitons in Perturbation Theory: Derivation of Maxwell's and Einstein's Equations*. Physical Review, 1965.

47. Gilbert N Lewis and Richard C Tolman. *The Principle of Relativity, and Non-Newtonian Mechanics*. Proceedings of the American Academy of Arts and Sciences, 1909.

48. Hendrik Lorentz et al. *The Principle of Relativity*. Methuen and Company, 1923.

49. Shin'ichirō Tomonaga. *On a Relativistically Invariant Formulation of the Quantum Theory of Wave Fields*. Riken Iho, 1943.

50. Julian Schwinger. *The Theory of Quantized Fields I*. Physical Review, 1951.

51. Richard Arnowitt and Stanley Deser. *Quantum Theory of Gravitation: General Formulation and Linearized Theory*. Physical Review, 1959.

52. Richard Arnowitt, Stanley Deser, and Charles W Misner. *Canonical Variables for General Relativity*. Physical Review, 1960.

53. Richard Arnowitt, Stanley Deser, and Charles W Misner. *Coordinate Invariance and Energy Expressions in General Relativity*. Physical Review, 1961.

54. Bryce DeWitt. *Quantum Theory of Gravity. I. The Canonical Theory*. Physical Review, 1967.

55. James Hartle and Stephen Hawking. *Wave Function of the Universe*. Physical Review, 1983.

56. Christian Deppner et al. *Collective-Mode Enhanced Matter-Wave Optics*. Physical Review Letters, 2021.

57. H1 Collaboration and ZEUS Collaborations. *Combination of Measurements of Inclusive Deep Inelastic e±p Scattering Cross Sections and QCD Analysis of HERA Data*. European Physical Journal C, 2015.

58. VD Burkert, L Elouadrhiri, and FX Girod. *The Pressure Distribution Inside the Proton*. Nature, 2018.

59. Claire Patterson. *Age of Meteorites and the Earth*. Geochimica et Cosmochimica Acta, 1956.

60. Léon Rosenfeld. *On the Quantization of Wave Fields*. Annalen der Physik, 1930.

61. Matvei Bronstein. *Quantum Theory of Weak Gravitational Fields.* Physikalische Zeitschrift der Sowjetunion, 1936.

62. Howard C Berg and Robert A Anderson. *Bacteria Swim by Rotating their Flagellar Filaments.* Nature, 1973.

63. Prashant K Singh et al. *CryoEM Structures Reveal how the Bacterial Flagellum Rotates and Switches Direction.* Nature Microbiology, 2024.

64. Renyi Liu and Howard Ochman. *Stepwise Formation of the Bacterial Flagellar System.* Proceedings of the National Academy of Sciences of the United States of America, 2007.

65. Adrián A Davín et al. *A Geological Timescale for Bacterial Evolution and Oxygen Adaptation.* Science, 2025.

66. Iain McGilchrist. *The Master and His Emissary.* Yale University Press, 2009.

67. Voltaire. *Treatise on Tolerance.* Cramer Brothers, 1763.

68. Montesquieu. *The Spirit of the Laws.* Barrillot & Fils, 1748.

69. John Locke. *Two Treatises of Government.* Awnsham Churchill, 1689.

70. Thomas Jefferson. *A Summary View of the Rights of British America.* Clementina Rind, 1774.

71. Second Continental Congress. *The Declaration of Independence.* John Dunlap, 1776.

72. Helen Andrews. *The Great Feminization.* Compact, 2025.

73. Alex Alma. *Bulletin/Novus: Nio av tio utrikesfödda har semestrat i sitt födelseland [Bulletin/Novus: Nine out of ten foreign-born have vacationed in their country of birth].* Bulletin, 2022.

74. Triggernometry. *Grooming Gang Survivor Tells Her Story.* YouTube, 2025.

75. R v Melia. *Far-right organiser found guilty of intent to stir up racial hatred through distribution of stickers.* Crown Prosecution Service, 2024.

76. Yvette Harding. *Hundreds of Churches Burned in Europe.* Assist News, 2024.

77. Heather Tomlinson. *Churches Are Burning Across Europe. But Why?* Premier Christianity, 2024.

78. Kamuran Samar. *Timeline: Deadly attacks on Christmas markets in Europe.* Euronews, 2024.

79. *ICE Boston, federal partners arrests illegal Ecuadoran national charged with more than 20 sex crimes against Massachusetts minor.* US Immigration and Customs Enforcement, 2025.

80. *ICE Boston arrests illegal Guatemalan national charged with forcibly raping Massachusetts minor.* US Immigration and Customs Enforcement, 2025.

81. *ICE arrests illegal Guatemalan alien charged with sex crime against Massachusetts child.* US Immigration and Customs Enforcement, 2025.

82. Joel S Migdal. *Strong Societies and Weak States.* Princeton University Press, 1988.

83. Joel S Migdal, Atul Kohli, and Vivienne Shue, eds. *State Power and Social Forces.* Cambridge University Press, 1994.

84. Vivienne Shue. *The Reach of the State.* Stanford University Press, 1988.

85. Lloyd I Rudolph and Susanne Hoeber Rudolph. *In Pursuit of Lakshmi.* University of Chicago Press, 1987.

86. Gretchen Livingston and Anna Brown. *Intermarriage in the US 50 Years After Loving v. Virginia.* Pew Research Center, 2017.

87. Jan H van de Beek et al. *Borderless Welfare State.* University of Amsterdam, 2021.

88. Finansministeriet Makropolitisk Center. *Indvandreres nettobidrag til de offentlige finanser i 2019.* Finansministeriet, 2023.

89. Steve Alder. *DOJ Unseals Criminal HIPAA Charges Against Surgeon Who Exposed Transgender Care at Texas Children's.* The HIPAA Journal, 2024.

90. Steve Alder. *DOJ Drops Charges Against Surgeon Who Exposed Continuing Transgender Care at Texas Children's.* The HIPAA Journal, 2025.

91. Tracy Campbell. *Deliver the Vote.* Carroll & Graf Publishers, 2005.

92. Edward B Foley. *Ballot Battles.* Oxford University Press, 2016.

93. John Fund and Hans von Spakovsky. *Who's Counting?* Encounter Books, 2012.

94. Erica Komisar. *Being There*. TarcherPerigee, 2017.

95. Jordan Peterson. *Maps of Meaning*. Routledge, 1999.

96. Jonathan Haidt. *The Righteous Mind*. Pantheon Books, 2012.

97. Karl Popper. *The Logic of Scientific Discovery*. Verlag von Julius Springer, 1934.

98. Francis Bacon. *Novum Organum*. John Bill, 1620.

99. John Locke. *An Essay Concerning Humane Understanding*. Thomas Basset, 1689.

100. Alfred Wegener. *The Origin of Continents*. Petermanns Geographische Mitteilungen, 1912.

101. Alfred Wegener. *The Origin of Continents and Oceans*. Friedrich Vieweg & Sohn, 1915.

102. Phoebus Levene. *The Structure of Yeast Nucleic Acid: IV. Ammonia Hydrolysis*. Journal of Biological Chemistry, 1919.

103. Erwin Chargaff. *Chemical Specificity of Nucleic Acids and Mechanism of their Enzymatic Degradation*. Experientia, 1950.

104. James Watson and Francis Crick. *Molecular Structure of Nucleic Acids: A Structure for Deoxyribose Nucleic Acid*. Nature, 1953.

105. Thomas Aquinas. *Summa Theologica*. 1274.

106. David Burrell. *Aquinas*. University of Notre Dame Press, 1979.

107. Sally Baden and Catherine Barber. *The Impact of the Second-Hand Clothing Trade on Developing Countries*. Oxfam, 2005.

108. Garth Frazer. *Used-Clothing Donations and Apparel Production in Africa*. The Economic Journal, 2008.

109. Andrew Brooks. *Clothing Poverty*. Zed Books, 2015.

110. Jordan Peterson. *We Who Wrestle with God*. Portfolio, 2024.

111. *What Percentage of Americans Are LGBTQ+?* Gallup, 2022–2026.

112. Gary J Gates. *LGBT Data Collection Amid Social and Demographic Shifts of the US LGBT Community*. American Journal of Public Health, 2017.

113. Tristan Bridges and Mignon R Moore. *Young Women of Color and Shifting Sexual Identities*. Contexts, 2018.

114. Engineering National Academies of Sciences and Medicine. *Understanding the Well-Being of LGBTQI+ Populations*. National Academies Press, 2020.

115. Gregory A Smith et al. *Decline of Christianity in the US Has Slowed, May Have Leveled Off*. Pew Research Center, 2025.

116. *How Religious Are Americans?* Gallup, 2024.

117. Melissa Deckman et al. *Religious Change in America*. Public Religion Research Institute, 2024.

118. Greg Lukianoff and Jonathan Haidt. *The Coddling of the American Mind*. Penguin Press, 2018.

119. Ray Dalio. *Principles for Dealing with the Changing World Order*. Avid Reader Press, 2021.

120. John P Incardona et al. *The Teratogenic Veratrum Alkaloid Cyclopamine Inhibits Sonic Hedgehog Signal Transduction*. Development, 1998.

121. Youngran Kim, Trudy Millard Krause, and Scott D Lane. *Trends and Seasonality of Emergency Department Visits and Hospitalizations for Suicidality Among Children and Adolescents in the US from 2016 to 2021*. JAMA Network Open, 2023.

122. Sally C Curtin, Matthew F Garnett, and Farida B Ahmad. *Provisional Numbers and Rates of Suicide by Month and Demographic Characteristics: United States, 2021*. NCHS Vital Statistics Rapid Release Reports, 2022.

123. Adam Smith. *The Wealth of Nations*. W Strahan and T Cadell, 1776.

124. Ernst Haeckel. *General Morphology of Organisms*. Georg Reimer, 1866.

125. MC & JC vs Indiana Department of Child Services. *Court of Appeals of Indiana*. Case No 22A-JC-49 decided October 21, 2022; rehearing denied December 22, 2022.

126. Todd Kolstad & Krista Cummins-Kolstad vs Montana Department of Public Health & Human Services. *13th Judicial District Court*. No DR-23-0240 (Feb 20, 2024) (child-protection case dismissed).

127. Jeff Younger–Anne Georgulas custody dispute. *Texas Supreme Court mandamus: In re Jeff Younger.* No 22-1137 (Texas Dec 30, 2022) (petition for writ of mandamus denied).

128. James Gibson. *The Ecological Approach to Visual Perception.* Houghton Mifflin, 1979.

129. Jessica L Irwin et al. *Maternal Prenatal Cortisol Programs the Infant Hypothalamic-Pituitary–Adrenal Axis.* Psychoneuroendocrinology, 2021.

130. Georgia Chalfun et al. *Perinatal Stress and Methylation of the NR3C1 Gene in Newborns - Systematic Review.* Epigenetics, 2022.

131. Steven Pinker. *The Blank Slate.* Viking, 2002.

132. Nim Tottenham et al. *Prolonged Institutional Rearing is Associated with Atypically Large Amygdala Volume and Difficulties in Emotion Regulation.* Developmental Science, 2010.

133. Martin H Teicher et al. *Childhood Neglect Is Associated with Reduced Corpus Callosum Area.* Biological Psychiatry, 2004.

134. J Douglas Bremner et al. *Magnetic Resonance Imaging-Based Measurement of Hippocampal Volume in Posttraumatic Stress Disorder Related to Childhood Physical and Sexual Abuse–A Preliminary Report.* Biological Psychiatry, 1997.

135. Michael D De Bellis et al. *Brain Structures in Pediatric Maltreatment-Related Posttraumatic Stress Disorder: A Sociodemographically Matched Study.* Biological Psychiatry, 2002.

136. Donald Hebb. *The Organization of Behavior.* John Wiley & Sons, 1949.

137. Richard Semon. *The Mneme.* Wilhelm Engelmann, 1904.

138. Karl Lashley. *In Search of the Engram.* Symposia of the Society for Experimental Biology, No. IV: Physiological Mechanisms in Animal Behaviour, 1950.

139. Sheena A Josselyn, Stefan Köhler, and Paul W Frankland. *Finding the Engram.* Nature Reviews Neuroscience, 2015.

140. Dheeraj S Roy et al. *Brain-Wide Mapping Reveals That Engrams for a Single Memory are Distributed Across Multiple Brain Regions.* Nature Communications, 2022.

141. Santiago Ramón y Cajal. *Texture of the Nervous System of Man and Vertebrates.* Imprenta y Librería de Nicolás Moya, 1899–1904.

142. F Caserta et al. *Determination of Fractal Dimension of Physiologically Characterized Neurons in Two and Three Dimensions.* Journal of Neuroscience Methods, 1995.

143. Sean M Polyn et al. *Category-Specific Cortical Activity Precedes Retrieval During Memory Search.* Science, 2005.

144. Steve Ramirez et al. *Creating a False Memory in the Hippocampus.* Science, 2013.

145. Teruhiro Okuyama et al. *Ventral CA1 Neurons Store Social Memory.* Science, 2016.

146. Akiko Hayashi-Takagi et al. *Labelling and Optical Erasure of Synaptic Memory Traces in the Motor Cortex.* Nature, 2015.

147. Marcus E Raichle and Debra A Gusnard. *Appraising the Brain's Energy Budget.* Proceedings of the National Academy of Sciences of the United States of America, 2002.

148. W Ritchie Russell and PW Nathan. *Traumatic Amnesia.* Brain, 1946.

149. Bryan D Devan et al. *Circadian Phase-Shifted Rats Show Normal Acquisition but Impaired Long-Term Retention of Place Information in the Water Task.* Neurobiology of Learning and Memory, 2001.

150. Rafal W Ameen et al. *Early Life Circadian Rhythm Disruption in Mice Alters Brain and Behavior in Adulthood.* Scientific Reports, 2022.

151. William Cheselden. *An Account of Some Observations Made by a Young Gentleman Who Was Born Blind or Lost His Sight So Early That He Had No Remembrance of Ever Having Seen and Was Couch'd between 13 and 14 Years of Age.* Philosophical Transactions of the Royal Society of London, 1728.

152. Marius von Senden. *Space and Sight.* Johann Ambrosius Barth, 1932.

153. Torsten N Wiesel and David H Hubel. *Single-Cell Responses in Striate Cortex of Kittens Deprived of Vision in One Eye.* Journal of Neurophysiology, 1963.

154. F Vargha-Khadem et al. *Differential Effects of Early Hippocampal Pathology on Episodic and Semantic Memory.* Science, 1997.

155. Brenda Milner. *Disorders of Learning and Memory after Temporal Lobe Lesions in Man*. Clinical Neurosurgery, 1972.

156. Suzanne Corkin. *What's New with the Amnesic Patient HM?* Nature Reviews Neuroscience, 2002.

157. Brenda Milner, Suzanne Corkin, and HL Teuber. *Further Analysis of the Hippocampal Amnesic Syndrome: 14-Year Follow-Up Study of HM*. Neuropsychologia, 1968.

158. William Beecher Scoville and Brenda Milner. *Loss of Recent Memory after Bilateral Hippocampal Lesions*. Journal of Neurology, Neurosurgery, and Psychiatry, 1957.

159. Dean F Mackinnon and Larry R Squire. *Autobiographical Memory and Amnesia*. Psychobiology, 1989.

160. Nancy L Rempel-Clower et al. *Three Cases of Enduring Memory Impairment after Bilateral Damage Limited to the Hippocampal Formation*. The Journal of Neuroscience, 1996.

161. Stuart Zola-Morgan, Larry R Squire, and David G Amaral. *Human Amnesia and the Medial Temporal Region: Enduring Memory Impairment Following a Bilateral Lesion Limited to Field CA1 of the Hippocampus*. The Journal of Neuroscience, 1986.

162. Ben Bowles et al. *Impaired Familiarity with Preserved Recollection after Anterior Temporal-Lobe Resection that Spares the Hippocampus*. Proceedings of the National Academy of Sciences of the United States of America, 2007.

163. Stefan Köhler and Chris B Martin. *Familiarity Impairments after Anterior Temporal-Lobe Resection with Hippocampal Sparing: Lessons Learned from Case NB*. Neuropsychologia, 2020.

164. R Adolphs et al. *Impaired Recognition of Emotion in Facial Expressions Following Bilateral Damage to the Human Amygdala*. Nature, 1994.

165. Raymond P Kesner and Jeanne M Novak. *Serial Position Curve in Rats: Role of the Dorsal Hippocampus*. Science, 1982.

166. Arthur P Shimamura, Jeri S Janowsky, and Larry R Squire. *Memory for the Temporal Order of Events in Patients with Frontal Lobe Lesions and Amnesic Patients*. Neuropsychologia, 1990.

167. Ofer Lahav. *Cosmological Parameters and Hyper-Parameters: The Hubble Constant from Boomerang and Maxima*. arXiv, 2000.

168. CL Bennett et al. *Nine-Year Wilkinson Microwave Anisotropy Probe (WMAP) Observations: Final Maps and Results*. The Astrophysical Journal Supplement Series, 2013.

169. Planck Collaboration. *Planck 2018 Results. VI. Cosmological Parameters*. Astronomy & Astrophysics, 2020.

170. SPT-3G Collaboration. *A Measurement of the CMB Temperature Power Spectrum and Constraints on Cosmology from the SPT-3G 2018 TT/TE/EE Data Set*. arXiv, 2022.

171. Thibaut Louis et al. *The Atacama Cosmology Telescope: DR6 Power Spectra Likelihoods and ΛCDM Parameters*. arXiv, 2025.

172. Wendy L Freedman et al. *Final Results from the Hubble Space Telescope Key Project to Measure the Hubble Constant*. The Astrophysical Journal, 2001.

173. A Sandage et al. *The Hubble Constant: A Summary of the HST Program for the Luminosity Calibration of Type Ia Supernovae by Means of Cepheids*. The Astrophysical Journal, 2006.

174. Adam G Riess et al. *A 2.4% Determination of the Local Value of the Hubble Constant*. The Astrophysical Journal, 2016.

175. Adam G Riess et al. *A Comprehensive Measurement of the Local Value of the Hubble Constant with 1 km s^{-1} Mpc^{-1} Uncertainty from the Hubble Space Telescope and the SH0ES Team*. The Astrophysical Journal Letters, 2022.

176. Adam G Riess et al. *The Perfect Host: JWST Cepheid Observations in a Background-Free Type Ia Supernova Host Confirm No Bias in Hubble-Constant Measurements*. The Astrophysical Journal Letters, 2025.

177. Santi Cassisi and Maurizio Salaris. *The 'Tip' of the Red Giant Branch as a Distance Indicator: Theoretical Calibration and the Value of H_0*. arXiv, 1997.

178. GA Tammann and B Reindl. *The Luminosity of Supernovae of Type Ia from Tip of the Red-Giant Branch Distances and the Value of H_0*. Astronomy & Astrophysics, 2013.

179. In Sung Jang and Myung Gyoon Lee. *The Tip of the Red Giant Branch Distances to Type Ia Supernova Host Galaxies. V. NGC 3021, NGC 3370, and NGC 1309 and the Value of the Hubble Constant*. The Astrophysical Journal, 2017.

180. Wendy L Freedman et al. *The Carnegie-Chicago Hubble Program. VIII. An Independent Determination of the Hubble Constant Based on the Tip of the Red Giant Branch*. The Astrophysical Journal, 2019.

181. Wendy L Freedman et al. *Status Report on the Chicago-Carnegie Hubble Program (CCHP): Measurement of the Hubble Constant Using the Hubble and James Webb Space Telescopes*. The Astrophysical Journal, 2025.

182. Vesto Slipher. *Nebulae*. Proceedings of the American Philosophical Society, 1917.

183. Edwin Hubble. *A Relation Between Distance and Radial Velocity Among Extra-Galactic Nebulae*. Proceedings of the National Academy of Sciences of the United States of America, 1929.

184. Licia Verde, Tommaso Treu, and Adam G Riess. *Tensions Between the Early and Late Universe*. Nature Astronomy, 2019.

185. Licia Verde, Nils Schöneberg, and Héctor Gil-Marín. *A Tale of Many H_0*. Annual Review of Astronomy and Astrophysics, 2024.

186. Kenneth J Zucker et al. *Sex-Typed Behavior in Cross-Gender-Identified Children: Stability and Change at a One-Year Follow-Up*. Journal of the American Academy of Child Psychiatry, 1985.

187. Kenneth J Zucker and Susan J Bradley. *Gender Identity Disorder and Psychosexual Problems in Children and Adolescents*. The Guilford Press, 1995.

188. Kelley D Drummond et al. *Follow-Up Study of Girls With Gender Identity Disorder*. Developmental Psychology, 2008.

189. Hanseatisches Oberlandesgericht Hamburg, Pressestelle. *Urteilsverkündung im sog. Stadtpark-Verfahren*. Pressestelle des Hanseatischen Oberlandesgerichts Hamburg, 2023.

190. Frank Chung. *Outrage as Eight of Nine Men Convicted of Gang Rape of 15-Year-Old in Germany Receive No Prison Time*. News Corp Australia, 2023.

191. Aristotle. *Politics*. 350 BCE.

192. James Surowiecki. *The Wisdom of Crowds*. Doubleday, 2004.

193. United Nations. *United Nations Global Principles for Information Integrity*. 2024.

194. Niles Eldredge and Stephen Jay Gould. *Punctuated Equilibria*. Freeman, Cooper & Co, 1972.

195. Ernst Mayr. *Systematics and the Origin of Species from the Viewpoint of a Zoologist*. Columbia University Press, 1942.

196. Preston E Cloud Jr. *Some Problems and Patterns of Evolution Exemplified by Fossil Invertebrates*. Evolution, 1948.

197. Stephen Jay Gould. *Wonderful Life*. WW Norton & Co, 1989.

198. Christopher D Whalen and Derek EG Briggs. *The Palaeozoic Colonization of the Water Column and the Rise of Global Nekton*. Proceedings of the Royal Society B, 2018.

199. Thomas Servais et al. *No (Cambrian) Explosion and No (Ordovician) Event: A Single Long-Term Radiation in the Early Paleozoic*. Palaeogeography, Palaeoclimatology, Palaeoecology, 2023.

200. Andrew H Knoll. *Paleobiological Perspectives on Early Eukaryotic Evolution*. Cold Spring Harbor Perspectives in Biology, 2014.

201. Susannah M Porter et al. *Early Eukaryote Diversity*. Paleobiology, 2025.

202. Bing Shen et al. *The Avalon Explosion: Evolution of Ediacara Morphospace*. Science, 2008.

203. M Gabriela Mángano and Luis A Buatois. *The Rise and Early Evolution of Animals: Where Do We Stand From a Trace-Fossil Perspective?* Interface Focus, 2020.

204. Charles D Walcott and Charles E Resser. *Addenda to Descriptions of Burgess Shale Fossils*. Smithsonian Institution, 1931.

205. J John Sepkoski Jr. *A Factor Analytic Description of the Phanerozoic Marine Fossil Record*. Paleobiology, 1981.

206. Derek EG Briggs, Richard A Fortey, and Matthew A Wills. *Morphological Disparity in the Cambrian*. Science, 1992.

207. Mark Webster. *A Cambrian Peak in Morphological Variation Within Trilobite Species*. Science, 2007.

208. Barry D Webby et al., eds. *The Great Ordovician Biodiversification Event*. Columbia University Press, 2004.

209. Thomas Servais et al. *The Great Ordovician Biodiversification Event (GOBE): The palaeoecological dimension.* Palaeogeography, Palaeoclimatology, Palaeoecology, 2010.

210. Christian Klug et al. *The Devonian Nekton Revolution.* Lethaia, 2010.

211. Marcello Ruta, Peter J Wagner, and Michael I Coates. *Evolutionary Patterns in Early Tetrapods. I. Rapid Initial Diversification Followed by Decrease in Rates of Character Change.* Proceedings of the Royal Society B, 2006.

212. Sarda Sahney, Michael J Benton, and Howard J Falcon-Lang. *Rainforest Collapse Triggered Carboniferous Tetrapod Diversification in Euramerica.* Geology, 2010.

213. Douglas H Erwin. *The Great Paleozoic Crisis.* Columbia University Press, 1993.

214. Massimo Bernardi et al. *Dinosaur Diversification Linked with the Carnian Pluvial Episode.* Nature Communications, 2018.

215. Luis W Alvarez et al. *Extraterrestrial Cause for the Cretaceous-Tertiary Extinction.* Science, 1980.

216. Alan R Hildebrand et al. *Chicxulub Crater - A Possible Cretaceous-Tertiary Boundary Impact Crater on the Yucatan Peninsula, Mexico.* Geology, 1991.

217. Thomas John Dixon Halliday, Paul Upchurch, and Anjali Goswami. *Eutherians Experienced Elevated Evolutionary Rates in the Immediate Aftermath of the Cretaceous–Palaeogene Mass Extinction.* Proceedings of the Royal Society B, 2016.

218. Maureen A O'Leary et al. *The Placental Mammal Ancestor and the Post–K-Pg Radiation of Placentals.* Science, 2013.

219. John Alroy. *The Fossil Record of North American Mammals: Evidence for a Paleocene Evolutionary Radiation.* Systematic Biology, 1999.

220. Richard M Bateman et al. *Early Evolution of Land Plants: Phylogeny, Physiology, and Ecology of the Primary Terrestrial Radiation.* Annual Review of Ecology and Systematics, 1998.

221. Eliott Capel et al. *The Silurian–Devonian Terrestrial Revolution: Diversity Patterns and Sampling Bias of the Vascular Plant Macrofossil Record.* Earth-Science Reviews, 2022.

222. Robin Hanson. *The Great Filter - Are We Almost Past It?* 1998.

223. Our World in Data. *Population – HYDE, Gapminder, UN – Long-run data.* HYDE (2023); Gapminder (2022); UN WPP (2024) – with major processing by Our World in Data. Original data: PBL Netherlands Environmental Assessment Agency, *History Database of the Global Environment 3.3*; Gapminder, *Population v7*; United Nations, *World Population Prospects*; Gapminder, *Systema Globalis*. Subset used: Europe, 1000 AD to present. Accessed 23 November 2025. Our World in Data, 2024.

224. Stan L Lindstedt and William A Calder III. *Body Size, Physiological Time, and Longevity of Homeothermic Animals.* The Quarterly Review of Biology, 1981.

225. Adam Hochschild. *Bury the Chains.* Macmillan, 2005.

226. William Hague. *William Wilberforce.* HarperPress, 2007.

227. Carole Peterson and Christy Roberts. *Like Mother, Like Daughter: Similarities in Narrative Style.* Developmental Psychology, 2003.

228. Paul H Mussen and Ann L Parker. *Mother Nurturance and Girls' Incidental Imitative Learning.* Journal of Personality and Social Psychology, 1965.

229. G Michael Hopf. *Those Who Remain.* CreateSpace, 2016.

230. Georg Cantor. *On a Property of the Collection of All Real Algebraic Numbers.* Journal für die reine und angewandte Mathematik, 1874.

231. Galileo Galilei. *Dialogues Concerning Two New Sciences.* Lodewijk Elzevir, 1638.

232. Tomoyasu Horikawa and Yukiyasu Kamitani. *Generic Decoding of Seen and Imagined Objects Using Hierarchical Visual Features.* Nature Communications, 2017.

233. Guohua Shen et al. *Deep Image Reconstruction from Human Brain Activity.* PLOS Computational Biology, 2018.

234. Yu Takagi and Shinji Nishimoto. *High-Resolution Image Reconstruction with Latent Diffusion Models from Human Brain Activity.* Proceedings of the IEEE/CVF Conference on Computer Vision and Pattern Recognition, 2023.

235. Hendrik Lorentz. *Electromagnetic Phenomena in a System Moving with any Velocity Less than that of Light.* Proceedings of the Academy of Sciences of Amsterdam, 1904.

236. James Clerk Maxwell. *A Dynamical Theory of the Electromagnetic Field*. Philosophical Transactions of the Royal Society of London, 1865.

237. Moritz Nagel et al. *Direct Terrestrial Test of Lorentz Symmetry in Electrodynamics to 10^{-18}*. Nature Communications, 2015.

238. AA Abdo et al. *Testing Einstein's Special Relativity with Fermi's Short Hard γ-Ray Burst GRB090510.* Nature, 2009.

239. Alfred Scharff Goldhaber and Michael Martin Nieto. *Photon and Graviton Mass Limits*. Reviews of Modern Physics, 2010.

240. Roger Penrose. *Gravitational Collapse and Space-Time Singularities*. Physical Review Letters, 1965.

241. Stephen Hawking and Roger Penrose. *The Singularities of Gravitational Collapse and Cosmology*. Proceedings of the Royal Society A, 1970.

242. Stephen Hawking. *Breakdown of Predictability in Gravitational Collapse*. Physical Review, 1976.

243. RFC Vessot et al. *Test of Relativistic Gravitation with a Space-Borne Hydrogen Maser*. Physical Review Letters, 1980.

244. Robert Brown. *A Brief Account of Microscopical Observations*. Philosophical Magazine, 1828.

245. Peter W Crockford et al. *The Geologic History of Primary Productivity*. Current Biology, 2023.

www.ingramcontent.com/pod-product-compliance
Lightning Source LLC
LaVergne TN
LVHW010553100826
845148LV00014B/2697

* 9 7 9 8 2 3 4 0 0 4 2 6 0 *